ALL·IN·ONE

MCITP SQL Server™ 2005 Database Developer

EXAM GUIDE

(Exams 70-431, 70-441, and 70-442)

Darril Gibson

New York • Chicago • San Francisco • Lisbon
London • Madrid • Mexico City • Milan • New Delhi
San Juan • Seoul • Singapore • Sydney • Toronto

The **McGraw·Hill** Companies

Cataloging-in-Publication Data is on file with the Library of Congress

McGraw-Hill books are available at special quantity discounts to use as premiums and sales promotions, or for use in corporate training programs. To contact a special sales representative, please visit the Contact Us page at www.mhprofessional.com.

MCITP SQL Server™ 2005 Database Developer All-in-One Exam Guide
(Exams 70-431, 70-441, & 70-442)

1 2 3 4 5 6 7 8 9 0 DOC DOC 0 1 9 8

ISBN: Book p/n 978-0-07-154675-1 and CD p/n 978-0-07-154676-8
of set 978-0-07-154669-0

MHID: Book p/n 0-07-154675-8 and CD p/n 0-07-154676-6
of set 0-07-154669-3

Sponsoring Editor	**Technical Editor**	**Composition**
Tim Green	*Glen E. Clarke*	*International Typesetting and Composition*
Editorial Supervisor	**Copy Editor**	
Jody McKenzie	*Mike McGee*	**Illustration**
Project Manager	**Proofreader**	*International Typesetting and Composition*
Aparna Shukla, International Typesetting and Composition	*Carol Shields*	**Art Director, Cover**
	Indexer	*Jeff Weeks*
Acquisitions Coordinator	*Broccoli Information Management*	
Jennifer Housh	**Production Supervisor**	
	James Kussow	

I'd like to dedicate this book to my wonderful sister Dawn Grzena. Though we've been separated by many miles since I packed my motorcycle into my van on my 18th birthday and headed out to seek my fortune, our Love has kept us close. She was there when I was initiated as a Chief in the U.S. Navy, and was there when I graduated from Troy State University. When my first book was published, she was as excited as I was. I'm thankful she's in my life.

ABOUT THE AUTHOR

Darril Gibson has been working with databases since the days of dBase, and Microsoft's SQL Server in particular since version 7.0. He's been a Microsoft Certified Trainer (MCT) for over nine years and specializes in delivering leading edge technical training. He's been involved in several writing projects, including technical editing a SQL Server 2005 book, and authoring the McGraw-Hill *MCITP Database Administrator All-In-One* book. Working with Keystone Learning, he developed several video training courses on topics such as A+, MCSE, and Exchange. He is currently working on a key government contract providing extensive training to Air Force personnel in support of a major Network Operations Support Center on a wide array of technologies, and he moonlights as adjunct faculty at a local college. He holds about 20 current certifications including MCT, MCTS: SQL Server 2005, MCITP: Database Administrator, MCITP: Database Developer, MCSE (NT 4.0, Windows 2000, Windows 2003), and MCSD (Visual Basic 6.0, .NET).

He is married to his wife of 15 years, Nimfa, and lives with her and three dogs in Virginia Beach. Whenever possible, all of them escape to a small cabin in the country on over 20 acres of land. Weekends are spent watching birds and wildlife and tending to flowers and roses that the local deer seem to think is their own private salad bar.

About the Technical Editor

Glen E. Clarke is a Microsoft Certified Systems Engineer (MCSE), a Microsoft Certified Database Administrator (MCDBA), a Microsoft Certified Training (MCT), Microsoft Certified IT Professional (MCITP), and a Microsoft Certified Solution Developer (MCSD). Glen holds a number of security certifications, including Prosoft's Security Analyst certification (CIWSA), SCP's Security Certified Network Specialist (SCNS), and the Security Certified Network Professional (SCNP). Glen is also an A+ Certified Professional, Network+ Certified Professional, and a Security+ Certified Professional. Currently, Glen works as an independent trainer and consultant, focusing on data recovery and network security auditing. He spends most of his time delivering courses on Windows Server, SQL Server, Exchange Server, Visual Studio .NET, security-related topics, Network+, and A+. Glen has worked on a number of certification titles, as both a technical editor and an author, and has authored the *Network+ Certification Study Guide, 3rd Edition* and co-authored *Mike Meyers Network+ Certification Passport, Second Edition* (both published by McGraw-Hill).

When not working, Glen loves to spend quality time with his beautiful wife, Tanya, and their three children, Sara, Brendon, and Ashlyn. He is an active member of the martial arts community, where he currently holds a first-degree black belt in Tae Kwon Do. You can visit Glen online at www.gleneclarke.com, or contact him at glenclarke@accesswave.ca.

CONTENTS

ACKNOWLEDGMENTS

Completing a book is a large project with several different phases, but none of them can be done alone. I'm very grateful for all the people that helped me along the way.

My agent, Carole McClendon, has opened many doors for me, including those that led to this book. Without her, instead of actively writing books, I'd probably still be writing endless proposals and reading endless rejection letters.

At McGraw-Hill, I'm thankful for the support and encouragement I've received from Tim Green, Senior Acquisitions Editor, and Jenni Housh, Acquisitions Coordinator. While many more people have been involved in the project, these two have been with me from beginning to end.

I also want to thank Glen Clarke for the insightful work he did as the technical editor.

INTRODUCTION

With mainstream Microsoft support of SQL Server 2000 ending on April 8, 2008, the importance of SQL Server 2005 continues to increase. Watching job advertisements, I'm seeing more and more job openings for database administrators and database developers, and an increase in SQL Server 2005 listed in the desired skills set.

As the Microsoft SQL Server 2005 market share grows, so does the demand for qualified DBMS experts to develop and maintain complex databases. Certifications are an ideal way to demonstrate knowledge and mastery of any product, including SQL Server 2005, and often certifications open up new doors and opportunities.

Whether you're trying to learn SQL Server from scratch, or upgrade your skills from SQL Server 2000, pursuing the MCITP certification is a great path to guide your studies. I've earned several certifications from Microsoft and I've found that by pursuing certifications, I'm able to learn a good mix of what's needed on the job and what Microsoft considers significant new enhancements to a product.

While this book will guide your studies to help you prepare for the MCITP certification, you'll also learn many job skills that can help you shine as a database developer.

MCITP: Database Administrator

To become a Microsoft Certified IT Professional (MCITP): Database Developer you need to pass three tests:

- **70-431 Technical Specialist**
  Microsoft SQL Server 2005—Implementation and Maintenance

- **70-441 Professional**
  Designing Database Solutions by Using Microsoft SQL Server 2005

- **70-442 Professional**
  Designing and Optimizing Data Access by Using Microsoft SQL Server 2005

When you pass the first test (70-431), you earn the Microsoft Certified Technical Specialist: SQL Server 2005 certification. When you pass the remaining two tests (70-441 and 70-442), you earn the MCITP: Database Developer certification.

As of this writing, to retain the MCITP certification, you need to recertify every three years. While other certifications, such as Cisco, require recertifying periodically, this is the first time Microsoft has included a recertification requirement.

Microsoft has two other MCITP certifications related to SQL Server 2005 that are not covered by this book. Keep on the lookout though: new books are always being written. The two other SQL Server 2005 MCITP certifications are:

- MCITP Database Administrator
- MCITP: Business Intelligence Developer

I've pursued several certifications over the years and know that the process of studying the objectives is an excellent way to guide my studies. It helps me learn the product, and when I'm pursuing Microsoft certifications, the objectives help me understand what Microsoft considers important in the product. I've written this book with this in mind. First and foremost, we cover the material to help you pass the tests, but you'll also walk away with knowledge you can use on the job.

While the questions at the end of each chapter are realistic, there is something to keep in mind for the 70-441 and 70-442 design exams. In the actual exam, you'll have three to five pages of text to read before you come to any questions. Part of your challenge in the design exams is to be able to identify what is relevant to the question within the scenario. For the questions at the end of each chapter, I have included only the relevant portion of a fictitious scenario. These end-of-chapter questions help to solidify your knowledge of the chapter's material, but they aren't the best option to prepare for the actual exams. For that, check out the test banks on the CD to see how the scenarios are put together and how the questions are used to force you to search through the scenario. Additionally, check out Appendix C to see how a design exam is put together.

The tests currently cost $125 each. As a Microsoft Certified Trainer, I occasionally receive discount vouchers that can be used to get a discount off the $125. I give these vouchers to students. As an owner of this book, I consider you a student. When the vouchers are available to me, I'll post them on mcitpsuccess.com for you to use.

One more thing. Finish the book and get certified, but don't think you're done learning. SQL Server 2005 is a very deep and robust product. If all you do is work with and manage SQL Server, I doubt you'll know it all before the next version comes out. I don't profess to know everything about SQL Server myself, and certainly don't claim this book will cover it all.

Registering for the Exam

To register for any Microsoft exam, visit the following web site:

www.microsoft.com/learning/mcpexams/register

While Microsoft testing has historically been available through both Prometric and Pearson Vue testing centers, Microsoft currently uses Prometric as their sole testing provider.

How to Use This Book

You can easily start on the first page of Chapter 1 and continue on until the last page in Chapter 15. That's the way I wrote the book and that's the way I envision using it to teach college classes. If you're not too interested in certification, but mostly want to immerse yourself in the product, this will work just grand.

If you're interested in certification, you may want to take a few preliminary steps before diving into the book.

First, you need to know what the objectives are for the exam. At the end of this introduction, I've included the objectives in a map that identifies where the objectives are covered. Keep in mind, however, that exam objectives do change, so I strongly encourage you to check out Microsoft's site and search for any differences. As of this writing, the text herein is accurate, but who knows what will have changed by the time you read this.

After you've reviewed the exam objectives, take a look at the appendices that cover the specific exam. There is an appendix for the 70-431 exam, another for 70-441, and another for 70-442. These appendices include some general notes on each exam and a list of concepts you should know and understand. These also include a listing of the chapters that cover material for each exam.

As you start each chapter, look at the Table of Contents to see if you're familiar with the topics. If you already know the content, feel free to jump to the back of the chapter and try the Test Preparation Questions. If you answer ALL of them correctly, feel free to skip the chapter. If not, go back and study the chapter.

Each chapter is laid out similar to how I would teach the topic in a classroom. For the important topics, I present it, show it, and then give you an opportunity to try it in an exercise. The method of showing is a little different in a book than in the classroom, but this is actually better for you. You can take as much time as you need to follow along.

The exercises are geared toward reinforcing your knowledge of the material in the chapter, but you can expect them to help you with the exams, too. Microsoft has included some excellent simulations on the 70-431 exam to ensure that people who pass the test are truly familiar with the product. If you can do the exercises and understand what you're doing, you should be able to handle the simulations on the actual tests.

As a supplement, I've included short training videos that show how to do some things within SQL Server 2005. Many times, a short demonstration can jumpstart your knowledge, and that's the purpose of these videos. Most are under five minutes and cover a simple concept you can view and then do on your own. These videos are included on the CD, or are available via download from the McGraw-Hill professional web site, www.mhprofessional.com. Click on the Computing tab and search for the book page in question. These may also help you with simulation questions on the exam by first watching how to do something and then doing it.

Sometimes while going through a chapter, you might like to have a different perspective on a topic. Toward the end of the chapter, you'll find Books Online topics listed in the BOL Topics section. Reading these will give you similar and sometimes additional information to help you better prepare for the tests.

Using the Self-Study Exercises, you can challenge yourself to see how much of the material you've actually retained. I envision instructors in the classroom using these when teaching from this book, so answers aren't provided. Suffice it to say though that frequently there is more than one way to accomplish a task. If you've done what's requested, the end result is what matters.

Next, do the Test Preparation Questions. If you're preparing for the 70-431 test, focus on the questions for that test. If you're preparing for the 70-441 or 70-442 exams, focus on those questions. Additionally, the CD-ROM has test banks for each of the three exams to help you prepare.

A word of caution. Just doing the questions on the CD-ROM without studying the book to understand why the right answers are right, and why the wrong answers are wrong is a recipe for failure. For success, both with the tests and on the job, study and understand the material, and know how to do the exercises in the book.

Conventions

Italics are used to amplify something within the text. This is frequently used when identifying database objects, or identifying something to press or click in exercises.

This book focuses on Microsoft SQL Server 2005. Occasionally, I'll shorten this to SQL Server. Unless otherwise specified, SQL Server refers to Microsoft's SQL Server 2005.

Reserved Words

Reserved words in SQL are those that have special meaning within SQL Server. They are used to define, manipulate, or access different objects with SQL Server. Throughout this book, I have often capitalized reserved words for better identification.

Some examples of reserved words are listed in Table 1.

TABLE	VIEW	PRIMARY KEY
CHECK	DEFAULT	FOREIGN KEY
SELECT	FROM	WHERE
FUNCTION	BACKUP	RESTORE

Table 1　SQL Server Reserved Words

Scripts

Throughout many of the chapters, Transact-SQL scripts are presented. While I strongly encourage you to type as many of the scripts yourself, there may be times when you want to have a workable script that you can cut and paste into the query window.

Scripts are included on the CD that comes with the book. You can also download scripts from mcitpsuccess.com. While every attempt has been made to ensure all the scripts in the book work, a typo may creep in. In the unlikely event you find a script that isn't working, please let me know at Darril@mcitpsuccess.com. I'll post script corrections on mcitpsuccess.com and if there are any other updates, I'll post them there as well.

 NOTE　Before you blame the script, make sure you check the case of the objects. A common frustration occurs when the collation is set to case sensitive (CS) and the script is not typed following the exact case of the objects. The error reports that the object does not exist.

Part of the reason I encourage you to type in the scripts is because you'll make mistakes. This isn't a bad thing. Indeed, it is a valuable learning experience. You'll make mistakes, troubleshoot them, and correct them, learning much along the way.

Icons

Throughout the book, you'll see a variety of different icons. These include:

 EXAM TIP This book is a preparation book to help you get certified, so exam tips on what to look for in the exam are included in every chapter. These tips include key information you'll need to know to successfully pass the exam.

 TIP Tips are added to provide extra information to save you effort, hassle, pain, or time. Tips often indicate how the material may apply on the job.

 NOTE Notes are added to clarify topics. They provide additional information and are used to clarify what may seem like a contradiction in the text.

 CAUTION Cautions are used to point out potentially harmful or risky situations when working with the technology.

Self-Study Exercises

Toward the end of every chapter, I include self-study exercises you can use to solidify knowledge you've gained in the chapter. Unlike the exercises within the chapter that include step-by-step instructions, these exercises are just task statements telling you what to do.

BOL Topics

After the exercises, you'll find a list of Books Online topics you can use as additional research. These topics are included to supplement and reinforce topics needed to successfully pass the certification tests.

The topics are listed using the BOL title. With BOL's search feature, you can enter the title in the Search box and the requested topic will usually appear first in the list.

Summary of What You Need to Know

In the Summary of What You Need to Know section, you'll find a short listing of core topics covered in the chapter for each exam. Most chapters include topics covered in all three exams. Some chapters only have topics for two exams, however. When preparing for a specific exam, use the summary section to guide your studying.

Sample Questions

Use the sample exam questions at the end of every chapter to test your knowledge of the material. If you think you have the material in the chapter mastered, go to the sample questions. If you get them all correct, you may indeed be ready. Additional exam questions are included on the test engine on the CD.

Objective Maps

The following three tables list all of the objectives for each of the three exams in the MCITP: Database Developer certification (70-431, 70-441, and 70-442). Additionally, each chapter is mapped to the specific chapter and section (or sections) where that topic is covered. When preparing for any of the tests, you can use these objective maps to remind you of the topics you need to know and specifically where to look to fill in any gaps in your knowledge.

Exam 70-431 Objective Map

Installing and Configuring SQL Server 2005	
Install SQL Server 2005.	Chapter 1, Installing SQL Server 2005
• Verify prerequisites.	Chapter 1, Installing SQL Server 2005
• Upgrade from an earlier version of SQL Server.	Chapter 1, Installing SQL Server 2005
• Create an instance.	Chapter 1, Installing SQL Server 2005
Configure SQL Server 2005 instances and databases.	Chapter 1, Configuring SQL Server 2005
• Configure log files and data files.	Chapter 1, Creating a Database Chapter 7, Filegroups
• Configure the SQL Server DatabaseMail subsystem for an instance.	Chapter 13, SQL Server Agent
• Choose a recovery model for the database.	Chapter 10, Recovery Models
Configure SQL Server security.	Chapter 8
• Configure server security principals.	Chapter 8, Security Principals
• Configure database securables.	Chapter 8, Database Securables
• Configure encryption.	Chapter 8, Encryption
Configure linked servers by using SQL Server Management Studio (SSMS).	Chapter 11, Linked Servers
• Identify the external data source.	Chapter 11, Linked Servers
• Identify the characteristics of the data source.	Chapter 11, Linked Servers
• Identify the security model of the data source.	Chapter 11, Linked Servers
Implementing High Availability and Disaster Recovery	
Implement database mirroring.	Chapter 10, Database Mirroring
• Prepare databases for database mirroring.	Chapter 10, Database Mirroring
• Create endpoints.	Chapter 10, Database Mirroring
• Specify database partners.	Chapter 10, Database Mirroring
• Specify a witness server.	Chapter 10, Database Mirroring
• Configure an operating mode.	Chapter 10, Database Mirroring
Implement log shipping.	Chapter 10, Log Shipping
• Initialize a secondary database.	Chapter 10, Log Shipping
• Configure log shipping options.	Chapter 10, Log Shipping

• Copy data from one table to another by using the SQL Server 2005 Integration Services (SSIS) Import and Export Wizard.	Chapter 15, SQL Server Integration Services (SSIS)
Manage replication.	Chapter 15, Replication
• Distinguish between replication types.	Chapter 15, Replication
• Configure a publisher, a distributor, and a subscriber.	Chapter 15, Replication
• Configure replication security.	Chapter 15, Replication
• Configure conflict resolution settings for merge replication.	Chapter 15, Replication
• Monitor replication.	Chapter 15, Replication
• Improve replication performance.	Chapter 15, Replication
• Plan for, stop, and restart recovery procedures.	Chapter 15, Replication
Maintaining Databases	
Implement and maintain SQL Server Agent jobs.	Chapter 13, SQL Server Agent
• Set a job owner.	Chapter 13, SQL Server Agent
• Create a job schedule.	Chapter 13, SQL Server Agent
• Create job steps.	Chapter 13, SQL Server Agent
• Configure job steps.	Chapter 13, SQL Server Agent
• Disable a job.	Chapter 13, SQL Server Agent
• Create a maintenance job.	Chapter 13, Maintenance Plans
• Set up alerts.	Chapter 13, SQL Server Agent
• Configure operators.	Chapter 13, SQL Server Agent
• Modify a job.	Chapter 13, SQL Server Agent
• Delete a job.	Chapter 13, SQL Server Agent
• Manage a job.	Chapter 13, SQL Server Agent
Manage databases by using Transact-SQL.	Chapter 2, Creating a Database Chapter 7, Index Maintenance, Statistics
• Manage index fragmentation.	Chapter 7, Index Maintenance
• Manage statistics.	Chapter 7, Statistics
• Shrink files.	Chapter 2, Creating a Database
• Perform database integrity checks by using DBCC CHECKDB.	Chapter 7, Index Maintenance
Back up a database.	Chapter 10, Database Backups
• Perform a full backup.	Chapter 10, Database Backups
• Perform a differential backup.	Chapter 10, Database Backups
• Perform a transaction log backup.	Chapter 10, Database Backups
• Initialize a media set by using the FORMAT option.	Chapter 10, Database Backups
• Append or overwrite an existing media set.	Chapter 10, Database Backups
• Create a backup device.	Chapter 10, Database Backups
• Back up filegroups.	Chapter 10, Database Backups, Restores

Restore a database.	Chapter 10, Restores
• Identify which files are needed from the backup strategy.	Chapter 10, Restores
• Restore a database from a single file and from multiple files.	Chapter 10, Restores
• Choose an appropriate restore method.	Chapter 10, Restores
Move a database between servers.	Chapter 10, Detach and Attach, Backups, Restores
• Choose an appropriate method for moving a database.	Chapter 10, Detach and Attach, Backups, Restores

Monitoring and Troubleshooting SQL Server Performance

Gather performance and optimization data by using the SQL Server Profiler.	Chapter 13, SQL Server Profiler
• Start a new trace.	Chapter 13, SQL Server Profiler
• Save the trace logs.	Chapter 13, SQL Server Profiler
• Configure SQL Server Profiler trace properties.	Chapter 13, SQL Server Profiler
• Configure a System Monitor counter log.	Chapter 13, SQL Server Profiler
• Correlate a SQL Server Profiler trace with System Monitor log data.	Chapter 13, SQL Server Profiler
Gather performance and optimization data by using the Database Engine Tuning Advisor.	Chapter 7, Database Engine Tuning Advisor (DTA)
• Build a workload file by using the SQL Server Profiler.	Chapter 13, SQL Server Profiler
• Tune a workload file by using the Database Engine Tuning Advisor.	Chapter 7, Database Engine Tuning Advisor (DTA)
• Save recommended indexes.	Chapter 7, Database Engine Tuning Advisor (DTA)
Monitor and resolve blocks and deadlocks.	Chapter 14, Locks and Deadlocks
• Identify the cause of a block by using the sys.dm_exec_requests system VIEW.	Chapter 14, Locks and Deadlocks
• Terminate an errant process.	Chapter 14, Locks and Deadlocks
• Configure SQL Server Profiler trace properties.	Chapter 13, SQL Server Profiler Chapter 14, Locks and Deadlocks
• Identify transaction blocks.	Chapter 14, Locks and Deadlocks
Diagnose and resolve database server errors.	Chapter 1, Troubleshooting the Installation or Operation
• Connect to a nonresponsive server by using the dedicated administrator connection (DAC).	Chapter 1, Connecting to SQL Server 2005
• Review SQL Server startup logs.	Chapter 1, Troubleshooting the Installation or Operation
• Review error messages in event logs.	Chapter 1, Troubleshooting the Installation or Operation

Monitor SQL Server Agent job history.	Chapter 13, SQL Server Agent
• Identify the cause of a failure.	Chapter 13, SQL Server Agent
• Identify outcome details.	Chapter 13, SQL Server Agent
• Find out when a job last ran.	Chapter 13, SQL Server Agent
Gather performance and optimization data by using DMVs.	Chapter 7, Index Maintenance Chapter 13, Dynamic Management VIEWs and Functions Chapter 14, Locks and Deadlocks

Creating and Implementing Database Objects

Implement a table.	Chapter 2, Tables
• Specify column details.	Chapter 2, Tables
• Specify the filegroup.	Chapter 3, Partitioning Tables Chapter 7, Filegroups
• Assign permissions to a role for tables.	Chapter 8, Security Principals, Database Securables
• Specify a partition scheme when creating a table.	Chapter 3, Partitioning Tables
• Specify a transaction.	Chapter 9, Transactions
Implement a VIEW.	Chapter 2, VIEWs
• Create an indexed VIEW.	Chapter 2, VIEWs Chapter 7, Index Design
• Create an updateable VIEW.	Chapter 2, VIEWs Chapter 6, Triggers
• Assign permissions to a role or schema for a VIEW.	Chapter 8, Security Principals, Database Securables
Implement triggers.	Chapter 6, Triggers
• Create a trigger.	Chapter 6, Triggers
• Create DDL triggers for responding to database structure changes.	Chapter 6, Triggers
• Identify recursive triggers.	Chapter 6, Triggers
• Identify nested triggers.	Chapter 6, Triggers
• Identify transaction triggers.	Chapter 6, Triggers
Implement functions.	Chapter 6, Functions
• Create a function.	Chapter 6, Functions
• Identify deterministic versus nondeterministic functions.	Chapter 6, Functions
Implement stored procedures.	Chapter 9
• Create a stored procedure.	Chapter 9, User-defined Stored Procedures
• Recompile a stored procedure.	Chapter 9, User-defined Stored Procedures
• Assign permissions to a role for a stored procedure.	Chapter 9, Security

Implement constraints.	Chapter 3, Constraints
• Specify the scope of a constraint.	Chapter 3, Constraints
• Create a new constraint.	Chapter 3, Constraints
Implement indexes.	Chapter 7, Indexes, Index Design
• Specify the filegroup.	Chapter 7, Index Design
• Specify the index type.	Chapter 7, Indexes, Index Design
• Specify relational index options.	Chapter 7, Index Design
• Specify columns.	Chapter 7, Index Design
• Specify a partition scheme when creating an index.	Chapter 7, Index Design
• Disable an index.	Chapter 7, Index Design
• Create an online index by using an ONLINE argument.	Chapter 7, Index Design, Database Engine Tuning Advisor (DTA)
Create user-defined types.	Chapter 2, Tables
• Create a Transact-SQL user-defined type.	Chapter 2, Tables
• Specify details of the data type.	Chapter 2, Tables
• Create a CLR user-defined type.	Chapter 2, Tables
Implement a full-text search.	Chapter 7, Full-text Indexes
• Create a catalog.	Chapter 7, Full-text Indexes
• Create an index.	Chapter 7, Full-text Indexes
• Specify a full-text population method.	Chapter 7, Full-text Indexes
Implement partitions.	Chapter 3, Partitioning Tables

Exam 70-441 Objective Map

Designing Database Testing and Code Management Procedures	
Design a unit test plan for a database.	Chapter 2, Creating a Database Chapter 9, User-defined Stored Procedures
• Assess which components should be unit tested.	Chapter 9, User-defined Stored Procedures
• Design tests for query performance.	Chapter 7, Index Design
• Design tests for data consistency.	Chapter 3, Constraints Chapter 9, User-defined Stored Procedures
• Design tests for application security.	Chapter 8, Designing the Security Strategy
• Design tests for system resources utilization.	Chapter 13, System Monitor
• Design tests to ensure code coverage.	Chapter 9, User-defined Stored Procedures
Create a performance baseline and benchmarking strategy for a database.	Chapter 13, System Monitor
• Establish performance objectives and capacity planning.	Chapter 13, System Monitor
• Create a strategy for measuring performance changes.	Chapter 13, System Monitor

• Create a plan for responding to performance changes.	Chapter 13, System Monitor
• Create a plan for tracking benchmark statistics over time.	Chapter 13, System Monitor
Create a plan for deploying a database.	Chapter 2, Creating a Database Chapter 15, Replication
• Select a deployment technique.	Chapter 2, Creating a Database Chapter 15, Replication
• Design scripts to deploy the database as part of application setup.	Chapter 2, Creating a Database
• Design database change scripts to apply application patches.	Chapter 2, Creating a Database
• Design scripts to upgrade database data and objects.	Chapter 4, Other DML Statements
Control changes to source code.	Chapter 8
• Set file permissions.	Chapter 8, Database Securables
• Set and retrieve version information.	Chapter 1, SQL Server Editions
• Detect differences between versions.	Chapter 1, SQL Server Editions
• Encrypt source code.	Chapter 8, Encryption
• Mark groups of objects, assign version numbers to them, and devise a method to track changes.	Chapter 3, Constraints

Designing an Application Solution for SQL Server 2005

Select and design SQL Server services to support business needs.	Chapter 11, 12, and 15
• Select the appropriate services to use to support business needs.	Chapter 11, Service Broker, Web Services and HTTP Endpoints Chapter 12, SQL Server Reporting Services (SSRS), Notification Services Chapter 15, Replication, SQL Server Integration Services (SSIS)
• Design a SQL Web services solution.	Chapter 11, Web Services and HTTP Endpoints
• Design a Notification Services solution to notify users.	Chapter 12, Notification Services
• Design a Service Broker solution for asynchronous database applications.	Chapter 11, Service Broker
• Design a Microsoft Distributed Transaction Coordinator (MS DTC) solution for distributed transactions.	Chapter 9, Transactions
• Design a Reporting Services solution.	Chapter 12, SQL Server Reporting Services (SSRS)
• Design an Integration Services solution.	Chapter 15, SQL Server Integration Services (SSIS)
• Design a SQL Server core service solution.	Chapter 1, Configuring SQL Server 2005
• Design a SQL Server Agent solution.	Chapter 13, SQL Server Agent
• Design a DatabaseMail solution.	Chapter 13, SQL Server Agent

• Specify a Reporting Services solution for distributing data.	Chapter 12, SQL Server Reporting Services (SSRS)
• Specify a Notification Services solution for distributing data.	Chapter 12, Notification Services

Designing Database Objects

Design objects that define data.	Chapter 2, 6, and 7
• Design user-defined data types.	Chapter 2, Tables
• Design tables that use advanced features.	Chapter 2, Tables Chapter 6, Triggers
• Design indexes.	Chapter 7, Index Design
• Specify indexed VIEWs to meet business requirements.	Chapter 7, Index Design
Design objects that retrieve data.	Chapter 2, 6, and 9
• Design VIEWs.	Chapter 2, VIEWs
• Design user-defined functions.	Chapter 6, Functions
• Design stored procedures.	Chapter 9, User-defined Stored Procedures
Design objects that extend the functionality of a server.	Chapter 6 and 9
• Design scalar user-defined functions to extend the functionality of the server.	Chapter 6, Functions Chapter 9, User-defined Stored Procedures
• Design CLR user-defined aggregates.	Chapter 6, CLR Integration
• Design stored procedures to extend the functionality of the server.	Chapter 9, User-defined Stored Procedures
Design objects that perform actions.	Chapter 6 and 11
• Design DML triggers.	Chapter 6, Triggers
• Design DDL triggers.	Chapter 6, DDL Triggers
• Design WMI triggers.	Chapter 6, Triggers
• Design Service Broker applications.	Chapter 11, Service Broker
• Design stored procedures to perform actions.	Chapter 9, User-defined Stored Procedures

Designing a Database

Design attributes.	Chapter 2 and 3
• Decide whether to persist an attribute.	Chapter 2, Computed Columns
• Specify domain integrity by creating attribute constraints.	Chapter 3, Constraints
• Choose appropriate column data types and sizes.	Chapter 2, Tables
Design entities.	Chapter 3, Data Integrity
• Define entities.	Chapter 3, Data Integrity
• Define entity integrity.	Chapter 3, Normalization and Normal Forms
• Normalize tables to reduce data redundancy.	Chapter 3, Normalization and Normal Forms
• Establish the appropriate level of denormalization.	Chapter 3, Normalization and Normal Forms

Exam 70-442 Objective Map

Designing Efficient Access to a SQL Server Service	
Design appropriate data access technologies.	Chapter 11, Data Access Methods
Design an appropriate data access object model.	Chapter 11, Data Access Methods
Design a cursor strategy for a data access component.	Chapter 14, Cursors
• Decide when to use cursors.	Chapter 14, Cursors
• Decide how to maximize cursor performance.	Chapter 14, Cursors
• Detect which applications are using cursors and evaluate whether to remove them.	Chapter 14, Cursors
Design caching strategies.	Chapter 11, Data Access Methods
• Select ADO.NET caching.	Chapter 11, Data Access Methods
• Design custom caching functionality.	Chapter 11, Data Access Methods
• Design a refresh strategy for cached data.	Chapter 11, Data Access Methods
Design client libraries to write applications that administer a SQL Server service.	Chapter 11, 12, 13, and 15
• Design server management objects (SMOs) applications.	Chapter 12, SQL Server Reporting Services (SSRS)
• Design replication management objects (RMOs) applications.	Chapter 15, Replication
• Design automation management objects (AMOs) applications.	Chapter 13, SQL Server Agent
• Design SQL Server Networking Interface (SNI) for asynchronous queries.	Chapter 11, Data Access Methods
Design queries that use multiple active result sets (MARS).	Chapter 11
• Decide when MARS queries are appropriate.	Chapter 11, Data Access Methods
• Choose an appropriate transaction isolation level when you use MARS.	Chapter 11, Data Access Methods
• Choose when to use Asynchronous queries.	Chapter 11, Data Access Methods
Designing a Database Query Strategy	
Write and modify queries.	Chapter 4
• Write queries.	Chapter 4, Select
• Modify queries to improve query performance.	Chapter 4, Select
Design queries for retrieving data from XML sources.	Chapter 5
• Select the correct attributes.	Chapter 5, Retrieving XML Data
• Select the correct nodes.	Chapter 5, Retrieving XML Data
• Filter by values of attributes and values of elements.	Chapter 5, Retrieving XML Data

- Include relational data, such as columns and variables, in the result of an XQuery expression. — Chapter 5, Retrieving XML Data
- Include XML attribute or node values in a tabular result set. — Chapter 5, Retrieving XML Data
- Update, insert, or delete relational data based on XML parameters to stored procedures. — Chapter 5, Retrieving XML Data
- Debug and troubleshoot queries against XML data sources. — Chapter 5, Retrieving XML Data

Design a cursor strategy.	Chapter 14
• Design cursor logic.	Chapter 14, Cursors
• Design cursors that work together with dynamic SQL execution.	Chapter 14, Cursors
• Select an appropriate cursor type.	Chapter 14, Cursors
• Design cursors that efficiently use server memory.	Chapter 14, Cursors
• Design cursors that minimize blocking.	Chapter 14, Cursors
• Design a strategy that minimizes or eliminates the use of cursors.	Chapter 14, Cursors

Designing Error-Handling Routines

Design code that validates input data and permissions.	Chapter 9, User-defined Stored Procedures, Security
Design code that detects and reacts to errors.	Chapter 9, Transactions
Design user-defined messages to communicate application events.	Chapter 9, Transactions

Designing a Transaction Strategy

Manage concurrency by selecting the appropriate transaction isolation levels.	Chapter 14, Transaction Isolation Levels
Design the locking granularity level.	Chapter 14, Transaction Isolation Levels
Design transaction scopes.	Chapter 14, Transaction Isolation Levels
Design code that uses transactions.	Chapter 14, Transaction Isolation Levels

Performance Tuning a Database and a Database Application

Optimize and tune queries for performance.	Chapter 7
• Evaluate query performance.	Chapter 7, Index Design
• Analyze query plans.	
• Modify queries to improve performance.	
• Test queries for improved performance.	
• Detect locking problems.	Chapter 14, Locks and Deadlocks
• Modify queries to optimize client and server performance.	Chapter 4, SELECT

• Rewrite subqueries to joins.	Chapter 4, SELECT
• Design queries that have search arguments (SARGs).	Chapter 4, SELECT
• Convert single-row statements into set-based queries.	Chapter 14, Cursors
Optimize indexing strategies.	Chapter 7
• Design an index strategy.	Chapter 7, Index Design
• Analyze index use across an application.	Chapter 7, Index Design, Statistics, Database Engine Tuning Advisor (DTA)
• Add, remove, or redesign indexes.	Chapter 7, Index Design, Database Engine Tuning Advisor (DTA)
• Optimize index-to-table-size ratio.	Chapter 7, Index Design
Scale database applications.	Chapter 3, 11, and 14
• Specify a data-partitioning model.	Chapter 3, Partitioning Tables
• Design queries that target multiple servers.	Chapter 11, Linked Servers
• Implement scale-out techniques like federated database, Service Broker, and distributed partitioned VIEWs.	Chapter 3, Partitioning Tables
• Design applications to distribute data and workloads transparently.	Chapter 11, Linked Servers Chapter 15, Replication
• Identify code or processes that can be moved to a different tier to improve performance.	Chapter 11, Data Access Methods
• Rewrite algorithms to improve efficiency.	Chapter 14, Cursors
Resolve performance problems.	Chapter 3, 13, and 14
• Analyze application performance across multiple users.	Chapter 13, System Monitor, SQL Server Profiler
• Capture workload information.	Chapter 13, SQL Server Profiler, SQL Trace
• Find out the causes of performance problems.	Chapter 13, System Monitor, SQL Server Profiler, SQL Trace
• Specify resolutions such as changing algorithms, scaling up and scaling out, and terminating a session.	Chapter 3, Partitioning Tables Chapter 13, System Monitor Chapter 14, Locks and Deadlocks
Optimize data storage.	Chapter 2 and 3
• Choose column data types to reduce storage requirements across the enterprise.	Chapter 2, Tables
• Design the appropriate use of varchar across the enterprise.	Chapter 2, Tables
• Denormalize entities to minimize page reads per query.	Chapter 3, Normalization and Normal Forms
• Optimize table width.	Chapter 2, Tables

Installing and Configuring SQL Server 2005

In this chapter, you will learn about:

- SQL Server editions
- Instances of SQL Server
- Installing SQL Server 2005
- Configuring SQL Server 2005
- Using configuration tools like the SQL Server Surface Area Configuration tool and SQL Server Configuration Manager
- Connecting to SQL Server via SSMS, SQLCmd, and dedicated administrator connections
- Examining the Installation
- Troubleshooting the installation
- Books Online

> *Whatever you do, or dream you can, begin it. Boldness has genius, magic, and power in it. Begin it now.*
>
> —*Goethe*

SQL Server 2005 is a powerful Relational Database Management System (RDMS) that is enjoying widespread use and growing market share. Learning SQL Server 2005 and becoming certified on it will open many more doors of opportunity for database administrators, or those seeking to become database administrators. This book will help you do both—learn it and become certified.

In this chapter, we'll start by installing and configuring SQL Server 2005. While I'll cover the various editions and operating systems, I fully expect most readers will install the SQL Server 2005 Evaluation edition on their desktop (Windows XP or Vista operating system) and learn it from there. To help you get started, I've included exercises on installing the evaluation edition on both platforms.

While some of you will have SQL Server on production servers, a production server is no place to play. If the production server installation blows up while you're experimenting and learning, it may become an opportunity to test the quality of your resume.

However, if your SQL Server installation blows up on your desktop, consider it an opportunity to repeat the installation—no big deal.

Let's be bold and get started.

SQL Server Editions

If tasked with purchasing SQL Server 2005, you'll need to ensure you are comfortable with the different versions, or editions, of SQL Server 2005. Each edition has unique capabilities and is designed to run in a specific environment as outlined in Table 1-1.

Edition	Comments
Enterprise	Designed to scale to the largest On-Line Transaction Processing (OLTP) database needs. Enterprise edition supports features such as database mirroring, database snapshots, and eight nodes in a failover cluster that are not supported by the Standard edition of SQL Server 2005.
Developer	Fully functional Enterprise version, but licensed for use as a development or test version, not as a production server.
Standard	Scaled-down version of SQL Server. Intended for small- to medium-sized organizations. Supports failover clustering of two nodes.
Workgroup	Designed for small organizations as an entry-level database.
Evaluation	A 180-day evaluation edition of Enterprise edition. If you don't have a copy of SQL Server 2005, you can use this to learn and evaluate it.
SQL Server Express	Free version that is integrated with Visual Studio 2005. Can be managed with SQL Server Management Studio Express.
SQL Server Compact	Previously called SQL Server 2005 Everywhere. Designed for mobile applications.

Table 1-1   SQL Server Editions

EXAM TIP   MCITP tests are primarily focused on Enterprise and Standard editions. While you need to be aware of all the editions for on-the-job requirements, for the test just focus on the key features of these two editions.

Table 1-2 compares many of the key features of SQL Server 2005 Standard and Enterprise editions.

I'd like to stress a couple of things about Table 1-2. First, while SQL Server 2005 Standard Edition supports clustering, it only supports two nodes. Second, "operating-system limit" means that whatever the operating system supports, this edition of SQL will support. If the operating system can support 8GB of RAM, these editions of SQL can support 8GB of RAM. Of course, this means we also need to understand the operating system features, capabilities, and limits.

Feature	SQL Server 2005 Standard Edition	SQL Server 2005 Enterprise Edition
Clustering	Two nodes	Eight nodes
Database Snapshots	No	Yes
Database Mirroring	Safety Full Only	Yes
Multi-Instances	50	50
Memory Enhancements	Few	Many
Max memory	Operating-system limit	Operating-system limit
Symmetric Multiprocessing (SMP)	Four CPUs	Operating-system limit

Table 1-2 SQL Server 2005 Feature Comparison

NOTE While SQL Server Books Online indicates that SQL Server 2005 is limited to only 16 instances, this was changed in July 2006. An MSDN (Microsoft Developer Network) article entitled "Maximum Capacity Specifications for SQL Server 2005" clarifies that 50 instances are now supported on all editions except Workgroup edition.

Operating Systems and Supported Benefits

SQL Server 2005 can be installed on many different Windows operating systems such as Windows 2000, Windows XP, Windows Vista, and Windows Server 2003, but chances are that your production SQL Server will be installed on a Windows Server. It is important to understand the features and limitations offered by the different editions of Windows Servers.

The Windows Server 2003 edition you choose depends on the capabilities that you need. Table 1-3 compares some of the capabilities of the different Windows Server 2003 editions.

Feature	Server 2003 Standard	Server 2003 Enterprise	Server 2003 Datacenter
Memory	4GB	64GB	128GB
Clustering	No	Eight nodes	Eight nodes
SMP	Four CPUs	Eight CPUs	32 CPUs

Table 1-3 Windows Server 2003 Feature Comparison

Let's look at an example of combining SQL Server 2005 features with the Windows Server 2005 editions features. If you install SQL Server 2005 Enterprise edition on Windows Server 2003 Standard, you'll be limited to 4GB of RAM because although SQL Server can handle more memory than 4GB, the Standard edition of Windows Server 2003 is limited to 4GB.

For learning purposes, you can install the Evaluation edition of SQL Server on your desktop operating system—Windows XP or Windows Vista.

 CAUTION If you're installing SQL Server 2005 on Windows Vista, you'll need to apply the SQL Server 2005 Service Pack 2 (SP2) after the installation for it to work properly. We'll do this in Exercise 1.2 later in this chapter.

Instances

SQL Server 2005 can handle hundreds of databases on a single server in a single installation. However sometimes it's necessary to create some separation between databases. Instead of installing SQL Server 2005 on a completely different server, we can install a separate *instance* of SQL Server on the same machine.

A separate instance of SQL Server is similar to a separate instance of any program you might launch. Say you open two documents in Word—one is a project document and the other is your résumé. You will have two separate instances of Word running. When you modify your résumé, it doesn't affect the project document.

Separate instances of SQL Server work the same way. By installing a separate instance, you can create databases in the different instances that are completely discrete from each other. This provides security separation such as creating logins in one instance without granting access to the other instance. Each instance is launched by its own SQL Server service that can be configured and manipulated without affecting the other. Additionally, separate instances can have many independent settings such as enabled services, settings for collations, and more.

The first instance installed on SQL Server 2005 is typically the *default instance*. Other instances are referred to as *named instances*. In Figure 1-1, you can see the default instance at the top with the name of the server: MCITPSUCCESS. The Named Instance is highlighted below it, intuitively named MCITPSUCCESS\MYNAMEDINSTANCE. You can label your named instance anything you like. Notice how each instance has a full set of folders (Databases, Security, Server Objects, and so on) that can be manipulated for that instance.

Figure 1-1

Multiple instances in SQL Server Management Studio

Identifying SQL Server 2005 Versions

On the job, you often need to be able to identify what version of SQL Server you're running and what service pack is installed. This information is readily available within SSMS, though it is somewhat coded.

Take a look again at Figure 1-1. Notice that the first line has the name of the server followed by some numbers—for instance, (SQL Server 9.0.3050).

The *9.0* refers to SQL Server 2005. SQL Server 7.0 was 7.0, SQL Server 2000 was 8.0, and SQL Server 2005 is 9.0.

The four-digit number after the version number refers to the release: A *1399* was the Release To Manufacturing (RTM) release; *2047* was SQL Server 2005 Service Pack 1. When SP2 was first released, it had a release number of *3042* (as in *9.00.3042.0*). Shortly thereafter came a critical update to SP2 with a release number of 3050. Notice that the numbers increase in value with each release. Because the release number shown in the figure (3050) is higher than Service Pack 2 (3042), I know that we have at least Service Pack 2 installed.

Look up Knowledge Base (KB) article 321185 on the Web for more information (search for "KB 321185" with your favorite search engine).

Security Impact

One of the primary reasons to create separate instances is for security factors.

As an example, let's consider two departments, the HR department and the R&D department. Both departments currently manage their own server with their own DBA (database administrator) groups. Each DBA group has full access to the server, can add logins, and manage all the server settings but cannot administer the server in the other department.

You're tasked with consolidating both departments onto the same server. If both were consolidated onto the same instance and each group still needed to be able to set instance level settings, then you'd be forced to grant the HR DBA group and the R&D DBA group full access to the server. You no longer have a separation of administration privileges between the two departments. Personnel information (such as salary data or Privacy Act data) would be available to DBAs in the R&D department, while proprietary research data would be available to DBAs in the HR department. More importantly, a server administrator can change settings that affect both departments now.

Instead, you could create two separate instances on one physical server—one as a default instance for the HR department and another as a named instance for the R&D department. You can then grant the HR DBAs full access to their instance, but they wouldn't have access to the R&D instance. Likewise, you'd provide full access for the R&D department DBAs to their instance, but they wouldn't have access to any of the HR databases in the HR instance.

In short, separate instances enable you to provide a separation of privileges and access.

Consolidating

You may be tasked with consolidating databases onto as few servers or as few instances as possible. Since SQL Server 2005 can run multiple databases at the same time, this is certainly possible.

When consolidating databases, you have two primary decision points: hardware and security. First, you must determine if the hardware can handle the load. Next, you determine whether the consolidation will violate any security practices you want to implement.

Hardware   Imagine having two identical servers, each hosting a single database. Both servers are averaging a Processor: % Processor Time of 10 percent. Putting both databases on one server causes the Processor: % Processor Time to increase to 20 percent. This is certainly acceptable.

Of course, we'd need to look at more than just the CPU when identifying performance issues. In any server, we have to look at the core four resources —memory, CPU, disk, and network. These would be the primary server resources we'd examine to determine if we could consolidate both databases onto a single server and if the server could handle the workload.

Security   Assuming we can consolidate the databases onto a single server from a hardware perspective, now we need to determine if we should put all databases onto a single instance, or create multiple instances. If we need to provide a separation between any databases, we would create a separate instance.

While an instance is not literally a separate server, it is easier to look at it this way. If you have one group of DBAs managing the first server and a different group of DBAs managing the second server, and you need to maintain this separation after the consolidation, you'd create different instances. If it's the same group of DBAs managing both servers, you can consolidate both servers onto a single instance and use database permissions to control which users can access which databases.

Additionally, you can have a lead group of database administrators that can access both instances. They would simply be added to the appropriate role to give them the permissions they need.

Installing SQL Server 2005

If you're going to learn SQL Server 2005, you need to install it. In this section, I talk about some basics and then guide you through the process of installing it on your system.

Microsoft provides two paths to test an evaluation copy of SQL Server 2005. You can download a 180-day evaluation version and install SQL Server 2005 from this download, or you can download a Virtual PC image that includes it already installed. Since the 70-431 test expects you to know how to install SQL, we're going to cover this method.

Prerequisites

You need to make sure your system supports SQL Server 2005 before attempting an installation. This includes both hardware and software prerequisites.

Hardware prerequisites state you need a Pentium III–compatible or faster CPU, 512MB or RAM or more, and about 800MB of disk space. SQL requires a minimum of 512MB for both Standard and Enterprise editions, but as they say, "don't try this at home." You're likely to see a very slow system. At least 1GB of RAM is recommended.

Software prerequisites are largely met by the operating system you are running. Windows 2000 (Server and Professional) requires Service Pack 4 or later. Windows XP requires Service Pack 2 or later. Windows 2003 requires Service Pack 1 or later. If you want to install Reporting Services, you'll need to install IIS and ASP.NET 2.0. We'll hold off installing IIS until we cover Reporting Services in Chapter 12. ASP.NET will be installed as part of IIS.

When installing SQL Server 2005, the setup program will check for several software components that are required by SQL Server. If they're not installed, it will install them. This includes Microsoft Windows .NET Framework 2.0, SQL Server Native Client, and SQL Server Setup support files.

Also, different operating systems have different service pack (SP) requirements. Since SQL Server 2005 was released after some current operating systems, service pack upgrades were issued so they would work optimally with SQL Server. Make sure you have the most recent service pack upgrade on your operating system and you'll be safe.

Windows Vista was released after SQL Server 2005. For SQL to run on Vista, you'll need to apply SQL Server's SP2 after the installation of SQL.

 CAUTION The scripting development environment and runtime engine that the Script task and Script component in SQL Server Integration Services (SSIS) use is incompatible with Windows Vista. If you are running Windows Vista, you won't be able to edit or debug scripts in SSIS packages that contain scripts. This may be changed in service packs beyond Service Pack 2.

When you start the installation, the prerequisites of your system are checked. If you don't meet them, you'll get an error saying you need to upgrade your system in order to do so. Thankfully, these errors usually are fairly easy to correct.

Downloading

If you don't have a copy of SQL Server 2005, you can download a free 180-day Evaluation edition. While this is documented in some places as a 120-day version, it's actually a 180-day version—Microsoft has given us a couple of extra months.

At this time, the link for the free download is www.microsoft.com/sql/downloads/trial-software.mspx, but it's subject to change at anytime. If you don't see SQL Server 2005 there now, use your favorite search engine and search on "download SQL Server 2005 Evaluation." Click the Microsoft link and follow the instructions. This will allow you to download the appropriate files. You can download a single executable file or an ISO image. Both are rather large at about 900MB to 1GB.

If you don't have a broadband link, Microsoft offers an option of mailing you the DVD for a nominal shipping and handling charge. If you're online with a 56K connection, it's probably worth your money to pay the few dollars for a DVD.

If you download the single executable file, you can double-click it and it will self-extract into the C:\SQLEval directory. You can then burn the contents to a DVD or launch it from here by double-clicking the Splash.hta file in the Servers directory.

Or, if you downloaded the ISO image, burn it to a DVD.

While you're downloading, you can also download the current service packs for SQL Server 2005. Just as with any product, it's best to run the most recent service pack. At this time, the link for SQL Server 2005 service packs is http://technet.microsoft.com/en-us/sqlserver/bb331754.aspx, but if this link has moved, a quick Internet search on "SQL Server 2005 SP download" should get you to the most recent service packs.

In this exercise, we'll install the SQL Server 2005 180-day Evaluation edition on Vista. In the next exercise, we'll go through the process on Windows XP Professional.

NOTE   Before beginning this exercise, you need to have downloaded the SQL Server 2005 evaluation edition and at least SQL Server 2005 Service Pack 2.

Exercise 1.1: Install SQL Server 2005
(on Windows XP or Windows Vista)

See how to install a separate instance of SQL Server in video 1-1.

NOTE   When installing SQL Server 2005 on Windows Vista, some minor differences will be apparent. These appear in the exercise as "Windows Vista only." If installing on Windows XP, simply ignore these extra steps.

1. Insert the DVD into your DVD drive. With autorun enabled, the SQL Server 2005 startup program will launch automatically. If autorun doesn't work, you can browse to the Servers folder on the DVD and double-click Splash.hta. You should see a display similar to Figure 1-2.

Figure 1-2
SQL Server 2005
installation splash
screen

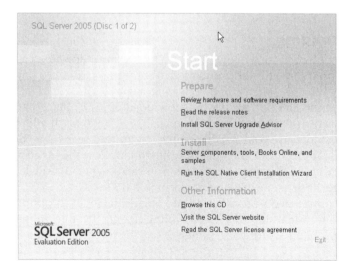

2. Under the Install section, click the entry marked Server Components, Tools, Books Online, And Samples.

   a. Windows Vista only: If the User Account Control dialog box appears, click Continue.

   b. Windows Vista only: The Program Compatibility Assistant dialog box pops up to let you know that SQL Server 2005 Service Pack 2 must be installed after SQL Server 2005 is installed. We will do this in this exercise. Click Run Program.

3. On the End User License Agreement page, if you agree, check the I Accept The Licensing Terms And Conditions box. Click Next.

4. On the Installing Prerequisites page, SQL Server will check your system for the necessary prerequisites. If any components are missing, the SQL Server Component Update will launch and install any necessary components. If necessary, click Install to begin the process. Once installation is completed, the Installing Prerequisites page will indicate success as shown in Figure 1-3. Click Next.

Figure 1-3
Prerequisites installed successfully

a. Windows Vista only: The Program Compatibility Assistant dialog box pops up again to let you know that Service Pack 2 must be installed after SQL Server 2005 is installed. Click Run Program.

5. On the System Configuration Check page, the installation program will scan your computer's configuration and determine if any components are missing or required for certain features. (This sometimes occurs very quickly, and you may miss seeing it.) Once scanning is completed, the program will launch the Welcome to the Microsoft SQL Server Installation Wizard page. Click Next to continue.

6. The System Configuration Check page (Figure 1-4 from a Windows Vista install) will list any issues you need to address. *Errors* must be resolved to continue with the installation. *Warnings* are informative. For example, you will likely see a warning that to support Reporting Services, you need to install IIS. Since we won't use Reporting Services until Chapter 12, we won't install IIS now. If desired, you can view the report, save the report to a file, copy the report, or even send it via e-mail. All of these options are available via the Report button. Click Next.

Figure 1-4
System
Configuration
Check showing
one warning and
zero errors

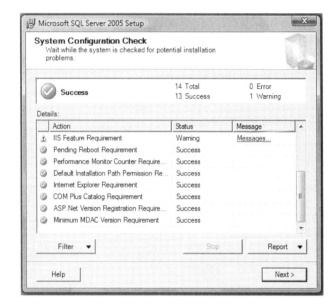

7. After a moment, the Microsoft SQL Server Installation wizard will launch.

8. On the Registration Information page, enter information in the Name and Company text boxes. Click Next.

9. On the Components To Install page, select SQL Server Database Services, Notification Services, Integration Services, and the box marked Workstation Components, Books Online And Development Tools, as shown in Figure 1-5. Click Advanced.

10. On the Feature Selection page, add the AdventureWorks Sample OLTP database, as shown in Figure 1-6. Click the + next to the Documentation, Samples, And Sample Databases tag. Click the + next to Sample Databases. Select the Will Be Installed On Local Hard Drive box for the AdventureWorks Sample OLTP database. Select the Sample Code and Applications and check the box marked Will Be Installed On Local Hard Drive. Click Next.

Figure 1-5

The Components to Install page

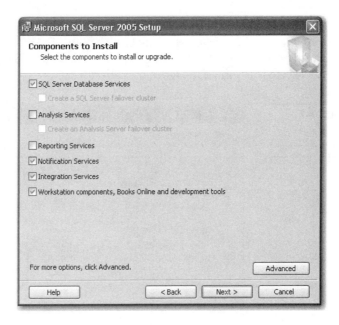

Figure 1-6

Selecting the AdventureWorks sample database

11. On the Instance Name page, leave Default Instance selected. Click Next.

12. On the Service Account page, select the Use The Built-In System Account box, and select Local System. Under Start Services At The End Of Setup, ensure SQL Server is selected, as shown in Figure 1-7. Select Next.

Figure 1-7

Selecting the
Service Account

EXAM TIP For a production server within a domain, you will typically use a domain user account, as Microsoft recommends. It will allow the service to access domain resources based on the permissions of the domain user account. For a development or training system, the built-in System account will suffice.

13. On the authentication mode page, ensure Windows authentication mode is selected, and click Next.

14. On the Collation Settings page, under SQL Collations, accept the default of Dictionary Order, Case-Insensitive, For Use With 1252 Character Set, as shown in Figure 1-8, and then click Next.

EXAM TIP The Collation setting defines the sorting behavior of the server. The setting on this page applies to the entire instance. However, we can change the collation on individual databases, tables, and columns. We can even set the collations used within a query.

15. On the Error And Usage Report Settings page, click Next.

Figure 1-8
Selecting the
Collation Settings

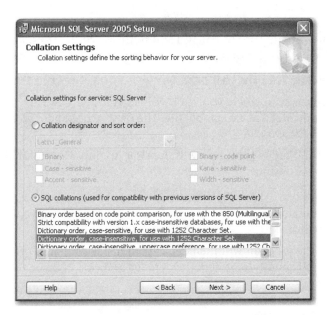

16. On the Ready To Install page, click Install. Be patient. This will take a while. Once complete, the Setup Progress page should look like Figure 1-9.

Figure 1-9
Setup Progress
successfully
completed

17. On the Setup Progress page, click Next.

18. On the Completing Microsoft SQL Server 2005 Setup page, read the summary notes and click Finish.

In the following exercise, we'll install a service pack to bring SQL Server 2005 up-to-date with all current patches and hotfixes. While this exercise uses SQL Server 2005 Service Pack 2, it should work the same with any service pack.

Exercise 1.2: Install SQL Server 2005 Service Pack

1. Browse to where you've downloaded the Service Pack and double-click the downloaded executable file. The file I've used here is SQLServer2005SP2-KB21896-x86-ENU.exe.

   a. Windows Vista only: If the User Account Control dialog box appears, click Continue.

2. On the Welcome page, click Next.

3. On the License Terms page, if you agree, check I Accept The Agreement. Click Next.

4. The program will then detect your installation and present a dialog box similar to Figure 1-10. Accept the defaults and click Next.

Figure 1-10

Feature Selection

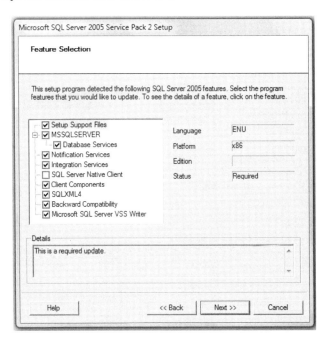

5. On the Authentication page, accept the default of Windows Authentication, and click Next.

6. On the Error and Usage Reporting Settings, deselect both check boxes, and click Next.

7. On the Running Processes page, give the SP upgrade time to detect what is running on your system. While you can click Next before it finishes, wait until the message appears saying Locked Files Found. This will likely show that MSSQLSERVER and MsDtsServer are running for the Database Services and Integration Services. You can either stop them via the Services applet, or reboot after the service pack is installed. We'll stop the MSSQL Service to prevent issues during the service pack install.

   a. On Windows XP: Select Control Panel | Administrative Tools | Services to launch the Services applet. Scroll down to the SQL Server (MSSQLServer) service. Right-click the service and select Stop. Scroll down to the SQL Server Integration Services service. Right-click the service and select Stop.

   b. On Windows Vista: Select Control Panel | System and Maintenance | Administrative Tools. Right-click Services and select Run As Administrator. On the User Account Control dialog box, click Continue. Scroll down to the SQL Server (MSSQLServer) service. Right-click the service and select Stop. Scroll down to the SQL Server Integration Services service. Right-click the service and select Stop.

8. On the Running Processes page, click Next.

9. On the Ready To Install page, click Install.

10. The Installation Progress page will progressively go through each product and install the upgrade. When a product is complete, a check box will be added to the Product. If the Computer Reboot Required screen appears, click OK. When all products are complete and the message Service Pack Completed appears, click Next.

11. On the Installation Complete page, click Next. Click Finish.

12. Windows Vista only: On the Additional Information page, review the information and ensure the check box marked Launch The User Provisioning Tool For Windows Vista After SP2 Installation Completes is checked. Click Finish.

NOTE   On most operating systems, members of the local administrators group are automatically mapped to the SQL sysadmin role granting them full access. This is not true for Windows Vista. The SQL Server 2005 User Provisioning Tool for Vista can be used to map users to the sysadmin role.

   a. On the SQL Server 2005 User Provisioning Tool for Vista, select your user account listed under Available privileges. Click the right arrow (>) to move this to the other pane: Privileges That Will Be Granted To... this account. On my test system named *Darril-PC*, I logged in under the account of *Darril* so the account is listed as Darril-PC\Darril, as shown in Figure 1-11. Click OK.

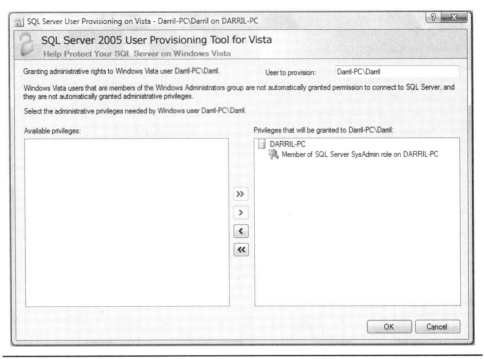

Figure 1-11   The SQL Server 2005 User Provisioning Tool for Vista

   TIP   To launch the SQL Server 2005 Provisioning Tool for Vista apart from the service pack, launch the Microsoft SQL Server 2005 Surface Area tool (Start | All Programs | Microsoft SQL Server 2005 | Configuration Tools | SQL Server 2005 Surface Area Configuration), and then click Add New Administrator.

Upgrading

It's also possible to upgrade to SQL Server 2005 from previous versions of SQL Server. You can upgrade from SQL Server 7.0 or SQL Server 2000 to SQL Server 2005.

As with operating systems, make sure you apply the most recent service pack upgrade to any SQL Server edition prior to the upgrade. Some features are no longer supported (such as those deprecated in SQL Server 2000), other features were deprecated in SQL Server 2005 (supported for backward compatibility, but not recommended for use), and other features have been replaced completely, such as Data Transformation Services (DTS), which was replaced by SQL Server Integration Services (SSIS).

Configuring SQL Server 2005

Microsoft SQL Server 2005 was developed with security in mind from the ground up. This is in line with Microsoft's mantra of $SD^3 + C$ (Secure by Design, Secure by Default, and Secure in Deployment and Communications).

This brings two important concepts out: (1) You don't have to worry about unneeded services being enabled by default; and (2) any needed services beyond the basics will need to be enabled. This allows SQL Server to run well after the initial installation.

For a small organization that is installing SQL Server for the first time, this is a godsend. Installing SQL and getting it up and running is relatively easy. For larger organizations, SQL Server 2005 provides a lot of depth where additional features can be enabled, or the configuration can be manipulated to get better performance for different applications.

In this section, we'll cover a few key configuration settings you should know as a SQL Server administrator.

Service Accounts

When you or I log on to a computer, we can launch an application and that application runs under the context of our user account. The rights and permissions available to that application can't exceed the rights and permissions we have as a logged-on user. Similarly, many services start before anyone logs on to the system. Each service starts under the context of a service account and the rights and permissions of the service are limited to the service account used to start the service.

The different service accounts available to start services are as follows:

- **Local System**   This specifies the local system account and does not require a password to connect to SQL Server on the local computer. Interaction with other servers is restricted.

- **Network Service**   This is a special built-in account that provides the same level of access to resources and objects as members of the Users group. Network resources are accessed using the credentials of the computer account. This is NOT recommended as the service account for SQL Server.

- **Local Service**   This is a special built-in account that provides the same level of access to resources and objects as members of the Users group. Network resources are accessed as a null session with no credentials.

- **Local User Account**   This is an account created on the local computer.

- **Domain User Account**   This is an account created in Active Directory in the Domain. Domain accounts can be granted specific rights and permissions as needed within the domain. For a production server, this is the recommended account used within a domain to start the SQL Server service and the SQL Server Agent service.

SQL Server runs with several different Windows services. For example, the SQL Server service is the database engine and must be running for users to both connect to and access databases. The SQL Server Agent service is used to manage jobs, run maintenance tasks, and more. Just as with any Windows service, each of the SQL Server services can start when the computer starts. The services do not need a user to log on and launch a program. Instead, a service can be configured to start automatically.

For this to be successful, the service starts under the context of a service account. The same way you can log on with a regular account and have certain privileges, or log on with an administrator account and have different privileges, the account you use with the service account will determine the privileges that each of the SQL Server services has when it starts. Of course, this begs the question: What account should you use for the service?

 EXAM TIP For the exam, it's expected that you're working in an enterprise- or a medium-sized organization within a domain. When configuring the service accounts in a domain, Microsoft recommends using a domain account so that access to network resources can be granted to the SQL services.

Microsoft recommends using the same domain account for the main SQL Server service and the SQL Server Agent service when using SQL Server in a domain environment. If network resources are not needed in a domain, a local user account can be used. Configuring a domain account will allow SQL Server to interact with other network services (such as when sending e-mail, replicating with other SQL Servers, or even interacting with a linked server) and perform many server-to-server activities.

If you were in a workgroup (instead of a domain), you could use the Local Service account as we did in the installation exercise. This is a special built-in account that allows the service to start and run. In general, it would *not* be used to access network resources; however, network resources that don't check credentials could be accessed.

Microsoft specifically recommends you do *not* use the Network Service for the SQL Server service and SQL Server Agent service. Instead, Microsoft recommends using a domain user account with minimal rights for the SQL Server service. This account does not need administrator account privileges.

Beware, however. Even though this domain account functions as a service account, it's a regular user account and is subject to all the same restrictions of a user account. If you work in a domain environment, you probably change your password regularly, and not because you come to work one day and say, "I think I'll change my password today." Instead, Group Policy settings force you to change your password after so many days. Common Group Policy settings force a password change after 45 or 90 days, but the domain administrator can change this to whatever she deems appropriate. Under such settings, a warning will inevitably pop up saying you need to change your password. You're usually given a few days to do so. If you don't, you get locked out and can't log in again until you change your password.

That works fine for you and me, but what about the domain account used to start your SQL services? The service doesn't know how to change the account's password. When the warning comes, it's ignored. So if you don't change the password for the service account, the account will be locked out and the services will no longer start.

Here's the scenario. You install and configure SQL Server and everything is working fine. About six weeks later, everything stops and you get a phone call. "SQL's broke" they say.

So what's the solution? When configuring domain accounts as service accounts, administrators have two primary choices to manage the password change issue: (1) Set the account properties so the password never expires. You should still change the password regularly, but account lockouts will be prevented. (2) Create a process where you regularly change the passwords of system accounts prior to expiration of the passwords. With either of these solutions, it's important to realize that the password must be changed in both Active Directory and in the Services applet so the passwords match.

One last comment on service accounts. The principle of least privilege needs to be applied. What's that mean? Give only the access needed. In the past, we often had to add service accounts to the local administrators group in order for general features to work. This is not the case today. Except for unique situations, it is not recommended to add the SQL Server service account to the local administrators group.

Services

Several different services are associated with SQL Server 2005, and you need to know what most of them are and what they do. Table 1-4 shows several key services and some of the associated features they power.

Service	Comments
SQL Server	Provides storage, processing and controlled access of data, and rapid transaction processing. Needed for SQL Server.
SQL Server Agent	Executes jobs, monitors SQL Server, fires alerts, and allows automation of some administrative tasks.
SQL Server Analysis Services	Supplies online analytical processing (OLAP) and data mining functionality for business intelligence applications. (MCITP focuses on OLTP.)
SQL Server Reporting Services	Manages, executes, renders, schedules, and delivers reports. This needs IIS as a supporting service.
SQL Server Integration Services	Provides management support for SQL Server 2005 Integration Services (SSIS) package storage and execution. Needed to create and run SSIS packages.
SQL Server Browser	Provides SQL Server connection information to client computers. Listens for incoming requests. Needed for a remote dedicated administrator connection (DAC).
SQL Server VSS Writer	Provides the interface to back up / restore Microsoft SQL server through the Windows VSS infrastructure. Used for backups with Volume Shadow Copy Service.

Table 1-4 SQL Server Services

EXAM TIP Make sure you're aware of the different services and their related features. For example, while the SQL Server Browser service does a lot more, administrators should know this is required for a remote dedicated administrator connection.

You can view these services the traditional way via the Services console. The following exercise can be used to configure a service in the Services console.

In this exercise, we'll configure the SQL Server Agent service to start automatically. The SQL Server Agent service is used to run maintenance jobs, respond to events by raising alerts, and notify users by using operators.

Exercise 1.3: Configure a Service via the Services Console

1. Launch the Services applet by choosing Start | Control Panel | Administrative Tools | Services.

   a. On Windows Vista: Select Control Panel | System and Maintenance | Administrative Tools. Right-click Services and select Run As Administrator. In the User Account Control dialog box, click Continue.

2. Scroll down to the SQL Server Agent service. You should see something similar to Figure 1-12.

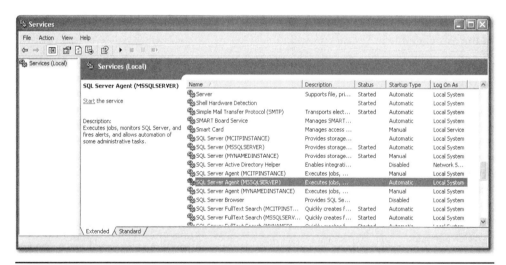

Figure 1-12   Services applet

You may notice that the figure shows three SQL Server Agent services, but you probably only have one SQL Server Agent service. That's because on my system, three separate instances of SQL Server are running: the default instance (MSSQLSERVER), an instance named MYNAMEDINSTANCE, and an instance named MCITPINSTANCE. This helps illustrate that separate instances have separate configurable services.

3. Double-click the SQL Server Agent service to open up the properties page for the service. On the General tab, change the Startup Type from Manual to Automatic.

4. Start the service by clicking Start. The properties page of the SQL Server Agent service should now look like Figure 1-13.

Figure 1-13
SQL Server Agent started and configured to start automatically

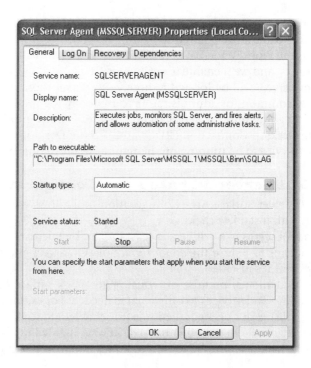

5. Select the Log On tab. If this is your desktop system where you followed Exercise 1.1, you'll notice the service is currently set to log on to the system by using the Local System account.

EXAM TIP While setting the service to use the Local System account will work for a development and learning system, it would typically be set to a domain account on a production server. For example, you could create a user account named SQLService in a domain named MCITP. You would then select This Account, enter **MCITP\SQLService**, and enter the password for the account. Of course, you could use any name for the user account, but naming the account SQLService is a little more intuitive than naming it Joe or Sally. It's a common practice to use the same account for both the SQL Server service (MSSQL) and the SQL Server Agent service.

---

6. Click OK. You have configured the SQL Server Agent service to start automatically.

7. Use the same procedure you just used with the SQL Server Agent service to enable and configure the SQL Server Browser service to start automatically. The SQL Server Browser service is a required service to access the dedicated administrator connection (DAC). We cover the DAC later in this chapter. If you look back at Figure 1-12, you'll notice that there is only SQL Server Browser service for the server, not one SQL Server Browser service per instance.

A couple of miscellaneous services you should be aware of include IIS and Terminal Services.

Internet Information Services (IIS) allows your computer to act as a web server. While it is commonly referred to as the "IIS service," the actual service in the Services applet is the World Wide Web Publishing service (W3SVC). This is required for Reporting Services, and we'll enable it in Chapter 12.

Many servers will be located remotely in a server room with extra physical security. It is very common for administrators to remotely log in to the server to administer it instead of going into the server room. Two tools built into Windows Server 2003 are Remote Desktop Connection (RDC) and Remote Desktops. Both require the Terminal Services service to be running on the remote server to operate.

The SQL Server Surface Area Configuration Tool

The SQL Server Surface Area Configuration tool allows you to configure features and services with just a few clicks.

This tool seems to be driven, at least in part, by Microsoft's $SD^3 + C$ philosophy. The whole idea is to reduce the *attack surface* of SQL Server and to enhance security from the moment it's installed.

The fundamental premise of reducing an attack surface of any IT product is to reduce features and services to only what is needed. For example, if Internet Information Services (IIS) is not needed, then it is not enabled. Since the service is not running, it can't be attacked. On the other hand, if IIS was enabled just in case it might be needed sometime later, it would be subject to attack and would require extra work to ensure it is protected.

The Surface Area Configuration tool is a security tool designed to help you limit—or enable—features, and limit services. By default, all but the basic features and services are disabled. The tool can be used to enable any features or services needed for the installation.

SQL Server Surface Area Configuration for Features

With SQL Server Surface Area Configuration for Features, you can enable or disable the features listed in Table 1-5.

Feature	Comments
Ad Hoc Remote Queries	Enable OPENROWSET and OPENDATASOURCE support
CLR Integration	Enable CLR integration
DAC	Enable remote DAC
Database Mail	Enable Database Mail stored procedures
Native XML Web Services	Enable HTTP endpoints
OLE Automation	Enable OLE Automation
Service Broker	Enable Service Broker endpoints
SQL Mail	Enable SQL Mail stored procedures
Web Assistant	Enable Web Assistant
Xp_cmdshell	Enable xp_cmdshell

Table 1-5 SQL Server Surface Area Configuration Features

Exercise 1.4: Launch SQL Server Surface Area Configuration for Features

Take a tour of the SQL Surface Area Configuration tool in video 1-4.

1. Choose Start | All Programs | Microsoft SQL Server 2005 | Configuration Tools | SQL Server Surface Area Configuration.

2. Select Surface Configuration For Features. You should see something similar to Figure 1-14.

Figure 1-14

The SQL Server Surface Area Configuration for Features screen

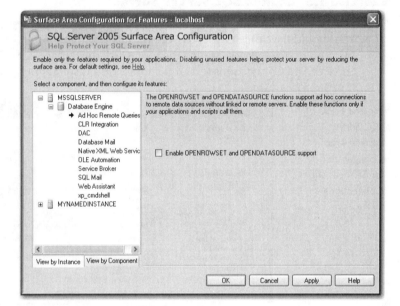

3. Click CLR Integration to see what this will enable or disable. Note the default setting is not enabled.

4. Click DAC to see what this will enable or disable. Note the default setting is not enabled.

5. Click SQL Mail and then Database Mail. Read what each will do, and note the default settings of both.

6. Click DAC and xp_cmdshell, and notice the default settings. At this point, you may notice a trend. None of these features is enabled. That's $SD^3 + C$ in action—secure by default.

7. Look at any other settings that interest you. Click Cancel to return to the main screen but leave the tool open for the next exercise.

SQL Server Surface Area Configuration for Services and Connections

In addition to configuring services via the Services console, you can also configure many SQL Server services via the SQL Server 2005 Surface Area Configuration tool. You don't have as many options with this tool, but you can change the startup type and start and stop the service.

The following exercise will lead you through changing the remote connections, examining the service states, and restarting the MSQLServer service.

Exercise 1.5: Launch SQL Server Surface Area Configuration for Services

1. You should have the SQL Server Surface Area Configuration tool open from the previous exercise. If not, launch the tool. Click the Surface Area Configuration For Services And Connections text. You should see a display similar to Figure 1-15.

Figure 1-15
SQL Server
Surface Area
Configuration
for Services and
Connections

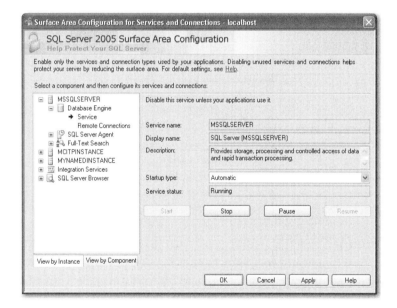

2. By default, the MSSQLServer | Database Engine | Service folder is selected. Note that the Startup Type is set to Automatic and the Service Status is Running.

3. Select Remote Connections. If you're using the Evaluation edition, this will be set to Local Connections Only. Instead, choose Local And Remote Connections, and below that select Using Both TCP/IP And Named Pipes, so your display is similar to Figure 1-16.

4. Click OK. In the Connection Settings Change Alert dialog box, click OK to acknowledge that you must restart your computer for this setting to take effect.

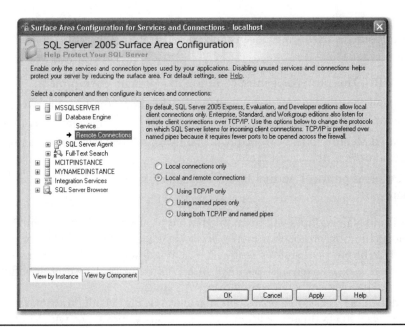

Figure 1-16 Enabling TCP/IP and Named Pipes

5. Click Surface Area Configuration For Services And Connections.

6. With the MSSQLServer | Database Engine | Service folder selected, click Stop to stop the service. After it has stopped, click Start to restart it. In Exercise 1.6, you'll see how this has enabled the TCP/IP protocol for this instance.

7. Select the SQL Server Agent Service. Note that the Startup Type is set to Automatic and that the Service Status is Running. This was done in Exercise 1.3 via the Services applet. As with many tasks in Microsoft products, you have more than one way to get the job done.

SQL Server Configuration Manager

You also have the capability of configuring protocols that your SQL Server will use for communication. If you're in a typical Server 2003 domain environment, you'll be using the TCP/IP protocol suite, but SQL Server does support other protocols.

EXAM TIP While several protocols are available, Microsoft tests often focus on Microsoft environments. In a typical Microsoft domain environment, you will have TCP/IP and Named Pipes enabled. If you need to choose between TCP/IP and Named Pipes, TCP/IP is more efficient, but often both will be enabled. One weakness with Named Pipes is in a WAN environment, which requires Named Pipes to create more connections, making it slower than TCP/IP, but it will often remain enabled unless performance degradation dictates it be disabled.

In the next lab, we'll see how we can use the SQL Server Configuration Manager to configure protocols used on a per-instance basis. The four protocols available are as follows:

- **TCP/IP**   This protocol is most common in a domain environment.
- **Named Pipes**   This protocol is also available in a domain or networked environment.
- **Shared Memory**   This protocol works only on a single machine. It is used when the network is not accessed.
- **VIA**   This protocol, Virtual Interface Adapter, is used with proprietary VIA hardware.

TCP/IP and Named Pipes will be enabled in a typical Microsoft environment. TCP/IP is the most common protocol on networks today. It's actually a full suite of protocols, and the TCP/IP protocol suite is required in a Windows 2003 domain environment. Named Pipes is a relatively fast protocol in a LAN network. However, it suffers from performance problems when traveling over WAN links.

Shared memory works only on a single machine. It is the default protocol when installing SQL Server 2005 Evaluation edition. VIA is proprietary and is used with VIA hardware.

When using TCP/IP, SQL will use TCP port 1433 to listen for connections by default. This is configurable in the SQL Server Configuration Manager, but if no port is listed, port 1433 is used.

 EXAM TIP   Port 1433 is the well-known port for SQL Server. If SQL Server traffic needs to traverse a firewall, port 1433 needs to be opened.

In the following exercise, we'll launch the SQL Server Configuration Manager and identify the status of the four supported protocols.

Exercise 1.6: Launch SQL Server Configuration Manager

1. Launch SQL Server Configuration Manager. Choose Start | All Programs | Microsoft SQL Server 2005 | Configuration Tools | SQL Server Configuration Manager.

2. Under SQL Server 2005 Network Configuration, select Protocols For MSSQLServer. You should see a display similar to Figure 1-17.

Figure 1-17
SQL Server
Configuration
Manager

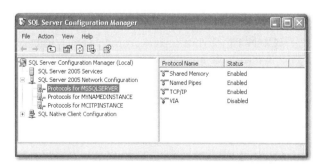

3. In the details pane, note that four protocols are listed: Shared Memory, Named Pipes, TCP/IP, and VIA. Notice that Shared Memory, Named Pipes, and TCP/IP all show a status of Enabled, and VIA shows a status of Disabled.

4. If your setting is different for any of the protocols, double-click the protocol and select Yes or No as needed for the Enabled property. Click OK.

On the Evaluation edition, Shared Memory is enabled by default. In the previous exercise, we enabled Named Pipes and TCP/IP with the SQL Server Surface Area Configuration For Services And Connections tool. This is what you would typically find on a production server.

Collations

Collations are simply the rules used to store and sort data. Different languages follow different sorting rules. Microsoft is an international company, so SQL Server can be found in just about any country.

The default collation is determined by the Windows Locale in the operating system. If you installed SQL Server on a system that was installed in the United States, it would default to a Latin1_General collation, and data would be interpreted and displayed using the 1252 (Latin1 ANSI) code page.

Collations can be set at the server level so the same collation applies to all databases. This is the default. If you have a database that needs to be stored with a different language, you can set the collation on the database level. You can also set the collation on individual columns and even override the collation in queries.

Connecting to SQL Server 2005

Now that SQL Server is installed and configured, we can connect to it. In this section, we'll discuss three primary ways to connect to SQL Server 2005: SQL Server Management Studio (SSMS), SQLCmd from the command line, and a dedicated administrator connection (DAC).

SQL Server Management Studio (SSMS)

Throughout this book, we'll be using SSMS to create, manipulate, monitor, and manage SQL Server instances, databases, and objects. While it certainly isn't the only tool available, it is the primary tool used by DBAs managing and maintaining a SQL Server implementation.

In the following exercise, we connect to SQL Server 2005 using SSMS.

Exercise 1.7: Connect to SQL Server Using SSMS

1. Choose Start | All Programs | Microsoft SQL Server 2005, right-click SQL Server Management Studio, and select Run As.

2. In the Run As dialog box, select The Following User, enter the username and password of an account with administrative privileges on your system, and click OK.

CAUTION It's *not* recommended to log on to your system with an account with administrative privileges. One reason is that if your system becomes infected with a virus while you're logged on, it will have your privileges. Instead, as a best practice, log on with a regular account, and then use secondary logon (Run As) to run programs that need elevated rights. The built-in administrators group has been placed into the sysadmin role by default, granting full access to your SQL Server. If you (or someone else) tried to launch SSMS with a different account and you weren't granted access, you wouldn't be able to connect. In Windows Vista, the User Account Control (UAC) feature prompts you any time elevated permissions are needed.

3. In the Connect To Server dialog box, notice that the Server Type is Database Engine, the Server Name is the name of your server, and the Authentication is Windows Authentication, as seen in Figure 1-18. Click Connect.

Figure 1-18
The SSMS
Connect To
Server dialog box

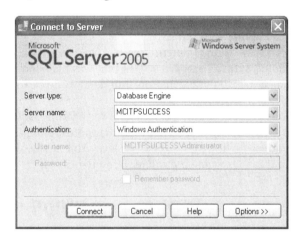

4. You will see SSMS open. You can leave it open. We'll explore SSMS in Exercise 1.9.

SQLCmd

SQLCmd is a command-line utility that allows you to enter Transact-SQL statements, system procedures, and script files from the command prompt, in the Query Editor (while in SQLCmd mode), and within a job in SQL Server Agent.

Once we explore Transact-SQL, the power of SQLCmd will be much more apparent. For now, just be aware that almost anything you can do with Transact-SQL, you can do from a script and launch it from SQLCmd.

The great strength of any command-line utility is that it can be automated. SQLCmd is no exception. Whether you need to automate the import of data with bcp, export data to an XML file, or perform maintenance of databases, such as detaching, copying, and reattaching databases in the middle of the night, you'll find that SQLCmd can help.

A less apparent benefit of SQLCmd is that you can use it to connect to SQL Server with the dedicated administrator connection when your SQL Server is not responding.

We'll show how to do some basic things with SQLCmd for the tests, but if you want to explore more, look up the Books Online article "sqlcmd Utility."

Dedicated Administrator Connection (DAC)

The dedicated administrator connection (DAC) allows you to access and troubleshoot an otherwise unresponsive SQL Server. Remember, the SQL Browser service needs to be running to enable DAC connections.

Two methods can be used to connect with the DAC: SSMS and SQLCmd.

 TIP It's important to remember that only an administrator can run the dedicated administrator connection (DAC). This means either that the account you are using is in the BUILTIN\Administrators group (automatically mapped to the sysadmin server role) or that your account had been added to the sysadmin role.

Documentation often suggests using the SA account. If you installed SQL Server following Exercise 1.1, this would not work since we selected Windows authentication mode and the SA account is disabled by default. In order for the SA account to work, the Server Authentication must be set to mixed mode (Windows and SQL Server authentication mode) and the SA account must be enabled.

In the following exercise, we connect to the dedicated administrator connection using SQLCmd.

Exercise 1.8: Connect to DAC with SQLCmd

1. Launch a command prompt with administrator privileges using the Run As command. (This can be done on Windows XP or Windows Vista by choosing Start | All Programs | Accessories, right-clicking Command Prompt, and selecting Run As, or Run As Administrator.)

2. At the command prompt, type **SQLCmd –S servername –A**, where *servername* is the name of your server. The –A specifies the dedicated administrator connection, or the administrator console, and must be capitalized. For example, if your server name was MCITPSuccess, you would enter **SQLCmd –S MCITPSuccess –A**.

 TIP If you don't know or remember your server name (the name of your computer), you can enter **hostname** at the command prompt to get it. If you've installed the default instance, just the server name is required in the SQLCmd statement. If you've installed a named instance and want to connect to the named instance, you'd enter the ***serverName\namedInstance***. For example, if your server name was MCITP and the named instance was MyNamedInstance, you would enter

```
SQLCmd -S MCITPSuccess\MyNamedInstance -A
```

While using spaces on the command line is sometimes tricky, the space after the –S switch can be included or omitted.

3. At this point, you have access to SQL Server with the DAC. Enter the following information on lines 1 and 2. Note that *1>* and *2>* are generated by SQLCmd. Don't reenter them.

```
1> SELECT @@Version
2> Go
```

Before you press ENTER on line 2, your display should look similar to Figure 1-19.

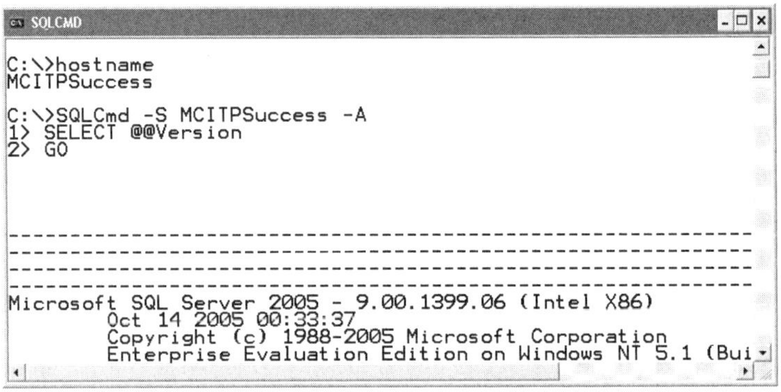

Figure 1-19
Using the command prompt to access the DAC

```
SQLCMD                                                        _ □ ×

C:\>hostname
MCITPSuccess

C:\>SQLCmd -S MCITPSuccess -A
1> SELECT @@Version
2> GO


--------------------------------------------------------------
--------------------------------------------------------------
--------------------------------------------------------------
--------------------------------------------------------------
Microsoft SQL Server 2005 - 9.00.1399.06 (Intel X86)
      Oct 14 2005 00:33:37
      Copyright (c) 1988-2005 Microsoft Corporation
      Enterprise Evaluation Edition on Windows NT 5.1 (Bui
```

4. You have just connected with DAC and entered a basic T-SQL command using the global variable @@*Version* to get the version information for your server. Press ENTER to see the results of the SELECT @@Version command.

5. Enter **Exit** and press ENTER to exit SQLCmd.

While this exercise shows how to get the version, you can execute any desired queries to diagnose problems and possibly terminate unresponsive sessions. For example, a transaction may have a lock on resources. This can be identified with DBCC OPENTRAN, SP_WHO, and terminated with KILL. We'll cover all of these commands as we move through the book. The point of the exercise is to show how to connect to SSMS via DAC.

Connect to DAC with SSMS

You can also connect to the DAC with SSMS. However, it's a little tricky because we can't use the Object Explorer with DAC.

First, launch SSMS as normal; however, don't try to connect. Instead, in the Connect To Server dialog box, click Cancel. If you try to connect here using the Admin: prefix from here (instead of clicking Cancel), you will get an error saying "Dedicated administrator connections are not supported (Object Explorer)."

After clicking cancel, you have SSMS open, but without any connections. Click the New Query button to create a new query window. Another Connect To Server dialog box will appear.

Change the Server Name when connecting to the server by adding the prefix of **Admin:**. In the Connect To Server dialog box, change the Server Name to **Admin:***server-Name\serverInstance* (where *serverName* is the name of your server and *serverInstance* is the name of the instance you want to connect to). For example, when connecting to the DAC on a server named MCITPSuccess with an instance of MyNamedInstance, you would enter **Admin:MCITPSuccess\MyNamedInstance**, as in Figure 1-20. To connect to the default instance on a server named MCITP, you'd enter **Admin:MCITP**.

Figure 1-20

Connecting to DAC with SSMS

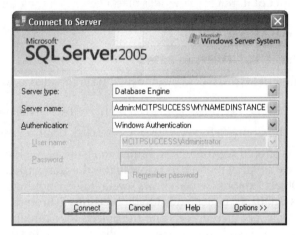

EXAM TIP Make sure you know about both methods of connecting to the Dedicated Administrator Connection—using SQLCmd and using SSMS.

In the following exercise, we'll connect to the dedicated administrator connection in SSMS.

Exercise 1.9: Connect to DAC with SSMS

1. Launch an instance of SSMS but do not click the Connect button.

2. On the Connect To dialog box, click Cancel.

3. Click the New Query button. In the Connect To dialog box, add **Admin:** to the front of the server name.

4. Click Connect. After a moment, the DAC connection will be established. Once you click Connect, you will have a new query window open with the dedicated administrator connection. Remember, the SQL Browser service must be running for the dedicated administrator connection to work properly. If the connection fails, instead of a new query window opening up, you will have an error message appear indicating an error occurred.

5. In the query window, enter the following script and press F5 to run it. The sys.dm_exec_sessions dynamic management view provides information on authenticated sessions on Microsoft SQL Server.

```
SELECT Session_id, login_time, cpu_time, memory_usage, reads, writes, login_name
FROM sys.dm_exec_sessions WITH (NOLOCK)

GO
```

6. Close the window.

Examining the Installation

Throughout the rest of this book, we'll spend a lot of time in SSMS covering just about every corner of it. But for now, let's take a get-acquainted tour with SSMS.

In this exercise, we explore some of the features and capabilities of SQL Server Management Studio (SSMS).

Exercise 1.10: Touring SSMS

Take a tour of SQL Server Management Studio in video 1-10.

1. IF SSMS is not open, launch SSMS from the Start menu as you would normally.

2. In the Connect To Server dialog box, click Connect using the default instance.

3. You should see something similar to Figure 1-21. Notice that across the top, you have a typical menu bar. Below that is the Standard toolbar. On the left you have Object Explorer, which shows several folders holding the SQL Server objects such as databases, tables, and stored procedures. Throughout this book, we'll touch on most of these folders and the objects they contain. On the right is the details pane. This will change based on what we are doing within SQL Server.

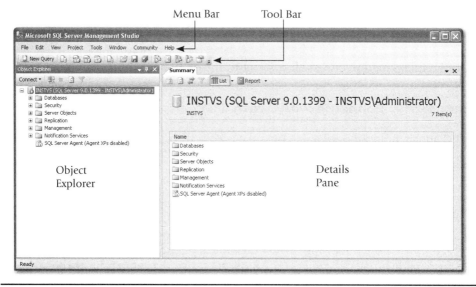

Figure 1-21 SSMS

4. Right-click anywhere on one of the toolbars to expose the context menu for the toolbars. Notice that Standard and SQL Editor toolbars are selected. Select the Help toolbar and notice an additional toolbar will appear with extra buttons.

5. Click the New Query button on the Standard toolbar. This will open a query window in the details pane that you can use to enter T-SQL commands.

6. In the query window, enter:

```
SELECT @@Version;
```

7. Hover over the Blue Check button (to the right of "! Execute"), and notice that the tooltip says "Parse." This button will *parse* your command, or in other words, check the syntax to make sure it can run—but that it does not run the commands. Click the Parse button.

8. If your syntax is correct, a results pane will open that says the "Command(s) completed successfully."

9. Click the "! Execute" button to run your query. In the results pane, you'll have a line that shows version information on your SQL Server. Note that you can also press F5 to execute the query. We'll cover Transact-SQL in much more depth in Chapter 4.

10. By default, your results are displayed in a grid. Some queries are displayed better in text. To change the results display, choose Query | Results To | Results To Text, as shown in Figure 1-22. Execute your query again and notice the different results in Figure 1-23. It's the same data, but just a little more readable.

Figure 1-22

Changing the query result output

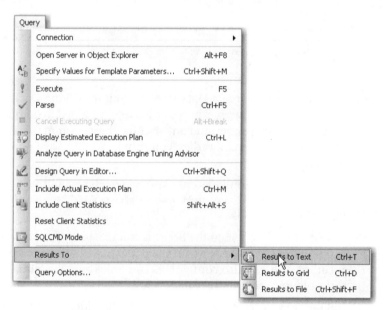

11. Right-click your instance name (the top line in Object Explorer) and click Properties. This opens the properties pages of this instance. Notice that you have several different properties pages that are accessible from this window, such as General, Memory, Processors, and more.

12. Click the Security properties page. This allows you to set the Server Authentication. With Windows authentication mode, only Windows accounts (that have been granted access) can access SQL Server. If you have non-Microsoft clients that need access to your SQL Server, you can change this to SQL Server And Windows authentication mode (also called mixed mode) and create SQL Server accounts. Click Cancel to exit the properties pages.

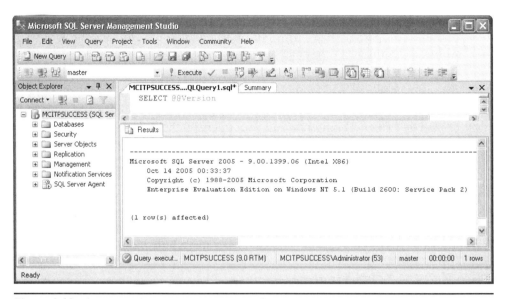

Figure 1-23 A query with results in text instead of in a grid

13. In Object Explorer, open Databases by double-clicking Databases or by clicking the + next to Databases. You will see a folder named System Databases, a folder for Database Snapshots, and any user databases you may have. If you followed the installation exercise earlier, you should see the AdventureWorks user database.

14. Open the AdventureWorks database folder. Here you'll see folders holding all the objects of the AdventureWorks database. We'll be in and out of this database throughout the book.

15. In Object Explorer, open the Security folder. Here you can add Logins to allow people access to the server (not the database—that's handled via Database Security). You can also configure Server Roles and Credentials. We'll explore the security topic more in the Chapter 9.

16. In Object Explorer, open the Server Objects folder. Here you'll find several different objects that are used for topics such as High Availability, Data Access, and Data Recovery.

17. Open the Replication folder. Replication is used to distribute copies or portions of your database to other servers. We'll cover this in more depth in Chapter 11.

18. Open the Management folder. As a database administrator, you'll probably find yourself spending a lot of time here. You can configure and monitor Maintenance Plans, review logs, identify locks, and much more. We'll cover elements in the Management folder throughout the book.

19. Click the Notification Services folder. Notice that there is no content yet. Notifications are used to program methods that will send messages in response to events. Notifications are a powerful new feature of SQL Server 2005 and will be covered more deeply in Chapter 12.

20. Click SQL Server Agent. If the service is not started, it will have a red down-arrow; if it is started and running, it will have a green up-arrow. If it's not running, right-click SQL Server Agent and select Start. Click Yes to confirm that you want to start the service. SQL Server Agent enables you to configure Jobs, Alerts, and Operators. We'll explore it in much more depth in Chapter 13.

System Databases

Every SQL Server instance has several system databases. System databases are used to store metadata for SQL Server. Metadata are data that describe themselves—in this example, the SQL configuration. As you make changes to SQL Server, the changes are stored in databases. These databases are not used by your applications, they are used by the SQL Server system—hence, the term System Databases. You can view the System databases in SSMS. These are introduced in Table 1-6.

System Database	Description
Master	Primary system database. Holds metadata on all other databases. Stores information such as logins, databases, and error messages.
MSDB	Holds SQL Server Agent information such as Jobs, Alerts, and Operators.
Model	This is the template or starting database of all new databases.
Distribution	Used for Replication.
Tempdb	Used as a workspace for temporary objects and intermediate result sets. Deleted upon shutdown. Re-created upon SQL startup.
Resource	Hidden by default. Only system database that is read-only. Contains copies of all system objects used by SQL Server that appear in each database.

Table 1-6   System Databases

Of course, these system databases are integral to the proper operation of your SQL Server. As an administrator, you should focus on the Master and MSDB databases, especially when it comes to protecting them with a disaster recovery plan.

Troubleshooting the Installation or Operation

If you've installed SQL Server and it's not working, or it was working and it's stopped, you'll want to know why as soon as possible. One of the first places to check is the logs. You have regular operating system logs and SQL Server logs that can help you.

Operating System Logs

No matter which Windows operating system you're using, you can access *Event Viewer* and view basic operating system logs. These include the System, Security, and Application logs. All three have information that can help you troubleshoot problems with your SQL server.

The System log holds system-level events such as when services start and stop, and can often give you insight into why your system may not be working. The Application log holds information logged specifically by applications such as SQL Server or Microsoft Exchange Server. The Security log holds auditing information.

SQL Server logs events to the application log, such as when SQL options are changed and when SQL services start and stop. Sometimes the reason SQL doesn't start is related to the authentication of the account starting the service. If the service can no longer authenticate (for example, because the domain account's password has expired), then the service using that account will fail. Events for this failure would be logged in both the system and the application log.

In this exercise, we'll launch Event Viewer and take a look at the available logs.

Exercise 1.11: View Event Viewer Logs

1. Choose Start | Control Panel | Administrative Tools | Event Viewer. Select the Application log. You should see a display similar to Figure 1-24.

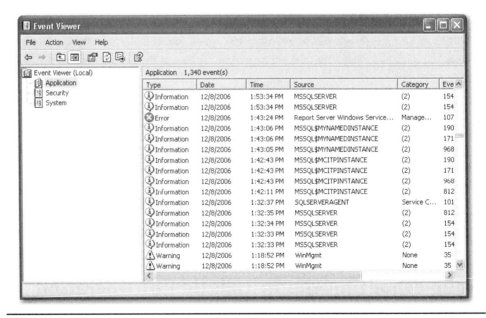

Figure 1-24 Viewing application events in Event Viewer

2. Scroll through the logs until you find an event with a source of MSSQLSERVER. Double-click the event to open it and read it.

3. Notice that some events are information (indicated by an icon of an *i* within a bubble), some are warnings (an exclamation mark in a yellow triangle), and some are errors (an *X* in a red circle).

4. Select the System log and browse through it. Note that since SQL Server is not an Operating System service, you won't find MSSQL Server source errors in the System log.

5. Select the Security log and browse through it. If auditing is not enabled on your system, you will not have any entries in the Security log.

TIP Some Event Viewer log entries are hard to interpret. If you come across one that looks a little cryptic, check out www.eventid.net. This has proven to be a great resource to a lot of techs.

SQL Logs

In addition to logs in Event Viewer, SQL Server logs information in different log files accessible via Windows Explorer or SSMS.

Installation Log

When you install SQL Server, it creates a summary.txt file in the following directory:

```
ProgramFiles\Microsoft SQL Server\90\Setup Bootstrap\LOG\
```

This log file has a listing of the log files that were created during the installation. If the installation failed, you can look here to get some clues to what went wrong. For any problems, the Install section will be labeled as "Failed" instead of "Successful."

Error Logs

Additionally, SQL Server maintains a series of error logs. These logs can be helpful in detecting any problems with SQL Server, especially related to an instance that doesn't want to restart. You can look at the logs directly via Windows Explorer in the following directory:

```
ProgramFiles\Microsoft SQL Server\MSSQL.1\MSSQL\LOG
```

TIP That .1 in the MSSQL.1 path may look like a typo, but it's not. The first instance is installed in the MSSQL.1 path. The second instance—surprise, surprise—is installed in the MSSQL.2 path. While the default instance is usually installed first, so it is usually installed in MSSQL.1, it isn't always MSSQL.1 It depends on when the default instance was installed.

Notice in Figure 1-25 that we have several instances. MSSQL.1 is where the first instance was installed, while MSSQL.5 is where the fifth instance was installed.

A new log is created each time SQL Server is restarted. The last six logs are retained by default. The current log is named ErrorLog with no extension. The most recent log

Figure 1-25
Windows
Explorer showing
folders for five
SQL instances

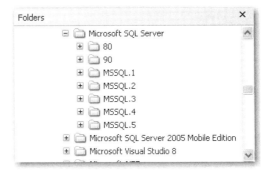

file is named ErrorLog.1, the previous one, ErrorLog.2, and so on. Each time SQL is restarted, the log files are named using the extension numbering system and a new log is created.

 EXAM TIP   Make sure you know the different logs available for troubleshooting an installation and operations of SQL Server. In addition to the system and application logs, the ErrorLog can provide valuable information. Remember, the most recent log does not have an extension.

You can also view the logs in SSMS in the Management | SQL Server Logs folder. It allows you to view the Current and the last six archived logs. Figure 1-26 shows the Management folder opened to view the SQL Server Logs folder.

Figure 1-26
SQL Server
Logs in SSMS

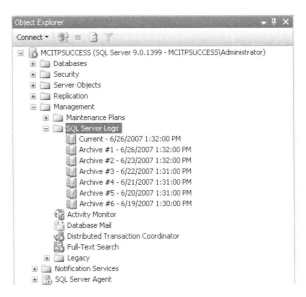

To view any of these logs, simply right-click the log and select View SQL Server Log. This will display the log contents in the detail pane.

Books Online

An invaluable tool in learning SQL Server 2005 is Books Online (BOL). I remember first using Books Online with SQL Server 7.0 and thinking this was the way that online help was supposed to be. It was robust and easy to use. If you had a question, you could usually find the answer there.

It was improved in SQL Server 2000 and again in SQL Server 2005. For just about any question you have on SQL, you can at least get a good start by spending a few minutes using BOL. I'll admit, though, that everyone isn't as big a fan as I am. You'd be hard-pressed to find any book that has all the answers on any given topic. Books Online is no exception. It doesn't answer every question for me, and it won't answer every question for you. Still, it's a great place to start, and when you need more, supplement your research on the Web.

This book is rather thick, but there's no way to cover everything there is to know about SQL Server 2005 here. That's not the intention of the book and I sure hope that's not what you're expecting. However, at the end of every chapter, I've included several topics in BOL that you can use to expand your knowledge related to the topics we've covered.

Books Online is occasionally updated. If you use your favorite search engine and enter **download SQL Server 2005 Books Online**, you'll find the link to download the most recent version. You'll likely find one that is much more recent than the one included with the evaluation copy of SQL Server 2005.

Additionally, Books Online can be installed on systems that don't have SQL Server 2005 installed. If you're using BOL as a study aid, you can download and install it on a system by itself.

In the following exercise, you'll launch Books Online and familiarize yourself with the interface.

Exercise 1.12: Learn Books Online

1. Launch Books Online by choosing Start | All Programs | Microsoft SQL Server 2005 | Documentation And Tutorials | SQL Server Books Online. You should see something similar to Figure 1-27.

   Notice the three tabs in the bottom-left corner: Index, Contents, and Help Favorites. The Index allows you to view all of the topics alphabetically, similar to an index in the back of this book, while the Contents page lets you read through Books Online as a book. However, few people have read Books Online from start to finish. If you click the + next to SQL Server 2005 Books Online, you'll see the "chapters" open up. You can then use this to help you focus on any topic you're exploring. Equally valuable are the many SQL Server 2005 tutorials available. I've found these quite welcome as a quick introduction to a new technology. The tutorials are easy to follow and include step-by-step instructions. Finally, any topic that interests you, you can add as a Help Favorite and easily find it here later.

Enter search   Add to Help Favorites

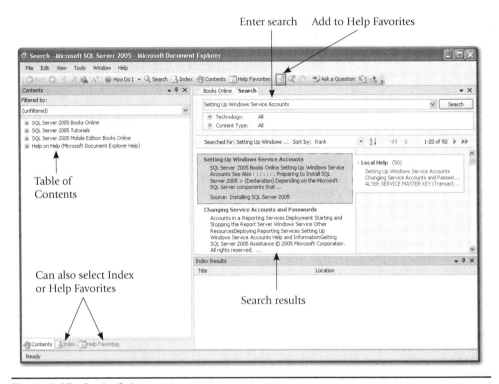

Figure 1-27   Books Online

2. Choose Tools | Options | Help | Online. You should see a display similar to Figure 1-28. If you don't have an always-on Internet connection, select "Try local first, then online" under When Loading Help Content. This will streamline your searches. Local content is very rich, while Internet content is a little more dynamic. In this book, I'll focus on the local content.

3. If the Search area is not available, click the Search button in the toolbar to make it appear. In the Search area, enter **Setting Up Windows Service Accounts** and either click Search or press ENTER. You'll see several topics open, as shown previously in Figure 1-27. In this example, the exact topic we're looking for is first. Obviously, it doesn't always work this way, but the same way you need to experiment with Google to get the best results, you'll have to do with BOL.

4. Double-click the Setting Up Windows Service Accounts summary content to pull up the article. The article opens as a tabbed document. Let's say this article intrigues you, but you don't have time to read it all now. Click the Add To Help Favorites button to add it to the favorites list.

5. In the bottom-left corner, click the Help Favorites tab. Notice the article you just saved is available here. You can delete a help topic saved here by right-clicking and selecting Delete. You can also save searches by clicking the Save Search button (located to the right of the Add To Help Favorites button) after doing a search.

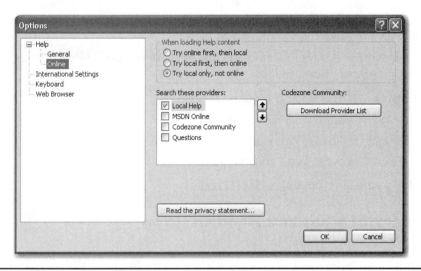

Figure 1-28   Setting Online Help options

6. Click the Search tab. Enter **Editions and Components of SQL Server 2005** and press ENTER. Save this to your favorites.

This book will help you learn quite a bit about SQL Server, but after you put this book down, BOL can provide many of your answers. The time you spend learning and mastering BOL is time well spent.

Chapter Review

In this chapter, we've covered the different editions of SQL Server and the different capabilities SQL Server offers according to what operating system it's installed on. You learned about the differences between a server and an instance of a server. We also covered installing, configuring, connecting to, and troubleshooting instances of SQL Server.

Additional Study

Self Study Exercises
Use these additional exercises to challenge yourself.

- Install a separate instance of SQL Server with only the SQL Server and SQL Server Agent services running. Use the existing instance as an example and configure the named instance with the same settings.
- Connect to your new instance using SSMS.
- Connect to your new instance using DAC from the command line and from SSMS.

- Using Windows Explorer, locate and view the SQL Error logs for your new instance. Identify the oldest log and the newest log.
- Launch the necessary tool to enable the network protocols Named Pipes and TCP/IP for your new instance.

BOL Topics

- Setting Up Windows Service Accounts
- Choosing a Network Protocol
- How to: View SQL Server 2005 Setup Log Files
- SQLCmd Utility Tutorial

Summary of What You Need to Know

70-431

This entire chapter has material covered in the 70-431 objectives. Pay special attention to the following topics:

- Installing and configuring SQL Server 2005 instances and databases
- Protocols and their uses
- Ports used by SQL Server 2005
- Tools used to troubleshoot the install or operation of SQL Server, such as SQL Server startup logs and error messages in event logs
- Dedicated administrator connection

70-441

Nothing in this chapter is within the 70-441 objectives.

70-442

Nothing in this chapter is within the 70-442 objectives.

Questions

70-431

1. You manage a SQL Server 2005 server that is used during the week days only. It was turned off after maintenance on Saturday. On Monday, the SQL Server service will not start. What logs could you view to help you identify the problem? (Choose all that apply.)

    A. The System log

    B. The Application log

    C. The Security log

    D. The SQL error log named ErrorLog

    E. The SQL error log named ErrorLog.1

    F. The SQL error log named ErrorLog.log

2. You are tasked with installing SQL Server 2005 on a server that will be used in a typical Server 2003 domain environment. What protocol(s) would you install? (Choose all that apply.)

    A. Unnamed Pipes

    B. Shared Memory

    C. TCP/IP

    D. Multiprotocol

3. What are the two ways to connect to the dedicated administrator connection for SQL Server 2005?

    A. Via SSMS and directly from the command line

    B. Via SSMS and via the SQLCmd command-line program

    C. Via SSRS and via the SQLCmd command-line program

    D. Via SSIS and directly from the command line

4. You are tasked with installing SQL Server 2005 on a server that will be used in a typical Server 2003 domain environment. Of the following, what protocol(s) would you install? (Choose all that apply.)

    A. Named Pipes

    B. Shared Memory

    C. Virtual Interface Adapter (VIA)

    D. Multiprotocol

5. You've installed a SQL Server 2005 server within a DMZ, but are unable to connect to it. You suspect a problem getting through the firewall. What port should you ask the system administrator to open on the firewall?

    A. 80

    B. 443

    C. 433

    D. 1433

6. You are called in to troubleshoot a SQL Server 2005 server that will not start after a massive power failure in your building. What would you view to help? (Choose all that apply.)

    A. The Security log in Event Viewer

    B. The System log in Event Viewer

    C. The ErrorLog.1 file in the
C:\Program Files\Microsoft SQL Server\MSSQL.1\MSSQL\LOG\directory

    D. The ErrorLog file in the
C:\Program Files\Microsoft SQL Server\MSSQL.1\MSSQL\LOG\directory

7. Users have complained that SQL has stopped responding on a server named MCITP. Logging on to the system, you find that you're unable to connect to SSMS normally. How else could you connect to the SQL Server? (Choose all that apply.)

    A. Use DAC with SQLCmd.

    B. Use DAC with SQL Server Agent.

    C. Use DAC with SSMS.

    D. Use DAC with SQL Profiler.

Answers

70-431

1. **A, B, D.** SQL Error logs are created each time a system is rebooted, and previous logs are renumbered with an extension between 1 and 6. The oldest log is named ErrorLog.6. The newest log is named ErrorLog with no extension. This log would be an excellent place to look. Additionally, the System and Application logs (viewable via Event Viewer) would be ideal places to look for any problems on a system.

2. **C.** TCP/IP is the primary protocol used in a Server 2003 domain environment. Named Pipes would be used in a LAN environment (there is no such thing as Unnamed Pipes). Shared Memory would be used on a single computer. Multiprotocol is not supported in SQL Server 2005.

3. **B.** The two ways to connect to the dedicated administrator connection (DAC) are from the SQLCmd command-line program and via the SQL Server Management Studio (SSMS) using the Admin: prefix when connecting. You can not connect to DAC directly from the command line without using SQLCmd, or by using SQL Server Reporting Services (SSRS) or SQL Server Integration Services (SSIS).

4. **A.** Named Pipes is the only choice here that would be used in a LAN environment. Shared Memory would be used on a single computer. VIA is proprietary. Multiprotocol is not supported in SQL Server 2005.

5. **D.** Port 1433 is the default listening port for SQL Server 2005. If traffic needs to get through a firewall, this port needs to be opened. Port 80 is the default port for HTTP, port 443 is the default port SSL, and port 433 is NNSP.

6. **B, D.** In Event Viewer, you can view the System log to see why a server won't start. The Application log would have information on applications such as SQL Server. The Security log contains auditing information. Assuming a default installation, the ErrorLog file (no extension) in the given directory would hold the most recently logged information on SQL Server. The ErrorLog.1 file is not the most recent log file.

7. **A, C.** The dedicated administrator connection (DAC) can be used to connect to a SQL server that is otherwise not responding. DAC can be used with SQLCmd or with SSMS, but not with SQL Server Agent or SQL Profiler.

SQL Server 2005 Database Basics

In this chapter, you will learn about:

- Tables
- Traditional data types
- New large value data types
- User-defined data types (including both T-SQL and CLR user-defined data types)
- Views
- Creating a database
- Schemas and naming conventions

> *Einstein argued that there must be simplified explanations of nature, because God is not capricious or arbitrary. No such faith comforts the software engineer.*
>
> —*Fred Brooks in* No Silver Bullet

Before we can get into the heavy topics of database development, we need to explain some of the basics for a database—things like tables, data types, and views. Tables and data types are the basics of any database. SQL Server also has *views*, which allow you to view any portion of a table or combination of tables.

Much of this may be very basic for an experienced database developer. If you fall in that category, you can breeze through most of this chapter. However, I encourage you to spend extra time in the New Large Value Data Types section. Included here is new information related to SQL Server 2005 that you don't want to skip.

Tables

Any database starts with a table. Tables hold the core of all our data. Simple databases can comprise one or just a few tables, while complex databases can hold hundreds of tables.

Let's say we want to create a database holding information about people in our company. It could be just a single table separated into different columns as shown in Table 2-1.

Column Name	Column Description
EmpID	Primary key to ensure we don't have duplicate rows
LName	Last name
FName	First name
HireDate	Date hired
BDay	Date of birth
SSN	Social security number
Street	Street address
City	City
State	State
Zip	ZIP code
Phone	Home phone
Department	Where they work
Salary	How much they earn
Picture	Graphics file
Resume	Word file of résumé, to show outside clients the employee's capabilities
ProjCompleted	XML file holding information on completed projects by employee

Table 2-1 Employee Table

The columns are determined by the data that is needed. In other words, we don't just decide we want a database. Rather, we have a need to store and retrieve data, so we organize the table based on that need. For example, your boss could say she needs to be able to regularly access a phone listing of all the employees.

You could simply create a Word document with this data, but the data is much easier to manipulate and retrieve if they are stored in a database.

By storing the data in a database table, we can easily re-sort the data by department, last name, salary, or any other column. Using full text search capabilities, we can search through text and binary columns to retrieve detailed information such as all the employees who have MCITP on their résumé.

We'll use this Employee table to build on other topics in this chapter.

Data Types

When we define columns in a table, we define the type of data we'll store there. Although we're focused on tables in this chapter, data types can also be defined elsewhere, such as in Transact-SQL scripts, functions, stored procedures, and more. Table 2-2 shows all the categories of data types; some will be available in tables, while others won't be.

Category	Description	Data Types
Character	This is text and string data such as you'd use for the LName, FName, and SSN columns.	Char, varchar, varchar(max), text
Unicode Character	Specifies data is stored in two bytes (instead of the one byte used to store non-Unicode character data) so they can be represented in multiple languages.	Nchar, nvarchar, nvarchar(max), ntext
Numerics (exact)	Numbers with exact amounts. Integers are whole numbers; decimal and numeric types support decimal points. Money is for currency. In our table, EmpID, Zip, and Salary could be defined as numerics (exact).	Bit, tinyint, smallint, int, bigint, numeric, decimal, smallmoney, money
Numerics (approximate)	Some scientific applications represent very large or very small numbers. They can use scientific notation and approximate the number.	Float, real
Date and time	Used to hold date and time data such as the date hired or the birth date.	Datetime, smalldatetime
Binary	This is data stored in other file formats such as graphics, PDF files, or Word documents. The *image* data type has been deprecated and replaced with varbinary(max). We can store any type of file in this data type.	Binary, image, varbinary, varbinary(max)
Other	Timestamp, uniqueidentifier, and XML data types are available in tables. The *xml* data type would be appropriate for the ProjCompleted column.	Cursor, timestamp, sql_variant, uniqueidentifier, table, xml

Table 2-2 Data Type Categories

Basic Data Types

The data types listed in Table 2-2 show the basic data types you'll use in your databases. For the most part, they are straightforward. If you want to store data such as a name, you'd store it in one of the character types. Numbers would be in one of the numerics, and so on.

However, we still have a lot of room to exercise some discretion. One of the most important things to keep in mind when deciding on a data type for a column is how much space the column will use in the database. Each data type uses a different amount of space in the database. The goal is to conserve space by using the appropriate data type for columns in your tables.

Saving Space   When creating a table, we want to use the least amount of space possible to hold the data. For example, if you need to go to the store for a gallon of milk, there's no need to rent a tanker truck to carry it. It would be inefficient and a lot more expensive than using a smaller vehicle.

 TIP In the following discussion, we'll come across four data types that look similar but have distinctive differences: char(), nchar(), varchar(), and nvarchar(). The difference between char() and nchar() [or varchar() and nvarchar()] is the *n*, which indicates that the data is stored in the Unicode format. Unicode supports a larger character set and is often used to display multiple languages. It takes twice as much storage space. The difference between char() and varchar() [or nchar() and nvarchar()] is that char() identifies a specific number of characters that will be stored, while varchar() identifies a variable number of characters that will be stored.

The Character data type is defined with a number such as nchar(25). This specifies that the data will always have 25 characters. How many characters are in a name? It varies, of course, so when defining columns such as the first name or last name columns, we'd use a variable number of characters (nvarchar) as in nvarchar(50). This specifies that the character data will use from 0 to 50 bytes—that is, it could be between 0 and 50 characters long. For something like a state abbreviation that is always two characters, nchar(2) would be perfect. If you don't know how much data space a column will take, we'd estimate the largest it would be and use that amount in nvarchar().

 TIP When using nvarchar, there is no harm in specifying a size larger than the largest you anticipate. For example, if the longest last name of any employee in your employee table is ten characters long, specifying a size of nvarchar(35) for the last name would allow for any new employee with an exceptionally long last name. If the maximum name length remained at 10 characters, nvarchar(35) and nvarchar(10) would take the same amount of space within the database. The difference is that a long name using more than 10 characters wouldn't fit into the nvarchar(10) properly. Since the data would be truncated, it would cause an error and fail. The name would fit into nvarchar(35) without incident. One of the great strengths of nvarchar is that SQL Server identifies how large the data actually is and only takes the amount of space needed.

For a name that needs to be presented with characters from different languages, we'd use nvarchar(50). This allows anywhere from 0 to 50 characters, but since it's specified as Unicode data, it will take up between 0 and 100 bytes of storage (twice as much as non-Unicode data). Why not nchar(50)? A name such as "Flintstone" would take 10 characters if stored as nvarchar(50), but would take a full 50 characters if stored as nchar(50).

Integers or whole numbers present us with many choices. Tinyint takes one byte and can hold numbers between 0 and 255. Bigint takes eight bytes and can accept numbers from -2^{63} to $2^{63}-1$ (about 9,223,372,036,854,775,807) or about 9EB (exabytes).

The difference between one byte and eight bytes might not seem like much, but imagine a table of two million rows. One column could take up 2MB or 16MB of space. The disk space taken isn't the only thing that is important, but rather how much disk space the database needs to search when performing queries. By using eight bytes when only one byte is needed, we force SQL Server to search through eight times as much data. Thus, you can expect a negative performance hit.

The time to think about optimizing a database isn't after it's created, but from the beginning, when designing the first column. Bottom line: Pick the smallest data type that will meet your needs.

Row Size   It's also important to understand how data is stored in SQL Server 2005. Figure 2-1 shows a simplistic view of how data is stored.

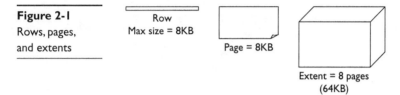

Figure 2-1
Rows, pages, and extents

Row
Max size = 8KB

Page = 8KB

Extent = 8 pages
(64KB)

First, the maximum size of any row is 8KB. This is because SQL Server stores data in pages and a page is 8KB. If your row size in a table is 6KB, you would only be able to store one row per page (with 2KB wasted space) and only eight rows per extent. For our two-million-row table, that would be 250,000 extents (2,000,000 divided by 8), or a size of about 16GB (250,000_64K).

In contrast, if your row was 100 bytes, you'd be able to store 80 rows on a page, and 640 rows per extent (80 rows_8 pages). The same two million rows would be stored in 3125 extents (2,000,000 divided by 640) and would take up about 200MB (3125_64KB).

So let's repeat the point. Row sizes should be as small as possible for the most efficient storage, searching, and management of data.

New Large Value Data Types

In SQL Server 2005, you have the capability to store data larger than 8KB by storing it outside of the row. SQL will create a pointer to this data within the row and store the data elsewhere in the database. In previous versions of SQL Server, only *text, ntext,* and *image* data could be stored out of the row. With SQL Server 2005, *varchar(max), nvarchar(max),* and *varbinary(max)* can also be stored out of the row and as a result can exceed the 8KB limitation.

Notice that in each of these, we are using the (max) specifier. The (max) specifier expands the storage capabilities of varchar, nvarchar, and varbinary data types to 2GB and stores the data outside the row.

Three columns in our Employee table that would likely benefit from this out-of-row storage are the Picture, Resume, and ProjCompleted columns. *Picture* could be a graphics file such as a JPEG. *Resume* could be a Word or PDF document. Both Picture and Resume could be stored as varbinary(max) columns. The *ProjCompleted* column is XML data. It could be stored as either XML data (if we wanted to use SQL's XML functionality) or varbinary(max).

EXAM TIP The varbinary(max) column is ideal for storing files that are not native to SQL, such as Word documents or PDF files. It replaces the image data type from previous versions of SQL Server, which has been deprecated and should no longer be used.

Figure 2-2 shows part of our Employee table and how it could be stored out of the row. The EmpID, FName, and LName columns would be stored in the row. For the Resume and Projs columns, only a pointer is stored, which identifies where the actual data is stored.

Figure 2-2
Data stored
out of the row

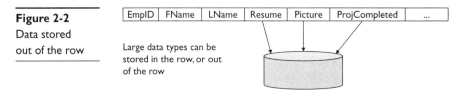

Large data types can be
stored in the row, or out
of the row

If the data to be stored are relatively small, we can choose to store it in the row instead of out of the row. SQL Server 2005 has an Out Of Row option that can be set at the table level. The stored procedure sp_tableoption is used to enable or disable storage of data out of the row. Setting this option allows data to be stored in the row as long as the data is shorter than what is specified in the sp_tableoption (256 bytes by default, but can be as large as 7000 bytes). If the data exceed this size, or there isn't enough room in the row for the data, they will be stored out of the row. For all the details of the sp_tableoption stored procedure, take a look at the Books Online article "sp_tableoption."

User-Defined Data Types

While the given data types will serve most purposes, you might have a need to create special data types. For example, while a standard ZIP code is five digits, the extended ZIP code is five digits—a dash and four digits, as in 23462-5555.

Instead of using the standard integer data type, we can create a user-defined data type to specify that the ZIP code should be entered as ten characters. This would prevent only a five-digit ZIP code from being entered. One of the primary reasons to create a user-defined data type is to ensure consistency in the way data is entered.

We can create two different kinds of data types

- *Transact-SQL* **user-defined data type**   This is a traditional user-defined data type created with T-SQL code.
- *CLR* **user-defined data type**   A CLR (Common Language Runtime) user-defined data type can be created using any .NET programming language such as C# or Visual Basic. CLR objects are especially useful when complex calculations are required.

TIP CLR integrated objects will be covered in much more depth in Chapter 6 and Chapter 9 with examples of creating external assemblies, registering the assembly within SQL Server, and creating SQL Server objects that reference and use the assembly.

Both T-SQL and CLR user-defined data types are explained in more depth on the following pages.

Before we can start creating database objects such as user-defined data types, we need to create a database.

In the following exercise, we'll create a simple database by using the model database as a template. Remember that the model database is a system database that is used as a template for all newly created databases.

Exercise 2.1: Create a Database

Watch video 2-1 to see a database being created in SQL Server Management Studio.

1. Open SSMS.

2. Click the New Query button.

3. Enter the following code in the query window:

```
USE Master;
GO
CREATE DATABASE Chapter2;
```

 TIP The preceding CREATE DATABASE statement has many options that are available. As written, it uses defaults for all of the options. For the full syntax, look at the Books Online article "Create Database (Transact SQL)."

4. Click the Execute button.

5. In the SSMS Object Explorer, open the Databases container to see that you have successfully created a database named Chapter2.

Alternatively, you could have right-clicked over the Databases folder in the SSMS and selected New Database. After entering a database name, click OK.

Later, we'll explore more of what we've done, but for now we've created a database we can use to start creating objects.

T-SQL User-Defined Data Types

T-SQL data types can be created using SSMS or Transact-SQL code. The syntax for creating the data type is:

```
CREATE TYPE [schema_name.] type_name
{
    FROM base_type
    [ ( precision [ , scale ] )  ]
    [ NULL | NOT NULL ]
  | EXTERNAL NAME assembly_name [ .class_name ]
} [ ; ]
```

We'll cover schemas later in this chapter, but in short, they allow us to group ownership of different database objects. The default schema is dbo. The base type is the data type our user-defined data type will be based on. Precision and scale are extra parameters used for decimal or numeric data types. EXTERNAL NAME is used for CLR-integrated user-defined data types.

As an example, if we wanted to create a user-defined data type for a ZIP code, we could use the following code:

```
CREATE TYPE Zip
FROM varchar(10) NOT NULL ;
```

Notice that this does nothing more than define the ZIP type as having a data type of varchar(10).

In the following exercise, we use the SSMS graphical user interface (GUI) to create a data type named ZIP Code.

Exercise 2.2: Create a T-SQL User-Defined Data Type

1. Open SSMS. In the Chapter2 database created in Exercise 2.1, open the Programmability folder, and then open the Types folder.

2. Right-click User-Defined Data Type, and select New User-Defined Data Type.

3. On the New User-Defined Data Type page, leave the default Schema as dbo. Enter Name as **ZipCode**. Change Data Type to **char**. Change Length to **10**. Your display should look similar to Figure 2-3.

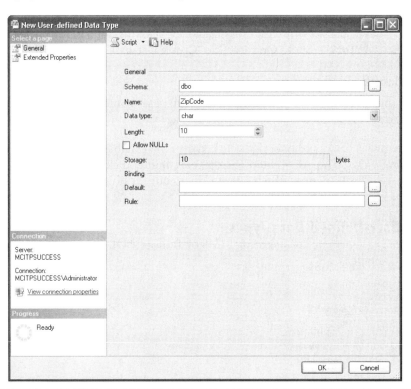

Figure 2-3   Creating a user-defined data type in SSMS

While the user-defined data type ensures that the data is entered as ten characters, it does not ensure they are entered as all numbers with a dash after the fifth number (#####-####). We could use a constraint to require a specific format, as we'll see in the Chapter 3, or we could create a CLR data type.

CLR User-Defined Data Types

Common Language Runtime (CLR) is integrated throughout SQL Server. It allows us to use any Microsoft.NET Framework language (C#, Visual Basic [VB], and so on) and to create an assembly that can be used by database objects. Creating CLR assemblies, our data types can have additional functionality via built-in methods. In Chapter 6 and Chapter 9, we'll create a CLR assembly in an exercise and use it with a database object.

 EXAM TIP   For any computation-intensive applications, CLR solutions provide significant performance gains. If you're faced with a scenario where advanced calculations must be performed, consider using a CLR solution over a T-SQL solution.

The database objects that can take advantage of CLR are triggers, stored procedures, functions, and data types.

XML Data Types

We can also store XML data types within SQL Server 2005. We'll explore the XML data type and methods of querying XML data in more depth in Chapter 5.

Creating Tables

With the knowledge we've gained from the chapter so far, let's redefine our table by adding data types. Table 2-3 shows one possible choice for the data types.

Note that you could choose other data types and still be correct. For example, any of the nvarchar() data types could have numbers different than 50. If you know that the longest department name is ten characters, you could choose to make this nvarchar(10).

The table can be created in two ways. One uses the SSMS graphical user interface (GUI), while the other uses Transact-SQL statements.

In the following exercise, we'll create a table using the GUI in SSMS. Before you start, you should have SSMS open and pointed to the Employee database created from the previous exercise.

Exercise 2.3: Create a Table in SSMS

1. Open the Chapter2 database by double-clicking it. Open the Tables folder by double-clicking it.

2. Right-click Tables and select New Table.

3. Under the Column Name, enter **EmpID.** Press TAB. Enter **in** to select int (for integer) data type. Clear the Allow Nulls check box to deselect this option. Press TAB to advance to the next row.

Column Name	Data Type	Column Description
EmpID	Integer	Primary key to ensure we don't have duplicate rows
LName	Nvarchar(50)	Last name
FName	Nvarchar(50)	First name
HireDate	Smalldatetime	Date hired
BDay	Smalldatetime	Date of birth
SSN	Nvarchar(11)	Social security number
Street	Nvarchar(50)	Street address
City	Nvarchar(50)	City
State	Nchar(2)	State
Zip	ZipCode (UDT)	ZIP code
Phone	Nchar(13)	Home phone
Department	Nvarchar(50)	Where they work
Salary	Money	How much they earn
Picture	Varbinary(max)	Graphics file
Resume	Varbinary(max)	Word file of résumé used to show outside clients the employee's capabilities
ProjCompleted	XML	XML file holding information on completed projects by the employee

Table 2-3   Employee Table with Data Types Defined

4. Under the Column Name, enter **LName**. Press TAB. Type in **varc** to select the nvarchar(50) data type. Note that it defaults to 50, but you can change it if your needs are different. Clear the Allow Nulls check box to deselect this option. Press TAB to go to the next row.

5. Complete the remainder of the columns so your display looks like Figure 2-4. Note that the ZipCode data type was created in Exercise 2.2.

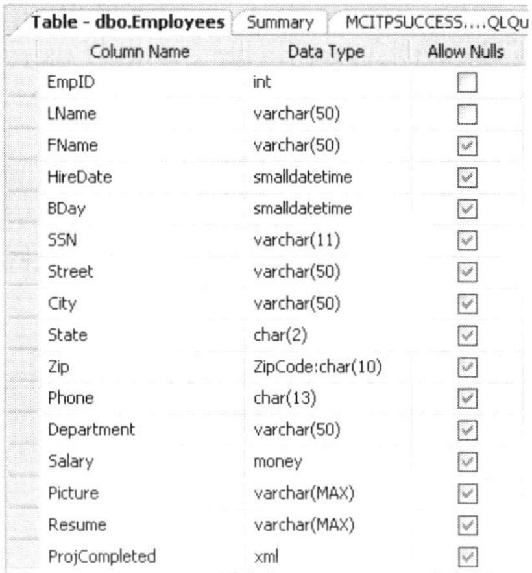

Figure 2-4
Creating a
table in SSMS

Column Name	Data Type	Allow Nulls
EmpID	int	☐
LName	varchar(50)	☐
FName	varchar(50)	☑
HireDate	smalldatetime	☑
BDay	smalldatetime	☑
SSN	varchar(11)	☑
Street	varchar(50)	☑
City	varchar(50)	☑
State	char(2)	☑
Zip	ZipCode:char(10)	☑
Phone	char(13)	☑
Department	varchar(50)	☑
Salary	money	☑
Picture	varchar(MAX)	☑
Resume	varchar(MAX)	☑
ProjCompleted	xml	☑

Table - dbo.Employees   Summary   MCITPSUCCESS....QLQu

6. Press CTRL+S to save the table. Alternatively, you could have selected File | Save Table1, or have right-clicked over the tab of the new table and selected Save Table1.

7. In the Choose Name dialog box, enter **Employees** and click OK.

Creating a Table with T-SQL

The same table we created in the previous exercise via SSMS can be created using a Transact-SQL script. The Books Online article "Create Table" shows the full syntax for creating a table using T-SQL. The basic syntax is:

```
CREATE TABLE TableName
column_name [data_type]        [ COLLATE collation_name ]        [ NULL | NOT NULL ]
[column_constraint]
[computed_column_definition]
[ table_constraint ]
[index_option]
```

As an example, the Employees table in the previous exercise could have been created with the following script:

```
CREATE TABLE Employees(
        EmpID int NOT NULL,
        LName varchar(50) NOT NULL,
        FName varchar(50) NULL,
        HireDate smalldatetime NULL,
        BDay smalldatetime NULL,
        SSN varchar(11) NULL,
        Street varchar(50) NULL,
        City varchar(50) NULL,
        State char(2) NULL,
        Zip dbo.ZipCode NULL,
        Phone char(13) NULL,
        Department varchar(50) NULL,
        Salary money NULL,
        Picture varchar(max) NULL,
        Resume varchar(max) NULL,
        ProjCompleted xml NULL
)
```

We'll cover more of the available options in the CREATE TABLE statement as we move through the book. In the following exercise, we create a table named Employees with T-SQL.

Exercise 2.4: Create a Table in T-SQL

1. With SSMS open, click the New Query button.

2. In the query window, enter the following text:

```
USE [Chapter2]
GO
CREATE TABLE [dbo].[EmployeesTSQL](
   [EmpID] [int] NOT NULL,
   [LName] [nvarchar](50) NOT NULL,
   [FName] [nvarchar](50) NULL,
   [HireDate] [smalldatetime] NULL,
```

```
[BDay] [smalldatetime] NULL,
[SSN] [varchar](11) NULL,
[Street] [varchar](50) NULL,
[City] [varchar](50) NULL,
[State] [char](2) NULL,
[Zip] [dbo].[ZipCode] NULL,
[Phone] [char](13) NULL,
[Department] [varchar](50) NULL,
[Salary] [money] NULL,
[Picture] [varchar](max) NULL,
[Resume] [varchar](max) NULL,
[ProjCompleted] [xml] NULL
)
```

 TIP In the script example, every identifier is delimited with brackets ([ ]). Since none of the identifiers have a space in them nor are any of the identifiers reserved words, this script could work without the brackets.

3. Click Execute to run your script.

4. Right-click Tables in your Employee database and select Refresh. You should see the dbo.Employees table that you created manually in the previous exercise and the dbo.EmployeesTSQL table created with the T-SQL Script.

5. If desired, you can create some sample data with the following INSERT statement:

```
Use Chapter2
Go
INSERT into Employees (EmpId,LName,FName,HireDate,Phone,Salary)
VALUES(1,'Gibson','Duane','Sep 9, 1964', '(757)555-5555',150000)
INSERT into Employees (EmpId,LName,FName,HireDate,Phone,Salary)
VALUES (2,'Villegas','Nimfa','Mar 31, 1962', '(757)555-4444',160000)

INSERT into EmployeesTSQL (EmpId,LName,FName,HireDate,Phone,Salary)
VALUES(1,'Grzena','Dawn','Apr 14, 1974', '(757)555-5555',170000)
INSERT into Employees (EmpId,LName,FName,HireDate,Phone,Salary)
VALUES (2,'Villegas','Nimfa','Mar 31, 1962', '(757)555-4444',160000)
```

Admittedly, we're a little ahead of ourselves here. In Chapter 4, we'll cover T-SQL statements in much more depth, but these exercises do give you some exposure to Transact-SQL.

Note that CREATE (as in CREATE Table) is a *Data Definition Language* (DDL) statement in Transact SQL. DDL statements define objects in the database, such as the CREATE command. Other DDL statements are ALTER and DROP. These are the same statements we'd use to create, modify, or drop any database objects (and even databases themselves). We used CREATE to create our table.

In contrast, *Data Manipulation Language* (DML) statements are used to manipulate the data by performing tasks such as add, delete, or modify the data. These include SELECT, INSERT, UPDATE, and DELETE. We used INSERT to add data to our table.

Notice a subtlety here: We don't delete objects; we drop them. We don't drop data; we delete them.

EXAM TIP If you see "DDL" or "DML" on your tests, don't be surprised if they are not spelled out as "Data Definition Language" and "Data Manipulation Language." You are expected to know that DDL is used for objects (and includes statements such as CREATE, ALTER, and DROP), while DML is used for data (and includes statements such as INSERT, UPDATE, and DELETE), even if all you see is the acronym of DDL or DML.

Nulls and Defaults

Nulls and defaults often work hand in hand within a table. Sometimes when creating a table, we want to make sure data is always entered in a column, so we specify the column as NOT NULL. Other times, we may want to allow the user to omit data, but still ensure some default information is entered into that column of the table. We can use NULL and DEFAULT definitions for both of these scenarios.

EXAM TIP Make sure you are familiar with the use of NULL and DEFAULT definitions. They are very valuable on the job and you can expect to see them on the tests.

Nulls

Data isn't always entered into a database immediately. For example, a new employee fills out a form, and later an intern enters the data into the database. As the intern comes across Pat Jones's employee form, he starts entering data and then comes to the Gender column. Is Pat male or female? For those who have watched certain vintage *Saturday Night Live* shows, you know that's a question that was never answered.

This is an excellent example of the need to support null data. What is the value of null? Just as the gender of Pat on *SNL* remains a mystery to many of us, we don't know the value of null. That's a very important point to grasp with null in this situation: Null is unknown.

When creating or altering a table, we need to specify whether NULL data is allowed on a column, or if something must be entered for the column. Primary keys require us to have data, so nulls are not allowed on a *primary key* column. Other columns are often left to your discretion to define as NULL or NOT NULL.

Default Definitions

The default data defined on the column are applied when a new row is added. If a DEFAULT is defined on a column and no data for the column is included with the INSERT, than the DEFAULT is used. Additionally, a DEFAULT can be used when altering a table. We'll see both examples in exercises in this section.

For example, let's say your company is in the state of California and 99% of your employees live in California. You could create a DEFAULT for the State column in the Employee table that specifies the state of CA. Now, any time an employee is added to the Employee table, you can leave the state blank and the state will default to CA.

Exercise 2.5 Create and Test a Default Definition

1. Create a table named Address with a DEFAULT Definition by running the following script:

```
USE Chapter2;
GO
CREATE TABLE dbo.Address
(
  AddressLine1 varchar(35) NULL,
  AddressLine2 varchar(35) NULL,
  City varchar(35) NULL,
  State char(2) NULL
        Constraint State_CA_def
        DEFAULT 'CA',
  Zip varchar(10) NULL,
)
```

2. Add a new address line, but leave the state blank.

3. In SSMS, right-click the Address table in the Chapter2 database and click Open Table.

4. Put your cursor in the last row in the AddressLine1 column and enter **232 Turning Court**. Press TAB twice and enter **San Francisco** as the City. Press TAB twice and enter **94102** as the Zip. Notice we are not entering data into the State column.

5. Click the X to close the table.

6. Right-click the Address table and click Open Table. Notice that the State has been entered as CA for California.

7. Close the table.

 TIP   In the previous exercise, a DEFAULT is created as part of the table definition. Defaults can also be created externally from the table, just as a user-defined data type can be created externally, and then bound to the table. For example, we could create a DEFAULT for a state as CA, and then bind this default to the Address table. However, this is no longer recommended. Microsoft has deprecated this feature in SQL Server 2005. Instead, we create DEFAULT definitions on the table by using the CREATE TABLE or ALTER TABLE commands.

Using Defaults with NULL

Another place that DEFAULT Definitions can be very useful is when adding columns to a table with the NOT NULL definition. If you try to add a column to a table with data using the NOT NULL argument, it will fail.

Think about it. If you add a column to a table that has existing data, the new column won't have any data, so it will be blank for each row. Typically, you would define a column as NOT NULL to ensure the column is filled in, but if you specify NOT NULL (meaning that it can't be blank), you would suddenly have a lot of rows that don't comply with the table definition (the rows that already exist in the table). SQL recognizes this, so the ALTER table definition will fail and give an error.

The only way to succeed with the task of adding a column with the NOT NULL setting after data is in the table is by adding a DEFAULT definition along with the NOT NULL. The default data could be something as simple as "Not Defined Yet."

 EXAM TIP A key point here is that DEFAULT definitions are valuable to use when you are adding new columns that won't accept NULL data. It is simply not possible to add a column using NOT NULL if the table has existing data, unless you use a DEFAULT definition.

The following exercise shows how adding a column using NOT NULL will fail without the DEFAULT, and then how the DEFAULT definition will allow it to succeed.

Exercise 2.6 Add a Column with and without a Default Definition

Watch the benefit of using DEFAULT with NULL in video 2-6.

1. Try to add a column named Country to your address table using the following script:

```
USE Chapter2;
GO
ALTER TABLE Address
    Add Country VARCHAR(50) NOT NULL;
```

2. Execute the script and notice the following error:

   ALTER TABLE only allows columns to be added that can contain nulls, or have a DEFAULT definition specified, or the column being added is an identity or timestamp column, or alternatively if none of the previous conditions are satisfied, the table must be empty to allow addition of this column. Column 'Country' cannot be added to non-empty table 'Address' because it does not satisfy these conditions.

   In other words, we already have a row with data from the previous exercise (232 Turning Court). If we add a Country column, it will be null for this row. However, the ALTER TABLE statement specifies that the Country column can't be null. Thus, we have a catch-22 situation. We'll see later in this exercise how we can use a DEFAULT to avoid this error.

3. It is possible to add columns *without* the NULL argument. Change the script to the following script (remove NOT in NOT NULL) and execute it.

```
USE Chapter2;
GO
ALTER TABLE Address
    Add Country VARCHAR(50) NULL;
```

4. Drop the column using the following script. We will add the column again using the NOT NULL argument and a DEFAULT definition in the next step:

```
USE Chapter2;
GO
Alter TABLE Address
Drop Column Country;
```

5. Create the new column with the DEFAULT using the following script:

```
USE Chapter2;
GO
ALTER TABLE Address
    Add Country VARCHAR(50) NOT NULL
  CONSTRAINT Country_USA_def
  DEFAULT 'USA';
```

6. After executing the script, right-click the Address table, and select Open Table. Notice that the Country column has been created and populated with 'USA' for each of the existing rows in the table.

Computed Columns

Tables in SQL Server 2005 can also have computed columns. A computed column is an expression that defines the value of the column. By default, data is not contained within the column, but instead it is a *virtual* column.

As an example, a parts table could have an InventoryCost column created as a computed column. The expression would be QuantityOnHand * Cost (assuming we have both these columns in the table).

Once created, computed columns can be used within T-SQL queries just like a regular column. T-SQL will be explored in much more depth in Chapter 4, but be aware that the computed columns can be included in SELECT lists, WHERE clauses, ORDER BY clauses, and more. Computed columns can't have data inserted or updated via INSERT or UPDATE statements.

The following script would create the InventoryCost computed column within a table. The bolded line shows the computed column.

```
USE Chapter2;
GO
CREATE TABLE ComputedColumnTest
(
      QuantityOnHand int NULL,
        Cost money NULL,
        InventoryCost AS (QuantityOnHand * Cost)
);
```

Persisted Column

A persisted column is a computed column that actually stores the computed data within the table, instead of computing the value of the data each time it is queried.

When data is inserted or updated into a table with a persisted computed column, SQL Server generates the value by using the formula of the computed column and storing the result with the rest of the table.

When should you use a persisted computed column over a nonpersisted computed column? Generally, simple operations or computations are quicker as nonpersisted computed columns. This is because processors and memory are quicker than disk I/O. For complex operations, a persisted computed column may be quicker. Additionally, a special case exists where you can use a persisted computed column to create an index. We'll explain this later in the section.

The only change to the script is to add the word PERSISTED to the end of the table definition.

```
USE Chapter2;
GO
CREATE TABLE ComputedColumnTestPersisted
(
        ComputedColumnTestID int NOT NULL,
        QuantityOnHand int NULL,
        Cost money NULL,
        InventoryCost AS (QuantityOnHand * Cost) PERSISTED,
CONSTRAINT PK_ComputedColumnTest_ComputedColumnTestID
PRIMARY KEY CLUSTERED (ComputedColumnTestID)
);
```

Guidelines with Computed and Persisted Columns

Some general guidelines to consider when using both computed and persisted columns relate to their cost in terms of resource usage. The whole purpose of using these features is to improve the performance of the database, but occasionally they can have a detrimental effect.

 EXAM TIP Use a computed column when data is derived from other columns using simple mathematical calculations. This is especially true for tables that hold relatively static data.

- Avoid the use of complex calculations or functions in computed columns.
  The overhead cost of complex calculations in any computed columns could result in poorer performance of the table.

- Avoid the use of persisted columns on dynamic data.
  A table with frequent inserts, updates, and deletes within a table will cause significant overhead on a persisted computed column as the data is constantly recalculated and stored. Generally, frequently queried data perform better as a persisted computed column, while frequently updated data perform better as a nonpersisted computed column.

- Use error-checking to protect against mathematic errors.
  As an example, a check for zero or null data before performing a divide will avoid a divide by zero error.

Indexed Computed Columns

An added benefit available to computed columns is that indexes can be created on them. We'll explore indexes in much more depth in Chapter 7, but for now be aware that an index can significantly improve the performance of a query. In short, an index in SQL Server works just like an index in the back of a book. Let's say we were looking for information on DEFAULTS. Which is quicker? Starting at the beginning of a book and checking every page from page 1 to the end of the book, or going to the index in the back of the book? Obviously, the index is quicker. Likewise, if SQL Server has an index available that it can search, the search will be much quicker.

The primary reason we'd create the index on a computed column is if we were frequently querying a *range* of data within the computed column. For example, if the computed column held InventoryCost and we frequently queried for rows that had an InventoryCost over a set dollar amount, an index would work well.

The biggest restriction on creating indexes on computed columns is that the computed column must be deterministic and precise.

Deterministic means the expression will always return the same result for a specified set of inputs. For example, 4 times 5 is always 20. As long as the numbers are 4 and 5, the answer will always be the same.

 EXAM TIP   If a computed column is frequently queried and filtered within a WHERE clause based on a range of data, you can generally improve performance by adding an index on the computed column. (However, you can NOT create an index on the computed column if the computed column is nondeterministic.)

Nondeterministic means the expression can return something different with a specified set of inputs. For example, 4 times Month(GetDate()) will be one thing this month, but something else next month.

 NOTE   The GetDate() function returns detailed information on today's date, such as the year, month, day, and time down to the millisecond. The Month() function returns an integer representing the month from a given date. Executing SELECT Month(GetDate()) in December would return the number 12, but running the same statement in July would return the number 7. Generally, any functions using dates are nondeterministic.

Precise means the number is not a floating or real number. You can not create an index on a nonpersisted column that is a floating or real number. However, if you make the computed column persisted, you can create an index on it.

 EXAM TIP   If a computed column is nondeterministic, indexes can NOT be created on the computed column. This includes both persisted and nonpersisted computed columns.

Collations

In Chapter 1, we briefly mentioned collations and how they are used to define the sorting behavior of the server. Collations can also be set at the database level, tables level, and individual column levels.

If data is to be stored within a column in a different collation than the database, they should be defined as a Unicode column. While storing the data as Unicode data will double the storage space, it ensures that data can be moved between columns seamlessly.

Imagine a company that regularly does business with Spanish-speaking countries. Most of the data is stored in Latin1_Gerneral_CI_AS collation (Case Insensitive and Ascending based on the Latin1_General collation). However, occasionally employee listings must be created using the Spanish collation.

Instead of re-creating the entire database in a different collation, a computed column could be created with the Modern_Spanish_CI_AS collation (Case Insensitive and Ascending based on the Modern_Spanish collation).

The following script shows how computed columns could be created on the EmployeesTSQL table with different collations created on the computed columns.

```
Use Chapter2;
Go
ALTER TABLE EmployeesTSQL
ADD FNameSpanish AS (FName)
COLLATE Modern_Spanish_CI_AS;
ALTER TABLE EmployeesTSQL
ADD LNameSpanish AS (LName)
COLLATE Modern_Spanish_CI_AS;
```

 EXAM TIP Computed columns can be created with a different collation. This will allow the data to be easily displayed differently without adding the additional storage.

To view the data in the different collation, we could use a simple SELECT, similar to the following. To allow you to see some data, use the INSERT statements first.

```
USE Chapter2;
Go
INSERT into EmployeesTSQL (EmpId,LName,FName,HireDate,Phone,Salary)
VALUES(1,'Grzena','Dawn','Apr 14, 1974', '(757)555-5555',180000);
INSERT into EmployeesTSQL (EmpId,LName,FName,HireDate,Phone,Salary)
VALUES (2,'Villegas','Nimfa','Mar 31, 1962', '(757)555-4444',180000);
GO
SELECT FNameSpanish, LNameSpanish
FROM EmployeesTSQL;
```

Additionally, if we needed to optimize the query to sort on the LNameSpanish column, we could create an index on the computed column.

Views

A VIEW in SQL Server allows us to access selected column and row data from one or more tables and reference that data by referencing the single view. A *VIEW* is a virtual table that represents one or more tables. It doesn't actually hold any data, but instead allows access to the data without accessing the table(s) directly. A VIEW has two primary purposes: to maintain security and to simplify access.

 EXAM TIP VIEWs can easily be created to combine data that need to be compared side by side. For example, if the current week sales data (in one column) needs to be compared to the weekly sales of the same week last year (from a separate column), a VIEW can be created to show this data side by side.

VIEWs enhance security because we can grant access to the view without granting access to the underlying table. Consider our employee data. Two columns jump out as data that we would want to protect: Salary and the Social Security Number.

While it is possible to grant permissions on a column level, this can be very tedious. Instead, we can create a VIEW including only the columns we want to show, and then grant access to the VIEW. This provides a level of security by ensuring that users that access the VIEW see only the columns we've included in the VIEW. They can't see other columns in the underlying table.

Further, users who are granted access to the VIEW do not need permissions to the underlying table. This is important because it prevents the possibility of users trying to bypass security by querying the table directly.

 TIP Using views to limit the columns available to users for security purposes is sometimes referred to as *vertical partitioning*.

As we'll see in Chapter 4, creating queries for one or more tables can get complex. However, just about any query we can create can be converted into a VIEW. This includes queries that join multiple tables.

Creating Views

It's relatively easy to create a basic VIEW. We'll create views using both SSMS and Transact-SQL statements based on the Employee table created earlier.

In the following exercise, we'll create a VIEW for a phone listing.

Exercise 2.7: Create a Simple View in SSMS

See how to create a view in SSMS by watching video 2-7.

1. If it's not already open, launch SSMS, double-click Databases, double-click the Chapter2 database created earlier, and double-click Views.

2. Right-click Views and select New View. In the Add Table dialog box, select Employees and then click Add.

3. Click Close. The Employees table should appear in the top portion of the screen known as the diagram pane.

4. In the Employees table, select LName, FName, and Phone by clicking the check box.

5. The middle area of the screen is known as the criteria pane. In the criteria pane, to the right of LName, under Sort Type, select Ascending. Your display should look similar to Figure 2-5.

Figure 2-5

Creating a
view in SSMS

TIP   In your research, you may read that ORDER BY can't be used in a VIEW. It can, but the TOP clause must also be included. The TOP clause allows us to retrieve the TOP number (as in top 5), or TOP PERCENT (as in top 10 percent). By using TOP (100) PERCENT, you can use the ORDER BY clause and return all rows.

Notice that in the top pane (diagram pane), you have the table you added. As you select columns to display, they appear in the middle pane (criteria pane). In the bottom pane (SQL pane), a T-SQL statement is built—the benefit is that you don't really need to type the T-SQL code for your VIEW. Simply use the visual interface and the SQL statement is built for you.

6. Press CTRL+S to save the VIEW.

7. In the Choose Name dialog box, enter **vw_EmpPhone**. Click OK.

8. With the VIEW created, we can view the data in it. Click the New Query button.

9. If the Connect to Server dialog box appears, accept the defaults and click Connect.

10. Enter the following T-SQL statements and then click Execute.

```
USE Chapter2;
GO
Select * from vw_EmpPhone
```

If you used the INSERT statements to enter some sample data when you created the table, you will be able to see a result set with your data. Even with no data, the VIEW will execute successfully; it just won't return any data.

We can also create views with T-SQL statements. The syntax of the CREATE VIEW statement is shown in the following code:

```
CREATE VIEW [ schema_name . ] view_name [ (column [ ,...n ] ) ]
[ WITH <view_attribute> [ ,...n ] ]
AS select_statement [ ; ]
[ WITH CHECK OPTION ]

<view_attribute> ::=
{
    [ ENCRYPTION ]
    [ SCHEMABINDING ]
    [ VIEW_METADATA ]       }
```

The different options for the CREATE VIEW statement are important to understand and will be explained in-depth later in this section. First, we'll create a basic VIEW using T-SQL statements in the following exercise.

Exercise 2.8: Create a View Using T-SQL

1. Use the same query window you used to create the VIEW in SSMS. Clear the lines you've entered. If you closed the query window, open another with the New Query button.

2. Enter the following T-SQL statements to create a simple VIEW:

```
USE Chapter2;
GO
CREATE VIEW dbo.vw_EmpSalary
AS
SELECT     TOP (100) PERCENT EmpID, LName, FName, Salary
FROM       dbo.Employees
ORDER BY LName;
```

Notice that the script is very similar to what you created in SSMS. We simply added the EmpID column and changed the third column from Phone to Salary.

3. Enter the following T-SQL statement to view the data from the view:

```
SELECT *
FROM vw_EmpSalary;
```

4. Highlight the statement you just entered, and then press F5 to execute just that line. You should have a result set based on data in your table.

5. It's also possible to see the original syntax that created the view with the sp_helptext stored procedure. Enter the following T-SQL statement to see the definition you just used to create this VIEW:

```
USE Chapter2;
GO
EXEC sp_helptext 'dbo.vw_EmpSalary ';
```

6. Enter the following T-SQL statements to create a more complex view within the AdventureWorks database. This VIEW is based on a SELECT statement joining columns from several tables.

 TIP If this SELECT statement looks a little challenging to you, don't be surprised. While it's common to join several tables together, they can look a little daunting if you don't see them often. We'll explore SELECT statements from simple to complex in Chapter 4.

```
USE AdventureWorks;
GO
CREATE VIEW dbo.vw_Employee_details
AS
SELECT
    e.EmployeeID
    ,c.LastName
    ,c.MiddleName
    ,c.FirstName
    ,e.Title AS [Job Title]
    ,c.Phone
    ,c.EmailAddress
    ,a.AddressLine1
    ,a.AddressLine2
    ,a.City
    ,sp.Name AS [State or Province]
    ,a.PostalCode
    ,cr.[Name] AS [CountryRegionName]
FROM HumanResources.Employee AS e
    INNER JOIN Person.Contact AS c
    ON c.ContactID = e.ContactID
    INNER JOIN HumanResources.EmployeeAddress AS ea
    ON e.EmployeeID = ea.EmployeeID
    INNER JOIN Person.Address AS a
    ON ea.AddressID = a.AddressID
    INNER JOIN Person.StateProvince AS sp
    ON sp.StateProvinceID = a.StateProvinceID
    INNER JOIN Person.CountryRegion AS cr
    ON cr.CountryRegionCode = sp.CountryRegionCode;
```

7. Enter and execute the following T-SQL statement to view the data from the VIEW.

```
SELECT *
FROM vw_Employee_details;
```

Updating Data in a VIEW

Even though views don't actually hold any data, you can still update the data in the underlying table(s)—usually. An exception is when you create a VIEW using a UNION statement. While this can still be modified, we'd use an Instead Of trigger as discussed in Chapter 6.

In the following exercise, we'll update the data using the VIEW.

Exercise 2.9: Update Data in a View

Watch video 2-9 to see how to troubleshoot a view if updates don't work.

1. With SSMS open, right-click the dbo.vw_EmpSalary VIEW and select Open View. If you don't see the VIEW, right-click Views and select Refresh. Your VIEW should look similar to that in Figure 2-6.

View - dbo.vw_EmpSalary	Table - dbo.Employees	Summary	MCITPSUCCESS....QLQuery3.sql*	
	EmpID	LName	FName	Salary
▶	1	Gibson	Duane	100000.0000
	2	Villegas	Nimfa	100000.0000
✳	NULL	NULL	NULL	NULL

Figure 2-6   A view opened for editing

2. At the bottom, where the nulls are, fill the columns with data such as your name and desired salary as a DBA. Make sure you enter a number in the EmpID column. This cannot be null.

3. Add the name of a friend.

4. Close the VIEW. You can do so by clicking the X at the top right of the tabbed document (not the X in SSMS).

5. Right-click the VIEW and select Open View to reopen it. You'll see that the data you entered has been saved.

6. Using the SSMS Object Explorer, browse to the Employees table. Right-click the Employees table and select Open Table. You can see here that by modifying the data in the VIEW, the data in the underlying table was modified.

VIEW Options

When creating views, you can specify different options that affect it. These are described next.

WITH SCHEMABINDING

One problem with views is that if the underlying tables are modified, it can break the VIEW. For example, our earlier Employee Phone VIEW is dependent on the LName, FName, and Phone columns. If someone was to add another phone column called

MobilePhone, and change the name of Phone to HomePhone, our VIEW would no longer work. When accessed, the VIEW would look for the Phone column, but since it no longer existed, it would error out.

To prevent the underlying table from being modified in such a way that our VIEW would break, we could specify the WITH SCHEMABINDING option when we create the VIEW.

WITH CHECK

To understand what the WITH CHECK option does, we first need to use a WHERE clause to create a VIEW that shows only a subset of rows. For example, we could create an Employee Salary VIEW based on the department and grant access to department managers for their department VIEW. The following definition will create a VIEW that an IT manager could use to view IT employee salary data:

```
USE Chapter2;
GO
CREATE VIEW dbo.vw_ITEmpSalary
AS
SELECT      LName, FName, Salary
FROM        dbo.Employees
WHERE Department = 'IT'
```

This works fine as it is. However, what if the manager accidentally modifies the department for one of her employees? While the employee still works in the IT department, since the record has been modified, the employee will no longer appear in the VIEW. Because the employee doesn't appear in the VIEW, the manager can't fix the record.

To prevent this from happening—in other words, to prevent data from being modified in such a way that it falls out of the VIEW—we can define it with the WITH CHECK option. If defined with the WITH CHECK option, the department in the preceding example could not be modified.

WITH ENCRYPTION

When a VIEW is created, the VIEW definition is kept in the sys.comments table of the database. If you don't want others to view the definition of the view, you can use the WITH ENCRYPTION option. Note that this is not encrypting the data, only the definition of the VIEW.

 EXAM TIP Views are very common in SQL Server, and only a few options relate to them. Make sure you know what the options are and when to use them.

Indexed View

Indexes can be created with views. We'll learn more about indexes in Chapter 7, but for now realize that indexes can improve the performance of tables and can also be created on views.

When creating an indexed view, you have to observe a few restrictions:

- All tables and user-defined functions must be referenced by two-part names.
- The VIEW must have been created using WITH SCHEMABINDING.
- If the VIEW uses any functions, the functions must use WITH SCHEMABINDING.
- If the VIEW uses any functions, the functions must be deterministic—that is, they cannot include any nondeterministic functions.

Of course, the last bulleted item begs the question: What is a nondeterministic FUNCTION? A *nondeterministic* FUNCTION returns different results when it's called at different times with the same parameters. For example, the GETDATE() FUNCTION returns one thing today, but will return something else tomorrow. A *deterministic* FUNCTION, on the other hand, always returns the same result whenever it is called with the same input values.

Creating a Database

While we created a basic database earlier, a lot more could have been done. We'll create a database using the GUI in SSMS and explore the different options that can be specified.

The data for a database is stored in two files. The primary database file ends with an extension of .mdf (master database file). Log files end with the extension of .ldf (log database file). If you create a secondary database file, it will end with the extension .ndf.

The .mdf or primary database file holds all of the database objects and data for the database. We'll explain the transaction log in depth in Chapter 10, but in short, it records DML activity (INSERT, UPDATE, and DELETE) against the database and helps maintain database integrity. For most applications, a single database file will meet your needs. However, in Chapter 7 we'll explain the benefits of creating multiple files in the Filegroups section.

 NOTE When the folks at Microsoft were trying to identify the three-character extension for the secondary data file, they briefly considered .sdf (secondary database file), but it was already being used for another file type. Someone at the table suggested that since .mdf was for the "master," they could use .ndf for "not the master." It stuck.

Locating the Files

By default, both the regular database file (.mdf) and the transaction log file (.ldf) of any database stored in the first instance of SQL Server are stored in the following directory:

```
C:\Program Files\Microsoft SQL Server\MSSQL.1\MSSQL\Data
```

If a database was created in the second instance of SQL Server, the files would be stored in the following:

```
C:\Program Files\Microsoft SQL Server\MSSQL.2\MSSQL\Data
```

Notice that the only difference is the MSSQL.1 for the first instance and MSSQL.2 for the second instance.

It's also possible that a database is stored somewhere else. A common optimization technique for a database is to store the database file on one drive and store the transaction log on another file. To verify where the database files are actually located, you can right-click the database within SSMS and select Properties | Files and then scroll over until the path is visible, as shown in Figure 2-7.

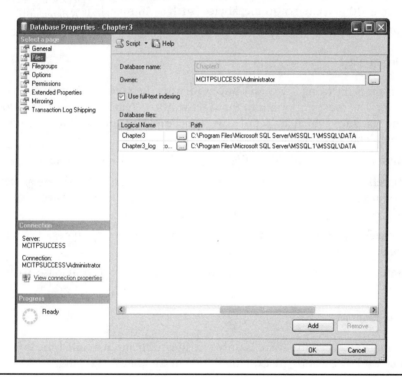

Figure 2-7 Viewing the path of the database files

EXAM TIP It's common to place the database files on a separate drive than the operating system, and the transaction log files on another drive. Make sure you know how to do this. This is demonstrated in the following exercise.

The details of why is much clearer once you understand what's going on in the transaction log, but for now be aware that we move the transaction log to improve performance and/or improve recovery capabilities.

Database Options

When creating a database, we're faced with choices with several options. We'll see these in the following exercise, but let's do an overview of them now.

The General page

- **Initial Size** This identifies the initial size of the data or transaction file. It doesn't indicate how much data is in the database, but instead just how big the data file is when created.

- **Autogrowth** Once data is added to a database, the data or transaction file can become full. If Enable Autogrowth is checked, the file will automatically resize itself based on the options specified. It can be set to grow by a specific percent (such as 10 percent), or in megabytes (such as 10 megabytes).

- **Path** This shows exactly where the data or transaction files are located.

The Options page

- **Automatic options** Several options identify the automatic operation of SQL Server. The most important of these is the Auto Create Statistics and Auto Update Statistics, which are set to True by default. Statistics will be explained in more detail in Chapter 7.

- **Cursor options** This identifies the default operation of cursors in SQL Server.

- **Miscellaneous options** ANSI standards can be manipulated here as well as several generic options. You can also set the operation of recursive triggers from this page. Triggers are covered in Chapter 6.

- **Recovery options** The Page Verify option identifies what types of checks are done upon reboot after a system crash.

- **State options** The State options identify the state of the database, such as Read-only.

The Filegroups page

- **Primary** By default, there is only one filegroup and it's called the Primary filegroup. Filegroups are explained fully in Chapter 7.

In the following exercise, we'll create a database within SSMS and modify many of the default options.

Exercise 2.10: Create a Database within SSMS

View the database properties in video 2-10.

1. With SSMS open, right-click Databases and select New Database.

2. In the New Database window, on the General page, enter the Database name as **Chapter2Test.** Notice that the two database files now are named Chapter2Test and

Chapter2Test_log. The initial size of these files is based on the size of the model database.

3. Change the size of the Chapter2Test Data file to 30MB and the size of the Chapter2Test_Log file to 10MB. Your display should look similar to Figure 2-8. While this sets the size of the files, the database still has no data. This just specifies how big the "placeholder" files are.

Figure 2-8
Creating a new database in SSMS

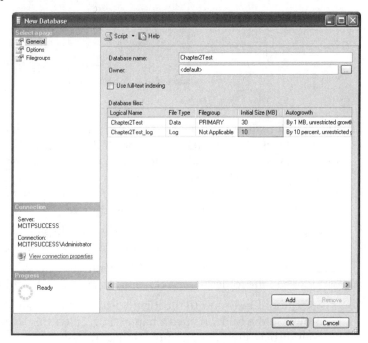

4. To the right of the Initial Size column is the Autogrowth column. This determines whether a database file or log file will grow as it fills up, and how it will grow. Click the ellipsis (. . .) button for the Autogrowth of the Chapter2Test data file. Verify the file is set to Enable Autogrowth and can grow to an unrestricted size. You should see something similar to Figure 2-9.

5. By using this dialog box, you can enable or disable autogrowth. As you add data to a database, the data file begins to fill up. If the amount of data approaches the size of the placeholder file, autogrowth options can allow the file to grow to hold more data. You can specify how the data files will grow, and also set a maximum size. Click OK.

 TIP If a database file or log file fills up and can't grow, it will become a read-only database. Because of this, autogrowth is typically enabled on a database. However, autogrowth can be a resource-intensive operation. DBAs strive to reduce the number of times a database will automatically resize itself by manually altering the size during off-peak hours and setting the amount it can grow by to a sufficiently large size.

Figure 2-9

Configuring auto-growth for a new database

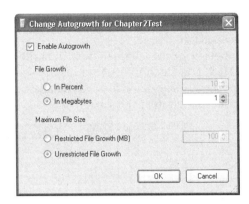

6. The default path of the database files is in the Program Files\Microsoft SQL Server\MSSQL.1\MSSQL\Data directory. If desired, you can change the location of the database files. In the next few steps, we will move the database and log files from their default location to another location. On a production server, we would move them to different drives, but for the purpose of this exercise, we'll just move them to another folder on the C: drive.

   a. Use the WINDOWS + E keys to launch Windows Explorer. Use Windows Explorer to create two directories named **Chapter2Data** and **Chapter2Log**.

   b. Select the ellipsis next to the data file Path. In the Locate Folder dialog box, browse to the folder named Chapter2Data. Select this folder and click OK.

   c. Select the ellipsis next to the log file Path. In the Locate Folder dialog box, browse to the folder named Chapter2Log. Select this folder and click OK. Your display should look similar to Figure 2-10.

   Under Select A Page, change the page being displayed from General to Options. Here, you can change many different options for your database. Notice the Recovery Model is set to Full. We will explain this further in Chapter 11, but for now realize that the Recovery Model is directly related to how the transaction log is used. Full allows you to use the transaction log to recover data in the case of a failure, but also requires you to manage the transaction log to prevent it from growing uncontrollably. Change the Recovery Model to Simple. The Simple recovery model causes the Transaction Log to be truncated automatically, reducing management requirements for the log file, but prevents the transaction log from being used in a recovery model.

7. Notice that Auto Create Statistics and Auto Update Statistics are both True. This ensures that indexes created in your database will work optimally. We'll explore statistics in more depth in Chapter 7. Auto Shrink is one of the options on this page. By default, this is set to False. If it's set to True, SQL Server periodically

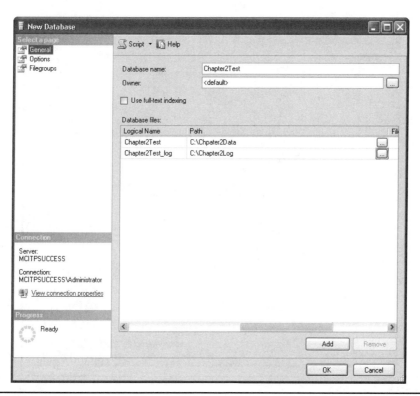

Figure 2-10   Changing the location of the data and log files

looks at the amount of data in the database files and shrinks the database files if they meet certain criteria. Your display should look similar to Figure 2-11.

8. Under Select A Page, change the page being displayed from Options to Filegroups. Here you can create additional filegroups, but for now we'll accept the default of one *Primary* filegroup.

9. Click the arrow to the right of Script and select Script Action To New Query Window. This will open a New Query window in SSMS with the T-SQL script to create the same database you are configuring in the GUI. If run, this script sets all the database options from all three pages in the GUI and creates a database. Review the script and compare it with the options selected in the GUI.

10. Return to the New Database dialog box, and click OK to add the Chapter2Test database.

11. Right-click Databases in SSMS and select Refresh.

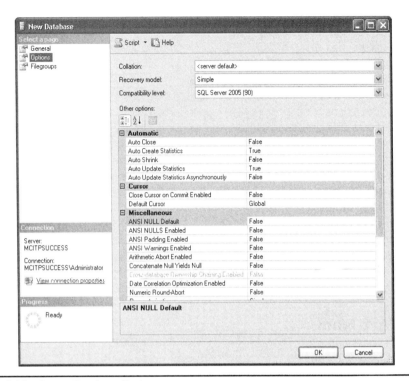

Figure 2-11 Setting Database Options

You can also create a database using T-SQL. As we've seen in earlier exercises, a database can be created with a simple statement such as:

```
CREATE DATABASE DatabaseName
```

The previous statement creates a database from the Model system database using all of the options and defaults set on the Model. To change some of these defaults, such as changing the location of the file or transaction files, you can do so by following the basic syntax of creating a database shown in the following template.

```
CREATE DATABASE database_name
    [ ON
        [ PRIMARY ] [ <filespec> [ ,...n ] ]
        [ , <filegroup> [ ,...n ] ] ]
    [ LOG ON { <filespec> [ ,...n ] } ]
    ]
    [ COLLATE collation_name ]
    [ WITH <external_access_option> ]
]
```

To see all of the possible arguments available, take a look at the Books Online article "Create Database (Transact-SQL)."

Schemas and Naming Conventions

The word *schema* has gone through a change in meaning within Microsoft's SQL Server 2005. I'm not a doctor, but we could almost say *schema* has a split personality.

In past versions, any time we referred to "schema" we were referring to the definition of the database or a database object. For example, the VIEW option WITH SCHEMABINDING refers to ensuring that any dependent object definitions are not changed. As we saw earlier in this chapter, WITH SCHEMABINDING is present in this version, so in this context, "schema" refers to the *definition* of the object.

"Schema" can also be found in the four-part naming structure of objects, and in this context, it refers to the name of a *container* or namespace (a term .NET developers are familiar with) of objects. (In past versions of SQL Server, it was the *owner*.)

A significant difference is that in past versions, individual users would be assigned ownership of objects and the object would be named with the username. For example, a VIEW created and owned by the user named Joe would be named Joe.vwEmpSalary. In SQL Server 2005, we add users to database roles and grant the roles ownership of schemas that contain groups of objects. Instead of using usernames (such as Joe) in the name of the object, we use the schema in the name of the object.

Four-Part Naming

As a database developer, you will be writing T-SQL statements that refer to objects such as tables, views, and stored procedures. Each object has a formal four-part name, though this is often shortened to a shorter one- or two-part name. The four-part name has the following format:

Server.database.schema.object

For example, for our Phone view in the Chapter2 database on a server named MCITPSuccess, the name would be MCITPSuccess.Chapter2.dbo.vw_EmpPhone.

In this case, we are using the default schema of dbo, which refers to database owner.

Server

The only time we specify the server is when we're trying to connect to a server external to the SQL Server that we're executing the query on. We can do this when accessing data on linked servers. For an *ad hoc query* (a query that's just going to be performed once and doesn't need a linked server created) against external OLE DB data sources, we can use the OPENROWSET or OPENDATASOURCE functions.

Database

This part of the object name is the database we want to access. If using the query window, often we employ the USE statement to set our context or to point to the database. When including the database in the query, it would look like this:

```
Select * from Chapter2.dbo.vw_EmpSalary
```

Notice that the server is omitted, so the query would use the local server instead of looking for an external server that we've created as a linked server.

We can also prefix a query with the USE command to set the context of the database as follows:

```
USE Chapter2;
GO
Select * from dbo.vw_EmpSalary
```

Schema

We use schemas to group together database objects with a common purpose. As mentioned earlier, you can also think of the schema as a container. We use a schema to grant access to a group of users based on their role membership.

For example, let's say we have a group of database administrators who manage all of the database objects related to sales. We could group these DBAs into a server role named SalesRole, as shown in Figure 2-12.

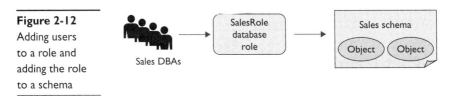

Figure 2-12
Adding users
to a role and
adding the role
to a schema

Now we can create a Sales schema, which will act as a container or namespace for all the Sales objects. To grant the Sales DBAs access to the objects in the Sales schema, we would assign ownership of the SalesRole role to the Sales schema, granting them full access.

If a new DBA is hired, she could easily be added to the SalesRole and be automatically granted access to the objects in the Sales schema. If one of the current Sales DBAs were to win the lottery and move on, you could easily remove him from the SalesRole without impacting any functionality.

This overcomes a significant problem we had in earlier versions of SQL Server. Before, if an employee who was assigned as an owner left the company, we couldn't drop the user until we reassigned ownership. By changing ownership, all queries that referenced the original owner would be broken. To get around this, Microsoft previously recommended that all objects be owned by one owner—dbo (database owner). This limited our flexibility.

By using schemas to group objects and assigning roles as the owner of a schema, we can add and drop users at will. We can even change the ownership of a schema by assigning different roles. Throughout all these changes, the schema will remain constant.

Object

The last part of the four-part name is the object. This includes the tables, views, triggers, functions, and stored procedures that the T-SQL code you are writing is referencing.

Naming Conventions

It's common to name objects by using a descriptive prefix appended to a meaningful name. For example, when creating our view earlier, we named it vwEmpPhone. Six months from now when we're looking at the name vwEmpPhone within a T-SQL script, we'll know that this is a view (*vw*) and it probably includes Employee Phone (*EmpPhone*) numbers. This is also commonly referred to as *self-documenting code*.

In contrast, I could have named the view *EP*. Six months from now, if I were to look at the name *EP* within a T-SQL script, I'd probably mutter "Huh?".

What prefixes should you use? Table 2-4 lists some common prefixes used for database objects. If you're the only DBA, you define the prefixes and the naming conventions that make sense to you. However, different environments come up with different naming conventions. As you move into an established environment as a DBA, part of your job is to identify what objects are being used and to follow the convention in place.

Prefix	Object
vw	View
usp	User-defined stored procedure
fn	User-defined FUNCTION
trg	Trigger

Table 2-4   Common Object Prefixes

As examples, Views could be named vwEmpPhone, vwEmpSalary, and so on. User-defined stored procedures might be named uspGetEmpManager, uspInsertNewCustomer, and so on. Functions would be named with the prefix of fn, while Triggers would be named with a prefix of trg. These aren't the only possibilities for prefix names. Typically, most environments already have a standard set of prefixes in use. What we need to do when working in any environment is identify the standard prefixes being used and name our objects similarly.

Chapter Review

The table is about the most basic object in a database and holds data in individual columns of rows. We define the data using data types, and SQL Server supports a wide range of data types, including large value data types (new to SQL Server 2005), T-SQL and CLR user-defined data types, and XML data types.

To focus the data, we can create views. To prevent our views from breaking from a modified table, we can use WITH SCHEMABINDING. To optimize a view, we can create an indexed view.

Schemas are a new feature in SQL Server 2005 and provide an improved method of granting ownership to groups of objects. Instead of assigning individual users ownership, we create a schema that acts as a container of objects, and then we add database roles to the schemas. The schema is part of the four-part naming convention as in *server .database.schema.table*.

Additional Study

Self Study Exercises

Use these additional exercises to challenge yourself:

- Create a database named Ch2Ex using T-SQL.
- Create a database named Ch2Ex2 using SSMS and change the size and location of the database files. Set the transaction log to be truncated automatically.
- Using SSMS, create a table within one of your new databases named Football with the following columns: FootballID, TeamName, DateNamed, WinLossRecord, and CurrentStanding. The WinLossRecord column will be an XML data type. Use your own judgment for other data types.
- Using T-SQL, create a table named Referees. Columns will include RefereeID, LastName, FirstName, and Picture. Allow only the FirstName to be null. The Picture column will hold actual photographs (pick the most appropriate data type).
- You realize that the amount of data in the WinLossRecord column is becoming very large for some Football teams. It can exceed 8K. Modify the Track data type to accommodate data beyond 8K.
- Add a column to the Football table named Owner. Ensure this owner can not be NULL.
- Create a user-defined data type for a new column. The data type will be team code with the first three letters of the team name, a dash, and a two-digit number.
- Create a VIEW including only the Football TeamName, the CurrentStanding, and the Owner name columns.
- Modify the VIEW so any changes to the underlying table will not break the VIEW.

BOL Topics

- Data Types (Transact-SQL)
- Using Unicode Data
- Using Large Value Types
- In-Row Data
- CREATE TABLE (Transact-SQL)
- Deterministic and Nondeterministic Functions
- Creating Indexes on Computed Columns
- CREATE VIEW (Transact-SQL)
- Creating Indexed Views
- Using Identifiers as Object Names
- User-Schema Separation

Summary of What You Need to Know

70-431

When preparing for the 70-431 test, make sure you know the topics in all the main sections of this chapter. The objectives specifically mention implementing tables, views, and user-defined data types, as well as configuring database properties such as log files and data files. Pay special attention to the information on views, data types, nulls, and defaults.

70-441

When preparing for the 70-441 test, make sure you know the topics in all the main sections of this chapter. The objectives specifically mention the basics of database design, designing user-defined data types, tables, computed columns, and views. Pay special attention to the information on views, data types, nulls, and defaults.

70-442

This chapter contains little related to the 70-442 test. The primary objective covered here discusses optimizing data storage types by choosing the appropriate data types and designing the appropriate use of varchar. When preparing for the 70-442 test, make sure you know about the large value types such as varchar(max), nvarchar(max), and varbinary(max). Additionally, make sure you understand the usage of computed columns.

Questions

70-431

1. Project Managers have asked you to modify the Projects table in a SQL Server 2005 database. They want a column added named ShortProjectName, and they want to ensure that this column is never left blank for new projects. How can you accomplish this? (Choose all that apply.)

   A. Create the new column and specify it as NULL.

   B. Create the new column and specify it as NOT NULL.

   C. Create a DEFAULT definition of 'Unnamed' for the column.

   D. Create a CHECK constraint of 'Unnamed' for the column.

2. You are tasked with modifying the Course table in a school's database. You need to add a Prerequisite column and ensure that nulls are not allowed. However, course prerequisites have not been identified for all courses yet. What would you do?

   A. Define the new column as NULL and use a TRIGGER to populate the data.

   B. Define the new column as NULL and use a FUNCTION to populate the data.

   C. Define the new column as NOT NULL and leave the columns empty.

   D. Define the new column as NOT NULL, with a default value of Not Identified.

3. You are creating a view to join the Temperature and Wind tables in your SQL Server 2005 database named Hurricanes. You need to ensure that modifications to the schemas of the underlying tables do not affect the VIEW. What should you do?

   A. Assign your assistant to check the VIEW on a daily basis.

   B. Create the VIEW using the WITH SCHEMABINDING option.

   C. Create a DML AFTER TRIGGER on each table to modify the VIEW if the schema is changed.

   D. Create a DML INSTEAD OF TRIGGER on each table to modify the VIEW if the schema is changed.

4. You are trying to optimize a VIEW by adding an index. However, it is not successful. What's the likely reason? (Choose all that apply.)

   A. The VIEW was created with a deterministic FUNCTION.

   B. The VIEW was created with a nondeterministic FUNCTION.

   C. The VIEW was created with the CHECK option.

   D. The VIEW was not created using WITH SCHEMABINDING.

5. Which of the following functions is nondeterministic and therefore can't be used in an indexed VIEW?

   A. GETDATE()

   B. DATEDIFF()

   C. DAY()

   D. MONTH()

6. The CREATE statement is one type of _____.

   A. DML statement

   B. DDL statement

   C. Evolutionary statement

   D. Spiritual statement

7. You are asked to add two new columns to the Customers table named PreferredCustomer (bit) and PreferredCustomerDiscount (decimal). Any preferred customers (the PreferredCustomer bit is a 1) should automatically get a discount (defined in the PreferredCustomerDiscount column). Currently, there aren't any PreferredCustomers identified. Preferred customers should automatically get a 10 percent discount. What should you do?

   A. Add the two columns, with a default of .10 for the PreferredCustomer and a default of 0 for the PreferredCustomerDiscount.

   B. Add the two columns, with a default of .10 for the PreferredCustomer and a default of 1 for the PreferredCustomerDiscount.

C. Add the two columns, with a default of .10 for the PreferredCustomer Discount and a default of 0 for the PreferredCustomer.

D. Add the two columns, with a default of .10 for the PreferredCustomer Discount and a default of 1 for the PreferredCustomer.

70-441

1. Sales data is partitioned into two tables—one for recent sales (the past six months) and one for older or archived sales data. You are tasked with creating a solution to allow managers to be able to see monthly sales data from the previous month and for the same period a year ago. What would you do?

   A. Create a view that joins data from both tables.

   B. Combine the data into a single table and query it.

   C. Create a trigger to identify when data is added and query the new data.

   D. Create indexes on the two tables based on the date and query the tables individually.

2. The price of a product depends on the status of the customer, and the status of the customer is based on the amount of business the customer does with the company. The Product table has a calculatedPrice column that performs complex calculations on a variety of columns from different tables. What should be created to determine the value for the calculatedPrice column and ensure it is returned as quickly as possible?

   A. A computed column

   B. A user-defined function to retrieve the data

   C. A DDL trigger to store the data

   D. A CLR user-defined data type

3. What database object would be commonly used to combine selected columns from two or more tables for both querying and updating?

   A. Table

   B. View

   C. Function

   D. Trigger

4. You are designing the Customers table used within a Sales database. The design document specifies that space is a concern for all tables. Which of the following data types would be a good choice for the LastName column in the Customers table?

   A. char(50)

   B. nchar(50)

    C. varbinary(50)

    D. varchar(50)

5. You are reviewing the design of a table that holds several columns of numeric data. One of the columns is derived from data in the numeric columns using a simple mathematical algorithm. How would you design the table?

    A. Implement a CLR user-defined data type.

    B. Implement a computed column.

    C. Implement a DDL trigger.

    D. Use one of the large value types to store the data.

70-442

1. You manage a SQL Server database that contains some employee resumes in PDF documents. Since the employees are consultants, the files are available to be downloaded. Many of these PDF documents include pictures of the employee, and the size of the PDF files is often several megabytes. What data type should be used to store the PDF files?

    A. Image

    B. varchar(max)

    C. nvarchar(max)

    D. varbinary(max)

2. The Referee table within the Football database has a column named picture which holds JPEG files. It was created in SQL Server 2000 and is using the image data type. You have upgraded the database to SQL Server 2005. Should the picture column be changed?

    A. No. The image data type is okay.

    B. Yes. It should be changed to the varbinary(max) data type.

    C. Yes. It should be changed to the varchar(max) data type.

    D. Yes. It should be changed to the XML data type.

3. You are tasked with optimizing a database by adding indexes. Which of the following computed columns can have indexes added to them? (Choose all that apply.)

    A. A computed column created from the Month function as Month(Birthdate)

    B. A computed column created from the GetDate() function

    C. A computed column based on the InventoryOnHand and Cost columns

    D. A computed column named ExtendedPrice based on the QuantityOrdered and Price columns

4. You are tasked with creating a solution that will allow names (LastName and FirstName) of customers in the Customers table of the MCITP database to be queried in the Modern_Spanish collation. It is currently stored in the Latin1_General collation and this capability needs to be retained. What do you do?

   A. Create a copy of the MCITP database on a different server with the Modern_Spanish collation.

   B. Create a copy of the MCITP database within the same instance as the MCITP database using the Modern_Spanish collation.

   C. Create a copy of the Customers table with the Modern_Spanish collation.

   D. Create a computed column on the names using the Modern_Spanish collation.

5. True or false? An index can be created on a computed column that has been created for a different collation.

   A. True

   B. False

Answers

70-431

1. **B, C.** The only way to ensure that a column is never null is to specify it as NOT NULL. However, this will fail unless a DEFAULT definition is also created populating the existing rows with a default value.

2. **D.** To ensure that nulls are not allowed, you would use the NOT NULL statement. Since nulls are no longer allowed, you would not be able to leave the column empty. Defining a default value of "not defined" would ensure the column is not null.

3. **B.** The WITH SCHEMABINDING option prevents underlying tables from being modified in such a way that would cause your view to break. While triggers could be used to identify whether tables have been modified, we would have to define a DDL TRIGGER, not a DML TRIGGER.

4. **B, D.** Indexed views can only be created on views that have been created with deterministic functions and using the WITH SCHEMABINDING option.

5. **A.** GETDATE() is nondeterministic. It will return one thing today and another tomorrow. However, all the other functions will return the same data as long as they have the same parameters passed in.

6. **B.** The DDL statements we mentioned in this chapter were CREATE, ALTER, and DROP.

7. **C.** PreferredCustomers haven't been identified, so the PreferredCustomer default should be set to 0. Customers that are identified should get a 10 percent discount, so the PreferredCustomerDiscount should be set to .10.

70-441

1. **A.** A view is the simple answer to this problem. There is no need to combine the data into a single table; it can be queried from two tables. A trigger wouldn't be used for queries. While indexes can improve the quality of queries, they aren't a requirement for queries.

2. **D.** A CLR user-defined data type would be best since complex calculations are required and performance is an issue. A computed column wouldn't be the best performance since the data would have to be recalculated each time the column is queried. Creating a function to retrieve it means we would have to use the function each time the column was queried. A DML trigger may be possible to store the data, but a DDL trigger would not work.

3. **B.** A view is used to combine selected columns from one or more tables. Just about any query that can be created against a database can be used to create a view. A table would only hold data from a single table. A function is a saved Transact-SQL or common language runtime (CLR) routine that returns a value. While a function could be used in this fashion, it wouldn't be as common as a view.

4. **D.** Varchar(50) is the best choice. It will use only the amount of space needed based on the length of the name. Char(50) and nchar(50) will use 50 bytes and 100 bytes, respectively, whether the LastName is 3 characters or 30 characters. Varbinary() is not appropriate for a text column.

5. **B.** We are using aggregated data from other columns in the table with a simple mathematical formula. A computed column would be the best choice. A CLR user-defined data type is useful for complex calculations, but this is not indicated here. A DDL trigger only works with Data Definition Language statements (CREATE, ALTER, DROP), so this wouldn't work here. There is nothing to indicate the size of the number would exceed 8K, so a large value type isn't needed.

70-442

1. **D.** Varbinary(max) is one of the new large value types and can store data up to 2GB in size. It is an ideal choice for any binary file. Image has been deprecated and should not be used. Varchar(max) and nvarchar(max) are for text files, but wouldn't be appropriate for a binary file.

2. **B.** The image data type is deprecated in SQL Server 2005, so ideally the data type should be changed. The varbinary(max) data type is most appropriate. Neither varchar(max) nor the XML data type would hold the JPEG data.

3. **C, D.** Indexes can not be created on computed columns that are nondeterministic. Computations based on the date (such as Month or GetDate functions) are nondeterministic.

4. **D.** A computed column can be created to display the data in the different collation. There is no need to create completely different databases or tables to achieve the result.

5. **True.** The primary restriction on creating indexes on computed columns is that the computed column must be nondeterministic and precise. Simply changing the collation would result in both a deterministic and precise result.

Database Design

In this chapter, you will learn about:

- Data integrity
- PRIMARY and FOREIGN KEY constraints
- Normalization and denormalization
- CHECK constraints
- Partitioning tables via horizontal partitioning or partition schemes
- Database design through an exercise

> *Beauty of style and harmony and grace and good rhythm depend on simplicity.*
>
> —*Plato*

Simplicity. No matter what you're designing—from a graceful garden to a dynamic database—much of the beauty comes from the simplicity of the design. In databases, we achieve simplicity by normalizing a database.

In Chapter 2, we presented basic data types and tables. In this chapter, we'll add multiple tables and show how the tables can be related with PRIMARY and FOREIGN KEYs. The normalization section of this chapter shows how you can reduce complex tables to their simplest form to ensure the functionality of a database. You'll see how some basic business rules can be enforced by implementing constraints and checks. And you'll learn how very large tables can be partitioned to increase performance of queries.

To help you solidify your understanding, we tie the chapter together with a database design exercise.

Data Integrity

One of the basic challenges of any databases is ensuring that we have quality data. A huge database with bogus and/or inconsistent data is only marginally better than no data at all. What we do with any database is implement different methods to ensure the integrity of the data.

Constraints are used to enforce data integrity by constraining, or restricting, the data that can be entered into a database. The different types of constraints that can be used to enforce data integrity are:

- **NOT NULL** This specifies that a column does not accept NULL values, or in other words, data must be entered. We covered NULL and NOT NULL in Chapter 2.

- **PRIMARY KEY** The PRIMARY KEY is used to ensure that each row within a table is unique. The PRIMARY KEY does not allow NULL values. (This will be covered in depth in this chapter.)

- **FOREIGN KEY** A FOREIGN KEY is used to create and enforce relationships between two tables. A FOREIGN KEY in one table typically references a PRIMARY KEY in another table (though it can also reference a column identified with the UNIQUE constraint). (FOREIGN KEYS will be covered in depth in this chapter.)

- **CHECK** The CHECK constraint allows us to limit the values that can be put into a column. We have a wide range of capabilities of limiting values that will be covered in more depth later in this chapter.

- **UNIQUE** The UNIQUE constraint is used to ensure that all values within a column are unique. This can be used on tables that have a PRIMARY KEY but need another column that must have each column unique. The UNIQUE constraint allows a NULL value.

We have three types of data integrity to consider in database design. These are outlined in Table 3-1.

Type of Integrity	Affects	Method
Domain	Columns	Data types, defaults, trigger constraints
Entity	Rows	PRIMARY KEY constraints
Referential	Relationships	PRIMARY KEY and FOREIGN KEY constraints

Table 3-1 Types of Data Integrity

With *domain integrity*, we try to ensure that the data entered is valid. We don't necessarily know that the data is accurate, but we can ensure it's valid. For example, if we have a phone number in a table, we could set the data type as char(13), and if someone accidentally entered the wrong number of characters, we'd know that the data isn't valid and we could restrict the entry. Constraints allow us to do more sophisticated checking than a basic data type, such as making sure the phone number is entered and formatted exactly how we want it, such as (# # #) # # # - # # # #, where # is any number between 0 and 9. If the parentheses and dash are entered where we specify and the numbers are entered where the number symbol is located, we know the data is valid and in the right format (though we still don't know if it is accurate).

Entity integrity affects the table and requires that all rows be unique. We enforce this with a PRIMARY KEY (PK) constraint.

Referential integrity ensures that created relationships between tables are maintained. It is maintained by creating relationships between tables with PRIMARY and FOREIGN KEYs—and among other checks, it ensures that data in a referenced table aren't deleted.

In the following sections, we'll first cover the primary and FOREIGN KEYs and then some other types of constraints.

PRIMARY KEYs

Each row within a table must be unique. This is referred to as entity integrity and is accomplished with the use of the PRIMARY KEY (PK) constraint. A PRIMARY KEY is a field or group of fields that uniquely identifies a row. Tables can have only one PK constraint, and it can't accept null values.

Consider our Employees table from Chapter 2. We can't afford to have two employees with all of their data the same. Even if you were to have two employees named John Smith, a PK such as EmployeeID would be used to enforce uniqueness between the two.

PRIMARY KEYs can be created using either numeric or character data types, though they are often defined as an *integer* data type with the IDENTITY property. Each time we add a new employee, the IDENTITY property will automatically create a new unique number for that employee. Identity needs two parameters, as in IDENTITY(100,1). The first number says what number to start with (referred to as the *seed*), and the next number says how much to increment for the next employee. With IDENTITY (100,1), the seed is 100 and the *increment* is 1; the first EmployeeID would be 100, and the next EmployeeID would be 101.

It's also possible to have a composite PK. What this means is that instead of using just a single column as the PK, we use two or more columns. This is frequently done in a junction table creating a many-to-many relationship between two tables. We'll discuss junction tables and many-to-many relationships later in this chapter.

Get Copies of the Scripts Online

This chapter covers many scripts, which are available on the accompanying CD. Updated scripts (if there is any need for updates) can be found at MCITPSuccess .com. Once you've downloaded them, you can easily cut and paste them into SSMS, but I strongly encourage you to type them in. You'll make mistakes, yes, but as you do, you'll learn. As you correct your typos, you'll learn more.

So why are the scripts available? Sometimes, especially after typing for a while, the smallest typos elude us. Instead of stopping in frustration, you can always cut and paste in the scripts, and if desired, compare yours side by side with the book scripts.

A simple DDL script to create an Employee table with the EmployeeID as the PRIMARY KEY is shown in the following code. Notice the PK is using the Identity property.

```
USE Master
CREATE DATABASE Chapter3;
GO
```

```
USE Chapter3;
GO
CREATE TABLE dbo.Employee
(
        EmployeeID int IDENTITY(100,1) NOT NULL,
        LastName varchar(35) NULL,
        FirstName varchar(35) NULL,
        CONSTRAINT [PK_Employee_EmployeeID] PRIMARY KEY CLUSTERED
        (
                EmployeeID
        )
)
```

Figure 3-1 shows what the table would look like in the SSMS graphical user interface (GUI). The key icon next to EmployeeID gives us a graphical representation of the column that is the PRIMARY KEY.

Figure 3-1
The Employee
table in SSMS

Column Name	Data Type	Allow Nulls
EmployeeID	int	☐
LastName	varchar(35)	☑
FirstName	varchar(35)	☑
		☐

EXAM TIP While it is possible to create tables in the SSMS GUI, what you'll often see on test questions is a script showing the structure of a table. You should be able to look at the script and be able to picture what the table looks like. This becomes a lot easier after you've typed in a few.

FOREIGN KEYs

A FOREIGN KEY (FK) is used to establish a relationship between two tables. The FK in one table will typically refer to the PK in the other table, (but could also refer to a UNIQUE constraint instead of a PK). This relationship provides referential integrity between the two tables.

While the primary purpose of the FOREIGN KEY constraint is to link the two tables together so that a row in one table is linked to a row in another table, it does more. It controls changes to data in both the PRIMARY KEY table and the FOREIGN KEY table. This will become clearer as we explore the FOREIGN KEY more.

Let's consider our Employee table. Notice that there are no address entries. We could have put the address, city, state, and zip columns in the Employee table, but imagine that our database has other tables for Customers, Suppliers, and Contractors. Each of these tables needs address information. The address information we put in one table, we would have to repeat in all the tables.

To reduce this redundancy, we create a separate table named Address and then relate the Employee and the Address table with a PK-to-FK relationship.

The Address table has a PK constraint named AddressID. We add an FK constraint named AddressID to the Employees table that references the AddressID field in the Address table. (We could also relate the Address table to the Customers, Suppliers, and Contractors tables.) This is done in the AdventureWorks database.

Let's take this a step further. Let's say we have an Employee record with an associated Address record. The employee leaves the company. If we deleted the employee record without deleting the address record, we would be left with an "orphan" record in the address table. This is unacceptable, and is actually prevented through referential integrity. The PK-FK relationship will prevent the deletion of the employee record as long as the associated address record exists.

You can use the following script to create the Address table. Note the creation of the PRIMARY KEY constraint, which is bolded:

```
USE Chapter3;
GO
CREATE TABLE dbo.Address
(
        AddressID int IDENTITY(1,1) NOT NULL,
        AddressLine1 varchar(35) NULL,
        AddressLine2 varchar(35) NULL,
        City varchar(35) NULL,
        State char(2) NULL,
        Zip varchar(10) NULL,
        CONSTRAINT [PK_Address_AddressID] PRIMARY KEY CLUSTERED
        (
             AddressID
         )
)
```

This isn't enough though. While we have both tables, they aren't connected. Think about an employee named Sally. When we enter Sally's address in the Address table, we need to make sure that it's connected to Sally's record in the Employee table.

To connect the two tables, we create a FOREIGN KEY constraint in the Employee table. The following is a script to modify the Employee table by adding the FK constraint, which is bolded:

```
USE Chapter3;
GO
Alter TABLE dbo.Employee
        ADD AddressID int NULL
        CONSTRAINT FK_Employee_Address FOREIGN KEY(AddressID)
             REFERENCES dbo.Address(AddressID)
```

Notice that we first add the column AddressID that we'll use as the FK, and then we create the constraint that REFERENCES the PK. Figure 3-2 shows the database diagram for the two related tables.

 TIP Notice that in the figure, the tables have a connector with a key icon on one side and an infinity symbol on the other. This identifies a one (the key side)-to-many (the infinity side) relationship between the tables. In Figure 3-2, one address could be linked to more than one employee (for example, if both a husband and wife are employees). This also gives a clear indication that we have a PK-to-FK relationship. Within the tables, the PK is identified with a key icon. While the FK isn't identified with an icon, since it's almost always created with the same name as the PK in the parent table, it's easy to identify. If we did not create a FOREIGN KEY constraint, there wouldn't be a line because a relationship between the tables would not exist.

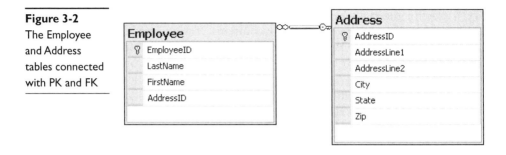

Figure 3-2
The Employee and Address tables connected with PK and FK

Let's look at a different example and see how we could connect two tables with an intermediate, or junction, table. Consider a company that sells books. Every time a sale is made, an invoice is created. The invoice might look like this:

```
INVOICE

   ORDERID:   15123              CUSTOMERID: 101
   DATE: Mar 30, 2008
   Items Purchased
   Item          Quantity      Item Price      Extended Price
   MCITP Dev     2             $69.95          $139.90
   Gardening     1             $14.95          $14.95
                                SubTotal             $154.85
                                Sales tax            $ 6.20
                                Total                $161.05
```

Three tables within a database that support this invoice might look like Figure 3-3, with the Orders, OrderDetails, and Products tables.

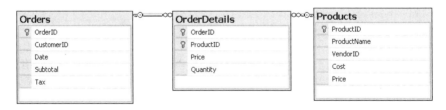

Figure 3-3   The Orders, OrderDetails, and Products tables

Notice that the OrderDetails table has a composite PK made up of both the OrderID and the ProductID. Additionally, the OrderID column in the OrderDetails table is an FK to the Orders table. The ProductID column in the OrderDetails table is an FK to the ProductID column in the Products table.

As a customer picks additional products for her order, the products are added to the OrderDetails table and thus added as detail lines on the invoice.

Imagine that the customer places the order over the phone with the intention of coming in to pick it up. The invoice has been created, and the Orders and OrderDetails tables hold the data from the invoice. All is good with the world, until… the customer calls and cancels the order.

If you delete the record from the Orders table, you could end up with "orphaned" records in the OrderDetails record—OrderDetails line items that don't relate to any existing order. This would be unacceptable. However, because we've created the FOREIGN KEY constraint on the OrderDetails table, referential integrity would prevent any attempt to delete the record in the Orders table as long as related records exist in the OrderDetails table. Instead, the database engine would return an error.

 EXAM TIP The FK constraint prevents orphaned records in child tables. In other words, records in the parent table cannot be deleted as long as records exist in the child table.

How do we delete the order then? Two ways:

- We could first delete the records in the child table (orderDetails), and then we could delete the record in the parent table (Orders).
- We could define the tables with the On Delete Cascade option.

Cascade Options

We can create Cascade options on the FOREIGN KEY constraint to cause the data deletions or updates in the parent table to *cascade* to the child table. Cascade options are defined as part of the FOREIGN KEY definition. For example, if we consider our Employees and Address tables created earlier, we may decide that if an Employee is deleted, we also want to delete the row in the Address table.

 EXAM TIP If we want to automate the deletions of records in FOREIGN KEY tables when a record in the PRIMARY KEY is deleted, we can define an On Delete Cascade option to have deletions cascade. We would define the cascade option on the FOREIGN KEY constraint.

We could alter the Employee table with the following script to implement cascading deletes from the Employees table to the Address table. First, we would drop the existing FK constraint and then re-create it with the ON DELETE CASCADE clause.

```
USE Chapter3;
Go
Alter TABLE dbo.Employee
      Drop Constraint FK_Employee_Address;
GO
Alter TABLE dbo.Employee
      ADD CONSTRAINT FK_Employee_Address FOREIGN KEY(AddressID)
            REFERENCES dbo.Address(AddressID)
                ON DELETE CASCADE
```

NOTE While this example does show us how to implement a cascading delete, it wouldn't be acceptable if we had multiple employees (such as a husband and wife) tied to the same address. If the husband was deleted, the wife's address would also be deleted. This is an excellent example of why cascading delete isn't the default.

If we consider our Orders and OrderDetails tables from the previous example, the OrderDetails table could be defined with an On Delete Cascade option on the FOREIGN KEY constraint. Now, if an order is deleted, all order detail records for this order would also be deleted.

We can also create an On Update Cascade, which causes updates in the PRIMARY KEY table to cascade down to the FOREIGN KEY table. This affects the related fields (PRIMARY KEY and FOREIGN KEY fields) only and since we rarely change the PRIMARY KEY data it wouldn't be used as often.

Consider this scenario: We have a PK of three digits on our Address table. The maximum number of addresses we can have is 1000 (0 to 999). The company grows and we decide to modify the PK of the address table to include the first three initials of the city followed by a six-digit number. If we modified the existing PRIMARY KEYs in the Address table, the Employee addresses would now be orphaned with FKs in the Employees table pointing to nonexistent PKs.

Instead, we could use On Update Cascade. When we modified the PK in the Address table, the change to the PK would be cascaded to the Employee table.

Validating Data with a FOREIGN KEY

Let's consider one more example of using PRIMARY and FOREIGN KEYs to help us ensure that only valid data is entered. Let's say we have customers only from the United States. We know that valid entries are limited to the 50 states.

We can create a table (named State) that contains one char(2) column (named State) set as the PK. We could then enter the two-letter abbreviation of all 50 states into this table, and create an FK from the Address table to this State table. Figure 3-4 shows a database diagram of these two tables.

Figure 3-4
Database diagram
of Address and
State tables

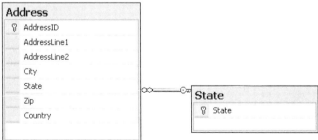

Now, whenever the state abbreviation is entered into the Address table, SQL Server compares the entry to the 50 valid entries in the State table. If someone makes a typo (such as *VS* instead of *VA* for Virginia), the FK constraint will prevent the data entry until it's corrected.

Of course, if the user enters *MA* instead of *VA* for Virginia, the database will allow it since *MA* is valid for Massachusetts. We can check to ensure the data is valid, but we can't make sure it's correct.

 EXAM TIP An FK constraint can be very effective in ensuring only valid data is entered. If the data doesn't exist in the child record, the entry fails. Compared with other methods, an FK constraint is often the most effective because it looks at the data *before* the data is entered. In contrast, DML triggers work on data after the data has been entered. Triggers can roll back the data entry, but that requires double work since the data is entered, and then undone.

The following exercise will demonstrate using a constraint for data validation.

Exercise 3.1: Enforce Integrity with an FK

1. Open SSMS if it isn't open already and create a New Query window.

2. If you didn't run the scripts described previously in this chapter, run them now:

    a. Run the script to create the Chapter3 database.

    b. USE Master
    CREATE DATABASE Chapter3;Run the script to create the Employee table.

```
USE Chapter3;
GO
CREATE TABLE dbo.Employee
(
        EmployeeID int IDENTITY(100,1) NOT NULL,
        LastName varchar(35) NULL,
        FirstName varchar(35) NULL,
        CONSTRAINT [PK_Employee_EmployeeID] PRIMARY KEY CLUSTERED
        (
                EmployeeID
        )
);
```

    c. Run the script to create the Address table.

```
USE Chapter3;
GO
CREATE TABLE dbo.Address
(
        AddressID int IDENTITY(1,1) NOT NULL,
        AddressLine1 varchar(35) NULL,
        AddressLine2 varchar(35) NULL,
        City varchar(35) NULL,
        State char(2) NULL,
        Zip varchar(10) NULL,
        CONSTRAINT [PK_Address_AddressID] PRIMARY KEY CLUSTERED
        (
                AddressID
        )
);
```

    d. Run the script to modify the Employee table by adding an AddressID column as an FK to the PK in the Address table.

```
Alter TABLE dbo.Employee
       ADD AddressID int NULL
           CONSTRAINT FK_Employee_Address FOREIGN KEY(AddressID)
               REFERENCES dbo.Address(AddressID);
```

3. Create a State table by using the following script:

```
CREATE TABLE dbo.State
(
  State char(2) NOT NULL,
    CONSTRAINT [PK_State_State] PRIMARY KEY CLUSTERED
    (
         State
    )
);
```

4. Populate the State table by executing the following INSERT statements:

```
INSERT INTO dbo.State VALUES('VA')
INSERT INTO dbo.State VALUES('NY')
INSERT INTO dbo.State VALUES('MA')
INSERT INTO dbo.State VALUES('NV')
INSERT INTO dbo.State VALUES('HI')
INSERT INTO dbo.State VALUES('CA')
```

    Notice this adds six entries for Virginia (VA), New York (NY), Massachusetts (MA), Nevada (NV), Hawaii (HI), and California (CA).

5. Create an FK in the Address table pointing to the State table by running the following script:

```
Alter TABLE dbo.Address
  ADD CONSTRAINT FK_Address_State FOREIGN KEY(State)
       REFERENCES dbo.State(State);
```

6. Add an address in the Address table with a valid state using the following INSERT statement:

```
INSERT INTO dbo.Address(AddressLine1, City, State, Zip)
VALUES ('565 Untraveled Path','Mossey','VA','23462')
```

    With this INSERT, we can see it's possible to add a record to the Address table:

7. Add an address with an invalid state with the following INSERT statement:

```
INSERT INTO dbo.Address(AddressLine1, City, State, Zip)
VALUES ('30 Degree Dr.','Frostproof','FF','73462')
```

    You should see an error similar to the following:

```
Msg 547, Level 16, State 0, Line 1
The INSERT statement conflicted with the FOREIGN KEY constraint "FK_
Address_State".
```

```
The conflict occurred in database "Chapter3", table "dbo.State", column
'State'.
The statement has been terminated.
```

8. By entering the following SELECT statement, you can verify the first row was added, but the second row was not:

```
SELECT * FROM Address
```

Table Relationships

As we've seen with the PRIMARY KEY and FOREIGN KEY sections previously, we can create relationships between tables. Usually, we match a PK in one table with an FK in another table in a one-to-many relationship. However, three different kinds of relationships actually exist.

- One-to-many relationships
- One-to-one relationships
- Many-to-many relationships

One-to-Many Relationships

In a one-to-many relationship, any row in the first table can have matches to many rows in the second table. For example, consider a company that sells products from several different manufacturers. Any single manufacturer (in the manufacturer table identified with the PK of ManufacturerID) could have many different products. However, any single product (in the product table identified with the PK of ProductID) can only have one manufacturer. We can see this in Figure 3-5.

Notice the icons in the connecting line in Figure 3-5. On the PK side, we can see a key (representing one) and on the FK side is an infinity symbol (representing many).

Figure 3-5 A one-to-many relationship

Many-to-Many Relationships

In the many-to-many relationship, any row in the first table can have matches to many rows in the second table. Additionally, any row in the second table can have matches to many rows in the first table.

Consider a publishing database. We could have a Book table listing titles and information on books, and an Author table holding information on authors. We can see this in Figure 3-6.

Figure 3-6
The Author and Book tables without a relationship

However, let's think about actual books and authors for a minute. Any book could be written by multiple authors, and any author could write multiple books. If we created a one-to-many relationship from the Book table to the Author table, it would work for a book with multiple authors, but any single author couldn't be related to multiple books. Likewise, if we created a one-to-many relationship from the Author table to the Book table, it would work for an author writing multiple books, but not for a book with multiple authors.

We need to create a many-to-many relationship. This is misleading though. We can not directly create a many-to-many relationship between two tables. Instead, we must define a third table (often referred to as a junction table).

The junction table has a one-to-many relationship with the first table, and then a second one-to-many relationship with the second table. We can see this in Figure 3-7.

Figure 3-7 A many-to-many relationship

EXAM TIP When designing a database where two tables need a many-to-many relationship between them, create a third connecting table, also known as a junction table. This junction table will have a composite PK key created from the PK from each of the two tables.

Earlier in this chapter, Figure 3-3 showed three tables common in a sales database: Orders, Products, and OrderDetails. Any order should be able to contain many products, while any product should be available for sale to many customers. This capability is achieved with the creation of the junction table of OrderDetails.

One-to-One Relationships

The least used relationship is the one-to-one relationship. Any single row in table one can have only a single matching row in table two. Additionally, any single row in table two can have only a single matching row in table one.

Since it's a one-to-one relationship, it's easier to simply store all the data in a single table. However, a few special circumstances can arise where it's beneficial to store data this way.

- You need to divide a table with many columns.
  You can get around the limitation of no more than 8K by dividing the table.

- Isolate columns into a separate table for security reasons.
  Sensitive data can be placed into a separate table with permissions used to control access to the table. This may be easier than using column level security on a single table.

- Store data that is short-lived.
  For example, during some types of migration, the data may be needed early in the migration but not in a later phase. When the later phase is reached, the second table could simply be deleted.

Figure 3-8 shows a diagram with two tables with a one-to-one relationship.

Figure 3-8
Two tables with
a one-to-one
relationship

Notice the icons in the connecting line in Figure 3-8. On the PK side, we can see a key (representing the one), and on the FK side is a key symbol (representing one).

Exploring Relationships in AdventureWorks

In the last chapter, we had a single Employees table in the Employee database. The AdventureWorks database has an Employee table also. However, since the database can store employee, customer, and vendor data, the AdventureWorks designers chose to create one table for all these types of people and then relate them to other tables using PK-to-FK relationships. The employee, customer, and vendors are stored in the contact table which is located in the person schema.

 TIP AdventureWorks is a very robust database with complex tables and relationships. How do you know what all the columns and tables are for? You look at the documentation. Thankfully, AdventureWorks is well documented in Books Online. Check out the topic "AdventureWorks Data Dictionary."

Rows in the Person.contact table can be identified as an employee-type person, a customer-type person, or a vendor-type person. We do this by creating relationships between the tables. Relationships are typically created between the PRIMARY KEY (PK) in one table and the FOREIGN KEY (FK) in another table.

In the next exercise, we'll create a database diagram in the AdventureWorks database that will show these relationships.

Exercise 3.2: Create a Database Diagram

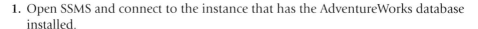

See how to create a diagram in SSMS in video 3-2.

1. Open SSMS and connect to the instance that has the AdventureWorks database installed.

2. Open Databases, open AdventureWorks, and then select Database Diagrams. Right-click Database Diagrams and select New Database Diagram.

3. Add the Contact(Person) table. Click Close.
   This is the Contact table in the Person schema (person.contact). Notice the key icon to the left of *ContactID*. This indicates this column is the PK. You'll typically see the PK first and it will end with *ID*. Most of the other columns are intuitive, such as FirstName and LastName. All columns are documented in Books Online in the "AdventureWorks Data Dictionary" article.

4. Right-click in the window and select Add Table. In the Add Table dialog box, add the Employee(HumanResources) table. Click Close. Arrange the tables so they look like Figure 3-9.

   We can see that these two tables are related based on the relationship connector. The relationships between the two tables are based on the ContactID PK in the Contact (Person) table and the ContactID FK in the Employee (HumanResources) table.

5. Hover over the connector between the two tables. It will have the name of the FOREIGN KEY right after the word "Relationship." The name is FK_Employee_ Contact_ContactID.

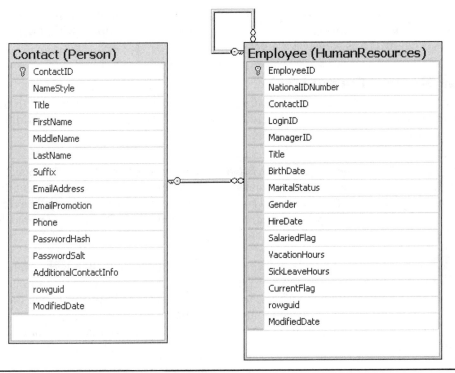

Figure 3-9 The Contact and Employee tables

6. Look at the Employee(HumanResources) table. Do you see any other FKs here? EmployeeID is the PK.

- ContactID is the FK pointing to the PK ContactID in the Contact table.

- LoginID is an FK pointing to a PK named LoginID in a table named Login.

- ManagerID is a little different. Managers are employees, too. Instead of creating a separate Manager table, we can create a relationship between the Employee table and itself. This is also called a *self-referencing table*. For example, Joe Employee is an employee with an EmployeeID of 101. Sally is Joe's manager; she's an employee with an EmployeeID of 202. In Joe's record, it will list the ManagerID as 202, pointing to Sally.

7. You can save your database diagram or just close it.

Normalization and Normal Forms

Normalization is the process of designing database tables to ensure that several database principles are followed. The database principles are referred to as *normal forms*. Edgar F. Codd wrote a paper in June 1970 entitled "A Relational Model of Data for Large Shared Data Banks," where the idea of normal forms was first introduced. Over the years, it was improved by Codd and others.

While more than three normal forms exist, the first three are the most quoted and most often used. The process of ensuring that your database complies with the normal forms is referred to as *normalizing* a database.

1st Normal Form (1NF)

First normal form (1NF) requires that all column values in a table be divided to their smallest element. In other words, all non-PRIMARY-KEY fields are atomic. Additionally, we would have no repeating groups.

 TIP *Atomic* doesn't mean explosive as in "atomic bomb." Instead, atomic refers to what was once understood to be the smallest possible element that can't be split—the atom. I know, I know; we can split atoms today. The term *atomic* was popularized before the practice of splitting atoms was commonly understood, and in some circles, it still sticks.

As an example, consider a name. You could have one name field; however, it could be split into first name, last name, and middle initial. A database with an entire name in the name field would be much harder to manipulate with simple functions such as sorting on the last name, or just querying the last name.

Consider Figure 3-10. This is a table used to build an invoice that does *not* comply with first normal form.

Figure 3-10
The InvoiceTable
that is not in 1NF

InvoiceTable

- OrderNumber
- CustomerName
- CustomerAddress
- Item1Name
- Item1Price
- Item1Qty
- Item2Name
- Item2Price
- Item2Qty

This table has a couple of problems:

- It has columns that can be divided (CustomerName and CustomerAddress).
- It has repeating groups of items, prices, and quantities. For a customer who wanted to purchase three or more items, the table wouldn't work. A customer could only purchase two or more unique items at a time.

The solution is to split the table into several related tables, as shown in Figure 3-11.

Figure 3-11
Normalized
tables to comply
with 1NF

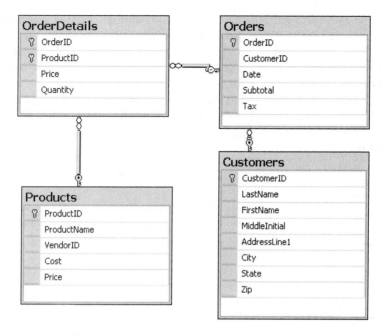

Now, each item within each table is reduced to its smallest element, and there are no repeating groups within individual tables. It doesn't matter if a customer wants to order 1 or 100 items. We would have one row in the Orders table, and as many items as desired in the OrderDetails table. Notice the OrderDetails table is using a composite PRIMARY KEY. Also, notice that the Orders and Products tables are connected with a junction table (OrderDetails) in a many-to-many relationship. The Customers table is related to the Orders table in a one-to-many relationship.

2nd Normal Form (2NF)

2nd normal form (2NF) applies to tables that have composite PRIMARY KEYs, where two or more attributes comprise the PRIMARY KEY. A table is said to be in second normal form if it is in first normal form and every non-PRIMARY KEY attribute is completely dependent on the whole PRIMARY KEY. In other words, if an attribute within the table is dependent on only one column of the composite PRIMARY KEY then it is NOT in second normal form.

Consider Figure 3-12 showing the OrderDetails table, which does *not* comply with 2NF because of the SupplierCity field.

Figure 3-12
An OrderDetails
table, which does
not comply with
2NF

The problem with this table is that the SupplierCity (the company that supplies this product to the company that then resells it) is not dependent on the whole PRIMARY KEY (both the OrderID and ProductID). Instead, the SupplierCity is dependent only on part of the PRIMARY KEY (ProductID). Another significant problem with this is that you'd be forced to enter the SupplierCity for every line entry on an order.

The solution would be to take the SupplierCity column out of the OrderDetails table and put it into a separate table such as a Suppliers table. It would then be referenced by the Product table using the PK of the Suppliers table: SupplierID. The database diagram of the normalized tables would look similar to Figure 3-13.

Figure 3-13

A normalized table with SupplierCity removed from the OrderDetails table

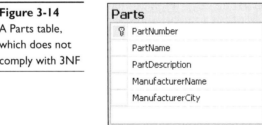

3rd Normal Form (3NF)

3rd normal form (3NF) requires there be no nontrivial functional dependencies of non-PRIMARY KEY attributes on something other than the PRIMARY KEY. In other words, fields within the table are only dependent on the PRIMARY KEY and not dependent on any non-PRIMARY KEY fields.

Consider Figure 3-14. It shows the Parts table, which does *not* comply with 3NF:

Figure 3-14

A Parts table, which does not comply with 3NF

Parts
🔑 PartNumber
PartName
PartDescription
ManufacturerName
ManufacturerCity

The problem is that the ManufacturerCity is dependent on the ManufacturerName as much as it's dependent on the PartNumber. Leaving it this way, we'd have to repeat the data entry for the ManufacturerCity and ManufacturerID for every single part. In addition to cramped fingers, we'd also get a fair share of typos where these are entered differently in different part numbers.

The solution would be to create a new table named Manufacturer, add the ManufacturerName column, columns for the address (street, city, state, zip), and reference that table with a PK and FK relationship on ManufacturerID. The database diagram of the Parts and Manufacturer tables would look similar to Figure 3-15.

Figure 3-15
A normalized
database with
the Manufacturer
table added

EXAM TIP To ensure that a table complies with 3NF, review each column and ask "Is this column dependent on the PK?" For example, consider an Orders table with the following columns: OrderID (PK), EmployeeID (FK), EmployeeLastName,.... EmployeeID identifies the employee that placed the order, so it is dependent on the OrderID. EmployeeLastName though is dependent on the EmployeeID, NOT the OrderID. More than likely, the EmployeeLastName column exists in the Employee table and should not be repeated in the Orders table.

Denormalization

While normalization of databases is an admirable goal, the truth is that we often denormalize a database for better performance. That is, we selectively break some of the rules to increase performance—queries to the database are slower on a normalized database than a database that is not normalized.

A classic example of a database optimized with denormalization starts with a table similar to the following Product shown in Figure 3-16.

Figure 3-16
A Product table

For example, let's say that management is very interested in the cost value of on-hand inventory and is requesting a report with this information on a daily basis. We could query the Product table, and for every product in the table, we could multiply the quantity (QtyOnHand) times the cost to give us an extended cost.

That's no big deal if you have only 200 products, but let's say you have 2 million products. The calculation has to occur on each of the 2 million rows in the table each time the report is run (daily in this example).

To optimize the table for this query, we could denormalize it by adding another column named ExtendedCost. We could use a script to initially populate the value of ExtendedCost in each row by multiplying Cost by QtyOnHand. To keep the data up to date, we could add triggers so that every time an item is added, or the quantity or cost is modified, the ExtendedCost is recalculated based on the QtyOnHand and the Cost fields. This would no longer be in 3NF because the ExtendedCost is dependent on the QtyOnHand and Cost fields instead of PartID. Said another way, ExtendedCost is redundant data; it already exists.

Some level of denormalization is common in both online transaction processing (OLTP) databases and online analytic processing (OLAP) databases. However, OLTP databases are mostly normalized because they are focused on inserts and modifications, which perform better in a normalized database. OLAP databases are commonly denormalized because they are focused on querying, and querying a database can be performed easier and quicker in a denormalized database.

 TIP   Denormalization is sometimes referred to as "flattening" a database. This is because denormalizing a database sometimes reduces the number of tables.

Generalization

A natural result of normalization is the creation of many tables. Generalization, on the other hand, is the process of combining similar entities together to form a single entity.

For example, generalization is used in the AdventureWorks database with tables to represent people, such as employees, customers, and vendors. Each of these tables could be created in the manner shown in Figure 3-17.

Figure 3-17
Three tables representing different types of people

Instead, generalization was applied within the AdventureWorks database. The Contact table was created that has all the general attributes of people, such as names and phone numbers. This general table is then related to the specific tables of Employee, VendorContact, and Individual (for customers). We can see this in Figure 3-18.

Figure 3-18
Generalization
applied with use
of a Contact table

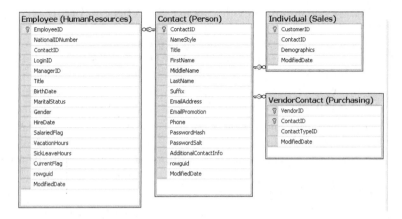

Additionally, a separate general Address table is created within AdventureWorks and related via junction tables. Each of the junction tables creates a relationship to the address table for the different contacts.

Generalization is used when a large number of entities (such as employees, customers, vendors) appear to be of the same type and have many of the same attributes (such as last name, first name, phone, address, and so on).

Careful though. Too much generalization can result in an overly complex design that is difficult to both manage and optimize.

CHECK Constraints

While PRIMARY KEYs and FOREIGN KEYs are constraints themselves, we have other types of constraints we can add. Just as with PKs and FKs, other constraints help us maintain and ensure different levels of data integrity. We covered the NOT NULL and DEFAULT constraints in Chapter 2. Here, we'll dig into the CHECK constraint.

A CHECK constraint adds significant functionality to the data type by further enforcing domain integrity. While the data type can ensure data is entered as text or numbers, we can create CHECK constraints to ensure that the data is entered in a certain format, or check for a value within a certain range. If the format is incorrect, the CHECK constraint disallows the insert or update. Additionally, CHECK constraints allow us to do checking and comparison of the data to make sure it falls within an acceptable range.

Using CHECK Constraints for Formatting

Sometimes we want data to be entered in a specific format. For example, we could desire that all phone numbers are entered as: (xxx)xxx-xxxx, or all social security numbers are entered as xxx-xx-xxxx. We saw in Chapter 2 how we could create a user-defined data type to ensure a specific number of characters are entered. Here, we'll see how a CHECK constraint can be used to ensure that the data is entered in a specific format.

CHECK constraints provide two significant benefits over other solutions.

- *Checks operate on the data before the modification is made.* Before the data is entered into the database, the CHECK will verify the format and reject the modification if it doesn't comply with the CHECK. Compare this to a trigger that checks the data *after* the modification and then must roll back the modification. We can see that the CHECK is much more efficient.

- *Checks work for all modifications.* Regardless of how the data is being modified (stored procedures, updates or inserts from an application, or ad-hoc queries), the CHECK will ensure the modification complies with the format.

 EXAM TIP A CHECK constraint provides the best performance when validating data for proper formatting. CHECK constraints examine the data before it is inserted or updated in the table and if it fails the check, the modification is prevented. DML triggers can provide similar functionality, except that triggers examine the data after the modification and then roll back the modification if unacceptable. Additionally, a CHECK constraint will check the data regardless of how the data was entered—such as through an application or an ad-hoc query.

In the next exercise, we'll create a CHECK constraint for a PhoneNumber column that ensures the phone number is entered in the correct format of a U.S. phone number (xxx)xxx-xxxx.

Exercise 3.3: Create and Test a CHECK Constraint

1. Open a New Query window in SSMS.

2. Add a Phone column to the Employee table in the Chapter3 database with the following script:

```
USE Chapter3;
GO
ALTER TABLE dbo.Employee
  ADD Phone char(13) NULL
```

3. Create a new CHECK constraint on the Employee table by running the following script:

```
USE Chapter3;
GO
ALTER TABLE Employee
  ADD CONSTRAINT ckPhone
  CHECK
  (Phone LIKE '([0-9][0-9][0-9])[0-9][0-9][0-9]-[0-9][0-9][0-9][0-9]')
```

Notice that this script will allow an open parentheses followed by three numbers, a closing parentheses followed by three more numbers, a dash, and then four more numbers. The opening and closing parentheses and the dash are all interpreted literally.

4. Add an employee to the Employee table with a valid phone number using the following INSERT statement:

```
INSERT into Employee (LastName,FirstName,Phone)
VALUES('Marx','Hi','(757)123-4567')
```

5. View the entry by entering the following SELECT statement and executing it:

```
SELECT * FROM Employee
```

You should see one line with the correct phone number.

6. Now we'll try to add an employee with the wrong format for the phone number. Enter and execute the following script:

```
INSERT into Employee (LastName,FirstName,Phone)
VALUES('Wright','Eilene','934.123.4567')
```

You should see an error similar to the following:

```
Msg 547, Level 16, State 0, Line 1
The INSERT statement conflicted with the CHECK constraint "chkPhone".
The conflict occurred in database "Chapter3", table "dbo.Employee",
column 'Phone'.
The statement has been terminated.
```

7. You can verify the entry wasn't successful by using the following script:

```
SELECT * FROM Employee
```

Using Check Constraint for Range Checking

Another popular way to use CHECK constraints is for range checking. In other words, we ensure that data entered is within a certain range. The following are a few examples:

- A new employee record has a hire date. We can ensure the hire date is not in the future by checking it against today's date. The concept is that if the hire date is in the future, it's not valid.

- A new employee record has a birth date. We can ensure the age of the employee is less than 120 years old. The concept is that if an employee's age is entered as more than 120 years old, it's not valid.

- A product table includes prices. We can ensure the price is never set below a minimum price. This employs a business rule that can protect us against a hacker who tries to set a price low, buy a couple of cases, and then put the price back to where it was.

We'll see an example of the CHECK constraint used for range checking in Exercise 3.4.

Using WITH CHECK and WITH NOCHECK

When a constraint is added to a table with an ALTER statement, by default it checks all the existing data. If you have data that violates the constraint, then the ALTER statement will fail and the constraint won't be added.

However, this feature can be turned off by using the WITH NOCHECK argument. The default is WITH CHECK, where the existing data is checked. WITH NOCHECK ignores the existing data. The constraint is only applied to any data entered after the constraint has been added.

 EXAM TIP When creating a CHECK constraint on an existing table and the existing data do NOT conform to the CHECK constraint, use the WITH NOCHECK argument. This allows the CHECK to be added and be applied to any future modifications, but will not check existing data.

Embedding Functions

One great feature of constraints is that you can embed functions in them. In Chapter 5, we'll explore functions in much greater detail, but for now be aware that functions are mini-program snippets we can use in a lot of different places with SQL.

 TIP One way to add functionality to a check is by using functions within the check. With SQL Server 2005, we can create T-SQL functions or CLR integrated functions (created with any .NET programming language). Using CLR integrated functions, you can add significant capabilities to a CHECK constraint, especially when complex computations are required.

SQL Server 2005 includes a whole range of built-in functions. For example, the GET-DATE() FUNCTION returns today's date. In addition to the built-in functions, SQL Server allows you to create your own user-defined functions.

Functions can be included in SELECT statements (covered in Chapter 4), triggers and stored procedures (covered in Chapter 5), CHECK constraints, and DEFAULT definitions.

The following exercise shows how to add some range checking constraints with and without NOCHECK, and with and without embedded functions.

Exercise 3.4: Create and Test a CHECK Constraint

1. Add a HireDate column and a BirthDate column to your Employee table using the following script. Note that HireDate is added as a smalldatetime data type, while BirthDate is added as a datetime data type.

 TIP The range of smalldatetime is restricted to January 1, 1990 through June 6, 2079. If there's a possibility you'll need to enter a date out of the range of January 1, 1990 to June 6, 2079, use the datetime data type, instead of the smalldatetime data type.

```
USE Chapter3;
GO
ALTER TABLE Employee
  ADD HireDate smalldatetime NULL,
  BirthDate datetime NULL;
```

2. Add a constraint to check that the HireDate is less than or equal to today's date using the following script. Notice that the GETDATE() FUNCTION is used to determine today's date.

```
USE Chapter3;
GO
ALTER TABLE Employee WITH NOCHECK
  ADD CONSTRAINT Ck_HireDate CHECK
  (HireDate  < GETDATE() OR HireDate = GetDate() );
```

Note that the WITH NOCHECK clause is added. This allows us to add the constraint without checking existing data. The default is WITH CHECK.

3. Add a constraint to verify that an employee's birthday is greater (more recent) than 120 years ago. Notice that we're using the DATEADD FUNCTION to subtract 120 years from today's date.

```
USE Chapter3;
GO
ALTER TABLE Employee
  ADD CONSTRAINT Ck_BirthDate CHECK
    (BirthDate > DATEADD(yyyy, -120, GETDATE() ) )
```

 NOTE The DATEADD built-in function is one of many built-in date functions. It allows us to add a number to part of a given date. We can add to the day, the month, or (as in the example) the year.

4. Add a Salary column to your Employee table with the following script:

```
USE Chapter3;
GO
ALTER TABLE Employee
  Add Salary money NULL
```

5. Create a constraint that ensures that any entered salary falls within the range of $20,000 to $200,000 using the following script. Notice that we're using the WITH NOCHECK option. If any data exists in the table, that data will not be checked with this constraint—only new data will be checked.

```
USE Chapter3;
GO
ALTER TABLE Employee WITH NOCHECK
  ADD CONSTRAINT Ck_Salary CHECK
    (Salary >= 20000 AND Salary <= 200000)
```

6. Verify operation of your constraints:

   a. Right-click the Address table and select Open Table. Identify a valid AddressID for one of the rows in the Address table. If a row doesn't exist, add one.

   b. Right-click the Employee table and select Open Table.

   c. Enter your name for LastName and FirstName. Press TAB.

d. Enter the AddressID you identified for AddressID in the preceding step. Press TAB.

e. Enter a date a week from now as the HireDate. You can use the format *d mmm yyyy* as in *1 Sep 2007*. Press TAB. While the data you entered is invalid, it isn't checked until the row is inserted. The row is inserted when we leave the row (step g following).

f. Enter a birth date as your actual birth date minus 100 years in the BirthDate column. Press TAB.

g. Simulate a salary of a well-compensated DBA, and enter a Salary of **300,000**. Press TAB. At this point, the system tries to insert the data and you get an error.

h. Read the error. It should be related to the CHECK constraint Ck_HireDate. Click OK to dismiss the error dialog box.

i. Correct the HireDate by changing the date to today's date. Press ENTER.

j. At this point, you get an error on the BirthDate column from the Ck_BirthDate constraint. Read the error and click OK. Correct the error by entering your actual birth date. Press TAB.

k. You'll now have an error on the Salary column from the ck_Salary constraint. Read the error and click OK. Correct the error by entering your salary as **200000**. Press TAB.

UNIQUE

The UNIQUE constraint allows a field besides the PK to be enforced as unique. The Department of Motor Vehicles (DMV) in the state where I live had an excellent example of a need for the UNIQUE constraint.

When I first moved to Virginia, my driver's license number was my social security number (SSN). Apparently, when they first designed their system, it was considered perfectly acceptable to use the SSN this way. However, in these days of identify theft, alarm bells should be going off whenever a social security number is being used or requested.

Imagining their database, I envision that they used the SSN as the PRIMARY KEY. SSNs are theoretically unique for living persons in the United States. Since an SSN card was often used as one piece of identification to get a driver's license, it was easy to use the SSN as a PK. And the PK within the database will enforce uniqueness if the quirk of a duplicate SSN were to crop up.

Years later, when the state recognized their error, they needed to be able to create a new number for the driver's license. However, the structure of the database was already established with the SSN used as a PK. Instead of completely redesigning the database, they could have simply added a new UNIQUE column for the driver's license number.

The UNIQUE constraint is very useful in this scenario. Since we can have only one PK and we're already using the SSN there, we can assign the UNIQUE constraint on the Driver's License Number column. The UNIQUE constraint ensures we don't have any duplicate driver's license numbers.

You can have more than one UNIQUE constraint, and unlike PKs, they can contain null data (but only one null). Additionally, UNIQUE constraints can be referenced by FOREIGN KEY constraints to link tables.

As an example, the following code could be used to add a UNIQUE constraint to the Driver table.

```
ALTER TABLE Driver
ADD DriverLicenceNumber VARCHAR(20) NULL
    CONSTRAINT DLN_unique UNIQUE;
```

Partitioning Tables

When tables get very large, often we consider partitioning them for optimization. What this means is that we divide the data so it is stored on more than one physical disk. This can make searching and the execution of frequently used queries much more efficient.

Two methods can be used to partition tables: horizontal partitioning and partition schemes. Horizontal partitioning has been available to us for a long time, but is more manual. Partition schemes are new to SQL Server 2005 and allow the system to automate the process of partitioning.

 EXAM TIP Horizontally partitioning tables is an invaluable technique used to manage large tables. While not all of us will manage tables large enough that they need to be partitioned, all test takers pursuing the MCITP: Database Developer certification need to be aware of the strategies available to partition data. Make sure you understand the big picture of why we partition tables and the benefits involved.

Horizontal Partitioning

In traditional horizontal partitioning, we divide the rows of the table into separate tables to make the size of the tables more manageable.

For example, a sales table could have sales data from four regions of the country (north, south, east, and west). Since each region is primarily interested in sales from their region, we can divide the sales table into four separate tables. This reduces the size of each table to only about 25 percent of the original size (assuming all regions are equal) and positively impacts the performance of all tables.

Each table would be defined the same way with the same columns. However, one column (we'll call it Region in this example) identifies which table the sales data is inserted into. The application that inserts the data would determine which region the sale occurred in and insert it into the appropriate table.

If headquarters needed to see sales from all regions, we could create a VIEW with a UNION statement to show all regions. This would pull the data from the four tables and present it as a single virtual table. This is referred to as a partitioned VIEW.

Partitioning by Date

A common choice of partitioning is based on dates. Consider an Orders table that has 10 million rows. Much of this data is referred to as historical data, and it includes orders placed more than six months ago. About 5 percent of the data is current data—orders from the past six months. Customer service personnel need to be able to access current data, but very rarely need to access historical data.

 EXAM TIP When recent data needs to be queried often from a very large table, the query can be optimized by partitioning the data by date. Older data can be moved to a different partition, reducing the amount of data that needs to be read for the query on the newer data.

If we leave the Orders table as a single table, then the customer service personnel have to wait until their queries can get through 10 million rows of data. This could be very inefficient. A way to optimize this is to horizontally partition the data by date.

We do this by creating two separate tables. The first table is the Orders table. The second table has the same definition as the Orders table, but has a different name, such as OrdersArchive.

We could run two queries on a monthly basis. The first query would read data from the Orders table; any data that is older than six months would be imported into the OrdersArchive table. The second query would delete any data in the Orders table older than six months (and was just imported into the OrdersArchive table).

Now when customer service personnel query the Orders table, it will only be about 500,000 rows. That's still a lot, but significantly less than the original 10 million.

Filegroups

While filegroups will be discussed in greater depth in Chapter 7, they deserve a mention here. By using filegroups, we can place the Orders table in one file on one disk and the OrdersArchive table in another file on another disk. However, we can't do this directly. Filegroups are the interim objects that allow us to place a table object on a specific drive.

Figure 3-19 shows the relationships between files and filegroups. Files can be created via SSMS or T-SQL statements, and their location can be changed after being created. Just as an Excel file would be stored on the hard drive, SQL Server databases use files that are stored on the hard drive to hold database objects.

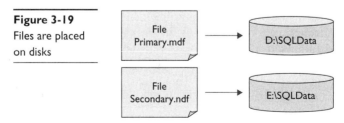

Figure 3-19
Files are placed
on disks

By default, we have one *file* (.mdf) and one *filegroup* (Primary). Additional files can be created and, by default, are associated with the Primary filegroup. We can also create additional filegroups and associate different files with filegroups.

In Figure 3-20, we can see the relationships among objects (such as tables), file-groups, and files. We can associate one file (such as orders.ndf on the D: drive) with a filegroup (such as fgSecond). Now we place a table named Orders into fgSecond; it will be stored on the D: drive. Similarly, we can associate another file (such as archive.ndf on the E: drive) with a different filegroup (such as fgArc). When we place the OrdersArchive table into fgArc, it will be stored on the E: drive.

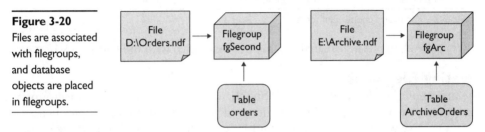

Figure 3-20

Files are associated with filegroups, and database objects are placed in filegroups.

When designing a table, we are not given the option of which file to place it in. We can only place database objects in filegroups.

Federations of Servers and Federated Databases

A federated database is a database that is spread across multiple servers, often in multiple geographical locations. A primary difference between horizontally partitioned databases and federated databases is that, the different partitions of federated databases are maintained on different servers that have a level of autonomy and can be independently managed.

The servers that hold the different parts of a federated database are referred to as a federation or federated database servers. A federation of database servers is used to spread the processing load across a group of servers. The data is horizontally partitioned allowing each of the servers to be independently managed, but distributed queries can be used to process requests on the entire database.

EXAM TIP When a large amount of data from a single database needs to spread across multiple locations, consider creating a federated database. A federated database can provide both scalability and load balancing.

Federated database servers are often used in the largest Web sites, with a multitier system to balance the processing load across multiple servers. This multitier system can provide very high levels of performance.

Partition Schemes

Partition schemes perform a function similar to horizontal partitioning, but are much more automated. New to SQL Server 2005, they partition a table based on ranges. Though appearing to be a single table, in truth they are spread across different file-groups (and normally spread across different disks) so overall I/O access to the database performs more efficiently.

The different elements of a partition scheme are listed in Table 3-2.

Partition Element	Purpose
Filegroups	Used to separate partitions onto different physical disks
Partition function	Identifies ranges of the different partitions
Partition scheme	Assigns partition functions to filegroups

Table 3-2 Partition Scheme Elements

Once the elements are created, a table can be created with the partition scheme.

Creating Filegroups

The first step in implementing a partition scheme is to create additional filegroups and files so we can actually spread the partitions across different files. In a production environment, we would have the different files on different disks, but in these exercises, we'll place them in the same drive. Since a partition scheme needs some data in order for us to see what it's doing, we'll use the AdventureWorks database.

 EXAM TIP Partitioning data is an effective method of retaining all the original data (as opposed to archiving it), while storing the data on separate physical disks. For example, archived data could be placed on one partition (stored on one physical disk), while current data could be stored on another partition (on another physical disk). With the data stored on different drives, queries for the different partitions are optimized due to multiple disks being accessed simultaneously.

In this first exercise, we'll create the filegroups necessary for our partition scheme.

Exercise 3.5: Create Filegroups in AdventureWorks

1. If it's not already open, open SSMS. Double-click Databases and double-click AdventureWorks to open up the AdventureWorks database.

2. Right-click AdventureWorks and click Properties.

3. Select the Filegroups Properties page. Notice one filegroup is named Primary. Click OK.

4. Create a New Query window and use the following script to add three new filegroups to the AdventureWorks database. Notice we are altering the database (not a database object), so our context is from the Master database.

```
USE master;
GO
ALTER DATABASE AdventureWorks ADD FILEGROUP Ch3FG1;
ALTER DATABASE AdventureWorks ADD FILEGROUP Ch3FG2;
ALTER DATABASE AdventureWorks ADD FILEGROUP Ch3FG3;
```

5. Use the following script to add three new files and associate them with the filegroups just created.

NOTE Note that the filename is in the MSSQL.1 path. If you are working with something other than the first instance installed on your system, you will need to change this to MSSQL.2 or some other path to be in the same directory with the rest of your databases in this instance. One way to determine where a database's files are located is to right-click the database and select Properties. Select the Files properties page, and scroll over to the Path heading.

```
USE master;
GO
ALTER DATABASE AdventureWorks
ADD FILE (NAME = 'Ch3F1',
         FILENAME = 'C:\Program Files\Microsoft SQL Server\MSSQL.1\MSSQL\DATA\
Ch3F1.ndf',
         SIZE = 1024KB, FILEGROWTH = 1024KB)
            TO FILEGROUP Ch3FG1
ALTER DATABASE AdventureWorks
ADD FILE (NAME = 'Ch3F2',
         FILENAME = 'C:\Program Files\Microsoft SQL Server\MSSQL.1\MSSQL\DATA\
Ch3F2.ndf',
         SIZE = 1024KB, FILEGROWTH = 1024KB)
            TO FILEGROUP Ch3FG2
ALTER DATABASE AdventureWorks
ADD FILE (NAME = 'Ch3F3',
         FILENAME = 'C:\Program Files\Microsoft SQL Server\MSSQL.1\MSSQL\DATA\
Ch3F3.ndf',
         SIZE = 1024KB, FILEGROWTH = 1024KB)
            TO FILEGROUP Ch3FG3
```

Creating a Partition Function

The partition function identifies the ranges where we'll separate the different partitions. For example, we could choose to have one partition hold all orders for years before 2001, the second partition could hold all orders between 2001 and 2002 (in other words, in the year 2001), and the last partition could hold all orders beyond 2001.

The syntax to create a partition function is:

```
CREATE PARTITION FUNCTION partition_function_name ( input_parameter_type )
AS RANGE [ LEFT | RIGHT ]
FOR VALUES ( [ boundary_value [ ,...n ] ] )
[ ; ]
```

The *Range* argument can be either *Range Left* or *Range Right*; if not specified, it's *Range Left*. This specifies which side of each given boundary (left or right), each boundary value belongs. This is subtle. Consider two boundaries of 5 and 10, something which gives us three ranges. The first is less than 5, the next is 5 to 10, and the third is > 10. However, what about the values of 5 and 10? Which range should 5 and 10 be in? If range left, 5 should be in the range of < 5 (to the left) and 10 should be in the range of 5 to 10 (to the left of 10).

For our preceding example, we'll use *Range Right* with the following values: *1/1/2001* and *1/1/2002*. Notice in the following table that the two values give us three ranges. The first range is everything to the left of the first value (< 1/1/2001). The second range is everything between the two values including the left value (> = 1/1/2001 and < 1/1/2002). The last range is everything to the right of the last value, including the last value (> = 1/1/2002). The values for the ranges are shown in Table 3-3.

Range	Values
1/1/2001	< 1/1/2001
1/1/2002	> = 1/1/2001 AND < 1/1/2002
(everything to the right of 1/1/2002)	> = 1/1/2002

Table 3-3   Function Ranges and Associated Values with the *Range Right* Argument (Used in the Example)

If instead, we chose *Range Left*, Table 3-4 would apply.

Range	Values
1/1/2001	< = 1/1/2001
1/1/2002	> 1/1/2001 AND < = 1/1/2002
(everything to the right of 1/1/2002)	> 1/1/2002

Table 3-4   Function Ranges and Associated Values with the *Range Left* Argument (NOT used in the example)

Creating the partition function is necessary before we can create the partition scheme. However, creating the function does not do anything in itself. It just sets us up to ultimately create the partition scheme.

In the following exercise, we'll create a partition function using the ranges in Table 3-3.

Exercise 3.6: Create a Partition Function in AdventureWorks

1. Create the partition function with the following script:

```
USE AdventureWorks;
GO
CREATE PARTITION FUNCTION pf_OrdersByDate (DateTime)
As RANGE RIGHT
For VALUES ('1/1/2001', '1/1/2002')
```

Notice the function is named pf_OrdersByDate. The *pf* is used to help us differentiate this as a partition function. This will help our script create a more meaningful partition scheme.

Creating a Partition Scheme

With the files, filegroups, and a partition function created, we can now associate the function with the filegroups. We do this with a partition scheme.

Remember that in the function, we specified two values, which actually created three ranges. When we specify the filegroups in the partition scheme, we need to specify three filegroups to hold the three ranges.

It is possible to have more than one partition on the same filegroup. You can even place all partitions on the same filegroup by specifying ALL.

The syntax to create a partition scheme is:

```
CREATE PARTITION SCHEME partition_scheme_name
AS PARTITION partition_function_name
[ ALL ] TO ( { file_group_name | [ PRIMARY ] } [ ,...n ] )
[ ; ]
```

In this exercise, we'll create the partition scheme by associating the partition function to the filegroups.

Exercise 3.7: Create a Partition Scheme in AdventureWorks

1. Create the partition scheme with the following script:

```
USE AdventureWorks;
GO
CREATE PARTITION SCHEME ps_OrdersByDate
AS PARTITION pf_OrdersByDate
TO (Ch3FG1, Ch3FG2,Ch3FG3)
```

Associating the Partition Scheme with a Table

The last step to make a partition scheme meaningful is to associate the partition scheme with a table.

In the following exercise, we'll create a simple table associated with a partition scheme and then populate it from an existing table. We'll then execute a script that can be used to demonstrate how the partition scheme has placed different pieces of the data on different filegroups.

Exercise 3.8: Associate the Partition Scheme with a Table

1. Create a table on the partition scheme with the following script:

```
USE AdventureWorks;
GO
CREATE TABLE dbo.SalesOrderHeaderPart(
   SalesOrderID int NOT NULL,
   OrderDate datetime not NULL,
   DueDate datetime not NULL
) ON ps_OrdersByDate(OrderDate)
```

2. Populate the data from the Sales.SalesOrderHeader table in AdventureWorks. The following script uses an INSERT. . . SELECT statement to pull data out of one table and insert it into another:

```
USE AdventureWorks;
GO
Insert dbo.SalesOrderHeaderPart
Select SalesOrderID,OrderDate,DueDate
FROM Sales.SalesOrderHeader
```

At this point, the data is populated in the table, and it is spread across the different partitions.

3. Execute the following query to see the data in the table. If AdventureWorks data has not been modified, you should see 31,465 rows returned (you can view this in the bottom right of the results pane).

```
Select * from dbo.SalesOrderHeaderPart
```

4. Execute the following query to see the data held in partition 1 (OrderDate less than 2001). If AdventureWorks data has not been modified, you should see 0 rows returned.

```
SELECT * FROM dbo.SalesOrderHeaderPart
WHERE $partition.pf_OrdersByDate (OrderDate) = 1
```

Notice that the $partition function allows us to determine which partition the data is held in by specifying "= 1". We simply include the name of the partition function (pf_OrdersByDate), the column the partition function has been created on (OrderDate), and the number of the partition we're interested in.

5. Execute the following query to see the data held in partition 2. If AdventureWorks data has not been modified, you should see 1379 rows returned.

```
SELECT *FROM dbo.SalesOrderHeaderPart
WHERE $partition.pf_OrdersByDate (OrderDate) = 2
```

6. Execute the following query to see the data held in partition 3. If AdventureWorks data has not been modified, you should see 30,086 rows returned.

```
SELECT *FROM dbo.SalesOrderHeaderPart
WHERE $partition.pf_OrdersByDate (OrderDate) = 3
```

7. Now we'll add three rows to our table and see how the partition scheme automatically puts the data into the right partition. Use the following script to insert three rows of data:

```
--Insert a row into partition 1
Insert dbo.SalesOrderHeaderPart (SalesOrderID, OrderDate, DueDate)
VALUES (99000, '1/1/1995', '1/1/1995')
--Insert a row into partition 2
Insert dbo.SalesOrderHeaderPart (SalesOrderID, OrderDate, DueDate)
VALUES (99000, '1/1/2001', '1/1/2001')
--Insert a row into partition 3
Insert dbo.SalesOrderHeaderPart (SalesOrderID, OrderDate, DueDate)
VALUES (99000, '1/1/2006', '1/1/2006')
```

8. Rerun the queries to show that the number of rows in each partition has incremented by one:

```
--Will now show 1 row
SELECT *FROM dbo.SalesOrderHeaderPart
WHERE $partition.pf_OrdersByDate (OrderDate) = 1
--Will now show 1380 rows
SELECT *FROM dbo.SalesOrderHeaderPart
WHERE $partition.pf_OrdersByDate (OrderDate) = 2
--Will now show 30,087 rows
SELECT *FROM dbo.SalesOrderHeaderPart
WHERE $partition.pf_OrdersByDate (OrderDate) = 3
```

Database Design Exercise

When teaching SQL in the classroom, I often use this scenario to help people move from the theoretical into the concrete. Instead of just thinking about how a database may be designed, we actually do it.

While a possible solution is provided at the end of the exercise, I strongly encourage you to try and solve the problem on your own before looking at the solution.

The Scenario

Imagine you are tasked with designing the database for an online testing site for practice tests. Someone else is designing the web site and will handle data entry. Your task is just to design the database. The application will be used by:

- **Program administrators**   Those who administer the database and program
- **Test administrators**   Those who create tests composed of test questions and answers
- **Test takers**   Those who take tests

The site will have multiple tests in multiple categories. For example, you could have a 70-431 test, a 70-441 test, and a 70-442 test all in the MCITP category. Each test would have a variable number of test questions, and each question would have an explanation (explaining why a test question was incorrect) and a reference.

Every question will have multiple answers (two for True/False and a variable number for multiple choice questions). The correct answer for each test question must be identified.

You must store history data for anyone who takes the test. These test history data will show the following for each test taken: which test was taken, who took it, when they took it, and their score.

Again, your job is not to create the application that uses the database, or even to create the data that goes into the database. All you need to do is design the database. However, an effective design will make the creation of the application much easier.

Using the previous paragraphs, determine the design. Use a pencil and paper to draw and label the tables. Identify the columns within each table. Use lines to identify relationships between the tables and identify PRIMARY KEYs and FOREIGN KEYs.

As a hint, my database solution uses seven tables. If you haven't created any tables yet, try to produce the answer with at least seven tables.

There is no single correct answer, so your solution may look slightly different from mine. The goal isn't to make sure you think like me, but to instead get you to think through the design of a database.

The Solution

You have finished the exercise, haven't you? No peeking until you've given it your best effort.

Hint

If you're stuck and unsure how to start, take a look at the explanation for creating the first two tables. Based on the knowledge you gain from creating these two tables, try to create the rest of the database design on your own. As a hint, my solution uses seven tables.

Creating the Person and Roles Tables

To start, read the first paragraph with the following bullets:

> The application will be used by:

- **Program administrators**   Those who administer the database and program
- **Test administrators**   Those who create tests composed of test questions and answers
- **Test takers**   Those who take tests

This tells me to create a user table. Since the word USER is a reserved word in SQL Server 2005, we could instead call it a Person table. The Person table might look like Figure 3-21.

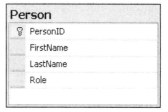

Figure 3-21 The Person table for the TestMaker database

Since we only have three roles, we could instead create a Role table and relate it to the Person table. This would prevent anyone from entering anything other than the three roles, or from shortening the roles to something else such as "Test Admin" instead of "Test Administrator." These two tables would look like Figure 3-22.

Figure 3-22 The Person and Roles tables related on the RoleID

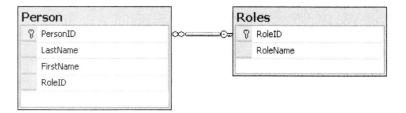

The first column I'd create in any table is the PRIMARY KEY. It's common to name this by adding a suffix of *ID* to the name of the table. We'd then create a relationship between the two tables using the RoleID column. The rest of the data would be determined by the given requirements. You may choose to add additional columns to the Person table such as Password, Email, Phone, or more, but the preceding tables will satisfy the basic requirements of the scenario.

Associated data in these two tables may look like Figures 3-23 and 3-24.

Figure 3-23
The Role table populated with the three possible roles

	RoleID	RoleName
▶	1	Program Administrator
	2	Test Administrator
	3	Test Taker
✳	*NULL*	*NULL*

Table - dbo.Roles Table - dbo.Person MCITPSUCCESS....

Figure 3-24
The Person table populated with one Program Administrator (RoleID of 1)

Table - dbo.Roles Table - dbo.Person MCITPSUCCESS..

	PersonID	LastName	FirstName	RoleID
	101	Gibson	Darril	1
▶✳	*NULL*	*NULL*	*NULL*	*NULL*

However, with these two tables designed this way, an individual could fill only one role. If you wanted to allow people to have more than one role, the tables could be designed in a many-to-many relationship with a third junction table. Figure 3-25 shows the tables redesigned with a junction table to allow individuals to fill multiple roles.

Figure 3-25   The Person and Roles tables in a many-to-many relationship

Creating the Tests and Category Tables
The next requirement comes from the following paragraph from the scenario:

> The site will have multiple tests in multiple categories. For example, you could have a 70-431 test, a 70-441 test, and a 70-442 test all in the MCITP category.

This tells me I need a Category table and a Tests table. Figure 3-26 shows how I designed them.

Figure 3-26
The Tests and Category tables

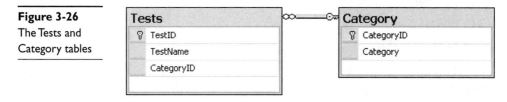

Again, the first column is the PK, and then the rest of the columns are determined by the requirements. We will create the relationship between the two tables on the CategoryID columns.

Data on a test might look like Figures 3-27 and 3-28.

Figure 3-27
The Category table populated with three possible categories

	CategoryID	Category
	101	MCTS
	102	MCITP Database Administrator
	103	MCITP Database Developer
▶*	*NULL*	*NULL*

Table - dbo.Tests **Table - dbo.Category** Table -

Figure 3-28
The Tests table populated with five possible tests

Table - **dbo.Tests** Table - dbo.Category Table - dbo.Roles

	TestID	TestName	CategoryID
	1	70-431	101
	2	70-441	103
	3	70-442	103
	4	70-443	102
	5	70-444	102
▶*	*NULL*	*NULL*	*NULL*

Creating the Question and Answer Tables

The rest of the scenario gives us some insight into how to create the Question and Answer tables.

> Each test question must have an explanation (explaining why a test question was incorrect) and a reference.

> Each question will have some answers (two for True/False and a variable number for multiple choice). The correct answer for each test question must be identified.

While you are designing the tables, it's good to bear in mind the process of a test taker. In other words, think about yourself taking a test. You might be presented with a question, and possible answers like the following:

Q. What type of key enforces uniqueness in a table?

A. PRIMARY KEY

B. SECONDARY KEY

C. FOREIGN KEY

D. SKELETON KEY

You choose A. After taking the test, you'd want to know if you were correct, perhaps an explanation of why you were correct, and possibly a reference where you could read additional information on the topic. A testing application may provide you with something like this:

Q. What type of key enforces uniqueness in a table?

A. PRIMARY KEY

B. SECONDARY KEY

C. FOREIGN KEY

D. SKELETON KEY

Correct answer: A.

You correctly chose answer A.

> Explanation: The PRIMARY KEY (PK) is used to enforce uniqueness. The FK creates a relationship between two tables, usually with a PK-to-FK link, but doesn't enforce uniqueness. There is no such thing as a SECONDARY Key. SKELETON Keys are for closets, not databases.

> Reference: See Chapter 3 of the All-In-One MCITP: Database Administrator book.

With this knowledge, we can create our Question and Answer tables. My design is shown in Figure 3-29.

Figure 3-29
Question and
Answer tables

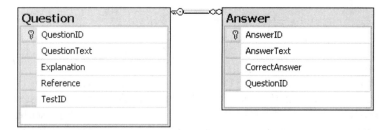

As with any table, the first column is the PK. The rest of the columns are determined by the requirements. We will create the relationship between the two tables on the QuestionID columns. Notice, we are also connecting the questions to specific tests with the TestID FOREIGN KEY in the Question table.

A populated row in the Question and Answer tables may look like Figures 3-30 and 3-31.

	QuestionID	QuestionText	Explanation	Reference	TestID
	501	What type of key enfor...	The PRIMARY KEY (PK) is used ...	See Chapter 3 o...	1
▸*	NULL	NULL	NULL	NULL	NULL

Tabs: Table - dbo.Roles Table - dbo.Person Table - dbo.Category **Table - dbo.Question**

Figure 3-30 The Question table with a single question

Figure 3-31

Figure 3-31

The Answer table
with answers
for the question
in the Question
table

Table - dbo.Answer		Table - dbo.Question	Table - dbo.Roles	Table - dbo.
AnswerID	AnswerText	CorrectAnswer	QuestionID	
101	PRIMARY KEY	True	501	
102	SECONDARY KEY	False	501	
103	FOREIGN KEY	False	501	
104	SKELETON KEY	False	501	
▶* NULL	NULL	NULL	NULL	

Creating the TestHistory Table

Lastly, we need to track a user's progress based on the following paragraph in the scenario:

> You need to store history data for anyone who takes the test. This test history data will show the following for each test taken: which test was taken, who took it, when they took it, and their score.

We can create a TestHistory table that looks similar to Figure 3-32.

Figure 3-32

The TestHistory
table

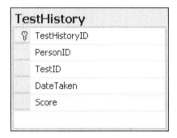

TestHistory
- 🔑 TestHistoryID
- PersonID
- TestID
- DateTaken
- Score

The first column is the PK. The PersonID ties to the Person table to determine the test taker. The TestID ties to the Test table to determine the test taken. The DateTaken and Score record when the test was taken and the test taker's score. Note that a user can take multiple tests in one day. If he were to earn the same score, all the columns would be identical except the TestHistoryID.

Figure 3-33 is a database diagram of the database using the design I came up with. Again, your design might look a little different and still meet the requirements of the scenario.

If your database design is different, it's not necessarily incorrect. Ask yourself these questions:

- Does it meet the objectives of the scenario?
- Is it normalized?
  - Are the tables atomic? Are tables reduced to their simplest components?
  - Does every column within a table depend on the key, the whole key, and nothing but the key?

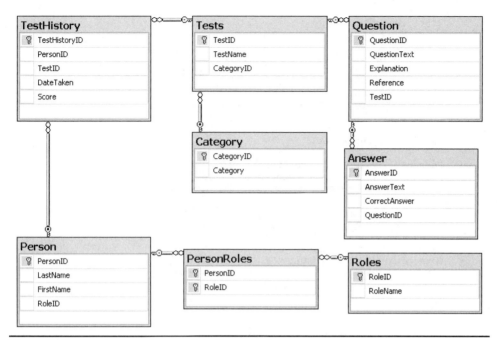

Figure 3-33 The database diagram of the Tester database

If the answer to all these questions is yes, great job! I bet you've done this before. If the answer to any of the preceding questions is no, tweak your design a little bit until it does meet these requirements.

If this is the first time you've done this, don't expect it to be perfect on the first try. The first time I did a summersault, it wasn't a pretty picture. However, after years of practice, I could finally roll over as well as anyone. It would have been foolish of me to think I could have done a perfect summersault the first time I tried. Likewise, the first time you try to design a database, it probably won't be perfect. No problem. Just tweak a little here and there, and eventually you'll have a workable design. You'll probably master it more quickly than I mastered summersaults.

The following is the script to create this database:

```
USE Master;
GO
CREATE DATABASE Tester;
GO
USE Tester
GO
CREATE TABLE dbo.Roles
(
        RoleID int NOT NULL,
        RoleName varchar(15) NULL,
    CONSTRAINT PK_RoleID PRIMARY KEY (RoleID)
)
```

```
GO
CREATE TABLE dbo.Person
(
        PersonID int NOT NULL,
        LastName varchar(15) NULL,
        FirstName varchar(15) NULL,
        RoleID int NULL
    CONSTRAINT PK_PersonID PRIMARY KEY (PersonID)
)
GO
CREATE TABLE dbo.PersonRoles
(
        PersonID int NOT NULL references dbo.Person,
        RoleID int NOT NULL references dbo.Roles,
    CONSTRAINT PK_PersonIDRoleID PRIMARY KEY (PersonID, RoleID)
)
GO
CREATE TABLE dbo.Category
(
        CategoryID int NOT NULL,
        Category varchar(30) NULL,
    CONSTRAINT PK_CategoryID PRIMARY KEY (CategoryID)
)
GO
CREATE TABLE dbo.Tests
(
        TestID int NOT NULL,
        TestName varchar(30) NULL,
        CategoryID int NULL references dbo.Category
    CONSTRAINT PK_TestID PRIMARY KEY (TestID)
)
GO
CREATE TABLE dbo.Question
(
        QuestionID int NOT NULL,
        QuestionText varchar(200) NULL,
        Explanation varchar(300) NULL,
        Reference varchar(200) NULL,
        TestID int NULL references dbo.Tests
    CONSTRAINT PK_QuestionID PRIMARY KEY (QuestionID)
)
GO
CREATE TABLE dbo.Answer
(
        AnswerID int NOT NULL,
        AnswerText varchar(100) NULL,
        CorrectAnswer bit NULL,
        QuestionID int NOT NULL references dbo.Question
    CONSTRAINT PK_AnswerID PRIMARY KEY (AnswerID)
)
GO
CREATE TABLE dbo.TestHistory
(
        TestHistoryID int NOT NULL,
        PersonID int NULL references dbo.Person,
        TestID int NULL references dbo.Tests,
        DateTaken datetime NULL,
        Score decimal(4,2) NULL
    CONSTRAINT PK_TestHistoryID PRIMARY KEY (TestHistoryID)
)
```

Chapter Review

With this chapter under your belt, you should have a good understanding of PRIMARY and FOREIGN KEYs and how they're used to create relationships between tables. We covered the different types of relationships (one-to-many, many-to-many, and one-to-one), normalization and how multiple tables are created to eliminate redundancy, and how occasionally databases are denormalized by adding redundancy. We covered other types of constraints such as CHECKs and defaults and when to implement them.

Very large tables of millions of rows can be partitioned. We covered the traditional horizontal partitioning tables and federations, and the new feature of implementing partition schemes. Lastly, we tied the chapter together with an exercise creating a database.

Additional Study

Self Study Exercises

Use these additional exercises to challenge yourself:

- Create a database named Ch3Ex.
- Create three tables named Books, Authors, and BookAuthors. Decide on the appropriate columns for each and create the appropriate relationships. Ensure you finish with a many-to-many relationship between the Books and Authors tables.
- If not created already, add a Phone column to the Authors table and create a CHECK constraint to ensure the phone is entered in the following format: xxx.xxx.xxxx.

BOL Topics

- PRIMARY KEY Constraints
- FOREIGN KEY Constraints
- AdventureWorks Data Dictionary
- ALTER TABLE (Transact-SQL)
- CHECK Constraints
- Functions (Database Engine)
- CREATE PARTITION SCHEME (Transact-SQL)
- Designing Partitions to Manage Subsets of Data

Summary of What You Need to Know

70-431

When preparing for the 70-431 test, make sure you understand the topics in all the main sections of this chapter. Spend extra time as needed to ensure you understand these topics:

- CHECK Constraints
- Partitioning Tables

70-441

When preparing for the 70-441 test, make sure you know the topics in all the main sections of this chapter. Understanding the uses of the PRIMARY KEY and FOREIGN KEY and the design of tables within a database to achieve a normalized database is essential to passing this test. You should recognize when, and how, to create a many-to-many relationship between tables, and the purpose and uses of cascading deletes and updates to child tables. Lastly, you should have a solid understanding of the different purposes and methods of partitioning large tables.

70-442

When preparing for the 70-442 test, make sure you have a solid understanding of the different uses of a FOREIGN KEY, the purpose and uses of cascading updates and deletes, and the purposes and methods of partitioning large tables.

Questions

70-431

1. You manage a SQL Server 2005 database named Hurricanes. It has a table of wind and temperature data by date and time and holds over 10 million rows. You are tasked with partitioning the data on a single server to increase performance and optimize maintenance. What should you do?

   A. Implement vertical partitioning.

   B. Implement horizontal partitioning.

   C. Implement a VIEW partition.

   D. Implement distributed partitioning.

2. You manage a database for an online retailer that has thousands of orders a day stored in an Orders table. The Orders table holds several years of data and has become quite slow. Is there any way to make it more efficient?

   A. No.

   B. Create a partitioning scheme that partitions the data by date.

   C. Create a partition function that maps filegroups to files.

   D. Vertically partition the table.

3. You need to ensure that any data that is entered into the Salary column of the Employee table falls within a range from $15,000 to $150,000. What should you create?

   A. DEFAULT

   B. CHECK Constraint

   C. DDL TRIGGER

   D. PRIMARY KEY Constraint

4. You are tasked with optimizing a query against the Orders table in the Sales database. The query only requests orders within the last 30 days, but the Orders table has orders from the last ten years. How can you optimize this query?

   A. Horizontally partition the table.

   B. Vertically partition the table.

   C. Create a clustered index on the OrderID column.

   D. Remove the clustered index.

70-441

1. You are designing a database that will be used for an international sales application. Products will have an English description but must be able to have a separate description in multiple different languages. How would you design the tables?

   A. Products table (ProductID, EngDescription, ForeignDescription, . . .)

   B. Products table (ProductID, Description, . . .)
      Languages table (LanguageID, LanguageName, Description, . . .)
      ProductLanguages table (ProductID, LanguageID, . . .)

   C. Product table (ProductID, Description, LanguageID, . . .)
      Languages table (LanguageID, LanguageName, Description, . . .)

   D. Products table (ProductID, EngDescription, ForeignDescription, . . .)
      Languages table (LanguageID, LanguageName, Description, . . .)

2. You are redesigning an Employee database. Besides the normal contact information, it must also list skills. Currently, it looks something like this:

   EmpID, LName, . . . Skill1, Skill2, Skill3

   The newly designed database needs to be normalized and each employee must have multiple skills assigned. What design would you choose?

   A. Employee1   table (EmployeeID, LName, . . ., SkillID)
      Skill1 table (SkillID, Skill)

   B. Employee2   table (EmployeeID, LName, . . ., SkillID1, SkillID2, SkillID3)
      Skill2 table (SkillID, Skill)

   C. Employee3   table (EmployeeID, LName, . . .)
      Skill3 table (SkillID, Skill)
      EmployeeSkill3 table (EmployeeID, SkillID, . . .)

   D. Employee3   table (EmployeeID, LName, . . ., SkillID1, SkillID2, SkillID3)
      Skill3 table (SkillID, SkillID1, SkillID2, SkillID3, . . .)

3. You are designing a Sales database that will be used to record orders and related details. Two of the tables are Orders and OrderDetails. The Orders table holds the details of the order. The OrderDetails table holds the individual line items

of the order. Which two actions will prevent orphaned child records in the OrderDetails table while also allowing deletes from the Orders table? (Choose two.)

A. A FOREIGN KEY constraint creating a references relationship between the Orders and OrderDetails table.

B. A cascade UPDATE between the two tables.

C. A PRIMARY KEY constraint creating a references relationship between the Orders and OrderDetails table.

D. A cascade DELETE between the two tables.

4. Your company subcontracts consultants to companies that need specific skills. You are designing a database for an application that will allow users to search for specific skills. Only identified skills can be associated with any individual consultant. How would you design the skill validation logic?

A. Use an INSERT trigger to compare the skill to Skills table.

B. Use a PK on the Consultant table to the FK in the Skills table.

C. Create an FK on the Consultant table to the PK in the Skills table.

D. Define the Consultant table with cascade Update.

5. You are designing a database that holds information on golf tournaments. The Tourney table holds tournament information on past, current, and future tournaments. You need to optimize performance for queries on past, current, and future tournaments while still ensuring that all the same information is retained. What should you do?

A. On a monthly basis run a stored procedure that removes past tournaments from the Tourney table.

B. Design a partitioned table that partitions the Tourney table into three partitions.

C. Create a SQL Server Report that shows the tourney table based on different queries.

D. Create a maintenance job to delete the past tournaments.

6. You are tasked with ensuring that data in the Employees table meet the following requirements:

• First names and last names can not be empty strings.

• E-mail addresses must be either NULL or in a valid format.

• E-mail addresses can't be changed from a valid format to an invalid format.

Data can be inserted and updated via an application or ad-hoc queries. What can be used to enforce these business rules while also ensuring the best possible performance? (Choose two.)

   A. Create a trigger to ensure the first and last names aren't empty strings.

   B. Create a CHECK to ensure the first and last names are not empty strings.

   C. Create stored procedures to INSERT and UPDATE e-mail addresses.

   D. Create a CHECK using a CLR integrated function to validate the e-mail addresses.

70-442

1. You are tasked with optimizing a query against the Orders table for the current month's sales. The orders table has millions of rows with several years' worth of data. When you query for the current month's data, query performance is exceeding 30 seconds. What should you do?

   A. Create a view on the data and use a where clause to filter by date.

   B. Create a partitioned table for the data, and partition the data by date.

   C. Create a federated database and partition the data by date.

   D. Create a clustered index on the TotalSales column.

2. In the HR database, you have an Employees table (holding information on employees) and an EmpBenefits table (holding the benefits chosen by any employee). This is accessed by an HR application used to add new employees and enter the benefits they have chosen. You need to ensure that benefits for an employee can't be added for an employee that doesn't exist. What should you do?

   A. On the EmpBenefits table, create a CHECK constraint to check for a valid EmployeeID.

   B. Create a trigger to roll back any inserts into the EmpBenefits table if an employee doesn't exist in the Employee table.

   C. On the Employee table, create a FOREIGN KEY constraint that references the EmpBenefits table.

   D. On the EmpBenefits table, create a FOREIGN KEY constraint that references the Employee table.

3. In the HR database, you have an Employees table (holding information on employees) and an EmpBenefits table (holding the different plans that can be chosen by any employee). An employee is able to choose one of the possible benefit plans. Employees that have left the company more than three years ago must be deleted. Currently, the record in the EmpBenefits table must be deleted before the record in the Employee table can be deleted. How can you change the database so records in the EmpBenefits table are automatically deleted when an Employee record is deleted?

   A. Alter the Employees table to implement cascading updates on the PK of the Employees table to the FK of the EmpBenefits table.

   B. Alter the Employees table to implement cascading deletes on the FK of the Employees table to the PK of the EmpBenefits table.

    C. Alter the EmpBenefits table to implement cascading Updates on the FK of the EmpBenefits table to the PK of the Employees table.

    D. Alter the EmpBenefits table to implement cascading deletes on the PK of the EmpBenefits table to the FK of the Employees table.

4. In the Sales database, phone numbers are frequently entered into the database incorrectly. You are tasked with ensuring that phone numbers are consistently entered as (xxx)xxx-xxxx where the x's represent numbers and the other characters are exactly as shown. Your solution should provide the best possible performance. What do you do?

    A. Use DML triggers to ensure the format is correct.

    B. Use DDL triggers to ensure the format is correct.

    C. Use a CHECK constraint to ensure the format is correct.

    D. Use stored procedures to format the phone number before the INSERT or UPDATE.

Answers

70-431

1. **B.** Horizontal partitioning can be used to move older data that isn't queried as often to a separate table. Views can be used for vertical partitioning (or allowing access to a select set of columns). Distributed partitioning is used to hold different partitioned tables on separate servers.

2. **B.** By creating a partitioning scheme based on the date, you can have older data on separate physical drives (based on files, filegroups, and partitions) and newer data in a smaller partition. The partition function creates the ranges, while the partition scheme maps the partitions to filegroups. Vertically partitioning the table (creating a VIEW) would not make it more efficient.

3. **B.** CHECK constraints can be used for range checking. A DEFAULT would put a default value in when a value isn't provided. A DDL TRIGGER can only be used with definition statements (such as CREATE, ALTER, and DROP), but couldn't check data. A PK enforces uniqueness in a table.

4. **A.** By horizontally partitioning the table on the date column, we can ensure that the partition we query has only recent orders. Vertically partitioning the table would be done with a VIEW to limit the columns available. Indexes could be helpful, but by default there is a clustered index on the PK and nothing indicates this is changed. Removing the clustered index wouldn't increase the performance of a query.

70-441

1. **B.** We need tables that will support multiple products and multiple languages. Additionally, any product must be able to be associated with multiple languages. This requires a many-to-many relationship. To support a many-to-many

relationship, we must have a junction table (ProductLanguages in this scenario). Only one answer supports a many-to-many relationship with a junction table.

2. **C.** The scenario requires a many-to-many relationship, so a junction table (EmployeeSkill3 here) must be included. Answer A would only allow one skill per employee. Answers B and D are not normalized.

3. **A, D.** An FK in the OrderDetails table to the PK in the Orders table will prevent an Order from being deleted in the Orders table if line items exist in the OrderDetails table. A cascade DELETE would allow any order deleted in the Orders table to delete related records in the OrderDetails table. A PK constraint enforces uniqueness, but does not create a relationship. A cascade UPDATE would only work with UPDATE statements, not delete.

4. **C.** An FK on the Consultant table to the PK in the Skills table would create referential integrity between the two tables and ensure that only valid skills are entered. Triggers are less efficient in this situation since they work on the data after it has been entered. Matching the PK in the Consultant table to an FK in the Skills table would ensure that every skill in the skills table is assigned to an existing Consultant, but not that every skill assigned exists in the Skills table. A cascade Update wouldn't provide referential integrity.

5. **B.** A partitioned table based on the status (past, current, or future) could be used to store the different parts of the table on three separate drives. This would optimize the queries, while still retaining all the information. Any solution that removes or deletes data is counter to the requirement that all the information should be retained. A SQL Server Report wouldn't optimize queries.

6. **B, D.** Since a CHECK constraint works on the data before the data modification, it is the best choice. Triggers will roll back the change after the data modification and thus result in double work and less-than-optimal performance. Stored procedures would work if we could guarantee that only the stored procedures were used for the data modifications. However, with ad-hoc queries used, we can't guarantee the stored procedures would be used.

70-442

1. **B.** A partitioned table, partitioned by date, will allow the recent sales data to be stored in one partition, and older data to be stored in another partition. This will significantly improve the query since a lot less data is queried. A VIEW would be created from the same faulty query, so this wouldn't improve performance. Spreading the data across several servers in a federation would constitute much more cost and work than required. A clustered index on the Date column may be a good solution, but a clustered index on the TotalSales column would not improve this query.

2. **D.** An FK constraint can be used to ensure that data isn't added to a child table if an associated record doesn't exist in the parent table. In this scenario, Employees is the parent table and EmpBenefits is the child table. By creating a PK-to-FK relationship from the Employees table to the EmpBenefits table,

we ensure an EmpBenefits record isn't created for an employee that doesn't exist. Using a CHECK constraint or a trigger would have a higher cost than a basic PK-to-FK relationship. Creating an FK on the Employee table referencing the EmpBenefits table would ensure that employees can't be added until they have picked benefits, but that isn't what's required in the scenario. While not explicitly stated in the question, the EmpBenefits table is a junction table creating a many-to-many relationship between the Employees table and the Benefits table.

3. **B.** The cascade option is created as part of the REFERENCES clause where an FK is created on the Employees table and references a PK on theEmpBenefits table.

   Since the question discusses the need to delete records of employees, a Cascade Delete statement must be used. The cascade option is not created on the EmpBenefits in this scenario since the FK exists on the Employees table. The cascade option is not created on the PK, but instead is created on the FK.

4. **C.** A CHECK constraint is the best choice since it verifies the change works on the data before the modification. A DML trigger would work, but it would only fire after the phone is entered and cause the modification to be rolled back. A DDL trigger doesn't work on data. Stored procedures would work as long as the stored procedures are the only method used to modify the data, but wouldn't work if the data was modified through other means.

Transact-SQL

In this chapter, you will learn about:

- Transact-SQL
- SELECT statements
- INSERT, UPDATE, and DELETE statements
- Advanced query techniques

> *The important thing is not to stop questioning.*
>
> —*Albert Einstein*

The database has the answers. All you have to do is ask. Of course, you need to know how to ask, and the method of asking in SQL Server 2005 is Transact-SQL. For those of you preparing to take the 70-431 or 70-442 tests, you'll need to know T-SQL's SELECT statement inside and out. When the DML statements are tested, they are tested rather deeply. T-SQL is not tested on the 70-441 test.

In this chapter, we'll start with the basics on the SELECT statement, expand to all the Data Manipulation Language (DML) statements of INSERT, UPDATE, and DELETE, and then cover some of the advanced querying techniques, such as Common Table Expressions (CTEs), INTERSECT and EXCEPT, PIVOT and UNPIVOT, and Ranking. We'll close with details on building transactions.

If you've been a database developer, you may have already done a lot of T-SQL development. Instead of reading the chapter from beginning to end, you may like to review the Advanced Querying techniques section toward the end of the chapter that introduces some concepts new to SQL Server 2005. Afterward, try out the practice test questions to see what you need to brush up on.

General Rules to Know

You should know some general rules before we jump into T-SQL. By being aware of these rules, you can avoid some problems later.

The ANSI Standard

First and foremost, be aware that Microsoft's T-SQL (and this book) will not follow all of the recommended ANSI standard practices. Transact-SQL is ANSI-compliant, meaning it can be written to comply with all of the ANSI recommendations, not that you will always find it that way. This is common with most database products—they comply with the ANSI standard to some extent, but generally they all have some unique capabilities that don't comply with the standard. As an example, T-SQL uses the GO statement, which is not part of the ANSI standard.

Further, if we were to scrutinize the ANSI standard for SQL, we'd find much complexity within it. For students who need a SQL primer (the goal of this chapter), the minutia of the ANSI standard may prevent them from learning the important elements of T-SQL.

Think of the SQL ANSI standard as a nonbinding recommendation. Different database management systems implement the standard in different ways. Our focus in this book is on Microsoft's implementation, which is referred to as *T-SQL*.

So, whether you're coming from an Oracle, DB2, MySQL, Access, or other Relational Database Management System (RDMS), or learning this from scratch, you will see a lot of similarities. Either way, expect to see enough differences to keep things interesting.

You should know about a standard that SQL Server 2005 is following that is related to the asterisk in SELECT statements. Previous versions of SQL Server supported the asterisk (such as *= for a LEFT OUTER JOIN or =* for a RIGHT OUTER JOIN) when representing JOIN statements, but these are not supported in SQL Server 2005 unless the compatibility level of the database is set to a lower version. We'll explore this more in the OUTER JOINS section in this chapter.

Delimiting Identifiers

"Delimiting identifiers" is a fancy way of saying "identifying names." If we have a table named Customer with a column named LastName, we can *identify* it with two types of *delimiters*: brackets and single quotes. It would look like *[LastName]* or *'LastName'*.

Using brackets is standard, so you'll probably see it this way most often, but single quotes can also be used if the QUOTED_IDENTIFIER option is on. This is one of the database options that can be viewed in the miscellaneous section of the database Options property page.

However, it's generally not necessary to delimit identifiers. Usually, we can omit the brackets and the single quotes, and based on where the identifier is in the statement, it will be identified correctly.

Two situations require you to delimit identifiers:

- If any spaces exist in the identifier, you *must* delimit the identifier. For example, [LastName] has no spaces so you do not need to include the square brackets, but [Last Name] does so you must delimit it. The delimiter in *LastName* can be omitted, but the delimiter in *[Last Name]* must be added.

- When using reserved keywords as an identifier, such as using the reserved word "View" to name a table used in a tourist database, [View] must be delimited when used. Using reserved words is not recommended and is only supported for backward compatibility. Consider this usage deprecated.

Case Sensitive and Case Insensitive

Is your database sensitive? I mean "case sensitive," as in does it care whether you enter or search data in mixed case, such as UPPERCASE and lowercase. If it is case sensitive and you don't use the exact case in your scripts as the objects are created in your database, the scripts won't work.

 NOTE If you installed AdventureWorks from the exercises in Chapter 1 and didn't modify the collation, the collation is set to case insensitive (CI). If you downloaded an AdventureWorks sample database from one of Microsoft's Web sites and installed it, you could have chosen a downloadable version that is case sensitive or case insensitive. If you're using a case sensitive collation, you can sometimes get unexpected errors that can be frustrating if you can't figure them out. The following section will help you determine the collation, and the errors you can expect if you're using a casesensitive collation.

From a workability perspective, it usually doesn't matter how you enter most of the commands in your scripts—as all uppercase or all lowercase, or following best practices. If the collation is set to CI (case insensitive), your scripts will work no matter what case you use. On the other hand, if the collation is set to CS (case sensitive) the data and the database objects must match or the queries will fail to retrieve what you're requesting.

If the collation is changed on the database, it changes the sensitivity of not only the data within the database, but also the naming of all objects within the database. This is the type of problem that has caused me to bang my head against the wall for hours until I figure out why a script that worked on one system doesn't work on another system. Hopefully, I can save you from needless head banging.

Consider the following script:

```
use adventureworks
go
select * from sales.salesorderheader
```

If the collation is set to CS, this script will fail with an error saying that sales .salesorderheader can't be found because the object within the AdventureWorks database is named Sales.SalesorderHeader. The object sales.salesorderheader is not the same as Sales.SalesorderHeader with a CS collation. It will work fine with the collation of CI.

Now look at the following script:

```
use AdventureWorks
go
select * from Sales.SalesOrderHeader
```

Notice that the only change is that the schema and table name both have a mixture of upper- and lowercase characters, matching the exact case found in AdventureWorks. This script will succeed with either collation.

To identify the collation of AdventureWorks in your database, do the following short exercise.

Exercise 4.1: Check Collation on the Database

1. Open SSMS. Double-click Databases to open the databases container.

2. Right-click AdventureWorks to view the properties page.

3. On the General page, in the Maintenance section, view the Collation. The *CS* in Latin1_General_CS_AS indicates that it is set to case sensitive, as shown in Figure 4-1.

Figure 4-1

AdventureWorks properties

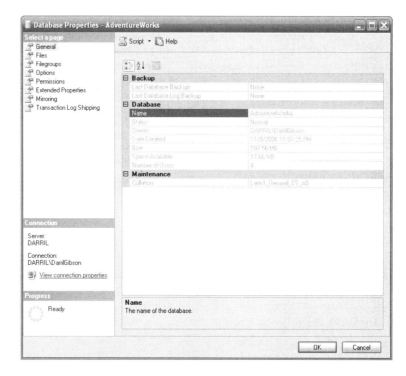

The SQL_Latin1_General_CP1_*CI*_AS indicates that the collation is set to *CI* or case *insensitive.* In other words, both uppercase and lowercase letters are interpreted the same.

 TIP What's most important to realize with the collation, especially when doing these exercises, is what case sensitivity setting you have on your database. If it's CI, the case doesn't matter. If it's CS, the case, especially the case of objects you enter in the scripts, *does* matter and can prevent your scripts from running.

4. Close the properties sheet and double-click System Databases to open the system databases container.

5. Right-click Master to view the properties page.

6. On the General page, in the Maintenance section, view the Collation. The *CI* in Latin1_General_CP1_*CI*_AS indicates that it is set to case insensitive, as shown in Figure 4-2.

Figure 4-2

Master database properties

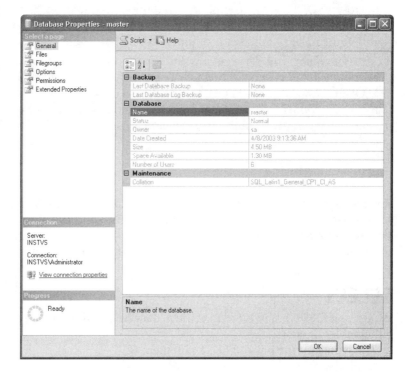

We are normally concerned with case sensitivity in the result sets of our scripts, and how the data will be sorted. However, it's just as important to realize that the objects within the database are also subject to the collation setting.

Before we move on, let's look at the same script but with "best practices" employed:

```
USE AdventureWorks;
GO
SELECT *
FROM Sales.SalesOrderHeader
```

Notice that the case of all objects (the database, the schema, and the table) matches the actual objects. Additionally, all reserved words (USE, SELECT, FROM) are listed as all uppercase. The ANSI standard recommends the usage of semicolons at the end of SQL statements. T-SQL within SQL Server 2005 will work with or without the semicolons, and even the BOL examples have a liberal sprinkling of examples with and without the semicolons.

Transact-SQL, or T-SQL, is the standard language used to manipulate the database and database objects. You learned in earlier chapters that there are different types of T-SQL statements, such as DML and DDL. You can use *Data Manipulation Language* (*DML*)

How Do You Say SQL? "Sequel" or "Ess-cue-el"?

Microsoft SQL Server is commonly pronounced as Microsoft "Sequel" Server. Likewise, Transact-SQL is pronounced "transact-sequel." However, more generically within the ANSI standard, it is pronounced as "ess-cue-el."

SQL is commonly understood to stand for *Structured Query Language*. In the 1970s, a group at IBM created a Structured English **Query** Language and briefly called it SEQUEL. However, since SEQUEL was held as a trademark by another company, the name was condensed to SQL. SQL was adopted as a standard by ANSI (American National Standards Institute) in 1986, and according to ANSI, the official pronunciation is "ess-cue-el."

statements to retrieve or modify the data in the database and use *Data Definition Language* (*DDL*) statements to manage the database objects. You have already been using DDL statements to create the database and other objects like tables and views. This chapter will focus on DML statements to retrieve, insert, update, and delete data.

SELECT

We use the SELECT statement to retrieve data from a database. It can be used against either tables or views.

The syntax for the basic SELECT statement is:

```
SELECT column list
FROM table or view
```

The Column List

The column list identifies the specific columns that we want in the output. To get all the columns, we can use the * as a wildcard as follows:

```
SELECT *
FROM table
```

Instead of retrieving all the columns, we usually restrict the columns we retrieve to specific columns. We can retrieve as many columns in the table as desired by simply adding the column names separated by commas. Of course, the columns in the select list must exist in the table.

```
SELECT Title, FName, LName, EmailAddress
FROM table
```

The header of the result set has the same name as the column. For example, the LName column will have a header of LName. While this may be acceptable most of the time, sometimes you might want to change the name of the column header in the result set. We do this by creating an *alias* with the *AS* keyword.

```
SELECT Title, FName AS [First Name],
 LName AS [Last Name], EmailAddress [Email Address]
FROM table
```

Notice that an alias can be identified with *AS* (such as, *FName* AS [*First Name*]) or without *AS* (for instance, *EmailAddress* [*Email Address*]). Both methods are successful, though the standard does specify use of the AS keyword.

FROM

The FROM clause identifies the table or view that contains the data and where the columns can be found.

As with all database objects, FROM clauses are fully identified with a four-part name: *server.database.schema.object*. We would only use the four-part name when accessing an object on another server (such as when accessing a linked server). All other times, the local server is assumed.

The database is often omitted in the clause. We first point to the database with the USE statement, and then can omit the database.

We can shorten the name to just a one-part name and identify only the object. However, we frequently include the schema when identifying tables in the FROM clause because tables often have different schemas in SQL Server 2005. If a schema is not identified for the object, dbo is the default schema used.

This script shows how to pull columns from the Person.Contact table:

```
USE AdventureWorks;
GO
SELECT Title, FirstName, LastName, EmailAddress
FROM Person.Contact;
```

 NOTE In the preceding script, the first line is *USE AdventureWorks*. This sets the context of the rest of the script to the AdventureWorks database. If this is omitted, SSMS defaults to the Master database. Since there is no Person. Contact table in the Master database, the preceding script would fail if pointed at Master.

Once you have set AdventureWorks as the database context in your query window, you won't need to do so again in the same query session. Your query window remains pointed at AdventureWorks. In the following examples, the *USE AdventureWorks* line is omitted, but unless specified otherwise, we are still using the AdventureWorks database.

Later in this chapter, we'll show how we can combine multiple tables in the FROM clause using the ON predicate.

In this exercise, we'll start using the SELECT statement. Imagine that someone is asking you to provide a listing of people in the database including their names and e-mail addresses.

Exercise 4.2: Use the SELECT Statement against AdventureWorks

1. Launch SSMS and create a new query window by clicking the New Query button.

2. Type in and execute the following script:

```
USE AdventureWorks;
GO
SELECT *
FROM Person.Contact;
```

This should give you a result set including all the columns and all the rows of the Contact table in the Person schema.

3. Queries are usually focused on specific information. Enter and execute the next script to return the title, name, and e-mail address of all the people in this table.

```
SELECT Title, FirstName, LastName, EmailAddress
FROM Person.Contact;
```

4. To change the column headers, add aliases to your statement with and without the AS keyword:

```
SELECT Title, FirstName AS [First Name], LastName [Last Name],
EmailAddress
FROM Person.Contact
```

WHERE

The previous queries return over 19,000 rows. Often, we need to limit our result set to something more manageable.

The WHERE clause allows us to add a search condition to our SELECT statement. This search condition filters the data based on exactly what we need. A SELECT statement with a WHERE clause would look like this:

```
SELECT Title, FirstName, LastName, EmailAddress
FROM Person.Contact
WHERE <search condition>
```

Many types of search operators are possible. They include:

- Comparison operators (=, <, <=, <>, and so on)
- String comparisons (LIKE, NOT LIKE)
- Logical operators (AND, OR, NOT)
- Ranges (BETWEEN and NOT BETWEEN)
- Lists of values (IN and NOT IN)
- Unknown Values (IS NULL and IS NOT NULL)
- Exists in Subquery (EXISTS and NOT EXISTS)

Avoiding the Negative

While search conditions allow us to filter on the negative (NOT, NOT LIKE, NOT IN, NOT EQUAL, and <>), it's generally not a good practice to do so. Proving something doesn't exist is harder than proving it exists in the real world. The query optimizer within SQL Server has the same problem. Queries that include the use of a negative search condition often force full table scans. A full table scan isn't such a big deal if your table has 300 rows. But for a very large table (say, 30 million rows), a table scan results in significantly poorer performance of the query than using nonnegative search condition queries.

Comparison Operators

Comparison operators allow us to compare data in the queried table or view and only return rows that meet our search condition. Comparison operators and their description are listed in Table 4-1.

Comparison Operator	Description
=	Equal to
<	Less than
>	Greater than
<=	Less than or equal to
>=	Greater than or equal to
<>	Not equal to (!= will work also)

Table 4-1   Comparison Operators Available in the WHERE Clause

For example, let's say you're asked to get a count of all orders that were made on July 4, 2004. The following query could be used, which combines the ">=" and the "<" operators within a Boolean AND statement.

```
SELECT COUNT(*) FROM Sales.SalesOrderHeader
WHERE OrderDate >= '2003/07/04' AND
OrderDate < '2004/07/04'
```

TIP   The COUNT(*) is a function used to count all rows within a table. We will explore this more in Chapter 6 and compare it with the COUNT(columnName) function.

You might be tempted to try a simple "=" comparison for the preceding problem, but it wouldn't work consistently with a date. Since a datetime data type can hold hours, minutes, seconds, and milliseconds, the following query would require the hours, minutes, seconds, and milliseconds to be the same—not just the year, month, and day.

```
SELECT COUNT(*) FROM Sales.SalesOrderHeader
WHERE OrderDate = '2004/07/27'        -- would not work consistently
```

 NOTE When using literal dates within a T-SQL statement, the date is enclosed between single quotes as with strings, and a separator is required between the year, month, and day.

Let's look at another example, where we're asked to get the e-mail address of all the contacts with a last name of Stone. We could enter the following query:

```
SELECT Title, FirstName, LastName, EmailAddress
FROM Person.Contact
WHERE LastName = 'Stone'
```

Notice that we put the name *Stone* in single quotes. This identifies it as string data. Similarly, if we were searching for contacts that were modified on or after June 29, 2004, we could use the following query:

```
SELECT Title, FirstName, LastName, EmailAddress
FROM Person.Contact
WHERE ModifiedDate >= '6/29/2004'
```

Notice that the date is also put into single quotes, but SQL Server recognizes it as a date. Numeric values don't need to be surrounded with quotes but instead are entered directly as numbers.

String Comparisons (LIKE, NOT LIKE)

String comparisons are great when you want to match patterns within a string, but not necessarily all of the string. The keyword to find words with a matching set of characters is LIKE, but the comparison allows us to use several different wildcard characters. Available wildcard characters are listed in Table 4-2.

Wildcard Character	Description
%	Any string of zero or more characters
_	Any single character
[]	Any single character within a range
[^]	Any single character not within a range

Table 4-2 Wildcard Characters Available with LIKE

An example of using LIKE to identify any contacts whose last name starts with *St* is shown next. Notice that the entire comparison string, including the wildcard, is enclosed in single quotes.

```
SELECT Title, FirstName, LastName, EmailAddress
FROM Person.Contact
WHERE LastName LIKE 'St%'
```

Similarly, we could search for any name that ends with *st* and then any other single letter with the following script:

```
SELECT Title, FirstName, LastName, EmailAddress
FROM Person.Contact
WHERE LastName LIKE '%st_'
```

It's also possible to embed functions within queries. Let's say our database is set with a casesensitive (CS) collation and we're looking for any contacts with a last name starting with *Mc* whether they've been entered as *MC, Mc,* or even *mc.* We could use the UPPER function that converts a string to all uppercase and then compare it with the LIKE predicate:

```
USE AdventureWorks
SELECT Title, FirstName, LastName, EmailAddress
FROM Person.Contact
WHERE UPPER(LastName) LIKE 'MC%'
```

Logical Operators (AND, OR, NOT)
Logical operators allow us to combine multiple expressions. We can use AND to meet multiple conditions, or we can use OR to meet one of multiple conditions.

The following script searches for contacts with the last name of *Smith* OR the first name of *John* and returns about 160 rows:

```
SELECT Title, FirstName, LastName, EmailAddress
FROM Person.Contact
WHERE LastName = 'Smith' OR FirstName ='John'
```

Similarly the following script searches for contacts with the last name of *Smith* AND the first name of *John* and returns only a single row:

```
SELECT Title, FirstName, LastName, EmailAddress
FROM Person.Contact
WHERE LastName = 'Smith' AND FirstName ='John'
```

Ranges (BETWEEN and NOT BETWEEN)
BETWEEN allows us to simplify the use of comparison operators. The biggest thing to remember about BETWEEN is that it is inclusive. In other words, if we are searching for a value between 5 and 10, it includes the values 5 and 10.

We can replicate the same search using comparison operators and logical operators. For example, *BETWEEN 5 and 10* is the same as *Value >=5 AND Value <=10.* The scripts that follow demonstrate both examples:

```
SELECT ContactID, Title, FirstName, LastName, EmailAddress
FROM Person.Contact
WHERE ContactID BETWEEN 5 and 10
SELECT ContactID, Title, FirstName, LastName, EmailAddress
FROM Person.Contact
WHERE ContactID >=5 AND ContactID <=10
```

Lists of Values (IN and NOT IN)

Using a list of values, we can greatly simplify complex OR statements. For example, say you are asked to retrieve a listing of contacts with first names of Sandy, Jay, Carla, or Ronald. Using the OR statement, your query may look like this:

```
SELECT ContactID, Title, FirstName, LastName, EmailAddress
FROM Person.Contact
WHERE FirstName = 'Sandy' OR FirstName = 'Jay' OR
      FirstName = 'Carla' OR FirstName = 'Ronald'
```

Instead, we can simplify this query with the IN operator by using the following query:

```
SELECT ContactID, Title, FirstName, LastName, EmailAddress
FROM Person.Contact
WHERE FirstName IN ('Sandy', 'Jay', 'Carla','Ronald')
```

The query optimizer would handle both statements (using OR or IN) the same way. However, for a DBA analyzing queries, the query using IN is much easier to read.

Unknown Values (IS NULL and IS NOT NULL)

Checking for NULL values within a query is sometimes required. For example, you might be asked to provide a listing of customers that have a phone number, or only customers that do not have phone numbers.

A common mistake when checking for null values is to try to use a comparison operator such as =. While the = comparison operator can be used to check for known values, the value of NULL is unknown, so a comparison operator will not work. Instead, we must use the IS NULL or IS NOT NULL comparison operators.

The following query can be executed against AdventureWorks and will check for any contacts in the Person.Contact table that don't have middle names listed (or in other words, that have a value of NULL for their middle name):

```
SELECT ContactID, Title, FirstName, MiddleName LastName, EmailAddress
FROM Person.Contact
Where MiddleName IS Null
```

 EXAM TIP Remember that we must use the IS NULL or IS NOT NULL function to check for NULL values. We cannot use a comparison to an empty string to determine if a value is NULL.

The ISNULL Function The ISNULL function is a handy function you should be aware of when working with NULL values. It allows you to query NULL data, but instead of outputting the value of NULL, you can replace NULL with a specified replacement value. This can be especially useful if you need to perform some mathematical calculation on the data such as SUM or AVG. The basic syntax is:

```
ISNULL ( check_expression , replacement_value )
```

In the following exercise, we'll create a table in the AdventureWorks database, modify it slightly, and view the differences in the data depending on whether we're looking at the data as NULL or if we are giving it a value of zero.

Exercise 4.3: See the ISNULL Function in Action

1. Open a New Query window in SSMS.

2. Identify the average list price of products in the Production.Product table in the AdventureWorks database with the following query.

```
USE AdventureWorks;
GO
SELECT AVG(ListPrice)
FROM Production.Product
```

Write down the list price here: _____. On my system, it is 438.6662.

 NOTE The list price column does not have null values. It does have several values that are 0.00, but the table definition does not allow the list price column to be null. We will create a copy of this table, alter it to allow nulls on the list price, and then modify the 0.00 to become null. We can then see the difference between using ISNULL and not using it.

3. Create a copy of the Production.Product table and name it NotRealProducts with the following query.

```
SELECT *
INTO dbo.NotRealProducts
FROM Production.Product
```

4. Alter the ListPrice column to accept nulls with the following query.

```
ALTER TABLE dbo.NotReaLproducts
   ALTER COLUMN [ListPrice] [money] NULL
```

5. Update the table to change the list price to NULL when it has a current value of 0.00 with the following query. Note that this uses an UPDATE statement that we will cover in more depth later in this chapter.

```
UPDATE NotRealProducts
Set ListPrice = NULL
WHERE ListPrice = 0
```

6. Now use the following query to identify the average list price of products in the NotRealProducts table.

```
SELECT AVG(ListPrice)
FROM NotRealProducts
```

Notice that the average price now is significantly higher. On my system, the average price is 727.2624. Why is this not the same as the average price before we changed the 0.00's to NULLs? This goes back to the old question of "What's the value of NULL?" We don't know. Since the value of NULL is unknown, it is not calculated in the average price. Any rows with a value of NULL are ignored, so about 200 rows are not included in the AVG calculation. This could cause problems in the real world if you want those records included in the average. As a solution, you may take the records with a NULL listprice and make them have a value of 0.00 so they are included in the result.

7. Enter the following query to get the average list price of all products. This query uses the ISNULL function to change the ListPrice value to 0.00 anytime it has a value of NULL. Note that this change is only within our query. It doesn't actually change the data within the table.

```
SELECT AVG(ISNULL(ListPrice, 0.00))
FROM NotRealProducts
```

You should have the same value as you wrote down in step 2 of this exercise. On my system, it is 438.6662.

8. Clean up AdventureWorks by dropping the NotRealProducts table with the following query.

```
DROP Table NotRealProducts
```

EXISTS in Subquery (EXISTS and NOT EXISTS)

We can use *subqueries* (a query within a query) with the EXISTS or NOT EXISTS clause to retrieve data based on the existence of the data within a subquery. The result of the subquery within the EXISTS or NOT EXISTS clause evaluates to TRUE or FALSE.

This sounds more complicated than it is. In AdventureWorks, we have the Person .Contact table, which lists all types of contacts (employees, customers, and vendors). Which of these contacts are employees? Only those that also exist in the Employees table.

Let's say you were asked to pull a listing (first name, last name, and e-mail address) of employees. One way to do this is with an EXISTS clause.

The HumanResources.Employee table lists all the employees and has a ContactsID column used as an FK to the Person.Contact.ContactsID PK. The following query will pull data out of the Person.Contact table as long as the ContactID exists in the Human-Resources.Employee table:

```
SELECT FirstName, LastName
FROM Person.Contact
WHERE EXISTS
      (SELECT *
       FROM HumanResources.Employee
        WHERE Person.Contact.ContactID =
          HumanResources.Employee.ContactID)
```

One way to evaluate this query is by looking at the internal query first. If a row evaluates to true in the internal query, the row in the external query will be returned. Later, we'll see how to do this with a JOIN statement.

Exercise 4.4: Use the WHERE Clause to Filter Data

1. Open SSMS and create a New Query window.

2. Retrieve all the information on all the products in the AdventureWorks database by entering the following script:

```
USE AdventureWorks;
GO
SELECT * FROM Production.Product
```

3. Use the following script to limit the columns displayed to just the product name, the product number, the cost, and the list price:

```
SELECT Name, ProductNumber, StandardCost, ListPrice
FROM Production.Product
```

4. Filter the result set by only listing products that have a cost greater than 0:

```
SELECT Name, ProductNumber, StandardCost, ListPrice
FROM Production.Product
WHERE StandardCost > 0
```

5. Find any parts that have a part number starting with CN:

```
SELECT Name, ProductNumber, StandardCost, ListPrice
FROM Production.Product
WHERE ProductNumber Like 'CN%'
```

6. Find any parts with a Standard Cost greater than $0 and less than $100:

```
SELECT Name, ProductNumber, StandardCost, ListPrice
FROM Production.Product
WHERE StandardCost > 0 AND StandardCost < 100
```

This script will return 111 rows if AdventureWorks hasn't been modified.

7. Retrieve a listing of parts with a cost BETWEEN $0 and $100:

```
SELECT Name, ProductNumber, StandardCost, ListPrice
FROM Production.Product
WHERE StandardCost BETWEEN 0.00 and 100
```

Notice this will return 311 rows because it is inclusive of $0 and $100.

8. Retrieve a listing of parts where the part number begins with the letter *A, B,* or *C.* Note that this query could be done in different ways, but the following script demonstrates the use of the EXISTS clause:

```
SELECT Name, ProductNumber, StandardCost, ListPrice
FROM Production.Product
WHERE EXISTS
   (Select * FROM Production.Product
    WHERE ProductNumber Like '[A-C]%')
```

ORDER BY

Sometimes you want to guarantee the order of your result set. For example, you may be retrieving a list of employees with their phone numbers. To be able to easily find the right employee, it would make it a lot easier if the results were sorted by last name.

The only way to guarantee a sort order is with the ORDER BY clause.

When you use the ORDER BY clause, the results are ordered in ascending order (lowest to highest) by default. You can change this to descending order by adding the keyword DESC after the ORDER BY clause, as shown in the following example:

```
SELECT Name, ProductNumber, StandardCost, ListPrice
FROM Production.Product
ORDER BY ListPrice DESC
```

Most data types can be ordered. In other words, I can order the results based on character data, date data, numerical data, and so on. There are exceptions. We *cannot* order results on these data types: *ntext*, *text*, *image*, and *xml*.

Columns in the ORDER BY clause don't have to be in the SELECT column list. In other words, we can sort on a column that doesn't appear in the result set. The exception is if we use the DISTINCT clause to eliminate duplicate rows. In this case, the column in the ORDER BY clause must be in the SELECT column list.

Limiting the Rows

You can limit the rows in your result set when using the ORDER BY clause by including the TOP statement. For example, if you want to retrieve the ten products with the highest prices, you could use the following query:

```
SELECT TOP 10 Name, ProductNumber, StandardCost, ListPrice
FROM Production.Product
ORDER BY ListPrice DESC
```

The TOP clause is directly related to the ORDER BY clause. If we wanted to identify the ten products with the lowest prices, we'd simply change the query to ascending by removing DESC or changing it to ASC. Remember, ASC is the default, so it doesn't need to be included.

In addition to limiting the rows to a set number, we can also limit the number of rows to a set percentage, as in the following query. Instead of getting ten rows as we did in the previous query, this query gives us 51 rows (10 percent of the 504 total rows available).

```
SELECT TOP 10 PERCENT Name, ProductNumber, StandardCost, ListPrice
FROM Production.Product
ORDER BY ListPrice DESC
```

 EXAM TIP The ORDER BY clause defaults to ascending (ASC) order (lowest to highest) if not specified. Often, when working with sales or other types of monetary data, we are looking for the data with the highest numbers first, such as the top five invoices or the top five sales people. In this case, we must specify the order as descending (DESC) so the data is represented from highest to lowest.

The Set Rowcount function is sometimes used within stored procedures or transactions. It will cause SQL Server to stop processing the query after the specified number of rows is returned. Unlike the TOP function, which can specify the number of rows or the percentage of rows, the Set Rowcount function can only specify the number of rows.

COLLATE

The collation can be set on a database, a table, a view, or a column. Additionally, we can specify use of a collation in a SELECT statement with the ORDER BY clause by adding the COLLATE argument. The benefit of using COLLATE in the ORDER BY clause is that we don't have to modify the underlying data to get the results we need.

For example, say you work in an international company based in New York with a SQL Server set with a SQL Latin1 CI collation. You restore a database backup from a branch office in Lithuania using the defaults on your server. What you've done is modified the database by changing the collation from Lithuania CS (CS for case sensitive) in the original to Latin1 CI (CI for case insensitive) on your server. If you run reports against this database, the ORDER BY clause will perform differently on your server than it would on the server in Lithuania.

Can you fix this? Of course.

By using the COLLATE argument in your ORDER BY clause, you can force the query to use the Lithuania CS collation in your query. It doesn't change the underlying database, and it's much quicker than rebuilding the database with the proper collation. Here's the syntax for including COLLATE in a SELECT statement:

```
SELECT TOP 10 Name, ProductNumber, StandardCost, ListPrice
FROM Production.Product
ORDER BY Name
COLLATE SQL_Lithuanian_Cp1257_CS_AS
```

 EXAM TIP If you look at the Books Online "What's New in SQL Server 2005" article, you'll see that Microsoft has added several *Database Engine International Enhancements.* While you may not work with complex languages such as Indic or Thai where the shapes of letters actually change depending on the characters around them, Microsoft does expect you to know that the database engine supports multiple collations and that they can be set on several levels: server, database, table, view, column, and query (using the COLLATE setting in the ORDER BY clause).

In the following exercise, we'll incorporate the ORDER BY clause into a SELECT statement.

Exercise 4.5: Use the ORDER BY Clause

1. Open SSMS and create a New Query window.

2. Create a listing of all employees and their phone numbers—ordered by Last Name—by entering and running the following query. This will create the result set in ascending order.

```
USE AdventureWorks;
GO
SELECT LastName, FirstName, Phone
FROM Person.Contact
ORDER BY LastName
```

Note that the keyword ASC is omitted because the default is in ascending order.

3. Change the order to descending order by adding the DESC keyword:

```
SELECT LastName, FirstName, Phone
FROM Person.Contact
ORDER BY LastName DESC
```

4. Return a listing that includes the customer ID, the salesperson ID, and the sales amount of the top five sales:

```
SELECT TOP 5 CustomerID, SalesPersonID, TotalDue
FROM Sales.SalesOrderHeader
ORDER BY TotalDue DESC
```

GROUP BY and HAVING

The GROUP BY clause allows us to organize the output rows into groups and summarize the data in those groups. In the previous example, we were able to identify information about individual sales. However, let's say we're interested in total sales for a customer, or total sales for a salesperson.

The Sales.SalesOrderHeader table has over 31,000 rows. What's not apparent is that these sales were generated by only 18 salespeople. Perhaps we're interested in how many sales each salesperson made. Instead of trying to count the information ourselves for each salesperson, we can query this information using the GROUP BY clause.

The GROUP BY clause is rather strict with the rules, as well as regarding which columns are allowed in the select list. Columns in the select list need to be in the GROUP BY clause, or they need to be aggregated with an aggregate function like COUNT.

In the following script, we are able to group the data by salesperson and provide summary data using the COUNT(*) function. The COUNT(*) function will count the actual number of rows in the SalesorderHeader column associated with each salesperson.

```
USE AdventureWorks;
GO
SELECT SalesPersonID, COUNT(*) AS 'Total Number of Sales'
FROM Sales.SalesOrderHeader
GROUP BY SalesPersonID;
```

Notice that you have only 18 rows returned, one for each of the 18 salespeople (including NULL), as shown in Figure 4-3.

COUNT(*) and COUNT(column)

It's common to use aggregate functions such as COUNT() with the GROUP BY clause, so while we're looking at GROUP BY, let's connect some knowledge on the COUNT function.

Figure 4-3

The GROUP

BY result

	SalesPersonID	Total Sales
1	NULL	27659
2	268	48
3	275	450
4	276	418
5	277	473
6	278	234
7	279	429
8	280	95
9	281	241
10	282	271
11	283	189
12	284	39
13	285	348
14	286	175
15	287	140
16	288	16
17	289	130
18	290	109

Earlier in this chapter, we encountered the COUNT(*) function, which is used to count all rows. The COUNT(COLUMN) function ignores NULL values.

In Figure 4-3, you may notice that one of the rows has NULL listed instead of a SalesPersonID. Some sales in the database do not have a SalesPersonID. Perhaps we're only interested in the number of sales by an actual sales person. We can modify the COUNT slightly to count only what exists in a specific column, instead of all the rows.

```
USE AdventureWorks;
GO
SELECT SalesPersonID, COUNT(SalesPersonID) AS 'Total Number of Sales'
FROM Sales.SalesOrderHeader
GROUP BY SalesPersonID;
```

The only difference between the output of this query and the previous query is that the value of NULL here is 0, whereas before it was over 27,000 sales. Here's a question for you. Which would take less computer resources: counting over 27,000 sales or ignoring them? Of course, the answer is obvious. Ignoring the sales attributed to the NULL employee takes fewer resources.

From a business perspective, there are times when the count of NULL is desired, and times when it isn't. Logical goals when creating any query include having it return the required information using the least number of resources. If you are only interested in identifying the number of sales attributed to actual salespersons, use the COUNT(SalesPersonID) function. If you actually need to identify the total number of sales and who made them, use COUNT(*).

HAVING

Let's imagine that the manager wants to personally recognize any salesperson that exceeds 100 individual sales. You can run the following script to do just that:

```
USE AdventureWorks;
GO
SELECT SalesPersonID, COUNT(SalesPersonID) AS 'Total Number of Sales'
FROM Sales.SalesOrderHeader
GROUP BY SalesPersonID
HAVING COUNT(SalesPersonID) > 100;
```

Notice in Figure 4-4 that this query returns only 13 rows, and since COUNT(SalesPersonID) was used instead of COUNT(*), the value of NULL was zero so it was not included.

Figure 4-4 The GROUP BY with HAVING clauses

	SalesPersonID	Total Sales
1	275	450
2	276	418
3	277	473
4	278	234
5	279	429
6	281	241
7	282	271
8	283	189
9	285	348
10	286	175
11	287	140
12	289	130
13	290	109

One way to think about the HAVING clause is by comparing it with the WHERE clause.

- The WHERE clause filters the rows of a SELECT statement based on some search condition.
- Likewise, the HAVING clause filters the rows of a GROUP BY clause based on some search condition.

Lastly, remember that the HAVING clause must be matched with a GROUP BY clause. We can not have a HAVING clause without a GROUP BY clause.

CUBE

The CUBE operator allows us to query an online transactional processing (OLTP) database but return results as a multidimensional cube. The multidimensional cube expands the queried columns and allows a manager to make better business decisions. It helps convert the data into more meaningful information.

In an online analytical processing (OLAP) database, we can reformat the entire database into cubes. These cubes are highly denormalized but optimized for querying based on business requirements.

The CUBE operator simulates the cubes in an OLAP database without rebuilding the entire database into cubes. To use the CUBE operator, we simply add WITH CUBE to the GROUP BY clause.

In the following exercise, we'll create a table and then query the results using the CUBE operator.

Exercise 4.6: Use the CUBE Operator

1. Open a New Query window in SSMS.

2. Create a database named Chapter4 and then create a table named Inventory in the database with the following script.

```
USE Master;
GO
CREATE DATABASE Chapter4;
GO
USE Chapter4;
GO
CREATE TABLE Inventory (
Item varchar(53) NOT NULL,
Color varchar(53) NULL,
Quantity int NULL
);
```

3. Populate the Inventory table with some data using the following INSERT statements.

```
INSERT INVENTORY VALUES ('Table', 'Red', 223);
INSERT INVENTORY VALUES ('Table', 'White', 54);
INSERT INVENTORY VALUES ('Table', 'Blue', 124);
INSERT INVENTORY VALUES ('Chair', 'Red', 210);
INSERT INVENTORY VALUES ('Chair', 'Blue', 101);
INSERT INVENTORY VALUES ('Chair', 'White', 23);
INSERT INVENTORY VALUES ('Stand', 'Red', 213);
INSERT INVENTORY VALUES ('Stand', 'Blue', 141);
INSERT INVENTORY VALUES ('Stand', 'White', 28);
```

4. Use a simple SELECT statement so we can view the data.

```
SELECT * FROM INVENTORY
```

This shows us all the inventory, but a business manager may be asking questions like "How many chairs do I have?" or "How many blue items do I have?" or "How many total pieces of inventory do I have?" We can get this type of summary data using the CUBE operator.

5. Run the following query to view the data with summary data.

```
SELECT Item, Color, SUM(Quantity) AS Quantity
FROM Inventory
GROUP BY Item, Color WITH CUBE;
```

Table 4-3 shows a partial result of the CUBE operator with only the extra rows generated by the CUBE operator added. Notice the NULL in the ITEM and COLOR columns. We can easily see that we have 334 chairs, 366 blue items, and a total of 1117 items (NULL in the Item and Color columns) in our inventory.

Item	Color	Quantity
Chair	NULL	334
Stand	NULL	382
Table	NULL	401
NULL	NULL	1117
NULL	Blue	366
NULL	Red	646
NULL	White	105

Table 4-3 Partial Result of CUBE

 EXAM TIP If you need summary data of the various columns displayed, use the CUBE operator. The CUBE operator generates NULL values in the result set that can be used to identify the summary data. The CUBE operator is used in conjunction with the GROUP BY statement.

6. A slight modification to the CUBE is the ROLLUP operator. Run the following query by replacing the CUBE opeator with the ROLLUP operator.

```
SELECT Item, Color, SUM(Quantity) AS Quantity

FROM Inventory

GROUP BY Item, Color WITH Rollup
```

In the result set, notice that the COLOR columns are not summarized. You have three less rows returned since there is no total for the Red, White, or Blue colors. The differences between CUBE and ROLLUP are:

- CUBE generates a result set that shows aggregates for *all combinations* of values in the selected columns.

- ROLLUP generates a result set that shows aggregates for a hierarchy of values in the selected columns.

Joins

Pulling data from one table at a time can only get us so far. At some point, we need to start pulling data from one or more tables.

In previous chapters, we covered how we use a PRIMARY KEY (PK) and a FOREIGN KEY (FK) to create relationships between tables. Now we discuss how to use those relationships to pull data from multiple tables simultaneously.

To join two tables, we use the ON statement to identify the PK and FK that hold the relationship.

The types of joins that SQL Server supports are listed in Table 4-4.

Type of Join	Description
Inner joins	Retrieves only data that exists in both tables based on the joined field.
Left outer joins	Retrieves all data in the left table, and only data that exists in the right table based on the joined field.
Right outer joins	Retrieves all data in the right table, and only data that exists in the left table based on the joined field.
Full joins (full outer joins)	Retrieves all data in both tables.
Cross joins	Creates a Cartesian product of the tables. Used to create sample databases with large volumes of data without too much effort.
Self-join	Joining a table to itself. This is sometimes required when retrieving data from a table that references the table (such as ManagerID of an Employee who is also in the Employee table as EmployeeID).

Table 4-4 Types of Joins

Inner Joins

First, we'll look at a simple query that joins two tables. The Production.Product table holds details on the ProductID such as the product name, product number, and ModelID. The Production.ProductModel table holds details on the ModelID such as the Model Name.

If we want a listing of products including the Model Name, we have to join the two tables. The following script first shows us what is in both tables, but without using the existing relationship. In reality, without connecting the two tables with a join, the two result sets aren't very useful.

```
USE AdventureWorks;
GO
SELECT Name, ProductNumber, ProductModelID
FROM Production.Product
SELECT ProductModelID,Name
FROM Production.ProductModel
```

Since the Production.Product and Production.ProductModel tables are related (on the ProductModelID column), they can be joined on the ProductModelID, as shown in the following example. This is the PK in the ProductModel table and is an FK in the Product table. To join the two tables in a SELECT statement, we could use the following script:

```
SELECT Production.Product.Name, Production.Product.ProductNumber,
       Production.ProductModel.Name AS 'Model Name'
FROM Production.ProductModel
INNER JOIN Production.Product
ON Production.ProductModel.ProductModelID =
   Production.Product.ProductModelID
```

Notice that the FROM statement is modified slightly by adding the INNER JOIN and the second table name. Next, we must identify the fields in each of the tables that hold the columns that define the relationship (ProductModelID in both tables in this example) with the ON clause.

TIP INNER JOIN is frequently shortened to just JOIN. You will see the two syntax choices used interchangeably, but most often, you'll just see JOIN.

A partial output of the previous script is shown in Figure 4-5.

Figure 4-5

Joining two tables

	Name	ProductNumber	Model Name
1	HL Road Frame - Black, 58	FR-R92B-58	HL Road Frame
2	HL Road Frame - Red, 58	FR-R92R-58	HL Road Frame
3	Sport-100 Helmet, Red	HL-U509-R	Sport-100
4	Sport-100 Helmet, Black	HL-U509	Sport-100
5	Mountain Bike Socks, M	SO-B909-M	Mountain Bike Socks
6	Mountain Bike Socks, L	SO-B909-L	Mountain Bike Socks

You can see that the JOIN statement identifies the first table (Production.Product) and the second table (Production.ProductModel). In addition, it identifies the PK and FK that will be used to join the tables in the ON clause (ProductModelID in each table).

We don't have to include the PK or FK in our select list. Often, this is meaningless data to end users. Instead, we just include what we want in the output. Notice that I used an alias in the select list for the Model Name. This is because we have two columns titled "Name," one in each table. To differentiate between the two in the output, I used an alias of 'Model Name' for the second. Since it has a space, I delimited it with single quotes.

Let's take a query that we used earlier to pull the top five sales out of the database. While it lists the CustomerID and SalesPersonID, you will very likely be requested to add actual names. The following query shows where we start:

```
SELECT TOP 5 CustomerID, SalesPersonID, TotalDue
FROM Sales.SalesOrderHeader
ORDER BY TotalDue DESC
```

Next, we'll modify the query to pull the data but also list the actual salesperson names. To help conceptualize the tables that are joined, let's look at the database diagram that shows the tables that hold the data we want. Figure 4-6 shows the relationships among the three tables. Notice that in the diagram the schema is shown in parentheses.

NOTE Notice in the diagram that the object and schema names are swapped from how they would appear in the four-part naming convention. For example, in the diagram the Contact table is listed as Contact(Person), but using the four-part name it would be listed as Server.AdventureWorks.Person.Contact, or shortened to Person.Contact.

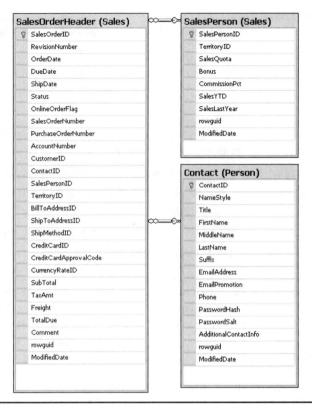

Figure 4-6   A database diagram of the Sales.SalesOrderHeader, Sales.SalesPerson, and Person.Contact tables

If you've used Microsoft Access, you may have used the Query By Example (QBE) window. SQL Server has a similar tool called the View Designer in SSMS that is used to create views. We used it in Chapter 2, and we'll use it again here to show how to easily build our SELECT statement joining multiple tables.

In the following exercise, we'll use the View Designer to create a listing of customers who have ordered products, including how much the orders were.

Exercise 4.7: Use the View Designer to Create Complex Joins

1. Open SSMS and then open the AdventureWorks database by double-clicking Databases and double-clicking the AdventureWorks database.

2. Right-click Views and select New View.

3. In the Add Table dialog box, choose the Contact (Person) table and click Add. Select the SalesOrderHeader (Sales) table and click Add. Click Close.

4. Arrange the tables so they look similar to Figure 4-7. Notice that the relationship is shown and points to the ContactID column in both tables.

Figure 4-7

Tables in the
View Designer

5. Now we'll select the columns we're interested in. It's important to select them in the order we want them to appear in the select list.

   a. In the Contact (Person) table, click the LastName and FirstName columns.

   b. In the SalesOrderHeader (Sales) table, click the CustomerID and TotalDue columns. Notice that two things have occurred as you've selected columns:

   • The columns are added into the column list pane in the center.

   • The SELECT statement is being built in the lower pane.

 TIP The View Designer has four panes. The top pane with the tables added is called the Diagram pane. The next pane with the selected columns listed is the Criteria pane. The third pane where the SELECT statement is being built is the SQL pane. Lastly, the Results pane displays your result set when the query is executed.

6. Add aliases to your column list:

   a. In the Alias column next to LastName, type in **Last Name** and press ENTER. Notice that it adds brackets around "Last Name" since there is a space. Observe how the SELECT statement changes.

   b. In the Alias column next to FirstName, enter **First Name.**

   c. In the Alias column next to CustomerID, enter **Customer Number.**

   d. In the Alias column next to TotalDue, enter **Order total**.

   Your display should look similar to Figure 4-8.

7. Test this SELECT statement using two methods. First, run it in the View Designer GUI by clicking the red exclamation mark (the Execute SQL button) on the menu bar, as shown in Figure 4-9.

8. We can also copy the query and paste it into any application where we want to run the query:

   a. Click in the pane holding the SELECT statement, and press CTRL+A to select it all.

   b. Press CTRL+C to copy the SELECT statement to the clipboard.

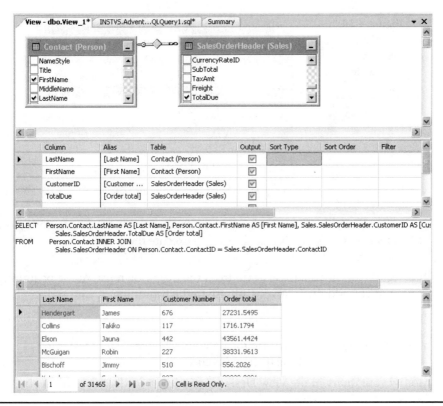

Figure 4-8 Building a SELECT statement in the View Designer window

Figure 4-9 The Execute SQL button in the View Designer toolbar

c. Open a New Query window by clicking the New Query button. If necessary, click Connect to connect to the default instance of your server.

d. Press CTRL+V to paste your script into the New Query window.

e. Notice the database that is currently being referenced in the New Query window is the *Master* database. This is in the Available Database drop-down list left of the Execute button on the toolbar, as seen in Figure 4-10.

f. Click the Execute button to execute the query. You receive an error message because the objects referenced do *not* exist in the Master database.

Figure 4-10

Selecting a different database in SSMS

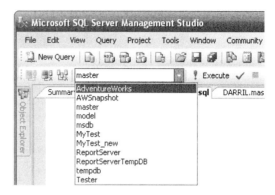

g. Use the Available Database drop-down list and select AdventureWorks, as in Figure 4-10. Click the Execute button to execute the query. This should be successful.

h. Select the Master database again from the drop-down list. At the beginning of your query, add the following phrase to the beginning of your script:

```
USE AdventureWorks
```

i. Run your query again. Notice the database changes from Master to AdventureWorks and the query runs successfully.

9. Modify your query in the View Designer window to order the result set by LastName and FirstName:

a. Switch to the View Designer window. In the Criteria pane, in the Sort Order column, in the LastName row, enter **1** as the Sort Order. Notice the Sort Type defaults to Ascending and the ORDER BY clause is added to your SELECT statement. Your display should look similar to Figure 4-11.

Figure 4-11

Setting the sort order in the View Designer

b. In the Sort Order column, in the FirstName row, enter **2** as the Sort Order. This causes the result set to be ordered by LastName. For any results that have the same LastName, the results will be ordered by FirstName. Notice also that the ORDER BY clause has been added.

c. Execute the query.

10. Filter your result set by looking only for contacts with a LastName of Smith or a FirstName of John:

a. In the View Designer window, in the Criteria pane in the Filter column of the LastName row, enter **Smith**. Notice that a WHERE clause is created. Your display should look similar to Figure 4-12. Execute the query and you'll see a result set for your view.

Figure 4-12
Adding a WHERE
clause with AND

Column	Alias	Table	Output	Sort Type	Sort Order	Filter
LastName	[Last Name]	Contact (Person)	☑	Ascending	1	= N'Smith'
FirstName	[First Name]	Contact (Person)	☑	Ascending	2	= N'John'
CustomerID	[Customer ...	SalesOrderHeader (Sales)	☑			
TotalDue	[Order total]	SalesOrderHeader (Sales)	☑			

```
SELECT    TOP (100) PERCENT Person.Contact.LastName AS [Last Name], Person.Contact.FirstName AS [First Name],
              Sales.SalesOrderHeader.CustomerID AS [Customer Number], Sales.SalesOrderHeader.TotalDue AS [Order total]
FROM      Person.Contact INNER JOIN
              Sales.SalesOrderHeader ON Person.Contact.ContactID = Sales.SalesOrderHeader.ContactID
WHERE     (Person.Contact.LastName = N'Smith') AND (Person.Contact.FirstName = N'John')
ORDER BY [Last Name], [First Name]
```

NOTE You may notice the SELECT statement doesn't just add Smith, but instead adds it as N'Smith'. The single quote is used to identify Smith as string data. The *N* prefix is used to identify the string data as Unicode data. Without the *N* prefix, the string is converted to the default code page of the database. While this may be acceptable for most situations, if you're using any type of different collation, you need to include the *N* prefix.

b. Remove the filter for the FirstName, and in the Or column for FirstName, enter **John**. Notice the WHERE clause is now modified with OR. Your display should look similar to Figure 4-13. Execute the query and you'll see a result set of many more rows than the earlier query.

Figure 4-13
Modifying the
AND to OR

Column	Alias	Table	Output	Sort Type	Sort Order	Filter	Or...
LastName	[Last Name]	Contact (Person)	☑	Ascending	1	= N'Smith'	
FirstName	[First Name]	Contact (Person)	☑	Ascending	2		= N'John'
CustomerID	[Customer ...	SalesOrderHeader (Sales)	☑				
TotalDue	[Order total]	SalesOrderHeader (Sales)	☑				

```
SELECT    TOP (100) PERCENT Person.Contact.LastName AS [Last Name], Person.Contact.FirstName AS [First Name],
              Sales.SalesOrderHeader.CustomerID AS [Customer Number], Sales.SalesOrderHeader.TotalDue AS [Order total]
FROM      Person.Contact INNER JOIN
              Sales.SalesOrderHeader ON Person.Contact.ContactID = Sales.SalesOrderHeader.ContactID
WHERE     (Person.Contact.LastName = N'Smith') OR
              (Person.Contact.FirstName = N'John')
ORDER BY [Last Name], [First Name]
```

OUTER JOINs

INNER JOINs allow us to pull data that exists in both tables, but sometimes we want to pull all the data from one of the tables in addition to what matches in both tables. These are referred to as OUTER JOINs. There are two types of outer joins: a *left outer join* and a *right outer join*.

A LEFT OUTER JOIN pulls all the data from the first table in the query (the one on the left), while a RIGHT OUTER JOIN pulls all the data from the second table in the query (the one on the right).

Earlier, we mentioned that the non-ANSI-compliant method of specifying a LEFT OUTER JOIN is *=, while the =* was used for a RIGHT OUTER JOIN. These methods are not supported in SQL Server 2005 unless the compatibility level is changed.

For example, a query similar to the following one may have been written in a previous version of SQL.

```
SELECT p.Name, pr.ProductReviewID
FROM Production.Product p,
Production.ProductReview pr
WHERE p.ProductID *= pr.ProductID
```

This query would return a listing of all the products in the Production.Product table and the ProductReviewID if it exists in the ProductReview table. Instead of a LEFT OUTER JOIN, it is using a WHERE clause with the *= operator.

To work within SQL Server 2005, it should instead be rewritten as follows:

```
USE AdventureWorks;
GO
SELECT p.Name, pr.ProductReviewID
FROM Production.Product p
LEFT OUTER JOIN Production.ProductReview pr
ON p.ProductID = pr.ProductID;
```

 EXAM TIP   In some SQL versions, a LEFT OUTER JOIN was represented as "*=" and a RIGHT OUTER JOIN was represented as "=*". This usage has been deprecated in SQL Server 2005. It is not ANSI-compliant and will not work with T-SQL within SQL Server 2005. It did work in SQL Server 2000, and if the compatibility level is set to 80, it will work in SQL Server 2005.

It is possible to get the query to work by setting a previous compatibility mode. For example, we could use the following query to set the compatibility mode to SQL Server 2000 (80), run the script, and then reset the compatibility mode to SQL Server 2005 (90).

```
sp_dbcmptlevel AdventureWorks, 80;
GO
SELECT E.EmployeeID, E.HireDate, J.Resume
FROM HumanResources.Employee AS E,
HumanResources.JobCandidate AS J
WHERE E.EmployeeID *= J.EmployeeID;
GO
sp_dbcmptlevel AdventureWorks, 90;
```

Table Aliases   You may have noticed that earlier queries in this chapter were rather long and cumbersome. One way they are often shortened is by using aliases.

TIP Alias: one word—two meanings. We've learned that aliases are used in the column list to give us a different header in the output. We can also use aliases in the SELECT list to avoid having to type out the name of the tables each time.

Let's take a look at the query we created in the View Designer:

```
SELECT Person.Contact.LastName AS [Last Name],
       Person.Contact.FirstName AS [First Name],
       Sales.SalesOrderHeader.CustomerID [Customer Number],
       Sales.SalesOrderHeader.TotalDue [Order Total]
FROM Person.Contact INNER JOIN
     Sales.SalesOrderHeader
ON Person.Contact.ContactID = Sales.SalesOrderHeader.ContactID INNER JOIN
     Sales.SalesPerson
ON Sales.SalesOrderHeader.SalesPersonID = Sales.SalesPerson.SalesPersonID
```

In the next script, we use aliases for the table names. Aliases are used for three tables, as shown in Table 4-5. The alias names are at your discretion. Using the first character in the table, or the first characters in the schema and the table, is common.

Table Name	Alias
Person.Contact	Pc
Sales.SalesOrderheader	soh
Sales.SalesPerson	sp

Table 4-5 Table Aliases

```
SELECT pc.LastName AS [Last Name],
       pc.FirstName AS [First Name],
       soh.CustomerID [Customer Number],
       soh.TotalDue [Order Total]
FROM Person.Contact AS pc INNER JOIN
       Sales.SalesOrderHeader soh
ON pc.ContactID = soh.ContactID
   INNER JOIN Sales.SalesPerson sp
ON soh.SalesPersonID = sp.SalesPersonID
```

 NOTE Students in the classroom often ask me: "How do I know what *pc* represents in the first line?" You must scan ahead to the FROM clause, looking for the initials of the alias such as *pc* or *soh*. I realize it's not natural; we'd expect to see the definition of *pc* before we see the abbreviation. The only thing I can say is that it gets easier with practice.

When using aliases in the column list, you can use the letters *AS* or leave them out. The same rule applies when using aliases to identify tables.

A Warning with Column Aliases While we covered column aliases earlier, it's worthwhile to point out a potential problem. First, let's remind ourselves what we mean by "column aliases" by looking at the following script:

```
SELECT SalesOrderID AS Invoice,
TotalDue [TotalDue],
OrderDate [Invoice Date]
FROM Sales.SalesOrderHeader
ORDER BY OrderDate
```

This works fine as written, but when we start creating more complex SELECT statements with embedded functions, we can get unexpected results if we're not careful. Notice that the TotalDue column in the SELECT list is being referenced with an alias of the same name of TotalDue. This is not good form and can create problems. The rule to remember is that the alias needs to be a separate name from any existing column. While this seems obvious, let's look at an example using the CONVERT function.

The CONVERT function allows us to convert data types from one form to another, and it's frequently used to change a date from a datetime data type to a varchar data type so that we can change the way it's displayed.

For example, the following script will cause the date to be displayed as *yyyy-mm-dd hh:m:ss:ms*.

```
SELECT GetDate()
```

Output: 2007-01-17 08:11:49.327.

Using the CONVERT function, we can have the date displayed in the U.S. format (style 101) as *mm/dd/yyyy* or in the ANSI format of *yy.mm.dd* (style 102):

```
SELECT CONVERT(varchar,GetDate(),101)
```

Output: 01/17/2007

```
SELECT CONVERT(varchar,GetDate(),102)
```

Output: 2007.01.17

Functions can be embedded into SELECT statements. Using the CONVERT function within a SELECT statement may look like the following:

```
SELECT SalesOrderID AS Invoice,
       TotalDue [Invoice Total],
CONVERT(varchar,OrderDate, 101)
FROM Sales.SalesOrderHeader
ORDER BY OrderDate
```

However, if you run this, you'll notice that the OrderDate column header is blank. It makes sense to provide an alias. Careful, though. The following script gives unexpected results because we are using the same alias name as a column name:

```
SELECT SalesOrderID AS Invoice,
       TotalDue [Invoice Total],
CONVERT(varchar,OrderDate, 101) As OrderDate
FROM Sales.SalesOrderHeader
ORDER BY OrderDate
```

EXAM TIP Beware of using the same name as an alias in the ORDER BY statement. Generally, we use the alias to give us a different, more readable name. Using the same name can give unexpected results.

Notice that we're using OrderDate in three places. First, it's the date column embedded in the CONVERT function. Next it's the alias of the converted column, which is of type varchar. Lastly, we are specifying the OrderDate in the ORDER BY clause.

Let's look at two possible dates: 01/01/2004 and 02/1/2001. Which one is first? It depends. If the data type is *date*, the year 2001 is before 2004. If the data type is *varchar*, than 01 is before 02, so 01/01/2004 is before 02/1/2001.

More than likely you want the output ordered by the *date* data type. The fix is to change the alias to something different, such as [Order Date] as shown in the following script:

```
SELECT SalesOrderID AS Invoice,
       TotalDue [Invoice Total],
CONVERT(varchar,OrderDate, 101) As [Order Date]
FROM Sales.SalesOrderHeader
ORDER BY OrderDate
```

UNION

The UNION operator is used to combine the results of two or more SELECT statements. The column lists in each of the SELECT statements must have the same structure in terms of data types, but they don't necessarily have to come from identical columns. In other words, if the first SELECT statement has a varchar data type in the first column, the second SELECT statement must have a varchar data type first.

For example, we could have the following two queries:

```
USE AdventureWorks;
GO
SELECT VendorID, Name
FROM Purchasing.Vendor
```

And:

```
USE AdventureWorks;
GO
SELECT ContactID, LastName
FROM Person.Contact;
```

The VendorID and the ContactID columns are both integer data types, while the Name and LastName are both varchar data types. The first SELECT statement queries the Purchasing.Vendor table (returning about 104 rows), while the second SELECT statement queries data from the Person.Contact table (returning about 19,970 rows).

Both statements can be combined together with a UNION operator, which would look like the following query and return over 20,000 rows.

```
USE AdventureWorks;
GO
SELECT VendorID AS ID, Name
FROM Purchasing.Vendor
```

```
UNION
SELECT ContactID, LastName
FROM Person.Contact
```

By default, the UNION operator removes duplicate rows from the result set. For example, if we queried an EmployeeWest table and an EmployeeEast table and used UNION to combine the two, if any individual existed in both tables, they would only appear once in the result set. The way the query optimizer identifies duplicates is by first sorting the result set and then eliminating the duplicates. However, you can't be sure of the sorted order; the only way to ensure the order of a result set is with the ORDER BY statement.

If duplicates are desired, ALL can be added to the UNION statement as follows:

```
SELECT VendorID AS ID, Name
FROM Purchasing.Vendor
UNION ALL
SELECT ContactID, LastName
FROM Person.Contact
```

Other DML Statements

Other Data Manipulation Language (DML) statements include UPDATE, INSERT, and DELETE, as shown in Table 4-6. Other DML statements are very similar to SELECT statements, so we won't add much here.

DML Statement	Description
UPDATE	Modify column(s) in a row
INSERT	Add new row(s)
DELETE	Eliminate row(s)

Table 4-6 DML Statements

UPDATE

To update columns within a row, we use the UPDATE statement. Under the hood, SQL actually deletes the original row and then re-creates the new row with the changed data.

If you look at Books Online, you'll see that the UPDATE statement can be quite complex, but for our discussion, we'll keep it simple. The basic syntax for the UPDATE statement is:

```
UPDATE tablename
SET column1 = value[, column2 = value, column3 = value]
WHERE search condition to limit the rows that are updated
```

Notice that we can set one or more columns in the SET portion of the UPDATE statement.

Let's say that JoLynn Dobney gets married to Jay Adams, and then JoLynn changes her name to JoLynn Adams. She's in the Person.Contact table, so we can find her with a SELECT statement:

```
USE AdventureWorks;
SELECT *
FROM Person.Contact
WHERE FirstName ='JoLynn' AND LastName = 'Dobney'
```

Executing the preceding script, we can see that she has a ContactID of 1070. Now we can change her last name to "Adams" with this UPDATE script. The SELECT statement allows us to verify that our update was successful.

```
UPDATE Person.Contact
SET LastName = 'Adams'
WHERE ContactID = 1070
SELECT *
FROM Person.Contact
WHERE ContactID = 1070
```

The UPDATE statement could be executed without the WHERE clause. However, just as the WHERE clause limits the rows in a SELECT statement, the WHERE clause limits the number of rows in the UPDATE statement. If you ran the UPDATE statement without the WHERE clause, it would change the last name of all people in the Person. Contact table to Adams!

INSERT

To add rows to a table, we use the INSERT statement. Rows that are inserted must obey the rules set up for the table. These include the proper data types and paying attention to NULLs, constraints, and triggers. While we haven't talked about triggers yet, we have covered NULLs, data types, and constraints.

Using the Object Explorer in SSMS, we can see the properties of the Person.Contact table, as shown in Figure 4-14.

Several columns are specified as NOT NULL, as shown in Table 4-7. Remember, if the column is specified as NOT NULL, NULLs are not allowed. However, if a default is specified, we can omit the data for this column and a default value will be entered.

Looking at Table 4-7, we can see that only four columns must be entered: FirstName, LastName, PasswordHash, and PasswordSalt. The rest can either be NULL or have a default or constraint that will populate them.

The basic syntax of the INSERT statement is shown next:

```
INSERT INTO table name (column1, column2, column3, etc.)
VAUES (value1, value2, value3, etc.)
```

If we are putting data into each column in the table, we can omit the column list. The exception is for a PRIMARY KEY defined with the IDENTITY constraint. This will

Figure 4-14
Using Object
Explorer in SSMS
to identify table
properties

always be left blank and created automatically by SQL Server. If we are omitting any columns that can be NULL or have defaults defined, we would omit them from both the column list and the value list. If included in the column list, data must be included in the value list.

Column with NOT NULL	Comment
ContactID	Created automatically with IDENTITY constraint
NameStyle	Has a default named DF_Contact_NameStyle
FirstName	Must be entered
LastName	Must be entered
EmailPromotion	Has a default named DF_Contact_EmailPromotion
PasswordHash	Must be entered
PasswordSalt	Must be entered
Rowguid	Has a default named DF_Contact_rowguid
ModifiedDate	Has a default named DF_Contact_ModifiedDate

Table 4-7 Person.Contact Non-NULL Columns

As an example, let's say we have a new employee. To add him to the Contact table, we could use the following script:

```
INSERT INTO Person.Contact
(FirstName, LastName,PasswordHash, PasswordSalt)
VALUES ('Darril', 'Gibson', 'P@ssw0rd','P@$$S@lt')
```

To verify that this was successful, we can use the following:

```
SELECT * FROM Person.Contact
WHERE FirstName = 'Darril'
```

DELETE

To eliminate (delete) rows, we use the DELETE statement. The basic syntax of the DELETE statement is:

```
DELETE FROM table
WHERE Column Name = Column Value
```

 CAUTION   If you omit the WHERE clause, you will delete *all* of the rows in the table. This is also known as an opportunity to test your disaster recovery plan, or worse, an opportunity to update your résumé.

Let's say that an employee won the lottery and is no longer working with us. We have been tasked with removing his record from the database. Before we delete the employee, it's a good practice to do a SELECT statement to verify that you are affecting the row(s) you want to affect:

```
SELECT * FROM Person.Contact
WHERE ContactID = 10
```

If this gives you just the row you're looking for, then modify the SELECT statement to be a DELETE statement, as shown next:

```
DELETE FROM Person.Contact
WHERE ContactID = 10
```

TRUNCATE TABLE

If you ever want to delete all the rows in the table, use the TRUNCATE TABLE statement. This works functionally the same as a DELETE statement without a WHERE clause. When you're done, all the rows in the table are gone.

The difference is that the DELETE statement will log each row deletion in the Transaction Log, while the TRUNCATE statement will just deallocate the pages where the rows were contained. The TRUNCATE statement is faster and uses fewer system resources since the deletion of each individual row is NOT logged into the transaction log.

The basic syntax for the TRUNCATE TABLE statement is:

```
TRUNCATE TABLE
    [ { database_name.[ schema_name ]. | schema_name . } ]
    table_name[ ; ]
```

In the following exercise, we'll go through the steps to add a vendor to the company by inserting a row into the Purchasing.Vendor table, modifying the row, and then deleting it.

Exercise 4.8: Insert, Update, and Delete Data with T-SQL

1. Open a New Query window in SSMS.

2. View the contents of the Purchasing.Vendor table using the following query. Notice the result set currently has 104 rows, as shown in Figure 4-15.

```
SELECT *
FROM Purchasing.Vendor
```

Figure 4-15

The Purchasing.
Vendor result set

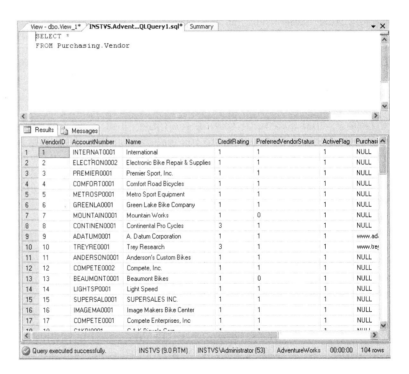

3. Open the AdventureWorks database (if it's not already opened) by double-clicking the Databases container and the AdventureWorks database.

4. Double-click the Tables container to open it, and then double-click the Purchasing.Vendor table to open it.

5. Double-click Columns to open the Columns container in the Purchasing. Vendor table. Notice that most columns are specified as NOT NULL. These either need to have data identified in an INSERT or have a default defined.

6. Double-click the Constraints container to open it. Notice that we have four constraints. The CK_Vendor_CreditRating ensures that a credit rating between 1 and 5 is entered. The other three are defaults for the ActiveFlag, ModifiedDate, and PreferredVendorStatus columns.

7. Double-click the Triggers folder. Notice the trigger named dVendor. This prevents a vendor from being deleted. Your display should look similar to Figure 4-16.

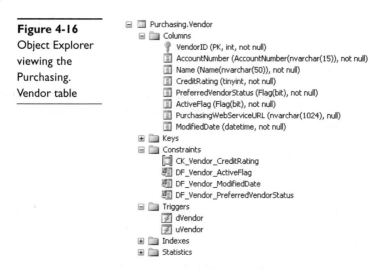

Figure 4-16
Object Explorer viewing the Purchasing. Vendor table

8. With the information we have, we can now build our INSERT statement. Table 4-8 summarizes the columns and shows that only three columns must be added.

Column	Comments
VendorID	Created with IDENTITY.
AccountNumber	Must be added. Specified as NOT NULL.
Name	Must be added. Specified as NOT NULL.
CreditRating	Must be added. Specified as NOT NULL. Constraint specifies range between 1 and 5.
PreferredVendorStatus	Specified as NOT NULL, but has DEFAULT specified if omitted.
ActiveFlag	Specified as NOT NULL, but has DEFAULT specified if omitted.
PurchasingWebServiceURL	Can be NULL.
ModifiedDate	Specified as NOT NULL, but has DEFAULT specified if omitted.

Table 4-8 The Purchasing. Vendor Table

Use the following INSERT statement to add the Acme Supplies Company with a credit rating of 1 and an account number of AcmeSupp101:

```
USE AdventureWorks
INSERT INTO Purchasing.Vendor
 (AccountNumber, Name,CreditRating)
VALUES('AcmeSupp101','AcmeSupplies',1)
```

9. Verify your vendor has successfully been added with the following SELECT statement:

```
USE AdventureWorks
SELECT *
FROM Purchasing.Vendor
WHERE AccountNumber = 'AcmeSupp101'
```

10. The vendor is experiencing some cash-flow problems, and their credit rating has been changed from 1 to 3. Use the following UPDATE statement to make this modification:

```
USE AdventureWorks
UPDATE Purchasing.Vendor
SET CreditRating = 3
WHERE AccountNumber = 'AcmeSupp101'
```

If you experiment with this script by changing the credit rating to 6 or something other than a number between 1 and 5, you'll see how the constraint prevents invalid data from being entered.

11. Verify the credit rating has been updated by rerunning the SELECT statement from step 9.

12. Let's assume the Acme Supplies Company was entered during testing. No company exists with that name. You are tasked with deleting the row for the Acme Supplies Company. Use the following DELETE statement to try and delete the row:

```
USE AdventureWorks
DELETE
FROM Purchasing.Vendor
WHERE AccountNumber = 'AcmeSupp101'
```

Running this script, you'll receive an error message like the following. This is because a trigger exists on the table.

```
Vendors cannot be deleted. They can only be marked as not active.
```

We'll explore triggers further in Chapter 5, but for now realize that since the trigger is preventing us from accomplishing our task, we can temporarily disable the trigger.

13. Use the following script to disable the trigger, delete the row, and then re-enable the trigger. Note that we are using two different methods to affect the trigger (DISABLE TRIGGER and ALTER TABLE).

```
USE AdventureWorks
Go
DISABLE TRIGGER dVendor ON Purchasing.Vendor
GO
DELETE
FROM Purchasing.Vendor
WHERE AccountNumber = 'AcmeSupp101'
GO
ALTER TABLE Purchasing.Vendor ENABLE TRIGGER dVendor
```

 EXAM TIP A trigger can be disabled in two ways. One is with the command *DISABLE TRIGGER triggername ON tablename*. The second is with the command *ALTER TABLE tablename DISABLE TRIGGER triggername*.

Advanced Query Techniques

When preparing for the 70-442 test, you'll need to understand the advanced query techniques available in SQL Server 2005. These include:

- Common Table Expressions (CTEs)
- EXCEPT and INTERSECT
- PIVOT and UNPIVOT
- Ranking functions

Common Table Expressions (CTEs)

Common Table Expressions (CTEs) are new to SQL Server 2005. They are used to provide a temporary result set within any DML statement. The CTE then works and appears as a table to the rest of the statement.

The CTE is similar to a derived table—it doesn't persist in the database, but instead lasts only for the duration of the query. However, the CTE can be self-referencing and can be referenced multiple times in the same query.

The following is a simple example of a CTE.

```
USE AdventureWorks
GO
WITH cteEmployees( FirstName, Lastname) AS
(
  SELECT FirstName, LastName
  FROM Person.Contact c JOIN HumanResources.Employee e
  On c.ContactID = e.ContactID
)
SELECT *
FROM cteEmployees
```

Notice the With line [*WITH cteEmployees(FirstName, Lastname)*] identifies the columns in our CTE as *FirstName, LastName*. The embedded SELECT statement can be just about any valid DML SELECT statement—the requirements are the same as for creating a VIEW. With the CTE created, we can now use it in a DML statement; we are retrieving the contents with a simple SELECT statement.

If after this query ran (or even after a GO statement), you again ran only the *SELECT* * *FROM cteEmployees* statement, you would get an error: *Invalid object name 'cteEmployees'*. It no longer exists.

The preceding example also shows the basic syntax structure for a CTE:

```
WITH CommonTableExpressionName [ ( column_list [,...n] ) ]
AS
(SELECT statement as CTE_query_definition )
```

Recursion with CTE

While a CTE can be recursive or nonrecursive, one of the great strengths of a CTE is its ability to reference itself and create a recursive CTE. A recursive CTE will be repeatedly executed until a complete result set is obtained. This is commonly done when accessing hierarchical data, such as when displaying employees in an organizational chart.

 EXAM TIP When hierarchical data needs to be displayed from a table that references itself, consider using a CTE to recursively access the table. A recursive query is one that references a recursive CTE. Three common examples of using recursive CTEs are 1) when creating an organizational chart of employees to show who reports to whom; 2) when creating a bill of materials where some parts are referred to as parents with subcomponents associated with them; and 3) when products are associated to parent categories. The recursive CTE can loop through the data and return a hierarchical display.

In earlier versions of SQL Server, the functionality of a recursive CTE was created by using temporary tables, cursors, and complex logic. In SQL Server 2005, the use of a recursive CTE makes this logic much simpler.

The Structure of Recursive CTE

The basic syntax of a recursive CTE is:

```
WITH cte_name ( column_name [,...n] )
AS
(
CTE_query_definition -- Anchor member is defined.
UNION ALL
CTE_query_definition -- Recursive member is defined referencing cte_name.
)
-- Statement using the CTE
SELECT *
FROM cte_name
```

Notice that the CTE query has two definitions. The first one (the anchor member) defines the query referencing the external table. It is followed by a UNION, UNION ALL, EXCEPT, or INTERSECT statement.

The next CTE definition references the CTE recursively. During the execution of the recursive CTE, the second query definition is run repeatedly until an empty set is returned.

In the following exercise, we'll create a table, populate it with data that can be arranged hierarchically, and then use a recursive CTE to retrieve and display the data.

Exercise 4.9: Use a CTE

1. Open a New Query window within SSMS.

2. Use the following script to create an Employees table in the Chapter4 database.

```
USE Chapter4;
GO
CREATE TABLE dbo.LincolnCabinet
(
  LincolnCabinetID int IDENTITY (100,1) NOT NULL,
  LastName varchar(50) NULL,
  FirstName varchar(50) NULL,
  MgrId int NULL references dbo.LincolnCabinet,
  Title varchar(50) NULL
    CONSTRAINT PK_LincolnCabinetID PRIMARY KEY (LincolnCabinetID)
);
```

Note that the MgrID references the LincolnCabinetID (the PK in the LincolnCabinet table).

3. With the table created, let's populate it with the following INSERT statements.

```
INSERT INTO LincolnCabinet (LastName, FirstName, MgrID, Title)
VALUES('Lincoln', 'Abraham', Null, 'President')
INSERT INTO LincolnCabinet (LastName, FirstName, MgrID, Title)
VALUES('Stanton', 'Edwin', 100, 'Secretary of War')
INSERT INTO LincolnCabinet (LastName, FirstName, MgrID, Title)
VALUES('Seward', 'William', 100, 'Secretary of State')
INSERT INTO LincolnCabinet (LastName, FirstName, MgrID, Title)
VALUES('Welles', 'Gideon', 100, 'Secretary of the Navy')
INSERT INTO LincolnCabinet (LastName, FirstName, MgrID, Title)
VALUES('Welles', 'Orson', 103, 'Grandson')
```

This shows President Abraham Lincoln at the top of the list as the President. Notice that the MgrID is Null since he doesn't directly report to any single person. Secretary of War Stanton, Secretary of State Seward, and the Secretary of the Navy all report directly to the President. Orson Welles was the grandson of Gideon Welles, so for the fun of it, we're putting him as reporting to Secretary of the Navy Gideon Welles.

4. With this done, let's query the table with a CTE. This CTE will allow us to recursively query the table to determine who works for whom in the hierarchy.

```
USE Chapter4;
GO
WITH cteReport (HierarchyOrder, MgrID, LincolnCabinetID, LastName, Title)
AS
(-- Anchor member definition
SELECT 0 AS HierarchyOrder, lc.MgrID, lc.LincolnCabinetID, lc.LastName,
lc.Title
FROM LincolnCabinet AS lc
WHERE MgrID IS NULL
UNION ALL
-- Recursive member definition
SELECT d.HierarchyOrder + 1, lc.MgrID, lc.LincolnCabinetID, lc.LastName,
lc.Title
```

```
FROM LincolnCabinet AS lc
INNER JOIN cteReport AS d
ON lc.MgrID = d.LincolnCabinetID
)
--Statement that executes the CTE
SELECT HierarchyOrder, LastName, Title, LincolnCabinetID, MgrID
FROM cteReport
```

TIP   If you try to run the query without using the statement to execute the CTE, you'll get the error: *Incorrect syntax near ')'*. Since the CTE is lost as soon as it's executed, the only time the CTE can be accessed is right after it's created. Thus, if it isn't accessed, it's perceived as an error.

After running this query, your display should look similar to Figure 4-17.

Figure 4-17

The result of a recursive CTE query against LincolnCabinet

	HierarchyOrder	LastName	Title	LincolnCabinetID	MgrID
1	0	Lincoln	President	100	NULL
2	1	Stanton	Secretary of War	101	100
3	1	Seward	Secretary of State	102	100
4	1	Welles	Secretary of the Navy	103	100
5	2	Welles	Grandson	104	103

5. We can also see a recursive CTE in action against the AdventureWorks database. The following query identifies who reports to whom and creates an organizational type of report.

```
USE AdventureWorks;
GO
WITH DirectReports (ManagerID, EmployeeID, Title, DeptID, Level)
AS
( -- Anchor member definition
    SELECT e.ManagerID, e.EmployeeID, e.Title, edh.DepartmentID, 0 AS
Level
    FROM HumanResources.Employee AS e
    INNER JOIN HumanResources.EmployeeDepartmentHistory AS edh
        ON e.EmployeeID = edh.EmployeeID AND edh.EndDate IS NULL
    WHERE ManagerID IS NULL
    UNION ALL
-- Recursive member definition
    SELECT e.ManagerID, e.EmployeeID, e.Title, edh.DepartmentID,
        Level + 1
    FROM HumanResources.Employee AS e
    INNER JOIN HumanResources.EmployeeDepartmentHistory AS edh
        ON e.EmployeeID = edh.EmployeeID AND edh.EndDate IS NULL
    INNER JOIN DirectReports AS d
        ON e.ManagerID = d.EmployeeID )
-- Statement that executes the CTE
SELECT ManagerID, EmployeeID, Title, Level
FROM DirectReports
INNER JOIN HumanResources.Department AS dp
    ON DirectReports.DeptID = dp.DepartmentID
WHERE dp.GroupName = N'Research and Development' OR Level = 0;
```

Your display should look similar to Figure 4-18.

Figure 4-18

A partial result of a recursive CTE query against AdventureWorks

	ManagerID	EmployeeID	Title	Level
1	NULL	109	Chief Executive Officer	0
2	109	12	Vice President of Engineering	1
3	12	3	Engineering Manager	2
4	3	4	Senior Tool Designer	3
5	3	9	Design Engineer	3
6	3	11	Design Engineer	3
7	3	158	Research and Development Manager	3

This last example is from the Books Online article entitled "Recursive Queries Using Common Table Expressions" and gives an excellent step-by-step explanation of what is occurring.

EXCEPT and INTERSECT

The EXCEPT and INTERSECT operators are new to SQL Server 2005. They can be used to compare the results of two or more SELECT statements and then return distinct values. The difference between the two is what is returned.

EXCEPT returns any distinct values from the left side query (the query preceding the EXCEPT operator) that aren't also on the right side query (the query after the EXCEPT operator). In other words, it looks for all the matches, and returns only what is an exception to the matches in the left query.

INTERSECT returns any distinct values that are returned by the queries on both sides of the INTERSECT. In other words, whatever exists on both sides of the INTERSECT will be returned. If one query returns the numbers 1, 2, 3, and the query on the other side returns the numbers 2, 3, 4, the numbers that will be returned are 2 and 3—or said another way, whatever exists on both sides.

The format of these queries is:

```
Query1 EXCEPT (or INTERSECT) Query2
```

Admittedly, "left" and "right" are a little misleading. If the query was written in a single line (as written in the previous code sample), then clearly Query1 is on the left and Query2 is on the right. However, queries are normally written in the following format:

```
Query1
EXCEPT (or INTERSECT)
Query2
```

Query1 is on the top, and Query2 is on the bottom. Still, Query1 is referred to as being on the left, while Query2 is considered to be on the right.

 EXAM TIP Any time you are seeking to identify the same distinct values that exist in two separate tables, use the INTERSECT operator. It can easily be used to provide a listing of any values that are repeated in both queries.

As an example, consider Tables 4-9 and 4-10, showing data of Customer1 and Customer2, respectively.

Table 4-9	LastName
Customer1	Smith
Table	Jones
	Johnson

Table 4-10	LastName
Customer2	Smith
Table	Jones
	Gibson

Now let's execute a query with the INTERSECT command against these two tables:

```
SELECT LastName FROM Customer1
INTERSECT
SELECT LastName FROM Customer2
```

The result is Jones and Smith.

The first query *SELECT LastName FROM Customer1* returns Smith, Jones and Johnson. The second query *SELECT LastName FROM Customer2* returns Smith, Jones, and Gibson. What's the same from both queries? Smith and Jones.

The EXCEPT command works a little differently.

```
SELECT LastName FROM Customer1
EXCEPT
SELECT LastName FROM Customer2
```

The preceding query will return the name Johnson. The names Smith and Jones both have a match in the two queries, but the name Johnson only exists in the left table, not in the right. It is an exception.

Can you guess what the result will be if you switch the tables? It won't be the same answer. Look at this query:

```
SELECT LastName FROM Customer2
EXCEPT
SELECT LastName FROM Customer1
```

Now, the query on the left is the Customer2 query. Again Smith and Jones have matches in both queries, but the exception in the Customer2 table is the name Gibson.

The EXCEPT and INTERSECT operators have just a couple of basic rules.

- The number and the order of the columns must be the same in all queries.
- The data types of the columns must be compatible.

PIVOT and UNPIVOT

The PIVOT and UNPIVOT relational operators are enhancements to T-SQL in SQL Server 2005. They can be used to rotate results, or said another way, change the result sets so that the columns become rows or the rows become columns. The result is called a cross-tab report and the query is called a cross-tab query.

A cross-tab query can restructure and recalculate data for different reporting or analysis requirements. It can be used to aggregate normalized data and present it in a more meaningful way. Although the same results were possible before SQL Server 2005, the introduction of PIVOT and UNPIVOT operators allows the code to be simpler.

While normalized data often works best for performance of a database, to retrieve the data and display it, we want something more like a spreadsheet similar to Microsoft Excel. PIVOT can take normalized data and display it like a spreadsheet. UNPIVOT can display data this is stored as a spreadsheet and display it in a normalized fashion.

 EXAM TIP If you need to create a cross-tab report, or need to display normalized data in a spreadsheet like format, use PIVOT to retrieve and reformat the output.

For example, let's say management is interested in how many purchase orders have been placed by certain employees named Pellow, Kurjan, Hagens, and Miller to specific vendors. We can query the Contact and Employee tables to get their EmployeeID (238, 241, 244, and 261, respectively).

Using the following SELECT statement, we could query this information from the Purchasing.PurchaseOrderHeader table. However, you can see from the output that it isn't very meaningful.

```
SELECT VendorID, PurchaseOrderID, EmployeeID
FROM Purchasing.PurchaseOrderHeader
WHERE EmployeeID IN ( 238, 241, 244, 261 )
ORDER BY VendorID
```

A partial result is listed in Figure 4-19.

Figure 4-19

The partial output of a query without PIVOT

	VendorID	PurchaseOrderID	EmployeeID
1	1	123	241
2	1	281	244
3	1	469	244
4	1	635	261
5	1	718	238
6	1	1130	238
7	1	1525	241
8	1	1683	244

Instead, we could reformat the query using PIVOT to list how many purchase orders were placed to specific vendors by these employees. We're still pulling the data out of the normalized Purchasing.PurchaseOrderHeader table, but we are presenting it in a much more meaningful way.

```
USE AdventureWorks;
GO
SELECT VendorID, [238] AS Pellow, [241] AS Kurjan, [244] AS Hagens, [261]
AS Miller
FROM
(SELECT PurchaseOrderID, EmployeeID, VendorID
FROM Purchasing.PurchaseOrderHeader) p
PIVOT
( COUNT (PurchaseOrderID)
FOR EmployeeID IN ( [238], [241], [244], [261] )
) AS pvt
ORDER BY VendorID
```

Figure 4-20 shows a partial output from this query. From a business perspective, a business manager may recognize the strength of changing which buyers purchase from which vendors. If instead of four buyers buying a company's product, all the purchases could be funneled to a single buyer so she can leverage a better price.

Figure 4-20

PIVOT partial output

	VendorID	Pellow	Kurjan	Hagens	Miller
1	1	4	5	5	4
2	2	5	5	5	4
3	3	4	5	5	4
4	4	5	5	5	4
5	5	5	4	4	5
6	7	4	4	4	5
7	8	5	5	5	4
8	10	6	5	5	4

The UNPIVOT operator could be used to reverse the process. It's similar to the PIVOT operator in that it allows you to rotate data and convert rows into columns. However, UNPIVOT is most useful when you have data stored in a spreadsheet fashion and you want to present it as normalized data.

Ranking

Sometimes, we may want our result sets ranked into some type of order. Such wishes are beyond a simple ORDER BY clause, which merely returns it in an order. Instead, we want a numerical output that shows exactly what the rank of each row is.

SQL Server 2005 provides four ranking functions that can be used to numerically rank the output. They are:

- RANK
- DENSE_RANK
- ROW_NUMBER
- NTILE

The data displayed from the database are the same for each ranking function. What changes is the Ranking column produced by the different functions. The difference in the RANK, DENSE_RANK, and ROW_NUMBER functions are based primarily on how duplicates are treated. NTILE divides the result set into a given number of groups. For example, let's imagine that we issued a query against a Sales database listing top sales people using the different ranking functions. Table 4-11 shows how the output would look.

Row	SalesPerson	MonthlySales	RANK	DENSE_RANK	ROW_NUMBER	NTILE(3)
I	101	$23,456	I	I	I	I
2	102	$23,321	2	2	2	I
3	103	$23,321	2	2	3	2
4	104	$14,123	4	3	4	2
5	105	$7,899	5	4	5	3

Table 4-11   Comparison of RANK, DENSE_RANK, ROW_NUMBER, and NTILE

The Row column is listed just for discussion purposes and wouldn't be part of the query. Notice that rows 2 and 3 have identical Monthly Sales, but other Monthly Sales are different.

The Rank column starts at 1 for the first row, and as long as the values are different, it will increment by one. Since rows 2 and 3 are the same, the rank of these rows is the same. However, the rank function still increments the value, so row 4 has a rank of 4. The rank of 3 is skipped since we had two ranks of 2.

EXAM TIP   If you want a numerical ranking and want the duplicate values to be counted in the ranked output so the ranking numbers are skipped, use the RANK function. If you don't want ranking numbers to be skipped, after duplicate values are encountered use the DENSE_RANK function.

DENSE_RANK is the same as the RANK function except values aren't skipped even if there's a tie. For example, rows 2 and 3 both have a rank of 2. The next row is listed with a rank of 3.

The ROW_NUMBER simply lists the row numbers. The values aren't evaluated for ties. Once an ORDER BY clause defines the order, the ROW_NUMBER function simply assigns row numbers.

NTILE divides the rows into groups, or buckets. Looking back at Table 4-11 we can see the result of the NTILE(3) function. NTILE(3) divides the five rows into three groups. Group one has two rows, group two has two rows, and group three has one row. Note that NTILE doesn't care about the values; rows 2 and 3 have identical totals but are divided into different groups. Instead, NTILE is primarily concerned with evenly dividing the number of rows as equally as possible. In our example from Table 4-11, we have 5 rows, so 5 divided by 3 = 1.667. Rounded up, we have two rows per group with only one row left for the last group. If instead we used NTILE(2), then we would have two groups. The number passed to NTILE defines how many groups we want and should be less than the total number of rows.

The syntax of each of the functions is shown in the following code listing. Notice that they all use the partition_by_clause and an order_by_clause. The NTILE function is the only function that receives an argument.

```
RANK ( )
        OVER ( [ <partition_by_clause> ] <order_by_clause> )
DENSE_RANK ( )
        OVER ( [ <partition_by_clause> ] <order_by_clause> )
ROW_NUMBER ( )
        OVER ( [ <partition_by_clause> ] <order_by_clause> )
NTILE (integer_expression)
        OVER ( [ <partition_by_clause> ] <order_by_clause> )
```

The optional <partition_by_clause> divides the result set produced by the FROM clause into partitions. The ranking function is then applied to the separate partitions. If the <partition_by_clause> is omitted, the ranking function is applied to the entire result set.

The <order_by_clause> determines the order in which the ranking function values are applied. The <order_by_clause> is not optional and must appear in the ranking function.

In the following exercise, we'll take a look at some queries using the ranking functions.

Exercise 4.10: Use Ranking Functions against the AdventureWorks Database

1. Open SSMS and then open a new query window.

2. Enter and execute the following query to return information on four specific customers. Notice that the partition_by_clause is omitted, so the ranking function applies to the entire result set.

```
SELECT CustomerID, SalesOrderID, SubTotal,
       RANK() OVER(ORDER BY SubTotal DESC) AS Rank
FROM Sales.SalesOrderHeader
WHERE CustomerID IN (599, 514, 638, 72)
ORDER BY SubTotal Desc
```

Your result set should look similar to Figure 4-21.

Figure 4-21

A partial RANK result set

	CustomerID	SalesOrderID	SubTotal	Rank
1	599	51131	224356.4831	1
2	638	46981	182344.2664	2
3	514	46616	182344.2664	2
4	72	47395	179754.1225	4
5	599	67305	140506.874	5

3. For comparison's sake, let's use this same query for each of the ranking functions. Add the bolded statements listed in the following code segment to your previous code and execute it.

```
SELECT CustomerID, SalesOrderID, SubTotal,
DENSE_RANK() OVER(ORDER BY SubTotal DESC) AS Dense_Rank,
ROW_NUMBER() OVER(ORDER BY SubTotal DESC) AS Row_Number,
NTILE(10) OVER(ORDER BY SubTotal DESC) AS NTile,
RANK() OVER(ORDER BY SubTotal DESC) AS Rank
FROM Sales.SalesOrderHeader
WHERE CustomerID IN (599, 514, 638, 72)
ORDER BY SubTotal Desc
```

Your code should look similar to Figure 4-22.

Figure 4-22

Partial output of the different ranking functions

	CustomerID	SalesOrderID	SubTotal	Dense_Rank	Row_Number	NTile	Rank
1	599	51131	224356.4831	1	1	1	1
2	638	46981	182344.2664	2	2	1	2
3	514	46616	182344.2664	2	3	1	2
4	72	47395	179754.1225	3	4	1	4
5	599	67305	140506.874	4	5	2	5
6	72	53506	129038.6978	5	6	2	6
7	72	50683	127012.8505	6	7	2	7
8	72	48336	121699.3439	7	8	3	8
9	599	61184	113451.8266	8	9	3	9
10	638	50222	112847.5701	9	10	3	10

4. The previous code snippets omitted the PARTITION BY clause, resulting in the ranking function being applied to the entire result set. In the following code, we'll add the PARTITION BY clause to partition the result set by the CustomerID. The bolded text shows what has changed from the first query.

```
SELECT CustomerID, SalesOrderID, SubTotal,
RANK() OVER(PARTITION BY CustomerID
ORDER BY SubTotal DESC) AS Rank
FROM Sales.SalesOrderHeader
WHERE CustomerID IN (599, 514, 638, 72)
ORDER BY CustomerID
```

Notice that this query ranks the invoices on a per-customer basis since we have partitioned the output by customer. Your display should look similar to Figure 4-23.

Figure 4-23

A partial listing of ranking function with the PARTITION BY clause

	CustomerID	SalesOrderID	SubTotal	Rank
1	72	47395	179754.1225	1
2	72	53506	129038.6978	2
3	72	50683	127012.8505	3
4	72	48336	121699.3439	4
5	72	71824	104178.6558	5
6	72	49479	96872.1497	6
7	72	58950	86699.2852	7
8	72	65237	64735.5898	8
9	514	46616	182344.2664	1
10	514	49828	106471.252	2

Chapter Review

In this chapter, we presented some basics on Transact-SQL and then added in some advanced query techniques. We covered the SELECT statement, adding the WHERE clause to filter the data, the ORDER BY clause to guarantee a sort order, the GROUP BY and HAVING classes to provide summary data, and the various JOIN clauses to combine data from multiple tables. We covered the other DML statements INSERT, UPDATE, and DELETE. For those readers preparing to take the 70-442 test, we also covered some advanced query techniques using common table expressions, EXCEPT and INTERSECT, PIVOT and UNPIVOT, and ranking functions.

Additional Study

Self Study Exercises

- Write a SELECT statement that retrieves a listing of all employees in Adventure-Works and includes their first and last names. Use aliases for the table names.

- Write a SELECT statement that includes all employees hired in the year 2001, ordered by Last Name from *Z* to *A*.

- Write a SELECT statement retrieving a list of all employees with birthdays in the next month. List the employees by name.

- Rewrite the following statement into an ANSI-compliant statement:

```
SELECT e.LastName, e.FirstName, a.City, a.StateEmployeeID
FROM Employee e, Address a
WHERE e.EmployeeID *= a.EmployeeID
```

- Add yourself as an employee using appropriate INSERT statements. Note that this requires an entry into the Contact table.

- Change the last name of Ms. Kim Abercrombie to Ziemba with an UPDATE statement.

- Use the DELETE statement to remove your record as a contact in Adventure-Works.

- Create a hierarchical result set from a query showing who works for whom in the AdventureWorks company. Use the Employee and Department tables.

- Write a query to list all employees by name, omitting any employees that don't have e-mail addresses listed in the database.

BOL Topics

- Working with Collations
- SELECT Clause (Transact-SQL)

- Search Condition (Transact-SQL)
- LIKE (Transact-SQL)
- ORDER BY Clause (Transact-SQL)
- COLLATE (Transact-SQL)
- GROUP BY (Transact-SQL)
- Join Fundamentals
- CAST and CONVERT (Transact-SQL)
- UPDATE (Transact-SQL)
- INSERT (Transact-SQL)
- DELETE (Transact-SQL)
- Recursive Queries Using Common Table Expressions
- Ranking Functions (Transact-SQL)
- Using PIVOT and UNPIVOT
- EXCEPT and INTERSECT (Transact-SQL)

Summary of What You Need to Know

70-431
When preparing for the 70-431 test, you need to be very proficient with T-SQL. This includes:

- Using and interpreting SELECT statements
- Using and interpreting other DML statements
- Using aliases
- Using Group By and Having statements

You should know how to work with transactions, including:

- BEGIN TRANSACTION
- COMMIT TRANSACTION
- ROLLBACK TRANSACTION

You should be familiar with TRY CATCH statements and how to catch errors within a T-SQL script.

70-441
Topics for the 70-441 test aren't included in this chapter.

70-442

When preparing for the 70-442 test, you must be thoroughly familiar with Transact-SQL statements. This includes both basic and advanced techniques. Expect to see complex T-SQL statements that must be analyzed and then either corrected or optimized. Keywords you should know include:

- SELECT
- WHERE
- NULL
- ORDER BY (including TOP)
- GROUP BY (including Having)
- CUBE
- PIVOT and UNPIVOT
- EXCEPT and INTERSECT
- WITH (common table expressions, including recursive common table expressions)
- RANK

Questions

70-431

1. You work in the Atlanta headquarters of your company managing a SQL Server 2005 server. You are tasked with providing a report on salespeople from the Madrid office ordered by last name and first name. You restore the Madrid office database onto your server and write a query to run the report. However, you notice that the salespeople are sorted differently in the Madrid office database. Management wants this report in the same order as the Madrid office database, as quickly as possible. What do you do?

   A. Rebuild the Madrid office database using the Madrid collation and rerun the report.

   B. Rewrite the query used to generate the report using the COLLATE keyword in the ORDER BY clause.

   C. Rewrite the query used to generate the report using the CONVERT keyword in the ORDER BY clause.

   D. Rewrite the query used to generate the report using the COLLATE keyword in the column list.

2. You are tasked with creating a query that will list car sales representatives and their total sales for the month. The report must only include those sales representatives who have exceeded sales of $90,000. Which query will accomplish these goals?

   A.

   ```
   SELECT sp.SalesPersonID, SUM (soh.TotalDue) as 'Monthly Sales'
   FROM Sales.SalesPerson sp JOIN Sales.SalesOrderHeader soh
   ON sp.SalesPersonID = soh.SalesPersonID
   WHERE MONTH(soh.OrderDate) = MONTH(GetDate())
   GROUP BY sp.SalesPersonID
   HAVING SUM(soh.TotalDue) > 90000
   ```

   B.

   ```
   SELECT sp.SalesPersonID, SUM (soh.TotalDue) as 'Monthly Sales'
   FROM Sales.SalesPerson sp JOIN Sales.SalesOrderHeader soh
   ON sp.SalesPersonID = soh.SalesPersonID
   WHERE MONTH(soh.OrderDate) = MONTH(GetDate())
   GROUP BY sp.SalesPersonID
   ```

   C.

   ```
   SELECT sp.SalesPersonID, SUM (soh.TotalDue) as 'Monthly Sales'
   FROM Sales.SalesPerson sp JOIN Sales.SalesOrderHeader soh
   ON sp.SalesPersonID = soh.SalesPersonID
   WHERE MONTH(soh.OrderDate) = MONTH(GetDate())
                  AND soh.TotalDue > 90000
   ```

   D.

   ```
   SELECT sp.SalesPersonID, SUM (soh.TotalDue) as 'Monthly Sales'
   FROM Sales.SalesPerson sp JOIN Sales.SalesOrderHeader soh
   ON sp.SalesPersonID = soh.SalesPersonID
   WHERE MONTH(soh.OrderDate) = MONTH(GetDate())
               AND soh.TotalDue >  90000
   GROUP BY sp.SalesPersonID
   HAVING SUM(soh.TotalDue) >= 90000
   ```

3. You are tasked with troubleshooting the following script. You expect the data to be ordered by *year, month, day*, with the newest year first. Instead, it's ordered by the *month, day, year*, starting with December. How can this be corrected?

   ```
   SELECT CustomerID, TotalDue, SaleDate,
          CONVERT(varchar, SaleDate, 101) as SaleDate
   FROM Sales
   ORDER BY SaleDate
   ```

   A. Add ASC to the ORDER BY clause.

   B. Add DESC to the ORDER BY clause.

   C. Add ASC to the ORDER BY clause, and change the alias to 'Sale Date'.

   D. Add DESC to the ORDER BY clause, and change the alias to 'Sale Date'.

4. A fellow developer is writing an application that will be used by management in a cell phone sales company. One of the things he wants to do is create a query that will identify any employees that exceeded total sales of a given dollar amount for a given timeframe. He's going to use variables inside the program but asks you to create the query using $4000 as the dollar amount, with the date range of July 1, 2007 to July 1, 2008, as the given timeframe. Which of the following queries will achieve this?

A.

```
SELECT e.LastName, SUM(o.TotalDue) AS 'Total Sales'
FROM Employee e
JOIN Orders o
ON e.EmployeeID = o.EmployeeID
WHERE o.OrderDate BETWEEN '07/01/2007' AND '07/01/2008'
GROUP BY e.LastName
HAVING SUM(o.OrderTotal) >= 4000
```

B.

```
SELECT e.LastName, SUM(o.TotalDue) AS 'Total Sales'
FROM Employee e
JOIN Orders o
ON e.EmployeeID = o.EmployeeID
WHERE o.OrderDate BETWEEN '07/01/2007' AND '07/01/2008'
GROUP BY s.LastName
```

C.

```
SELECT e.LastName, SUM(o.TotalDue) AS 'Total Sales'
FROM Employee e
JOIN Orders o
ON e.EmployeeID = o.EmployeeID
WHERE o.OrderDate BETWEEN '07/01/2007' AND '07/01/2008'
                                    AND o.TotalDue >= 4000
GROUP BY s.LastName
```

D.

```
SELECT e.LastName, SUM(o.TotalDue) AS 'Total Sales'
FROM Employee e
JOIN Orders o
ON e.EmployeeID = o.EmployeeID
WHERE o.ordertotal = 4000
    AND o.OrderDate BETWEEN '07/01/2007' AND '07/01/2008'
GROUP BY s.LastName
HAVING SUM(o.TotalDue) >= 4000
```

70-442

1. You are tasked with creating an employee report showing who reports to whom in a hierarchical display. In the Employee table, a field named MgrID exists

which identifies the employee's manager. A partially populated Employee table looks similar to Figure 4-24.

Figure 4-24
A partially populated Employee table

	EmployeeID	LastName	FirstName	MgrId	Title
1	100	Gibson	Darril	NULL	CEO
2	102	Smith	Joe	101	Dept MGR
3	103	Johansen	Maria	101	Dept MGR
4	104	Johnson	Sally	103	Sales Person
5	101	Grzena	Dawn	100	VP

Your report should look similar to Figure 4-25.

Figure 4-25
A report

	MgrID	EmployeeID	LastName	Title	Hierarchy
1	NULL	100	Gibson	CEO	0
2	100	101	Grzena	VP	1
3	101	102	Smith	Dept MGR	2
4	101	103	Johansen	Dept MGR	2
5	103	104	Johnson	Sales Person	3

Which of the following queries will achieve the required results?

A.

```
SELECT * FROM Employees Order by Hierarchy
```

B.

```
SELECT MgrID, EmployeeID, LastName, Title, Order as Hierarchy
FROM Employees
Order by EmployeeID
```

C.

```
SELECT e.MgrID, e.EmployeeID, e.LastName, e.Title, 0 AS Hierarchy
FROM Employee AS e
WHERE MgrID IS NULL
UNION ALL
SELECT e.MgrID, e.EmployeeID, e.LastName, e.Title, Hierarchy + 1
FROM Employee AS e
```

D.

```
WITH cteReport (MgrID, EmployeeID, LastName, Title, Hierarchy)
AS
( SELECT e.MgrID, e.EmployeeID, e.LastName, e.Title, 0 AS Hierarchy
FROM Employee AS e
WHERE MgrID IS NULL
UNION ALL
SELECT e.MgrID, e.EmployeeID, e.LastName, e.Title, d.Hierarchy + 1
FROM Employee AS e
```

```
INNER JOIN cteReport AS d
ON e.MgrID = d.EmployeeID)

SELECT *
FROM cteReport
```

2. You are rewriting code that was ported over from another database and needs to be ANSI-compliant. How would you rewrite the following SELECT statement?

```
SELECT c.LastName, c.FirstName, e.EmployeeID
FROM Person.Contact c, HumanResources.Employee e
WHERE c.ContactID =* e.ContactID
```

A.

```
SELECT c.LastName, c.FirstName, e.EmployeeID
FROM Person.Contact c RIGHT OUTER JOIN
HumanResources.Employee e
ON c.ContactID = e.ContactID
```

B.

```
SELECT c.LastName, c.FirstName, e.EmployeeID
FROM Person.Contact c LEFT OUTER JOIN
HumanResources.Employee e
ON c.ContactID = e.ContactID
```

C.

```
SELECT c.LastName, c.FirstName, e.EmployeeID
FROM Person.Contact c, HumanResources.Employee e
AS LEFT OUTER JOIN
ON c.ContactID = e.ContactID
```

D.

```
SELECT c.LastName, c.FirstName, e.EmployeeID
FROM Person.Contact c, HumanResources.Employee e
AS RIGHT OUTER JOIN
ON c.ContactID = e.ContactID
```

3. You have been tasked with creating a query that can identify those employees who have received company awards. The Employees table lists all employees, and the Awards table lists all employees who have received a company award. What operator should you use?

   A. PIVOT

   B. EXCEPT

   C. INTERSECT

   D. UNION

4. You are tasked with identifying how many purchase orders were placed by the four different buyers in your company. You want to create a cross-tabulation

query that returns the number of orders each buyer has placed with a listing of each company where they've purchased products. What specific T-SQL command would be needed to create this cross-tab report?

A. PIVOT

B. EXCEPT

C. INTERSECT

D. VIEW

5. A manager has asked you to create a query that will list the top invoices, including the salesperson. The query should list the salesperson's position based on their top sale and would look similar to the sample report shown in Figure 4-26. If two sales persons have the same subtotal for the top sale, they should be assigned the same position.

Figure 4-26

A sample report

	Position	SalesPersonID	SalesOrderID	SubTotal
1	1	281	51131	224356.4831
2	2	285	46616	182344.2664
3	2	286	46981	182344.2664
4	4	275	47395	179754.1225

What operator would allow you to create the Position column?

A. RANK

B. ROW_NUMBER

C. DENSE_RANK

D. NTILE

6. Management wants a query that will tell them what the highest sales were for the day. They will run it at any time of the day and will provide a variable representing a percentage of records to view. An entry of 100 would indicate 100 percent of the records, while 10 would represent 10 percent of the records. The variable will be passed in and declared as @Percent. Which of the following queries would achieve your goals?

A.

```
SELECT TOP (@Percent) PERCENT TotalDue, OrderDate
FROM Sales.SalesOrderHeader
ORDER BY TotalDue DESC
```

B.

```
SET rowcount @Percent
SELECT TotalDue, OrderDate
FROM Purchasing.PurchaseOrderHeader
Where OrderDate = GetDate()
ORDER BY TotalDue DESC
```

C.

```
SELECT TOP (@Percent) PERCENT TotalDue, OrderDate
FROM Sales.SalesOrderHeader
Where OrderDate = GetDate()
ORDER BY TotalDue
```

D.

```
SELECT TOP (@Percent) PERCENT TotalDue, OrderDate
FROM Sales.SalesOrderHeader
Where OrderDate = GetDate()
ORDER BY TotalDue DESC
```

7. You are troubleshooting a query that an assistant has been unable to get to work. The query is trying to retrieve a listing of customers that don't have phone numbers listed in the Customer database. The query is:

```
SELECT LastName, FirstName, Phone
FROM Customer
WHERE Phone = NULL
```

What would you do to make the query work?

A. Replace WHERE Phone = NULL with WHERE Phone ='' '

B. Replace WHERE Phone = NULL with WHERE IS NOT NULL

C. Replace WHERE Phone = NULL with WHERE Phone IS NULL

D. Before the query, issue the following SET statement: SET ANSI_NULLS ON

8. You work at a car dealership that has several different locations and are tasked with creating a cross-tab report that will list sales by year for different car dealerships. You only want data for the years 2006 and 2007. Which code segment would you use?

A.

```
SELECT pivot.DealershipID, pivot.2006, pivot.2007
FROM (
SELECT ds.DealershipID ,ds.SalesOrderAmt ,YEAR(ds.OrderDate) AS Year
FROM Sales.DealerSales ds
) AS ds
PIVOT (
SUM(SalesOrderAmt) FOR Year IN (2006,2007)
) AS pivot;
```

B.

```
SELECT ds.DealershipID, ds.SalesOrderAmt
FROM Sales.DealerSales ds
WHERE YEAR(ds.OrderDate) = 2006
EXCEPT
SELECT ds.DealershipID, ds.SalesOrderAmt
FROM Sales.DealerSales ds
WHERE YEAR(ds.OrderDate) = 2007
```

C.

```
SELECT ds.DealershipID, ds.SalesOrderAmt
FROM Sales.DealerSales ds
WHERE YEAR(ds.OrderDate) = 2006
INTERSECT
SELECT ds.DealershipID, ds.SalesOrderAmt
FROM Sales.DealerSales ds
WHERE YEAR(ds.OrderDate) = 2007
```

D.

```
SELECT ds.DealershipID, ds.SalesOrderAmt
FROM Sales.DealerSales ds
WHERE YEAR(ds.OrderDate) = 2006
UNION ALL
SELECT ds.DealershipID, ds.SalesOrderAmt
FROM Sales.DealerSales ds
WHERE YEAR(ds.OrderDate) = 2007
```

9. You are asked to review code within an application to ensure it conforms with ANSI standards. You come across the following code:

```
SELECT c.CustomerID, c.LastSaleDate, s.YrTotalSales
FROM Customer c
Sales s
WHERE c.CustomerID *= s.CustomerID
```

What would you change to ensure it complies with ANSI standards?

A. Nothing. It is ANSI-compliant as it is.

B.

```
SELECT c.CustomerID, c LastSaleDate, sYrTotalSales
FROM Customer AS c
FULL OUTER JOIN Sales AS s
ON c. CustomerID = J. CustomerID
```

C.

```
SELECT c. CustomerID, c. LastSaleDate, s.YrTotalSales
FROM Customer AS c
INNER JOIN Sales AS s
ON c. CustomerID = s. CustomerID
```

D.

```
SELECT c. CustomerID, c.Hiredate, s.YrTotalSales
FROM Customer AS c
LEFT OUTER JOIN Sales AS s
ON c. CustomerID = s. CustomerID
```

10. You need to reproduce a report that provides summary data of your furniture store's inventory. A partial output of your desired result is shown in Table 4-12, with the NULLs representing summary data.

Item	Color	Quantity
Chair	NULL	334
Stand	NULL	382
Table	NULL	401
NULL	NULL	1117
NULL	Blue	366
NULL	White	105
NULL	Red	646

Table 4-12 Partial Output of a Query against Furniture Store Inventory

What operators would you include in the SELECT statement to accomplish this goal? (Choose all that apply.)

A. ROLLUP

B. CUBE

C. GROUP BY

D. ORDER BY

Answers

70-431

1. **B.** The COLLATE keyword can be used to change the collation within a SELECT statement, but can only be used in the ORDER BY clause, not the column list. CONVERT is used to convert from one data type to another. Rebuilding the entire database would be possible if you have a lot of time on your hands, but is not the best choice for "as quickly as possible."

2. **A.** Answer A is the only one that will achieve the desired goals. B doesn't limit the results to reps that have exceeded sales of $90,000. C and D limit the results to only individual sales exceeding $90,000.

 TIP When answering questions like this, it's a good idea to look for what's the same, and then what's different. For example, each of the answers has identical lines for the first four lines. Your task is then to just interpret the remaining lines.

3. **D.** With the alias the same as the ORDER BY clause, the date will be sorted in the converted format of varchar instead of with the original value of datetime. Changing the alias will solve this. By default, the ORDER BY statement will cause data to be sorted in ascending order (ASC). Adding DESC will change this to descending.

4. **A. Answer** B does not check for the dollar amount of $4000. Answers C and D include o.OrderTotal >= 4000 (or o.OrderTotal = 4000) in the WHERE clause. This will restrict any totals added to the sum to only the individual orders that equal or exceed $4000, not the total sales for the given time frame.

70-442

1. **D.** This is an excellent example of use of a recursive CTE in a recursive query. We need to loop through the Employees table multiple times to identify who works for whom. This is done by placing SELECT after the UNION All statement within the CTE. Since the table has no Hierarchy column, it can't be referenced unless it's created. To prove this to yourself, create and populate an Employee table as shown in the display and try the preceding queries.

2. **A.** The "=*" needs to be replaced with RIGHT OUTER JOIN. LEFT OUTER JOIN would replace "*=". The RIGHT OUTER JOIN clause would be placed between the two tables (not after the two tables).

3. **C.** The Intersect operator will list all results that exist on both the left side and the right side of the query. For example, the query could be SELECT EmployeeID FROM Employees INTERSECT SELECT EmployeeID FROM Awards. EXCEPT will list only what exists on the left side, but that does NOT exist on the right side. PIVOT is a relational operator used to manipulate a table-valued expression into another table.

4. **A.** PIVOT would allow a cross tabulation report as the scenario requests. EXCEPT and INTERSECT can compare two queries but wouldn't provide the results requested. A VIEW is an object, not a T-SQL command.

5. **A.** The RANK operator can return a sequential integer for each row, with duplicate values assigned the same rank, but still be counted as a row value. In the figure, four rows are listed as 1, 2, 3, and 4. The Subtotal for rows 2 and 3 are the same, so the position for both is tied for second and displayed as 2. Position 3 is skipped due to the tie, and the next position is 4. ROW_NUMBER would assign each a sequential integer as Position of 1, 2, 3, and 4. DENSE_RANK is similar to RANK but does not skip numbers. The preceding display would have positions of 1, 2, 2, and 3. NTILE groups the result into a specified number of groups and would assign incrementing integers to each successive group.

6. **D.** To view the top percentage of orders for a specific date, you must specify the date, and in the Order By clause, specify DESC for descending. GetDate() is used to show today's sales. Answer A omits the WHERE clause to specify the date.

The Set Rowcount would specify the exact number of rows to limit the query to, not the percentage of rows. If ASC or DESC is omitted, the ORDER BY clause will default to ASC or ascending, resulting in the lowest sales for the day.

7. **C.** To check for a NULL value, use the IS NULL function. A comparison to an empty string will not work. Using IS NOT NULL will return a listing of customers with phone numbers. When SET ANSI_NULLS is ON, all comparisons against a null value evaluate to UNKNOWN.

8. **A.** This question is much easier than it seems, and could be asked another way: What operator would you use to create a cross-tab report? The answer is we'd use the PIVOT operator in a cross-tab query. Only one query includes the PIVOT operator. EXCEPT returns all the distinct values from the left side query except for what exists on the right side. INTERSECT returns distinct values that exist on both sides of the query, while UNION operators return all the data from both queries.

9. **D.** The *= in the WHERE clause is equivalent to a LEFT OUTER JOIN, but this usage is not ANSI-compliant. A RIGHT OUTER JOIN would be equivalent to a =*.

10. **B, C.** To get the summary data shown, use the CUBE operator. The CUBE operator must be used with the GROUP BY operator. Only the CUBE or the ROLLUP operator could be used, but the ROLLUP operator would not show the summary data for all possible combinations. None of the columns are in any order, so the ORDER BY clause would not be needed.

XML

In this chapter, you will learn about:

- XML data
- Storing XML
- Retrieving XML

> We only see a little of the ocean,
> A few miles distance from the rocky shore;
> But oh! out there beyond – beyond the eye's horizon
> There's more – there's more.
> We only see a little of God's loving,
> A few rich treasures from his mighty store;
> But oh! out there beyond – beyond our life's horizon
> There's more – there's more.
>
> —*Unknown*

Though it's composed of only three short letters—XML—don't be fooled. There is a lot to the topic of Extensible Markup Language (XML). While reading several of Dr. Michael Rys's XML papers on Microsoft's site, I came across a line that stuck with me. I may be paraphrasing, but the message was, "Don't try to learn it all, it simply isn't possible."

XML is one of those topics where we need to learn only that which we need. Don't try to master all of the possibilities and intricacies of XML if you just want to use a simple XML function. When the need to learn *more* comes up, *then* learn more. Unless your job is nothing but XML, there's no way you'll master all its topics and subtopics. With that in mind, don't expect this chapter to make you a master of XML. My goal here is to offer the basics on what you need to know for the certification exams. But be assured, there's more, there's more.

XML Overview

Extensible Markup Language (XML) is like UPC bar codes were years ago. They started creeping in, and some people in the know said, "Get used to them. They'll be everywhere." It's the same with XML. It was originally designed to simply be used as a document format, but due to its ease of use, extensibility, and easy readability by both machines and humans, it has become a popular format for storing and sharing data. Soon, XML will be everywhere. A primary reason (and distinctive benefit) as to why XML enjoys such widespread use is because it easily describes the data contained within an XML file.

One of the great strengths of XML is its simplicity. At its core is an XML file, which is just a plain text file. As a plain text file, it's highly portable and can be read by a number of different environments. XML files can be both exported and imported by most database systems, and can be easily transported over the Internet.

With the introduction of the XML data type in SQL Server 2005, it's possible to add entire XML data files as XML text into a column within a row.

One thing to understand about XML is its terminology. So, let's define a few things:

- **Elements**   The name in the start and end tags is the element. Since we can make the element name whatever we want it to be, it is usually named to describe the data. Elements can include only the element name, or include both attributes and values. The first example shows an element with only the element name:

  ```
  <elementName> … </elementName>
  <Author>Darril Gibson</Author>
  ```

- **Attribute**   Attributes within an element are used to specify additional information about the element. As the preceding examples show, attributes are optional in an element.

- **Value**   Values are associated with Attributes and must be enclosed in quotes to comply with rules to ensure the XML is well-formed.

  The following example shows an element with attributes and values included:

  ```
  <elementname attributeName = "Value">
  <Author FirstName="Darril">Gibson</Author>
  ```

- **XML Namespace**   A special type of XML attribute that is placed within an XML tag. The attribute prefix is xmlns:. The namespace suffix is unique within the application and follows the colon (:). A Uniform Resource Identifier (URI) or Uniform Resource Locator (URL) is commonly used. Within any application, it is very possible to have elements the same, such as <description> for a Parts table, and <description> for a Products table. The XML namespace differentiates between the two elements. The namespace for the AdventureWorks.Production. ProductModel Instructions column is shown in the following XML snippet:

  ```
  <root xmlns="http://schemas.microsoft.com/sqlserver/2004/07/adventure-
  works/ProductModelManuInstructions">
  ```

- **XML Schema Definition (XSD)**   This is an instance of an XML schema. It defines the structure of an XML document in terms of the elements, the attributes, data types, and relationships.

XML Data

XML data is data that is stored using XML tags. These tags can be associated with an XML schema that identifies the tags, but an XML schema is not required. If you've been exposed to HTML, you'll be able to understand XML formatting a little more easily, but even if you're not familiar with HTML, the basics of XML are still easy to grasp.

HTML is a programming construct used to format web pages. All web browsers can interpret HTML to display different elements of the web page. For example, a heading can be identified with the <H1> element. All data between the <H1> and </H1> tags will be displayed as a Header 1. If you want text on a web page to be displayed as bold text, you would surround it with <strong> and </strong>. The <strong> is the opening (or starting) of bold text, and when you are ready to turn bold off, you simply use the closing tag, which has a / at the beginning of it—in this example, </strong> would turn bold off.

XML data is similar to HTML in that it uses tags. However, a significant distinguishing factor between XML and HTML is that HTML is used to identify *how we display* the data, while XML is used to *describe* the actual data.

For example, an XML document used to hold information on completed projects could contain the following information:

- Project Name
- Start Date
- End Date
- Manager
- Scope
- Comments

We could take the entire XML document (properly formatted XML text) and store it in a column of a table. Let's say we have an Employee table and we want to include appropriate project information for employees. We could add a ProjCompleted column. Data stored in the ProjCompleted column might look like the following:

```
<ProjCompleted><ProjectName>Employee Database</ProjectName><StartDate>Jan
2, 2008</StartDate><EndDate>Feb 1, 2008</EndDate><Manager>Darril Gibson</
Manager><Scope>Create full database including all tables and associated data-
base objects.</Scope> <Comments>Intern will be tasked to complete data entry
after database is created.</Comments></ProjCompleted>
```

The same data is displayed a little more intuitively next:

```
<ProjCompleted>
  <ProjectName>
      Employee Database
  </ProjectName>
  <StartDate>
      Jan 2, 2008
```

```
</StartDate>
<EndDate>
      Feb 1, 2008
</EndDate>
<Manager>
      Darril Gibson
</Manager>
<Scope>
      Create full database including all tables and associated database
objects.
</Scope>
<Comments>
      Intern will be tasked to complete data entry after database is
created.
</Comments>
</ProjCompleted>
```

XML has several strengths that contribute to its increasing popularity:

- *XML is a common language.*   Most databases can easily import an XML document as a basic text document, no matter what database it came from. For example, a database exported from an Oracle database into an XML document can be imported into SQL Server. Of course, SQL Server can export data into an XML document so it can be imported into any other database server that recognizes XML.

- *XML can easily go through firewalls.*   Using SOAP (Simple Object Access Protocol) messages, an XML document can use the same protocol (HTTP) that HTML documents use. Firewalls are typically already configured to allow HTTP through (on port 80). SOAP messages take advantage of this and pass XML documents through the same port. Anyone who's tried to convince a security-conscious systems administrator to open another port appreciates the simplicity of XML.

Well-formed XML

In order for an XML document to be considered correct, it must be well-formed. XML parsers check XML documents to ensure they are well-formed and can either accept or reject them. We'll see later how the XML data type includes an XML parser and rejects XML data that is not well-formed.

A well-formed document must conform to several rules, most of which are listed next:

- Non-empty elements must have both a start-tag and an end-tag. For example, a <letter> start-tag must have a matching </letter> end-tag. End-tags include a backslash as the first character.

- Empty elements must be marked with a self-closing tag (a backslash as the last character). As an example, this tag <end /> both opens and closes.

- Tags must be properly nested. Non-root elements must be completely contained within another element. As an example, the following would be acceptable:

```
<Address>
  <city> </city>
```

```
    <state> </state>
  </Address>
```

However, the following would *not* be acceptable. Notice how the city tag is opened before the state tag, but then closed within the state tags.

```
<Address>
  <city>
  <state></city>
  </state>
</Address>
```

- All attribute values must be contained within either single quotes or double quotes, such as <element attribute="value">.

- The document must comply with character encoding. UTF-8 is the default. In general, special characters are not allowed.

While not a well-formed rule, it's also important to realize that XML is case sensitive, thus <Root> does not equal <root>. Because of this, it's best to adopt conventions and follow them closely when working with XML. For example, sometimes XML is written as all lowercase to avoid any syntax errors.

Storing XML Data

When storing XML data, we have the choice of storing it as an XML data type or as an nvarchar(max) data type. If stored as XML, we can retrieve and manipulate the data as XML data and we can also type the data.

This becomes a primary decision point when deciding the data type used to store XML data. Will we be using SQL Server 2005 tools to retrieve and manipulate the XML data, or will an external application be pulling the entire document and manipulating it externally?

If SQL Server will be used to retrieve and manipulate the data, the XML data type must be used. This allows SQL Server to validate and parse the data and also gives us access to several XML methods that can be used to interact with the XML data.

 EXAM TIP It's important to know when to use the XML data type and when to use the (n)varchar(max) data type to store XML data. If the XML data will be queried or manipulated within SQL Server 2005, use the XML data type. If it will be manipulated externally and simply stored within SQL Server as a single file, use the (n)varchar(max) data type.

On the other hand, if an external application will do all the manipulation, the best choice is (n)varchar(max). Extra overhead exists in the validation and parsing of XML data for the XML data type that is simply not necessary if an external application will be doing all the work. Both the XML data type and (n)varchar(max) allow storage of data as large as 2GB.

TIP   Remember, the choice between using nvarchar(max) and varchar(max) is dependent on the data. If we will be storing Unicode data (an extended character set used to support multiple languages), we must use nvarchar(max) since this utilizes twice as much storage space for each character.

In this section, we'll cover the XML data type, typed versus untyped XML, and how to create a schema collection to type our data.

The XML Data Type

The XML data type allows us to store full XML documents and fragments within a SQL Server database column. Fragments are XML documents that are missing a single top-level element. XML documents stored as an XML data type are limited to no more than 2GB, but since an XML document is straight text, this is quite large.

Let's say we have an Employee table, with a ProjCompleted column that will hold XML data. If we've made a decision that we will query and manipulate the XML data within this column from SQL Server, then we would choose to store the ProjCompleted data as an *xml* data type. On the other hand, if design considerations specify that the XML data will only be manipulated externally, we could store the data as nvarchar(max).

If the data is stored as an XML type, we have some added capabilities, such as SQL Server automatically determining whether the data is well-formed or valid. SQL also provides several XML methods for querying and shredding XML data. If we have no need for these capabilities, nvarchar(max) is a better choice.

TIP   Shredding is a common term that refers to processing XML data. Said another way, mapping XML elements and/or attributes into relational data is called shredding.

Reasons for choosing the XML data type over another data type—such as varchar(max) or varbinary(max)—include:

- You want to share, query, and modify your XML data within the database (instead of in an external application).
- You want SQL Server to guarantee that the data is well-formed.
- You want the data types validated according to your defined XML schema.
- You have both relational data and XML data, and you want interoperability to exist between both in your application.
- You want to index the XML data for efficient query processing.

Typed vs. Untyped XML

Just as how a table we create within a database has various data types defined, XML data can also have data types defined. In other words, XML tags are either not defined (untyped), or they can be defined by anyone. To define XML tags, we create an XML schema collection and associate it with our XML data.

Consider the following project data in XML format. If we leave it as untyped, then anything can be entered into any of the fields.

```
<ProjCompleted>
  <ProjectName>Employee Database</ProjectName>
  <StartDate>2008-01-02abc</StartDate>
  <EndDate>2008-02-02</EndDate>
  <Manager>Darril Gibson</Manager>
  <Scope>
    Create full database including all tables and associated database
objects.
  </Scope>
</ProjCompleted>
```

Notice the typo in the StartDate node? Instead of a date of *2008-01-02* it's a character string of *2008-01-02abc*. Since this is untyped data, no data integrity checks are performed, and so this error would not be caught. However, the XML parser would still check the data to ensure they are well-formed.

 TIP The XML *date* data type would be entered as *yyyy-mm-dd* with a Z at the end. For example, June 29, 2008, would be entered as **2008-06-29Z**. Without the z at the end, the date would not be interpreted as a date.

Even though this XML data can be stored in a column, think of it as its own table. If we were to create it as a table, it might look like Figure 5-1.

Figure 5-1
An XML schema displayed as a typed table

Column Name	Data Type	Allow Nulls
ProjectName	varchar(50)	☑
StartDate	datetime	☑
EndDate	datetime	☑
Manager	varchar(50)	☑
Scope	varbinary(200)	☑
		☐

Table - dbo.ProjCompleted   INSTVS.Advent...QLQuery2.sql*

Notice that in the table, we identify the data in the columns with a data type. And once the data type is defined, the database system enforces data entry to just that data type. The StartDate could only be entered as a datetime data type, but if a typo were to occur, the DBMS would identify the error and reject the entry. The same validation occurs once we type the XML data.

XML Schema Collection

The way we type the XML data is by creating an XML schema collection to define the data that will be in our XML data type. We then associate the schema collection to our XML column.

The CREATE XML SCHEMA COLLECTION can be very complex. In our example, we're going to keep it rather simple. However, we don't want to corrupt the Adventure-Works database, so we'll create our own database.

In this exercise, we'll create a test database, add a table with an untyped XML data type, and insert some XML data into it.

Exercise 5.1: Create a Database and Table for XML Testing

1. Create a database named XMLTest using the following script:

```
CREATE DATABASE XMLTest
```

2. Create a table named Project by using the following script:

```
USE XMLTest;
GO
CREATE TABLE Project
(
  ProjectID int IDENTITY(1,1) NOT NULL,
  ProjectData xml NOT NULL
  CONSTRAINT [PK_Project_ProjectID] PRIMARY KEY CLUSTERED
  (ProjectID)
 )
```

Notice we've created a primary key on the ProjectID column with the IDENTITY property so that the primary key will be populated automatically.

3. Insert a column of untyped data into the Project table with the following script:

```
--Insert untyped data
DECLARE @xmlInsert XML
SET @xmlInsert =
'<project>
  <projectname>Employee Database</projectname>
  <startdate>1994-06-10abc</startdate>
  <enddate>2008-05-05def</enddate>
  <manager>Darril Gibson</manager>
  <scope>Create database for employees</scope>
</project>'
INSERT INTO Project
VALUES (@xmlInsert)
```

Note that the dates have trailing letters that make them invalid as a date. Since the data isn't typed, the system allows the data entry.

4. Try to insert a column of untyped data that is NOT well-formed into the Project table. The following script is the same as the previous script except that the <manager> tag is not properly closed. Since the XML is not well-formed, the data entry is rejected.

```
--Insert untyped data
DECLARE @xmlInsert XML
SET @xmlInsert =
```

```
'<project>
  <projectname>Employee Database</projectname>
  <startdate>1994-06-10abc</startdate>
  <enddate>2008-05-05def</enddate>
  <manager>Darril Gibson<manager>
  <scope>Create database for employees</scope>
</project>'
INSERT INTO Project
VALUES (@xmlInsert)
```

5. Delete the invalid data by using the following script:

```
DELETE FROM Project
```

The CREATE XML SCHEMA COLLECTION command is used to import the schema components into a database. Using this command, we can identify the namespace for our schema, the element name, and the data types for each individual element of our XML document.

The basic syntax is:

```
CREATE XML SCHEMA COLLECTION [ <relational_schema>. ]
                        sql_identifier AS Expression
```

In the next exercise, we'll create an XML schema collection and associate it with our XML column, causing the column to be typed.

Exercise 5.2: Create an XML Schema Collection and Associate It with Our Table

1. Use the following script to create an XML schema collection in the XMLTest database:

```
USE XMLTest;
GO
CREATE XML SCHEMA COLLECTION dbo.xmlProjectSchemaCollection AS
'<?xml version="1.0"?>
<xs:schema xmlns:xs="http://www.w3.org/2001/XMLSchema">
<xs:element name="project">
    <xs:complexType>
     <xs:sequence>
     <xs:element name="projectnumber" type="xs:int"/>
     <xs:element name="projectname" type="xs:string"/>
     <xs:element name="startdate" type="xs:date"/>
     <xs:element name="enddate" type="xs:date"/>
     <xs:element name="manager" type="xs:string"/>
     <xs:element name="scope" type="xs:string"/>
     </xs:sequence>
    </xs:complexType>
</xs:element>
</xs:schema> '
```

2. To view the schema collection, use the following script:

```
SELECT xml_schema_namespace('dbo','xmlProjectSchemaCollection')
```

3. To associate the schema collection to the ProjectData column in the Project table, we'd use this script:

```
USE XMLTest;
GO
ALTER TABLE Project
ALTER COLUMN ProjectData XML (dbo.xmlProjectSchemaCollection)
```

At this point, we have our table without any data, but it is associated with the schema collection we've created for it.

In the following exercise, we'll store XML data into our table. We begin by creating a variable of XML data type, then populating that variable, and ultimately inserting it into the table.

Exercise 5.3: Enter XML Data into Our Table

1. Use the following script to enter a row with XML data into the Project table:

```
USE XMLTest;
GO
DECLARE @xmlInsert XML
SET @xmlInsert =
'<project>
  <projectnumber>101</projectnumber>
  <projectname>Employee Database</projectname>
  <startdate>2007-06-30Z</startdate>
  <enddate>2008-05-29Z</enddate>
  <manager>Darril Gibson</manager>
  <scope>Create database for employees</scope>
</project>'
INSERT INTO Project
VALUES (@xmlInsert)
```

2. Use the following script to try to enter a row with *invalid* XML data into the Project table:

```
USE XMLTest;
GO
DECLARE @xmlInsert XML
SET @xmlInsert =
'<project>
  <projectnumber>101</projectnumber>
  <projectname>Employee Database</projectname>
  <startdate>2007-06-30abc</startdate>
  <enddate>2008-05-29Z</enddate>
  <manager>Darril Gibson</manager>
  <scope>Create database for employees</scope>
</project>'
INSERT INTO Project
VALUES (@xmlInsert)
```

This will result in the following error:

```
XML Validation: Invalid simple type value: '2007-06-30abc'. Location:
/*:project[1]/*:startdate[1]
```

3. Use the following script to query your table:

```
SELECT * FROM Project
```

4. Write down the ProjectID number displayed in the previous SELECT statement. It will probably be 2 unless you've experimented some. We'll use this ProjectID in the next step.

5. Use the following script to pull only the XML column from just one row. Use the ProjectID you recorded in the previous step. Of course, our table only includes one row, but it's very likely a populated table would have many more.

 TIP   The following query uses the XML query method. We'll explore the XML methods in more depth later in this chapter.

```
USE XMLTest;
GO
SELECT ProjectData.query('project/projectname')
FROM Project
Where ProjectID=2
```

Retrieving XML Data

With any database, we need to be able to retrieve the data. With XML, we have two perspectives. One is that we have regular relational data, but it needs to be exported in an XML format. This is done with the FOR XML clause and it can be executed in four different modes. The second perspective is that we have stored XML data and we need to be able to retrieve and manipulate this XML data. This is done with five different XML methods, or the OPENXML statement.

In this section, we'll explore the FOR XML clause and the uses and benefits of each of the four different modes. We'll follow it with the uses of the different XML methods, including a short introduction to XPath and XQuery.

FOR XML

SQL Server 2000 had support for XML starting with the basic FOR XML clause. The FOR XML clause returns the result set as an XML data type, which can then be exported. It is added to the end of a SELECT statement. The FOR XML clause can have four different modes:

- Raw
- Auto
- Explicit
- Path

Each of the four different modes provides different capabilities and each has different complexities. The Raw and Auto modes are the simplest to use, but don't provide much flexibility. The Explicit and Path modes are a little more complex, but offer more flexibility in how the data is returned. Let's explore the four different modes and identify the differences in each.

 EXAM TIP The FOR XML statement remains an excellent method of creating XML text output when retrieving data from your SQL Server database with a select statement. The different modes provide different capabilities, but at the core is the FOR XML statement. When tasked with efficiently creating XML output from relational data, consider using the FOR XML statement.

FOR XML RAW

Raw mode is used to transform rows into XML elements using the generic identifier <row>.

The following is a simple SELECT statement pulling some data out of the Person .Contact table. The result looks like Figure 5-2.

```
USE AdventureWorks;
GO
SELECT ContactID, FirstName, LastName
FROM Person.Contact
WHERE ContactID=6 or ContactID=8;
```

Figure 5-2
The result of a simple SELECT statement

Now, let's add the FOR XML RAW statement to convert this same result set into an XML result set:

```
SELECT ContactID, FirstName, LastName
FROM Person.Contact
WHERE ContactID=6 or ContactID=8
FOR XML RAW;
```

The result looks like the following. It's the same data but is now in an XML format that can easily be exported for any need.

```
<row ContactID="6" FirstName="Frances" LastName="Adams" />
<row ContactID="8" FirstName="Carla" LastName="Adams" />
```

Notice how each row is a full XML tag. If we want to divide the rows into separate elements, we can add the ELEMENTS directive, as shown in the following statement. The ELEMENTS directive can be used with any of the four modes.

```
SELECT ContactID, FirstName, LastName
FROM Person.Contact
WHERE ContactID=6 or ContactID=8
FOR XML RAW, ELEMENTS;
```

```
<row>
  <ContactID>6</ContactID>
  <FirstName>Frances</FirstName>
  <LastName>Adams</LastName>
</row>
<row>
  <ContactID>8</ContactID>
  <FirstName>Carla</FirstName>
  <LastName>Adams</LastName>
</row>
```

FOR XML AUTO

AUTO mode returns the query results as nested XML elements. It doesn't provide as much control over the output, but as we can see in the following query, it names the rows based on the table where the data has been retrieved from.

This query is used to list names of two employees and requires a join on the Person.Contact table and the HumanResources.Employee table. In the following query, two tables are used to show how the different tables are identified in the result set.

```
SELECT Person.Contact.ContactID, Person.Contact.FirstName,
       Person.Contact.LastName, HumanResources.Employee.EmployeeID
FROM Person.Contact INNER JOIN
HumanResources.Employee
ON Person.Contact.ContactID = HumanResources.Employee.ContactID
WHERE Person.Contact.ContactID=1209 or Person.Contact.ContactID=1030
FOR XML AUTO;
```

The result is shown next. Notice that this is similar to FOR XML RAW except that instead of naming the rows "row," they are named according to the table "Person.Contact". The column from the HumanResources.Employee table is embedded within the row, but has a different node to show that it's from a related table.

```
<Person.Contact ContactID="1209" FirstName="Guy" LastName="Gilbert">
  <HumanResources.Employee EmployeeID="1" />
</Person.Contact>
<Person.Contact ContactID="1030" FirstName="Kevin" LastName="Brown">
  <HumanResources.Employee EmployeeID="2" />
</Person.Contact>
```

FOR XML Explicit

When we need more control over the output than either RAW or AUTO modes can provide, we may want to use the EXPLICIT mode. EXPLICIT mode is more complex to write, but provides the most flexibility. Typically, we work backwards when creating a query using EXPLICIT mode. In other words, we first identify the output we want.

For example, let's say an application requires the data in the following format:

```
<Employee EmpID="289">
  <Name FName="Rachel" LName="Valdez" />
</Employee>
<Employee EmpID="290">
  <Name FName="Lynn" LName="Tsoflias" />
</Employee>
```

The following is the script to create the required XML output. Notice the "Select 1" tag creates the structure populating the Employee <EmpID=xxx> tag, but leaving the FName and LName elements as null. The SELECT 2 statement creates the inner tag <Name FName="xxx" LName="xxx" />, matching it with the structure created in the SELECT 1 statement. The UNION ALL clause is used to bring them together.

```
SELECT 1    as Tag,
       NULL as Parent,
       EmployeeID as [Employee!1!EmpID],
       NULL       as [Name!2!FName],
       NULL       as [Name!2!LName]
FROM   HumanResources.Employee E, Person.Contact C
WHERE  E.ContactID = C.ContactID
UNION ALL
SELECT 2 as Tag,
       1 as Parent,
       EmployeeID,
       FirstName,
       LastName
FROM   HumanResources.Employee E, Person.Contact C
WHERE  E.ContactID = C.ContactID
ORDER BY [Employee!1!EmpID],[Name!2!FName]
FOR XML EXPLICIT
```

As you can see, this is much more complex even for a simple XML output. However, that's a common theme whenever we want to do it our way. Thankfully, the EXPLICIT tag allows the possibility to create just about any output you may want, but it will likely take some time. If you want to explore this in more depth, take a look at the Books Online article, "Using Explicit Mode."

The FOR XML PATH

The PATH mode offers a flexibility similar to the EXPLICIT mode, but with greater simplicity. It let's us easily mix elements and attributes in our statement.

As an example, let's look at the following query:

```
USE AdventureWorks;
GO
SELECT ProductModelID, Name, Instructions
FROM Production.ProductModel
WHERE ProductModelID=47
```

This gives us the results shown in Figure 5-3. Notice that the output is a mixture of regular data and an XML column.

Figure 5-3 The results of a simple query

If we clicked the link to the XML data (under the Instructions) column, a new tabbed window would open in SSMS, allowing us to view the XML data. If instead we wanted to combine the output into a single XML output file, we can modify the query as follows:

NOTE In order to retrieve data from an XML column, we need to use one of the XML methods. The following statement uses the *query* method, which will be explored with all of the XML methods later in this section.

```
SELECT ProductModelID,Name,
    Instructions.query('declare namespace
    ModelID="http://schemas.microsoft.com/sqlserver/2004/07/adventure-
works/ProductModelManuInstructions";
    /ModelID:root/ModelID:Location ')
FROM Production.ProductModel
WHERE ProductModelID=47
FOR XML PATH
```

Notice that the Instructions column has been modified to query the XML data with a statement that is similar to XPath-like syntax. A logical question is, "Where does the schema definition come from that is used to declare the namespace?" It actually comes from the first line in the Instructions XML column (xmlns="http…").

XSINIL

Just as any table can have NULL columns, an XML data type may include some elements that are null. Sometimes we want null columns to appear and sometimes we don't. By using the XSINIL (think "nil, null, nothing") parameter in a FOR XML statement, we can ensure that all columns appear, even if some are NULL or blank.

EXAM TIP The XSINIL argument can be used in the FOR XML statement to ensure that NULL values are included in the output. It can also be used within the ELEMENTS directive of a XML schema definition as XSI:NIL.

Let's take a look at two examples in the AdventureWorks database to demonstrate XSINIL. In this first example, we won't use the XSINIL argument.

```
USE AdventureWorks;
GO
SELECT ProductID, Name, Color
FROM Production.Product
FOR XML RAW, ELEMENTS;
```

The following shows how two of the rows look in the result set. Notice that Product 316 (the Blade) does not have a Color, so a node for the color is omitted. Product 317 (the Crankarm) does have a color, so the node is shown.

```
<row>
  <ProductID>316</ProductID>
  <Name>Blade</Name>
</row>
```

```
<row>
  <ProductID>317</ProductID>
  <Name>LL Crankarm</Name>
  <Color>Black</Color>
</row>
```

Now let's look at how we could add the XSINIL argument.

```
USE AdventureWorks;
GO
SELECT ProductID, Name, Color
FROM Production.Product
FOR XML RAW, ELEMENTS XSINIL
```

The result set is a little different. Product 316 now has a node for the color, but it lists it as xsi:nil="true" to indicate NULL.

```
<row xmlns:xsi="http://www.w3.org/2001/XMLSchema-instance">
  <ProductID>316</ProductID>
  <Name>Blade</Name>
  <Color xsi:nil="true" />
</row>
<row xmlns:xsi="http://www.w3.org/2001/XMLSchema-instance">
  <ProductID>317</ProductID>
  <Name>LL Crankarm</Name>
  <Color>Black</Color>
</row>
```

XML Methods

SQL Server provides several methods that allow us to query and manipulate XML data stored in a column using the XML data type. These are outlined in Table 5-1.

Method	Description
Value	Use to retrieve a single value from within a SQL column.
Nodes	Use to shred XML data into relational data.
Query	Use to query an XML column.
Modify	Use to specify XML DML statements.
Exist	Use to determine if an XML query returns data.

Table 5-1 XML Methods

All of these can be embedded in a SELECT statement as part of an XQuery, as we'll see later in this section. The format is:

```
XMLdoc.Method(XQuery)
```

Once we describe the methods, we'll take a look at plugging an XQuery expression in with them to actually pull the data.

Value

The Value method can be used to retrieve a value of SQL type from an XML column. This is what we'd use to extract a specific value from an XML column. It allows us to create SELECT queries that either combine or compare XML data with non-XML data.

In the following example, we create a variable named *@myXML* and populate it with a simulated XML column. The XML column holds information on project number 101 and project number 102.

Next, we create a variable named *@ProjName* and populate it with the name of the project from the second project in the SET statement.

The SELECT statement prints the name for us. The result should look like Figure 5-4.

Figure 5-4

Using the Value method to pull a single value

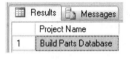

```
DECLARE @myXML xml
SET @myXML =
'<Root>
<Project ProjectNumber="101" ProjectName = "Employee Database"
  StartDate ="2008-06-30Z" EndDate = "2008-07-29Z"
  Manager = "Darril Gibson">
</Project>
<Project ProjectNumber="102" ProjectName = "Build Parts Database"
  StartDate ="2008-08-30Z" EndDate = "2008-09-29Z"
  Manager = "Justin Case">
</Project>
</Root>'
DECLARE @ProjName varchar(50)
SET @ProjName = @myXML.value('(/Root/Project/@ProjectName)[2]', 'nvarchar(50)' )
SELECT @ProjName AS [Project Name]
```

Query

The Query method can be used to pull XML data from an XML column, as we did in earlier examples. The Query method frequently uses XQuery language expressions that are similar to SELECT statements. As with XML in general, XQuery expressions have a lot of depth, allowing you to do exactly what you want to do, even if it does take some time to create the query.

In the Nodes section, we'll show an example combining the Value and Query methods to pull multiple values out of an XML document.

We saw a simple example of the query method in Exercise 5.3.

```
USE XMLTest;
GO
SELECT ProjectData.query('project/projectname')
FROM Project
Where ProjectID=2
```

The result is shown in Figure 5-5.

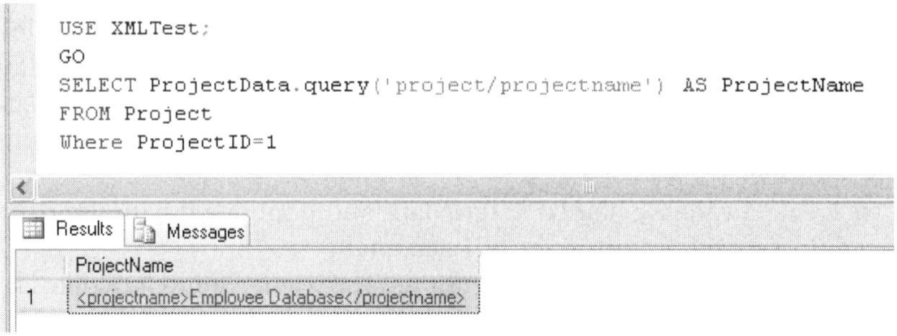

```
USE XMLTest;
GO
SELECT ProjectData.query('project/projectname') AS ProjectName
FROM Project
Where ProjectID=1
```

Results	Messages

	ProjectName
1	<projectname>Employee Database</projectname>

Figure 5-5   The result of a query using the Query method

Another example of the Query method is shown in the Nodes section.

Nodes

The Nodes method is used to shred an XML column into relational data. In other words, if you have an XML column filled with data, you can use the Nodes method to pull out the data and present that data in a meaningful way. The general syntax of the Nodes method is:

```
Nodes (XQuery) as Table(Column)
```

However, before we can use the Nodes method, typically we're going to pull some data out of an XML document using the Value or Query method. The following query shows how we can use the Nodes method. It starts by creating an XML document and then uses a SELECT statement to pull the data from the XML document.

```
DECLARE @myXML xml
SET @myXML =
'<Root>
  <Project ProjectNumber="101">
    <ProjectName>Employee Database</ProjectName>
    <StartDate>2008-06-30Z</StartDate>
    <EndDate>2008-07-29Z</EndDate>
    <Manager>Darril Gibson</Manager>
  </Project>
  <Project ProjectNumber="102">
    <ProjectName>Build Parts Database</ProjectName>
    <StartDate>2008-08-30Z</StartDate>
    <EndDate>2008-09-29Z</EndDate>
    <Manager>Justin Case</Manager>
  </Project>
</Root>'
SELECT
  MyTable.cols.value('@ProjectNumber', 'int') AS ProjectNumber,
  MyTable.cols.query('StartDate') AS StartDate,
  MyTable.cols.query('EndDate') AS EndDate
FROM @myXML.nodes('/Root/Project') MyTable (cols)
```

Notice that the value and query section refer to the MyTable(x) definition created in the Nodes section. The Nodes method defines the table name of the resulting rowset—in this case, we're calling it simply MyTable. By using a single column name of cols in the MyTable definition, we can identify multiple columns in the SELECT statement using the same cols identifier.

The result of the preceding query is shown in Figure 5-6.

	ProjectNumber	StartDate	EndDate
1	101	\<StartDate\>2008-06-30Z\</StartDate\>	\<EndDate\>2008-07-29Z\</EndDate\>
2	102	\<StartDate\>2008-08-30Z\</StartDate\>	\<EndDate\>2008-09-29Z\</EndDate\>

Figure 5-6   The result of a query using the Nodes method

The query combines the Value and Query methods to pull data out of the XML document and then displays them with the Nodes method.

 EXAM TIP   The Nodes method is an ideal solution when XML data needs to be shredded so that the different elements can be manipulated and/or stored independently. Used with the Value method, it can be very effective at comparing XML data and non-XML data and putting the XML data into a relational format.

Modify

The Modify method lets you execute XML Data Manipulation Language (DML) statements against XML columns. This allows us to modify parts of an XML data type while retaining the integrity of the overall XML data. While the XQuery language allows us to query the XML data, it doesn't let us modify it.

XML DML statements include:

- Insert
- Delete
- Replace Value Of

Exist

Exist works the same way that the EXISTS clause works in a SELECT statement. Used within an XQuery language expression, it will return a 1 if true, indicating that the embedded XQuery has a non-null result set. We can use this to pull rows based on the value of individual attributes within the XML column. We'll see an example of the Exist method in the XQuery section.

The basic syntax of the Exist method is shown in the following code. The XQuery portion is an XQuery expression or a string literal.

```
exist (XQuery)
```

As an example, the following simple query checks for the existence of a specific project start date using an XQuery. Since the element exists, the SELECT statement returns a 1.

```
DECLARE @myXML xml
DECLARE @ExistResult bit
--The following line creates the XML
SET @myXML = '<root ProjDate = "2008-01-01Z"/>'
--The Exist method checks the XML path against a given value
--In this case we're comparing the XML path against a given date
SET @ExistResult =
            @myXML.exist('/root[(@ProjDate cast as xs:date?) eq xs:
date("2008-01-01Z")]')
--It populates the @ExistResult with a 1 if the node exists, or a 0 if not
SELECT @ExistResult
```

XPath

XPath was created as a solution to finding information embedded within an XML document. It identifies the path to the XML data we are seeking and is typically included in an expression to identify specifically which element or attribute we are seeking. We've been using XPath expressions within our XML methods.

Let's take a look at a simple XPath expression compared against our earlier ProjCompleted XML data column. I've added an extra element within the start date to show a deeper XPath expression and have omitted the majority of the XML document for reasons of space.

```
<ProjCompleted>
  <ProjectName>
      Employee Database
  </ProjectName>
  <StartDate>
    <ScheduledStartDate>09012007Z<ScheduledStartDate>
    <ActualStartDate>09312007Z<ActualStartDate>
  </StartDate>
  ...
</ProjCompleted>
```

The XPath Expression to the actual start date of a project in this XML column would be:

```
ProjCompleted/StartDate/ActualStartDate
```

By using the XPath expression in an XQuery, we can drill down to the exact data we need within an XML column or document.

XQuery

With the basics of the XML methods covered, we can now tie things together using XQuery. With XQuery, data can be extracted and manipulated from XML documents. XQuery uses XPath syntax to address specific parts of an XML document. It's actually a full query langauge designed by the W3C specifically to query XML data, and the full language specification can be viewed at www.w3.org/tr/xquery.

An XQuery expression can be made up of literals, variables, path expressions, context item expressions, functions, and constructors.

- **Literal** This is a numerical or string value. Strings must be enclosed in quotation marks.

- **Variable** This is a reference to a specified value.

- **Path expression** This descibes the location of elements within the XML hierarchy. They can be relative or absolute paths.

- **Context item expression** This is a method used to reference a value within the current element in XML data.

- **Function** Numerous XQuery functions are available for use when accessing data in XML columns or variables.

- **Constructor** This is anXQuery component that enables the definition of XML structures.

To see this in action, let's look at how we can pull demographic sales data out of the AdventureWorks database. The Sales.Store table has a column named Demographics, which is XML data.

```
USE AdventureWorks;
GO
SELECT Demographics
FROM Sales.Store
WHERE CustomerID = 10
```

The preceding query returns XML data, which looks like the following:

```
<StoreSurvey
xmlns="http://schemas.microsoft.com/sqlserver/2004/07/adventure-works/StoreSurvey">
  <AnnualSales>800000</AnnualSales>
  <AnnualRevenue>80000</AnnualRevenue>
  <BankName>Primary International</BankName>
  <BusinessType>BM</BusinessType>
  <YearOpened>1988</YearOpened>
  <Specialty>Mountain</Specialty>
  <SquareFeet>21000</SquareFeet>
  <Brands>4+</Brands>
  <Internet>DSL</Internet>
  <NumberEmployees>11</NumberEmployees>
</StoreSurvey>
```

Let's say that instead of getting all of the XML data, we wanted only a specific piece of data from within the XML column, such as the Annual Revenue. Going by the earlier XML methods available to us, the method that lets us view a single value is the Value method.

The following query shows how an XQuery statement can be embedded within a SELECT statement to pull a specific value:

```
SELECT Name, Demographics.value
        ('declare namespace ss=
        "http://schemas.microsoft.com/sqlserver/2004/07/adventure-works/
StoreSurvey";
        (/ss:StoreSurvey/ss:AnnualRevenue)[1]','money') AS AnnualRevenue
FROM Sales.Store
WHERE CustomerID = 10;
```

The Value method in the previous example has two parameters: the XPath and the data type. We're first declaring the namespace as ss (from StoreSurvey) and then identifying the path as /ss:StoreSurvey/ss:AnnualRevenue. We're using the data type of money. If instead we wanted the data type to be expressed as a numeric, we could have replaced money with numeric (12,2), where the first number indicates the number of digits in the output and the second number indicates the number of decimal points.

The result should look like Figure 5-7.

Figure 5-7 The result of XQuery using the Value method

If instead of looking at just one individual row, we wanted to list all rows that meet a certain condition, we could use the Exists method. For example, let's say we wanted to identify all the stores that exceeded one million dollars in annual sales.

The following query has an Exists method in the WHERE clause to look at the specific data identified in the XPath portion of the XQuery statement. This query returns 396 rows.

```
SELECT CustomerID, Name
FROM Sales.Store
WHERE Demographics.exist('declare namespace
        ss="http://schemas.microsoft.com/sqlserver/2004/07/adventure-works/
StoreSurvey";
        /ss:StoreSurvey/ss:AnnualSales[. > 1000000]') = 1
ORDER BY Name;
```

Remember, our goal in this chapter is not to make you an expert at constructing XML queries, but to instead help you see a little of what's possible. You should know the capabilities of the five XML methods and how they can fit into a SELECT statement.

Using OPENXML to Shred XML Data

We've covered using the Nodes XML method to shred XML data. Another method available is the OPENXML statement. It allows us to query an XML document and display it either in a table format or as a rowset.

OPENXML is a tool within T-SQL that we can use to shred XML data and create a rowset view similar to a table. Let's look at an example that allows us to view all the elements. In this example, we'll create an XML document that shows two orders (but it could just as easily have 200 orders or more). With the document created, we'll then use OPENXML to shred it and display it.

```
--First we create the XML document in memory as a string
DECLARE @XmlDoc nvarchar(1000)
SET @XmlDoc = N'<ROOT>
<Customer CustomerID="HPOTTE" ContactName="Harry Potter">
   <Order OrderID="10248" CustomerID="HPOTTE" EmployeeID="17"
         OrderDate="2008-09-01T00:00:00">
     <OrderDetail ProductID="211" Quantity="1"/>
     <OrderDetail ProductID="342" Quantity="3"/>
   </Order>
</Customer>
<Customer CustomerID="RWEASE" ContactName="Ron Weasely">
   <Order OrderID="10283" CustomerID="RWEASE" EmployeeID="19"
         OrderDate="2008-03-30T00:00:00">
     <OrderDetail ProductID="172" Quantity="5"/>
   </Order>
</Customer>
</ROOT>'

-- Next we parse the document with sp_xml_preparedocument
DECLARE @DocHandle int
EXEC sp_xml_preparedocument @DocHandle OUTPUT, @XmlDoc
-- Now we shred it with OPENXML
SELECT *
FROM OPENXML (@DocHandle, '/ROOT/Customer/Order')
     WITH (CustomerID  varchar(10),
           OrderID varchar(20),
           OrderDate datetime)
--Last we clean up
EXEC sp_xml_removedocument @DocHandle
```

The result should look similar to Figure 5-8.

Figure 5-8
The OPENXML
result

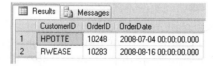

	CustomerID	OrderID	OrderDate
1	HPOTTE	10248	2008-07-04 00:00:00.000
2	RWEASE	10283	2008-08-16 00:00:00.000

The sp_xml_removedocument system stored procedure is a house-cleaning procedure that removes the XML document from memory and invalidates the document handle.

Notice a couple of things here. First, the @DocHandle is used to identify the name of the XML document that was parsed. OPENXML requires the use of sp_xml_preparedocument to parse a document before it can be used.

Next is the rowpattern, or the path of the data we're trying to retrieve. If the rowpattern was shortened to '/ROOT/Customer' than attributes within the Order node ('/ROOT/Customer/Order') couldn't be retrieved. It is possible to use wildcards here such as '/ROOT/*/*'.

The WITH clause identifies the columns we want to retrieve and display. These columns must exist in the XML document and be reachable via the rowpattern. If the columns don't exist or are not reachable, the result will show NULL for that column.

There are a lot more possibilities with OPENXML. Our goal here is just to introduce to you OPENXML, and especially to make sure you understand that it can be used to shred an XML document. While our example showed using OPENXML with a document that we created, it can just as easily be used to shred a document we receive from outside sources such as vendors or partners.

XMLReader and XMLWriter

The .NET Framework Class Library provides two significant tools that allow interaction with XML data in a SQL Server 2005 database. This is the XMLReader object and the XMLWriter object. While we'll cover different methods of accessing data in more depth in Chapter 11, these two objects deserve a mention in the XML chapter.

The XMLReader object provides fast, non-cached, forward-only access to data. If there is no need for an in-memory use of the data, the XMLReader object is often the best choice for retrieving large quantities of XML data.

 EXAM TIP   When XML files need to be created as fast as possible while using a minimum amount of memory, consider using the XMLReader object. This is an improvement in the .NET Framework 2.0, where previously a DataSet object had to be created to temporarily store the data.

Where the XMLReader object excels at reading large quantities of XML data, the XMLWriter object excels at writing XML data. The XMLReader provides a fast, non-cached, forward-only means of generating streams or files containing XML data.

Both commands are used within .NET languages such as Visual Basic .NET or C# .NET.

XML Indexes

In Chapter 7, we'll explore indexes in much greater depth, but in this section we'll cover indexes that can be applied to the XML data type. While Chapter 7 more fully explains how this is done, for now it's important to realize that by creating indexes it allows SQL Server to query the data more efficiently.

The first index created on an XML data type is a primary XML index. While a primary index by itself may improve performance of some queries, often secondary XML indexes are created to improve specific types of query performance. Secondary XML indexes can only be created after a primary XML index has been created. Secondary XML index types include PATH, VALUE, and PROPERTY.

Primary XML Indexes

XML data is stored as a Binary Large Object (BLOB). Without an index, the BLOB must be shredded (processed) at runtime which can be very time consuming depending on the size of the BLOB. By creating a primary XML index, the data is shredded into rows that are more easily searched by the database engine.

The primary XML index includes the primary key of the base table and various node information from the XML BLOB. This index can be useful in improving queries especially if the queries specify the Exist() method in the WHERE clause.

As an example, the following query would benefit from a primary XML index. It returns information from the <summary> element stored in the CatalogDescription column of the ProductModel table in AdventureWorks. The WHERE clause includes the Exist method to return only product models that have a <Features> description included.

```
USE AdventureWorks;
GO
WITH XMLNAMESPACES
('http://schemas.microsoft.com/sqlserver/2004/07/adventure-works/ProductMod-
elDescription' AS "PD")
SELECT CatalogDescription.query('
  /PD:ProductDescription/PD:Summary
') as Result
FROM Production.ProductModel
WHERE CatalogDescription.exist ('/PD:ProductDescription/PD:Features') = 1
```

The preceding query returns six lines in the result set. However, each non-null row in the CatalogDescription column must be shredded and examined for the existence of the Features element. If a primary XML index was available, it could be searched for the Features element much quicker and with fewer resources. This example shows how a primary XML index can help queries using the Exist method. For other types of queries, secondary XML indexes can be used.

PATH Secondary XML Indexes

The PATH secondary XML index is built on the Path and Node values of the XML data. If queries are based on path expressions, this index may provide better performance than simply creating the primary XML index. Examples of path expressions are:

- **/root/Location**   This specifies only a path.
- **/root/Location/@LocationID[.="19"]**   This is where both the path and the node value ("19" in this example) are specified.

As an example, the following query would be improved with a PATH secondary XML index:

```
USE AdventureWorks;
GO
WITH XMLNAMESPACES
('http://schemas.microsoft.com/sqlserver/2004/07/adventure-works/ProductMod-
elDescription' AS "PD")
```

```
SELECT CatalogDescription.query('
  /PD:ProductDescription/PD:Summary
') as Result
FROM Production.ProductModel
WHERE CatalogDescription.exist
('/PD:ProductDescription/@ProductModelID[.="19"]') = 1
```

VALUE Secondary XML Indexes

For queries that are value-based and where the path is not fully specified (or includes a wildcard such as *), the VALUE secondary XML index might obtain better results than just the primary XML index.

Examples of values are listed in the following bullets. Notice the first one has a wild-card in the path, while the second one does not have a path.

- /Root/ProductDescription/@*[. = "Mountain Bike"]
- //ProductDescription[@Name = "Mountain Bike"]

 EXAM TIP When XML data are to be queried looking for specific values or specific data contained within the XML data, consider using the VALUE secondary XML index. This will provide the best performance when the path is not known.

Before we do the query to pull the data, let's take a look at the AdditionalContactInfo XML column in the Person.Contact table with the following query:

```
USE AdventureWorks;
GO
SELECT AdditionalContactInfo
FROM PERSON.CONTACT
WHERE ContactID = 2
```

After clicking the XML result, you'll see a result similar to the XML nodes shown next. The entire listing is not shown here for reasons of brevity.

```
<AdditionalContactInfo
xmlns="http://schemas.microsoft.com/sqlserver/2004/07/adventure-works/ContactInfo"
xmlns:crm="http://schemas.microsoft.com/sqlserver/2004/07/adventure-works/
ContactRecord"
xmlns:act="http://schemas.microsoft.com/sqlserver/2004/07/adventure-works/
ContactTypes">
  These are additional phone and pager numbers for the customer.
  <act:telephoneNumber>
    <act:number>
      206-555-2222
    </act:number>
    <act:SpecialInstructions>
      On weekends, contact the manager at this number.
    </act:SpecialInstructions>
  </act:telephoneNumber>
  <act:telephoneNumber>
    <act:number>
      206-555-1234
    </act:number>
```

```
    </act:telephoneNumber>
    <act:pager>
      <act:number>
        206-555-1244
      </act:number>
      <act:SpecialInstructions>
        Do not page between 9:00 a.m. and 5:00 p.m.
      </act:SpecialInstructions>
    </act:pager>
. . .
</AdditionalContactInfo>
```

What if we were looking for someone with a phone number of 206-555-1234? Certainly, we can see from the following listing that ContactID has this phone number, but it would be challenging if we had 1000 contacts to look through. There are actually multiple nodes where this can exist. With this in mind, the VALUE XML secondary index is ideal in helping with the query, which is listed next:

```
USE AdventureWorks;
GO
WITH XMLNAMESPACES (
  'http://schemas.microsoft.com/sqlserver/2004/07/adventure-works/ContactInfo'
AS CI,
  'http://schemas.microsoft.com/sqlserver/2004/07/adventure-works/Contact-
Types' AS ACT)
SELECT ContactID
FROM   Person.Contact
WHERE  AdditionalContactInfo.exist
('//ACT:telephoneNumber/ACT:number[.="206-555-1234"]') = 1
```

Notice that it's checking for the existence of a specific value (206-555-1234) and the path is not fully specified. It finds this in the XML data column of Contact ID 2.

The VALUE secondary XML index is the default index created when a secondary index is created. We'll see this in the next exercise.

PROPERTY Secondary XML Indexes

Queries that use the Value method to retrieve one or more values may benefit from a PROPERTY secondary XML index. This index includes the primary key, Path, and Node values from the primary XML index.

As an example, the following query uses the Value method to retrieve ProductModelID and ProductModelName attribute values for a specific product (with ProductModelID 35):

```
WITH XMLNAMESPACES
('http://schemas.microsoft.com/sqlserver/2004/07/adventure-works/ProductMod-
elDescription' AS "PD")
SELECT
CatalogDescription.value('(/PD:ProductDescription/@ProductModelID)[1]', 'int')
as ModelID,
CatalogDescription.value('(/PD:ProductDescription/@ProductModelName)[1]',
'varchar(30)') as ModelName
FROM Production.ProductModel
WHERE ProductModelID = 35
```

The result should look similar to Figure 5-9.

Figure 5-9   The result of a query that would benefit from a Property secondary XML index

To understand the query, it's worthwhile looking at the ProductDescription element and the values that are included. This node is listed next. Notice it has the ProductModelID and ProductModelName values embedded as attributes in the ProductDescription node.

```
<p1:ProductDescription
xmlns:p1="http://schemas.microsoft.com/sqlserver/2004/07/adventure-works/
ProductModelDescription"
xmlns:wm="http://schemas.microsoft.com/sqlserver/2004/07/adventure-works/
ProductModelWarrAndMain"
xmlns:wf="http://www.adventure-works.com/schemas/OtherFeatures"
xmlns:html="http://www.w3.org/1999/xhtml"
ProductModelID="35" ProductModelName="Touring-2000">
```

It's relatively easy to create an XML index. As an example, here's a quick exercise to create an XML index on the JobCandidate table in AdventureWorks.

Exercise 5.4: Create an XML Index

1. Open an instance of SSMS.

2. Use the Object Explorer to browse to the Databases | AdventureWorks | Tables | HumanResources.JobCandidate table.

3. Right-click the HumanResources.JobCandidate table and select Modify. Your display should look similar to Figure 5-10. Notice that the Resume column is an XML data type and has Content.HumanResources.HRResumeSchemaCollection associated with it.

	Column Name	Data Type	Allow Nulls
⚷	JobCandidateID	int	☐
	EmployeeID	int	☑
	Resume	xml(CONTENT HumanResources.HRResumeSchem...	☐
	ModifiedDate	datetime	☐

Figure 5-10   Viewing the HumanResources.JobCandidate table

4. Right-click anywhere over the Resume column and select XML Indexes…

5. In the XML Indexes dialog box, click Add. Your display should look similar to Figure 5-11. Notice that in the General properties, the Is Primary section has a value of "Yes," indicating this is a primary XML index.

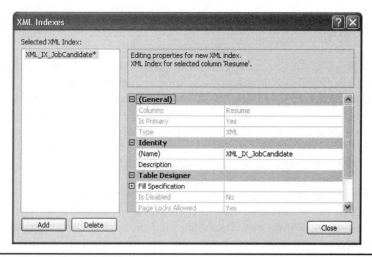

Figure 5-11   Creating a primary XML index

6. Click the Close button to close the XML indexes dialog box.

7. Right-click over the Table tab and select Save JobCandidate. That's it. An XML index has been created.

8. To create a secondary XML index, right-click anywhere over the Resume column, and then select XML Indexes...

9. In the XML Indexes dialog box, click Add. Your display should look similar to Figure 5-12. Notice that in the General properties, the SecondaryIndex is set to Value. You can change this by selecting the drop-down box and choosing Property, Value, or Path. However, VALUE is the index we want. Click Close.

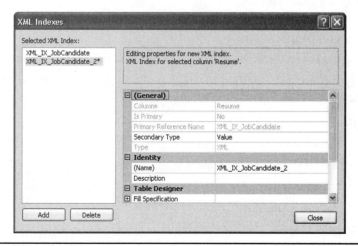

Figure 5-12   Creating a VALUE secondary XML index

Chapter Review

In this chapter, we presented some basics on XML. SQL Server supports the XML data type, which allows XML documents to be as large as 2GB. If we want SQL Server to parse and validate our XML data, we should use the XML data type. If we aren't going to use any of the XML capabilities within SQL Server (such as when an external application manages the XML data) we would use the (n)varchar(max) data type instead of the XML data type. The (n)varchar(max) data type can also be as large as 2GB, but it doesn't have any of the overhead of parsing and validating XML data.

When we want to retrieve relational data but display it in an XML format, we'd use FOR XML within the SELECT statement. When we want to retrieve and/or manipulate XML data stored in an XML data type, we'd use one of the five XML methods: Value, Nodes, Query, Modify, and Exist. The Value method retrieves any single value within the XML document we need. The Nodes method is used to shred XML data into relational data. The Exist method works just like T-SQL EXISTS, but allows us to check for the existence of certain values within an XML document.

Lastly, if XML data is frequently queried, we can create XML indexes to optimize specific types of queries on XML data. We first must create a Primary XML index, however.

If we further want to improve queries, we can consider one of the different secondary XML indexes. For example, the VALUE secondary XML index can be used to optimize queries that look for specific values or specific data contained within XML columns.

Additional Study

Self-Study Exercises

- Write a query to pull all of the employees out of AdventureWorks but provide the output in XML format.
- Identify the best data type to use for XML documents that will be manipulated in an external application.
- Identify the best XML method to use to shred XML data into relational data.
- Identify the best XML method to use to pull a single value out of an XML data column.

BOL Topics

- XML Best Practices
- Basic Syntax of the FOR XML Clause
- XML Data Type Methods
- Indexes on XML Data Type Columns
- Retrieving Data Using the XMLReader

Summary of What You Need to Know

70-431

When preparing for the 70-431 test, you should have an understanding of such basics as:

- How to store XML data (which data type to use)
- Use of XSINIL
- XML methods (such as Nodes and Value)

70-441

When preparing for the 70-441 test, you should have an understanding of such basics as:

- How to store XML data (which data type to use)
- How to optimize XML queries with XML indexes
- XML methods

70-442

This entire chapter covers material for the 70-442 test.

Questions

70-431

1. You are creating a query to pull data from a SQL Server 2005 database and pass it to an application as an XML document using the FOR XML statement. Some of the data in the document contain null values. How can you ensure that all columns in the XML schema are passed to the XML document even if the columns are blank?

   A. This will be done automatically.

   B. Add the INCLUDE NULLS argument to the FOR XML statement.

   C. Add the XSINIL argument to the FOR XML statement.

   D. This cannot be done.

2. You are designing a Jobs database which will be used by an external application to match job candidates with consulting jobs. Job candidate data needs to be stored in an XML format that could be as large as 2MB in size. The application will insert, retrieve, and manipulate the XML documents. The retrieved documents must be identical to the originals. What data type should you use to store the XML documents?

   A. XML

   B. Varchar(max)

   C. Varchar(8000)

   D. Varchar(2000000)

3. You are tasked with writing a query that returns data out of the Sales database. The result set needs to include data from the Customer and CustomerHistory tables. Some of the data is stored in XML data type columns. Your query needs to return a result set that includes data from relational fields and attribute values from the XML data type columns. Which two XML methods should you use? (Choose two.)

   A. Value

   B. Nodes

   C. Query

   D. Modify

   E. Exist

70-441

1. You are tasked with designing the database for an application that will be used to manage stock portfolios of customers. Customers' stock portfolios can be queried by both brokers and customers. It should be returned as a document that contains as many as 20,000 characters. Only certain tags are allowed and it must be possible to easily retrieve specific data instead of the entire document. What should you choose? (Choose all that apply.)

   A. Use the nvarchar(max) data type to store the data.

   B. Use the XML data type to store the data.

   C. Use a trigger to verify that correct tags are used.

   D. Use an XML collection to verify that correct tags are used.

2. Hurricane and tropical storm information is stored in a SQL Server 2005 database named Weather. During a storm, many different attributes about the storm need to be stored, and they can change frequently. The attributes are not the same for each named storm. This data must be easily searchable in the database by using Transact-SQL. The information ranges from several bytes to several kilobytes in size. You design a table named StormInformation with the following columns to hold this information:

   ```
   StormID          StormAttributes
   ```

   What data type should you use for the StormAttributes column?

   A. A user-defined data type

   B. Varchar(max)

   C. Nvarchar(max)

   D. XML

3. The StockPortfolio database has an XML column named CustomerAttributes. One or more financial goals (such as "Rainy Day Fund," "Retirement," or "College Fund"), can be entered into this XML column as different nodes. Sales people often need to search for goals that are embedded in the XML data. When a customer's record is searched for goals, the native XML data must be queried without loss of performance. What action (or actions) would you perform to create a supporting indexing strategy? (Choose all that apply.)

A. Create a clustered index on the CustomerAttributes column.

B. Create a non-clustered index on the CustomerAttributes column.

C. Create a Primary XML index on the CustomerAttributes column.

D. Create a Path Secondary XML index on the CustomerAttributes column.

E. Create a Value Secondary XML index on the CustomerAttributes column.

F. Create a Property Secondary XML index on the CustomerAttributes column.

4. Data from your database are regularly exported to an XML file and shared with a business partner. Occasionally, the business partner is unable to import this data and they state that the XML file is improperly formatted. Management suspects the problem is due to the file not being imported within the given time constraints. Management has asked that the original XML data be retained so it can be viewed later. What should you do?

A. Create an archive table and store the data in an XML column.

B. When necessary, retrieve the original data from the original tables.

C. Use a stored procedure to retrieve the data originally, and if needed again, run the stored procedure again.

D. After any XML file is exported, back up the database and use this as an archive.

70-442

1. One of the things that the StockPortfolio application does is collect stock prices throughout the day. At any time, this data can be queried, requiring an XML text file as an output. This file must be created as fast as possible, while using a minimum amount of memory. What would you suggest?

A. Use a SELECT statement to retrieve the data. Use an XMLReader object to read the XML data.

B. Use a SELECT statement to retrieve the data. Store the result in a DataSet object and read it from there.

C. Use a SELECT ... FOR XML statement to retrieve the data. Use an XMLReader object to read the XML data.

D. Use a SELECT ... FOR XML statement to retrieve the data. Store the result in a DataSet object and read it from there.

2. You are tasked with creating a stored procedure that will accept an XML parameter, and then store the different elements in a relational table structure. What should you use within the stored procedure?

A. FOR XML Explicit

B. The Nodes method

C. The Value method

D. The Exist method

3. Your sales database includes customer data from an XML data type column. You need to create a query that contains the values of CustomerID, LastName, FirstName, and Phone columns. The report should be ordered by LastName. What should you use to create this output?

A. The Nodes and Value method of the XML data type

B. FOR XML PATH

C. The Modify method of the XML data type

D. The Query method of the XML data type

4. You manage a database named StockPortfolio. It contains a table named Purchases with an XML column named PurchaseHistory, which is shown in the following XML snippet:

```
<purchasehistory>
  <purchasedate>… </purchasedate>
  <stockpurchased>…  </stockpurchased>
  <stockpurchased>…  </stockpurchased>
  . . .
</purchasehistory>
```

You need to design a query that will display the total number of different stocks purchased. Which of the following would you use?

A.

```
SELECT PurchaseID,
SUM(PurchaseHistory.value('count(/purchasehistory/stockpurchased)', 'INT'))
AS NumberOfDifferentStocksPurchased
FROM Purchases
GROUP BY PurchaseID;
```

B.

```
SELECT PurchaseID,COUNT(PurchaseHistory.modify('count(/purchasehistory/
stockpurchased)', 'INT'))
AS NumberOfDifferentStocksPurchased
FROM Purchases
GROUP BY PurchaseID;
```

C.

```
SELECT PurchaseID,SUM(PurchaseHistory.exist('/ purchasehistory/
stockpurchased')
AS NumberOfDifferentStocksPurchased
FROM Purchases
GROUP BY PurchaseID;
```

D.

```
SELECT PurchaseID,COUNT(PurchaseHistory.exist('/ purchasehistory/
stockpurchased')
AS NumberOfDifferentStocksPurchased
FROM Purchases
GROUP BY PurchaseID;
```

5. You are creating a query to search the Resume column from the JobCandidates tables. The Resume column is stored in an XML data type column. Your query must search the Resume column and only return résumés that contain a specific search phrase that will be passed in as a variable (@skill). The Full-Text search feature is not enabled on your database. Which of the following code segments would meet your goals?

A.

```
SELECT Description
FROM Product
WHERE CONTAINS(Description,@skill)
```

B.

```
SELECT Description
FROM Product
WHERE CAST(Description AS
nvarchar(max))LIKE N'%' + @skill + N'%'
```

C.

```
SELECT Description
FROM Product
WHERE PATINDEX(@skill,
CAST(Description as nvarchar(max)) > 0
```

D.

```
SELECT Description FROM Product WHERE
Description.exist('/Description[contains(., sql:variable
("@skill"))]') = 1
```

Answers

70-431

1. **C.** The XSINIL will include NULLS in the output when included with the FOR XML clause. It is not done automatically, and there is no INCLUDE NULLS argument.

2. **B.** The maximum size of a row is 8KB, so one of the large value data types [XML or (n)varchar(max)] must be used. Since the external application will do all the work with the XML, it's best to store it as (n)varchar(max) to avoid the overhead of the XML data type. Varchar(8000) wouldn't be enough space to hold 2MB, and varchar(20000000) isn't valid.

3. **A, B.** This problem requires both retrieving individual values and shredding the XML document into a relational result set. The two methods that can achieve this are the Value and the Nodes methods.

70-441

1. **B, D.** This is two questions. What data type should you use and how can you ensure data integrity? It's over 8K, so it can only be nvarchar(max) or an XML data type, and since we need to be able retrieve specific data (such as with XQuery), the XML data type is needed. Since only certain tags are allowed it must be typed, so an XML collection is used.

2. **D.** The XML data type is the best choice. Many different attributes can easily be stored in different nodes, and XML data can easily be retrieved from the database. A user-defined type wouldn't be able to accommodate varied attributes in each storm. varchar(max) and nvarchar(max) would be stored outside the database and wouldn't allow the data to be easily queried.

3. **C, E.** Since the goals have multiple values and can be in multiple nodes, the path is not known. This makes the Value Secondary XML the ideal choice. Before creating a secondary XML index, a Primary XML index must be created.

4. **A.** The original XML file must be retained. Since it is created from data exported from the database, the only way to ensure we have the original XML file is to create a copy. The simplest way to do this is by creating an archive table and storing the XML file in either an XML column or a nvarchar(max) column. Backing up the entire database each time an XML file is exported would be too labor- and resource-intensive.

70-442

1. **C.** To retrieve the data in an XML format, we need to use the SELECT … FOR XML statement. Since performance is important while using a minimum amount of memory, the best choice is an XMLReader object. A DataSet object stores the data in memory first.

2. **B.** The Nodes method can be used to shred XML data into relational data. If it was a single element (instead of elements) we were retrieving from the XML parameter, the Value method might be a better choice. The Exist method is used to determine whether an XML query will return any data. FOR XML is used to provide an XML output.

3. **A.** The nodes can be used to shred XML data into relational data, and can be combined with the Value method. The Exists method is used to determine if an XML query returns any data. FOR XML is used to provide an XML output.

4. **A.** In order to identify this count, we start with the Value method to drill down into the stockpurchased element. The Modify method is used to change the data, but we only want to query it, not modify it. The Exist method only tells us whether the element exists—returning either a 1 or a 0—so it couldn't tell us how many times the stockpurchased element was repeated.

5. **D.** The Exist XML method is ideally suited to this task. We want to search an XML column and return data based on whether or not certain data exist. The CONTAINS predicate can only be used when full-text is enabled. Both LIKE and PATINDEX (searches for a pattern) may achieve the same results, but they wouldn't be as effective in searching an XML column as an XML method.

Advanced Database Objects

In this chapter, you will learn about:

- Built-in functions
- User-defined functions
- DML triggers
- DDL triggers
- CLR-integrated database objects

> *Anyone who has never made a mistake has never tried anything new.*
>
> —*Albert Einstein*

We covered many of the basic database objects in earlier chapters. Now we'll discuss some of the advanced database objects: functions, triggers, and CLR integration. All of these objects work together to give DBAs many choices in solving a broad range of problems. You'll learn the benefits of each of these objects and how to use them to solve a wide variety of problems.

If you've never tried them before, expect to make some mistakes as you type them in. That's not a bad thing. It is instead proof that you're moving forward and trying new things.

Functions

Functions are available in almost every advanced programming language today. You remember from grade school that to get the sum of a group of numbers, you would simply add them all together. However, instead, the SUM built-in function can do that for us against a result set with very little coding on our part, and it's just one of many built-in functions available in SQL Server.

While SQL Server includes a wealth of built-in functions, at times you may need to create your own. In such cases, you can use T-SQL code to create user-defined functions.

In this section, we'll cover some built-in functions, and then explore what is necessary to create your own user-defined functions.

An Overview of the Functions

The available built-in functions fall into several different categories. Table 6-1 lists the types of functions, with a general description of functions within the category. Each category has between four and dozens of individual functions. Scalar functions actually include ten subcategories of functions themselves.

Types of Functions	Description
Aggregate	Works on a group of data, but returns a single value.
Scalar	Works on a single piece of data and returns a single value.
Rowset	Returns a rowset that can be referenced like a table.
Ranking	Returns a ranking value for rows within a partition.

Table 6-1 Types of Functions

It's beyond the scope of this book to cover every built-in function, but we will go through a few to show you how to explore these on your own.

A key feature of functions is that they can be used within a SELECT statement. This allows us to provide very complex results in our query, and do so with the ease of just calling a function. Functions can accept input (though it's not always required), and then return an output. As we see in Table 6-1, the output is as varied as our needs.

Built-in Functions

The best way to understand built-in functions is to explore a few of them.

AVG

The AVG function allows us to retrieve the average of a group of values while ignoring NULL values. For example, let's say the boss has asked you to let her know the average price of existing products. You could spend days counting and adding or you could look in Books Online for aggregate functions and then enter the following query:

```
Use AdventureWorks;
GO
SELECT AVG(ListPrice)
FROM Production.Product;
```

This results in a price of 438.662.

 TIP A great feature of the AVG function is that it automatically ignores the NULL value. This is different than a price of 0, which would be counted.

Some of these prices are 0.00, indicating that a price hasn't been identified. If we want to exclude them from our list, we could enter the following query to identify the average list price of all products with a list price that isn't 0, and thus come up with 727.2624:

```
Use AdventureWorks;
GO
SELECT AVG(ListPrice)
FROM Production.Product
WHERE ListPrice > 0;
```

MAX and MIN

The MAX and MIN functions can be used to identify the maximum or minimum values within a column. Usually we would use these on numerical columns, but they can also be used on character data. When used on character data, they return the maximum or minimum based on the collation.

For example, to identify the product that has the maximum list price, we can execute the following query. It will search all of the items in the table and return the highest value.

```
USE AdventureWorks;
GO
SELECT MAX(ListPrice) AS 'Maximum List Price'
```

FROM Production.Product;To identify the minimum price, we could substitute MAX with MIN as shown in the following query:

```
SELECT MIN(ListPrice) AS 'Minimum List Price'
FROM Production.Product;
```

Both MAX and MIN ignore any NULL values.

COUNT(*) and COUNT(expression)

The COUNT functions can be used to determine how many items exist in a group. For example, let's say we're interested in how many employees worked at AdventureWorks. A quick search in Books Online finds the COUNT function and allows us to build the following query. The COUNT(*) will count every row in the table and let us know we have 290 employees.

```
USE AdventureWorks;
GO
SELECT Count(*)
FROM HumanResources.Employee;
```

If desired, we can substitute the wild card (*) with an expression such as a column name. For example, let's say I'm interested in knowing how many sales each person actually had. We can use the COUNT(expression) function with the GROUP BY clause to get the information we need. The following query is an example that will work against the AdventureWorks Database:

```
SELECT SalesPersonID, COUNT(SalesOrderID)
FROM Sales.SalesOrderHeader
GROUP BY SalesPersonID
```

One key difference between COUNT(expression) and COUNT(*) is that COUNT(expression) will ignore fields with NULL values, while COUNT(*) will count all fields in the column. For example, in the following query, we only count fields that have data in the Color column. There are 256 products with a color, while the rest have NULL in the Color field.

```
SELECT COUNT(Color)
FROM Production.Product;
```

 EXAM TIP The Count(*) function will count all rows in a table or a result set, while the Count(expression) function will count only the rows that have a value in the specified expression. The Count(expression) function allows you to avoid counting rows that have a NULL value in specific columns.

COALESCE

Coalesce is a function that can be used as an expression within a T-SQL statement. It returns the value of the first non-NULL value from multiple choices. As an example, consider an employee database that has an Employee table similar to Table 6-2.

LastName	FirstName	CellPhone	HomePhone
Flintstone	Fred	555-9998	555-1111
Flintstone	Wilma	NULL	555-1111
Rubble	Barney	555-9999	NULL
Rubble	Betty	NULL	NULL

Table 6-2 Employee Table for COALESCE Example

Notice that some employees have a home phone number listed, some have cell numbers listed, some have neither, and some have both. We could generate a query similar to the following code to list the first non-NULL phone number:

```
SELECT LastName, FirstName,
       COALESCE(CellPhone,HomePhone) as Phone
FROM Employee
ORDER By LastName;
```

Notice that both the CellPhone and HomePhone numbers are in the query, with CellPhone listed first. If a CellPhone number exists, it will be retrieved, while the HomePhone number will be ignored. If CellPhone is NULL, the listing will retrieve the HomePhone number. If neither phone numbers exist (both values are NULL), the statement will return a NULL.

The result set from the previous script would look like Table 6-3.

LastName	FirstName	Phone
Flintstone	Fred	555-9998
Flintstone	Wilma	555-1111
Rubble	Betty	NULL
Rubble	Barney	555-9988

Table 6-3 Output from the COALESCE Query

The COALESCE statement works similar to a CASE statement. A Case statement will use the first statement in the list of statements that is true. The following code checks for a value in the CellPhone column and uses it if it is not NULL. If not, it'll use the HomePhone value if a value exists in the HomePhone column. Last, if both the CellPhone and the HomePhone are NULL, it gives the variable @Phone a value of NULL.

```
CASE
    WHEN (CellPhone IS NOT NULL) THEN @Phone=CellPhone
    WHEN (HomePhone IS NOT NULL) THEN @Phone=HomePhone
    ELSE @Phone=Null
END
```

Date and Time Functions

SQL Server includes many date and time functions that can be used to perform operations on date or time values and then return values. These are listed in Table 6-4. They can be very useful when we want to manipulate dates such as identifying the month or year of a given date.

GetDate	Returns current system date and time.
DateAdd	Adds an interval to a given date.
DatePart	Returns a specific part of the date, such as year, month, and day. Returns this as an integer.
DateName	Returns a specific part of the date in a character string.
Month	Returns the month of a given date.

Table 6-4 Date and Time Functions

These examples are used in Chapter 9 as we demonstrate how to create stored procedures. The following script shows simple examples of how these functions could be used:

```
-- Returns today's date
SELECT GETDATE() AS Today
-- Returns the month (as an integer) for today's date
```

```
SELECT MONTH(GETDATE()) As [Month Integer]
-- Returns today's date plus 30 days
SELECT DATEADD(day, 30, GETDATE()) AS [Add 30 Days to today]
-- Returns the month (as an integer) for today's date
SELECT DATEPART(month, GETDATE()) AS [Month as Integer]
-- Returns the month (as a string) for today's date
SELECT DATENAME(month, GETDATE()) AS [Month as Name]
-- Returns the weekday name (as a string) for today's date
SELECT DATENAME(weekday, GETDATE()) AS [WeekDay Name]
```

Running the previous script will result in an output similar to Figure 6-1.

Figure 6-1

The result of

Date functions

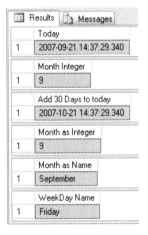

String Functions (UPPER, LTRIM, RTRIM, LEN)

Several string functions provide useful methods of manipulating string data. For example, if we have a database with the collation set to Case Sensitive and we want to ensure that any comparisons don't pay attention to the case, we could use UPPER. The following script compares the first name converted to all uppercase, with the name "kim" converted to all uppercase, and returns ten rows:

```
SELECT FirstName, LastName, Phone
FROM Person.Contact
Where UPPER(FirstName) = UPPER('kim');
```

Sometimes data within a database has trailing or leading spaces. We can clean up the output (or clean up the data before inputting it into our database) with LTRIM and RTRIM, which remove leading and trailing spaces. For example, let's say we've found that some of the names being entered into the Person.Contact table are entered with leading spaces.

Let's simulate this with the following INSERT statement. Notice that both the first and last names have leading spaces.

```
INSERT INTO Person.Contact
(FirstName, LastName,PasswordHash, PasswordSalt)
VALUES ('  Harry', '  Potter', 'P@ssw0rd','P@$$S@lt');
```

The following query would not find this entry. Even though we have an employee with the first name of Harry, he can't be located without eliminating the leading spaces.

```
SELECT * from Person.Contact
WHERE FirstName = 'Harry';
```

Instead, we'd use this query with the LTRIM function:

```
SELECT * from Person.Contact
WHERE LTRIM(FirstName) = 'Harry';
```

The LEN function can be very useful when we are trying to identify the maximum length of a column. It returns the number of characters of a specified string, excluding trailing blanks.

For example, we may realize that the Name column in the Product table has been created using a char(100) definition. We suspect that 100 characters is much longer than required, but want to verify the length of the longest product name in the table before we redefine the column with varchar(). Thus, the following query could be used:

```
SELECT Max(LEN(Name))
FROM Production.Product
```

In the following exercise, we'll explore some of the date functions.

Exercise 6.1: Use Built-in Functions

1. Launch a New Query window in SSMS.

2. Use the following script to create a database named Chapter6 and a table within it named AuditAccess:

```
CREATE Database Chapter6;
GO
USE Chapter6;
GO
CREATE TABLE dbo.AuditAccess
(
   AuditAccessID int IDENTITY(1,1) NOT NULL,
   UserName varchar(50) NOT NULL,
   LoginTime datetime NULL,
   CONSTRAINT [PK_AuditAccess_AuditAccessID] PRIMARY KEY CLUSTERED
   (
         AuditAccessID
   )
);
```

3. Use the following query with a scalar system function to identify the system user that is currently logged on (that would be you!) based on the Windows logon name. This typically takes the format of *domain\user* in a domain, or *computer\user* in a workgroup.

```
SELECT SUSER_SNAME()
```

4. We can embed functions into DML statements. In the following query, we are using the SUSER_SNAME() function to identify the user and create a log entry saying the user is logged in. We can also use the GETDATE() function to identify now as the day and time of login. The SELECT statement shows that we have successfully added these entries.

```
INSERT INTO AuditAccess VALUES('Bozo','1-5-2008');
INSERT INTO AuditAccess VALUES('Krusty','1-6-2008');
INSERT INTO AuditAccess VALUES(SUSER_SNAME(),'1-7-2008');
INSERT INTO AuditAccess VALUES(SUSER_SNAME(),GETDATE());
GO
SELECT * FROM AuditAccess;
```

You should get a result similar to that in Figure 6-2.

	AuditAccessID	UserName	LoginTime
1	15	Bozo	2008-01-05 00:00:00.000
2	16	Krusty	2008-01-06 00:00:00.000
3	17	MCITPSUCCESS\Administrator	2008-01-07 00:00:00.000
4	18	MCITPSUCCESS\Administrator	2007-07-13 17:18:01.873

Figure 6-2   The results after inputting data into the AuditAccess table

Function Efficiency

Even though functions are easy to use for complex operations, it's sometimes important to realize that there is a resource cost associated with using functions. In other words, if you have a choice of using a simple comparison with a query, or using a function, your choice should be the simple query.

As an example, let's say we want to identify how many sales occurred for July 1, 2004. Many methods would help us achieve this goal. However, some are better than others.

The following methods are compared both for accuracy and duration. I don't mean to imply that these methods are the only way to achieve the desired result; I chose them simply for reasons of comparison. For the queries that will work, the following code is added so we can verify how long it takes. The Print statement appears in the messages tab of the output query.

```
Declare @start datetime, @end datetime
Set @start = GetDate()
```

Then, after the SELECT statement, I added the following code:

```
Set @end = GetDate()
Print 'Code took ' + Str((DATEDIFF(ms ,@start,@end) ), 3,0) + ' milliseconds
to run.'
```

The results of all the methods are shown in Table 6-5.

Method	Results
Compare date with =	Does not work accurately.
Compare with >= and <	0 milliseconds (The most efficient method)
Compare with CONVERT function	33 milliseconds
Compare with YEAR, MONTH, DAY functions	16 milliseconds
Compare with DATEDIFF function	16 milliseconds

Table 6-5 Comparison of Different Queries

Method 1: Comparing Dates with the = Operator This first method uses the = operator to compare the specific date with the date listed in the OrderDate column.

```
USE AdventureWorks;
GO
SELECT COUNT(*) FROM Sales.SalesOrderHeader
WHERE OrderDate = '20040701'
```

While this method looks acceptable on the surface, it won't consistently work in a live database. The date includes time information. In AdventureWorks, the time is all at 00:00:000 (minutes, seconds, milliseconds), but in a live database you can fully expect the time to be accurate based on the entry.

If you created the AuditAccess table in the Chpater 6 database, you can see this with the following scripts. The first script adds a row with the current date and time entered into the LoginTime row.

```
USE Chapter6;
GO
INSERT INTO AuditAccess VALUES(SUSER_SNAME(),GETDATE());
```

Next, we'll query the table using the GetDate function for today:

```
SELECT * FROM AuditAccess
WHERE LoginTime = GetDate()
```

The preceding query returns zero rows since the time is not exact.

Method 2: Comparing Dates with the >= and < Operators The second method fine-tunes the first method so it accurately returns the correct results. It still does simple comparisons in the WHERE clause without using a function and is the most efficient.

EXAM TIP   When creating queries, the most efficient method is to use a simple comparison. It may be possible to create a complex query using several embedded functions, but if efficiency is your goal, consider omitting the functions.

```
USE AdventureWorks;
GO
Declare @start datetime, @end datetime
Set @start = GetDate()
SELECT COUNT(*) FROM Sales.SalesOrderHeader
WHERE OrderDate >= '20040701' AND
OrderDate < '20040702'
Set @end = GetDate()
Print 'Code took ' + Str((DATEDIFF(ms ,@start,@end) ), 3,0) + ' milliseconds
to run.'
```

This query is the best. It accurately returns 37 rows, and by clicking the Messages tab (as shown in Figure 6-3), it shows it took 10 milliseconds to run. If you run it again, it'll probably report 0 milliseconds since the data is already in cache.

Figure 6-3

The Messages tab
of a query result

```
USE AdventureWorks;
GO
Declare @start datetime, @end datetime
Set @start = GetDate()
SELECT COUNT(*) FROM Sales.SalesOrderHeader
WHERE OrderDate >= '20040701' AND
OrderDate < '20040702'
Set @end = GetDate()
Print 'Code took ' + Str((DATEDIFF(ms ,@start,@end) ), 3,0)
    + ' milliseconds to run.'
```

Results Messages

```
(1 row(s) affected)
Code took  10 milliseconds to run.
```

NOTE   I've listed the times I received on my test system for comparison, but the times on your system will likely be different. What's important is to compare them to each other rather than to my specific times. Additionally, once the data is in cache, all of the queries will run quicker. By running the query twice, you are assured of seeing what the timing of the query would be if the data was in cache.

Method 3: Comparing Dates with the CONVERT Function   This

method also finetunes the first method to ensure that only the date is compared and not the time. It uses the CONVERT function to convert the date to a string in the format: yyyymmdd. While accurate, the CONVERT function takes considerably longer than the second method.

```
Declare @start datetime, @end datetime
Set @start = GetDate()
SELECT COUNT(*) FROM Sales.SalesOrderHeader
WHERE CONVERT(CHAR(8), OrderDate, 112)
= '20040701'
```

```
Set @end = GetDate()
Print 'Code took ' + Str((DATEDIFF(ms ,@start,@end) ), 3,0) + ' milliseconds to run.'
```

This query accurately returns 37 rows and took 33 milliseconds to run.

Method 4: Comparing Dates with YEAR, MONTH, and DAY

Functions   This method uses three different date functions to achieve the results. While it is accurate, it is slower than the direct comparison.

```
Declare @start datetime, @end datetime
Set @start = GetDate()
SELECT COUNT(*) FROM Sales.SalesOrderHeader
WHERE YEAR(OrderDate) = 2004 AND
MONTH(OrderDate) = 07 AND DAY(OrderDate) = 01
Set @end = GetDate()
Print 'Code took ' + Str((DATEDIFF(ms ,@start,@end) ), 3,0) + ' milliseconds to run.'
```

This query accurately returns 37 rows and took 16 milliseconds to run.

Method 5: Comparing Dates with DATEDIFF Functions   This last method shown also returns an accurate result, but takes longer than the direct query. It uses the DATEDIFF function to compare the given date with the OrderDate.

```
Declare @start datetime, @end datetime
Set @start = GetDate()
SELECT COUNT(*) FROM Sales.SalesOrderHeader
WHERE DATEDIFF(day, OrderDate, '20040701') = 0
Set @end = GetDate()
Print 'Code took ' + Str((DATEDIFF(ms ,@start,@end) ), 3,0) + ' milliseconds
to run.'
```

This query accurately returns 37 rows and also took 16 milliseconds to run.

Deterministic vs. Nondeterministic

Understanding the difference between deterministic functions and nondeterministic functions is especially important when creating indexes on a VIEW. Indexes can't be created on a VIEW if the VIEW references a nondeterministic function. Of course, this begs the question: What is a nondeterministic function?

A nondeterministic function can return different data when the function is executed at different times. Table 6-6 shows a listing of nondeterministic functions.

@@CONNECTIONS	@@CPU_BUSY	@@DBTS
@@IDLE	@@IO_BUSY	@@MAX_CONNECTIONS
@@PACK_RECEIVED	@@PACK_SENT	@@PACKET_ERRORS
@@TIMETICKS	@@TOTAL_ERRORS	@@TOTAL_READ
@@TOTAL_WRITE	CURRENT_TIMESTAMP	GETDATE
GETUTCDATE	GET_TRANSMISSION_STATUS	NEWID
NEWSEQUENTIALID	RAND	TEXTPTR

Table 6-6   Nondeterministic Functions

The simplest example is the GETDATE function. When run, it will retrieve the date, including the time (hours, minutes, seconds, and milliseconds), but if run again just a short time later, some part of the time will be different. Therefore, GETDATE is a nondeterministic function.

A deterministic function will return the same value each time it is run, as long as the provided parameters remain the same. Table 6-7 shows a listing of deterministic functions.

ABS	ACOS	ASIN	ATAN
ATN2	CEILING	COALESCE	COS
COT	DATELENGTH	DATEADD	DATEDIFF
DAY	DEGREES	EXP	FLOOR
ISNULL	ISNUMERIC	LOG	LOG10
MONTH	NULLIF	PARSENAME	POWER
RADIANS	ROUND	SIGN	SIN
SQUARE	SQRT	TAN	YEAR

Table 6-7 Deterministic Functions

As an example, the Year function will return the year from a given date. The following query will always return the number 2008 since the query always includes the parameter '01/01/2008':

```
SELECT YEAR('01/01/2008')
```

If a different date was passed in to the function (in other words, a different parameter was passed in), we'd get a different result, of course, but part of the definition of a deterministic function is that it returns the same data as long as the parameters are the same.

User-Defined Functions

While SQL Server provides many built-in functions, there's no way it can provide the functions needed for every possible situation. Instead, SQL gives you the ability to create your own user-defined functions.

User-defined functions can be:

- Used in T-SQL statements such as SELECT and INSERT
- Used in external applications
- Embedded in another user-defined function
- Used to parameterize a VIEW (VIEWs can't accept parameters, but you can create a function that accepts a parameter and works like a view)
- Used to define a column or a CHECK constraint on a column
- Used in place of a stored procedure

Functions can also be written in any .NET programming language, as discussed later in the CLR section.

As with built-in functions, user-defined functions can accept input and will provide output. As an example, let's say we want to identify the state based on a ZIP code. We could have a table populated with that information, so now all we'd have to do is build a function to query it.

To see this in action, we need to create the table and populate it with some data, as shown in the following script:

```
--Create the table
USE Chapter6;
GO
CREATE TABLE dbo.ZipState
(
        ZipStateID int IDENTITY(1,1) NOT NULL,
        ZipCode int NOT NULL,
        State char(2) NOT NULL,
        CONSTRAINT [PK_ZipState_ZipStateID] PRIMARY KEY CLUSTERED
        (
                ZipStateID
         )
);
--Populate the table
INSERT INTO ZipState (ZipCode, State) VALUES(23462,'VA');
INSERT INTO ZipState (ZipCode, State) VALUES(94562,'CA');
INSERT INTO ZipState (ZipCode, State) VALUES(74562,'OK');
INSERT INTO ZipState (ZipCode, State) VALUES(54562,'WI');
```

Of course, in an actual table you'd have much more data, and you'd probably update it regularly using a method such as a web service. You could then regularly query the service and keep the data within your table up-to-date. However, for our needs these few rows will work.

Ultimately, we want to be able to find the state by providing just the ZIP code. A simple SELECT statement for this may look like the following:

```
SELECT fn_GetState(zip) as State;
```

First, we have to create a function named GetState(). We do this using the following script:

```
USE Chapter6;
GO
CREATE FUNCTION dbo.fn_GetState(@zip int)
RETURNS char(2)
AS
BEGIN
  DECLARE @State char(2)
  SELECT @State = State
  FROM ZipState
  WHERE ZipCode = @zip
  Return @State
END;
```

Notice that we identify the function with a two-part name of *schema.functionName* when it's created. The input parameter is named *@zip,* and we're expecting to get an integer data type to represent the ZIP code. This is based on what is in the base table we created earlier.

The output of the function is determined by the RETURN statement. The value of *@State* is embedded in the SELECT statement and will hold the value of the state based on the ZIP code.

 TIP   Notice that the value returned is contained within the *@State* variable. That's the value returned in place of the function's name when we call the function.

The next step is to use the function in a statement:

```
SELECT dbo.fn_GetState(23462) as State;
```

You should see something similar to Figure 6-4.

Figure 6-4
The result after executing a user-defined function

As long as the ZIP code that we pass into the function exists in the State table, we'll get a state in the results.

But what if we pass in a ZIP code that isn't recognized? The following query will return a value of NULL:

```
SELECT dbo.fn_GetState(11111) as State;
```

If we want a more user-friendly response, we can modify our function. Any time we want to modify a database object, we would use an ALTER statement. The reason why we do not DROP and then CREATE the object again is to preserve the permissions on the original object.

```
USE Chapter6;
GO
ALTER FUNCTION dbo.fn_GetState(@zip int)
RETURNS char(2)
AS
BEGIN
  DECLARE @State char(2)
  SELECT @State = State
  FROM ZipState
  WHERE ZipCode = @zip
  IF (@State IS NULL)
      SET @State = 'NA'
  Return @State
END;
```

Now, any time a ZIP code doesn't exist in the database, instead of returning a value of NULL, it will return a value of *NA* for "Not Available." We can see this by executing the following script:

```
USE Chapter6;
GO
SELECT dbo.fn_GetState(11111);
```

In the next exercise, we'll use the AuditAccess table we created in the earlier exercise. We'll add some data to the table and then create a function used to query specific information on this data.

Exercise 6.2: Create and Use User-Defined Functions

1. Open a New Query window in SSMS.

2. Use the following script to add some lines to the AuditAccess table. The first three rows are added with literal data. The last row is added using built-in functions. Notice that in the last INSERT we are using the GETDATE() function.

```
USE Chapter6;
GO
INSERT INTO AuditAccess VALUES('Harry','07-02-2008');
INSERT INTO AuditAccess VALUES('Ron','07-03-2008');
INSERT INTO AuditAccess VALUES('Hermione','07-05-2008');
INSERT INTO AuditAccess VALUES(SUSER_SNAME(),GetDate());
SELECT * FROM AuditAccess;
```

Execute the INSERT statements several times to add several rows for each user into your table.

3. Now we'll create a user-defined function that can determine whether a user has ever logged in before, as well as how many times the user has logged in:

```
USE Chapter6;
GO
CREATE FUNCTION dbo.fn_CountLogins(@UserName varchar(50))
RETURNS int
AS
BEGIN
  Declare @Logins int
  SELECT @Logins = COUNT(*) FROM AuditAccess
    WHERE UserName = @UserName
  Return @Logins
END;
```

 EXAM TIP User-defined functions can be used to return *scalar information* (a single answer) based on queries that review multiple rows (even millions of rows).

4. To execute the function, use the following script:

```
DECLARE @UserName varchar(50);
SET @UserName = SUSER_SNAME();
```

```
SELECT dbo.fn_CountLogins(@UserName) AS UserName;
SELECT dbo.fn_CountLogins('Harry') as 'Harry'
```

You should see a display similar to Figure 6-5.

Figure 6-5

Output from
a user-defined
function

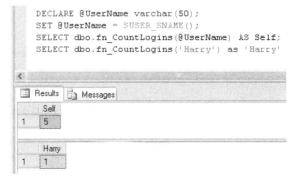

Triggers

Triggers provide a lot of power for database developers. They allow us to enforce business rules and ensure data integrity. We can audit changes to data, changes to database objects, roll back unacceptable changes, and much more.

Since triggers are created on tables, they allow us to control or respond to data modifications at the table level. In other words, a trigger can be programmed to respond to any INSERT, UPDATE or DELETE statement that occurs on a table. This is especially useful if the data is being modified via different methods such as with a stored procedure from one application or direct DML statements from another application.

New to SQL Server 2005 are Data Definition Language (DDL) triggers that respond to DDL statements such as CREATE, ALTER, and DROP. These can be very useful when auditing the creation and modification of objects within the server and objects within individual databases.

An Overview of Triggers

A *trigger* is a special type of stored procedure that executes automatically in response to other actions. We'll cover stored procedures in depth in Chapter 8, but in essence stored procedures are groups of T-SQL that we can group together and fire with one execution statement. Unlike stored procedures, triggers can't be executed directly. Instead, they are only executed in response to an event.

Triggers are associated with specific actions (such as UPDATE, INSERT, and DELETE) on a table. An UPDATE trigger configured on a table or VIEW will fire in response to any UPDATE on the table or VIEW. Likewise, an INSERT or DELETE trigger configured on a table or VIEW will fire in response to an INSERT or DELETE on the table or VIEW.

One great benefit of a trigger is that it will execute no matter what is causing the action. If you want to monitor updates to the data, a trigger will catch the change if the table was updated from a function, stored procedure, a direct UPDATE statement, or any other method.

Triggers are primarily AFTER triggers, meaning they fire after an UPDATE, INSERT, or DELETE. However, DML triggers can also be configured as INSTEAD OF triggers. An INSTEAD OF trigger will cause the trigger to fire instead of the DML statement that fired it.

Both DML and DDL triggers can be configured as outlined in Table 6-8. Note that only DML triggers can be configured as INSTEAD OF triggers.

Primary Type	T-SQL Statements	Type
DML	INSERT, UPDATE, DELETE	AFTER, INSTEAD OF
DDL	CREATE, ALTER, DROP	AFTER

Table 6-8 Types of Triggers

Triggers are not intended to return data.

DML Triggers

Data Manipulation Language (DML) triggers work on the following DML statements:

- INSERT
- UPDATE
- DELETE

Triggers are associated with tables. In other words, I can create an INSERT trigger on the Employees table, and then, whenever an INSERT occurs on the Employees table the trigger fires.

One of the strengths of triggers is that they will fire no matter how the modification was done. For example, I may want to ensure that before a customer is deleted, checks are done to ensure the customer is no longer active. If I create a stored procedure or a function to perform the checks before the deletion, I'm only guaranteed the checks are done if the stored procedure or function is used. If the deletion is done with a DELETE statement, the checks aren't done.

However, since I can create a DELETE trigger on the table that will fire no matter what executes the DELETE statement, it will catch all attempts to delete the customer record.

Two *temporary* tables exist to allow triggers to examine what just occurred. These are listed in Table 6-9 along with the commands that can access these temporary tables.

DML Command	Temporary Table	Description
DELETE	Deleted	Holds data that was just deleted.
INSERT	Inserted	Holds data that was just inserted.
UPDATE	Inserted Deleted	Holds a copy of the data after the update. Holds a copy of the data before the update.

Table 6-9 Trigger Temporary Tables

INSERT Trigger

The steps for an INSERT trigger are:

1. An INSERT statement is executed on a table.

2. The inserted data is placed into the *inserted table.*

3. The INSERT trigger fires.

An INSERT trigger fires in response to any INSERT statement on the table. An example of using an INSERT trigger is to record the date the record was created.

Earlier in this chapter, we created the StateZip table. Let's make a slight modification to the table by adding a CreationDate column of data type datetime. Since we have data in the table, we'll allow NULL data.

```
USE Chapter6;
ALTER TABLE dbo.ZipState
ADD CreationDate datetime NULL;
```

Now we can create an INSERT trigger on the column. First, let's review the syntax of an UPDATE statement. The following UPDATE will use the GetDate function to get today's date and change the CreationDate column to today's date. However, we don't want to do that with every row. We only want to do it with rows that have just been added and that exist in the temporary *inserted* table, so we join the existing table with the inserted table.

```
UPDATE z
SET CreationDate = GetDate()
FROM ZipState as z INNER JOIN inserted AS i
ON i.ZipStateID = z.ZipStateID;
```

 NOTE The *inserted* and *deleted* tables can't be accessed directly. If we try to run the previous UPDATE statement by itself, it will fail, but only because the *inserted* table isn't accessible. Triggers can access the *inserted* and *deleted* tables immediately after the DML statement. Additionally, DML statements have an OUTPUT clause (described in Chapter 8) that can access these tables.

Now that we've fleshed out the syntax of the UPDATE, we simply need to wrap it with a CREATE trigger statement. The bolded portion in the following script is all we need to add:

```
USE Chapter6;
GO
CREATE TRIGGER trgRecordCreationDate
ON ZipState
AFTER INSERT
AS
```

```
UPDATE z
SET CreationDate = GetDate()
FROM ZipState as z INNER JOIN inserted AS i
ON i.ZipStateID = z.ZipStateID;
```

Now whenever an INSERT is executed on the ZipState column, this trigger will fire and add the current date to the CreationDate column. Let's see it work by entering a row into your table. First, we insert a row:

```
INSERT INTO ZipState (ZipCode, State) VALUES(23752,'VA');
```

Now we can check to see what was done:

```
SELECT * FROM ZipState;
```

Figures 6-6 and 6-7 show what has happened during the process. First, the INSERT statement fires and updates the table. When the table is updated, the inserted data is entered into the inserted table.

INSERT INTO ZipState (ZipCode, state)
VALUES(23752,'VA');

	ZipState ID	ZipCode	State	CreationDate
Data inserted into ZipState table	1	23462	VA	NULL
	2	94562	CA	NULL
	3	74562	OK	NULL
	4	23752	VA	NULL

	ZipState ID	ZipCode	State	CreationDate
Data inserted into inserted table	4	23752	VA	NULL

Figure 6-6 The INSERT statement updates the ZipState table and *inserted* table.

Next, the INSERT trigger fires and updates the data in the table by adding the current date.

Trigger fires → UPDATE CreationDate = GetDate() . . .

	ZipState ID	ZipCode	State	CreationDate
Zip state table updated	1	23462	VA	NULL
	2	94562	CA	NULL
	3	74562	OK	NULL
	4	23752	VA	20070901

Figure 6-7 The INSERT trigger fires and updates the new row.

 TIP The *inserted* table only holds the data from the last INSERT statement. Data is not held in the table permanently. The same applies to the *deleted* table. Data is not appended, but instead data from only the last statement is in the table.

The DELETE Trigger

The DELETE trigger works in a similar fashion to the INSERT trigger, but only on DELETE statements for the table. The steps for a DELETE statement are:

1. The DELETE statement is executed on a table.

2. The deleted data is placed into a *deleted* table.

3. The DELETE trigger fires.

As an example, let's create a DELETE trigger on the AuditAccess table created earlier in the Chapter6 database. Since we have created the AuditAccess table to record anyone who has logged in to the system, we may choose to disallow any deletions from this table. We can enforce this business rule with a DELETE trigger:

```
USE Chapter6;
GO
CREATE TRIGGER trgPreventDeletion
ON AuditAccess
AFTER DELETE
AS
RAISERROR ('Audit access entries cannot be delcted', 16, 10) WITH LOG
ROLLBACK TRANSACTION;
```

The RAISERROR statement provides feedback to the user about the error. We can put any text desired in here. The WITH LOG statement will cause the error to be logged into the application log that is viewable with Event Viewer.

 TIP The DELETE statement that fires this trigger starts an implicit transaction. By using the ROLLBACK TRANSACTION statement, we are rolling back the DELETE statement.

Let's try it. First, we can see if we have any data in the AuditAccess table by using the following SELECT statement:

```
USE Chapter6;
SELECT * FROM AuditAccess;
```

I have some clown named Krusty in my table. Let's try to delete his entries:

```
DELETE FROM AuditAccess
WHERE UserName = 'Krusty'
```

Figure 6-8 shows the error message logged from the RAISERROR statement in the application log. Messages can be configured to be logged automatically with any RAISERROR statement, or by using the WITH LOG statement in the RAISERROR statement.

Using the SELECT * FROM AuditAccess statement, we can see that the data has not been deleted.

Figure 6-8

The error message shown in Event Viewer

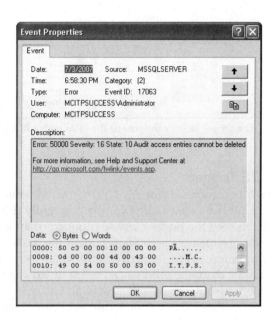

Figure 6-9 shows how the DELETE trigger responded to the DELETE statement. First, the DELETE statement executes and deletes the row or rows. All the rows that are deleted are placed into the deleted table.

Figure 6-9

The DELETE trigger in action

AuditAccess table

AuditAccessID	UserName	LoginDate
1	Hoot	2007-07-02
2	Darril	2007-07-03
3	Squeaky	2007-07-05
4	Krusty	2007-02-02

DELETE FROM AuditAccess
WHERE UserName = 'Krusty'

Data deleted from AuditAccess table

AuditAccessID	UserName	LoginDate
1	Hoot	2007-07-02
2	Darril	2007-07-03
3	Squeaky	2007-07-05

Data inserted into deleted table

AuditAccessID	UserName	LoginDate
4	Krusty	2007-02-02

Next, the trigger fires, as we can see in Figure 6-10, and then the trigger rolls back the DELETE statement and logs an error message. With the transaction rolled back, the row is returned to the table.

Figure 6-10 The trigger returns the row to the table with a ROLLBACK TRAN

The UPDATE Trigger

An UPDATE trigger monitors for any UPDATE statements on the table.

As an example, let's say that the company recently suffered a SQL injection attack. The attacker changed the price of several products to .01 and bought two cases of gold-plated widgets at a penny each. Management has tasked you with ensuring that the price of any product can't be reduced by more than 10 percent. Further, they have specified that no more than one product can be modified at a time.

Since the price would be modified with an UPDATE statement, we can use an UPDATE trigger to enforce this business rule. AdventureWorks is populated with data in the Production.Product table, and we can use it as an example.

The following trigger will be created on the Production.Product table, so the trigger needs to be created with the same schema of Production:

```
USE AdventureWorks;
GO
CREATE TRIGGER Production.trgPriceControl
ON Production.Product
AFTER UPDATE
AS
IF (SELECT COUNT(*) FROM inserted) > 1
Begin
     RAISERROR ('No more than one product can be updated at a time.', 16,
10) WITH LOG
        ROLLBACK TRAN
    RETURN  -- Exit script
End
DECLARE @NewPrice decimal
DECLARE @OldPrice decimal
SET @NewPrice = (SELECT ListPrice from inserted)
SET @OldPrice = (SELECT ListPrice from deleted)
IF @NewPrice < (@OldPrice * .9)      -- more than 10% reduction
Begin
        RAISERROR ('Unauthorized price change attempted.', 16, 10) WITH LOG
    ROLLBACK TRAN
End
```

The first IF statement checks to see how many rows are in the inserted table. If more than one row exists, we give an error, roll back the DELETE, and exit.

The second IF statement compares the new and old prices. If the new price is reduced by more than 10 percent of the original price, an error is given and the transaction is rolled back.

Let's give it a try. First, see which products are available with prices:

```
SELECT * FROM Production.Product
WHERE ListPrice > 0
```

Now we'll try to change the prices of all the products. In the following script, I'm starting with a BEGIN TRAN statement as a safety net in case I've done something wrong with the trigger. If the trigger doesn't fire, I can just enter ROLLBACK TRAN to get the data back to normal.

```
BEGIN TRAN
UPDATE Production.Product
SET ListPrice = .01
SELECT * FROM Production.Product
WHERE ListPrice > 0
```

The SELECT statement should not fire since the transaction should be rolled back by the trigger. Instead, it should give an error saying we can only change the price of one product at a time. If the SELECT statement executes, it indicates the trigger didn't fire as expected and we've just changed the price of all products to .01. Enter ROLLBACK TRAN to undo the change.

Now let's try to change the price of just one product:

```
Begin Tran
UPDATE Production.Product
SET ListPrice = .01
WHERE ProductID = 514
```

This should fail with an error indicating "Unauthorized price change attempted."

Figure 6-11 shows how the UPDATE trigger uses both the inserted and deleted tables. The original data is preserved in the deleted table, and the new data is held in the inserted table.

Figure 6-11
A DELETE
trigger using both
inserted and
deleted tables

ProductID	ProductNumber	...	ListPrice
511	RM-R600		101.25
512	RM-R800		75.45
513	RM-T801		15.43
514	SA-M198		133.34

Product table

Data updated in product table

```
UPDATE Production.Product
SET ListPrice = .01
WHERE ProductID = 514
```

Data added to inserted table

ProductID	ProductNumber	...	ListPrice
514	SA-M198		.01

Data added to deleted table

ProductID	ProductNumber	...	ListPrice
514	SA-M198		133.34

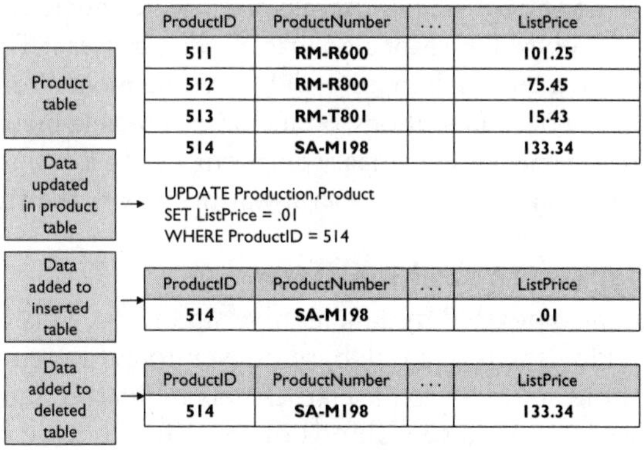

In Figure 6-12, we can see how the trigger can compare the contents of the two tables, and if necessary, roll back the transaction.

Figure 6-12

A DELETE trigger in action

ProductID	ProductNumber	. . .	ListPrice
514	SA-M198		.01

Data added to inserted table

ProductID	ProductNumber	. . .	ListPrice
514	SA-M198		133.34

Data added to deleted table

Trigger fires and compares prices

• New updated list price in inserted table
• Original list price in deleted table
• Data compared and rolled back if unacceptable

ProductID	ProductNumber	. . .	ListPrice
511	RM-R600		101.25
512	RM-R800		75.45
513	RM-T801		15.43
514	SA-M198		133.34

Data rolled back in product table

Using Triggers for Auditing

Triggers are very effective as a tool to audit changes in data. If you need to identify key details on who modified data and when, a trigger is a perfect choice.

Unlike stored procedures or functions, triggers will catch DML statements no matter how they are entered. As a reminder, DML statements can be executed using a number of different methods:

- An ad hoc DML statement
- Within a stored procedure
- Within a function
- Within another trigger

EXAM TIP   DML triggers are ideal for auditing data changes, since they will capture the change no matter what causes it. For example, an UPDATE trigger on a table will capture UPDATE statements from stored procedures, ad hoc queries, applications, or any other possible method of sending an UPDATE statement to a database. In comparison, trying to use a stored procedure to audit data changes would only work if the change was made with the stored procedure.

Using Triggers to Archive Data

Triggers can also be used in data archive situations. This includes moving inactive data to different tables within a database or even to a different database.

For example, let's say we have an Orders table. If it had all the orders since the company opened, it may have millions of rows. Instead, we could create a solution where the data is moved to an archive table after the order is considered closed.

We could use a Boolean flag called blnOrderClosed and set it based on business guidance. For example, management might consider the order closed as soon as the order is shipped, or perhaps 30 days after the order is shipped. Other business logic within an application could also be used to set the blnOrderClosed flag, but the point is that it will be set sometime.

Knowing the flag will be set through an UPDATE statement, we could create an UPDATE trigger on the table. In the UPDATE trigger, we check to see if the column being updated is blnOrderClosed. If so, we can INSERT the row into an ArchiveOrders table and delete it from the Orders table.

Using Triggers to Cancel Deletes

A DML trigger can be useful in ensuring that data isn't deleted from a table. For example, we may have a customer table and want to ensure that customers are never deleted. Instead, the database design is set up to indicate the customer is no longer active. This can be a Boolean column named Active where 1 indicates the customer is active and a 0 indicates the customer is inactive.

By creating a DELETE trigger on the Customer table, we would catch all attempts to delete a customer. We would roll back the deletion and instead mark the Active column to indicate the customer is inactive. We could also create an error message to indicate that customers can not be deleted, but instead should be set to inactive.

We can demonstrate this capability in the AdventureWorks database. Let's say we want to ensure that Job Candidates aren't deleted from the HumanResources.JobCandidate table, but are instead marked as inactive. First, we need to create an Inactive column. The following script does this:

```
USE AdventureWorks;
GO
ALTER TABLE HumanResources.JobCandidate
Add Inactive bit NULL
```

Next, we can create the trigger. Notice in the following code that we're using an INSTEAD OF trigger. Instead of allowing the DELETE, the UPDATE statement is issued to mark the Job Candidate as inactive.

```
USE AdventureWorks;
GO
CREATE TRIGGER trgPreventDeleteJobCandidate
ON HumanResources.JobCandidate
INSTEAD OF DELETE
AS
UPDATE HumanResources.JobCandidate
 SET Inactive = 1
 FROM HumanResources.JobCandidate as c INNER JOIN deleted AS d
 ON c.JobCandidateID = d.JobCandidateID;
RAISERROR ('Job Candidates cannot be deleted. Candidate marked as inactive
instead.', 16, 10) WITH LOG
```

To test, the trigger, first add a Job Candidate:

```
INSERT INTO HumanResources.JobCandidate
          (EmployeeID, ModifiedDate ,Inactive)
VALUES    (1, GetDate(), 1)
GO
SELECT * FROM HumanResources.JobCandidate
```

More than likely, the JobCandidateID of the last row in the JobCandidate table is 14. Whatever the last JobCandidateID is, write it down here: _____.

Now let's try to delete the row we just created. The following code assumes the Job-CandidateID you identified was 14.

```
DELETE FROM HumanResources.JobCandidate
WHERE JobCandidateID = 14;
GO
SELECT * FROM HumanResources.JobCandidate
```

If you look at the Results tab, you'll see that the row you tried to delete was not deleted. Additionally, you'll see that the inactive column is now a 1.

Triggers vs. Constraints

It's useful to compare triggers against constraints. Both have the primary benefit of ensuring that a desired operation is caught no matter how the data is modified. However, they both have their individual strengths.

EXAM TIP Triggers will catch modifications from all sources. If a database is updated through a variety of different sources (such as through functions, stored procedures, or applications) consider using a trigger. The trigger will catch all of the modifications.

For example, if I want to ensure that the value of a birth date column is in a certain range of dates, both a trigger and a constraint could successfully be used. Now, if the date is modified via a stored procedure, a T-SQL query, or an application, the modification can be checked and either prevented or rolled back if it's out of range. In comparison, a stored procedure could be created to check the data before doing a modification, but we can't ensure the stored procedure is the only method used to update the data.

Constraints work on the modification before the data is updated. AFTER triggers work on the modification after the update. From a performance perspective, this is significant. If we can use a constraint, we eliminate rework. Triggers to roll back the data change add work.

My wife and I have been doing some painting at our home. I could go to the paint store, pick out the paint, paint the room, and then see if my wife likes the color. If she doesn't like it, I'll either never hear the end of it, or I'll be repainting that room in the color of her choice. That would be how the trigger adds *rework* if it's used to roll back data entries. No thank you.

Instead, I bring my wife to the store to pick a color. If I reach for the neon green, she calmly shakes her head preventing my error just as a database constraint would prevent needless rework on the database. Ultimately, we pick a color both of us like. If she's happy, I'm happy. As Bob Spiker, a sharp (though philosophical) system engineer student once shared with me, "Happy wife. Happy life." Use constraints as your first choice in preventing invalid data entry, and use triggers to enforce more complex business logic and to add customized error messages.

While constraints perform the best, their capability is frequently limited. Consider the following information when deciding to use a constraint or a trigger.

- DML triggers support all the functionality of constraints, but they can also contain complex processing logic using T-SQL code.

- DML triggers can include customized messages and complex error handling. Constraints can only use standard system error messages.

- Referential integrity will be maintained through constraints (FK and PK) much more efficiently than with triggers.

- Triggers can take action based on referential integrity errors enforced through constraints (such as sending the data to another table).

Embedding Functions and Other Database Objects

While our examples with triggers were relatively straightforward, you can get quite sophisticated with triggers. For instance, you can embed built-in or user-defined functions, raise error messages, execute stored procedures, and more.

One easy way to remember what can be done with a trigger is to think of it as a special type of stored procedure. Almost anything that can be embedded within a stored procedure can be embedded with a trigger. The significant difference is that triggers are not intended to return data and can't be called directly.

In the following exercise, we'll create a DML trigger to move data based on a flag being set. First, we'll create an archive table to store inactive users. Next, we'll modify our AuditAccess table to include a Boolean flag for InactiveStatus. Then, we'll add a trigger to move the data if the Boolean flag is true. Lastly, we'll test it.

Exercise 6.3: Create a DML Trigger to Archive Data

1. Open a New Query window in SSMS.

2. Use the following script to create a table named ArchiveAuditAccess. Since we will import the data directly from the AuditAccess table, we'll remove the PRIMARY KEY constraint from the table. Notice we are using the *bit* data type for InactiveStatus. If a user is inactive, we'll set this to a 1. Further, if we put a user into this archive table and the bit is not set, we'll use a default of 1.

```
USE Chapter6;
CREATE TABLE dbo.ArchiveAuditAccess
(
  ArchiveAuditAccessID int NOT NULL,
  UserName varchar(50) NOT NULL,
  LoginTime datetime NULL,
  InactiveStatus bit NULL
    CONSTRAINT [DF_Inactive] DEFAULT 1
);
```

3. Now we'll modify the original AuditAccess table by adding the same InactiveStatus field with the following script:

```
ALTER TABLE dbo.AuditAccess
ADD InactiveStatus bit NULL;
```

4. To verify that our tables are what we want, enter the following SELECT statements. The ArchiveAuditAccess table should be empty, but with four columns, while the AuditAccess table should have data that we entered during an earlier exercise.

```
SELECT * FROM ArchiveAuditAccess
SELECT * FROM AuditAccess
```

5. Now we'll create our trigger. To keep things simple, first we'll make sure that only one row is modified at a time. The following script will create the trigger:

```
CREATE TRIGGER trgArchiveInactiveUsers
ON AuditAccess
AFTER UPDATE
AS
IF (SELECT COUNT(*) FROM inserted) > 1
Begin
    RAISERROR ('Only one user can be modified at a time.', 16, 10) WITH
LOG
    ROLLBACK TRAN
    RETURN
End
```

6. To test it, let's try to set the inactive status on all users to 0. The following script should cause our error to be raised:

```
UPDATE AuditAccess
SET InactiveStatus = 0
```

7. Now we can modify the trigger to add a check to see if the bit has been modified to 1. If it has, we'll insert all the rows for the user into our ArchiveAuditAccess table and delete all of the rows for this user from the AuditAccess table. The bolded text that follows is what is added to the script:

```
ALTER TRIGGER trgArchiveInactiveUsers
ON AuditAccess AFTER UPDATE
AS
IF (SELECT COUNT(*) FROM inserted) > 1
Begin
    RAISERROR ('Only one user can be modified at a time.', 16, 10) WITH
LOG
    ROLLBACK TRAN
    RETURN
End
IF (SELECT InactiveStatus FROM inserted) = 1
Begin
    DECLARE @UserName varchar (20)
    SET @UserName = (SELECT UserName FROM inserted)
    -- Add the rows to the Archive table
      INSERT INTO ArchiveAuditAccess
      SELECT * FROM AuditAccess
      WHERE UserName = @UserName
    -- Delete the rows from the source table
    DELETE FROM AuditAccess
      WHERE UserName = @UserName
    RAISERROR ('User has been archived', 16, 10)
End
```

TIP If you created the trgPreventDeletion as demonstrated earlier in this chapter, you can disable it with the following command so this exercise will work:

```
DISABLE TRIGGER trgPreventDeletion ON AuditAccess;
```

8. Let's give it a try. The following script updates the bit to a 1 and should fire your trigger:

```
UPDATE AuditAccess
SET InactiveStatus = 1
WHERE AuditAccessID = 1
```

9. To see what has been modified, use this script:

```
SELECT * FROM ArchiveAuditAccess
SELECT * FROM AuditAccess
```

INSTEAD OF

Most triggers are AFTER triggers. In other words, they fire after the DML statement has occurred. DML triggers can also be created as INSTEAD OF triggers. Just as the name implies, an INSTEAD OF trigger will fire instead of the DML statement that triggered it.

INSTEAD OF triggers are not available for DDL triggers.

For Updateable Views

The classic reason to use an INSTEAD OF trigger is for a VIEW that can't otherwise be updated. Most VIEWS can be updated. Let's first look at a simple VIEW:

```
CREATE VIEW vwStockQuotes AS
SELECT Symbol, Date, High, Low, ClosingPrice, SharesSold
FROM Stocks
```

NOTE This script won't run against any databases we've been working with. It's used as an example only.

As new stock data is received we can insert them into the VIEW and they will be inserted into the underlying table. However, if these are stock data, a single table could easily comprise millions of rows.

Instead of a single table, we could divide the data into two (or more) tables and use a UNION clause to combine the data in a distributable VIEW. Let's say we horizontally partition the stock table into two tables: StocksAL (for all the stocks that start with the letters A through L), and StocksKZ (for all the stocks that start with the letters K through Z). We could further optimize the partitioned table by storing the different partitions on different physical disks.

Our distributed VIEW would be created with a script like the following:

```
CREATE VIEW vwStockQuotes AS
SELECT Symbol, Date, High, Low, ClosingPrice, SharesSold
```

```
FROM StocksAL
UNION
SELECT Symbol, Date, High, Low, ClosingPrice, SharesSold
FROM StocksKZ
```

 NOTE This script will not run against any databases we have been working with. It is used as an example only.

While this VIEW would work great for viewing the data, the data cannot be updated through the VIEW because of the UNION clause. Let's say that, occasionally, the Shares-Sold column needs to be updated to account for only finalized sales. Unfortunately, VIEWs created with a UNION clause can't be directly updated. The VIEW isn't intelligent enough to know that an update to SharesSold for the MSFT stock on a given date would need to update the StocksKZ table. Instead, we would create an INSTEAD OF trigger.

 EXAM TIP Distributed VIEWs can not be updated directly since they are created with a UNION clause. To update data in a distributed VIEW, use a DML INSTEAD OF trigger.

By creating an INSTEAD OF trigger on the VIEW, we can cause any updates to execute the trigger instead of trying to do the update to the VIEW directly. The trigger would include logic to determine which base table to update.

Exercise 6.4: Create an INSTEAD OF DML Trigger to Use with a Distributed VIEW

1. Create a New Query window in SSMS.

2. Use the following script to create a table named State and populate it with some data. We'll use this as a lookup table to verify that a state exists.

```
USE Chapter6;
GO
CREATE TABLE dbo.State
(
   StateID char(2) NOT NULL,
   CONSTRAINT [PK_State_StateID] PRIMARY KEY CLUSTERED
   (
         StateID
   )
);
GO
--Populate the table
INSERT INTO State VALUES('VA');
INSERT INTO State VALUES('CA');
INSERT INTO State VALUES('OK');
INSERT INTO State VALUES('WI');
```

3. We'll now create two ZipState tables (one for ZIP codes that start with the numbers 1 through 5, and the other for ZIP codes that start with

numbers 6 through 9) and establish a relationship between the tables on the StateID columns. After creating the tables, we'll populate them with some data.

```
CREATE TABLE dbo.ZipState1To5(
  ZipState1To5ID int IDENTITY(1,1) NOT NULL,
  ZipCode int NOT NULL,
  State char(2) NOT NULL,
    CONSTRAINT FK_State_State1To5 FOREIGN KEY(State)
        REFERENCES dbo.State(StateID),
  CONSTRAINT [PK_ZipState_ZipState1To5ID] PRIMARY KEY CLUSTERED
  (
        ZipState1To5ID
  )
);
GO
CREATE TABLE dbo.ZipState6To9(
  ZipState6To9ID int IDENTITY(1,1) NOT NULL,
  ZipCode int NOT NULL,
  State char(2) NOT NULL,
    CONSTRAINT FK_State_State6To9 FOREIGN KEY(State)
        REFERENCES dbo.State(StateID),
  CONSTRAINT [PK_ZipState_ZipState6To9ID] PRIMARY KEY CLUSTERED
  (
        ZipState6To9ID
  )
);
--Populate the tables
INSERT INTO ZipState1To5 (ZipCode, State) VALUES(23462,'VA');
INSERT INTO ZipState1To5 (ZipCode, State) VALUES(44562,'WI');
INSERT INTO ZipState6To9 (ZipCode, State) VALUES(94562,'CA');
INSERT INTO ZipState6To9 (ZipCode, State) VALUES(74562,'OK');
```

4. Create a distributed VIEW using the two tables with the following script:

```
CREATE VIEW vwZips AS
    SELECT ZipState1To5ID AS ZipStateID, ZipCode, State
    FROM ZipState1To5
UNION
    SELECT ZipState6To9ID, ZipCode, State
    FROM ZipState6To9
```

5. To view the data from the VIEW, use the following query:

```
SELECT * FROM vwZips
```

6. Create an error by trying to modify the data via the VIEW. We can do this with the following script. (This script will produce an error similar to Figure 6-13.)

Figure 6-13

An error from UPDATE into the distributed VIEW

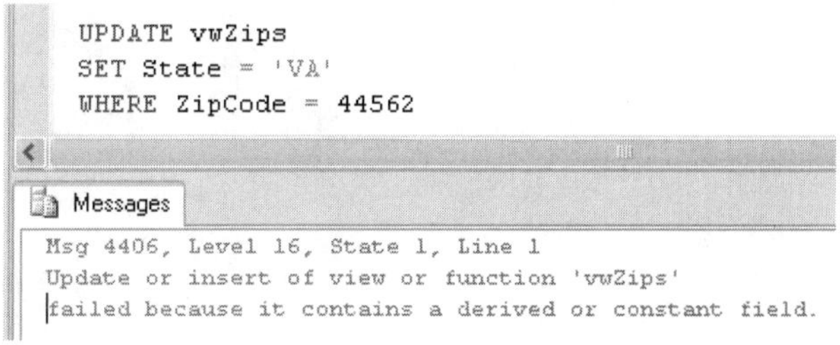

```
UPDATE vwZips
SET State = 'VA'
WHERE ZipCode = 44562
```

```
Messages
Msg 4406, Level 16, State 1, Line 1
Update or insert of view or function 'vwZips'
failed because it contains a derived or constant field.
```

```
UPDATE vwZips
SET State = 'VA'
WHERE ZipCode = 44562
```

7. To prevent the error, we'll create an INSTEAD OF trigger to update the correct underlying table. The following script will create the trigger:

```
CREATE TRIGGER trgUpdateVwZips
ON vwZips
INSTEAD OF UPDATE
AS
DECLARE @Zip int
DECLARE @State char(2)
--Get the zip and state from the inserted table
Set @Zip = (SELECT ZipCode FROM inserted)
Set @State = (SELECT State FROM inserted)
If @Zip < 60000
   --ZipCode is in the ZipState1To5 table
   UPDATE ZipState1To5
        SET State = @State
        WHERE ZipCode = @Zip
ELSE
   --ZipCode is in the ZipState6To9 table
   UPDATE ZipState6To9
        SET State = @State
        WHERE ZipCode = @Zip
```

Modify the data by using an UPDATE against the VIEW. We'll first use a SELECT statement to see what the data is before the UPDATE, and then after the update use another SELECT statement. After executing the following query, your display should look similar to Figure 6-14. Note that when the trigger fires the output is red. This is normal.

Figure 6-14

A successful update of a distributed VIEW with an INSTEAD OF trigger

```
SELECT * FROM vwZips;
UPDATE vwZips
SET State = 'WI'
WHERE ZipCode = 44562;
SELECT * FROM vwZips
```

	ZipStateID	ZipCode	State
1	1	23462	VA
2	1	94562	CA
3	2	44562	VA
4	2	74562	OK

	ZipStateID	ZipCode	State
1	1	23462	VA
2	1	94562	CA
3	2	44562	WI
4	2	74562	OK

```
SELECT * FROM vwZips;
UPDATE vwZips
SET State = 'WI'
WHERE ZipCode = 44562;
SELECT * FROM vwZips
```

Using INSTEAD OF for Failed Imports

Another possible reason to use INSTEAD OF triggers is when data will be imported to a table, but you know that some of the data will not meet the constraint testing.

For example, let's say that you regularly import data received from several different business partners into a table named SalesLeads. Your goal is to import the data into a table, but you find that the data often have typos or other inconsistencies that cause it to fail. Some are as simple as the state abbreviation being misspelled, causing it to fail a referential integrity check with another table. Others have a Boolean column randomly defined as *True, T, Yes, Y,* or *1,* instead of one single definition.

Using the DML INSTEAD OF trigger, we can cause a different action to occur instead of the failed import. The INSTEAD OF trigger would examine the data for each row before the INSERT. If the data was acceptable, it would allow the INSERT. If the data wasn't acceptable, it would instead insert the data into a temporary table.

In the following exercise, we'll create an INSTEAD OF DML trigger that moves data into a temporary table if it fails certain types of checks. Imagine that the company you work for just discovered that many entries aren't getting added to the AuditAccess table because the INSERT statements are failing constraint checking. You are tasked with creating an INSTEAD OF trigger to instead insert this data into a temporary table to be examined later.

Exercise 6.5: Create an INSTEAD OF DML Trigger to Record Errors

1. Create a New Query window in SSMS.

2. If you didn't do the previous exercise, use the following script to create a table named State and then populate it with some data. We'll use this as a lookup table to verify that a state exists.

```
USE Chapter6;
GO
CREATE TABLE dbo.State
(
   StateID char(2) NOT NULL,
   CONSTRAINT [PK_State_StateID] PRIMARY KEY CLUSTERED
   (
         StateID
     )
);
GO
--Populate the table
INSERT INTO State VALUES('VA');
INSERT INTO State VALUES('CA');
INSERT INTO State VALUES('OK');
INSERT INTO State VALUES('WI');
```

3. Next, we'll create a ZipState table (similar to what was created in a demonstration earlier in this chapter), and establish a relationship between the tables on the StateID columns. After creating it, we'll populate it with some valid data.

CAUTION   If you created the ZipState table while following along earlier in the chapter, you must first drop it using the DROP TABLE dbo.ZipState command.

```
CREATE TABLE dbo.ZipState(
  ZipStateID int NOT NULL,
  ZipCode int NOT NULL,
  State char(2) NOT NULL,
       CONSTRAINT FK_State_State FOREIGN KEY(State)
         REFERENCES dbo.State(StateID),
  CONSTRAINT [PK_ZipState_ZipStateID] PRIMARY KEY CLUSTERED
  (
       ZipStateID      )
);
GO
--Populate the table
INSERT INTO ZipState (ZipStateID, ZipCode, State) VALUES(1,23462,'VA');
INSERT INTO ZipState (ZipStateID, ZipCode, State) VALUES(2,94562,'CA');
INSERT INTO ZipState (ZipStateID, ZipCode, State) VALUES(3, 74562,'OK');
INSERT INTO ZipState (ZipStateID, ZipCode, State) VALUES(4, 54562,'WI');
```

4. Simulate an error by trying to enter data with a state that doesn't exist (MM) in the referenced table. The following line will produce an error similar to Figure 6-15:

```
INSERT INTO ZipState (ZipStateID, ZipCode, State)
              VALUES(5, 54562,'MM');
```

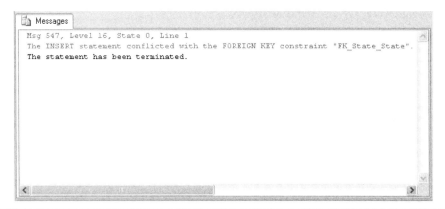

Figure 6-15   An error from INSERT

5. To prevent the error, we'll create an INSTEAD OF trigger to move it into an error table. First, create the error table with this script:

```
CREATE TABLE dbo.ZipStateError(
  ZipStateErrorID int IDENTITY(1,1) NOT NULL,
```

```
    ZipCode int NOT NULL,
    State char(2) NOT NULL,
    CONSTRAINT [PK_ZipState_ZipStateErrorID] PRIMARY KEY CLUSTERED
    (
          ZipStateErrorID
    )
);
```

6. Create the INSTEAD OF trigger by using the following script:

```
CREATE TRIGGER trgZipStateError
ON ZipState
INSTEAD OF INSERT
AS
DECLARE @State char(2)
DECLARE @Count int
SET @State = (SELECT State FROM inserted)
SET @Count = (SELECT Count(StateID) FROM State WHERE StateID = @State)
IF @Count = 0
-- Insert the data into the error table
BEGIN
    INSERT INTO ZipStateError
      SELECT ZipCode, State From inserted
    RAISERROR ('ZipStateError entry added ', 16, 10) WITH LOG
END
ELSE
-- Insert the data into the regular table
    INSERT INTO ZipState SELECT ZipCode,State, GetDate() FROM inserted
```

7. Before we try to enter bad data, let's look at our table contents with the following SELECT statements. The ZipState table should have four entries, while the ZipStateError table should be empty.

```
SELECT * FROM ZipState
SELECT * FROM ZipStateError
```

8. Reenter the line that failed before:

```
INSERT INTO ZipState (ZipStateID, ZipCode, State)
            VALUES(5, 54562,'MM');
```

Note that when the trigger fires, the output is red. This is normal.

9. By rerunning the same SELECT statements again, we can see that the data was not entered into the ZipState table, but was instead entered into the ZipStateError table:

```
SELECT * FROM ZipState;
SELECT * FROM ZipStateError;
```

DDL Triggers

An exciting new feature available in SQL Server 2005 is the use of DDL triggers. DDL triggers are very much like DML triggers except that they work on DDL statements and have a different scope.

DDL triggers can only be configured as AFTER triggers, not INSTEAD OF triggers.

DDL Triggers New to SQL Server 2005

Traditionally in Microsoft SQL Server, we only had Data Manipulation Language (DML) triggers which worked on DML statements such as INSERT, UPDATE and DELETE. Microsoft SQL Server 2005 introduced Data Definition Language (DDL) triggers which work on DDL statements such as CREATE, ALTER, DROP, and more.

From an auditing perspective this is huge. Now we can use a DDL trigger to audit the creation, modification, or deletion of server objects, such as databases or logins, and any objects within a database.

For example, management may want to know whenever a database is created, deleted, or modified. You can create a DDL trigger with a server scope designed to capture all executions of CREATE DATABASE, ALTER DATABASE, or DROP DATABASE statements. Depending on how it's written, the DDL trigger can log data such as the exact syntax of the executed statement, who executed it, and when. As a new feature that is listed on the test objectives, expect them to be heavily tested whenever they're listed on the objectives. They are explicitly listed on the 70-431 and 70-441 objectives, and indirectly on the 70-442 objectives. Ensure you understand the scope (server and database), the statements that cause them to be fired (CREATE, ALTER, DROP, and more), and some of the uses.

DDL Trigger Statements

Data Definition Language (DDL) triggers only fire in response to DDL statements. These include:

- CREATE
- ALTER
- DROP

As we discussed earlier, DML triggers can be configured on a table. Once an UPDATE trigger is configured, any UPDATE statement issued against the table fires the trigger.

DDL triggers are a little more specific. Instead of just writing a DDL CREATE trigger on the server to monitor all CREATE statements, we must specify what objects we're interested in with statements such as CREATE_DATABASE or CREATE_TABLE. Notice how intuitively these events are named. The CREATE DATABASE statement (with a space between the two words) will raise the CREATE_DATABASE event (with an underscore between the two words).

DDL triggers can be created for server-level events (such as CREATE DATABASE or CREATE LOGINS). They can also be created for database-level events (such as CREATE TABLE or CREATE VIEW). If you think about the SSMS Object Explorer, the difference becomes straightforward. If your actions affect objects within a database (such as tables, VIEWs, indexes, triggers, functions, and others), then it is a database-level event.

If the actions affect the instance, but not an existing database (such as databases, end-points, logins, and so on), then it is a server-level event.

We can also specify groups of DDL events to capture. For example, Figure 6-16 shows the DDL events that can be grouped together with a Server scope. By creating a trigger and specifying the DDL SERVER LEVEL EVENTS, it will capture all the possible DDL server events. Similarly, we can specify DDL DATABASE LEVEL EVENTS to capture all possible DDL events for a database.

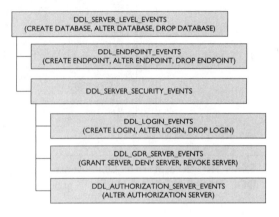

Figure 6-16
DDL SERVER
LEVEL EVENTS

DDL_SERVER_LEVEL_EVENTS
(CREATE DATABASE, ALTER DATABASE, DROP DATABASE)

DDL_ENDPOINT_EVENTS
(CREATE ENDPOINT, ALTER ENDPOINT, DROP ENDPOINT)

DDL_SERVER_SECURITY_EVENTS

DDL_LOGIN_EVENTS
(CREATE LOGIN, ALTER LOGIN, DROP LOGIN)

DDL_GDR_SERVER_EVENTS
(GRANT SERVER, DENY SERVER, REVOKE SERVER)

DDL_AUTHORIZATION_SERVER_EVENTS
(ALTER AUTHORIZATION SERVER)

EXAM TIP   To capture all DDL events at the server level, specify the DDL_SERVER_LEVEL EVENTS group in the DDL trigger definition. To capture all DDL events at the database level, specify the DDL_DATABASE_LEVEL_EVENTS group in the DDL trigger.

Notice the hierarchy in Figure 6-16. By specifying DDL_SERVER_LEVEL_EVENTS, it includes the CREATE DATABASE, ALTER DATABASE and DROP DATABASE statements, and all of the child events (ENDPOINT_EVENTS and SERVER_SECURITY EVENTS). Likewise, it's possible to specify DDL_SERVER_SECURITY_EVENTS, which would include all the LOGIN events, all of the GDR_SERVER events, and all of the AUTHORI-ZATION_SERVER events. Or, if desired, we can specify a particular event such as the CREATE LOGIN event.

DDL Trigger Scope

DDL triggers can be *server*-scoped or *database*-scoped.

Server-scoped triggers will respond to server-based DDL statements (such as CREATE DATABASE). Server-scoped triggers are stored in the Master database.

A database-scoped DDL trigger will monitor DDL statements executed on the database (such as ALTER TABLE). Database-scoped triggers are stored in the database.

Figures 6-16 through 6-20 show the DDL_DATABASE_LEVEL EVENTS. Obviously, many more events are associated with the database than with the server. But just as the server-level events have a hierarchy, the database-level events have a hierarchy. By specifying the DDL_DATABASE_LEVEL_EVENTS, all of the events listed in Figures 6-17 through 6-21 would be included.

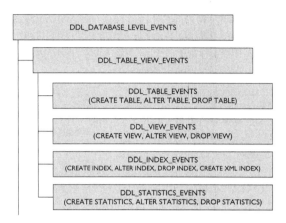

Figure 6-17
Database-level
and Table-View
DDL events

 EXAM TIP To capture all DDL events at the database level, specify the DDL_DATABASE_LEVEL EVENTS group in the DDL trigger definition.

As an example of a DDL trigger that can capture all database-level events, the following code can be used to create a database-level DDL trigger. First, let's create a table to capture the event.

```
USE Chapter6;
GO
CREATE TABLE DatabaseAudit
(
        AuditID int IDENTITY(100,1) NOT NULL,
        AuditEvent varchar(max) NULL,
        CONSTRAINT [PK_DatabaesAudit_AuditID2] PRIMARY KEY CLUSTERED
        (
                AuditID
        )
)
```

Next, we'll create the trigger with the following code:

```
Use Chapter6;
GO
CREATE TRIGGER trig_All_ddl_database
ON DATABASE FOR
DDL_DATABASE_LEVEL_EVENTS
AS
    PRINT 'Database DDL Trigger Fired.'
    INSERT INTO DatabaseAudit (AuditEvent)
    VALUES (EVENTDATA().value('(/EVENT_INSTANCE/TSQLCommand/CommandText)[1]',
'nvarchar(max)'))
```

To see the result of the trigger, create a table within the database using the following code. Since the CREATE TABLE statement is within the DATABASE LEVEL EVENTS (as shown in Figure 6-17), it will be captured.

```
USE Chapter6;
GO
CREATE TABLE TestTable
(
        TestID int IDENTITY(100,1) NOT NULL,
        TestData varchar(max) NULL,
);
GO
SELECT * FROM DatabaseAudit;
```

Figure 6-18 shows more DDL events under the DDL_DATABASE_LEVEL events.

Figure 6-18

Database-level database object DDL events

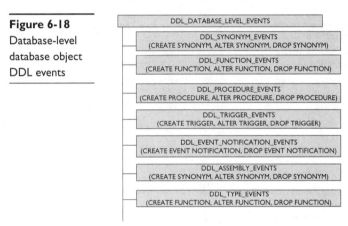

On a smaller scale, we could specify the DDL_DATABASE SECURITY EVENTS, and the DDL trigger would capture all the events listed in this hierarchy, which is shown in Figure 6-19. Figure 6-20 shows the SSB events under the DDL_DATABASE EVENTS. Figure 6-21 shows the XML Schema Collection and Partition events.

Figure 6-19

Database-level and database security DDL events

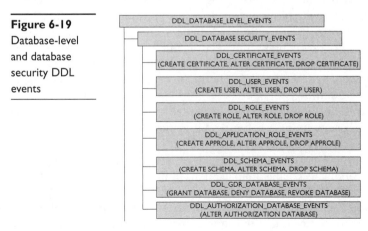

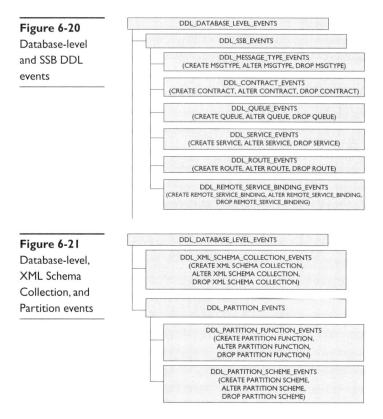

Figure 6-20
Database-level and SSB DDL events

Figure 6-21
Database-level, XML Schema Collection, and Partition events

Using DDL Triggers for Auditing

One of the primary purposes of a DDL trigger is to use it for auditing changes to either the server or a database.

Change management has become an important concept to grasp and implement within the IT community. The Gartner Group has released information from studies that indicate that as much as 80 percent of outages are due to people and processes. Only about 20 percent of outage durations are due to actual hardware failure. The other 80 percent is attributable to things like unauthorized changes, changes being made without following procedures, lack of procedures, human error, and other operator error or process failures.

With change management policies and procedures in place, when a need for a change occurs, instead of just implementing it, the process is slowed down so the impact of the change can be examined.

For example, modifying the schema of a table by deleting what appears to be an unused column, or renaming a column so it is more intuitive, may seem like a harmless change. However, this change will adversely affect any other database objects referencing that column. A critical stored procedure or a frequently queried VIEW could suddenly stop working. A change management policy would allow key players to examine the change using tools such as sp_depends to identify any object dependencies.

In addition to change management policies and procedures, an auditing strategy can be implemented that records the changes, including who did it and when they did it.

By creating an ALTER_TABLE trigger, you could catch any statements that altered a table and record the auditing information. Once the change is caught, the trigger can be programmed to record it in a table within the database, record it in a table in a special auditing database, use tools like Database Mail to immediately send an e-mail to the appropriate personnel, or even roll back the change.

 EXAM TIP Consider DDL triggers to audit schema changes to a database, or changes at the server level. A DDL trigger can catch the change and then record it (such as in a database table), notify DBAs with Database Mail, and/or roll back the change.

In the following exercise, we'll create a DDL trigger that will prevent any changes to tables by monitoring the ALTER TABLE statement. As with any trigger, you can change the content of the trigger to do what you want.

Exercise 6.6: Create a DDL Trigger to Prevent Changes to Tables

1. Open a New Query window in SSMS.

2. Use the following query to create a database-scoped trigger to monitor for the ALTER TABLE statement. The trigger will then give an error and roll back the statement.

```
USE Chapter6;
GO
CREATE TRIGGER NoTableChanges
ON DATABASE
FOR ALTER_TABLE
AS
    RAISERROR ('Tables cannot be altered in this database.', 16, 1)
    ROLLBACK;
```

3. Try to alter a table within the database with this statement:

```
ALTER TABLE dbo.ZipState
ADD NewColumn varChar(20) NULL;
```

The ALTER TABLE statement fails and is rolled back by the trigger.

In the following exercise, we'll create a DDL trigger that will monitor for the creation of databases and log the SQL script used to create the database in the application log. We could just as easily create an audit database and log the creation of databases in a table within the audit database.

Exercise 6.7: Create a DDL Trigger to Monitor the Creation of Databases

1. Open a New Query window in SSMS.

2. Use the following query to create a server-scoped trigger to monitor for the CREATE DATABASE statement. The trigger gives feedback, saying the event occurred, and then logs it into the application log.

```
CREATE TRIGGER ddl_trig_Create_DB
ON ALL SERVER
```

```
FOR CREATE_DATABASE
AS
    DECLARE @Statement nvarchar(max)
    Set @Statement = 'Database created with this statement: '
    Set @Statement = @Statement + (SELECT EVENTDATA().value('(/EVENT_
INSTANCE/TSQLCommand/CommandText)[1]','nvarchar(max)'))
SELECT @Statement
RAISERROR (@Statement, 16, 10) WITH LOG
```

3. Use the following statement to create a database and see the trigger in action:

```
CREATE DATABASE DeleteMe
```

4. Open the application log in Event Viewer to view the results. You should see something similar to Figure 6-22.

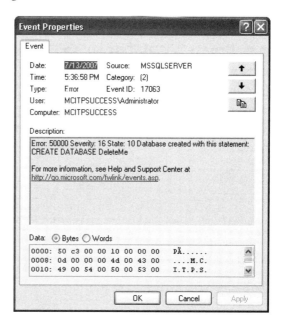

Figure 6-22
A CREATE DATABASE event logged from DDL trigger

Triggers vs. Event Notifications

Briefly, event notifications can be used to log and review changes or activity within the database, or to perform limited actions (such as send an e-mail) in response to an event. The Event Notification service is external to SQL, but easily works with SQL Server.

Sometimes event notifications are a better alternative to triggers. For a brief comparison, take a look at Table 6-10.

Disabling Triggers

Suppose you want to disable a trigger. For example, you may have an INSTEAD OF trigger that does significant analysis on inserted rows to determine if they should be

Triggers	Event Notifications
Respond to DML or DDL statements.	Respond to DDL or TRACE events.
Can include T-SQL or CLR managed code.	Do not run code, but instead just send an XML message to a Service Broker service.
Processed synchronously as part of a transaction.	Processed asynchronously. Not part of the transaction that caused the notification.
Must be processed locally.	Can be processed on a remote server.
Can roll back the transaction.	*Cannot* roll back the transaction.
Can be used with EXECUTE AS.	*Cannot* be used with EXECUTE AS.

Table 6-10   Triggers vs. Event Notifications

imported into the table or inserted into a different table. You are preparing to do a bulk import of data that you've sanitized and know should be in this table. You could disable the INSTEAD OF trigger to speed up the bulk import.

Triggers can be disabled in two ways:

- Disable the trigger directly:

```
DISABLE TRIGGER trgTriggerName ON tablename --(DML only)
DISABLE TRIGGER trgTriggerName ON DATABASE --(or ALL SERVER) (DDL Only)
```

- Alter the table and disable the trigger:

```
ALTER TABLE tablename DISABLE TRIGGER trg_TriggerName
```

Of course, you could drop a trigger completely, but if you needed it again in the future, you'd have to re-create it.

In the following exercise, we'll disable some of the triggers we've created in previous exercises.

Exercise 6.8: Disable DML and DDL Triggers

1. Open a New Query window in SSMS.

2. Enter the following text to disable the DML trigger created on the AuditAccess table:

```
DISABLE TRIGGER trgPreventDeletion on AuditAccess
```

3. Use the following script to disable the DML trigger created in AdventureWorks on the Production.Product table:

```
USE AdventureWorks;
GO
ALTER TABLE Production.Product DISABLE TRIGGER trgPriceControl
```

4. Enter this script to disable the server-scoped DDL trigger that is monitoring the creation of databases:

```
DISABLE TRIGGER ddl_trig_Create_DB
ON ALL SERVER
```

5. Use the following script to disable the database-scoped DDL trigger that is preventing the altering of tables:

```
USE Chapter6;
DISABLE TRIGGER NoTableChanges
ON DATABASE
```

Recursive and Nested Triggers

I looked up *recursion* in the dictionary once, and it gave a brief explanation and then said, "See Recursion." I was there for hours as I kept looking up *recursion* again and again. Not really, but hopefully you see the point. Recursion is the process of a procedure calling itself, and in effect repeating the same thing over and over. To be meaningful, recursion in a program includes a check to see if the program should do it again, or determine whether it's already done.

Recursive triggers allow both indirect and direct recursion. *Indirect* recursion is where an update to Table1 fires a trigger that affects Table2 that fires a trigger that updates Table1 again. *Direct* recursion is where an update to Table1 fires a trigger that affects Table1 again and then fires the trigger again.

Only 32 levels of recursion, or nested triggers, are allowed. If the triggers exceed 32, all nested triggers are rolled back. Recursion can get quite complex quickly. And if not programmed correctly, it can be quite expensive in terms of processing. Because of this, it's common to see recursion turned off.

To disable direct recursion, use the ALTER DATABASE statement with the RECURSIVE_TRIGGERS setting. To disable indirect recursion, use the sp_configure command to set the nested triggers server option to 0. It's also possible to set the properties of the server to allow or disallow nested triggers in the properties of the instance within SSMS.

INSTEAD OF triggers are not called recursively. Consider an INSERT INSTEAD OF trigger. An INSERT statement tries to insert a row. Instead, the trigger fires and examines the data. If it passes the check, it inserts the data into the row. The second INSERT does not fire the INSTEAD OF trigger.

In the following exercise, we'll set the server to allow nested triggers.

Exercise 6.9: Disable Nested Triggers within an Instance

1. Launch SSMS.

2. Right-click the instance and select Properties.

3. On the Select A Page pane, choose Advanced.

4. In the Miscellaneous settings, modify the Allow Triggers To Fire Others setting to False. Your display should look similar to Figure 6-23.

Figure 6-23
Disabling nested triggers within an instance

Common Language Runtime (CLR) Integration

New to SQL Server 2005 is the integration of Common Language Runtime (CLR) code into SQL Server. This lets us create CLR-based database objects. In other words, we can create CLR programs (such as Dynamic Link Libraries or DLLs) in programs outside of SQL Server 2005. Then, this CLR program can be integrated into SQL Server 2005 by creating an object such as a CLR-integrated stored procedure.

We are able to use C#, Visual Basic, or any other .NET programming language to create stored procedures, triggers, user-defined types, and user-defined functions. By using a full-featured programming language, we can get much more sophisticated in our code than T-SQL allows. Further, CLR is managed code giving us many benefits related to code safety and security.

One of the biggest benefits of CLR-integrated code is the performance gain we enjoy when doing complex calculations, or the significant manipulation of text type data. Any time we need to perform computation-intensive operations, CLR code will execute much more quickly than straight T-SQL.

EXAM TIP   If complex comparisons, advanced calculations, or significant text manipulation are required, consider using a CLR-integrated database object, such as a function created as a CLR-integrated function.

Another benefit of a CLR-integrated object is its ability to access files outside of the database. While some extended stored procedures can be used to access external files, this feature has been deprecated in SQL Server 2005 and is normally restricted due to security issues. However, instead of having an extended stored procedure access external files, a CLR-integrated object can be created to access the external files.

EXAM TIP When replacing extended stored procedures, consider using CLR-integrated objects created from managed code (a .NET language such as Visual Basic or C #).

And, of course, we have the benefit of flexibility when using a .NET programming language. Assemblies created in a robust programming language such as C# or Visual Basic can do just about anything that is needed.

The MCITP tests don't require you to create CLR-integrated database objects—only to know that they exist and what the benefits are. However, let's take a quick look at the process of creating a CLR stored procedure.

Five steps are required to create a CLR stored procedure:

1. Create a class in a .NET Framework language. This could be C#, VB, or any other language you choose. The code executed in the CLR integrated function would be defined as a static or shared method within a class.

2. Build the assembly.

3. Register the assembly in SQL Server.

4. Facilitate the use of CLR-enabled code in the database.

5. Create a SQL Server object (such as a function or stored procedure) that references the registered assembly.

The first three steps of the process would be similar if we were creating any type of CLR-integrated objects (triggers, functions, stored procedures, or user-defined data types). In the next exercise, we'll see an example of creating a CLR-integrated function. In Chapter 9, we'll create a CLR-integrated stored procedure in an exercise.

Execution Context

Security can become a concern when dealing with CLR-integrated objects. Since they are created completely external to SQL Server, there's no way of knowing exactly what they are doing (unless you view the code). SQL Server protects itself by creating CLR-integrated objects using the SAFE permission, which prevents it from accessing anything external to SQL Server. However, if you want to change this, it can be done (we'll see how in Exercise 6.10). Additionally, you may want your function, stored procedure, or other object to execute with elevated permissions. This can also be done using the EXECUTE AS clause.

One of the big benefits of many programmable database objects is that you can grant permissions to users to access them without having to grant users access to underlying tables. For example, we can grant access to a VIEW without explicitly granting access to the underlying table.

A couple of exceptions exist, however. We'll explore permissions more in the security chapters, but for now consider that some objects—like tables, VIEWs, and stored procedures—can be granted individual permissions like INSERT, UPDATE, and EXECUTE. Nevertheless, some other actions can't be granted individually.

For example, TRUNCATE TABLE can't be granted to users. Instead, a user must be granted the ALTER permission on a table in order to truncate a table.

NOTE TRUNCATE TABLE will delete all the data in a table. However, unlike the DELETE statement that logs the deletion of each individual row in the transaction log, the TRUNCATE TABLE statement removes all the pages for the table, and afterward shows no record of which rows were deleted.

One of the core principles of security is the Principle of Least Privilege. In other words, we only grant users the permission they need to do the job. Granting ALTER permission on a table might be much more than we want to grant.

To get around this, we can use the EXECUTE AS clause to execute a function, stored procedure, trigger, or CLR-integrated object in the context of another user. EXECUTE AS can be used for stored procedures, queues, triggers, and most functions to alter the execution context.

In addition to identifying the user that the object will execute as, we can also identify specific permissions that are allowed. The permissions available in the EXECUTE AS clause are listed in Table 6-11.

Permission	Description
SAFE	Most restrictive. Allows access internal to the database and server only.
EXTERNAL_ACCESS	Same as SAFE permission, but can also access external resources, such as files, network shares, and the Registry.
UNSAFE	Unrestricted. Can access anything in or out of SQL Server, including unmanaged code.

Table 6-11 Execution Context Permissions

EXAM TIP If you need to grant access to external files, CLR-integrated objects can be created using the EXTERNAL_ACCESS permission. SAFE will not grant access to external files, and UNSAFE is too much access.

We'll explore the EXECUTE AS clause in more detail in Chapter 8. This previous explanation just shows the permissions we can set to allow our assemblies to access data outside of the database or to restrict access. Some examples of EXECUTE AS will be shown in Chapter 8.

The following exercise creates and compiles a basic dynamic link library (DLL) in Visual Basic, adds the DLL to a database as an assembly, creates a function using the assembly, and executes the function.

Exercise 6.10: Create a CLR Assembly

1. Press WINDOWS+E to open Windows Explorer. Browse to the root of C:\ and create a folder named MCITPSuccess.

2. In the MCITPSuccess folder, create a new text document. Double-click the New Text Document and enter the following code into it:

```
Imports Microsoft.SqlServer.Server
Imports System.Data.SqlClient
Public Class WeekdayClass
    <SqlFunction(DataAccess:=DataAccessKind.Read)> _
        Public Shared Function fn_Happy(ByVal dt As _
            System.Data.SqlTypes.SqlDateTime) As String
        If dt.IsNull Then
            Return WeekdayName(Weekday(Today()))
        Else
            Return WeekdayName(Weekday(dt))
        End If
    End Function
End Class
```

 NOTE The WeekdayClass class has only one function named fn_Happy. It will accept a date, or default to today's date. It uses three date functions (WeekdayName, Weekday, and Today) to determine what day of the week it is. It then outputs the name of the weekday for the date.

3. In Notepad, select File | Save As...

4. In the Save As dialog box, enter the File name as "happy_dll.vb", including the quotes.

 NOTE By entering the quotes around the file name, you save it with the extension of vb. Without the quotes, it would be saved as a text file and the rest of this procedure wouldn't work. The Visual Basic file (happy_dll.vb) will be compiled to create a dynamic link library (DLL) file.

5. Using Windows Explorer, browse to the C:\WINDOWS\Microsoft.NET\ Framework\ directory. Identify the full name of the folder that holds the v2 framework and write it down here: _____. In Figure 6-24, you can see it as v2.0.50727.

Figure 6-24
Framework v2

```
⊟ 🗀 Microsoft.NET
  ⊟ 🗀 Framework
      🗀 v1.0.3705
    ⊞ 🗀 v1.1.4322
    ⊞ 🗀 v2.0.50727
```

6. Press WINDOWS+R to open the run line. Enter **cmd** to access the command line.

7. At the command line, enter the following command. If your Framework version is different, substitute the correct directory identified in step 5. This directory holds the Visual Basic compiler (vbc) we will use to compile our program.

```
cd c:\WINDOWS\Microsoft.NET\Framework\v2.0.50727
```

8. Enter the following command to compile the Visual Basic file you saved as happy_dll.vb:

```
vbc /target:library c:\MCITPSuccess\happy_dll.vb
```

9. Using Windows Explorer, verify that a file named happy_dll.dll has been created in your MCITPSuccess folder.

10. Open SSMS and create a new query window.

11. If a Chapter6 database doesn't exist, create it with the following script:

```
USE Master;
GO
CREATE Database Chapter6
```

12. Enter the following query to create an assembly in the Chapter6 database:

```
USE Chapter6;
GO
CREATE ASSEMBLY assyMCITPSuccess
FROM 'c:\MCITPSuccess\happy_dll.dll'
WITH PERMISSION_SET = SAFE
```

13. Using SSMS, browse to the Chapter6 | Programmability | Assemblies container. Right-click the Assemblies container and click Refresh. Your display should look similar to Figure 6-25, showing that the assyMCITPSuccess assembly has been created.

Figure 6-25

The assyMCITP-Success assembly

14. Right-click the assyMCITPSuccess assembly and select Properties. Your display should look like Figure 6-26. Change the permission to External Access and click OK. This will fail. Read the error and click OK. Click Cancel.

Figure 6-26 The Properties page of assyMCITPSuccess assembly

NOTE Before the permissions can be changed, the owner of the assembly must have the appropriate permission and the database must have the TRUSTWORTHY database property turned on, or the assembly must be signed with a certificate or key using the appropriate permission. The TRUSTWORTHY database property is used to indicate whether or not the SQL Server instance trusts the database and the contents within it. TRUSTWORTHY can be turned on with the following command:

```
ALTER DATABASE Chapter6
    SET Trustworthy ON
```

15. Enter the following script to create a user-defined function that will access the assembly:

```
USE Chapter6
GO
CREATE FUNCTION udfHappy(@dt as datetime)
RETURNS NVARCHAR(4000)
AS EXTERNAL NAME assyMCITPSuccess.WeekdayClass.fn_Happy
```

Note the structure of the external name. First is the assembly we created in SQL Server, next is the name of the class within the DLL created from the Visual Basic file (pointed to by the assembly), and last is the function within the class.

16. Before we can execute the stored procedure, we must enable execution of the user code in the .NET Framework. Execution of CLR code is disabled by default. Use the following script to set the 'clr enabled' option to on:

```
USE master;
GO
EXEC sp_configure 'show advanced option', '1';
GO
EXEC sp_configure 'clr enabled', '1';
RECONFIGURE;
```

17. Test the function using the following query:

```
USE Chapter6;
GO
SELECT  'Happy ' + dbo.udfHappy(NULL) + '!'
SELECT  'Happy ' + dbo.udfHappy('01/01/2008') + '!'
```

Chapter Review

Advanced database objects give database administrators a significant amount of flexibility when implementing database solutions. In this chapter, we covered functions, triggers, and CLR integration.

SQL Server 2005 provides us with a wealth of built-in functions. A successful DBA knows generally what these are, and more importantly, knows how to find more information when it's time to use them. When the built-in objects don't meet our needs, we can create our own built-in functions and stored procedures.

Triggers are very effective at implementing auditing strategies, whether auditing the change of data or changes to the database or server. DML triggers monitor change of the data by responding to INSERT, UPDATE, and DELETE events. DDL triggers monitor changes to the server or databases by responding to CREATE, ALTER, and DROP events.

Many database objects can be integrated with CLR. Assemblies can be created in any .NET programming language, registered within SQL server, and embedded in stored procedures, triggers, user-defined data types, and many functions.

Additional Study

Self-Study Exercises

- Use BOL to look up and execute the following built-in functions: UPPER, SYSTEM_USER, and COUNT.

- Create a user-defined stored procedure for each of the built-in functions you just looked up and executed.

- Create a trigger on a table to monitor whenever data is changed in a table. Log who did it and when, into a separate table.

- Create a trigger to identify when a database is created and log an entry in the application log.
- Create an INSTEAD OF trigger on a VIEW.

BOL Topics

- Functions (Transact-SQL)
- User-Defined Functions (Database Engine)
- Understanding DDL Triggers
- Designing DDL Triggers
- DDL Events for Use with DDL Triggers
- Introduction to Common Language Runtime (CLR) Integration
- CLR Integration Security

Summary of What You Need to Know

70-431

This entire chapter includes information required for the 70-431 test. However, if there is a focus of the test it would be on triggers, so be sure you understand the use of triggers, especially the difference between DDL and DML triggers, and their associated options.

You should understand the general purpose and usage of functions and CLR integration as well.

70-441

While all the material in this chapter can be found on the 70-441 test, the heaviest focus is on triggers. Expect to see questions on both DML and DDL triggers. Functions—including creating your own user-defined functions—should also be understood well.

70-442

The 70-442 objectives state that candidates should be expert in troubleshooting programming objects (such as triggers and functions). While you can expect questions from any topic in this chapter, you probably will not see many.

Questions

70-431

1. You assist in the management of a gaming web site with SQL Server 2005 as a back-end database. You are tasked with creating a function that returns scalar information about the activity time of any user currently logged in. How can you do this?

    A. Create a function that returns a number representing the number of hours the user has been logged in for the current day.

    B. Create a function that returns a list of values representing the days the user has been logged in.

    C. Create a function that returns a list of values representing the number of hours a user has been logged in for each day of the current month.

    D. Create a function that launches a trigger that subtracts the current time from the original logged in time.

2. You are tasked with importing weather data into your SQL Server 2005 database named Hurricanes, from an Access database. The Hurricane database includes a Hurricanes table with a StateCode foreign key column and a StateAffected table with a StateCode primary key column. A primary/foreign key relationship has been defined between the tables on the StateCode column. Referential integrity will ensure that records can't be added to the Hurricanes table with a StateCode that does not exist in the StateAffected table. However, you want to ensure that the import succeeds even if the StateCode doesn't exist in the StateAffected table. What can you do?

    A. Nothing. This can't be overwritten. You must ensure the imported data is in the correct format.

    B. Create a DML INSTEAD OF trigger that writes the failed records to a file or table.

    C. Create a DML AFTER trigger that writes the failed records to a file or table.

    D. Create a DDL INSTEAD OF trigger that writes the failed records to a file or table.

3. Someone recently made changes to the structure of some tables in a database that you manage on a SQL Server 2005 database, and it resulted in a critical application no longer working. The CEO wanted to know who made the change, but it was not possible to identify who did it. The CEO dictated a company policy that now mandates that all changes to the database schema be tracked. What should you do?

    A. Update your résumé before they discover it was you.

    B. Implement a DDL trigger.

    C. Implement a DML trigger.

    D. Create a function to modify the schema.

4. Which of the following statements can be used to temporarily disable a trigger? (Choose two.)

    A. ALTER TABLE *tablename* DISABLE TRIGGER trg_*TriggerName*

    B. ALTER TRIGGER trg_*TriggerName* Disable

    C. DROP TRIGGER trg_*TriggerName*

    D. DISABLE TRIGGER trg_*TriggerName* ON *tablename*

5. You are involved in a project creating a scientific web application with a back-end database running SQL Server 2005. The application must quickly display the results of calculation-intensive operations and support as many as 500

simultaneous users. You are tasked with ensuring that the database processes calculations as quickly and efficiently as possible. What should you do?

A. Implement CLR-stored procedures in the database.

B. Implement compiled Transact-SQL queries in the application.

C. Implement Reporting Services in the application.

D. Buy a bigger processor.

70-441

1. You need to define a function that will determine if a row within a table can be deleted. The function will need to verify complex string values and perform advanced calculations. What should you create?

A. Create a function as a stored procedure.

B. Create a function as a trigger.

C. Create a function as a CLR integrated function.

D. Create a function from T-SQL.

2. Your Sales database is using an extended stored procedure to call an external COM component to recalculate bonus information for sales personnel when orders are placed by a sales person. The Bonus information is in a calculated column. You are asked to eliminate the use of the extended stored procedure. What would you do?

A. Write a new extended stored procedure to call the COM component. Write a trigger to execute the extended stored procedure when a sale occurs so as to update the Bonus column.

B. Rewrite the COM component in a .NET language. Write a trigger to call the new component when a sale occurs so as to update the Bonus column.

C. Create a CLR-integrated user-defined function to call the COM component. Create an UPDATE trigger to execute the function when a sale occurs to update the Bonus column.

D. Write a stored procedure to call the COM component and have the COM component update the Bonus column when a sale occurs.

3. You are tasked with ensuring that sales records are not deleted from the Sales database unless a specific routine is run to ensure several conditions are met. The routine performs string manipulation and advanced calculations. Users modify the Sales database using several different methods. What should you do?

A. Create a stored procedure to run the routine and then delete the records if the conditions are met.

B. Create a user-defined function to run the routine and then delete the records if the conditions are met.

    C. Create a DELETE trigger to run the routine and then roll back the deletion if the conditions are not met.

    D. Create a DDL trigger to run the routine and then roll back the deletion if the conditions are not met.

4. Last week, a DBA made a minor modification to a table within the Sales database which effectively broke some key VIEWs used by management. You are tasked with ensuring that the CIO is immediately notified of any changes to the Sales database. How can you do this?

    A. Create DML triggers that use Database Mail to send an e-mail message to the CIO as soon as the DML statement is executed.

    B. Create DDL triggers that use Database Mail to send an e-mail message to the CIO as soon as the DDL statement is executed.

    C. Create DML triggers that use SQL Mail to send an e-mail message to the CIO as soon as the DML statement is executed.

    D. Create DDL triggers that use SQL Mail to send an e-mail message to the CIO as soon as the DDL statement is executed.

5. You are tasked with creating a solution that will audit all changes to any database objects. These changes must be kept permanently. What should you do?

    A. Create DML triggers to write the auditing information to a table.

    B. Create DDL triggers to write the auditing information to a table.

    C. Create functions to write auditing information to an audit log.

    D. Create stored procedures to write auditing information to an audit log.

6. You manage a Sales database. Any customer that buys something is added to the Customer table and the sale is added to the Orders table associated with the customer's PK. The customers table has an Active column to indicate if the customer is active or inactive. Data must never be deleted from the Orders table, and referential integrity must be maintained. How should you handle customer deletions?

    A. Use a cascade delete.

    B. Redesign the database so the customer is not related to the Orders table.

    C. Use a trigger to roll back the deletion and change the Customer from Active to Inactive.

    D. Use a trigger to change the customer from Active to Inactive before deleting the customer.

7. You manage a testing database and must ensure that any changes to the data in the TestHistory table are audited. What should you do?

A. Create DDL triggers to capture changes to the data and write the changes to another table in the database.

B. Create DML triggers to capture changes to the data and write the changes to another table in the database.

C. Ensure that database users are denied permission on the TestHistory table.

D. Write a stored procedure to change the TestHistory data and also write the changes to another table in the database.

70-442

1. You are writing a query that will list Employees and their phone numbers. Some employees have home phone numbers, some have cell numbers, and some have both listed in the table. You want to list the cell number if it exists, but if not, you want to list the home number. What function would you use in your query?

A. COALESCE

B. IFNULL

C. NULLIF

D. The CLR function

2. You need to create a query that will identify the number of orders with an order date of July 4, 2004. An index has been created on the OrderDate column in the Sales.SalesOrderHeader table. The OrderDate column is a datetime data type. Which of the following queries would be the most efficient?

A.

```
SELECT COUNT(*) FROM Sales.SalesOrderHeader
WHERE OrderDate >= '20040704' AND
OrderDate < '20040704'
```

B.

```
SELECT COUNT(*) FROM Sales.SalesOrderHeader
WHERE CONVERT(CHAR(8), OrderDate, 112)
= '20040704'
```

C.

```
SELECT COUNT(*) FROM Sales.SalesOrderHeader
WHERE YEAR(OrderDate) = 2004 AND
MONTH(OrderDate) = 07 AND DAY(OrderDate) = 04
```

D.

```
SELECT COUNT(*) FROM Sales.SalesOrderHeader
WHERE DATEDIFF(day, OrderDate, '20040704') = 0
```

3. You are tasked with creating a solution that will capture the creations, deletions, and modifications of all database objects in the Testing database. What would be the easiest way to accomplish this?

   A. Create a DML trigger using the DDL_SERVER_LEVEL_EVENTS event group using SERVER as the scope.

   B. Create a DML trigger using the DDL_DATABASE_LEVEL_EVENTS event group using DATABASE as the scope.

   C. Create a DDL trigger using the DDL_SERVER_LEVEL_EVENTS event group using SERVER as the scope.

   D. Create a DDL trigger using the DDL_DATABASE_LEVEL_EVENTS event group using DATABASE as the scope.

4. You need to create a solution that will allow data to be modified in an Investments database via a distributed VIEW. What will allow you to do this?

   A. Nothing extra is needed. Data can be modified directly in a VIEW.

   B. Create a DML trigger on the VIEW to update the underlying table.

   C. Create a DDL trigger on the VIEW to update the underlying table.

   D. Create an INSTEAD OF trigger on the VIEW to update the appropriate underlying table.

5. After analyzing the performance of the Portfolio database, you realize that a large number of read and writes are occurring. Stock names are created using the char(200) data type in the Stocks table. You've verified that future stock names will not be any larger than any existing stock name, and you suspect that char(200) is larger than it needs to be. What can you do to identify the best size for the StockName column?

   A. Execute the following query:
      SELECT MIN(StockName) FROM Stocks

   B. Execute the following query:
      SELECT MAX(StockName) FROM Stocks

   C. Execute the following query:
      SELECT MAX(Len(StockName)) FROM Stocks

   D. Execute the following query:
      SELECT COUNT(StockName) FROM Stocks

Answers

70-431

1. **A.** Scalar functions return a single value. Lists are not scalar, and a trigger cannot be fired from a function.

2. **B.** DML INSTEAD OF triggers can cause a different action to occur instead of the action that caused them. In this case, an INSERT DML INSTEAD OF trigger can be configured to examine the data, and if it won't import correctly, instead write the data to another table. A DML AFTER trigger wouldn't work because referential integrity would prevent the data entry. DDL triggers work on DDL statements, not DML statements.

3. **B.** DDL triggers are new in SQL Server 2005 and can be set to fire on DDL statements such as CREATE, ALTER, and DROP. DML triggers work on DML statements, not DDL statements. Creating a function wouldn't provide any auditing capability.

4. **A, D.** The two valid statements to disable a trigger are on the trigger or the table. Dropping the trigger would remove it permanently, not temporarily. Disable is not a valid option with the ALTER TRIGGER statement.

5. **A.** CLR-integrated database objects (such as stored procedures) are especially favored with calculation-intensive operations. There's no such thing as compiled T-SQL queries. Reporting Services wouldn't speed up the calculations. Spending money on a bigger processor when an existing solution is possible isn't the best way to endear yourself to management.

70-441

1. **C.** Since the function will perform advanced calculations and verify complex string values, a CLR-integrated function is appropriate. Functions are separate objects than stored procedures or triggers, so a function can't be created as one of these objects. A T-SQL function is possible but wouldn't perform as well as a CLR-integrated function.

2. **C.** In the original scenario, an UPDATE trigger is firing an extended stored procedure, which calls the external COM component. We need to eliminate the extended stored procedure. There is no indication the COM component needs to be eliminated. A CLR-integrated object can access an external file and is a good alternative to using extended stored procedures.

3. **C.** Since the database is updated through a variety of sources, a DELETE trigger would be the only method out of those shown that would catch all deletions. Creating a stored procedure or a user-defined function would work if there was a way to ensure that deletions always used the stored procedure or function, but since users modify the database using different methods, a trigger would be the best choice. A DDL trigger does not work on DELETE statements.

4. **B.** Table modifications would be done with the DDL statement ALTER. DML triggers only catch DML statements (INSERT, UPDATE, and DELETE).

5. **B.** DDL triggers can capture changes to database objects. DML triggers, on the other hand, will capture changes to the data, but not to the objects. Functions and stored procedures could be used, but would not ensure that all changes are captured.

6. **C.** Data must never be deleted from the Orders table and referential integrity must be maintained; therefore customers should never be deleted since deleting the customer would violate referential integrity. A trigger could be used to roll back customer deletion attempts. The Customer and Orders table are associated with each other (more than likely with a Customer / CustomerID [PK] and Orders / CustomerID [FK] relationship). A cascade delete would cause a customer deletion to delete associated rows in the Orders table. If the Customer table is not related to the Orders table, there would be no way to know whose orders are in the Orders table.

7. **B.** DML triggers can capture all data changes and write the audited information to a separate table. DDL triggers won't capture changes to the data. Denying access to the table won't audit the changes, but would instead prevent the changes. A stored procedure wouldn't capture the change if it occurred through another method such as a simple UPDATE statement.

70-442

1. **A.** COALESCE will return the first non-NULL expression among multiple choices in a query. There is no IFNULL function within T-SQL, and NULLIF is used to compare two expressions and, if they are the same, return a value of NULL. A CLR function would be useful for complex computations, but not for a simple retrieval of existing data.

2. **A.** When comparing dates, the most efficient method is using a simple comparison. While functions can be used to achieve the desired results, a simple comparison is much quicker.

3. **C.** The DDL_SERVER_LEVEL_EVENTS event group encompasses all DDL events at the server level. DML triggers would not capture DDL events. DDL_DATABASE_LEVEL_EVENTS would not capture CREATE DATABASE events.

4. **D.** Since the VIEW is a distributed VIEW, we can assume multiple tables are used to build the VIEW via a UNION clause. This VIEW can not be updated directly. An INSTEAD OF trigger can be created to examine the DML statement (UPDATE, INSERT, or DELETE) and instead of updating the VIEW, it will identify the correct underlying table to modify.

5. **C.** Stock names are likely no more than 30 characters long, but the only way to know for sure is to check the length with the LEN function. MAX(LEN(StockName)) will identify the maximum length. MAX will only identify the StockName that is alphabetically the last one, while Min will identify the first one listed alphabetically. Count will identify how many stocks are in the table.

Optimizing Databases

In this chapter, you will learn about:

- Optimizing databases with indexes
- Optimizing indexes
- Statistics
- Full-text catalogs and indexes
- Database Engine Tuning Advisor (DTA)
- Index maintenance
- Database Console Command (DBCC)
- Use of filegroups

> *Architects know that some kinds of design problems are more personal than others. One of the cleanest, most abstract design problems is designing bridges. There your job is largely a matter of spanning a given distance with the least material. The other end of the spectrum is designing chairs. Chair designers have to spend their time thinking about human butts.*
>
> —*Paul Graham*

When optimizing a database, we need to think about design and how the database is used. A simple design goes far, but for greater harmony in the application we need to know how the data is being used—that is, how it is being queried.

By understanding how data is being queried, we now have a much better understanding of what indexes to add. And adding indexes is where we get the best gains in performance—but only if we add the *right* indexes. Though it might be difficult at times, I love doing this much more than I think I'd enjoy designing chairs.

Indexes

At the back of this book is an index. If you were trying to look up information on stored procedures, you could turn to the index and it would tell you on which pages to find that information.

But what if the book had no index? We'd have to start on page 1 and continue through each page until we found stored procedures mentioned. However, if we found stored procedures mentioned on page 44, would we be done? Not at all. They could also be mentioned in several other places throughout the book, so we would need to check each page until we reached the end. However, with an index, we would know exactly which pages have information on stored procedures and we could go directly to those pages.

Similarly, indexes in databases help the query optimizer find information. The query optimizer (sometimes called the query engine) shown in Figure 7-1, does a great deal under the hood in SQL Server. When a query is submitted to a database, the query optimizer parses it (makes sure it's syntactically correct), resolves it (makes sure database objects exist), and then optimizes it. A significant part of the optimization process is to determine if indexes exist that would relate to the query and decide if they are useful.

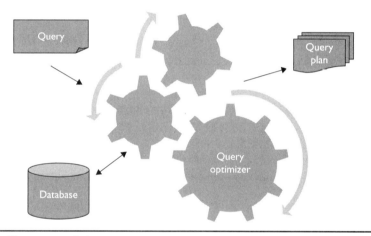

Figure 7-1 The query optimizer

For example, consider a parts table of over five million parts and the requirement to find the price of a blue widget with a part ID of 101. The following query would be able to find this information quite quickly:

```
SELECT Price from Parts WHERE PartID = 101;
```

The query optimizer would check for indexes on the referenced columns (Price and PartID) in the referenced table (Parts). The PartID column is the PK and, by default, PKs are created with a clustered index. The query optimizer would determine that the index on the PartID column would help it find the data the quickest and so would include it in the query plan.

 EXAM TIP Adding indexes to frequently queried data will significantly improve the performance of the queries that use that data. When tasked with improving query performance, investigate the possibility of adding indexes to frequently queried data.

On the other hand, let's say we don't know the part ID of our blue widget. We could then use the following query:

```
SELECT Price from Parts WHERE Name = 'Blue Widget';
```

If there is no index on the Name column, the query optimizer would have to check all five million rows of the table. This is referred to as a *table scan* and obviously is much slower than the first example where we would use an index.

SQL Server supports two primary types of indexes that we'll discuss in this section: clustered and nonclustered. The absence of an index on a column is referred to as a *heap*. In chapter 5 we presented XML indexes, and later in this chapter we'll present full-text indexes.

Clustered

A clustered index is similar to a dictionary or a phone book. The data is ordered in the same way the index is ordered.

For example, if you were to look up the word "success" in the dictionary, once you reached the word, you would also be on the same page as the definition of the word. You wouldn't need to look further.

The white pages of a phone book work the same way. Thinking about a phone book helps to emphasize that we can only order the book in one way (or at least only one way at a time). If you were looking up Ms. Olive Yewe, once you found her you would also have her address and phone number:

Yewe, Olive   476 Lovers Lane   555-5555

Many years ago, I sold real estate for a short time. I worked in an office with several salespeople and we were assigned territories. We had a special phone book that was ordered by street names, and it would give the name of who lived there and their phone number. I was able to do mass mailings with this information, or if I was feeling especially masochistic, I could try to call everyone on a street in my territory.

The key point here is that it was a completely separate phone book, ordered in a completely different way. In other words, we can't have one physical phone book that is simultaneously organized by both last name *and* street name.

Similarly, we can have only one clustered index on a table. One physical table can't be ordered in two different ways simultaneously. It *is* possible to create a completely separate copy of the table and order it in a different way, but for one table we can only have *one* clustered index.

 TIP You can have only one clustered index on a table. A single table can only be ordered one way at a time.

A clustered index orders the data within a table in the same order as the clustered index.

By default, the PRIMARY KEY is created as a clustered index. As a reminder, the PRIMARY KEY must have an index, and the index is what enforces uniqueness on the PRIMARY KEY.

Best Use of Clustered Indexes

Since a table can only have one clustered index, the column chosen as the clustered index deserves some special consideration. Additionally, the performance of a clustered index is generally faster than a nonclustered index since the data is actually organized in the order of the clustered index.

You can often get the best performance from a clustered index in the following situations:

- **PRIMARY KEY queries**   The PK is created as a clustered index by default. This is because it will often provide the best performance. Joins combine multiple tables based on PK-to-FK relationships. If the PK wasn't a clustered index, the query optimizer would need to perform lookups to find the underlying data.

- **Range queries**   These queries search using ranges of data (such as between two different dates, or between two different prices). For example, imagine we frequently query a Sales table based on the OrderDate. By creating a clustered index on the OrderDate column, we actually order the table based on the OrderDate column. Once the first date in the range is found, the following rows are automatically in the range until the high end of the range is reached.

- **Queries that use ORDER BY**   If you frequently must create reports and have the data in a specific sorted order, it will help the performance of the query if the data starts out in a sorted order. For example, if you frequently create reports that are ordered by the CustomerLName, then creating a clustered index on the CustomerLName column will improve the performance of this report.

Nonclustered

A nonclustered index is similar to the index at the back of the book. By looking up a word or phrase, such as stored procedures in the index, we can identify where information on stored procedures is located.

Let's point out something obvious. If you look at the back of this book, you can see that the index is much thinner than the book's full thickness. Even if you had to search each page of the index, it would be much quicker than searching each page of the book. But you don't need to search each page of the index, because it is ordered alphabetically.

 EXAM TIP   By creating indexes on a table, we can improve the performance of queries that would use that index. Only one clustered index is allowed, but multiple nonclustered indexes can be created depending on the optimization goals.

When executing queries, the query optimizer can use nonclustered indexes the same way we use a book's index. Think back to our five-million-row parts table and the query that searches based on the name:

```
SELECT Price from Parts WHERE Name = 'Blue Widget';
```

If there was no index on the Name column, this search would require a table scan—meaning all five million rows of the parts table would have to be examined. However, if we were to create an index on the Name column, we could streamline this query.

Looking at Figure 7-2, we can see how data from the Parts table might be stored in SQL Server. In Chapter 2, we mentioned that pages are 8KB in size (limiting rows to no more than 8KB). We store eight pages within an extent, making extents 64KB in size. When SQL Server reads data off the disk, it reads full extents at a time. The Parts table is stored in 11 contiguous extents, in a total of 84 pages.

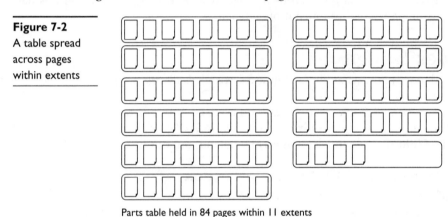

Figure 7-2
A table spread across pages within extents

Parts table held in 84 pages within 11 extents

Now imagine that we need to search for a blue widget. Without the index, we'd have to search through 11 extents (or 704KB). With the index shown in Figure 7-3, we only have to search one extent (64KB). Obviously, it's quicker to search 64KB than 704KB.

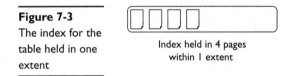

Figure 7-3
The index for the table held in one extent

Index held in 4 pages within 1 extent

Five million rows would likely be much more than 11 extents. If we were going to display this realistically for a five-million-row parts table, we would have Figure 7-2 spread across several pages in this book with many more extents. However, for this example, we'll keep the number of extents small.

We can have up to 249 nonclustered indexes on a table. However, there is a point of limited returns. Consider Figures 7-2 and 7-3 again. If we had indexes on every column, the size of the indexes would be as big as the size of the table.

As we'll see later in this chapter, indexes also incur some overhead. If it costs more in resources to maintain an index than we are getting in performance gains, it doesn't make sense to use the index.

Full-Text Indexes

Full-text indexes allow us to do full-text searches on individual columns. By enabling full-text indexes, we can perform sophisticated searches on text type data. We'll explore these in much more depth later in the chapter.

XML Indexes

Both primary and secondary XML indexes can be created on the XML data type column. The first index created on an XML data type column must be a primary XML index.

Since the XML data type can be as large as 2GB, having an index on this data can make XML path searches much more efficient.

Index Design

Now that we know what kinds of indexes exist, let's discuss some of the basics of index design.

Remember, we don't create indexes on every column of a table. The cost is too high. Additionally, we can have only one clustered index. The clustered index is typically set on the PRIMARY KEY. It's set that way by default, but can be changed if necessary.

When and Why to Create an Index

Since it's not feasible to create indexes on all columns, but some indexes are worthwhile, we must decide which columns to create the indexes on. Indexes are created on PKs to enforce uniqueness, but beyond that, the primary reason to create an index on a column is to optimize queries that are used often.

If a column is rarely used in a query, it is not a good candidate for an index.

 EXAM TIP You should have a solid understanding of when to create indexes and when not to create indexes. The following bulleted list identifies columns that are good candidates for indexes and thus should be committed to memory.

Columns that are good candidates for indexes are:

- **Primary keys and foreign keys.**   PKs must have indexes, and clustered indexes are created by default. FKs are used in join operations, so it is very common to have indexes created on FKs.

- **Columns that are frequently referenced in queries.**   If the column is frequently referenced in a query, then having it in an index can speed up the queries.

- **Columns that are searched for ranges of key values (with WHERE clauses).**   A range of key values includes clauses such as *WHERE @Value > 100 or WHERE*

@*Value BETWEEN 10 and 20*. This allows the query optimizer to limit the number of pages that need to be searched.

- **Columns that need to be sorted (used in the ORDER BY clause).**   Consider a table named Parts. Business practices require a report ordered by PartName to be called almost daily. If we created a clustered index on the PartName column, the Parts table would already be ordered and the query optimizer wouldn't need to do another sort operation.

- **Columns that are frequently grouped together during aggregation (for example, AVG function).**   Consider our Parts table. Let's say it's 300MB in size. If we frequently needed to determine the average cost, we could create a nonclustered index on this column. The size of this index (only one column of the Parts table) would be significantly less than 300MB, perhaps 20MB. Now instead of having to search through 300MB of data to determine the average price, the query optimizer only has to search through 20MB.

Some columns should *not* be indexed. These include:

- Columns that are seldom referenced in queries.
- Columns that aren't selective, or have few unique values. For example, gender would be either *M* or *F*, making for only two values, so an index wouldn't be very useful.
- Large Object (LOB) data types cannot be used as the key column in an index. They can instead be used as part of a composite index. LOB data types include text, ntext, varchar(max), nvarchar(max), varbinary(max), xml, and image.

In the following exercise, we'll create an index on the last name in the Person .Contact table via the GUI in SSMS.

Exercise 7.1: Create an Index in SSMS

See how to create an index within SSMS in video 7-1.

1. Launch SSMS and access the AdventureWorks database.
2. Double-click Tables within the AdventureWorks database. Double-click the Person.Contact table, and then double-click Indexes. Your display should look similar to Figure 7-4.

   Notice that four indexes have been created: one clustered, two nonclustered, and one Primary XML.
3. Right-click Indexes and select New Index.
4. In the Index name, enter **idx_LastName.** Ensure the Index Type is set as Nonclustered.
5. Click Add. In the Select Columns From 'Person.Contact' dialog box, check the box next to LastName. Your display should look similar to Figure 7-5. Click OK.

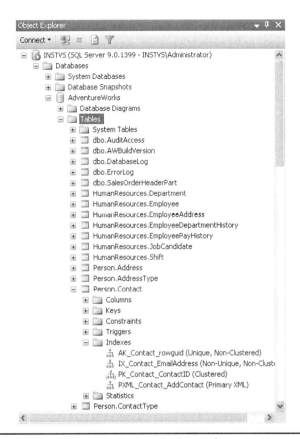

Figure 7-4   Object Explorer looking at indexes in the Person.Contact table

Figure 7-5
Adding a column
to the index

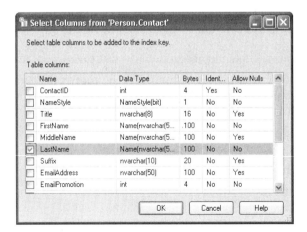

6. Click Options to access the Options properties page. We'll accept the defaults, but I want to point out a couple of these settings. You can also view them in Figure 7-6.

- Automatically Recompute Statistics is checked.

- Store Intermediate Sort Results In tempdb is checked.

- Set Fill Factor is *not* checked.

- Use Index is checked, indicating this index will be enabled.

Figure 7-6

Index options

7. Click OK to create the index.

Composite Index

Indexes can be composed of more than one column. When it does use more than one column, we refer to it as a composite index. We might use a composite index to increase the selectivity of the index (make the entries more unique) or to cover a query.

When creating a composite index, one column is referred to as the *key* column, and the other columns are referred to as the *included* columns. When creating a composite index, it is best to use the less common column as the key column because statistics are only derived and maintained on this column. Statistics aren't maintained on included columns. We'll discuss statistics more fully later in this chapter.

Covering a Query

Covering a query with an index is done to increase the performance of a specific query. One index will include all the referenced columns of the covered query.

For example, consider a Customer table that's 800MB in size. Salespeople frequently run a query that pulls a contact name (first name and last name) and phone number from the Customer table based on the CustomerID.

Let's say the Customer table is actually 15 columns wide. However, we are referencing only four columns in the query: CustomerID, FirstName, LastName, and Phone.

We could create a composite index of all four columns referenced in the query. Now whenever this query is run, instead of searching through the entire 800MB table, the smaller composite index (perhaps 500KB) could be searched. Figure 7-7 shows the comparison of the table and the index. Clearly, the query optimizer can search the smaller index for data quicker than it can search the entire table.

Figure 7-7

A comparison of a full table and a covering index

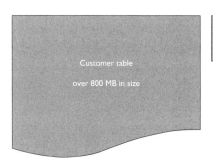

Covering a query can provide significant performance gains for specific frequently run queries. However, since both the data in the index and the data in the underlying table must be updated, there is a maintenance cost involved. Only the most frequently run queries should be covered by a composite index.

EXAM TIP A covering index can be used to optimize the most frequently used queries. Covering a query with an index involves adding all of the referenced columns in the query to the index. This allows the query optimizer to look at the smaller index only and not the larger table. The T-SQL statement used to include additional columns in the index is INCLUDE.

In this next exercise, we'll cover a query by creating a composite index using T-SQL statements. The columns we'll include in the index are LastName, FirstName, and EmailAddress. Since LastName is less common than FirstName and is likely to be included in the WHERE clause to narrow the search, the LastName column will be the key column.

Exercise 7.2: Cover a Query with a Composite Index Using T-SQL

1. Launch a New Query window in SSMS. Press CTRL+M or select the Query menu and then choose Include Actual Execution Plan.

2. Enter and execute the following query. This is the query we are planning to optimize by covering it with an index.

```
USE AdventureWorks;
GO
SELECT LastName, FirstName, EmailAddress
FROM Person.Contact;
```

3. Select the Execution Plan tab and observe the execution plan the query optimizer used. Your display should look similar to Figure 7-8.

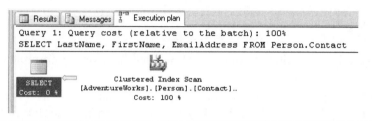

Figure 7-8 The execution plan of the e-mail address query

4. Hover over the clustered index scan icon in the plan to observe the details of this plan step. Your display should look similar to Figure 7-9.

Figure 7-9
Details of the clustered index scan step

Clustered Index Scan	
Scanning a clustered index, entirely or only a range.	
Physical Operation	Clustered Index Scan
Logical Operation	Clustered Index Scan
Actual Number of Rows	19973
Estimated I/O Cost	0.416458
Estimated CPU Cost	0.0221273
Estimated Operator Cost	0.438586 (100%)
Estimated Subtree Cost	0.438586
Estimated Number of Rows	19973
Estimated Row Size	165 B
Actual Rebinds	0
Actual Rewinds	0
Ordered	False
Node ID	0

Object
[AdventureWorks].[Person].[Contact].
[PK_Contact_ContactID]
Output List
[AdventureWorks].[Person].[Contact].FirstName,
[AdventureWorks].[Person].[Contact].LastName,
[AdventureWorks].[Person].[Contact].EmailAddress

NOTE The goal of a covering index is to cover a query. When it's created, we want to ensure it is used. Looking at the execution plan before and after creating our covering index will help us verify the index is being used as desired.

5. Use the following script to drop the existing index created in Exercise 7.1:

```
USE AdventureWorks;
GO
DROP INDEX idx_LastName
ON Person.Contact;
```

6. Use the following script to create the new composite index that will cover the query:

```
USE AdventureWorks;
GO
CREATE NONCLUSTERED INDEX idx_LastFirstNameEmail
   ON Person.Contact (LastName)
       INCLUDE ( FirstName, EmailAddress);
```

We could specify different options in the query, but for this example we'll accept the default options.

7. In SSMS, select Indexes under the Person.Contact table, and press F5 to refresh the display. You should see the idx_LastFirstNameEmail index has been created.

8. Right-click the index and select Properties. Notice on an existing index that additional properties pages have been created. We'll explore the fragmentation page later.

9. In the query window, enter the following script. This is the same script entered earlier.

```
USE AdventureWorks;
GO
SELECT LastName, FirstName, EmailAddress
FROM Person.Contact;
```

10. Select the Execution Plan tab. Notice that the scan type this time was an index scan instead of the clustered index scan shown earlier. Hover over the index scan icon. Your display should look similar to Figure 7-10.

Figure 7-10

Details of the index scan step

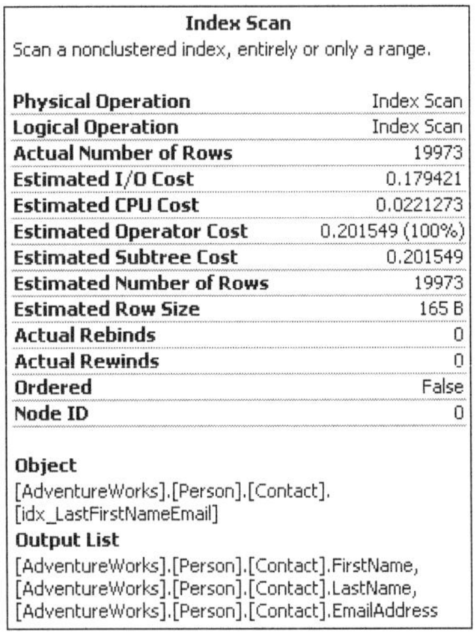

Index Scan	
Scan a nonclustered index, entirely or only a range.	
Physical Operation	Index Scan
Logical Operation	Index Scan
Actual Number of Rows	19973
Estimated I/O Cost	0.179421
Estimated CPU Cost	0.0221273
Estimated Operator Cost	0.201549 (100%)
Estimated Subtree Cost	0.201549
Estimated Number of Rows	19973
Estimated Row Size	165 B
Actual Rebinds	0
Actual Rewinds	0
Ordered	False
Node ID	0

Object
[AdventureWorks].[Person].[Contact].
[idx_LastFirstNameEmail]
Output List
[AdventureWorks].[Person].[Contact].FirstName,
[AdventureWorks].[Person].[Contact].LastName,
[AdventureWorks].[Person].[Contact].EmailAddress

When looking at the execution plan, notice several costs are listed. These identify the cost of individual operators, the cost of an operator and all previous operators read from right to left (known as a subtree), and the cost of all the operators in the plan (the cost of the query). The Estimated I/O cost typically refers to disk activity, though it can also include memory activity. The Estimated Operator Cost is the sum of the Estimated I/O cost and the Estimated CPU cost.

TIP Expect differences in the numbers shown in Figures 7-9 and 7-10 from what you see on your computer. Nonetheless, the key point here is that some of the costs in the second operation (Figure 7-10) are significantly less than the costs in the first scan (Figure 7-9). Pay particular attention to the Estimated I/O Cost, the Estimated Operator Cost, and the Estimated Subtree Cost. Additionally, by looking at the details of the step (under "Object"), we can verify that the index we created to cover this query was actually used.

Analyzing Queries

TIP Analysis of queries can fill a book by itself. For this chapter and to help you prepare for the tests, we are keeping it simple. In the statistics section, we'll present some basics on viewing the execution plan, an integral tool when analyzing queries in depth.

By looking at queries frequently used on our database, we can identify the best indexes to create. In our earlier example of the Parts table, the PK (and the clustered index) is on the PartID column. For the following query, the index is perfect:

```
SELECT Price from Parts WHERE PartID = 101;
```

As another example, let's say the company runs a report every Monday using the following query:

```
SELECT * FROM Employees ORDER BY LastName
```

In this query, we are pulling all the rows from the Employees and then sorting them by last name. If the table were already sorted by last name by having a clustered index on the LastName column, then this query would run quicker because the data is retrieved in a sorted order. In contrast, if the table were sorted on another column (such as the EmployeeID column), than once the data was pulled from the table it would need to be sorted, thus taking additional time and processing power. In other words, if we wanted to optimize this query, we would change the clustered index on the PK to a nonclustered index and create a clustered index on the LastName column. This would sort the entire table based on LastName. Now when we run this query, the data is already sorted, and another sort operation isn't required.

This process has trade-offs, though. While reordering the table by LastName would increase the performance of this query, it may negatively impact the performance of other queries. Later in this chapter, we'll explore using the Database Engine Tuning Advisor (DTA) to help us with query analysis.

The Leaf and Nonleaf Levels

An index typically has several levels. The bottom level has the most detail and is referred to as the *leaf* level. The top level is the *root*. Levels in the middle are referred to as *intermediate* levels. In Figure 7-11, we can see the leaf level (the lowest level of the index) and the root level (nonleaf level).

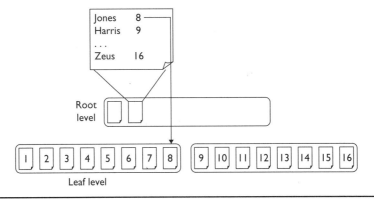

Figure 7-11 The leaf and nonleaf levels of an index

In this example, if we were looking for an employee with the last name of June, we could look in the root level. This shows that page 8 starts with Jones and page 9 starts with Harris. June is between Jones and Harris, so June must be in page 8.

Fill Factors

Is that glass half full or half empty? I'm not trying to see if you're an optimist, but instead want to give you an image of the fill factor. It identifies how full (or how empty) index pages are when the index is first created. The fill factor is specified in percent. A fill factor of 60 indicates pages are 60 percent full when first created (with 40 percent free space). A fill factor of 100 equates to 100 percent full.

TIP An index page with zero data isn't possible. If there's no data, there's no page. However, a fill factor of 0 can be specified; a fill factor of 0 is interpreted as 100 percent full. Any percentage between 0 and 100 is valid.

Actually, "100 percent full" is a little misleading. Pages set at 100 percent full have room to insert one more row. What happens after that next row is inserted? The page splits.

Page Splits

Let's take a look at our Employees table. If we used the EmployeeID as the PK with an IDENTITY (1,1), then any new employees would have an EmployeeID of the last new employee incremented by one. If the last employee was 101, the next one would be 102. New employees would always be entered at the end.

However, let's say we created a nonclustered index on the LastName column. Part of the Employee table may be in page 6 of the extent, as shown in Figure 7-12.

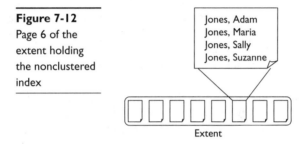

Figure 7-12

Page 6 of the extent holding the nonclustered index

Jones, Adam
Jones, Maria
Jones, Sally
Jones, Suzanne

Extent

This page would hold a lot more than four rows, but for brevity's sake, let's say this page is currently full. We add an employee named Johnny Jones. Alphabetically, we can see he needs to go into this page, but there is no more room. Instead, the page is split.

In Figure 7-13, we can see that SQL Server has located a free page in another extent. It splits the index in half and puts half of the index information into the free page in the new extent and leaves half of the index in the original page in the original extent.

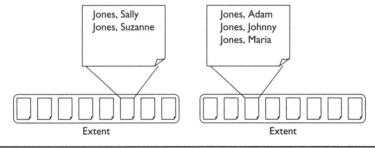

Jones, Sally
Jones, Suzanne

Jones, Adam
Jones, Johnny
Jones, Maria

Extent   Extent

Figure 7-13   A page split between two extents

Page splits occur whenever a page fills up. If we anticipate many inserts that would cause page splits, we would create the index with a fill factor less than 100.

Let's put this information together with an example. Consider a sales table that records sales. The clustered index is on the Date column so the entire table is ordered by date. There's also a nonclustered index on the customer LastName column. What causes a page split on the LastName index?

If the index starts 100 percent full, then after two orders with customer names that would go into the same page, a page split would occur. To prevent page splits, we could change the fill factor to 80 percent so it would take longer for a page split to occur. But what if page splits still occur with the fill factor set to 80 percent? Maybe we should then change the fill factor to something lower, say 50 percent or 20 percent.

Of course, this brings up another question. Why don't we just set the fill factor to a low number, such as 20 percent for all the indexes? The answer is because there's a maintenance cost. Just as page splits impact performance, leaving pages empty makes the indexes larger. An index with a fill factor of 50 percent makes the index twice as large

 TIP The fill factor becomes a significant factor in the ultimate size of the index. Consider an index that's 20MB with a fill factor of 100 percent. How big would the index be if we set the fill factor at 50 percent, or allowed the pages to be half full? It would be twice as large.

Part of your goal when determining the fill factor is striking a balance between (1) having the pages as full as possible and (2) having the least amount of page splits. One of the ways to determine how many page splits are occurring is by measuring fragmentation.

Fragmentation A side effect of page splits is fragmentation of the index. The more page splits you have, the more fragmented an index becomes. We can see this in Figure 7-14.

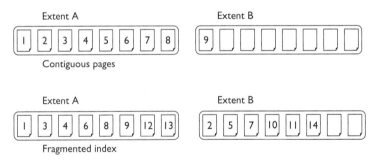

Figure 7-14 A fragmented index

When the index is first created, the pages are created one right after another (page 1, page 2, page 3, and so on) within extents. As each page split occurs, many of the pages are moved to other extents, and the pages are no longer in order.

Suppose we had to read all the data in the fragmented index shown in Figure 7-14. While the data is in only two extents, to be in order, we'd have to switch between extents as we reached the end of almost every page. We'd start in page 1 in Extent A, then switch to Extent B for page 2, then switch back to Extent A for page 3.

Switching extents can be resource-intensive if done constantly. Later, we'll talk about monitoring indexes for fragmentation and what can be done to fix it once it occurs.

But if you want to prevent fragmentation, use a fill factor appropriate for the number of inserts you expect so you can prevent, or at least minimize, page splits.

Pad Index

In Figure 7-11, we showed how the index actually has multiple levels. The leaf level of the index is what will be split the most. However, for a very heavily modified database, it's also possible that the root level or intermediate levels of the index are being split.

If we want to specify a fill factor for the nonleaf levels of the index, we specify the pad index option. The pad index option directs the system to use the same percentage as the fill factor when filling the nonleaf levels of the index.

Calculating Size

One of the key factors to consider when designing an index is how much space it will take. To calculate this, you must consider many factors:

- Fill factors
- The number of columns in the index
- The fixed data size
- The number of variable-length columns
- The average variable-length data size
- The estimated number of rows
- Clustered index keys

I realize the preceding bulleted list may look daunting, but really only three concepts are present, and they can be calculated with this simple formula:

$(S * R) / F$

- S = The size of the index row
- R = The number of rows in the index
- F = The fill factor

The Size of the Index Row

To determine the size of an index row, we identify the size of the columns in the index. If our index is just the PRIMARY KEY displayed as an integer, it is four bytes long. That's the size of an index row.

If we used a composite index of last name and first name, it would be a little different. The LastName column may be defined as an nvarchar(50), and the FirstName column may be defined as a nvarchar(35). But as nvarchar, it only uses the space it needs.

We can easily calculate the average length used by any nvarchar column by using the AVG and LEN functions. The following script will calculate the average length of both the FirstName and LastName columns in the Person.Contact table in AdventureWorks:

```
USE AdventureWorks
SELECT AVG(Len(FirstName)) FROM Person.Contact
GO
SELECT AVG(Len(LastName)) FROM Person.Contact
```

This script shows us the average length of the first name is five characters and the average length of the last name is five characters. Since these are stored as nvarchar (instead of varchar), they take twice as much space so the characters can be displayed in different languages. Our index row size (S) is 20 bytes. This is calculated as $(5 * 2)$ for the first name + $(5 * 2)$ for the last name.

As long as we're talking about the length of the columns, let's add that columns with very long data types aren't good candidates for an index. For example, a column named Comments with a data type of varchar(400) should not be indexed (unless you are using a full-text index). If the index takes a significant amount of space compared to the actual table, any small performance gains we get out of creating the index is typically negated by the maintenance overhead.

The Number of Rows

To count the rows in the Person.Contact table, we can use the following script:

```
USE AdventureWorks
SELECT Count(*) FROM Person.Contact
```

This shows us we have about 19,000 rows (R).

The Fill Factor

We discussed the fill factor earlier. Since the fill factor describes how full the pages within the index are (and indirectly how much empty space is reserved) when they're created, it is a significant factor in calculating the size. If we anticipate many INSERTS into the table, we could choose to set a fill factor of 50 percent. If we didn't anticipate many inserts, we could set a higher fill factor such as 70 percent or 80 percent.

50 percent fill factor:

20 bytes * 19,974 rows = 399,480 bytes

399,480 bytes / 50% fill factor = 798,960 bytes

or 80 percent fill factor:

20 bytes * 19,974 rows = 399,480 bytes

399,480 bytes / 80% fill factor = 499,350 bytes

tempdb

In Chapter 1, we discussed different system databases. One, the tempdb database, deserves some special consideration here when designing and building the indexes.

As a reminder, the tempdb database is used as a workspace for temporary objects and intermediary results sets. Note that this database is recreated from scratch each time SQL Server starts.

Take a look at the properties of the tempdb database. In Figure 7-15, we can see the default options for the tempdb database. It starts at 8MB and then as more space is needed, it will grow by 10 percent.

Figure 7-15

tempdb

properties

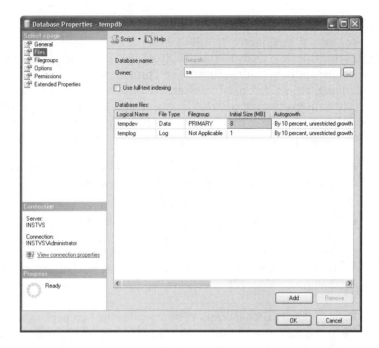

We saw in Exercise 7.1 that the Store Intermediate Sort Results In tempdb box is checked by default when an index is created. If we were creating the index with a script, it would be specified as SORT_IN_TEMPDB, but this is also ON by default. This means that when an index is rebuilt, the tempdb database will be used for temporary storage.

This is an important point. Since the tempdb database will be used by default when creating or rebuilding indexes, it needs to be at least as big as the largest index when the database starts. If it isn't large enough, it will have to resize itself. Depending on the difference between the initial size and the largest index, it may have to resize itself multiple times.

It is best to change the initial size of the tempdb database to a size just a little larger than the largest index.

TIP   If you have to frequently rebuild indexes and you leave the default of sorting the results in tempdb, you want to have the initial size of the tempdb set to a little bit larger than the largest index.

If tempdb doesn't start at the size it needs to be, then Autogrowth will cause it to grow to the size needed. If it starts at 8MB and needs to grow to 1GB in size, it will have to resize itself about 50 times!

While this will work, it is much more resource-intensive to have the database constantly resize itself than to set it to the size it needs to be originally.

Creating an Indexed VIEW

As we learned in Chapter 2, VIEWs don't actually hold data, but instead are virtual tables that can help us focus the data from existing tables. We can use them to provide vertical partitioning (hide columns) and provide a layer of security since permissions to underlying tables don't need to be granted when granting access to the VIEW.

If we want to optimize a VIEW, we can create an index on the VIEW. This is referred to as creating an *indexed VIEW*. Indexes on VIEWs are created as unique clustered indexes.

An indexed VIEW gets the best performance gains in two situations:

- **The data in the VIEW is frequently read but rarely updated.**   If the data in the index is frequently changed, then the overhead of index maintenance takes away from the performance gains.

- **The VIEW is used to produce aggregations of data (such as SUM, AVG, and so on).**   Since the index materializes the VIEW, the indexed VIEW can be searched instead of having to search the base table(s) to produce the aggregations. The size of the indexed VIEW would typically be significantly smaller than the base table(s).

 EXAM TIP   Indexed VIEWs provide the best performance gains when used to produce aggregations on a large amount of data, and on data that is frequently read but not frequently updated.

Indexed VIEWs are a little picky. While we covered this in more detail in Chapter 2, remember that several prerequisites must be met when creating indexed VIEWs. These include the following:

- Tables must be referenced by two-part names (for instance, *schema.tablename*) in the VIEW definition. Included functions must also be referenced with a two-part name.

- The VIEW must be created using the WITH SCHEMABINDING option. Included functions must also use the WITH SCHEMABINDING option.

- The VIEW can only reference tables, not other VIEWs.

- All base tables referenced by the VIEW must be in the same database as the VIEW and have the same owner as the VIEW.

- The VIEW must be deterministic.

- Several SET options must be configured according to specific rules.

 EXAM TIP   Some of the basic rules for creating indexes on VIEWs are that:
1) They must be created with the SCHEMABINDING option.
2) Objects must be referenced with a two-part name (for example, *schema.table*).
3) The VIEW must be deterministic (it *cannot* contain any nondeterministic functions).
4) All base tables referenced by the VIEW must be in the same database as the VIEW and have the same owner as the VIEW.

Statistics

My statistics class in college was one of the most challenging classes I had—mostly because they seemed to talk in a different language. I was able to squeak by, but statistics is not my forte. The good news is that all of the heavy lifting needed for statistics is done by the database engine. We don't have to be statistical experts, but instead just need to know how SQL Server is using statistics and how they are maintained.

SQL Server uses statistics to determine how useful an index is when it's creating a query plan. Before we explore that further, let's look at statistics in general.

Statistics is an area of mathematics concerned with masses of data. It examines a sample of the whole population in order to interpret or predict information on the whole population. Imagine it snows in your city. Once the snowstorm is over, the weather forecaster says you've received 18 inches of snow.

I doubt that the weather forecaster went all over the city with a ruler measuring how thick the snowfall was at five million different places within the city. Instead, he might have five or ten measuring tools scattered throughout the city and by looking at those measurements, he can fairly accurately say what happened throughout the entire city.

In this example, the whole population is the amount of snow that fell on every inch of the city. A portion of the whole population (the sample) is the measurements by the five or ten measuring tools scattered throughout the city.

Similarly, the query analyzer within SQL Server uses statistics to determine how dense or how selective an index is for any given query. Instead of looking at all five million rows of an index, the query analyzer can look at the statistics (maybe 300 rows) of the index and make decisions on the usefulness of the index.

Statistics in SQL Server

Let's assume you execute a query in SQL Server. The query optimizer:

- Parses it (makes sure it's syntactically correct)
- Resolves it (makes sure the referenced objects exist)
- Optimizes it (identifies the best plan and the best indexes to use)
- Executes it

How does the query optimizer know which index to use during the optimization phase? It uses statistics on the index to determine the density and selectivity. Ideally, the indexes with the highest selectivity and lowest density are chosen for use when executing the query.

Density

The density refers to the percentage of *duplicate* rows in an index. Let's say we have a database of the Smith family. Almost every member of the Smith family has the last name of Smith. If we had an index on the LastName column, it would be very dense and not very useful for most queries, as shown in Table 7-1.

LastName	FirstName	...
Smith	Adam	
Smith	David	
Smith	Emily	
Smith	John	
Smith	Mary	
Smith	Sally	
...	...	
Toth	William	

Table 7-1   Sample Data from the Smith Family

An index can be very dense for one query and not very useful, or not dense for another query making it very useful. Consider this query looking for John Smith:

```
SELECT * FROM FamilyTable WHERE LastName = 'Smith' AND FirstName = 'John';
```

In this case, the index is not useful and the query optimizer probably would not look at it. Let's look at another query on the same table:

```
SELECT * FROM FamilyTable WHERE LastName = 'Toth' AND FirstName = 'William';
```

In this case, we have only one row that meets the query, so the index is not dense for this query and would be used.

Alternatively, consider a PK on a table. A PK must be unique, so the density of an index on the PK is very low. PK indexes are frequently used because the density is always low.

Selectivity

Selectivity refers to the percentage of rows accessed or returned by a query. Let's look at the Smith family table again, but this time with the PK added, as shown in Table 7-2.

FamilyID	LastName	FirstName	...
1	Smith	Adam	
2	Smith	David	
3	Smith	Emily	
4	Smith	John	
5	Smith	Mary	
6	Smith	Sally	
	...	...	
1000	Toth	William	

Table 7-2   The Smith Family Table with PK

Consider this query:

```
SELECT * FROM FamilyTable WHERE FamilyID = 5;
```

The result of this query is one person and only one. This index is very selective for this query and so the index would likely be used.

Consider this query:

```
SELECT * FROM FamilyTable WHERE FamilyID > 990;
```

Our table is 1000 rows, and the query returns only ten rows or 1 percent of them. Again, our index is very selective for this query and would likely be used.

For a query that isn't selective, consider this query:

```
SELECT * FROM FamilyTable WHERE FamilyID < 900;
```

This query will return 899 rows or 90 percent of the table. Instead of searching the index to find a row, and then getting the row's data, the query optimizer might choose to do a table scan instead. While table scans aren't very efficient when we need to identify one of 1000 rows, they are efficient when we need to identify 90 percent of a table.

Statistics on an Index

Now that we understand selectivity and density, let's cover which statistics are actually created.

Assume you have an Orders table with five million rows. The query optimizer wants to know how dense an index is, or how selective an index is for a given query. If it had to search the entire five million rows of each possible index, it may take longer to calculate which index to use than it actually takes when using a single index.

In Figure 7-16, we can see the OrderID index in comparison with the statistics on the index. The actual index is five million rows, but the statistics on the index is only 300.

Row #	OrderID	Row #	OrderID
1	1001	1	1001
2	1002	2	10,016,667
3	1003	3	10,033,334
4	1004	. . .	. . .
. . .	. . .	. . .	. . .
901	100,901	100	100,166,670
902	100,902	101	100,183,337
. . .	. . .	. . .	. . .
4,999,999	1,004,999,999	299	10,04,983,333
5,000,000	1,005,000,000	300	10,05,000,000

OrdersID index
5,000,000 rows

Statistics on OrdersID index
300 rows

Figure 7-16   Statistics created on the Orders table

In this example, we are using a step of 300 with an even distribution of 16,667. The first sample is 1, the next sample is 16,667, and samples are taken all the way to the 300th sample of 5,000,000. Now by looking at the 300 rows in the statistics, the query optimizer is able to determine that the index is highly selective.

TIP   In the classroom, I'm often asked how many rows are actually needed in the statistics to make it work correctly. My response: "When it comes to mathematics, there are *three* types of people—those that are good at math and... those that aren't. You can guess which group I'm in." Thankfully, we don't have to be good at statistics or math to use statistics effectively in SQL Server.

Statistical experts have worked with the SQL Server programmers to determine what is required to make sure that statistically significant samples are taken. What we need to do is ensure that the system is creating and maintaining statistics automatically with the AUTO CREATE STATISTICS and AUTO UPDATE STATISTICS settings.

The Query Plan

Once the query optimizer identifies the best methods to use to execute the query, it creates a query plan. You can view the query plan in SSMS by pressing CTRL+M or by selecting the Query drop-down menu and choosing Include Actual Execution Plan before executing the plan. Once the query is executed, an additional tab appears in the output and a graphical view of the execution plan can be viewed.

Using the following query, we can see the execution plan:

```
USE AdventureWorks;
GO
SELECT * FROM HumanResources.vEmployee
WHERE EmployeeID = 101
```

In Figure 7-17, we have executed the query and selected the execution plan in the output pane. There's a lot to this plan, but we're going to keep it simple and just look at the beginning. These plans work from right to left, so in the figure I've scrolled to the far right of the bottom plan.

Figure 7-17

Viewing a partial execution plan

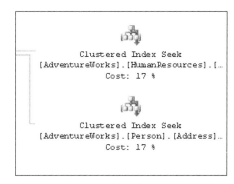

We can see that the plan starts with two clustered index seeks. If we hover over either of these, details pop up on the operation. Figure 7-18 shows the details from the top clustered index seek first illustrated in Figure 7-17.

Figure 7-18

Viewing the details of an execution plan operation

Clustered Index Seek

Scanning a particular range of rows from a clustered index.

Physical Operation	Clustered Index Seek
Logical Operation	Clustered Index Seek
Estimated I/O Cost	0.003125
Estimated CPU Cost	0.0001581
Estimated Operator Cost	0.0032831 (17%)
Estimated Subtree Cost	0.0032831
Estimated Number of Rows	1
Estimated Row Size	11 B
Ordered	True
Node ID	6

Object
[AdventureWorks].[HumanResources].
[EmployeeAddress].
[PK_EmployeeAddress_EmployeeID_AddressID] [ea]
Output List
[AdventureWorks].[HumanResources].
[EmployeeAddress].AddressID
Seek Predicates
Prefix: [AdventureWorks].[HumanResources].
[EmployeeAddress].EmployeeID = (101)

Notice that the index is identified in the Object as *PK_EmployeeAddress_EmployeeID_AddressID* in the AdventureWorks database, the HumanResources schema, and the EmployeeAddress table.

If we've created this index for this view and it's normally used, but is not being used now, we have a problem. Another possibility is that the index is being used, but is performing much slower than normal. For either of these problems, we need to view and possibly update the statistics.

Viewing and Updating Statistics

When an index is created, the settings to automatically create statistics and automatically update statistics are both enabled by default. As the index is updated, the statistics become out-of-date. SQL Server monitors the changes, and when a threshold is reached, the statistics are updated.

TIP For 95 percent of SQL Server databases, AUTO CREATE STATISTICS and AUTO UPDATE STATISTICS settings are enabled. This allows SQL to create and update these automatically. These are the recommended settings, and for the most part you won't have to worry about them—unless someone changes them to disabled.

To view statistics on an existing database, we can use the Database Console Command (DBCC) SHOW_STATISTICS. In addition to giving us information on the current distribution statistics for the table, it also lets us know when the statistics were last updated.

An On-the-Job Scenario

I worked with a customer that did a detailed, time-consuming weekly report. Most weeks, the report took about 30 minutes. Occasionally, it took about three hours to run. Everything seemed to be the same on the different runs, so we started looking at the statistics.

What we found was that due to modifications to the database (INSERTs, UP-DATEs, DELETEs), the statistics were far enough out-of-date to cause the report to run significantly slower. However, the statistics weren't far enough out-of-date for the query optimizer to realize they were out-of-date.

To solve the problem, we scheduled a job to update statistics on the tables in this report. We had the job run in the early morning of the day the report was run and never had the problem again.

Remember, though, updating the statistics on this table will cause any stored procedures that use these statistics to be recompiled. Resist the temptation to write a script to update the statistics on all tables and effectively flush all of your stored procedures from cache.

The basic syntax for the DBCC SHOW_STATISTICS command is:

```
DBCC SHOW_STATISTICS (tableName, indexName)
```

The DBCC SHOW_STATISTICS command provides three result sets as outlined in Table 7-3.

Result Set	Description
STAT_HEADER	Basic information on the statistics including when they were updated.
DENSITY_VECTOR	Statistical information related to density and selectivity.
HISTOGRAM	Details on the statistics.

Table 7-3 SHOW_STATISTICS Result Sets

If we suspect the statistics are too old and are out-of-date, we can update statistics with the UPDATE STATISTICS command. The basic syntax for the UPDATE STATISTICS command is:

```
UPDATE STATISTICS tableName
```

The preceding command will update the statistics on all indexes on a table. If we want to target a specific index within a table, we can add it to the statement as follows:

```
UPDATE STATISTICS tableName, indexName
```

If we want to update the statistics on every table within the database, we can execute the sp_updatestats system stored procedure. This is a drastic step though and would be both time-consuming and resource-intensive. About the only time we'd want to do that is if we found that statistics were disabled on the database and we just enabled them. This stored procedure would then update all of the statistics.

EXAM TIP A common symptom indicating statistics may be out-of-date is when queries begin to run slower than normal. If the statistics are found to be missing or out-of-date, two methods can be used to manually update them. One, the UPDATE STATISTICS (table name, optional index name) is used to update statistics on a specific index or all the indexes on a specific table. Second, the system stored procedure sp_updatestats can be used to update all the statistics on all tables within a database.

Out-of-Date Statistics

As we mentioned previously, the two database settings related to statistics—AUTO CREATE STATISTICS and AUTO UPDATE STATISTICS—are enabled by default and it would be rare to change these settings. However, just because it's rare, doesn't mean you won't see it. You may indeed come upon a database where the automatic feature of statistics has been disabled and now the database is performing slowly.

First, it's important to realize that on an OLTP database, disabling these two options will eventually result in your database performing slower. Depending on how much activity your database has, you may see the slowdown very quickly and over time, but either way a slowdown is coming.

We mentioned using the DBCC SHOW_STATISTICS command. This will instantly show you whether the statistics are out-of-date. Another way the error can jump out at you is in the Execution Plan. Out-of-date or missing statistics are indicated with the table name in red text in the execution plan.

EXAM TIP If the Execution Plan shows table names in red text, it indicates that statistics are either missing or out-of-date. You can right click the table and choose to update the statistics if desired. To reenable automatic creation and updating of statistics on the database, select the database properties and set AUTO CREATE STATISTICS and AUTO UPDATE STATISTICS properties to TRUE. You can also execute the following script to set these properties to TRUE:

```
ALTER DATABASE AdventureWorks
SET AUTO_CREATE_STATISTICS ON
ALTER DATABASE AdventureWorks
SET AUTO_UPDATE_STATISTICS ON
```

In the following exercise, we view existing statistics and show how to manually update them.

Exercise 7.3: View and Update Statistics Using T-SQL Statements

1. Launch SSMS.

2. Turn off the AUTO CREATE STATISTICS and AUTO UPDATE STATISTICS options via the database properties page.

   a. Right-click the AdventureWorks database and select Properties. Select the Options page.

   b. Verify that that the AUTO CREATE STATISTICS option and AUTO UPDATE STATISTICS option are both set to TRUE.

   c. Change both options to FALSE. Your display should look like Figure 7-19. Click OK.

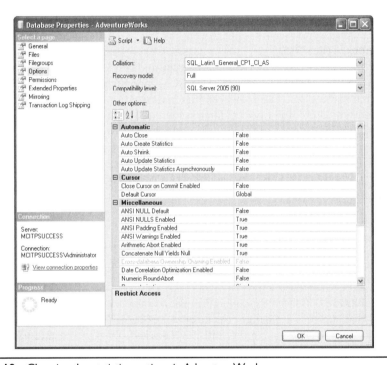

Figure 7-19   Changing the statistics options in AdventureWorks

3. Turn the AUTO CREATE STATISTICS and AUTO UPDATE STATISTICS options ON via a T-SQL script.

   a. Create a New Query window in SSMS.

   b. Enter and execute the following script:

```
ALTER DATABASE AdventureWorks
  SET AUTO_CREATE_STATISTICS ON
ALTER DATABASE AdventureWorks
  SET AUTO_UPDATE_STATISTICS ON
```

4. Right-click the AdventureWorks database and select Properties. Select the Options page and verify the AUTO CREATE STATISTICS and AUTO UPDATE STATISTICS options are both set to TRUE.

5. Use the following script to view the statistics on an index in the Person.Address table in the AdventureWorks database. Your display should look like Figure 7-20.

```
USE AdventureWorks;
GO
DBCC SHOW_STATISTICS ('Person.Contact', AK_Contact_rowguid);
```

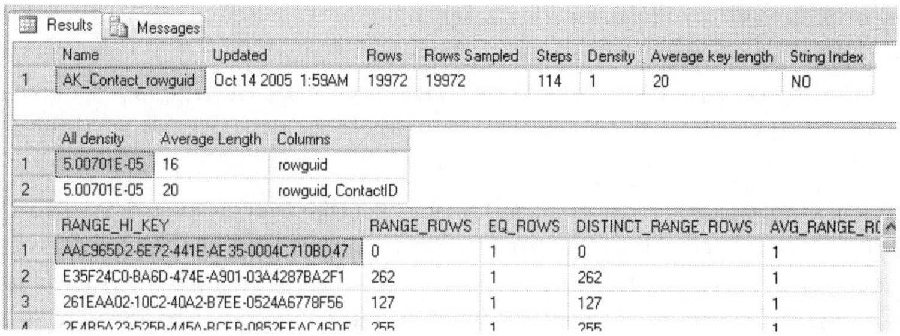

	Name	Updated	Rows	Rows Sampled	Steps	Density	Average key length	String Index
1	AK_Contact_rowguid	Oct 14 2005 1:59AM	19972	19972	114	1	20	NO

	All density	Average Length	Columns
1	5.00701E-05	16	rowguid
2	5.00701E-05	20	rowguid, ContactID

	RANGE_HI_KEY	RANGE_ROWS	EQ_ROWS	DISTINCT_RANGE_ROWS	AVG_RANGE_R(
1	AAC965D2-6E72-441E-AE35-0004C710BD47	0	1	0	1
2	E35F24C0-BA6D-474E-A901-03A4287BA2F1	262	1	262	1
3	261EAA02-10C2-40A2-B7EE-0524A6778F56	127	1	127	1
4	2E4B5A23-525B-445A-BCFB-0852FEAC46DF	255	1	255	1

Figure 7-20   Output of DBCC SHOW STATISTICS

6. Look at the first query result set in Figure 7-20. It's a single row and includes the Updated column. The Updated column shows the last time the statistics were updated. This row also includes the number of steps in the statistics. Even though there are over 19,000 rows in the index, only 114 steps (or 114 rows) are required in the statistics.

7. Execute the following script to update the statistics on the Person.Address table and display them again:

```
USE AdventureWorks;
GO
UPDATE STATISTICS Person.Contact;
GO
DBCC SHOW_STATISTICS ('Person.Contact', AK_Contact_rowguid );
```

8. Look at the Updated column in the first result set. It should be today's date.

9. Execute the following script to update the statistics on all the tables in the AdventureWorks database:

```
USE AdventureWorks;
GO
sp_updatestats;
```

The Impact of Updating Statistics

Updating statistics can be processor-intensive. In the previous exercise, we only had about 19,000 rows, but if your table has over five million rows then updating the statistics can impact performance.

For very large databases, you may find it necessary to take control of when the statistics are updated. For example, let's assume our Orders table has about five million rows and is heavily updated. By regularly using DBCC SHOW_STATISTICS, we realize that some statistics are updated about once a week and often during peak times.

Instead of allowing the statistics to be updated during peak times, we could create a job to update these statistics in the middle of the night once a week.

A side effect of updating statistics is that any queries or stored procedures that reference tables that include the indexes will be recompiled.

Assume we chose to update the statistics on all the indexes on the Orders table. All the queries and stored procedures that reference the Orders table and are currently in cache created their execution plan based on the old statistics. SQL assumes that if the statistics needed to be updated, they must have been out-of-date, so the existing plans based on these out-of-date statistics must also be out-of-date. Thus, they are flushed from cache.

I have run across situations on the job where a DBA has created a script to manually update all the statistics on all tables in a database on a regular basis (such as weekly). This also purges the cache of all cache-stored procedures, and the next time each stored procedure is run, it must be recompiled. This could negatively impact performance depending on the number of stored procedures kept in cache. A more judicious use of manually updating statistics is only updating the statistics that need to be updated. Often, this is none.

 TIP   A sudden jump in the number of stored procedures being recompiled could indicate that statistics have been updated.

Information on SQL Server Queries

When troubleshooting performance issues you may also wish to use some of the SET commands. With these you can gain insight into the different performance characteristics of queries. Listed in the following bullets are some of the SET commands you may find useful.

SET STATISTICS IO ON   SET STATISTICS IO ON will cause SQL Server to display statistical type information on the disk activity generated by T-SQL statements. This is in the form of how many pages are read from the disk (physical reads) and how many pages are read from memory (logical reads).

As an example, if you wanted to know how much disk activity was caused by a specific query, you could use the following T-SQL code:

```
SET STATISTICS IO on;
GO
SELECT * FROM Person.Contact;
```

SET SHOWPLAN_ALL   SET SHOWPLAN_ALL gives you information on the execution plan (in text). When SET SHOWPLAN_ALL is on, queries are not executed but instead only the execution plan is shown. This is sometimes done to document the execution plan at a moment in time for use as a baseline. When performance issues are encountered, the current plan can be compared to the previous plan.

SET STATISTICS TIME   SET STATISTICS TIME displays the number of milliseconds it takes to parse, compile, and execute statements.

Full-Text Indexes

Full-text indexes can be created on textual data to increase performance and capabilities with searches. The steps for enabling and creating full-text indexes on a database are:

1. Verify the database is enabled for full-text searches.

2. Create a full-text catalog.

3. Create full-text indexes.

The following data types can be included in a full-text index: *char, varchar, nvarchar, varchar(max), varbinary(max), XML,* and *image.* Clustered or nonclustered indexes aren't useful with full-text searches.

Consider a column named Resume that is defined with the varbinary(max) data type in the Employee table. Employees can submit their résumé as a Word document, and the entire Word document can be placed into the table.

 NOTE   SQL Server can't automatically search a Word document because it is in Word format instead of simple text. However, with the use of filters many different types of documents can be searched. This includes Word, Excel, PDFs, and many more formats. For more information see the "Filters" Books Online article.

Now, by creating a full-text index on the Resume column, we can search for specific text phrases within the documents. If you're looking for an employee with experience in SQL Server 2005, you can search specifically for "SQL Server 2005" in your searches.

To create full-text catalogs and full-text indexes, the database must be full-text enabled. By default, a database is enabled for full-text searches, but you can use the following command to verify it hasn't been changed:

```
SELECT DATABASEPROPERTYEX('AdventureWorks','IsFullTextEnabled')
```

Full-Text Catalogs and Full-Text Indexes

To enable full-text searching, we would first create a full-text catalog and then create a full-text index on the column where we want to enable full-text searches.

EXAM TIP   To support full-text searches, we must create a full-text catalog for the database and then create a full-text index on the appropriate column within a table. For example, if we want to search a JobSkills column within the Employees table in the HR database, we would first create a full-text catalog on the HR database, and then create a full-text index on the JobSkills column in the Employees table.

The full-text catalog is where the full-text indexes reside. By default, a database would not have any full-text catalogs. If full-text indexes are desired, we first create one or more full-text catalogs.

For most databases one catalog is enough. However, if we have an exceptionally large full-text index, we may choose to create a special catalog just for it.

Only one full-text index is allowed per table. Additionally, the full-text index uses a UNIQUE index for referencing the other data in the table. The PK can be used since it has a UNIQUE index created on it by default.

Full-Text Queries

With a full-text catalog in the database and a full-text index on a column, we can now execute sophisticated queries using the CONTAINS and FREETEXT predicates. Without full-text catalogs and indexes, we can only use the LIKE statement in the WHERE clause.

The CONTAINS predicate allows us to find inflectional forms of words. For example, searching for the word "drive," the full-text search will also locate the words "drives," "driven," "drove," and "driving." We can search for phrases, use wildcards, and even use proximity terms to only return words that are near other words.

 EXAM TIP The CONTAINS predicate can be used to search text-based columns looking for both exact matches and fuzzy matches such as inflectionally generated words. To use the CONTAINS predicate, a full-text index must exist on the column.

In the following exercise, we'll create a full-text catalog on the AdventureWorks database, create a full-text index, and then query it.

Exercise 7.4: Work with Full-Text Indexes

1. Open a New Query window in SSMS.

2. Use the following query to verify that full-text searches are enabled on AdventureWorks:

```
USE AdventureWorks;
SELECT DATABASEPROPERTYEX('AdventureWorks','IsFullTextEnabled')
```

The result set should be a *1*, indicating it is full-text enabled. If it is a *0*, indicating it is disabled, execute the sp_fulltext_database stored procedure as shown next, to enable it:

```
EXEC [AdventureWorks].[dbo].[sp_fulltext_database] @action = 'enable'
```

3. Just because full text is enabled though, doesn't mean we have full-text indexes. Enter and execute the following script and observe the error.

```
SELECT *
FROM HumanResources.JobCandidate
WHERE CONTAINS(Resume, ' "mechanical engineering" ');
```

The error indicates we cannot use a CONTAINS or FREETEXT predicate because it is not full-text indexed.

4. Use the following script to create a full-text catalog on the AdventureWorks database.

```
USE AdventureWorks;
CREATE FULLTEXT CATALOG ftCatalog as DEFAULT
```

5. The HumanResources.JobCandidate table has a Resume column of data type XML. Before we can create the full-text index on it, we need to identify the name of the index on the PK. Using the SSMS Object Explorer, browse to the indexes in the HumanResources.JobCandidate table to identify the name. You can see this in Figure 7-21.

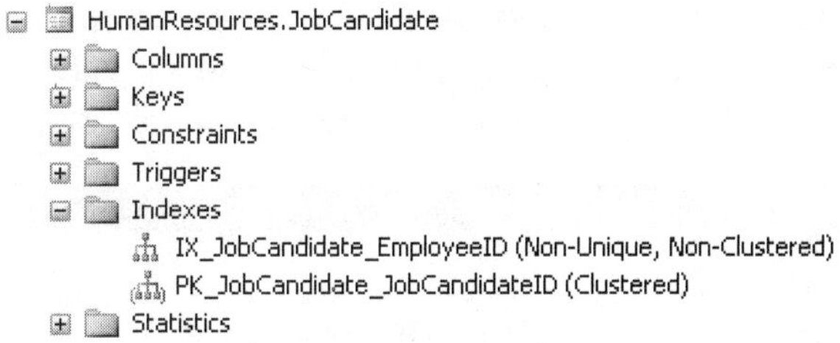

Figure 7-21

Identifying the index name using the Object Browser in SSMS

```
HumanResources.JobCandidate
    Columns
    Keys
    Constraints
    Triggers
    Indexes
        IX_JobCandidate_EmployeeID (Non-Unique, Non-Clustered)
        PK_JobCandidate_JobCandidateID (Clustered)
    Statistics
```

6. Use the following script to create the full-text index on the HumanResources .JobCandidate table using the existing PK:

```
CREATE FULLTEXT INDEX ON HumanResources.JobCandidate(Resume) KEY INDEX
PK_JobCandidate_JobCandidateID;
```

7. Now we can query the data within the table. Suppose we're looking for a candidate with mechanical engineering experience. Execute the following query to find that person:

```
SELECT *
FROM HumanResources.JobCandidate
WHERE CONTAINS(Resume, ' "mechanical engineering" ');
```

8. Imagine we are looking for all job candidates with experience in selling. To ensure we get all possible candidates no matter what verb tense of the word sell is used in the column (sell, sold, selling), we can specify FORMSOF and INFLECTIONAL. The following query will return all verb tenses of sell and sale:

```
SELECT *
FROM HumanResources.JobCandidate
WHERE CONTAINS(Resume, ' FORMSOF (INFLECTIONAL, sell, sale) ');
```

Database Engine Tuning Advisor (DTA)

For a complex database with dozens or hundreds of tables, it isn't so easy to identify the best indexes to create. The Database Engine Tuning Advisor (DTA) can be used to provide a little more science to this monumental task.

The DTA replaces the Index Tuning wizard from SQL Server 2000. It can be used to:

- Recommend indexes (clustered and nonclustered) to create
- Recommend indexes to drop
- Recommend indexed VIEWs
- Analyze the effects of the proposed changes
- Provide reports summarizing the changes and the effects of the changes

Setup and Configuration

You can launch DTA from SSMS. It can be selected from the Tools drop-down menu. Once you launch it, you will be prompted to identify the instance you want to connect with. You will then see a display similar to Figure 7-22.

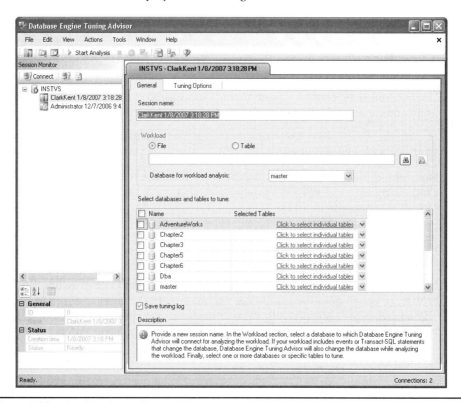

Figure 7-22   Database Engine Tuning Advisor

If you've run DTA before, the previous results will appear in the left pane. At any time you can review the recommendations from previous runs. In the right pane, DTA starts in the General properties page. The session name defaults to the username and the date and time the session was created.

Workload

The workload is what we are measuring. It is a set of T-SQL statements that is executed against the database we are tuning. Workloads can be derived from trace files or trace tables, a T-SQL script file, or XML files.

In many environments where a production server exists that can't be taken offline, a test bed is created. Ideally, this server will have similar hardware and up-to-date databases (created from recent backups).

We'll cover SQL Profiler in Chapter 13, but one of the things we can do is run SQL Profiler on a test server and capture all the activity on an instance of a production server. Each statement executed against the production server can be captured and then saved in either a trace file or trace table. If you do this during live activity, you can create a file duplicating actual activity on your production server. This is a realistic workload file.

One of the drawbacks of files captured with SQL Profiler is that the files can be quite large. This is one of the reasons we'd save it on a test bed server. Executing DTA on the production server with this large trace file might cause it to bog down. So instead we'd execute DTA on the test server.

Tuning Options

This page is divided into three sections.

- **Physical Design Structures (PDS) in use database.** This allows you to choose which indexes and/or indexed VIEWs to recommend.

 TIP   The first time I came across the phrase "Physical Design Structures" (PDS), I spent a good deal of time trying to define it. To save you some searching, *Physical Design Structures* are simply indexes and indexed VIEWs.

- **Partitioning strategy to employ.** Here you can allow the DTA to recommend partitioning. Partitioning strategies can be recommended based on two different goals: performance or maintenance:
- **Full partitioning** will recommend partitions for the *best performance* of the workload.
- **Aligned partitioning** will recommend partitions with the added goal of making the partitions *easy to maintain.*
- **Physical Design Structures to keep in the database.** You can specify whether you want existing indexes or indexed VIEWs to be kept.

Recommendations

Once DTA is run, it provides recommendations. You can immediately apply the recommendations, save the recommendations as a T-SQL script file, or evaluate the recommendations.

In the following exercise, we'll have DTA analyze a query to determine if the database could benefit from an added index when running it. We'll allow it to recommend partitions based on best performance. Since we're running only a single query, we'll keep existing Physical Design Structures.

Exercise 7.5: Run DTA

1. Launch SSMS.

2. From the Tools drop-down menu, select Database Engine Tuning Advisor. Click Connect.

3. Create a workload file that will be used by DTA:

   a. Using Windows Explorer, browse to the root of C:\ on your hard drive.

   b. With C:\ selected, right-click in the right-hand pane, point to New, and select New Text Document.

   c. Rename the text file **Workload.sql**. In the Rename Warning dialog box, click Yes.

CAUTION If file extensions are *not* showing in Windows Explorer, the New Text Document file will be saved as Workload.sql.txt. This is not what you want. To enable file extensions to be shown within Windows Explorer, select Tools | Folder Options | View tab, and deselect the Hide Extensions For Known File Types check box.

---

   d. Right-click Workload.sql file and click Edit. If the Edit option is not available, click Open and Select Notepad. Enter the following script into the file:

   ```
   USE AdventureWorks;
   Go
   SELECT * FROM Sales.Customer
   ```

   e. Save and close the file.

4. In DTA, on the general page, accept the default session name. In the Workload section, ensure File is selected and type in **c:\Workload.sql** to use the file you just created as the workload.

5. In the Select Databases And Tables To Tune section, click the link next to AdventureWorks labeled Click To Select Individual Tables. Select the Customer table in the Sales schema.

6. For the Database For Workload Analysis section, select AdventureWorks. Your display should look similar to Figure 7-23.

7. Click the Tuning Options tab. Our goal is to identify only missing nonclustered indexes, keep existing indexes, and to allow recommendations for partitions based on best performance.

   a. In the section Physical Design Structures (PDS) To Use In Database, select Nonclustered Indexes.

   b. In the Partitioning Strategy To Employ section, select Full Partitioning. This will allow it to recommend partitions based on best performance.

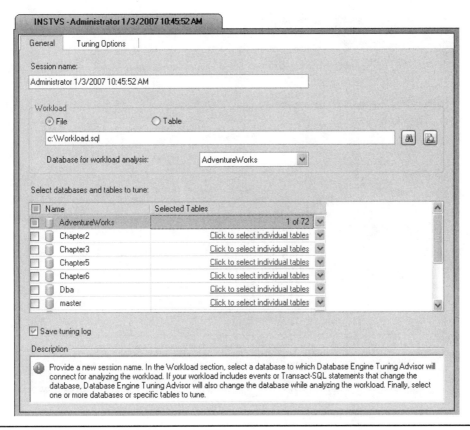

Figure 7-23   The General options page in DTA

c. In the section titled Physical Design Structures (PDS) To keep In Database, select Keep All Existing PDS. Your display should look similar to Figure 7-24.

8. Click the Advanced Options button. Notice that you can have DTA suggest online or offline recommendations. Accept the default of All Recommendations Are Offline, and then click OK.

9. Click the Start Analysis button to begin the analysis. After a moment, the DTA will complete and provide recommendations.

10. On the Recommendations tab, you'll see that an index is recommended.

11. Click the Actions drop-down menu and select Save Recommendations. In the Save As dialog box, browse to c:\ and name the file **DTARecommendations.sql**.

12. Using Windows Explorer, browse to the root of c:\ and open the DTAR ecommendations.sql file. Notice that it includes a script to implement the recommendations.

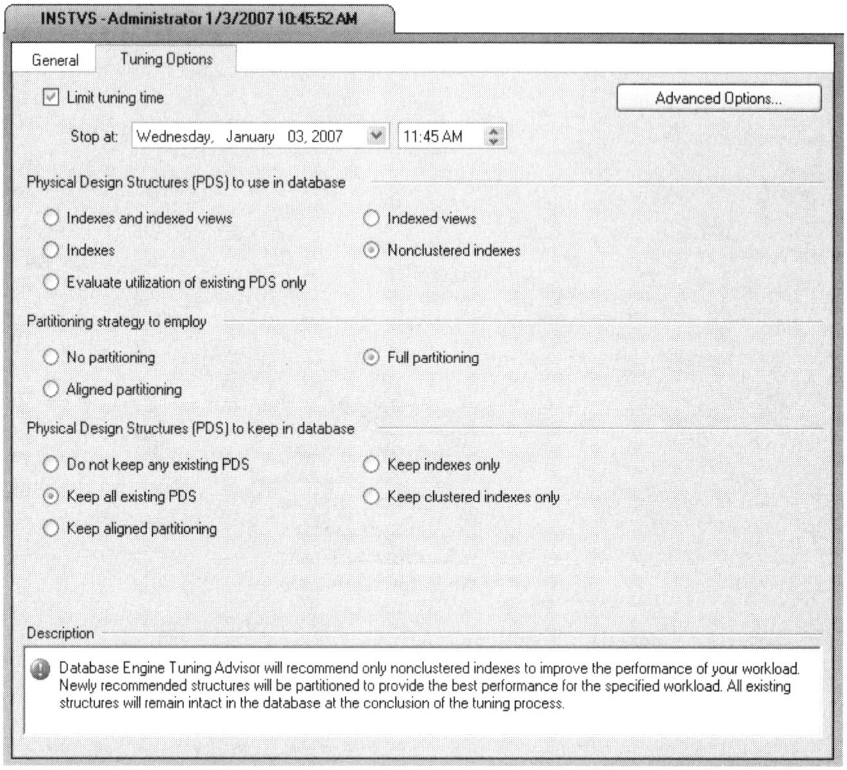

Figure 7-24 DTA tuning options

Index Maintenance

While SQL Server does keep the indexes up-to-date as the table is updated, indexes can become fragmented due to page splits, as we mentioned earlier. The same way your hard drive slows down when it gets too heavily fragmented, the database can slow down when indexes become fragmented.

Additionally, indexes can be created on a database but might never be used. Even though the index isn't being used, it still incurs overhead to maintain it. An occasional search of a database to ensure that all created indexes are being used is worthwhile. We would drop unused indexes to eliminate the needless overhead.

Dynamic Management VIEWs and Functions

In SQL Server 2005, many dynamic management VIEWs (DMVs) and functions have been created to allow us to view key information within SQL. Dynamic management Views and functions have two primary scopes:

- **Server-scoped** VIEW SERVER STATE permission is required on the server.
- **Database-scoped** VIEW DATABASE STATE permission is required on the database.

Dynamic management VIEWs and functions have to be referenced with two-part names. The schema is consistently the sys schema, so you will see them referenced as *sys.ViewName* or *sys.FunctionName*.

In this section, we'll present a couple of DMVs that can be used when maintaining indexes. In Chapter 13, we'll present a more comprehensive view of DMVs, along with an introduction into Dashboard Reports available in SQL Server 2005 SP2.

Fragmentation

The more page splits an index experiences, the more fragmented it becomes. An index can experience *logical* fragmentation (where pages are out of order) and *extent* fragmentation (where extents are out of order).

Both types of fragmentation can be easily identified with the sys.dm_db.index_physical_stats dynamic management function.

 TIP The DBCC SHOWCONTIG command has been deprecated in SQL Server 2005 and replaced with the sys.dm_db_index_physical_stats dynamic management function.

To view the fragmentation on all indexes of all databases, the following command can be used:

```
SELECT * FROM sys.dm_db_index_physical_stats (NULL, NULL, NULL, NULL, NULL);
```

While you can use BOL to look up any of the columns in the output, a couple of them deserve special mention:

- **Index_id**   This identifies the type of index it is.

0	No index (heap)
1	Clustered index
2–249	Nonclustered index

- **Avg_fragmentation_in_percent**   Ideally, this number will be as close to 0 as possible, indicating the index is not fragmented. Any number greater than 10 percent denotes fragmentation that may be causing performance problems and should be investigated.

- **Avg_page_space_used_in_percent**   This identifies how full a page is. By comparing this to the FILLFACTOR, you can get an idea of how much activity the index is experiencing.

Defragmenting a Fragmented Index

If you find an index that is fragmented, you have three choices to resolve the problem: reorganize the index, rebuild the index, or re-create the index.

- **Reorganize** This uses the ALTER INDEX REORGANIZE statement, which reorganizes the leaf level of the index. It is always done ONLINE. Statistics are not updated during this operation.

- **Rebuild** This uses the ALTER INDEX REBUILD statement. It can be done ONLINE or OFFLINE, but defaults to OFFLINE. To achieve availability similar to the reorganize option, you could rebuild indexes online.

 EXAM TIP Make sure you understand which method causes the index to remain online and which method causes it to be offline.

- REORGANIZE is always ONLINE.

- REBUILD defaults to OFFLINE, but can be specified to be kept ONLINE.

- **Re-create** The index can be dropped and re-created from scratch. This is the most comprehensive method and is always done OFFLINE.

Space Needed to Rebuild Indexes Generally, the amount of space needed to rebuild is little more than the size of the index. If you are rebuilding several indexes (such as all indexes on a table), you want to make sure you have enough space to accommodate the largest index. In SQL Server 2005, it is common to use the tempdb when rebuilding indexes. Because of this, the initial size of the tempdb database is an important consideration. Set it to be a little larger than the largest index.

Tracking Usage

To easily determine how useful an index is, you can use the sys.dm_db_index_usage_stats dynamic management VIEW. It identifies how many times an index was used for different operations since the last boot of the SQL Server.

The syntax to execute this VIEW is:

```
SELECT * FROM sys.dm_db_index_usage_stats
```

If an index is not being used at all, it won't even appear in this VIEW. The first time an index is used, a row is added to the VIEW and the counters are initialized to zero. If your system has been up and operational for a while, but an index is not being used at all, you should consider dropping it.

In the following exercise we'll take a look at some of the information on indexes in the AdventureWorks database and reorganize one.

Exercise 7.6: Perform Index Maintenance

See how to rebuild indexes using both a fill factor and a pad index in video 7-6.

1. Open a New Query window in SSMS.

2. Execute the following query to view the usage statistics on all the indexes in AdventureWorks. Notice that we're using the DB_ID function to specify only the AdventureWorks database.

```
SELECT * FROM
sys.dm_db_index_physical_stats
  (DB_ID('AdventureWorks'), NULL, NULL, NULL, NULL);
```

3. See if you can find an index with an avg_fragmentation_in_percent greater than 10. In my version of AdventureWorks, the fourth row has a fragmentation of about 67 percent. The object_id identifies the source table. Write down the index_id and the object_id.
index_id _____ object_id _____

4. To identify the table that the index is associated with, use the following query. Use the object_id you just identified in step 3 in the WHERE clause. (I used 30623152, but yours may be different.)

```
USE AdventureWorks;
GO
SELECT * FROM sys.objects
WHERE object_id = 30623152
```

Notice the name of the table. On my system, the table name is StoreContact. This table is in the Sales schema.

5. Now let's see if this index is ever used. Execute the following query to view the usage statistics:

```
USE AdventureWorks;
GO
SELECT * FROM sys.dm_db_index_usage_stats
WHERE database_id = DB_ID();
```

More than likely, you will not see the object_id you identified in step three in your result set. This indicates this index has not been used.

6. Execute the following query to use the index. If your table is something other than Sales.StoreContact, you will need to execute a query on your table.

```
SELECT CustomerID, ContactID from Sales.StoreContact
```

7. Look at the usage statistics again using the following query. You'll see a row added for your index.

```
SELECT * FROM sys.dm_db_index_usage_stats
WHERE database_id = DB_ID();
```

8. We have been tasked to defragment this index, but it must remain online. To do so, we'll reorganize the index with the following query:

```
USE AdventureWorks;
GO
ALTER INDEX IX_StoreContact_ContactID
ON Sales.StoreContact
REORGANIZE;
```

EXAM TIP   You can also use SSMS to perform many of these functions by right-clicking the index. On the job that may be how you do things because point-and-click is certainly a lot easier if you know which index you want to look at. However, on the MCITP: Database Developer tests expect to see a lot of T-SQL statements.

System Monitor Counters

System Monitor will be covered in more depth in Chapter 13, but for now be aware that it can be used to check the performance of a server. It includes some counters that can be used for index maintenance and two of these are listed in the following text. If you are tasked with maintaining a SQL Server, you will want to include these two counters in your baseline:

- **SQL Server:Access Methods object**   This object searches through and measures allocation of SQL Server database objects. This includes the number of index searches or number of pages that are allocated to indexes and data. The default counter for this object is the Full Scans/sec counter. A full scan indicates that the entire table is being accessed instead of the index being used. This could be due to the statistics being out-of-date, or because an index doesn't exist.

- **SQL Server:SQL Statistics object**   Counters in this object monitor requests sent to an instance of SQL Server. By monitoring the number of batches received, or query compilations and recompilations, you can learn how quickly SQL Server is processing user queries, and how effectively the queries are being processed. The default counter for this object is the Batch Requests/sec. The Batch Requests/sec counter provides information on how many SQL batch requests SQL is receiving. It can be an ideal measure to determine how much work SQL is performing. A number of batch requests indicates good throughput.

NOTE   SQL Statistics is not measuring index statistics, but instead statistics on SQL itself. If you want to measure general statistics on SQL Server, use the SQL Server:General Statistics object.

DBCC

The Database Console Commands (DBCCs) provide methods to check on several elements of a database. As with the dynamic functions and VIEWs, there are too many commands to cover each one. Instead, we'll cover a few.

While not completely replaced, there seems to be a trend within SQL Server 2005 to replace many of these with dynamic functions and VIEWs.

DBCC commands belong to one of four primary categories, as shown in Table 7-4.

Category	Description
Maintenance	Maintenance tasks on databases, indexes, or filegroups.
Informational	Gather and display information on different server or database objects.
Validation	Check on databases and various database objects.
Miscellaneous	Miscellaneous tasks.

Table 7-4 DBCC Categories

Several of the more common DBCC commands are listed in Table 7-5. At a minimum, a successful DBA would be familiar with these. Several have been discussed in the text previously.

DBCC Command	Description
CHECKDB	Checks the integrity of the database and all the objects in the database. This includes allocation, structural, and logical integrity.
CHECKFILEGROUP	Checks the integrity of all the tables within a filegroup.
CHECKTABLE	Checks the integrity of a table or VIEW.
HELP	Gives information on any DBCC command.
SHOW_STATISTICS	Shows current distribution statistics for a specific index.
OPENTRAN	Shows information on the oldest active transactions (active, distributed, and nondistributed).
SHRINKFILE	Shrinks the size of a data or log file.
SHRINKDATABASE	Shrinks the size of the database.
SQLPERF	Shows information on transaction log usage.

Table 7-5 Common DBCC Commands

 TIP DBCC CHECKDB (to check database integrity), DBCC OPENTRAN (to check for open transactions within a database), and DBCC SQLPERF (to get information on the transaction log) are still widely used commands within SQL Server 2005.

Microsoft has deprecated several DBCC commands. Table 7-6 lists several of the DBCC commands you may have used in SQL Server 2000 that are now deprecated. Avoid using these.

Deprecated Command	Alternative Recommendation
INDEXDEFRAG	Use ALTER INDEX.
DBREINDEX	Use ALTER INDEX.
DBREPAIR	Use DROP DATABASE.
SHOWCONTIG	Use sys.dm_db_index_physical_stats.

Table 7-6 Deprecated DBCC Commands

Filegroups

The last method of optimizing a database we'll discuss in this chapter is filegroups. The majority of databases will have a single filegroup that holds a single file (the .mdf file). However, we can add additional files and filegroups to optimize the performance of a database.

As a reminder, a file is created for the database when the database is created (named *databaseName*_data, by default). All database objects (tables, VIEWs, indexes, and so on) are physically stored in the file. This data file is kept logically in a filegroup. By default, the first filegroup is named Primary and is often referred to as the *primary filegroup*.

The transaction log is a separate file and is not kept in a filegroup at all.

While database objects are physically stored in the data file, we can't choose which file an object is stored in, at least not directly. What we can do is pick which filegroup a database object is stored in. By creating a new file (perhaps on a different drive) and placing it into a new filegroup, we can manipulate where database objects are located. In large databases, we can create additional files and/or filegroups for the following purposes:

- **Performance**   Placing tables that are frequently joined on separate filegroups (that have files located on separate physical drives) can allow parallel scans from two drives simultaneously. Additionally, placing a single large table on one filegroup allows us to move it to a separate physical drive.

- **Recoverability**   Creating multiple files and filegroups, we can create a backup scheme that backs up filegroups.

- **Partitioning**   As discussed in Chapter 3, we can create a partitioning scheme that stores some portions of a table on one filegroup, and other portions of the table on another filegroup (using different files on different drives for each of the filegroups).

Filegroup Possibilities

Three possibilities exist for filegroup association with files. Understanding these possibilities makes it easier to understand how to use filegroups for optimization. The possibilities are:

- One file and one filegroup
- Multiple files and one filegroup
- Multiple files and multiple filegroups

One File and One Filegroup

Take a look at Figure 7-25. This shows the AdventureWorks database stored on one file: AdventureWorks_data.mdf. The database file is associated with one filegroup: Primary.

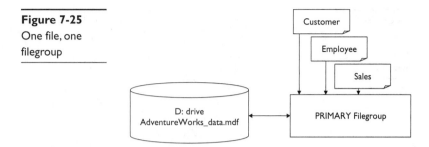

Figure 7-25
One file, one filegroup

In this scenario, we can't control where database objects will be stored. They will all be stored in the AdventureWorks_data.mdf file, which is in the Primary filegroup.

This is the scenario that the majority of databases will use. It is only when they become very large that we need to look for optimization strategies.

Multiple Files and One Filegroup

We can create a second file and place it on a different disk drive, as shown in Figure 7-26. Notice the extension of the secondary file is .ndf. The second file starts out empty, but as data is added, deleted, and modified, SQL Server strives to equalize the amount of data stored in each file. With the two files located on two separate drives within the filegroup, this subsequently equalizes the data stored on both drives.

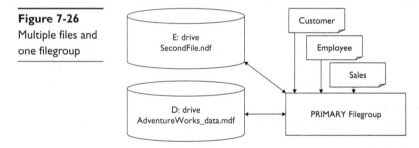

Figure 7-26
Multiple files and one filegroup

Ideally, over time 50 percent of the data will be in the AdventureWorks_Data.mdf file (on one drive) and 50 percent of the data will be on the SecondFile.ndf file (on a separate drive).

Remember though, we can't pick which file an individual database object is stored in. The only thing we can do is pick the filegroup. Since all database objects will be stored in the Primary filegroup, SQL determines where the data is stored. The contents of the Customer, Employee, and Sales tables will be spread across both drives.

Multiple Files and Multiple Filegroups

The third possibility is to create multiple files and multiple filegroups. We can see this in Figure 7-27. In this example, we have a secondary filegroup named Secondary.

Figure 7-27
Multiple files
and multiple
filegroups

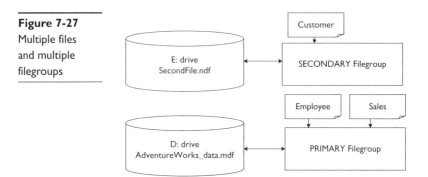

By creating the Secondary filegroup and associating the SecondFile.ndf file with the Secondary filegroup, we can specify which objects are placed on which drive.

In the figure, we have specified the Secondary filegroup for the Customer table. This causes the Customer table to be on the E: drive. The Employee and Sales tables have been placed on the Primary filegroup. This causes these tables to be placed on the D: drive.

EXAM TIP When tasked with optimizing a database by placing objects (such as a single extremely large table) on another physical disk, we would use filegroups. By creating a secondary filegroup, we can create file (or files) on different physical disks and associate the database object with this filegroup. The net effect is that the large object is located on a different physical disk.

Again, we can't associate database objects such as a table with a file directly. Instead, we can only associate the objects with the filegroup. In this exercise, we'll demonstrate that by creating a filegroup, a file, and creating a table on a different filegroup.

Exercise 7.7: Create Files, Filegroups, and Associate Tables with a Filegroup

1. Launch SSMS and create a New Query window.

2. Execute the following script to create a database and a table:

```
CREATE Database Chapter7;
GO
USE Chapter7;
```

3. Use the following script to create a second file named SecondFile.ndf and a second filegroup named Secondary:

```
ALTER DATABASE Chapter7 ADD FILEGROUP Secondary;
ALTER DATABASE Chapter7
ADD FILE (NAME = 'SecondFile', FILENAME = 'C:\Program Files\Microsoft
SQL Server\MSSQL.1\MSSQL\DATA\ SecondFile.ndf',
  SIZE = 1024KB, FILEGROWTH = 1024KB)
        TO FILEGROUP Secondary
```

NOTE Of course, the path that you add this second file to is dependent on the location of the first instance of SQL Server. For example, if you installed the first instance on the D: drive, change the *C:* to *D:*.

4. Create a table on the Secondary filegroup with this script. Notice that we can only specify the filegroup, not the file.

```
CREATE TABLE dbo.Customer(
  CustomerID int IDENTITY(1,1) NOT NULL,
  Notes varchar(50) NOT NULL,
  CONSTRAINT [PK_Customer_CustomerID] PRIMARY KEY CLUSTERED
  (
        CustomerID
  )
)ON SECONDARY
```

5. Using the GUI, view the properties of the Customer table:

   a. In SSMS, right-click Databases and click Refresh. Open the chapter7 database. Open the Tables folder.

   b. Right-click the Customer table and select Properties. Your display should look similar to Figure 7-28. Notice in the Storage section, the Secondary filegroup is listed. There is no property for a file, only a filegroup.

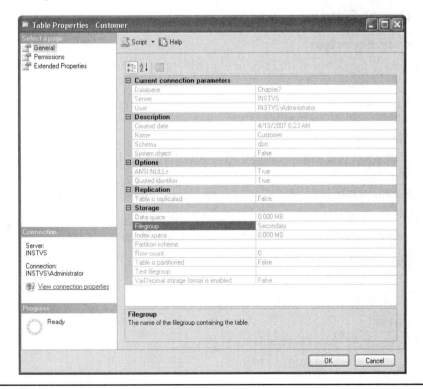

Figure 7-28 The Customer table properties

Chapter Review

In this chapter, we covered some important concepts related to optimizing databases. Indexes are central to any optimization strategy.

We can create one clustered index (indexid of 1) on tables, and multiple nonclustered indexes (indexid of 2 to 249). If we want to use sophisticated queries (such as with the CONTAINS predicate) against textual data, we can implement full-text catalogs and indexes. To help us determine what indexes are needed, we can use the Database Engine Tuning Advisor.

SQL Server uses statistics on indexes to determine their usefulness. These are automatically created and automatically updated by default. We can manually update the statistics on a table with the UPDATE STATISTICS command or manually update all the statistics in a database with the sp_updatestats system stored procedure.

Indexes can become fragmented, so sometimes they require intervention. Some dynamic management views and functions can help us look at the details on statistics, and if necessary, we can update the statistics.

Lastly, we talked about the three possibilities of configuring files and filegroups, and how we can do so for performance, recoverability, or partitioning reasons. For example, a large table can be placed on a different physical disk through the use of filegroups.

Additional Study

Self-Study Exercises

- Create a nonclustered index on the modifiedDate column of the Sales.Customer table.
- Change the clustered index on the Sales.SalesOrderHeader table from the Sales OrderID column to the OrderDate column to optimize searches based on a range of dates.
- Create a full-text index on the Document column of the Production.Document table.
- View the statistics on all the indexes in the AdventureWorks database.
- Update the statistics on the production.product table.
- Update all the statistics on the AdventureWorks database.
- Move the Sales.SalesOrderDetail table to a file in a different directory. (This will take several steps.)
- Check the structural integrity of the AdventureWorks database.

BOL Topics

- Clustered Index Design Guidelines
- Creating Indexes (Database Engine)

- Creating Indexes with Included Columns
- Designing Indexed Views
- Reorganizing and Rebuilding Indexes Full-Text Search Fundamentals
- Dynamic Management Views and Functions
- Tools for Performance Monitoring and Tuning
- Checklist for Analyzing Slow-Running Queries
- sys.dm_db_index_physical_stats
- sys.dm_db_index_usage_stats
- ALTER INDEX (Transact-SQL)
- SQL Server, SQL Statistics Object
- DBCC (Transact-SQL)
- DBCC SHOW_STATISTICS (Transact-SQL)
- UPDATE STATISTICS (Transact-SQL)
- sp_updatestats

Summary of What You Need to Know

70-431
This entire chapter includes information required for the 70-431 test.

70-441
This entire chapter includes information required for the 70-441 test. Pay special attention to all the information dealing with clustered, nonclustered, and covering indexes.

70-442
This entire chapter includes information required for the 70-442 test. Pay special attention to all the information dealing with clustered, nonclustered, full text, and covering indexes. You should also know the information on statistics and filegroups.

Questions

70-431

1. You work for a company that processes over 50,000 transactions daily in the Orders table. The Orders table requires a clustered index on the OrdersID column. A highly used query queries orders by date. What can you do to improve this query?

   A. Create a clustered index on the date column.

   B. Create a nonclustered index on the date column.

   C. Move the Orders table to its own filegroup.

   D. Change the clustered index to a nonclustered composite index.

2. You manage a SQL Server 2005 database named Hurricanes and discover that all indexes of the Temperature table are heavily fragmented, thus decreasing performance. You must decrease the fragmentation of the indexes without taking the Temperature table offline. What should you do?

A. DBCC DEFRAG INDEXES.

B. Defragment the disks on the server.

C. ALTER INDEX ALL on Hurricane REBUILD.

D. ALTER INDEX ALL on Hurricane REORGANIZE WITH (LOB_COMPACTION=ON).

3. You have created a VIEW on the Employees table using the following Transact-SQL statement:

```
CREATE VIEW vw_Birthday AS
SELECT LastName, FirstName, Birthday FROM Employees;
```

You are tasked with creating an index on the vw_Birthday VIEW. What must you do prior to creating the index? (Choose two.)

A. Alter the VIEW and include the WITH INDEXING clause.

B. Alter the VIEW and include the schema name with the column names.

C. Alter the VIEW and include the WITH SCHEMABINDING clause.

D. Alter the VIEW and include the schema name with the table name.

4. Users are complaining that reports are running quite slowly. You determine that some statistics are missing and others are out-of-date. What Transact-SQL statement can you use to correct the problem?

A. DBCC CHECKTABLE

B. ALTER INDEX REORGANIZE

C. UPDATE STATISTICS

D. DBCC CREATE STATISTICS

5. You manage a SQL Server 2005 database used to identify and track prospects for IT recruiting. It includes a Prospect table with a Resume column. You need to implement full-text searching so you can run reports by querying text in the Resume column. Which of the following must you do? (Choose two. Each correct answer implements part of the solution.)

A. Create a clustered index on the Resume column.

B. Create a full-text catalog.

C. Create a nonclustered index on the Resume column.

D. Create a full-text index on the Resume column.

70-441

1. You manage a Stock database used as a back-end for a web site. The Web Developer is complaining that some of the pages where users query for stock information are taking more than 15 seconds to return. The queries are based on stock name, stock symbol, and price. What can you do to improve the performance?

    A. Create indexes on the commonly queried columns.

    B. Create a stored procedure to retrieve the commonly queried data.

    C. Create a function that returns the queried data.

    D. Create a trigger to fire the sp_IncreasePerformance system stored procedure whenever data is queried by the web application.

2. You are tasked with optimizing a VIEW named vwStockPerformanceHistory that is frequently read but rarely updated. The VIEW is usually queried by using an ORDER BY clause and it produces a statistical summary based on the PriceChange column. The VIEW uses deterministic functions. How can you optimize this VIEW?

    A. Create a full-text index on the PriceChange column.

    B. Create an index on the PriceChange column on the base table.

    C. Create an index on the PriceChange column on the VIEW.

    D. Change the deterministic functions to nondeterministic functions and create an index on the PriceChange column on the VIEW.

3. You manage a web application that uses a Stock database. Customers frequently query the Orders table of the Stock database for information on open orders. Most queries to the Orders table are related to specific customers. How can you ensure that these queries are optimized?

    A. Ensure that these queries are only accessed via a VIEW.

    B. Change the Customer PK column so it has an index.

    C. Ensure that the queries are only executed via a stored procedure.

    D. Specify an index on the Customer FK in the Orders table.

4. You manage a stock portfolio database accessible via a web application. Through analysis you have identified the two most often executed queries. One retrieves customer information and their total portfolio amount. The second retrieves a listing of stocks in their portfolio including the current value. How can you provide the best possible optimization for these queries?

    A. Ensure that each table queried has a clustered index on the PK.

    B. Ensure that the tables accessed by these queries have their statistics rebuilt nightly.

    C. Ensure that the tables accessed by these queries have their statistics removed.

    D. Create covering indexes for these queries.

  5. You are tasked with optimizing a distributed VIEW that pulls data from multiple servers. The VIEW uses deterministic functions. You've verified the VIEW's performance is very slow. What can you do?

    A. Make the VIEW an indexed VIEW.

    B. Change the VIEW so it uses nondeterministic functions and make it an indexed VIEW.

    C. Add indexes to the underlying tables of the VIEW.

    D. Rewrite the VIEW as a stored procedure.

70-442

  1. You are analyzing the execution plan for a slow-running query in the StockPortfolio database and you notice the tables are displayed in red. You've verified that indexes exist on the query. What can you do to resolve the problem? (Choose all that apply.)

    A. Set the AUTO CREATE STATISTICS database property to True or execute the following command:

```
ALTER DATABASE AdventureWorks
    SET AUTO_CREATE_STATISTICS ON
```

    B. Set the AUTO UPDATE STATISTICS database property to True or execute the following command:

```
ALTER DATABASE AdventureWorks
    SET AUTO_UPDATE_STATISTICS ON
```

    C. Execute the following command for each table in the database:

```
UPDATE STATISTICS (tablename)
```

    D. Execute the following command:

```
Exec sp_updatestats
```

    E. Change the Display Text color to Blue in the execution plan.

  2. You are developing a script that will be frequently used within an application. It will accept start and end dates and return a list of sales within those dates. The following script shows what you've created. For now, you are using test dates, but in the final version the script will be created as a stored procedure with parameters.

```
USE AdventureWorks;
GO
DECLARE @StartDate datetime
```

```
DECLARE @EndDate datetime
Set @StartDate = '01/01/2001'
Set @EndDate = '12/31/2001'
SELECT CustomerID, TotalDue, OrderDate
FROM Sales.SalesOrderHeader
WHERE ORDERDATE BETWEEN @StartDate and @EndDate
```

During testing, you realize the script is unacceptably slow. How can you improve the performance of this script?

A. Create an indexed VIEW using the OrderDate and CustomerID columns.

B. Create a clustered index on the OrderDate and TotalDue columns.

C. Create a nonclustered index on the OrderDate column and use the INCLUDE clause to include the CustomerID and TotalDue columns.

D. Create a nonclustered index on the OrderDate column.

3. You have been called in to improve the performance of a database. The design ensured the database fully complied with 3NF. You've identified a core set of queries that are used most often. Each of these joins two or more tables. After some review, you realize no additional indexes have been added to the database and decide to optimize the indexing strategy but also ensure that index maintenance is minimized. What do you do?

A. Add nonclustered indexes to cover all the queries.

B. Create indexes on all the PKs used in the core set of queries.

C. Create indexes on all the FKs used in the core set of queries.

D. Convert all of the core queries into indexed VIEWs.

4. You are tasked with improving the performance of the following frequently run query. The query receives the @OrderMonth value as a parameter, but for testing you are assigning a value.

```
DECLARE @OrderMonth datetime
Set @OrderMonth = 2
SELECT SalesOrderID, OrderDate, CustomerID
FROM Sales.SalesOrderHeader
WHERE MONTH(OrderDate) = @OrderMonth
```

What two steps can you take to improve the performance of this query? (Each answer presents part of the solution.)

A. Create a nonclustered index on the OrderDate column.

B. Create a clustered index on the OrderDate column.

C. Create a computed column in the Sales.SalesOrderHeader table using MONTH(OrderDate).

D. Create a nonclustered index on the MONTH(OrderDate) column.

E. Create a clustered index on the MONTH(OrderDate) column.

F. Create a covering index to cover the query.

5. You are asked to help analyze a database and make recommendations for improvements. Currently, you are analyzing the Employees table. Table 7-7 shows a partial layout of the Employees table.

Column	EmployeeID	LName	FName	Address	Phone	...
Data type	Int	char(50)	char(50)	char(500)	char(20)	...
Index type	nonclustered	nonclustered	nonclustered	clustered		...

Table 7-7 The Employees Table Layout

Based on the number of rows, you've identified that the Employees table and its indexes use too much memory. What can you do to improve the memory usage?

A. Rebuild the clustered index, changing the fill factor from 100 to 50.

B. Rebuild the nonclustered indexes, changing the fill factor from 100 to 50.

C. Change the clustered index to a different column with a smaller data type.

D. Change the EmployeeID column from a nonclustered index to a clustered index.

6. A table named PriceChanges logs all the price changes for each stock throughout the day, including the opening and closing price. This table is using a considerable amount of disk space and you are tasked with moving it to another disk. How would you accomplish this?

A. Move all the indexes to another filegroup.

B. In the properties of the table, specify a different disk location.

C. Move the table to a different server.

D. Move the table to another filegroup.

7. As part of a StockPortfolio database, you have created a query used to create a customer activity report. This query displays stocks sold and stocks purchased for a given date period. The OrderDate column is used in the WHERE clause to filter the report. You are tasked with improving the performance of this query. Of the following, which two actions should you do? (Each correct answer presents part of the solution.)

A. Create a clustered index on the OrderDate column.

B. Create a clustered index on StockPortfolio.

C. Use BETWEEN in the WHERE clause.

D. Order the results using the ORDER BY clause.

8. You are writing a query that will search a product description column looking for specific attributes. The results must include exact matches, inflectionally generated words, and synonyms. What would you include in your query?

    A. LIKE

    B. CONTAINS

    C. PATINDEX

    D. NEAR

9. You are tasked with creating a query that will return rows based on all verb tenses of a word in the Description column of a table. What must be done to achieve this? (Choose two. Each correct answer presents part of the solution.)

    A. Use the LIKE operator in the WHERE clause.

    B. Use the CONTAINS operator in the WHERE clause.

    C. Use the VERB operator in the WHERE clause.

    D. Create a clustered index in the Description column.

    E. Create a nonclustered index in the Description column.

    F. Create a full-text index in the Description column.

Answers

70-431

1. **B.** To optimize the query, we create an index on the date column. Since the OrdersID column must have a clustered index and we can have only one clustered index, the only other choice is a nonclustered index.

2. **D.** To decrease the fragmentation, we would either rebuild or reorganize the indexes. Reorganize is always done online (leaving the table available). Rebuild can be done online if the WITH (ONLINE = ON) clause is used. Defragmenting disks doesn't affect indexes. LOB_COMPACTION simply says that for any composite indexes with large object (LOB) data types, compact the pages holding them.

3. **C, D.** Two of the basic rules for creating indexes on VIEWs are (1) they must be created with the SCHEMABINDING option, and (2) objects must be referenced with a two-part name (schema.table). There is no WITH INDEXING clause. The schema name would be with the table or VIEW names, not with the column names.

4. **C.** The UPDATE STATISTICS command is the command to use to manually update statistics on a table or a VIEW. DBCC doesn't have a CREATE STATISTICS command. DBCC CHECKTABLE will check the integrity of all the pages and structures, but does not create or update statistics. ALTER INDEX REORGANIZE will defragment the index, which is not called for in this scenario.

5. **B, D.** To enable full-text searching, you would first create a full-text catalog and then create a full-text index on the column where you want to enable full-text searches. Clustered or nonclustered indexes will not help.

70-441

1. **A.** Adding indexes for frequently queried data will improve the performance of queries that use the index. Neither a stored procedure nor a function will improve the performance of these queries. There is no such thing as an sp_IncreasePerformance system stored procedure.

2. **C.** An indexed VIEW will provide significant performance gains when created on a VIEW that is frequently read but not updated, and when the VIEW is used to perform aggregations. The vwStockPerformanceHistory VIEW does both. Indexed VIEWs require referenced functions to use deterministic functions.

3. **D.** Since the queries are related to specific customers, there must be an FK-to-PK relationship between the Orders table and the Customers table (more than likely on a column named CustomerID). In the Customers table, the CustomerID column is the PK (and an index is automatically created on it to enforce uniqueness), and in the Orders table the CustomerID column is the FK. Adding an index to the CustomerID column in the Orders table would improve the performance. Neither a VIEW nor a stored procedure would be able to ensure these queries are optimized.

4. **D.** A covering index can be used to optimize a specific query by including all the columns referenced by the query in the index. By default, statistics are maintained automatically by SQL Server 2005 and it's rare that we need to take control of this when they are rebuilt. We certainly would not want to remove the statistics.

5. **C.** Adding indexes to the underlying tables will improve the performance. Making the VIEW an indexed VIEW might sound good, but a distributed VIEW can NOT have indexes created on it. All base tables referenced by the VIEW must be in the same database as the VIEW and have the same owner as the VIEW. Rewriting the VIEW as a stored procedure wouldn't improve the underlying performance of the queries.

70-442

1. **A, B, C, D.** The execution plan warns about out-of-date or missing statistics by displaying the table name in red text. Statistics should be set to automatically be created and automatically updated. To ensure they are all up-to-date, either the UPDATE STATISTICS command could be entered against every table (the hard way), or the sp_updatestats system stored procedure could be executed (the easy way). Execution plans don't have properties such as Display Text that can be manipulated.

2. **C.** By creating a nonclustered index and including all the columns in the query, we cover the query. Now, when this query is executed, only the index will be searched for the data instead of the entire table. An indexed VIEW may also work if it included all columns. Any other indexes that don't include all the

columns would still require accessing the underlying table. They may provide some performance gains but not as much as the covering index.

3. **C.** The core set of queries join two or more tables, and the database is in 3NF (highly normalized). Tables would logically be joined on PK-to-FK relationships. Creating indexes on the FKs would improve the performance of the core set of queries. PKs already have an index (they must to enforce uniqueness). Covering all the queries with indexes, or converting all the queries into indexed VIEWs would add a significant amount of index maintenance overhead.

4. **C, F.** Covering this query with a covering index would be the best solution. There are few referenced columns and it is a frequently running query. By creating a computed column on the MONTH(OrderDate) and including it in the covering index it becomes materialized in the index. While indexing the OrderDate column would provide some gains, it wouldn't be as much as covering the query.

5. **C.** Having an index on a column with a char(500) data type would consume a lot of memory. Ideally, you would either reduce the size of this column or remove the index from the column. A fill factor of 100 is 100 percent full (only one more row can be added). A fill factor of 10 is 10 percent full (or 90 percent empty), which would consume more memory. Changing an index from nonclustered to clustered would not change the memory consumption.

6. **D.** To move a database object such as tables and/or indexes to another physical disk, we must use filegroups. We'd create a secondary filegroup and add a file (or files) from a different physical disk to the filegroup. We can then associate the table with a filegroup to effectively move it to another disk.

7. **A, C.** Two ways to optimize a query with a range of data is to create a clustered index on the range column and use BETWEEN in the WHERE clause. StockPortfolio is the name of the database and an index can't be placed on an entire database. Using the ORDER BY clause will cause the results to take longer since an additional sorting operation will be required.

8. **B.** The CONTAINS predicate can be used to search text-based columns looking for both exact matches and fuzzy matches. An inflectionally generated word is derived from a stem. For example, the word ride is the inflectional stem of rides, rode, riding, and ridden. CONTAINS requires a full-text index on the column. LIKE can be used on text-based data that do not have full-text indexes, but it will only find exact matches, not inflectional words or synonyms. PATINDEX works on text-based data and can find the starting position of an exact match of a specified expression. The NEAR keyword can work within a CONTAINS clause to identify text near other text.

9. **B, F.** The CONTAINS operator can be used to search character type data and return inflectional forms of a word (verb tenses). LIKE can not return verb tenses. There is no VERB operator. The CONTAINS operator requires a full-text index on the searched column.

Security

In this chapter, you will learn about:

- Server security basics
- Authentication modes
- Security principals such as server logins and database users
- Server roles and database roles
- Securables such as tables, VIEWs, and stored procedures
- Permissions
- Encryption

> *Never underestimate the time, expense, and effort an opponent*
> *will expend to break a code.*
>
> —*Robert Morris*

It's been said that the only way to keep your computer 100 percent safe and secure is to power it down, unplug it from the network, and bury it in the sand. Safe and secure? Yes. Usable? No. When it comes to security, we must constantly strive for a balance between security and usability by practicing risk management.

In this chapter, we'll cover some basic security concepts in SQL Server 2005, including authentication modes, security principals, and securables. Security principals are users, roles, or groups that can be granted access to different securables. Securables, on the other hand, are resources that can have their access regulated, such as databases, stored procedures, tables, and so on.

Think of any database you might manage. People must be able to access it. You create security principals (users or roles) to allow that access—first to the server with a login, and then to the database with a user or role. Next, you need to restrict or widen access to different parts of the database. You will manipulate the permissions or access constraints of the database object (the securable) to grant the specific access desired.

Server Security Basics

Before users have access to the database, they must have access to the server. This is done by creating server logins, and then mapping the server login to a database user or role. Take a look at Figure 8-1 for the big picture. Two important points should be grasped here:

- Without access to the server, there is no access to a database (unless we use an advanced method such as an application role).

- Granting access to the server does not automatically grant access to a database (unless we enable the guest account).

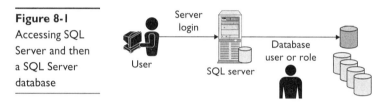

Figure 8-1
Accessing SQL
Server and then
a SQL Server
database

The first step toward configuring SQL security is creating the login. The types of logins we can create are dependent on the authentication mode of SQL Server.

Authentication Modes

Two primary authentication modes are available with SQL Server:

- **Windows Authentication**   A user logs into the domain (or local computer) and this credential is mapped to a login account on SQL Server. The user only has to provide credentials to the operating system, not SQL Server. A separate SQL login account is not required.

- **SQL Server and Windows Authentication (Mixed Mode)**   Allows use of either Windows Authentication or SQL Server Authentication. SQL Server Authentication requires the creation of a separate login account on the SQL server.

Windows Authentication

To understand how Windows Authentication works, take a look at Figure 8-2. The user first logs in to the domain (circle 1) and is authenticated by a domain controller. When the user has been authenticated, the login service creates and returns a security token for the user (circle 2) that includes items such as the security identifier (SID) of the user account. The token also includes the SIDs of any groups where the user is a member.

At some point, the user tries to access SQL Server and presents the security token for authentication (circle 3). SQL Server checks the user's token to see if either the user account or one of the group SIDs in the token maps to a server login. If so, SQL Server grants the user access to the server. With Windows Authentication, the user does not need to resupply credentials.

Figure 8-2
Windows
Authentication
in a domain

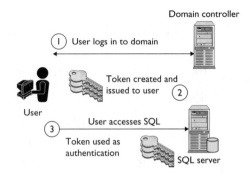

Windows Authentication provides several benefits:

- Utilizes Kerberos security protocol
- Provides password policy enforcement with complexity validation for strong passwords
- Provides support for account lockout
- Supports password expiration

While the previous explanation discussed a user in a domain, everything would work similarly for a user with a local computer account. Instead of a user's credentials being validated by a domain controller using Active Directory when first logging on, the user's credentials would be validated by the local computer using the local Security Account Manager (SAM) database. Unlike Active Directory, the local SAM does not use Kerberos.

SQL Server and Windows Authentication (Mixed Mode)

If SQL Server and Windows Authentication (commonly called "Mixed Mode") is selected, then access can be granted using either Windows Authentication or by creating SQL Server login accounts.

Using SQL Server Authentication and creating SQL logins can be useful to grant access to users who are running non-Windows systems (such as UNIX or Linux) and don't have Windows accounts.

The Windows Authentication part of Mixed Mode works the same way it does in Windows Authentication. For SQL Server Authentication, we must create a SQL Server login (something we'll explain how to do later in this chapter).

TIP While Microsoft recommends using Windows Authentication whenever possible. On the job, the choice between Windows Authentication and Mixed Mode authentication isn't always so easy. Even some Microsoft applications (such as Project Server) require SQL Server to be running in Mixed Mode. However, the server can be set to Mixed Mode with the majority of the accounts accessing SQL Server being Windows accounts. The biggest thing to ensure when in Mixed Mode is that the sa account (a SQL built-in system administrator account available only in Mixed Mode) has a strong password that is changed regularly, or the account is disabled completely.

In the following short exercise, we'll change the authentication mode from Windows Authentication to Mixed Mode. This will allow us to create SQL Server logins in the next exercise.

Exercise 8.1: Check the Authentication Mode

View the server properties in video 8-1.

1. Launch SSMS and connect to the default instance of SQL Server running on your system.

2. Right-click your server instance and select Properties.

3. In the Server Properties dialog box, in the Select A Page pane, choose Security. Your display should look similar to Figure 8-3.

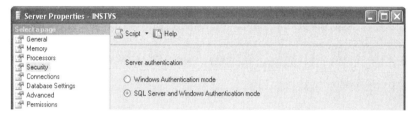

Figure 8-3   Server Security properties

4. If it is not already set, choose the SQL Server And Windows authentication mode option, and then click OK.

   a. If this is a change, a dialog box will appear saying the changes won't take effect until SQL Server is restarted. Click OK.

   b. If the warning dialog box appeared, right-click the server instance in SSMS and select Restart to restart the service. Click Yes in the verification dialog box. If an additional verification box appears to restart SQL Server Agent, click Yes.

The sa Account

A special login account is the sa account. "sa" is short for "system administrator." The sa account is only available for use in Mixed Mode authentication and is disabled by default. The sa account is a member of the sysadmin role and has full administrative control of all objects in the instance. Once enabled, it offers enormous power, so it should be protected with a strong password.

In early implementations of SQL Server, the sa account was enabled on some systems with blank passwords. This became an easy backdoor for hackers, and many systems were compromised.

With Microsoft's SD^3+C mantra (Secure by Design, Secure by Default, and Secure in Deployment and Communications), the sa account starts out disabled, and if you try to enable it later and set it with a blank password, you get a warning. When installing SQL Server, the installation wizard won't let you continue until you set a strong password for the sa account.

Creating Logins

To grant access to a server, we create logins. This login can then be mapped to a database user to grant access to individual databases. In this section, we'll cover the different methods used to create the login. Once a login is created, server-level permissions can be granted to the login.

If the server is set to Windows authentication mode, we can only use Windows logins. If the server is in Windows authentication mode and a user tries to connect to the SQL Server with a SQL login account, the user will get an error message.

 EXAM TIP The error "Login failed: the user is not associated with a trusted SQL Server connection" often indicates the server is in Windows authentication mode and the user is trying to access the server with a SQL Server login (not a Windows login).

If the server is in Mixed Mode authentication, we can use either Windows or SQL logins.

Windows logins can be created for Windows user accounts or Windows groups. Later in this chapter, we'll cover groups in more depth, but for now realize that by creating a login for a Windows group, you grant identical access to all users in that Windows group.

We can create the logins via the graphical user interface (GUI) or with T-SQL statements.

Creating Logins with the GUI

To create the login with the GUI, use the SSMS object browser to open the server Security container. Figure 8-4 shows the Logins container within the server Security container.

Figure 8-4

Logins within the server Security container

By right-clicking the Logins container and selecting New Login, you can create a new Login. Figure 8-5 shows the Login—New dialog box.

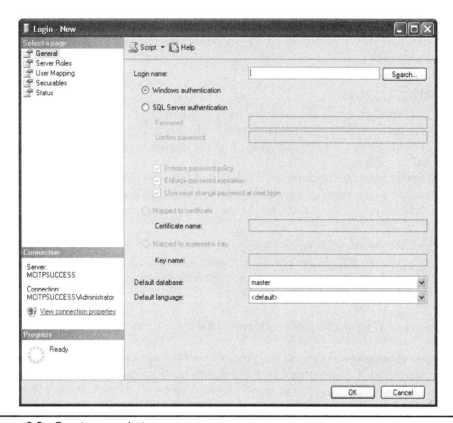

Figure 8-5 Creating a new login

Several properties can be configured and are worth noting on this page:

- **Login name** This is different depending on if you are creating a SQL login or a Windows login.
  - **SQL login** You choose the login name.
  - **Windows login** This is the actual name of the user or group account in Windows. If in a domain, it takes the form of *domain\userName*. If in a work-group, it takes the form of *computer\userName*.
- **Authentication** You can choose Windows Authentication or SQL Server Authentication. The choice affects the login name as just described. For a SQL login, you can create the name, but not so with a Windows login name.
- **Password policy settings** This allows the system to enforce password policies (if SQL is running on Windows Server 2003) for SQL Server login accounts. We'll explain several additional elements of password policies later, but the following are the basics:

- **Enforce password policy** This requires use of the same complexity of passwords for a SQL Server login that Windows employs.

- **Enforce password expiration** This uses the same expiration rules as those in Windows.

- **User must change password at next login** This forces the user to change the password at the next login.

 TIP The password policy and the password expiration can be enabled on a SQL Server 2005 implementation running on Windows XP, but full support for these features is not available on Windows XP. The full functionality depends on the NetValidatePasswordPolicy API (application programming interface), which is available in Windows Server 2003, but not Windows XP. As an example of a feature that doesn't function on Windows XP, weak passwords are accepted for SQL Server logins when SQL Server is installed on XP, but not on Windows Server 2003 when the Password Policy settings are enabled.

Selecting the User Must Change Password At Next Login setting will cause an error on a Windows XP system until it is deselected, but other functionality may go unnoticed.

- **Certificate and keys** These properties allow you to associate a login with a specific certificate or key.

- **Default database** This identifies which database the user will try to connect to when first connecting to the server. This does *not* grant Connect permission to the database.

- **Default language** This identifies the default language for the login.

While the authentication mode is important for any users who wish to log in, it doesn't matter what authentication mode the server is running in when creating logins. In other words, if the server is in Windows authentication mode, you can still create a SQL Server login. However, this SQL Server login couldn't be used until the authentication mode is switched to Mixed Mode.

Creating Logins with T-SQL Statements

Logins can also be created using T-SQL statements. The basic syntax is:

```
CREATE LOGIN loginName WITH PASSWORD = 'password'
```

The new password policy features can also be enabled with the Login creation script using the following clauses:

- **CHECK_POLICY** This specifies that Windows password policies are applied on this login. The syntax is CHECK_POLICY = ON. This is ON by default.

- **CHECK_EXPIRATION** This specifies that the password expiration policy should be enforced on this login. The syntax is CHECK_EXPIRATION = ON.

- **MUST_CHANGE**   SQL will prompt the SQL Server login for a new password the first time the new login is used.

The syntax used to create a new login with the password policy disabled would be:

```
CREATE LOGIN Sally WITH PASSWORD = 'password',
CHECK_POLICY = OFF
```

Password Policy

The Password Policy is an excellent new security feature of SQL Server 2005. As long as we're running SQL Server 2005 on a server running Windows Server 2003, we can use this to enforce password complexity and password expiration policies on SQL Server logins.

Notice we can only use this on SQL Server logins. Whenever possible, we use Windows accounts for logins, and Windows manages the password security for these accounts. With SQL Server 2005, we can now enforce some password security measures for SQL Server logins that simply weren't available before.

Parts of this Password Policy do work if running Windows XP, but for full implementations of the features, it needs to be running on a Windows Server 2003 product.

To use any of the settings, either Enforce Password Policy or CHECK_POLICY must be enabled. With CHECK_POLICY ON, CHECK_EXPIRATION can also be on. However, CHECK_EXPIRATION *cannot* be enabled without CHECK_POLICY being enabled.

Password Complexity   Checking the box to Enforce Password Policy or using the With Check option will enforce password complexity. This means that passwords must meet the following conditions:

- They do *not* contain all or part of the user's account name.
- They are at least six characters long.
- They contain three of the following types of characters:
  - Uppercase letters
  - Lowercase letters
  - Numbers (0–9)
  - Non-alphanumeric characters (@, %, *, and so on)

Password Expiration   When Password Expiration is enabled, logins will be prompted to change their passwords after some time limit has passed. Password Expiration follows the Maximum Password Age set in Group Policy.

In the following exercise, we'll create logins via the GUI and T-SQL statements.

Exercise 8.2: Create Logins

1. Create a Windows user account named Geri.

   a. To launch Computer Management, click Start, right-click My Computer, and select Manage.

   b. Open Local Users And Groups within the System Tools snap-in. Your display should look similar to Figure 8-6.

Figure 8-6

Creating a new user in Computer Management

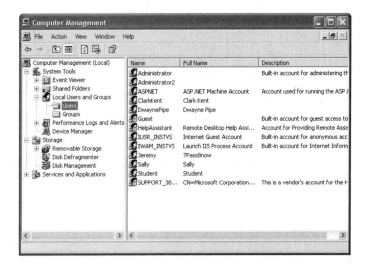

c. Right-click Users and select New User.

d. Enter **Geri** as the User Name and **P@ssw0rd** in the Password and Confirm Password boxes. Deselect the User Must Change Password At Next Logon box. Click Create. Click Close. Close Computer Management.

2. Open an instance of SSMS with administrative account access.

3. Open the Logins container within the Server Security container.

4. Create a login for the Geri user account using the GUI.

a. Right-click Logins and select New Login.

b. In the Login—New dialog box, choose Search | Advanced | Find Now.

c. Select the Geri account created in step 1. Click OK twice. Your display should look similar to Figure 8-7 with your computer name instead of the MCITPSuccess computer name. If you were to click OK, you would create the Geri account, but at this point you would click *Cancel* instead of OK. We're going to create the same account with T-SQL statements.

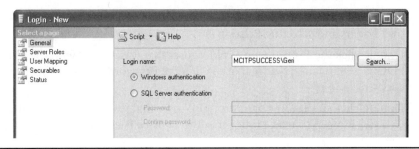

Figure 8-7   Creating a Windows login in GUI

5. Create a Windows login using T-SQL statements:

   a. Determine your computer name. Press WINDOWS+R to access the Run command. (The WINDOWS key is the Windows Logo key between the CTRL and ALT keys on the left side of the space bar on most keyboards.) Enter **CMD** and click OK. At the command prompt, enter **Hostname** and press ENTER. Write down the name of your computer _____. Close the command prompt window.

   b. Open a New Query window in SSMS.

   c. Use the following script to create a Windows login for the Geri account created in step 1. Substitute your computer name identified in step a. earlier in place of *yourComputerName*:

   ```
   CREATE LOGIN [yourComputerName\Geri] FROM WINDOWS
   ```

CAUTION Make sure you use the delimiters *[ ]* in the *computername\ username* in the preceding statement. Without the delimiters, the \ is misinterpreted and results in an error.

6. Create a SQL Server login that uses T-SQL statements with a weak password using the following script:

   ```
   CREATE LOGIN TSQL_LoginWeakPW
   WITH PASSWORD = 'password', CHECK_POLICY = OFF
   ```

7. Create a SQL Server login using T-SQL statements with a strong password:

   ```
   CREATE LOGIN TSQL_LoginStrongPW2
   WITH PASSWORD = 'P@ssw0rd'
   ```

TIP The default for CHECK_POLICY is On if it is not provided in the script. This conforms with Microsoft's SD³+C security philosophy.

8. View the logins you created:

   a. In the SSMS Object Explorer, refresh the Logins container by right-clicking over Logins and selecting Refresh.

   b. Double-click the TSQL_LoginWeakPW user that was created with the CHECK_POLICY=OFF clause. Notice that the Enforce Password Policy setting is *not* checked.

   c. Double-click the TSQL_LoginStrongPW user that was created without the CHECK_POLICY clause. Notice that the Enforce Password Policy setting is checked.

Server Roles

In the previous chapter, we saw that a database has several built-in database roles. By adding a user to one of these roles, we automatically granted the user the associated privileges granted to the database role.

We have similar roles at the server level. By adding a login to a server role, we automatically grant the user all the privileges associated with the server role. Server roles including short descriptions are listed in Table 8-1.

Server Role	Description
SysAdmin	Allows full access to anything and everything within the SQL instance. Members of the BUILTIN\Administrators Windows group (local administrators) are automatically a member of the sysadmin role. Within a domain, the domain admins group is automatically added to the local administrators group.
ServerAdmin	Can modify serverwide configuration options and shut down the server.
SecurityAdmin	Can manage logins and login properties, including resetting passwords. Can GRANT, DENY, and REVOKE permissions at the server level and database level.
BulkAdmin	Can run the BULK INSERT command.
DbCreator	Can CREATE, ALTER, DROP, and RESTORE any database.
ProcessAdmin	Can terminate processes running on SQL Server.
SetupAdmin	Can add and remove linked servers. Can execute some stored procedures.
DiskAdmin	Can manage disk files.

Table 8-1   Server Roles

Two roles that stand out are the sysadmin role and the serveradmin role. Their differences are important, but may not be obvious. Think of the sysadmin role as having the keys to the entire SQL kingdom. Membership in this role grants full access to the SQL Server instance. The serveradmin role is a little less intuitive. Based on the name, you might think you can do anything as a member of this role, but you can only modify settings.

Notice, I stopped short of saying full access to the *server* when talking of the sysadmin role. Why is that?

Remember in Chapter 1 when we introduced instances? One of the primary reasons to create a separate instance is to have a security separation. A user in the sysadmin role in the default instance has full and complete control over that instance. However, if a separate named instance was created, the first user would have zero access to that named instance. Each instance has its own set of server roles that only apply to the instance, not the full server.

However, anyone in the local administrators group or who logs on as a local administrator will be granted full access to all instances on the server. This is because the administrators group is automatically added to the sysadmin role in each instance of a server on Windows XP and Windows Server 2003 products.

Checking Effective Permissions

We have the ability to check effective permissions on any securable. As an example, right-click the instance, choose Properties, and then select the Permissions tab. Your display should look similar to Figure 8-8. This page shows that Geri is granted Connect permissions. However, this is a little misleading.

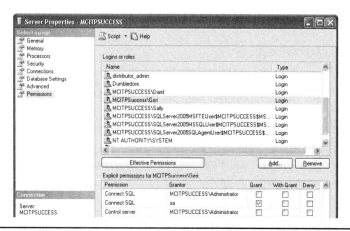

Figure 8-8 Server-level permissions

It's not apparent, but I have added Geri to the serveradmin role. The display of her permissions only shows what's been explicitly granted to her, not her serveradmin permissions. By clicking the Effective Permissions button, I can view all the permissions assigned directly to her and granted through all of her role memberships. Figure 8-9 shows Geri's effective permissions as a member of the serveradmin role.

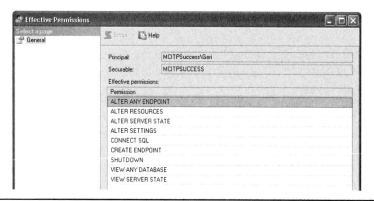

Figure 8-9 Effective permissions including role permissions

Groups

From a system administrator perspective, groups allow us to easily organize users so we can ultimately grant them permissions. More specifically, within a Windows Domain we have *global* groups, which are used to organize users, and *domain local* groups, which are used to assign permissions for resources.

In small organizations, domain local groups can be bypassed completely, and for this discussion that's what we'll do. We'll stick to global groups. Take a look at Figure 8-10 for a big-picture view of what we're doing. The global group G_MCITP_DBAs will be created and managed by a network administrator of the Windows domain.

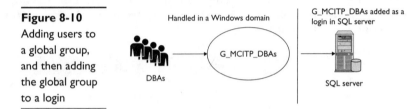

Figure 8-10
Adding users to a global group, and then adding the global group to a login

Handled in a Windows domain

DBAs → G_MCITP_DBAs

G_MCITP_DBAs added as a login in SQL server

SQL server

We have a group of five users who are responsible for database administration on the MCITP server. They all log in to the domain to do regular work and occasionally need to access the MCITP SQL Server to administer it. While we could create logins on the SQL Server for each of these users, it would be a whole lot easier to just add one global group as a login on the SQL Server.

Since the system administrator is already managing the global group G_MCITP_DBAs, our job becomes much easer. By adding the Windows group as a login, we have several benefits:

- New DBAs added to the G_MCITP_DBAs global group are automatically added to the login on the server and have the same access as other administrators.

- Group management is probably already being done by system administrators. No additional work needs to be done by us.

- We don't have to manage users individually.

In the following exercise, we'll add a Windows group, add a user to the group, and grant access to the group on the SQL Server. We'll then verify the access for the user.

TIP While we will use local groups in this exercise, the process works the same way when using global groups in a domain. If you have the benefit of access to a domain where you can create your own global groups, go ahead and create domain global groups. However, it's anticipated that most readers won't have a domain that they can manipulate.

Exercise 8.3: Work with Windows Groups

1. Open Computer Management by clicking Start, right-clicking My Computer, and selecting Manage.

2. Create three new user accounts:

    a. Open the Local Users And Groups container by double-clicking Local Users And Groups.

    b. Right-click the Users container and click New User.

    c. In the New User dialog box, enter **Dawn** as the User Name. Enter **P@ssw0rd** in the Password and Confirm Password text boxes. Deselect the User Must Change Password At Next Logon box. Your display should look similar to Figure 8-11. Click Create.

Figure 8-11
Creating a
Windows user

    d. Repeat the process for two additional users named **Nimfa** and **Darril**. Click Close.

3. Right-click over Groups and select New Group.

4. In the New Group dialog box, enter **G_MCITP_DBAs** as the Group Name. Enter **Database Administrators for the MCITP SQL Server** as the Description.

5. Add the three users to this group:

    a. Click Add.

    b. In the Select Users dialog box, click Advanced.

    c. Click the Find Now button.

    d. While holding down the CTRL key, select the three users created earlier: Dawn, Nimfa, and Darril. Click OK.

e. In the Select Users dialog box, click OK. Your display should look similar to Figure 8-12. Click Create, and then click Close.

Figure 8-12

Creating a new group for DBAs

6. With the users added to the G_MCITP_DBAs group, we can now add the group to the SQL server. Open an instance of SSMS.

7. Open the Logins container within the Security container for the server.

8. Right-click Logins and select New Login.

9. On the Login—New page, click the Search button to the right of the Login Name text box.

10. In the Select User Or Group dialog box, click the Object Types button. Make sure the Groups box is checked as shown in Figure 8-13. Click OK.

Figure 8-13

Selecting Groups as an object type

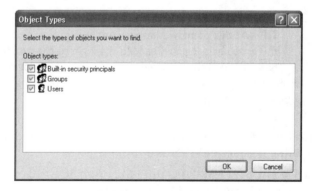

11. In the Select User Or Group dialog box, click the Advanced button.

12. Click Find Now. Browse to the G_MCITP_DBAs group and select it. Click OK, and then click OK again.

13. Ensure that Windows Authentication is selected. Your display should look similar to Figure 8-14.

Figure 8-14   Adding a Windows group as a login

14. In the Select A Page pane, choose Server Roles. Enable the sysadmin role. Your display should look similar to Figure 8-15. Click OK.

Figure 8-15   Adding a login to a server role

TIP   At this point, we have a Windows group with three users. We've added the group as a login and added the login to the sysadmin role. Even though we haven't added these individual user accounts as logins to the server, each of these users now has sysadmin privileges in the instance by being a member of the Windows group that was assigned the login.

15. Now let's verify that one of these users truly has sysadmin privileges. Start another instance of SSMS as one of the users.

    a. Choose Start | All Programs | Microsoft SQL Server 2005, right-click over SQL Server Management Studio, and select Run As.

    b. In the Run As box, select The Following User and enter **Dawn** as the User Name and **P@ssw0rd** as the Password. Click OK.

    c. In the Connect To Server dialog box, select the default instance and click Connect.

    d. Open a New Query window in SSMS.

16. Execute the following script to identify the user that is currently logged on:

```
SELECT SUSER_SNAME();
```

Notice that the user (not the group) is displayed. This allows you to grant access to multiple users with a single group, but still identify specific users. For example, you may have a need to audit who is modifying data or who is modifying table definitions. You can use triggers with the suser_sname() function to identify the specific user.

17. Additionally, you can use the individual Windows account for the execution context. Remember, we did not add a login for the Nimfa account to the SQL Server. Instead, we added the Group G_MCITP_DBAs, and Nimfa is a member of the G_MCITP_DBAs group. Execute the following script to show we can use the EXECUTE AS clause to identify users of groups that have been granted access:

```
EXECUTE AS LOGIN = 'yourComputerName\Nimfa';
SELECT SUSER_SNAME();
IF IS_SRVROLEMEMBER ('sysadmin') = 1
Print 'You are in the sysadmin role'
REVERT
GO
EXECUTE AS LOGIN = 'yourComputerName\Darril';
SELECT SUSER_SNAME();
IF IS_SRVROLEMEMBER ('sysadmin') = 1
Print 'You are in the sysadmin role'
```

    TIP The Print command sends the output to the Messages tab, and the SELECT statement sends the output to the Results tab. You won't see both results in the same display, but instead must select the different tabs in the results pane.

18. Execute the following script to identify the role memberships of the current user:

```
IF IS_SRVROLEMEMBER ('sysadmin') = 1
Print 'You are in the sysadmin role'
```

Security Principals

Don't be scared by the term *security principals*. This is just another way of saying who we can grant permissions to. Security principals can be created from three different sources, as outlined in Table 8-2. Notice that the different principals have different scopes. Both the Windows-level and SQL Server–level scopes have access to the server, but only the database-level principals have access to the database objects. What isn't apparent is that the server-level principals must be mapped to the database-level principals to actually grant database access.

Scope	Principals
SQL Server level	SQL Server login.
Windows level	Local user, Local group, Domain user, Domain group.
Database level	Database user, Database role, Application role.

Table 8-2 The Scope of Security Principals

Overall, the following are the steps required to grant users access to a server, a database, and objects within the database:

1. Create a login to the server. This provides access to the server and can be created from a Windows-level (such as a Windows user account or group) or SQL Server–level security principal.

2. Database user is created within a database and associated with the server login.

3. Object permissions are granted within the database.

I'd like to stress a critical piece of information here. Access to the server does *not* mean access to all databases. We could have 100 different databases hosted on a server. Just because someone has been granted login access to the server doesn't automatically grant them access to all of these databases. It's very conceivable that single logins are mapped to single databases.

We use database-level security principals (users and roles) to grant users access to individual databases. Further, granting someone access to the database does *not* grant them access to everything *in* the database.

There's a lot to comprehend here, but if you can grasp the bigger picture, the details will come together. To help bring it into focus, we'll do an exercise that demonstrates many of these concepts. For now, simply focus on the results of the steps—what works and what doesn't work—which will help you gain a big-picture perspective. After you complete this chapter, I invite you back to do this exercise again. On the second time through, you should gain a better understanding of some of the details. Then you can create a different user, such as Sally2.

In the following exercise, we'll demonstrate the differences among access to the server, access to a database, and access to individual objects within a database.

Exercise 8.4: Access AdventureWorks

1. Create a Windows user account named Sally:

   a. Click Start, right-click My Computer, and select Manage to launch Computer Management.

   b. Open Local Users And Groups within the System Tools snap-in.

   c. Right-click Users and select New User.

d. Enter **Sally** as the User Name and **P@ssw0rd** in the Password and Confirm Password boxes. Click Create | Close. Close Computer Management.

2. Create a login in SQL Server for the Sally account:

   a. Open SSMS using an account that has administrative privileges, and connect to the default instance of SQL Server.

   b. Open the Security container. Open the Logins container.

   c. Right-click Logins and select New Login.

   d. In the Login—New dialog box, click the Search button.

   e. In the Select User Or Group dialog box, click the Advanced button. Click the Find Now button. Scroll down to the Sally account created in step 1 and select it. Click OK, and then click OK.

 TIP The username is represented as *computerName\userName*. If you knew your computer's name, you could just enter the data here without searching, and a domain account would be added as *domainName\userName*.

   f. Change the Default Database from Master to AdventureWorks. Your display should look similar to Figure 8-16.

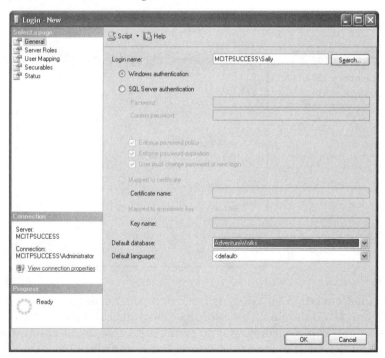

Figure 8-16   Creating a server login account

   g. In the Login—New dialog box, click OK. Leave the SSMS window open.

TIP While it may seem as though we have just granted Sally permission to the AdventureWorks database, we haven't. By setting the default database, all we have done is set her connection to point to the AdventureWorks database. Currently Sally has *no* permissions on the AdventureWorks database except what has been granted to the Public role. Since the Public role has not been granted any permission, if she tries to connect to the server her connection attempt will fail.

3. Using the following steps, open another instance of SSMS and try to connect to it using the Sally account just created. This will fail.

   a. Choose Start | All Programs | Microsoft SQL Server 2005. Right-click over SQL Server Management Studio and click Run As.

   b. Select The Following User and in the User Name box enter **Sally**. For the Password enter **P@ssw0rd**.

NOTE For a standalone computer or one in a workgroup, you can enter either the username only, or the computer name and username in the format of *computerName\username*. For example, if the computer name was MCITP, we could use *MCITP\Sally*.

Your display should look similar to Figure 8-17. Click OK.

Figure 8-17
Launching SSMS
using Run As

   c. In the Connect To Server dialog box, select your default instance and click Connect. You should get an error since the connection tries to connect to the AdventureWorks database, but no permissions exist on AdventureWorks for Sally. Click OK, but leave the Connect To Server dialog box open.

4. Use the following steps to change the default database from AdventureWorks to Master for the Sally Login:

   a. In the first SSMS window (the one open with administrative privileges), right-click the Sally login and select Properties.

   b. Change the Default database from AdventureWorks to Master. Click OK.

5. Connect to SSMS using the Sally account. This will succeed.

   a. In the Connect To Server dialog box that you left open in step 3c, ensure the default instance is still selected and click Connect. You should successfully connect to the instance as Sally.

6. View the permissions on the Master database:

   a. Open the Databases container.

   b. Open the System Databases container.

   c. Right-click the Master database and select Properties. On the Select A Page pane, choose Permissions. Scroll down to the Connect permission. Your display should look similar to Figure 8-18.

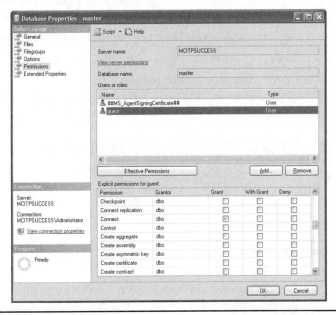

Figure 8-18   The Guest account is granted Connect permission to the Master database

---

TIP   The Guest account is created automatically in all databases, but is disabled by default on all databases except the Master. Any user granted login access to the server is automatically granted the same access as the Guest account on each of the databases in the server. Since the Guest account is enabled in the Master database by default, a new login is able to connect to the server as long as they connect to the Master database.

7. Use the original SSMS connection with full administrative permissions to create a database user named Sally in the AdventureWorks database. Map the database user named Sally to the server login named Sally.

TIP With two instances of SSMS open, it's easy to get confused about which one is which. However, by looking at the end of the instance name in Object Explorer (see Figure 8-19), you can identify the instance by the username. Use this to verify which instance you're viewing when switching back and forth between instances.

Figure 8-19 Verifying the instance by using Object Explorer

a. If not open, open the Databases container in the original SSMS connection. Open the AdventureWorks container. Open the Security container.

b. Right-click Users and select New User. For the User Name, enter **Sally_dbUser**.

c. Click the ellipsis (…) button to the far right of Login Name.

d. In the Select Login dialog box, click Browse.

e. In the Browse For Objects dialog box, select the checkbox next to Sally and click OK. Your display should look similar to Figure 8-20. Click OK.

Figure 8-20 Creating a user within a database

8. Use the original SSMS connection with full administrative permissions to open a new query window, and execute the following stored procedure. You should have a result set of four rows.

```
USE AdventureWorks;
GO
EXEC uspGetEmployeeManagers 1;
```

9. Use Sally's SSMS connection to execute the same stored procedure. This will fail. You should get an error indicating that Sally doesn't have Execute permission on the stored procedure. This verifies that while Sally has been granted login access to the server, she does not have access to the database.

10. Use Sally's SSMS connection to try to access the Person.Contact table using the following script. This also fails because Sally doesn't have SELECT permission on the Person.Contact table.

```
SELECT *
FROM Person.Contact
WHERE LastName = 'Gilbert'
```

11. Use the original SSMS connection to grant Sally Execute permissions on the uspGetEmployeeManagers stored procedure:

   a. Open the Programmability container in the AdventureWorks database.

   b. Open the Stored Procedures container. Right-click the dbo.uspGetEmployeeManagers stored procedure and select Properties.

 TIP By using the command *sp_helptext uspGetEmployeeManagers*, you can see that the stored procedure uses a complex join of several tables, including the Person.Contact table.

   c. In the Select A Page pane, select Permissions. Click Add.

   d. In the Select Users Or Roles dialog box, click Browse. Select Sally and click OK, and then click OK.

   e. In the Explicit Permissions For Sally_dbUser area, select Grant for the Execute permission. Your display should look similar to Figure 8-21. Click OK.

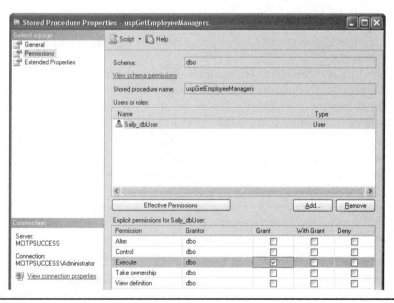

Figure 8-21   Granting the Execute permission for a stored procedure

12. Use Sally's SSMS connection to execute the same stored procedure again. It should succeed this time.

```
USE AdventureWorks;
GO
EXEC uspGetEmployeeManagers 1;
```

13. Use Sally's SSMS connection to try to access the Person.Contact table with the SELECT statement. It should still fail.

```
SELECT *
FROM Person.Contact
WHERE LastName = 'Gilbert'
```

Exercise Comments   This exercise demonstrated some key security principles and may raise a couple of questions. Let's answer them:

- *Why were we able to do anything in the first SSMS connection?*
  In the first connection we are connected with a user account that has administrative privileges. The account is a member of the built-in administrators group. This group is automatically added to the sysadmin role and members of the sysadmin role have full permissions on the server.

 NOTE   For those of you who may be using Vista, the preceding note isn't true. Vista users are not members of the sysadmin role by default. Users must be mapped to the sysadmin role with the SQL Server 2005 User Provisioning Tool for Windows Vista.

- *Why is a user able to connect to the Master database even though a user account doesn't exist?*
  When a Login is created, it is automatically mapped to the Guest account for every database. By default, the Guest account is enabled in the Master database, so connections to the Master database are allowed. However, the Guest account is disabled in all other databases by default.

- *After permissions were granted on the stored procedure, why did it work but the SELECT statement on the actual tables not work?*
  Permissions granted on stored procedures that use DML statements (such as SELECT) allow access to any objects that the stored procedure accesses, but only through the stored procedure. To grant SELECT access to the table directly the SELECT permission must be granted.

Database Users

As we saw in the previous exercise, database users are created within a database in order to grant access to a database. When created, the database user is mapped to a server login.

The syntax to create a login and a database user with T-SQL statements is shown next:

```
CREATE LOGIN Sally_TSQL
    WITH PASSWORD = 'P@ssw0rd ';


USE AdventureWorks;
CREATE USER Sally_TSQL_dbUser
    FOR LOGIN Sally_TSQL;
```

It is possible to create a database user without a login. Doing so will prevent the database user from connecting to any other databases on the server as the Guest. Further, the database user can never be mapped to a login. While a user without a login can't be used to log in to the server, it can be used for impersonation. The following code creates a database user without a login, grants permissions, and then uses the EXECUTE AS clause to run code under the context of our new user:

```
-- Create the user in the database
CREATE USER Steve WITHOUT Login
-- Grant the user permissions on a table
GRANT SELECT ON Person.Contact TO Steve
--Use the EXECUTE AS clause to execute in the context of a user
EXECUTE AS USER = 'Steve'
SELECT * FROM Person.Contact
REVERT
```

Database users can be created to represent single users or multiple users. If we have five users that need access to a database, we might choose to create five logins and five separate database users.

However, if we have 500 users within a domain who need access to a database, creating 500 separate logins and 500 separate database users is likely more work than we're interested in. So, we can do this an easier way.

On the domain level, we can ask the system administrator to create a global group that includes these 500 users. More than likely, one already exists. We then create a login with this group. With a single login representing the 500 users, we can create a single database user mapped to this login and assign the appropriate permissions.

If we have some users who need different permissions than the group of 500, we would either add these users to specific database roles or create additional database users.

The Guest Account

The Guest account is created by default in every database and is disabled by default. Every login added to the server automatically has the same access as the Guest account, as long as the Guest account has been enabled. The purpose of the Guest account is ease of administration.

Consider a simplistic implementation of SQL Server within a small business that hosts a single central database. One Windows group that includes all employees of the business could be used to create a single login. By enabling the Guest account and granting permissions to this account, nothing else needs to be done. Granted, additional users with elevated permissions will likely be added, but for the most part this does make it easy to implement.

Within SQL Server 2005, Microsoft has implemented SD³+C: Secure by Design, Secure by Default, and Secure in Deployment and Communications. Because of this, the Guest account is disabled by default. If you look at the Guest account in any database, you can see a small red down-arrow indicating it is disabled (see Figure 8-22). The arrow is subtle, but it's there.

Figure 8-22

The Guest account disabled

To enable the Guest account in any database, use the following script:

```
USE database;
GO
GRANT CONNECT TO GUEST;
```

To disable the Guest account within a database, use the following script:

```
REVOKE CONNECT TO GUEST;
```

dbo

The dbo user exists in every database. *dbo* stands for database owner and is a member of the db_owner role. The dbo can do anything and everything in the database. The sysadmin server role maps to the db_owner role, allowing someone in the sysadmin server role to be able to manage any and all databases on the server.

Reminder: anyone in the local Windows administrators group is automatically mapped to the sysadmin server role, and thus, also has full access to all databases.

Database Roles

SQL Server 2005 includes both fixed database and fixed server roles that can be used to easily grant users the specific rights and permissions needed to accomplish a wide variety of tasks. We covered the server roles earlier in this chapter.

Database roles are referred to as *fixed* because they automatically exist in each database. By adding users to any of these roles, the user has the added rights and permissions of these roles. We can also create our own database roles to meet specific needs.

For those of you coming from a system administration background, roles work the same way as Windows groups. Windows has built-in groups that can be used for streamlined administration. If someone needs to have full and complete access to a server, we can add her to the Administrators group. If she needs to be able to back up and restore data on that server, we can add her to the Backup Operators group. Roles within SQL Server work the same way.

Table 8-3 summarizes the fixed database roles.

Database Role	Description
db_owner	Keys to the kingdom for the database. Can perform all configuration and maintenance activities on the database including dropping the database.
db_securityadmin	Can modify role membership and manage permissions.
db_accessadmin	Can manipulate database access. Can add or remove access for Windows logins, Windows groups, and SQL Server logins.
db_backupoperator	Can back up the database.
db_datareader	Can read all data from all user tables.
db_datawriter	Can add, delete, or change data in all user tables.
db_denydatareader	Explicitly denied the ability to read any data in user tables.
db_denydatawriter	Explicitly denied the ability to write any data to user tables.
db_ddladmin	Can execute DDL commands (CREATE, ALTER, DROP) within the database.
Public	Default role. Every database user is a member of the Public role.

Table 8-3   Fixed Database Roles

For the most part, the database roles are intuitive. Not a lot needs to be added to the information in Table 8-3. However, there is an important point to remember with the roles. If a user is a member of multiple roles, the permissions are cumulative. For example, if a user is a member of the db_datareader role and the db_datawriter role, the user has the permissions granted by both roles.

The Principle of Least Privilege

The Principle of Least Privilege states that we should give users the permissions they need, but no more. This principle has been around for a long time and transcends IT. The military follows a Need-To-Know principle that works the same way. Individuals are given exactly what they need to know for a topic or mission, but no more.

If users need to read data, we grant SELECT permission on the specific tables or views they need to read. We don't grant SELECT permission on all tables and views in the database. We don't just add users to the db_datareader role if they only need to read a few of the tables or views.

From a usability perspective, it is much easier to just put everyone into the sysadmin server role or db_owner database role. Then we don't have to manage security. However, usability isn't the only consideration. Security is very important.

When creating a security policy and identifying which roles to create and which roles to add users to, keep the Principle of Least Privilege in mind.

The Public Role

The Public role deserves special mention. Every database user is a member of the Public database role. We can use this to grant all database users the same permissions by granting the permissions to the Public role.

Earlier, we talked about using the Guest account for easy administration on smaller implementations of SQL Server. This works fine if we want to grant access to a database for all users who have access to the server. We can grant login access for a group of users, enable the Guest account in all the databases, grant appropriate permissions to the Guest account, and we're in business.

But what if we want only a specific group of users that can access the server to have access to a specific database? The Public role can be used to accomplish this.

Assume we have a small company with two key departments: *Sales* and *Research and Development*. All the users in the Sales department are in the G_Sales Windows global group. All the users in the Research and Development department are in the G_RnD Windows global group.

Our SQL Server has two databases (RnD and Sales). The Research and Development department needs access to the RnD database and the Sales. The Sales department, on the other hand, needs access to the Sales database. However, we don't want sales personnel to be able to access the RnD database.

For the users in the Research and Development department, we can create a database user named RnD_Users in the RnD database mapped to the G_RnD global group. We then grant the appropriate permissions to the Public role, and since the RnD_Users are in the database, they have the permissions assigned to the Public role. Since the Sales users don't have access to the RnD database, they would not have access to the RnD database. We can see this in Figure 8-23.

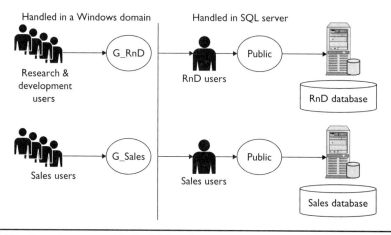

Figure 8-23   Managing access with the Public role

We could similarly map the Sales users to the Sales database and assign appropriate permissions to the Public role. Now all the users in the G_RnD global group have the appropriate permissions to the RnD database, but none of the Sales users have access.

A logical question is, "Why not just grant permissions to the RnD_Users group instead of the Public role?" This would work until we needed to grant permissions to an additional group. Assume we are tasked with granting several managers the same permissions as the users in the Research and Development department. With what we've done so far, all we'd have to do is grant the managers access to the database, and they'd be in the Public role with the appropriate permissions.

If we had granted the permissions to the RnD_Users group instead of to the Public role, we would now have to assign the appropriate permissions to the Managers group. Thus, we'd now have a dual-entry problem. Any time we change the permission for one group, we'd have to change the permission for the other group, and the potential for problems would increase.

In this scenario, the Guest account is not enabled in the RnD database. If it were, then all the users in the Sales department would have access to the RnD database—a scenario we don't want.

User-Defined Database Roles

While the existing fixed database roles are great for their intended purpose, they can't meet all possible needs. For some purposes, we need to create our own database role where we can grant the specific permissions needed

If you have any type of separation of database access, the use of user-defined database roles is invaluable. By creating our own roles, we can specify the specific permissions we need on any database objects. With the database role created, we can add users to the roles, and based on their role memberships, they will have the assigned permissions.

Earlier, we compared the fixed database roles with built-in Windows groups. Within Windows Domains we also have the ability to create our own Global and Domain Local groups. Creating our own database roles works the same as creating our own groups in a domain.

In the following exercise, consider this scenario. You have hired a consultant to come in and rewrite several stored procedures. You need to grant her full access to these specific stored procedures, but you don't want to grant her any other access. You'll create a special database role and grant permissions for this role to do anything with the specific stored procedures.

Exercise 8.5: Create a Database Role

1. Connect to an instance of SSMS.

2. Open the AdventureWorks database. Browse to the Security | Roles | Database Roles container within AdventureWorks. Open the Security container, the Roles container, and then the Database Roles container. Your display should look similar to Figure 8-24.

3. Right-click Database Roles and select New Database Role.

4. On the Database Role–New page, enter the Role Name as **spManager**.

5. In the Role Members area, click Add. In the Select Database User Or Role dialog box, click Browse. In the Browse For Objects dialog box, select the Sally_dbUser database user created in the earlier exercise. Click OK, and then click OK again in the next window.

Figure 8-24
The Database
Roles container

 NOTE While we are only adding a single user to the role in this exercise, in practice you will likely be adding several users to a role. However, even if you're only adding one user to a role, it is still useful to create the role. We assign permissions to the role. While Sally is in the role, she has the permissions. If Sally gets promoted and moves on and Joe is added to the role, he now has the same permissions Sally had. If we add or change the role membership later, we can easily do so, and the permissions are already set. If we had assigned permissions only to the user, then we'd have to repeat all the steps for every new user.

Your display should look similar to Figure 8-25. Click OK.

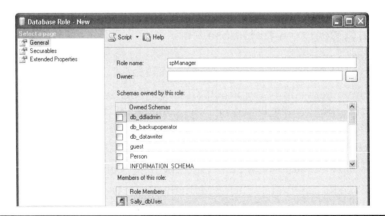

Figure 8-25 Adding a database role

6. Within AdventureWorks, open the Programmability | Stored Procedures container.

7. Right-click the dbo.uspGetBillOfMaterials stored procedure and select Properties.

8. In the Select A Page pane, click Permissions.

9. In the Users Or Roles section, click Add. In the Select Users Or Roles dialog box, click Browse. In the Browse For Objects dialog box, select the spManager database role. Click OK, and then click OK.

10. In the Explicit Permissions For spManager section, check the box under Grant for each of the permissions. Your display should look similar to Figure 8-26. Click OK.

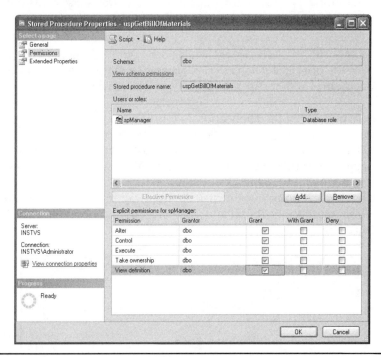

Figure 8-26 Setting permissions on the uspGetBillOfMaterials

We could then repeat steps 7–10 on each stored procedure that needs to be modified.

Application Roles

Application roles can be created to set specific permissions for applications. Application roles do not have any members and are activated with the sp_setapprole stored procedure, which includes both the application role name and a password.

Consider a business that uses a database named Hurricanes. The database has a wide range of weather data related to hurricanes. An application named Hurricane Tracking is used to access the database, and hundreds of people use the Hurricane database within your company.

Instead of granting the hundreds of users access to SQL Server, one application role can be created for the Hurricane Tracking program. Within the program, the sp_setapprole stored procedure is executed, and access is granted to the database for the application role.

This can be a method of controlling access. If you only want to grant access to the database through a specific application, the application role can be created for this purpose. No additional permissions would be granted to the users, so the only way the users can access the database is through the application.

 EXAM TIP If all user access is to be done through an application, consider the use of an application role. The application role is activated within the application with the sp_setapprole system stored procedure.

The primary purpose of the application role is to grant and control access to a database through the role. At the same time, we can deny access to the database through any other means, by simply not granting access to the database to any other principal besides the application role. It's important to note that, when an application role is activated for a user their individual permissions are not valid.

To create an application role, right-click the Application Roles container (*database* | Security | Roles | Applications Roles) and select New Application Role. Enter the name of the application role and a password, as shown in Figure 8-27.

Figure 8-27   Creating a new application role

The next step would be to assign specific permissions for the application role. For example, if you wanted the application to be able to execute all stored procedures within the Sales schema, and also run SELECT statements against all tables and views in the Sales schema, we can grant EXECUTE and SELECT permissions to the role within the Sales schema. Figure 8-28 shows us doing just that.

Schemas

A schema is a collection of database entities within a single namespace. With the use of schemas, different groups of database objects (tables, views, stored procedures, and so on) can be grouped together into a common namespace.

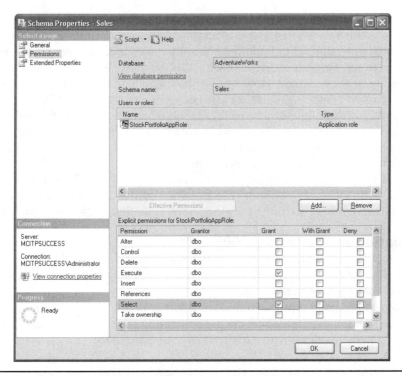

Figure 8-28   Granting permissions to the app role in the Sales schema

For example, consider the AdventureWorks business. They have a Sales department, and the database has tables and other objects directly related to sales. We can create a Sales schema with the express purpose of organizing the sales objects within this namespace.

The concept of schemas in this context is new to SQL Server 2005, and is largely used to resolve a problem database administrators faced in previous editions of SQL Server. In the four-part name of a database object, the schema is the third part:

serverName.databaseName.schemaName.objectName

In SQL Server 2000, the four-part name looked like this:

serverName.databaseName.owner.objectName

The Problem with SQL Server 2000 Object Names
Every database object needs an owner. Let's say I create a table named Employees in the Certification database on the SQL Server 2000 server named MCDBA. The four-part name would look like this:

MCDBA.Certification.darrilgibson.Employees

This might work fine for a long time. Perhaps I've even created dozens of objects with myself as the owner. Then a wonderful thing happens. I win the lottery! Instead of writing stored procedures, I'm looking for worthy causes to share my wealth with.

Needless to say, I am no longer managing this database. You come in and take over responsibility of the database. However, all these database objects have my name on them. You couldn't delete my database user because I own all of the objects. If you were to change the owner name of any of these objects, relationships between them and other objects would be broken. You would have to change the database owner name on all of the objects and on all of the definitions of the objects. At the very least, you could expect a long weekend of changing and testing.

To avoid the problem, Microsoft's recommendation was for all database objects to be owned by the dbo user. With all objects owned by the dbo, the problem could be avoided. However, this also limited organization capabilities within the database.

The Solution in SQL Server 2005

With the creation of schemas in SQL Server 2005, users don't own objects. Instead, we define a schema as a namespace that encompasses a group of database objects—one or more users than own a schema.

Dropping a user isn't a problem because the user doesn't own the object. If necessary, we grant ownership of the schema to another user. The use of schemas also allows permissions to be managed with a higher degree of granularity.

TIP   Users don't own objects. Users own schemas and schemas are used to name objects. With this understanding, a four-part name would never include the name of a user. The third part of the four-part name should only include the schema name.

Schema Permissions

Schemas have specific permissions that can be assigned. These are relatively standard permissions, but the great strength here is that by granting specific permissions to a schema, we grant the same permissions to all objects in the schema.

Figure 8-29 shows the permissions that can be assigned to schemas. For example, if I assign the SELECT permission within the Person schema to a specific use or role, then that user or role will now have SELECT permissions for all the tables and VIEWs in the Person schema.

Figure 8-29
Schema
permissions

Permission	Grantor	Grant	With Grant	Deny
Alter	dbo	☐	☐	☐
Control	dbo	☐	☐	☐
Delete	dbo	☐	☐	☐
Execute	dbo	☐	☐	☐
Insert	dbo	☐	☐	☐
References	dbo	☐	☐	☐
Select	dbo	☐	☐	☐
Take ownership	dbo	☐	☐	☐
Update	dbo	☐	☐	☐
View definition	dbo	☐	☐	☐

EXAM TIP By granting the appropriate permissions on the schema, we can allow access to the underlying tables and VIEWs without expressly granting access to the underlying tables and VIEWs. This also applies to any database objects, such as stored procedures or functions. Instead of granting execute permissions to any stored procedure or function within the schema, the Execute permission can be granted to the schema, and the permission will be applied to all stored procedures and functions within the schema.

Similarly, if we want to grant execute permissions to all stored procedures and functions within the schema, we can grant the Execute permission to the schema. In the following exercise, we'll demonstrate this with the Sally_dbUser account created earlier.

Exercise 8.6: Grant Permissions to a Schema

1. If not already open, open an instance of SSMS and create a new query window.

2. Enter and execute the following script to impersonate Sally_dbUser within the AdventureWorks database.

```
EXECUTE AS USER = 'Sally_dbUser'
SELECT * FROM Person.Contact
REVERT
```

Note that this fails since Sally_dbUser does not have permissions on the Person.Contact table.

3. Grant Sally_dbUser SELECT permissions on the Person schema.

   a. Using the SSMS Object Explorer, browse to the Person schema in the Databases | AdventureWorks | Security | Schemas folder.

   b. Right-click the Person schema and select Properties. Click the Permissions page.

   c. Click the Add... button.

   d. In the Select Users Or Roles dialog box, enter **Sally** and click the Check Names button to find all the users starting with "Sally."

   e. In the Multiple Objects Found dialog box, select the check box next to Sally_dbUser. Click OK, and then click OK.

   f. In the Schema Properties dialog, select the check box for Grant Select Permission. Your display should look similar to Figure 8-30. Click OK.

4. Enter and execute the following script to impersonate Sally_dbUser within the AdventureWorks database.

```
EXECUTE AS USER = 'Sally_dbUser'
SELECT * FROM Person.Contact
REVERT
```

This now succeeds even though this user does not have direct permissions on the underlying table.

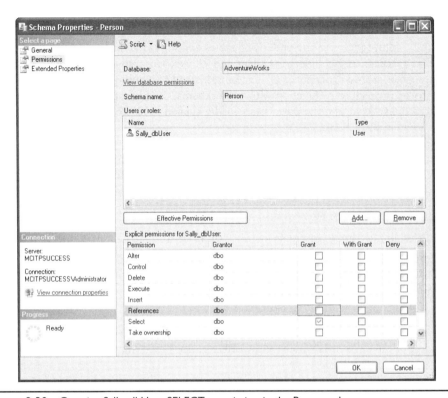

Figure 8-30   Granting Sally_dbUser SELECT permission in the Person schema

5. Enter and execute the following script to try and execute a stored procedure as Sally.

```
EXECUTE AS USER = 'Sally_dbUser'
EXEC dbo.uspGetEmployeeManagers 1
REVERT
```

This fails since Sally does not have the Execute permission on this stored procedure.

6. Grant the Sally_dbUser user the Execute permission on the dbo schema.

   a. Using the SSMS Object Explorer, browse to the Person schema in the Databases | AdventureWorks | Security | Schemas folder.

   b. Right-click the dbo schema and select Properties. Choose the Permissions page.

   c. Click the Add… button.

   d. In the Select Users Or Roles dialog box, enter **Sally** and click the Check Names button to find all the users starting with "Sally."

    e. In the Multiple Objects Found dialog box, select the check box next to the Sally_dbUser user. Click OK, and then click OK.

    f. In the Schema Properties dialog, select the check box for Grant Execute Permission. Click OK.

7. Enter and execute the following script to try and execute the same stored procedure as Sally with the dbo Execute permission.

```
EXECUTE AS USER = 'Sally_dbUser'
EXEC dbo.uspGetEmployeeManagers 1
REVERT
```

This now succeeds.

Database Securables

Database securables are objects we can secure with permissions. We grant specific permissions to principals on an object granting or denying access. Many of the securables are listed below:

- Columns
- Database
- Functions
- Schema
- Server
- Service broker queues
- Stored procedures
- Synonyms
- Tables
- VIEWs

Some securables are contained within others creating nested hierarchies, or "scopes." The three scopes are Server, Database, and Schema. Permissions assigned to the scope are inherited by the objects within that scope, but not inherited to objects outside the scope. The previous exercise demonstrated this concept. By granting permissions to a schema, the identical permissions were applied to objects within the schema.

Permissions

The actual permissions that can be assigned to all the objects are quite lengthy. If you want to view a complete list, take a look at the Permissions topic in Books Online. However, we need to cover some generic concepts related to permissions.

Individual permissions can be granted, denied, or revoked:

- **Granted**   You are explicitly given this permission.
- **Denied**   You are explicitly denied this permission.
- **Revoked**   This removes any permissions that have been granted or denied.

Grant and Deny are straightforward, but the Revoke permission frequently trips people up. Revoke has a negative connotation and implies something is being taken away. However, revoke doesn't always mean access is no longer granted.

Consider a table named Employee. We can grant Sally SELECT permission on the Employee table by selecting the check box in the Grant column in the Select row. We can see this in Figure 8-31. This allows Sally to execute SELECT statements against the table.

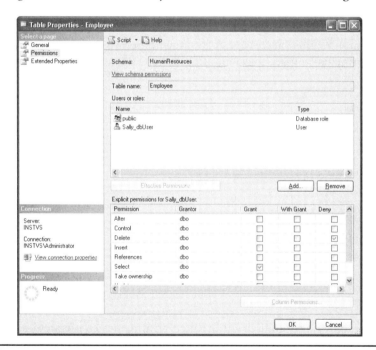

Figure 8-31   Employee table permissions

Notice that in Figure 8-31, we've selected the Deny check box in the Delete row. Thus, Sally is explicitly denied the permission to execute DELETE statements against this table. If the Public role were *granted* Delete permission and Sally were *denied* Delete permission, then Delete would take precedence.

If we were to revoke either the Select or Delete permissions, they would be removed and there would be no check box. On the surface this implies no access. However, if the Public role were granted Select or Delete permissions, the user would still have Select or Delete permissions even though the individual user permissions were revoked or removed.

TIP Between the Grant and Deny permission, you can see the With Grant permission. The With Grant permission grants the user or role the ability to also grant the associated permissions to others.

When a user has multiple permissions assigned, such as when a user is a member of multiple roles, the effective permission is a combination of all permissions assigned. Any deny permission overrides any grant permission.

Permissions can be assigned via the GUI (as shown in this chapter) or with T-SQL statements of GRANT, DENY, and REVOKE.

Permission Conventions

Permissions follow two primary conventions no matter what securable they apply to:

- Permissions follow a hierarchical structure. For example, granting Control permission on the database grants Control to all objects within the database.

- Permissions are named using core naming conventions. While we'll delve into specific permissions of some objects, these naming conventions apply to all securables.

The naming conventions of permissions are listed next.

- **CONTROL**   This grants ownership-like capabilities.

- **ALTER**   This grants the ability to change properties (except ownership) of a specific object. ALTER includes any type of modification, including CREATE and DROP.

- **ALTER ANY (object type)**   This grants ALTER permission on any type of named object. ALTER ANY can be used on any database securable or on any server securable.

- **CREATE**   This grants the ability to create an object. CREATE can be granted on a server securable, database securable, or schema-contained securable.

- **TAKE OWNERSHIP**   This grants the ability to take ownership. Once owned, anything can be done to an object, including changing the permissions.

- **IMPERSONATE**   This grants the ability to impersonate a user or login.

- **VIEW DEFINITION**   This grants the ability to view the metadata on an object.

- **BACKUP and DUMP**   These are synonymous and allow backups of the database, though DUMP has been deprecated.

- **RESTORE and LOAD**   These are synonymous and allow restores of the database, though LOAD has been deprecated.

Tables and VIEWs

Both tables and VIEWs can have the same possible permissions assigned. These are listed in Table 8-4.

Permission	Description
Alter	Can execute ALTER statements.
Control	Full control on the object just as an owner would have.
Delete	Can execute DELETE statements.
Insert	Can execute INSERT statements.
References	Can reference this table using the REFERENCES clause. This is needed when using JOINs within a SELECT statement on PK and FK relationships. Remember, the FK is defined with the REFERENCES clause.
Select	Can execute SELECT statements.
Take Ownership	Enables the ability to take ownership. Once owned, the user has full control on the object.
Update	Can execute UPDATE statements.
View Definition	Can execute commands to view metadata on the object.

Table 8-4 Table and VIEW Permissions

Just as with any database object permissions, these permissions can be granted, denied, or revoked via the GUI or via T-SQL statements to any user or role in the database.

By granting permissions to a VIEW, we can provide column-level security to a table. This is much easier than explicitly granting and denying permissions on individual table columns. Consider an Employee table with the following columns:

- EmployeeID
- LastName
- FirstName
- SSN
- Salary
- Phone

The SSN (social security number) and Salary data might be important to protect. However, we need users to be able to retrieve names and phone numbers. So, what do we do?

We create a VIEW on the following columns:

- LastName
- FirstName
- Phone

We grant Select permission on the VIEW, but not on the underlying table. Now users can execute queries against the VIEW and get employee phone numbers, but they do not have access to sensitive data.

In the following exercise, we'll create a VIEW and verify that permissions on the VIEW are all that are needed to access the underlying table.

Exercise 8.7: Grant Permissions to a VIEW

Watch video 8-7 to see how to grant permissions to objects within SSMS.

1. If not open, launch an instance of SSMS and open a new query window.

2. Enter the following text to impersonate the Sally_dbUser user and try to access the Production.Product table:

```
EXECUTE AS USER = 'Sally_dbUser'
SELECT * FROM Production.Product
SELECT * FROM Production.ProductInventory
REVERT
```

   This will fail since Sally does not have access to the Production.Product table, or the Production.ProductInventory table.

3. Enter the following text to create a VIEW of products that have inventory levels lower than the reorder point:

```
CREATE VIEW vwLowInventoryProduct
AS
SELECT p.ProductID, p.Name, p.ProductNumber, p.ReorderPoint,
pi.Quantity
FROM Production.Product AS P
INNER JOIN Production.ProductInventory AS pi
ON p.ProductID = pi.ProductID
WHERE p.ReorderPoint > pi.Quantity
```

4. Grant Sally SELECT permission on this VIEW with the following script:

```
GRANT SELECT ON vwLowInventoryProduct
TO Sally_dbUser
```

5. Execute the following script to show that Sally is able to view the underlying data with SELECT permission on the VIEW, but without any permission on the underlying tables:

```
EXECUTE AS USER = 'Sally_dbUser'
SELECT * FROM vwLowInventoryProduct
REVERT
```

Stored Procedures and Functions

Stored procedures and functions have similar permissions. These are outlined in Table 8-5.

Permission	Description
Alter	Can execute ALTER statements.
Control	Full control on the object just as an owner would have.
Execute	Allows execution of a stored procedure or function.
Take Ownership	Gives the ability to take ownership. Once owned, the user has full control on the object.
View Definition	Can execute commands to view metadata on the object.

Table 8-5   Stored Procedures and Functions Permissions

Functions also have the References and Select permissions. These work the same way in a function as they would in a table or a VIEW.

In an earlier exercise in this chapter, we saw that granting the Execute permission on a stored procedure without granting the Select permission on the underlying table is enough to grant access. We'll explore this further in Chapter 9.

This concept works the same with functions. If a function accesses an underlying table, only the Execute permission on the function is required. Individual permissions on the underlying table are not required.

CLR Assemblies

CLR assemblies have three specific permissions that can be assigned. We mentioned these in Chapter 6 and they will come up again in Chapter 9 with stored procedures. The permissions can be defined when the assembly is registered with the SQL Server instance or set from the property page of the assembly, as shown in Figure 8-32.

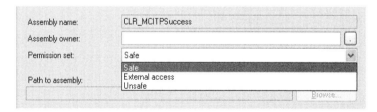

Figure 8-32   CLR assembly permissions

As a reminder, the three permission sets associated with CLR assemblies were:

- **Safe**   Only access to internal data is allowed.

- **External Access**   This allows access to external resources such as files, network environmental variables, and the Registry.

- **Unsafe**   This allows unrestricted access to resources within and outside SQL Server.

The permission set is defined in the CREATE ASSSEMBLY statement with the following syntax:

```
USE database;
GO
CREATE ASSEMBLY assemblyName
FROM 'path to dll file'
WITH PERMISSION_SET = SAFE
```

By default, CLR assemblies will be set to Safe, so it is possible to see an assembly created without the WITH PERMISSION SET statement. In order to be changed to something other than Safe, the database's TRUSTWORTHY property must be turned ON. This property is set to OFF by default. The TRUSTWORTHY property is used to indicate whether the SQL Server instance trusts the database and the contents within it.

If external resources need to be accessed, then the database should be set to TRUSTWORTHY with the following script:

```
ALTER DATABASE databaseName
    SET Trustworthy ON
```

Once done, the permissions can be changed via the property page.

Ownership Chaining

When multiple database objects access each other in order, it's referred to as a chain. For example, a simple chain could be created by a VIEW named vwEmployee that accesses the Employee and Contact tables. We can see this in Figure 8-33.

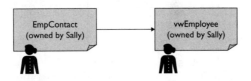

Figure 8-33 A chain created by a VIEW with both objects owned by the same user

In Figure 8-33, we can see that Sally owns the VIEW. Since she also owns the EmpContact table, she is able to grant access to the vwEmployee and the access is chained to the underlying table.

This isn't always the case. Take a look at Figure 8-34. Here we can see that Sally owns the VIEW, but does not own the underlying table EmpSalary. In this case, if Sally grants access to another user, the access isn't automatically granted to the underlying table. Instead, permissions on the EmpSalary table are checked when the VIEW is accessed.

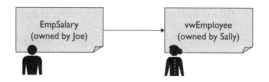

Figure 8-34 A chain created by a VIEW with both objects NOT owned by the same user

If Sally grants access to the vwEmployee VIEW to Joe, then when Joe accesses the VIEW, the permissions on the EmpSalary data will be checked. Assuming that Joe has access besides just being the owner, then Joe will be able to access the VIEW and the underlying data in the table. However, if Sally granted access to someone else that didn't have access to the EmpSalary table, then they still wouldn't be able to access the data in the table. This would be referred to as a broken ownership chain.

Cross-Database Ownership Chains

A cross-database ownership chain can exist when ownership chaining is allowed between different databases within an instance. This is disabled by default, but if it *was* enabled it would work like Figure 8-35.

Figure 8-35
A cross-database
ownership chain

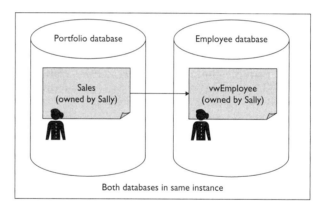

In Figure 8-35, we can see that Sally owns the VIEW vwEmployee in the Employee database and also owns the Sales table in the Portfolio database. In this case, she could grant ownership to the vwEmployee VIEW and users would not need additional permissions on the Sales table. Instead, Sally's ownership would be chained between the objects in the databases. Again, this is disabled by default. To enable cross database chaining on an instance, you can use the following command:

```
ALTER DATABASE AdventureWorks
  SET DB_CHAINING ON
```

Once this command is executed, you can verify that the option has been changed by looking at the Options property page of the database. It should look like Figure 8-36.

Notice that this option is dimmed indicating it can only be viewed on this page, not changed from this page.

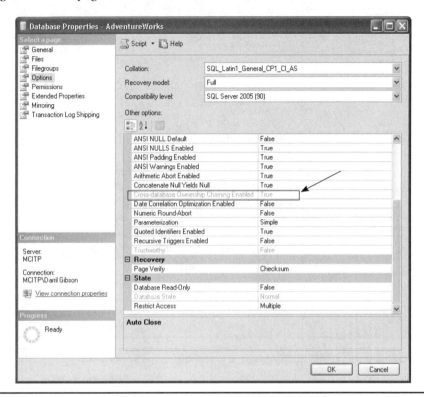

Figure 8-36   Cross-Database Ownership Chaining Enabled set to True

---

EXAM TIP   To enable ownership chaining between databases in a single instance of SQL Server, enable cross-database ownership chaining on each database involved in the chain.

This option should be set on each database involved in the chain. Only members of the sysadmin role can modify the DB_CHAINING setting. As an alternative, cross-database ownership chaining can be enabled on the instance and it will be applied to all databases on the instance. Setting it at the instance can be done on the Security property page of the instance, as shown in Figure 8-37.

Designing an Execution Context Strategy

The topic of designing an execution strategy came up in Chapter 6, but deserves some clarification here. In SQL Server 2005, we have the ability to specifically identify the execution context of T-SQL code that is run. We did this in Exercises 8.3 and 8.7 using the EXECUTE AS clause. It can also be done within stored procedures, triggers, and

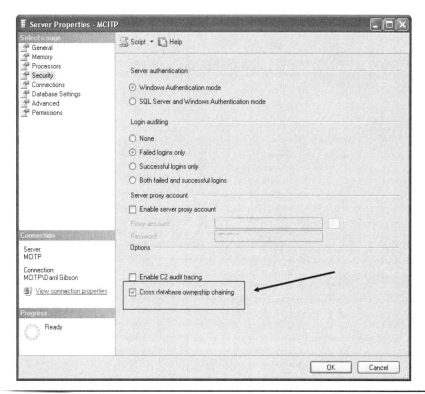

Figure 8-37   Enabling cross-database ownership chaining on the Server Instance

many functions. In other words, we can specify which user's account will be used when the code is run.

While execution context concepts apply to all these modules, let's focus our discussion on a stored procedure. It will work the same way for other modules.

Consider this scenario. On a regular basis, we import data into a staging table from an external database. Immediately before importing the data, we truncate the staging table. We use a stored procedure to do this and a DBA will execute the stored procedure.

In this case, either the DBA needs elevated permissions to truncate the staging table and import the data, or the stored procedure needs elevated permissions. However, since there isn't a Truncate permission available, we'd have to grant the DBA ALTER permissions on the database to allow him to truncate the table.

Instead of granting ALTER permissions, we use the EXECUTE AS clause, in effect creating our own specialized permissions for this code.

The EXECUTE AS clause has several contexts that the stored procedure can be configured to run under. The choices are:

- User Name
- Caller

- Self

- Owner

User Name This specifies that the stored procedure will run under the context of any specified database user or server login.

Caller This specifies that the stored procedure will run as the user that executes the stored procedure. In this case, the user executing the stored procedures must have all the required permissions on all referenced objects. Caller is the default for stored procedures when the EXECUTE AS clause is not added.

Self This specifies that the stored procedure will run under the context of the user creating or altering the stored procedure. Self is the default for queues.

Owner This specifies that the module will run under the context of the owner of the module. If the module doesn't have an owner, the owner of the schema of the module will be used.

So how could we create our stored procedure for the staging table? We have multiple possibilities. Obviously, whoever executes the stored procedure needs Execute permissions on the stored procedure. Other EXECUTE AS permissions are shown next.

- **Execute As User_name** We would define the stored procedure using the Execute As User_name clause, and designate a user with appropriate permissions on the staging table. Anyone with the Execute permission on the stored procedure could execute it.

- **Execute As Caller** Ensure the DBA executing the stored procedure has appropriate permission on the staging table. Only someone with the ALTER permission on the staging table could successfully execute the stored procedure that truncates it.

- **Execute As Self** Ensure the person who created the stored procedure has appropriate permissions on the staging table. Anyone with the Execute permission on the stored procedure could execute it.

- **Execute As Owner** Ensure that the owner of the schema of the stored procedure has appropriate permissions on the staging table. Anyone with the Execute permission on the stored procedure could execute it.

Database-Level Permissions

The permissions that can be assigned at the database level are quite numerous. However, they follow the same naming conventions as other permissions previously mentioned.

Most of the database permissions fall into the categories of basic DDL commands, such as CREATE, ALTER, and DROP. The Create permission maps to the CREATE DDL statement. The Alter permission maps to the ALTER and DROP DDL statements.

A key database permission outside of the DDL statements is *Connect*, which we saw earlier. This permission grants users access to the database and makes them members of the Public role.

Security Catalog VIEWs

SQL Server provides several security catalog VIEWs that can be used to view security information on several different levels, as well as inspect information on permissions assigned to securables, principals granted access, members of roles (database or server), and demographic information on keys and certificates.

These same VIEWs are also useful for documenting the state of the permissions and securables at any given time, or in other words, in creating a *security baseline.* By creating a security baseline, you can later compare the current state to the baseline and identify what has been changed.

The three categories of security catalog VIEWs are:

- Database-level views
- Server-level views
- Encryption views

As an example, the following queries can be run using a few of these VIEWs to get different security information on your server or database:

```
-- List all users and roles in a database
SELECT * FROM Sys.database_principals
-- List all users and roles in a server
SELECT * FROM Sys.server_principals
-- List all SQL server logins
SELECT * FROM  Sys.sql_logins
```

For more information on these views, look up the Books Online article, "Security Catalog Views (Transact-SQL)."

Designing the Security Strategy

We've covered many of the key security principles in this chapter and earlier chapters. Designing a sound security strategy is the process of adhering to these principles. Let's review them here.

Services

One of our primary security goals is to reduce the attack surface of the server. We do this by making sure that unneeded services are not running. In Chapter 1, we covered the services that are required.

If you need a service, than by all means make sure it's running. However, if you don't need a service, don't start it—the more services running on a system, the more doorways are available to a hacker. Table 8-6 is a review of some of the key features and their required services.

Feature	Required Service
SQL Server	SQL Server service.
SQL Server Agent	SQL Server Agent service.
Dedicated administrator connection	Browser service.
Reporting services	IIS, ASP .NET 2.0.
Notifications	Notification service.
Backup with volume shadow copies	SQL Writer Service.

Table 8-6   Key Services Associated with Key SQL Server 2005 Features

Auditing

To track what is occurring on a system, we need to enable auditing on the SQL Server. Auditing can occur on many levels.

In Chapter 6, we covered the use of triggers for auditing. We can use triggers to audit activity at the instance level or down to the database level. If we want to know if someone has created a database, modified a table's schema, or even added or modified data within a database, we can use triggers.

DML triggers can be used to audit database activity where the data is being modified. DDL triggers can be used to audit activity where the database schema is being modified or where server-level changes are taking place.

Encryption

Encryption isn't a new feature in SQL Server 2005, but as easy as encryption was to break in SQL Server 2000, it might as well be new. It's been rebuilt from the ground up using certificates and supports a wide variety of encryption algorithms.

The capabilities of encryption go way beyond what I'm including in this small section. The goal here is to provide enough exposure so you can see the basics. One thing I want to clarify right away is that this topic refers to encrypting the data. We also have the capability of encrypting database object definitions (the source code for VIEWs, functions, and stored procedures), making it harder for someone to see the definition of our objects. However, this encryption topic shows how that actual data can be encrypted, and at such a high level of confidence that it can't be easily broken.

 TIP   An ideal way to protect data from accidental disclosure is to encrypt it within a database. Any type of sensitive data (such as credit card information, privacy act information, patient information, and so on) can be encrypted at the column level to protect it.

SQL Server 2005 uses a hierarchical encryption and key management infrastructure where each layer encrypts the layer below it using a combination of certificates and keys. Take a look at Figure 8-38 for an overview of the encryption hierarchy.

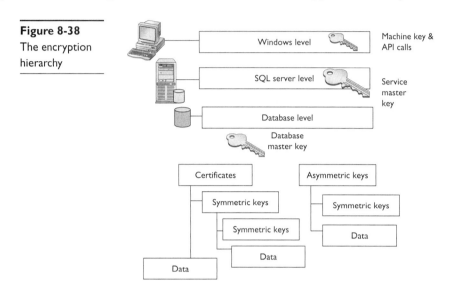

Figure 8-38 The encryption hierarchy

The Windows operating system provides a local machine key and data protection Application Program Interface (API) calls. When needed, the SQL Server service master key is created from these resources. There is only one service master key for the server.

For any databases that need encryption, a *database master key* is created from the service master key. Certificates, symmetric keys, and asymmetric keys are created from the database master key and can be used to encrypt and decrypt the data.

Keys and Algorithms

Keys are used to encrypt and decrypt the data with a specific algorithm. I've found in the classroom that these concepts are not always understood, so I'll explain them briefly here.

When I was a kid in school, a friend and I used to create coded messages. We'd let each other know what the key was on any given day. I could create an encrypted note using the key, and he could then decrypt it and read it using the same key. If it fell into the enemies' hands (the teachers!), they wouldn't have a clue what it was.

Consider the following phrase: "MCITP Success." We can encrypt it with this key and algorithm: Key = 3; Algorithm = Increment the letter with the key to encrypt— Decrement the letter with the key to decrypt.

With a key of *1*, the encrypted *M* would be *N*, the *C* would be *D*, and so on. With a key of *2*, the *M* would be *O*, the *C* would be *E*, and so on. Since we have a key of *3*, the *M* is a *P*, and the *C* is *F*.

The entire phrase is encrypted to "PFLWS Vxffhvv."

Obviously, modern encryption uses more complex keys and algorithms, but the concepts are the same. In this context, the key we used was considered a symmetric key. In other words, symmetric encryption uses the same key to both encrypt and decrypt.

Symmetric Keys and Asymmetric Keys

A *symmetric* key is a single key that is used for both encryption and decryption.

An *asymmetric* key is a combination of two keys commonly referred to as *public* and *private*. The public key and the private key are a matched set. One key is used to encrypt the data, and another is used to decrypt the data. A *certificate* holds and shares the public key. Certificates created and used within SQL Server follow the X.509 standard.

Generally, asymmetric encryption is much more resource-intensive than symmetric encryption. Because of this, asymmetric encryption is typically used just to create a symmetric key that will be used for a session, not to encrypt the whole session.

Let's explore a generic example that you've probably used. Suppose you want to purchase a book from a commercial web site such as MCITPSuccess.com. As soon as an HTTPS session is started, MCITPSuccess.com sends you a certificate. Embedded in the certificate is a public key.

If the public and private keys are used to encrypt the entire session, it will use too many resources and be too slow. So the goal is to create a symmetric key that both the server and the web browser at the client know, without letting anyone else know what it is.

Remember, the public key embedded in the certificate is matched to a private key held at MCITPSuccess.com. Data encrypted by the public key can only be decrypted by the private key.

Your browser creates a key that will be used as the symmetric key. Let's say it picks 151 (though it will pick something much more complex). Your browser knows the key, but the MCITPSuccess.com server doesn't. Your browser encrypts the symmetric key of 151 with the MCITPSuccess.com public key, resulting in an encrypted symmetric key of "F5&^aPl," which is then sent across the Internet in this encrypted format.

If anyone intercepts this data, they can't read it; the only key that can decrypt it is the private key held at MCITPSuccess.com. MCITPSuccess.com receives the encrypted key, decrypts it, and now your browser and the MCITPSuccess.com server know the symmetric key is 151. The rest of the session is encrypted and decrypted with this symmetric key.

To summarize the basic steps in a typical purchase you might make from a web site:

- You connect to the web site and the web site sends your browser a certificate containing a *public* key.

- Your browser uses the site's public key to encrypt a key the browser creates. Your browser sends its newly encrypted key to the web site.

- The web site uses its *private* key to decrypt the browser key for use as a symmetric key. Both browser and web site now use this symmetric key to encrypt and decrypt their transaction data.

Algorithms

SQL Server 2005 supports several encryption algorithms. These include DES, Triple DES, RC2, RC4, 128-bit RC4, DESX, 128-bit AES, 192-bit AES, and 256-bit AES. These are well-respected encryption algorithms and will not be easily broken.

 NOTE AES algorithms are not supported on Windows XP or Server 2000.

Of course, the stronger the encryption the more resources will be consumed on the server. The choice of the algorithm needs to be a balanced decision, considering both the importance of the data and the available resources. Additionally, it would be rare to encrypt an entire database. Instead, key columns (such as columns holding credit card information or privacy act information) would be chosen for encryption.

Encrypting Data

The steps required to enable and use encryption with a symmetric key are:

1. Create a database master key.
2. Create a symmetric key.
3. Open the key.
4. Encrypt the data within the column with the key.
5. Close the key.

Creating a Database Master Key

The first step in encrypting data is creating a database master key. This key will be used to encrypt the data and/or other keys if desired.

If this is the first database master key created on the server, then the service master key will be automatically created during this step. The service master key is the root of the SQL Server encryption hierarchy. All database master keys are encrypted with the service master key.

The command to create the database master key is straightforward:

```
CREATE MASTER KEY ENCRYPTION BY PASSWORD = 'password'
```

The database master key only needs to be created once for the database.

Creating Certificates and Keys

Once the database master key has been created, we can create certificates, symmetric keys, and/or asymmetric keys.

By creating a certificate, we offer symmetric keys protection from compromise. The certificate is used to encrypt and decrypt symmetric keys when needed. The basic syntax to create a certificate is:

```
CREATE CERTIFICATE certificateName
   WITH SUBJECT = 'description'
```

Certificates follow the X.509 standard. Private keys generated by SQL are 1024 bits long, and the keys can be from 384 bits to 3456 bits if generated from an external source. The private key is associated with the public key that is embedded in the certificate. The private key is encrypted from the database master key by default.

Either symmetric keys or asymmetric keys can be created to encrypt the data. As described earlier, an asymmetric key uses a key pair (public and private)—one to encrypt the data, and the other to decrypt it. A symmetric key uses a single key to both encrypt and decrypt the data.

The basic syntax to create a symmetric key from a certificate is:

```
CREATE SYMMETRIC KEY keyName ENCRYPTION BY encrypting mechanism
```

The possible encrypting mechanisms are certificate, password, symmetric key, or asymmetric key.

Encrypting Data

Once the keys are created, it becomes a rather straightforward process to encrypt the data. This is broken down into three steps:

1. Open the key.

2. Encrypt the data.

3. Close the key.

By opening the key, it is decrypted and made available for use. The command to open a key is:

```
OPEN SYMMETRIC KEY keyName DECRYPTION BY decryption_mechanism
```

The decryption mechanism is the same one specified when creating the key. In other words, if we created the key with a password, we would decrypt the key with a password.

With the key open, we can encrypt the data by using the EncryptByKey function. The EncryptByKey function has two required parameters:

- **Key_GUID** This is the GUID of the key used to encrypt the text. It can be identified as the actual GUID, or by listing the name of the open key.

- **Clear text** This is the actual text to be encrypted.

The partial syntax for the EncryptByKey function is:

```
EncryptByKey(Key_GUID(' keyName '), ' Data to encrypt ')
```

Once the data has been encrypted, the key should be closed. If not closed, it will remain open for the entire session.

In the next exercise, we will create the necessary keys to encrypt data, use them to encrypt a column of data, and then use them to view the decrypted data.

Putting It All Together

Obviously, the topics in this chapter aren't disjointed technologies. They are intended to be used as part of a comprehensive security strategy.

Let's say you are tasked with creating a strategy designed to accept customers' credit cards, immediately encrypt them so they are never stored in clear text, and then—when necessary—retrieve them. How would you do this?

First create a user in the database, and grant the permissions necessary to use the certificates and keys with full access to the database objects. One possibility would be to add this user to the db_owner database role. For a large database, you may choose to spread the permissions among multiple accounts (that is, one user or database role to execute the stored procedure to encrypt the data, another user or role to execute the stored procedure to decrypt the data, and another user or role with full control to manage schema changes).

Next, create a stored procedure (usp_InputCustomer) dedicated to accepting customer information as input parameters and storing it in the appropriate table. The credit card information would be encrypted within this stored procedure. Define this stored procedure with the EXECUTE AS clause identifying the user that was placed in the db_owner role.

The customer information could be gathered from a web page, or a phone representative could be collecting it and typing it into a Windows program. Depending on how the data is collected and entered, you need to grant Execute permission to a user or role on the usp_InputCustomer stored procedure. Since the stored procedure was defined with the EXECUTE AS clause, no additional permissions are needed on the underlying tables, certificates, or keys.

Now create another stored procedure that can be used during a purchasing phase. This stored procedure would accept the customer ID as the input and then output the unencrypted credit card information that can be used to purchase merchandise. Again, define the stored procedure with the EXECUTE AS permission using the User account that is a member of the db_owner role.

Lastly, grant the Execute permission on the purchasing stored-procedure to the appropriate user or role that needs it during the purchasing phase.

If this process is done via the Web, at no time will any database users ever see the unencrypted credit card information. The customer enters it into a page, and it's immediately encrypted before being stored.

If other customer information is needed, VIEWs can be created with the appropriate permissions to allow access to the specific columns needed, but not those displaying the encrypted data.

Exercise 8.8: Use Encryption

1. Open SSMS and create a New Query window.

2. Use the following script to create a new database named Chapter8 and a table named Customers in the database:

```
USE Master;
GO
CREATE DATABASE Chapter8;
GO
USE Chapter8;
Go
CREATE TABLE dbo.Customer
(
    CustomerID int IDENTITY(1,1) NOT NULL,
    LastName varchar(50) NOT NULL,
    FirstName varchar(50) NOT NULL,
    CreditCardNumber nvarchar(20) NULL,
    EncryptedCreditCardNumber varbinary(128) NULL,
    CONSTRAINT [PK_Customer_CustomerID] PRIMARY KEY CLUSTERED
    (
            CustomerID
    )
);
```

 CAUTION Encrypted data needs to be stored in a varbinary column. If you try to store it in a varchar column similar to the source data, you won't be able to decrypt it.

3. Use the following script to add four lines of data to the Customer table and then view them:

```
INSERT INTO Customer VALUES(' Jetson ', ' George ', ' 1234-5678-1234
',NULL);
INSERT INTO Customer VALUES('Jetson', 'Elroy', '9876-5432-9876',NULL);
INSERT INTO Customer VALUES('Simpson', 'Homer', '1029-3847-5765',NULL);
INSERT INTO Customer VALUES('Simpson', 'Bart', '5678-1234-5678',NULL);
SELECT * FROM Customer;
```

4. Create the keys and certificate necessary for the encryption:

   a. Create a database master key with the following code:

   ```
   CREATE MASTER KEY ENCRYPTION BY PASSWORD = 'P@ssw0rd'
   ```

 NOTE If this is the first time a database master key is being created on the server, this command will also automatically create a service master key. This will be transparent.

   b. Create a certificate that will be used to encrypt the symmetric key. Use the following command. Be patient, because it may take a moment.

   ```
   CREATE CERTIFICATE CreditCardCert
       WITH SUBJECT =  'Customer Credit Card Numbers'
   ```

    c. Create a symmetric key from the certificate with the following command:

```
CREATE SYMMETRIC KEY CreditCardKey1 WITH ALGORITHM = DES
    ENCRYPTION BY CERTIFICATE CreditCardCert;
```

  5. Open the key and encrypt the data with the following commands:

    a. Open the symmetric key that will be used to encrypt the data:

```
OPEN SYMMETRIC KEY CreditCardKey1
    DECRYPTION BY CERTIFICATE CreditCardCert;
```

    b. Encrypt the data with the following command:

```
UPDATE Customer
Set EncryptedCreditCardNumber =
                EncryptByKey(Key_GUID('CreditCardKey1'),CreditCardNumber)
SELECT * FROM Customer;
```

    c. Close the symmetric key with the following command:

```
ClOSE SYMMETRIC KEY CreditCardKey1
```

  6. To view the unencrypted data, we need to open the symmetric key, decrypt the data, and then close the symmetric key:

    a. Open the symmetric key with the following command. Notice that the syntax is exactly the same whether using it for encryption or decryption.

```
OPEN SYMMETRIC KEY CreditCardKey1
    DECRYPTION BY CERTIFICATE CreditCardCert;
```

    b. Decrypt the data with the following command:

```
SELECT CustomerID, LastName, FirstName, CreditCardNumber
, CONVERT(nvarchar, DecryptByKey(EncryptedCreditCardNumber))
    AS 'Decrypted Credit Card Number'
    FROM Customer
```

 CAUTION You must convert the decrypted data to an nvarchar data type (not varchar). Trying to display it as varchar will render it indecipherable.

    c. Close the symmetric key:

```
ClOSE SYMMETRIC KEY CreditCardKey1
```

  7. Alternatively, you can use the following command, which automatically opens the symmetric key and uses it to decrypt the data in a single command:

```
SELECT CustomerID, LastName, FirstName, CreditCardNumber,
    CONVERT(nvarchar, DecryptByKeyAutoCert(cert_ID('CreditCardCert'),
        NULL, EncryptedCreditCardNumber))

    AS 'Decrypted Credit Card Number'
    FROM Customer
```

Backing Up Keys

Once keys have been created and used to encrypt data, they become very valuable. In our previous exercise, we kept the original unencrypted data so it could easily be displayed side by side with the decrypted data. However, in a production environment, we'd encrypt the data and not keep unencrypted copies of the original.

Now the only way to get the data into a readable state is by using the keys. This makes it extremely important to have backups of the keys, and backups of these keys are just as important as backups of the original data.

We'll cover backups in more depth in Chapter 10. For now, just remember that while backing up the database by itself does include normal database objects, it does not include the keys. To back up the keys, additional steps must be taken.

Regular backup strategies should be employed to protect the backups. This includes storing one copy onsite in an NTFS-protected partition, and storing another copy off-site to protect against major disasters.

 EXAM TIP A best practice when using encryption is to include the service master key and any database master keys in the backup plan. Just backing up the database doesn't include the encryption keys.

In the following exercise, we'll create backups of the service master key and the database master key.

Exercise 8.9: Back Up the Service Master Key and the Database Master Key

1. If not already open, open a New Query window in SSMS.

2. Use the following command to create a backup of the service master key created in the previous exercise:

```
BACKUP SERVICE MASTER KEY TO FILE =
   'c:\svcMasterKey.bak' ENCRYPTION BY PASSWORD = 'P@ssw0rd'
```

 NOTE Note that we're backing this up to the root of c:\. You can just as easily back it up to another drive, or a folder. Simply enter the full path where you want it backed up. Of course, this is only half the battle. Once the key is backed up locally it needs to be included in a disaster recovery plan, so the backed up keys are safely stored with other backups.

---

3. Use the following command to create a backup of the database master key created in the previous exercise:

```
BACKUP MASTER KEY TO FILE =
   'c:\dbMasterKey.bak' ENCRYPTION BY PASSWORD ='P@ssw0rd'
```

4. To back up the certificate use the following command:

```
BACKUP CERTIFICATE CreditCardCert TO FILE = 'c:\CreditCardCert.bak'
   WITH PRIVATE KEY ( FILE = 'c:\CreditCardKey1',
   ENCRYPTION BY PASSWORD = 'Pa$$w0rd' );
```

Chapter Review

In this chapter, we covered the basics of SQL Server 2005 security starting at the server level and then working down to the database and ultimately the data level.

We started by learning the two different authentication modes (Windows Authentication, and SQL Server and Windows Authentication), when to use each, and how to change modes. We created logins to match Windows users, Windows groups, and simple SQL logins.

In the "Security Principals" section, we spent a lot of time going over the different principals, such as database users, database roles, and schemas. We then learned about database securables, permissions, and ownership chaining. We closed out the chapter with detailed information on encryption and how to encrypt data within the database.

Additional Study

Self-Study Exercises

- Change the authentication mode.
- Add a server login.
- Add a user to a database.
- Add the user to the db_owner role.
- Create a view and grant access to the view without granting access to an underlying table.
- Create a database master key.
- Encrypt a single column of data within a table and verify that you succeeded.

BOL Topics

- CREATE LOGIN (Transact-SQL)
- Server-Level Roles
- Principals
- Application Roles
- Securables
- User-Schema Separation
- Permissions
- Ownership Chains
- EXECUTE AS Clause (Transact-SQL)
- CLR Integration Security
- How to Encrypt a Column of Data

Summary of What You Need to Know

70-431

When preparing for the 70-431 test, make sure you understand the following topics, including how to manipulate them within SSMS:

- Authentication mode
- Security principals
- Securables
- CLR permissions
- Encryption

70-441

This entire chapter covers material for the 70-441 test, but you might want to pay special attention to the following topics:

- Permission chaining and database chaining
- Use of permissions on objects to control access (for example, granting permission to a VIEW, function, or stored procedure while denying direct access to underlying tables)
- Use of roles to control access
- Methods of encrypting data (and source code)

70-442

No objectives for the 70-442 test are included in this chapter

Questions

70-431

1. A developer has created a CLR assembly that reads data from a file. You need to register it, but should only grant the privileges needed. What security permission should you choose?

    A. SAFE

    B. UNSAFE

    C. EXTERNAL_ACCESS

    D. sa

2. You are tasked with registering an assembly with a SQL Server 2005 server that you manage. It contains a CLR function that reads data from a file, manipulates it, and then sends it to the database. You need to register it with the CREATE

ASSEMBLY statement following the Principle of Least Privilege. Which of the following should you choose?

A. SAFE

B. UNSAFE

C. EXTERNAL_ACCESS

D. Full Control

3. What database role provides full access to all database securables?

A. db_sa

B. db_owner

C. db_accessadmin

D. db_sysadmin

4. The Hurricane database has been created with the defaults. The server is in Windows Authentication Mode. What is needed to access the Hurricane database? (Choose all that apply.)

A. A SQL Server login

B. A server login

C. A database user account

D. Access to the Public role

5. You create a VIEW that shows only three of the seven columns in the Employee table. What permissions are required on the Employee table to allow modifications?

A. SELECT

B. ALTER

C. SELECT AND ALTER

D. NONE

6. A fellow DBA has created a login named hpotter by using the following Transact-SQL script:

```
CREATE LOGIN hpotter WITH PASSWORD = 'MC!TPSucc3$$'
```

However, when hpotter tries to log in, he receives the following error message:

```
"Login failed. The user is not associated with a trusted SQL Server
connection."
```

What's the likely problem?

A. The authentication mode is set to SQL Server and Windows Authentication and needs to be changed to Windows authentication mode.

B. The authentication mode is set to Windows Authentication and needs to be changed to SQL Server and Windows authentication mode.

C. The authentication mode is set to SQL Server and Windows Authentication and needs to be changed to SQL Server authentication mode.

D. The authentication mode is set to Windows Authentication and needs to be changed to SQL Server authentication mode.

7. A CLR function is being written by another developer that will read data from a comma separated value (CSV) file, perform some calculations on the data, and then return a value to a SQL Server 2005 database. You are tasked with registering the assembly named Calc. What code will you use?

A.

```
CREATE ASSEMBLY calc
FROM 'c:\calc\calc.dll'
WITH PERMISSION_SET = SAFE
```

B.

```
CREATE ASSEMBLY calc
FROM 'c:\calc\calc.dll'
WITH PERMISSION_SET = EXTERNAL_ACCESS
```

C.

```
CREATE ASSEMBLY calc
FROM 'c:\calc\calc.dll'
WITH PERMISSION_SET = UNSAFE
```

D.

```
CREATE ASSEMBLY calc
FROM 'c:\calc\calc.dll'
```

70-441

1. A stored procedure named usp_AddStockToPortfolio is used to add stock purchases to a customer's portfolio based on stock purchase orders. The stored procedure will access data in tables stored in another database within the SQL Server instance. To succeed, what should be done? (Choose two. Each correct answer presents part of the solution.)

A. Set the EXECUTE AS option of the stored procedure to use the sysadmin role.

B. Ensure that the stored procedure and underlying tables are owned by the same user.

C. Enable the DB_CHAINING option on each database.

D. Enable the DB_CHAINING option on the instance of SQL Server.

2. You are designing an application that will be used by AlwaysUp Airline customers at kiosks in the airport. Customers should be able to purchase tickets, check reservations, reserve seating, and check in. The kiosks will connect to a back-end SQL Server 2005 database named AlwaysUp by using Windows authentication through a Windows security group named G_AlwaysUpKiosk. Stored procedures have been created to access the appropriate data within the KioskApp schema. Customers should not have direct access to any database tables. What would you do? (Choose all that apply.)

A. Create a database role named Kiosk.

B. Grant the Kiosk role Connect permission to the AlwaysUp database.

C. Add the G_AlwaysUpKiosk group to a server login and map the login to the Kiosk database role.

D. Add the Kiosk database role to the G_AlwaysUpKiosk group.

E. Grant Execute permissions to the Kiosk role on the KioskApp schema.

F. Grant Execute permissions to the Kiosk role for the appropriate stored procedures.

3. You are designing the StockPortfolio database that will be used by different internal Windows applications. Users should access the database through these client applications and will not need direct access to database objects. What should you do?

A. Design the solution so stored procedures are used for all database access.

B. Design the solution so the client applications use an application role.

C. Map Windows users to the db_owner fixed database role.

D. Map Windows users to the db_datareader and db_datawriter fixed database roles.

4. Your company is required to keep an audit history on all stock purchases and sales and this data is regularly audited by a government agency. The company just had some problems with a government audit of data and an internal auditing department has been created to identify problems before the next government audit. You need to ensure the following requirements are followed:

- Internal auditors must be able to run ad hoc queries against the database using their own tools.

- Audit data must be readable by only the company auditors.

- Only database administrators can have direct access to tables within the database.

You have created audit tables containing the appropriate auditable data. What else should you do?

A. Grant the auditors access to the audit tables and do nothing else.

B. Grant the auditors access to the audit tables. Create VIEWs of the audit tables and grant the auditors access to those VIEWs.

C. Deny access to the audit tables to the auditors. Create VIEWs of the audit tables and grant access to those VIEWs to the auditors.

D. Deny access to the audit tables to the auditors. Create stored procedures to allow the auditors access to the data.

5. You manage a database named StockPortfolio. Customers routinely transfer money into their accounts from their bank accounts when purchasing stocks, and money is transferred to their bank account when stock is sold. This data is stored in the CustomerBanking table. Management wants you to provide the best possible protection for the customer's banking information. What can you do?

A. Encrypt the columns holding the banking information in the CustomerBanking table.

B. Encrypt the CustomerBanking table in the database.

C. Encrypt the StockPortfolio database.

D. Encrypt the server instance.

Answers

70-431

1. **C.** To grant access to external files, you should grant EXTERNAL_ACCESS permission to grant the ability to access external system resources such as files, networks, environmental variables, and the Registry. SAFE is the most restrictive and only grants access to local data. UNSAFE allows assemblies unrestricted access. sa is a built-in login, not a permission.

2. **C.** The three choices are: (1) SAFE—only internal computation and local data access are allowed; it's the most restrictive; (2) EXTERNAL_ACCESS—it's safe, with the additional ability to access external system resources such as files, networks, environmental variables, and the Registry; and (3) UNSAFE—it allows assemblies unrestricted access and can call unmanaged code. There is no Full Control permission.

3. **B.** The db_owner has access to all database securables. The db_accessadmin can add or remove access but doesn't have access itself. There is no db_sa or db_sysadmin database role.

4. **B, C.** A login is needed to provide access to the server, and a database user account is needed to access a database. A user can't be added to the Public role directly. If the guest account is enabled on a database, connect access is provided. Once connect access is provided to the database, a user is automatically a member of the Public role. However, the guest account is disabled by default so it couldn't be used in this scenario. A SQL Server login would only be useful if the server was in Mixed authentication mode, not Windows authentication mode.

5. **D.** Permissions only need to be granted on the VIEW.

6. **B.** The login script has created a SQL Server login. In order for this to work, the authentication mode must be set to "Windows and SQL Server Authentication" mode. There is no such thing as "SQL Server Authentication" mode. There is only "Windows Authentication" and "SQL Server and Windows Authentication" modes.

7. **B.** To access the external files, the permission set should be set to External Access. The default is Safe and would prevent the assembly from accessing the CSV file. Unsafe provides too much access and wouldn't be recommended.

70-441

1. **B, C.** The DB_CHAINING option needs to be set to ON for each database. This will enable cross-database ownership chaining. Additionally, make sure the same user either owns, or is in a role that owns all objects in the chain. While cross-database ownership chaining can be enabled on the instance, thus applying it to all databases, this is not the DB_CHAINING option. Membership in the sysadmin role is not necessary.

2. **A, C, F.** We would add the Windows group to a server login and then add the server login to a database user or role. Since stored procedures have been created within the KioskApp schema expressly for this purpose, we can grant the execute permission to the schema without having to grant the execute permission for each of the stored procedures.

3. **B.** Since access to the database should only be through the client applications, an application role should be used. While stored procedures can be a good method to control access, using them would require direct access to at least the stored procedure database objects. Mapping users to any of the roles would provide direct access.

4. **C.** It might seem as though there are conflicting goals in this scenario: Auditors need to be able to run ad hoc queries, but only database administrators can have direct access. However, by creating views for the auditors that they can use for their ad hoc queries, both goals can be met. By granting access to the view, data can be retrieved from the table without granting access to the base table.

5. **A.** Column-level encryption is the best choice. Since encryption is a CPU-intensive operation, you would only want to encrypt what is necessary. It's not possible to encrypt the entire instance.

Stored Procedures

In this chapter, you will learn about:

- Stored procedure uses and benefits
- Stored procedure types
- Transactions
- Error handling including TRY CATCH
- Creating user-defined stored procedures
- Stored procedure security
- CLR-integrated stored procedures

> *Success is more a function of consistent common sense than it is of genius.*
>
> *—An Wang*

Stored procedures are powerful. We have the capability of encapsulating complex business logic, enhancing security, preventing SQL injection attacks, reducing network traffic, and much more through the use of stored procedures. And once created, all you have to do is grant Execute permission to allow users to run them—no matter how complex the logic or how many tables are accessed.

Students have heard me say this many times: The difference between good database developers and great database developers is their ability to create stored procedures.

Your stored procedures don't need to be complex to be great. There's a lot to be said for consistently creating simple logic. While you may occasionally create the master-piece that shows your true genius, that isn't required to be successful. To paraphrase the founder of Wang Labs, success is achieved more often from consistent common sense than it is of genius.

An Overview of Stored Procedures

I love stored procedures. We can create wonderful, powerful, seemingly magical T-SQL code with stored procedures. While some people argue that SQL isn't a true programming language, with stored procedures we get pretty darn close.

A stored procedure can have as many, or as few, lines of code as you need to do the job. It can include variables, transactions, complex error messages, DDL or DML statements, and much more. You can pass parameters in, and get data back as either scalar values or table-type result sets from stored procedures.

Many of the benefits of stored procedures are listed in Table 9-1 and outlined in the following pages. Throughout the chapter, we'll dig deeper into these topics, but understanding the overall benefits of stored procedures helps to grasp the big picture.

Benefit	Description
Hides the complexity of operations	A single stored procedure can have hundreds of T-SQL lines.
Enhances network traffic	Instead of sending hundreds of lines of code over the network, a single command and single result are used.
Enhances security	Users can be granted execute permission on a stored procedure without the need to grant permissions on any underlying objects.
Protects against SQL injection attacks	Parameterized stored procedures can check parameters for embedded malicious code.
Adds modularity to SQL Server	Stored procedures can be reused as needed after initial creation. Stored procedures can call other stored procedures.

Table 9-1   Stored Procedure Benefits

Used for Optimization

Stored procedures can be used to encapsulate complex business logic within them that have literally hundreds of lines of code. When executed, instead of sending these hundreds of lines of code over the network from a batch, only one statement needs to be sent, such as Exec usp_RunHundredsOfLinesOfCode. From a network perspective, this can save bandwidth.

Additionally, stored procedures are optimized and compiled when they are first run. The plan is stored in cache and when the stored procedure is run again, the compiled plan is used, thus saving a significant amount of computer resources since it doesn't need to be recompiled.

Figure 9-1 shows the process a stored procedure goes through from creation to execution. When first created, the stored procedure is parsed—checked for syntactical accuracy. Unlike a regular batch, the database isn't checked to ensure that objects (such as tables, VIEWs, or other stored procedures) the stored procedure references actually exist. Instead, name resolution is delayed.

The first time the stored procedure is executed (and anytime it is recompiled), the database engine optimizes the stored procedure. One of the big decision points is which indexes to use based on factors such as statistics, and the density and selectivity of indexes for the specific queries. The result of this optimization process is a plan for the stored procedure. That plan is then compiled and stored in cache.

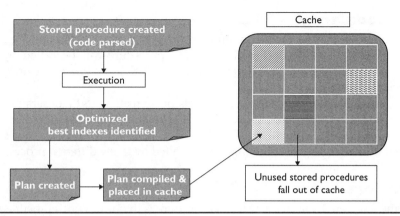

Figure 9-1 A stored procedure life cycle

SQL Server's cache holds more than just stored procedures. It can also contain plans for functions, triggers, temporary tables, and any T-SQL query. If it was a perfect world, you'd have 64GB of RAM and everything would be optimized once when first executed, placed in cache, and rarely need to be optimized again.

If your server is like most though, memory is a precious resource with limitations, so unused stored procedure plans typically fall out of cache and need to be recompiled the next time they are run. However, a stored procedure that is frequently used may stay in cache almost the entire time the server is up and operational.

Security

Stored procedures can enhance a database's security since granting the Execute permission to a stored permission negates the need to grant permissions to underlying tables. Using stored procedures in this way can protect the base tables from direct modification.

With no permission to the base tables, users cannot make modifications to the table except through the stored procedure. In this way, we provide a layer of security to the base tables and can also ensure that business rules are enforced since the data are only modified through the stored procedure.

Encapsulating the logic within a module and only providing access to the module is sometimes cited as a best practice. This is similar to the way a VIEW or a function can be used to provide access to underlying tables without granting direct permission to the underlying object.

Using parameterized stored procedures (stored procedures that accept parameters) is considered a core defense against SQL injection attacks. Since the parameters are interpreted differently within a stored procedure then they would be if used to build a dynamic SQL statement, SQL injection attacks can be prevented.

Additionally, parameters within a stored procedure can be validated. In other words, using code within the stored procedure, the parameters can be checked to ensure they are valid.

Adds Modularity

Stored procedures can be reused by different processes within the database as many times as needed. A single well-defined stored procedure can be called by several different processes. The advantage to the developer is that the procedure doesn't need to be recreated.

They can be created with T-SQL statements or by using a .NET programming language, as described in the CLR section later. By creating a CLR-integrated stored procedure, we can take advantage of a full-fledged programming language, but still fully integrated into a single procedure that can be called by many different processes.

Limitations

One of the few limitations with a stored procedure is that it can't be embedded within a SELECT statement. As a comparison, functions can be embedded in a SELECT statement as:

```
SELECT dbo.fn_CountLogins(@UserName) AS 'Self';
```

However, trying to embed a stored procedure in a SELECT statement results in a syntax error:

```
SELECT * from sp_helpdb --  will result in error
SELECT sp_helpdb as 'HelpDb'  -- will result in error
```

Instead, stored procedures are executed as follows:

```
Exec sp_helpdb;
```

Types of Stored Procedures

Though three types of stored procedures exist, only two are typically used today.

- **System Stored Procedures**   These are stored procedures included within SQL Server. They encapsulate the logic to perform several different types of actions. System stored procedures start with the prefix of sp_.

- **User-Defined Stored Procedures**   These are the stored procedures we can create on our own for specific jobs. Almost any T-SQL statement can be included in a user-defined stored procedure. User-defined stored procedures should not start with the prefix sp_, and often use the prefix of usp_.

- **Extended Stored Procedures**   Extended stored procedures are DLLs that SQL Server can dynamically load and run. They have historically been a security risk and so are often disabled. Use of extended stored procedures in SQL Server 2005 is deprecated.

System Stored Procedures

SQL Server includes many system-supplied stored procedures that start with the prefix *sp_*. It's impossible to know all of them instantly, but you will work with more and more of them as your experience with SQL grows.

One way to familiarize yourself with some of the system stored procedures available is by looking at Books Online. In the following exercise, we'll use BOL to explore some system stored procedures.

Exercise 9.1: Look Up and Use System Stored Procedures

1. Open up Books Online by clicking Start | All Programs | Microsoft SQL Server 2005 | Documentation and Tutorials | SQL Server Books Online.

2. Click the Index tab at the bottom left.

3. In the Look For box, enter **sp_**.

   You should have a display similar to Figure 9-2. If you're trying to look up a specific stored procedure, this is often the easiest way.

Figure 9-2

Using Books Online to find system stored procedures

4. In the Look For box, enter **sp_server** and double-click the sp_server_info link. This opens the help article for the sp_server_info stored procedure. The article gives an overview on the stored procedure, the syntax, and then detailed information on the parameters.

5. Open a New Query window in SSMS.

6. Enter the following stored procedure name and click the Execute button. This executes the stored procedure.

```
sp_server_info
```

7. To execute a stored procedure within a script, use the EXEC command to execute it. Enter the following script to make sure it will *not* work by just clicking the Execute button:

```
USE AdventureWorks;
sp_server_info;
```

8. Add the EXEC command to make certain it will work:

```
USE AdventureWorks;
EXEC sp_server_info;
```

9. Some stored procedures can be used to give you information on objects within SQL Server. Use the following command to show what user databases exist in your system:

```
Exec sp_helpdb;
```

10. Many stored procedures are designed to work with or without parameters—in other words, the parameters are optional. The same sp_helpdb stored procedure that lists all databases when parameters aren't provided will do something different when the name of a database is provided as a parameter:

```
Exec sp_helpdb AdventureWorks;
```

11. In Chapter 7, we covered optimizing databases and mentioned the stored procedure sp_updatestats. This can be used to update the statistics on all tables within a database and is useful if automatic updating of statistics was inadvertently disabled. Enter the following command and execute it to view the definition of the sp_updatestats stored procedure:

```
sp_helptext sp_updatestats
```

12. In Chapter 13, we'll cover using SQL Server Agent to monitor events and send alerts. One of the things SQL Server Agent can do is monitor the Event Viewer log and respond when a specific event occurs. To facilitate this, sometimes we want to create our own message. Use BOL to look up sp_addmessage. We'll use this later in the chapter in the "Error Catching" section.

Extended Stored Procedures

Extended stored procedures have been available in past versions of SQL Server, but are considered deprecated in SQL Server 2005. Extended stored procedures are identi-fied with *xp_* at the beginning. They could call modules outside of SQL, typically by accessing a DLL. However, they presented significant security risks and were frequently blocked by DBAs. In SQL Server 2005, CLR-integrated stored procedures should be created instead. We'll cover CLR-integrated stored procedures later in this chapter.

User-Defined Stored Procedures

A user-defined stored procedure is any stored procedure we create to do specific jobs. They can contain input parameters, allowing us to pass specific information into the stored procedure. They can have output parameters that let them return multiple values (though they can't be used in a SELECT statement). One stored procedure can call other stored procedures.

Just about any T-SQL statement can be included within a stored procedure. Very often, batches of T-SQL code are created within transactions within a stored procedure. Transactions are often embedded into stored procedures, so before we start creating our own user-defined stored procedures, let's cover some basics on transactions.

Transactions

Transactions are an integral part of any database. They allow us to group together several statements that are acted on as a whole. In other words, all the statements succeed as one, or if any one of them fails, they all fail as a whole.

In Chapter 10, we'll cover the transaction log and how it tracks transactions, but for now you should be aware that the transaction log keeps a record of every change to a database. This includes the DML statements of INSERT, UPDATE, and DELETE.

Instead of writing these changes to the database directly, the changes are written to the transaction log. We can see this in Figure 9-3.

Figure 9-3   Writing to the transaction log

Then, sometime later (often within a second), the transaction log is "checkpointed," and data in the log is written to the database, as shown in Figure 9-4. Among other things, this protects the database from becoming corrupted due to a power failure.

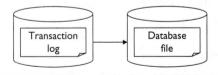

Figure 9-4   Checkpointing committed transactions to the database

If the system does crash, upon power-up the transaction log is reviewed, and any transactions that haven't been checkpointed are now written to the database. This happens automatically.

We can also use this process to group transactions together and prevent them from being committed to the database until we're ready. We start a transaction with a BEGIN TRANSACTION (or BEGIN TRAN) command. We can then include any T-SQL code we want, including DML statements such as INSERT, UPDATE, and DELETE. We can include decision points (such as with an IF statement) and either roll back the transaction or commit it. The transaction isn't actually written to the database until a COMMIT TRANSACTION statement is reached. If desired, we can also issue a ROLLBACK TRANSACTION to undo the entire transaction.

When checkpoints occur, the only transactions written to the database are those that have been committed. By default, any INSERT, UPDATE, and DELETE statement is considered committed as soon as it's executed since SQL Server works in autocommit mode by default.

An Overview of Transactions

Consider a transaction at the ATM where you're going to withdraw money from your account. Suppose you insert your ATM card, enter your PIN, and specify how much money you want to withdraw. The system checks your balance, gives you your money, and then debits your account. Usually, everything works fine.

However, today it checks your balance, gives you your money, but just before it debits your account, the system loses power. Oh, no! Is this acceptable?

To the bank, it's not. They've lost money. Actually, the way the bank would set up the transaction is shown in the following pseudo-code:

```
Check Balance
If Balance NOT OK, exit
BEGIN TRAN
  Debit Account
  Distribute Money
COMMIT TRAN
```

Note that we are grouping the "Debit Account" and "Distribute Money" statements together as a single transaction. The idea is that either they both succeed together, or neither succeeds.

Now, imagine that the system lost power just after debiting your account, but before giving you your money. Is this acceptable? Absolutely not!

However, upon power-up the system would see that a BEGIN TRAN was recorded without a matching COMMIT TRAN. The "Debit Account" statement would then be rolled back.

Commit Transaction

To see a simple example of this in action, we'll change Ms. Catherine R. Abel's last name from Abel to Cain to signify a marriage. Note that at the end of the UPDATE statement, the data isn't considered committed because a BEGIN TRANSACTION statement hasn't had a matching COMMIT TRANSACTION yet.

```
USE AdventureWorks;
GO
BEGIN TRANSACTION
  UPDATE Person.Contact
  SET LastName = 'Cain'
  WHERE ContactID = 2
  -- data not committed yet
COMMIT TRANSACTION
```

A more realistic example would be where we have more than one statement in the transaction. For example, in AdventureWorks we have parts held in multiple locations. To see this, execute the following script:

```
SELECT * FROM
Production.ProductInventory
WHERE ProductID = 1
```

This shows that ProductID has parts in three separate locations. Imagine that we are moving ten of these from the first location to the second location. This requires one UPDATE to decrement ten from the first location, and a second UPDATE to add ten to the second location. However, if either statement fails while the other succeeds, our inventory will be out of sync. We need to ensure they both succeed, or both fail, as a single transaction. The following script will accomplish this:

```
USE AdventureWorks;
GO
BEGIN TRANSACTION
        UPDATE Production.ProductInventory
                SET Quantity = Quantity - 10
                WHERE ProductID = 1 AND LocationID=1
        UPDATE Production.ProductInventory
                SET Quantity = Quantity + 10
                WHERE ProductID = 1 AND LocationID=6
COMMIT TRANSACTION
```

We can then rerun the SELECT statement for ProductID of 1 and verify the changes have occurred:

```
SELECT * FROM
Production.ProductInventory
WHERE ProductID = 1
```

Transactions that are begun should be either committed or rolled back. For example, the following script starts a transaction, inserts a row into a table, but then never commits or rolls back the statement. This leaves the data uncommitted and can cause a wide variety of problems.

```
USE AdventureWorks;
GO
BEGIN TRAN
  INSERT INTO Person.Contact
```

```
  (FirstName, LastName,PasswordHash, PasswordSalt)
    VALUES ('Harry', 'Potter', 'P@ssw0rd','P@$$S@lt')
-- This leaves an open transaction that can be closed with
-- ROLLBACK TRAN
```

One of the most significant problems that can occur with an uncommitted transaction is with the transaction log. We'll cover the transaction log in much more detail in Chapter 10, but for now be aware that when a checkpoint event occurs, committed data within the log is written to the database. Then, when the log is backed up, the log is truncated. In other words, the space used to hold committed transactions that have been written to the database is freed up. If the log has a long-running transaction that is not committed, the transaction log will continue to grow until it either fills the disk or it reaches its maximum size. If the transaction log is full and can't grow any more, the database becomes a read-only database.

If you suspect you have open transactions, you can use the DBCC OPENTRAN statement to identify them. As an example, the following code begins a transaction but doesn't commit it, and then uses DBCC OPENTRAN to view the open transaction.

```
BEGIN TRAN
  INSERT INTO Person.Contact
  (FirstName, LastName, PasswordHash, PasswordSalt)
  VALUES ('Harry', 'Potter', 'P@ssw0rd', 'P@$$s@lt')
  DBCC OPENTRAN
```

The results are shown in Figure 9-5. To close the transaction without committing the change, we can enter the following command:

```
ROLLBACK TRAN
```

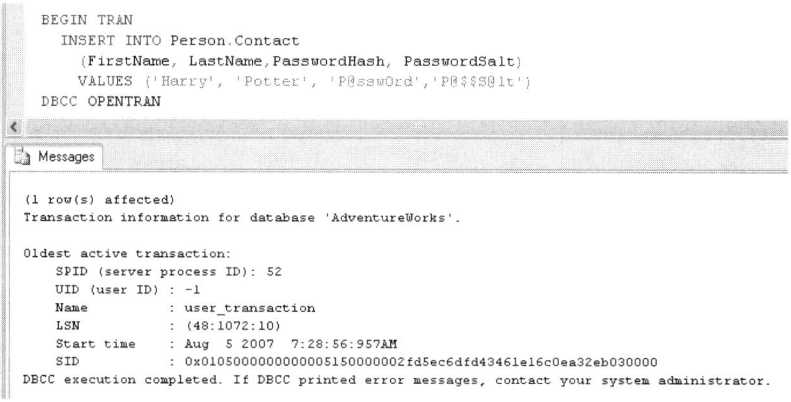

Figure 9-5 Result of DBCC OPEN with a transaction open

To identify additional details on the open transaction (before it's rolled back), the sp_who command can be executed using the server process ID (SPID) identified in the DBCC result. For example, Figure 9-5 shows an SPID of 52, so we can execute the following command to get more information on that process, such as the user that executed it.

```
Exec sp_who 52
```

 EXAM TIP   Any time you have a BEGIN transaction, you need to have either a COMMIT transaction or a ROLLBACK transaction. If not, you are left with open transactions. Open transactions can cause a wide variety of problems, such as a transaction log that continues to grow, taking up resources. If you suspect you have open transactions, you can use the DBCC OPENTRAN statement in the database where you suspect the open transactions exist.

If you entered the previous script with the BEGIN TRAN but did not execute the ROLLBACK TRAN, you can undo it with the following script, which will also verify there are now no open transactions in the database.

```
USE AdventureWorks;
GO
ROLLBACK TRAN;
DBCC OPENTRAN
```

ROLLBACK TRANSACTION

The ROLLBACK TRANSACTION (or ROLLBACK TRAN) statement undoes all the T-SQL actions since the BEGIN TRAN statement. Typically transactions have some type of decision logic included within them to check for certain conditions. Based on the results of the check, the transaction can either be committed or rolled back.

Let's take the example of moving products from one location to another, as shown in the following script.

```
USE AdventureWorks
BEGIN TRANSACTION
        UPDATE Production.ProductInventory
                SET Quantity = Quantity - 10
                WHERE ProductID = 1 AND LocationID=1
        UPDATE Production.ProductInventory
                SET Quantity = Quantity + 10
                WHERE ProductID = 1 AND LocationID=6
COMMIT TRANSACTION
```

As long as the UPDATE doesn't try to subtract more parts from a location than are currently listed there, this will work fine. However, let's say that LocationID 1 for ProductID of 1 actually contains a zero quantity. If we try to subtract 10 from the current quantity, we end up with a negative number. That's unacceptable. Either we have parts there, or we don't.

We could modify our script to check for valid data (perhaps in an IF statement), and if it's not valid, we can roll back the transaction. We'll show that solution in the next section.

IF, BEGIN, END, and RETURN

To make our script work, we need to add some commands to our repertoire.

The IF statement can be used to do general decision-making. The IF statement works logically the same way it works in the English language. For example, IF I have money, I can buy milk. IF I don't have money, I can't buy milk. (Feel free to substitute your beverage of choice.)

Logically, we could write this as:

```
IF money > 0
        'Buy milk'
Else
        'Don't buy milk'
```

One quirk about T-SQL is that anytime we have more than one statement that should execute if the condition is true, we have to enclose the statements to execute within a BEGIN and END pair, as shown next.

```
IF money > 0
        BEGIN
                'Buy milk'
                'Celebrate'
        END
```

If instead we omitted the BEGIN and END statements, then it would not work as expected. We would buy milk only if we had money, but we would always celebrate.

```
IF money > 0
        'Buy milk'              --Executes only if we have money
'Celebrate'                     --Always executes
```

Lastly, the RETURN statement can be used to unconditionally exit a script or a procedure. This can be useful if we've detected an error and we don't want to execute any more code in the script, or even if we've detected a logical condition and want to exit based on business rules. As an example, consider the following pseudo-code:

```
IF money > 0
        BEGIN
                'Buy milk'
                'Buy eggs'
        END
ELSE
        RETURN
'Celebrate'
```

Notice that if we have money, we'll buy milk and eggs and then we'll celebrate. However, if we don't have money, we won't buy milk and eggs, and the RETURN causes us to exit, so we won't celebrate either.

EXAM TIP If you need to conditionally exit a stored procedure, consider using the RETURN clause. This can let you ensure specific code isn't executed based on certain conditions.

Now, back to our original goal. In our script, we want to check whether the quantity is a negative number, and if so, roll back the transaction.

We'll use the IF statement with BEGIN and END. Since only the first UPDATE is subtracting numbers, we would only need to check its result. If the result is a negative number, we would roll back the TRANSACTION and exit the script with RETURN.

```
BEGIN TRANSACTION
      UPDATE Production.ProductInventory
            SET Quantity = Quantity - 1000
      WHERE ProductID = 1 AND LocationID=1
      If (SELECT Quantity
            FROM Production.ProductInventory
            WHERE ProductID =1 and LocationID=1) < 0
      BEGIN
            ROLLBACK TRANSACTION
            RETURN
      END
      UPDATE Production.ProductInventory
            SET Quantity = Quantity + 1000
            WHERE ProductID = 1 AND LocationID=6
COMMIT TRANSACTION
```

> **TIP**   This business objective could be achieved in multiple ways. For example, we could use triggers to roll back negative quantities, or use constraints to prevent the quantity from being a negative number. The previous script isn't intended to imply that this is the only way to accomplish the objective, but instead to demonstrate the logic and syntax of transactions, including **BEGIN, ROLLBACK, COMMIT,** and **RETURN.**

In the following exercise, we'll create a transaction, roll back a transaction, and commit a transaction, using the RETURN statement to do so.

Exercise 9.2: Use Transactions

Video 9-2 shows this exercise from beginning to end.

1. Open a New Query window in SSMS.

2. Run the following script to see that the beginning price of the LL Mountain Seat Assembly (ProductID 514) is $133.34.

   ```
   USE AdventureWorks;
   GO
   SELECT ProductID, Name, ListPrice
   FROM Production.Product
   WHERE ProductID = 514;
   ```

3. Update the price with a 10 percent increase. Without a transaction defined, the update is committed immediately.

   ```
   BEGIN TRAN
     USE AdventureWorks;
     GO
   ```

```
UPDATE Production.Product
SET ListPrice = ListPrice * 1.1
WHERE ProductID=514
SELECT ProductID, Name, ListPrice
FROM Production.Product
WHERE ProductID = 514
```

Notice that we haven't added either a ROLLBACK or COMMIT for the transaction, so it's still open. With it open, we have locked the row so no one else can view it. However, if we stay in our current connection (the New Query window in SSMS), we are able to see the change, even it if isn't committed. Your display should look similar to Figure 9-6.

Figure 9-6
The query
has executed
successfully, but
the transaction
hasn't been
committed

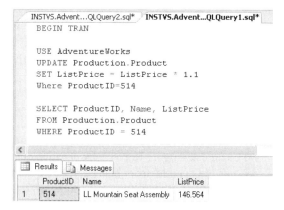

4. Open a New Query window, and enter the following script to see that the open transaction (and the associated lock) prevents others from viewing the data:

```
--Window 2
USE AdventureWorks;
GO
SELECT ProductID, Name, ListPrice
FROM Production.Product
WHERE ProductID = 514;
```

The query will not finish. Your display should look similar to Figure 9-7. Notice that at the bottom left of the query window, an icon continues to move in a circle (indicating action) and the text never changes from "Executing query..."

Figure 9-7 A query that won't complete due to an open transaction in another connection

5. Go back to the first window where the BEGIN TRAN statement exists. Enter the following command to roll back the transaction, and then view the ListPrice to see that it has returned to the original price of $133.34.

```
ROLLBACK TRAN;
SELECT ProductID, Name, ListPrice
FROM Production.Product
WHERE ProductID = 514;
```

6. Select the second query window. With the first transaction completed (with either a ROLLBACK or COMMIT), you'll see that the second transaction is now released. It has successfully completed.

7. Use the following query to change the ListPrice by adding a 10 percent increase. The difference here is that we are checking to see if the new price is more than $1000, and if so, we will provide feedback with the PRINT command, roll back the transaction, and then exit the transaction with the RETURN statement.

```
BEGIN TRAN
  UPDATE Production.Product
  SET ListPrice = ListPrice * 1.1
  WHERE ProductID=514
  IF (SELECT ListPrice
    FROM Production.Product
    WHERE ProductID=514) > $1000
  BEGIN
    PRINT 'Price is > $1000.  This UPDATE needs special approval'
    ROLLBACK TRAN
    RETURN
  END
  SELECT ProductID, Name, ListPrice
  FROM Production.Product
  WHERE ProductID = 514
COMMIT TRAN
```

8. Go to the second window and run the same script as before to see that the change has been implemented: You'll see that this succeeds.

```
--Window 2
SELECT ProductID, Name, ListPrice
FROM Production.Product
WHERE ProductID = 514;
```

9. To see this get rolled back, change the dollar amounts in the first window's script from $1000 to $100, as shown in the following script. The only thing that is different is bolded.

```
BEGIN TRAN
  UPDATE Production.Product
  SET ListPrice = ListPrice * 1.1
  WHERE ProductID=514
  IF (SELECT ListPrice
    FROM Production.Product
    WHERE ProductID=514) > $100
  BEGIN
```

```
      PRINT 'Price is > $100.  This UPDATE needs special approval'
      ROLLBACK TRAN
      RETURN
   END
   SELECT ProductID, Name, ListPrice
   FROM Production.Product
   WHERE ProductID = 514
COMMIT TRAN
```

Execute this script and you'll see the feedback message from the PRINT command displayed. If you use the DBCC OPENTRAN command, you can verify that a transaction is not open.

10. Using the following script, return the price to normal so if anyone wants to buy this, they won't be overcharged:

```
UPDATE Production.Product
SET ListPrice = 133.24
Where ProductID=514
SELECT ProductID, Name, ListPrice
FROM Production.Product
WHERE ProductID = 514
```

Implicit vs. Explicit Transactions

Explicit transactions are those that start with BEGIN TRAN and end with COMMIT TRAN or ROLLBACK TRAN. Implicit transactions are those that start a transaction just by issuing a command. They must also be ended with either a COMMIT TRAN or ROLLBACK TRAN command, but don't have a BEGIN TRAN command.

Implicit transactions can be set to ON with the following command:

```
SET IMPLICIT_TRANSACTIONS ON
```

Implicit transactions will remain on for the entire connection or until a SET IM-PLICIT TRANSACTIONS OFF command is received. When OFF, the system works in autocommit mode, meaning that statements will execute and commit without the need for a COMMIT TRAN or ROLLBACK TRAN command.

 EXAM TIP   If implicit transactions are set to ON, ensure that any of the commands listed in the following table have an associated COMMIT TRAN or ROLLBACK TRAN command. Otherwise, the transaction will be rolled back when the connection is closed.

When implicit transactions are set to ON, any of the commands listed in Table 9-2 will require either a COMMIT TRAN or ROLLBACK TRAN command.

ALTER TABLE	CREATE	DELETE	DROP
FETCH	GRANT	INSERT	OPEN
REVOKE	SELECT	TRUNCATE TABLE	UPDATE

Table 9-2   Commands Requiring COMMIT TRAN or ROLLBACK TRAN When in Implicit Transaction Mode

By default, SQL Server 2005 works in autocommit transaction mode. In other words, any of the statements in Table 9-2 will automatically commit after being executed without the need for a ROLLBACK TRAN or COMMIT TRAN statement.

Creating Savepoints

Savepoints can be used as a method to roll back a portion of a transaction. In other words, we can create a savepoint in the middle of a transaction, and then sometime later roll back to the savepoint instead of rolling back the entire transaction.

For example, let's use our stock inventory modification where we are moving parts from one location to another. The inventory may show that only 40 widgets exist in location A1, but there's actually a quantity of 100. The inventory in the database is incorrect. We can move 100 widgets into location B2 from location A1, and we want the inventory to accurately reflect the new quantity there. However, taking 100 from 40 would result in a negative number, so we may choose to roll back that part of the transaction.

Savepoints are primarily useful when we don't expect errors to occur. In our example, it's unlikely that we're suddenly going to find an extra 60 widgets that we didn't know about, so it would be uncommon to roll back to the savepoint.

 EXAM TIP When you need to be able to roll back part of a transaction while keeping the rest of the transaction intact, consider using savepoints. Transaction savepoints allow us to roll back only a portion of a transaction.

The following exercise shows how we could create a savepoint that allows part of a transaction to be rolled back, while other parts of the transaction are committed.

Exercise 9.3: Create a Savepoint

1. Launch SSMS and create a new query window.

2. Enter and execute the following script to view the current quantity of the Production.ProductInventory table:

```
USE AdventureWorks;
GO
SELECT * FROM Production.ProductInventory
WHERE ProductID = 1;
```

In my current version of AdventureWorks, I have quantities of:

- LocationID 1   408
- LocationID 6   324
- LocationID 50   353

3. Enter and execute the following script to move a quantity of 1000 of ProductID from Location 1 to Location 6. Notice that we only have a quantity of 408 in Location 1, so taking away 1000 would result in an unwanted negative value.

We can check for the negative value condition and roll back to an interim savepoint named NegativeQtyCheck.

```
BEGIN TRANSACTION
  UPDATE Production.ProductInventory
  SET Quantity = Quantity + 1000
  WHERE ProductID = 1 AND LocationID = 6
--We want the previous UPDATE to complete, but we want the ability to
--rollback the following transaction.  The savepoint gives us that
ability.
  SAVE TRANSACTION NegativeQtyCheck;
  UPDATE Production.ProductInventory
  SET Quantity = Quantity - 1000
  WHERE ProductID = 1 AND LocationID = 1
--Here we check for a negative condition and rollback to the savepoint
--if the negative condition exists
  if (SELECT Quantity
        FROM Production.ProductInventory
        WHERE ProductID = 1 and LocationID = 1) < 0
  ROLLBACK TRANSACTION NegativeQtyCheck
--Now we review the results
SELECT * FROM Production.ProductInventory
WHERE ProductID = 1;
```

Your result should look similar to Figure 9-8. Notice that the first UPDATE is reflected (showing the quantity in location increased by 1000), but the second UPDATE has been rolled back (leaving the quantity as 408). This is a little misleading though. The first UPDATE actually isn't committed to the database yet, but is viewable in this connection.

Figure 9-8

Results after rollback to the savepoint

	ProductID	LocationID	Shelf	Bin	Quantity
1	1	1	A	1	408
2	1	6	B	5	1324
3	1	50	A	5	353

4. Check for an open transaction using the following command:

```
DBCC OPENTRAN
```

This shows that the transaction is still open. The first UPDATE is after a BEGIN TRANSACTION, but it has neither been committed nor rolled back, even though the savepoint has been rolled back.

5. Execute the following code to roll back the transaction. Observe the output.

```
ROLLBACK TRAN
SELECT * FROM Production.ProductInventory
  WHERE ProductID = 1
```

Your display should look like Figure 9-9, showing that the inventory is back the way it started.

Figure 9-9

Results of the table after the transaction is rolled back

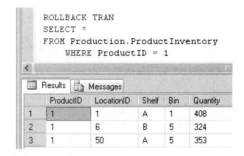

```
ROLLBACK TRAN
SELECT *
FROM Production.ProductInventory
    WHERE ProductID = 1
```

	ProductID	LocationID	Shelf	Bin	Quantity
1	1	1	A	1	408
2	1	6	B	5	324
3	1	50	A	5	353

6. A more complete script for the update of the two locations is shown in the following script. Notice the bolded text is all that has been added to the script from step 3.

```
BEGIN TRANSACTION
   UPDATE Production.ProductInventory
   SET Quantity = Quantity + 1000
   WHERE ProductID = 1 AND LocationID = 6
--We want the previous UPDATE to complete, but we want the ability to -
--rollback the following transaction.  The savepoint gives us that
ability.
   SAVE TRANSACTION InventoryMove;
   UPDATE Production.ProductInventory
   SET Quantity = Quantity - 1000
   WHERE ProductID = 1 AND LocationID = 1
--Here we check for a negative condition and rollback to the savepoint
--if the negative condition exists
      If (SELECT Quantity
          FROM Production.ProductInventory
          WHERE ProductID = 1 and LocationID = 1) < 0
   ROLLBACK TRANSACTION InventoryMove  -- rollback to savepoint
--Now COMMIT the transaction. Even if the second UPDATE is rolled back
--the first UPDATE succeeds and is committed.
COMMIT TRANSACTION
```

7. Execute the following code to verify that no transactions are still open:

```
DBCC OPENTRAN
```

8. Execute the following code to verify the update has been completed as expected:

```
SELECT * FROM Production.ProductInventory
   WHERE ProductID = 1
```

The quantities should be as follows:

- LocationID 1   408
- LocationID 6   1324
- LocationID 50   353

9. If desired, execute the following script to put the inventory back to the original values:

```
UPDATE Production.ProductInventory
SET Quantity = 324
WHERE ProductID = 1 AND LocationID = 6
```

Creating Marked Transactions

Sometimes, you want to ensure that two or more databases within the same instance remain logically consistent in the case of failure. We'll cover database recovery in more detail in Chapter 10, but for now realize that creating a marked transaction will allow you to recover both databases to exactly the same logical point. This is only possible if the recovery model is set to Full- or Bulk-logged.

As an example, consider whether you have multiple databases within the same instance. One database (Orders) is used for most of the online order processing. Another database (Archive) is designed to provide archive logging for all the databases on the server. If we want to create a transaction affecting the Orders and Archive databases, while ensuring that we could recover them both up to the start of the transaction, we would create a transaction using a mark.

 EXAM TIP If you are creating a transaction that affects two databases in the same instance and want to be able to recover both databases to the same logical time (the start of the transaction), consider using the WITH MARK clause in the transaction.

To add a mark to a transaction, we give the transaction a name and add the clause WITH MARK as follows:

```
BEGIN TRANSACTION TranName WITH MARK ' ArchiveOrders'
```

Notice that the transaction has a name (TranName) and the mark has a name ('ArchiveOrders'). This mark becomes a potential recovery point for each of the databases involved in the transaction. If the Orders and Archive databases are updated within the transaction, then the mark goes into the transaction log of each of these databases. This prevents the need to do simultaneous backups of the databases.

Using the OUTPUT Clause

Sometimes we may want to verify the results of our DML statements within a transaction. We can use the OUTPUT clause to return information from each row affected by an INSERT, UPDATE, or DELETE statement after the statement has been executed. We can use this information to send back a confirmation message, log the results in an archive log, or use it to check and enforce business requirements.

For example, let's say we manage a Stock Portfolio database. One of the business rules states that users can not purchase any more than five stocks in any single transaction. You can program some code into a stored procedure to verify this is enforced. As a part of the INSERT statement, the results of the INSERT is moved into a temporary table and the table can then be examined.

The following code shows how this may be implemented:

 NOTE This code does not work against an existing database but is shown as an illustration.

```
USE StockPortfolio;
GO
BEGIN TRAN
--Create a temporary table to hold the result of the INSERT
DECLARE @VerifyStocks table(
      CustomerID int,
      StockName varchar(4),    --Unique stock code
      Date datetime,           --Date of order
      Qty int,                 --Quantity of shares ordered
      Price);                  --Purchase price of stock
--Insert the order from the Shopping cart
 --Include the OUTPUT clause in the INSERT statement
INSERT INTO StockPurchaseOrder
   OUTPUT INSERT CustomerID, StockName, Date, Qty, Price INTO @VerifyStocks
      SELECT CustomerID, StockName, Date, Qty, Price
      FROM ShoppingCart;
--Count the number of rows in the temporary table and make a decision
IF (SELECT COUNT (*) FROM @VerifyStocks) > 5
   ROLLBACK TRAN
Else
   COMMIT TRAN
```

If you're an experienced developer, you may look at this and ask why we didn't just count the number of items in the shopping cart. If there's nothing in the shopping cart table, we wouldn't even start the transaction. That certainly would be a more logical method of approaching this.

However, what if the data is passed to the stored procedure in a more complex format? For example, consider an order passed into a stored procedure as an XML parameter that includes data to be inserted into both a StockPurchaseOrderHeader table and a StockPurchaseOrderItems table. The stored procedure can shred the data and then insert it into the appropriate tables. If the OUTPUT clause is used, we can check to see if more than five rows are added and then roll back the transaction.

Error Catching

In Microsoft .NET languages like C# and Visual Basic, a programming construct known as TRY...CATCH (hereafter, "TRY CATCH") has been available for exception handling. A similar feature is now available in T-SQL.

TRY CATCH in SQL Server 2005 has two blocks. The TRY block performs some action, and if an error occurs, code within the CATCH block runs. If the TRY block performs successfully, the CATCH block does not run.

The syntax is straightforward:

```
BEGIN TRY
   Code we want to run
END TRY
BEGIN CATCH
   Code to run if an error occurs
END CATCH
```

We can use our earlier example where we're moving products from one bin to another. While our IF statement checks for a negative inventory, many more possible errors can occur with an UPDATE statement. Instead of writing IF statements for all possible errors, the CATCH block will catch errors and allow us to roll back the transaction.

Let's say we have used a CHECK CONSTRAINT to implement a business rule on the quantity column. The CHECK doesn't allow any updates that would result in a negative quantity. The following script creates the CHECK CONSTRAINT on our table:

```
ALTER TABLE Production.ProductInventory
ADD CONSTRAINT CK_Quantity
CHECK (Quantity >= 0)
```

If we try to update the quantity with the following script after the constraint has been added, it will result in a negative value and an error based on our constraint will occur:

```
UPDATE Production.ProductInventory
SET Quantity = -1000
WHERE ProductID = 1 AND LocationID = 1
```

The resulting error is shown in Figure 9-10.

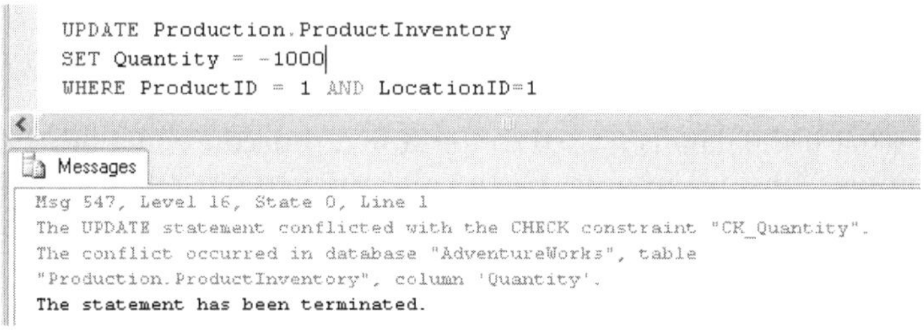

```
UPDATE Production.ProductInventory
SET Quantity = -1000
WHERE ProductID = 1 AND LocationID=1
```

Messages

```
Msg 547, Level 16, State 0, Line 1
The UPDATE statement conflicted with the CHECK constraint "CK_Quantity".
The conflict occurred in database "AdventureWorks", table
"Production.ProductInventory", column 'Quantity'.
The statement has been terminated.
```

Figure 9-10   An error from constraint violation

Instead, we can run our update with TRY CATCH blocks. This script has changed in a couple of ways:

- The IF statement has been removed.
- TRY CATCH blocks have been added.

```
BEGIN TRY
   BEGIN TRANSACTION
UPDATE Production.ProductInventory
```

```
          SET Quantity = Quantity -  1000
    WHERE ProductID = 1 AND LocationID = 1
    UPDATE Production.ProductInventory
          SET Quantity = Quantity + 1000
          WHERE ProductID = 1 AND LocationID = 6
    COMMIT TRANSACTION
END TRY
BEGIN CATCH
   ROLLBACK TRANSACTION
          PRINT 'Transaction rolled back'
END CATCH
```

EXAM TIP   One of the key benefits of the CATCH block within a TRY CATCH construct is the ability to roll back the transaction. When using a TRY CATCH block to catch errors within a transaction, make sure you have a ROLLBACK TRANSACTION statement in the CATCH block. It's also common to include an error message within the CATCH block to provide feedback to the user.

Since subtracting 1000 from the quantity results in a negative quantity, the CHECK CONSTRAINT throws an error. When the error occurs, control of the script passes to the CATCH block and the entire transaction is rolled back.

If you run this script without the PRINT statement showing the transaction was rolled back, you'll see the message "Command(s) completed successfully," which can be misleading. The command did complete successfully because the error was caught; however, an error did occur, causing the command to be rolled back. Some kind of user feedback is typically included in a CATCH block.

How you actually want the error to appear depends on the application. The good news is that the error is much cleaner, and you have rolled back the transaction. You can verify nothing has been updated by querying the table again:

```
SELECT * FROM Production.ProductInventory
WHERE ProductID = 1
```

The @@ERROR Function

The @@ERROR function is a useful tool to check to see if an error occurred in the last executed T-SQL statement. If the last statement was successful, it will hold a value of 0. If the last statement was not successful, it will hold the number of the error.

It's common to use a check similar to:

```
IF @@ ERROR <> 0
  -- An error occurred in last statement, execute error code
ELSE
  -- @@ Error = 0, execute success code
```

As an example, let's say we tried to delete an Employee from the HumanResources .Employee table. This would be prevented due to a DELETE trigger on the table, but we could observe the error with the following script:

```
DELETE FROM HumanResources.Employee
    WHERE EmployeeID = 1;
GO
PRINT 'Error Number: ' + CAST(@@ERROR AS VARCHAR(8));
```

The result wold be similar to Figure 9-11.

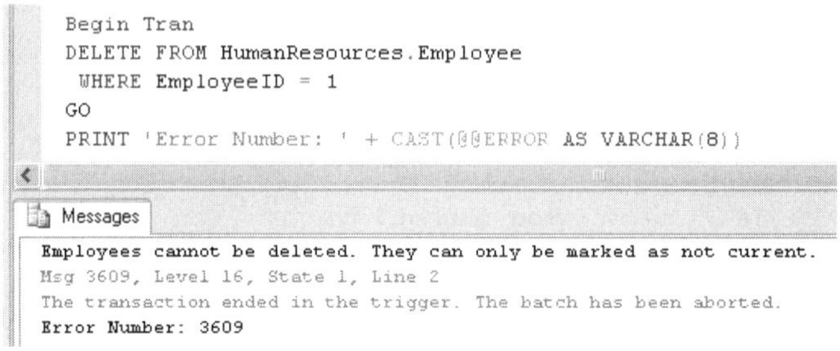

```
Begin Tran
DELETE FROM HumanResources.Employee
  WHERE EmployeeID = 1
GO
PRINT 'Error Number: ' + CAST(@@ERROR AS VARCHAR(8))
```

Messages

```
Employees cannot be deleted. They can only be marked as not current.
Msg 3609, Level 16, State 1, Line 2
The transaction ended in the trigger. The batch has been aborted.
Error Number: 3609
```

Figure 9-11   Checking the value of an @@Error

In the following script, we'll successfully execute a T-SQL statement and then check the value of the error number:

```
SELECT * FROM HumanResources.Employee
  WHERE EmployeeID = 1;
GO
PRINT 'Error Number: ' + CAST(@@ERROR AS VARCHAR(8));
```

By clicking the Messages tab, we can see the error has a value of 0, indicating success.

```
(1 row(s) affected)
Error Number: 0
```

An important point to remember is that the @@Error only holds the value based on the last executed statement. For example, if we executed two successive T-SQL statements (such as a DELETE and then a SELECT), the @@Error would only hold the value based on the results of the SELECT statement. Thus, the result of the DELETE statement is lost.

In the following script, we try to delete a record. If we checked the @@Error right away, it would return an error number other than 0 indicating an error occurred. Instead, we execute another T-SQL statement and then check the value of the @@Error. Since the SELECT statement succeeds, the value of the @@Error is 0 and the script erroneously reports success.

```
DELETE FROM HumanResources.Employee
 WHERE EmployeeID = 1
GO
SELECT * FROM HumanResources.Employee;
GO
IF @@Error <> 0 -- we have an error
  PRINT 'Error Number: ' + CAST(@@ERROR AS VARCHAR(8));
ELSE -- value = 0
  PRINT 'Successfully deleted record' -- erroneous logic
```

In the following exercise, we'll implement error checking with TRY CATCH blocks to roll back a transaction. First, we'll try it without a TRY CATCH block so we can see how SQL will handle the errors.

Exercise 9.4: Catch Errors

1. Open a New Query window in SSMS.

2. You are tasked with writing a script to change the List Price of products. The List Price will be entered as a variable. Enter the following script to simulate this without the use of TRY CATCH blocks.

 NOTE This script will fail due to the existence of the CK_Product_ListPrice constraint, which prevents products from having a negative List Price.

```
DECLARE @ProductID int, @ListPrice money
SET @ProductID = 1
SET @ListPrice = -1.00
UPDATE Production.Product
SET ListPrice = @ListPrice
WHERE ProductID = @ProductID
```

Your display should look similar to Figure 9-12. Notice that this error is rather messy.

```
DECLARE @ProductID int, @ListPrice money
SET @ProductID = 1
SET @ListPrice = -1.00
UPDATE Production.Product
SET ListPrice = @ListPrice
WHERE ProductID = @ProductID
```

Messages

```
Msg 547, Level 16, State 0, Line 4
The UPDATE statement conflicted with the CHECK constraint
 "CK_Product_ListPrice". The conflict occurred in database
"AdventureWorks", table "Production.Product", column 'ListPrice'.
The statement has been terminated.
```

Figure 9-12 The error when trying to update the list price to a negative value

3. By using the TRY CATCH blocks, we can check for the error and provide a much cleaner error response. Enter and execute the following code:

```
DECLARE @ProductID int, @ListPrice money
SET @ProductID = 1
SET @ListPrice = -1.00
BEGIN TRY
  BEGIN TRANSACTION
    UPDATE Production.Product
```

```
        SET ListPrice = @ListPrice
        WHERE ProductID = @ProductID
    COMMIT TRANSACTION
END TRY
BEGIN CATCH
  If @ListPrice < 0
        PRINT 'List Price cannot be a negative number.'
  ROLLBACK TRANSACTION
END CATCH
```

Your display should look like Figure 9-13. Notice this is a much cleaner error message.

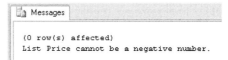

Figure 9-13
A result of
CATCH

```
(0 row(s) affected)
List Price cannot be a negative number.
```

4. Run the following script to verify that the update didn't occur:

```
SELECT *
FROM Production.Product
WHERE ProductID = 1
```

5. Now use the same script from step 3 with one minor change. Set the @ListPrice variable to 1.23 (a positive number). Change this line and rerun the script.

```
SET @ListPrice = 1.23
```

6. Use the following SELECT statement to verify the change occurred:

```
SELECT *
FROM Production.Product
WHERE ProductID = 1
```

Raising Errors

It's possible to raise errors within our code. We can create our own user-defined error message (starting at number 50001), or build our own messages dynamically. User-defined error messages are stored in the sys.messages catalog view. To view all of the messages, you can execute the following code. Messages with a message_id less than 50000 are used by SQL Server.

```
SELECT * FROM sys.messages
WHERE message_ID > 50000
```

To add our own messages to the sys.messages table, we can use the sp_addmessage system stored procedure, as shown in the following code:

```
USE master
GO
EXEC sp_addmessage 50001, 16,
    'Uh Oh.  Something bad happened.';
```

Of course, we could change the text to anything we want it to be. However, with this error message created we can now raise the error. The basic syntax to raise an error follows:

```
RAISERROR (error number (or 'text'), severity, state)
```

The actual command to raise the error number 50001 that we created with the sp_addmessage stored procedure would be:

```
RAISERROR(50001, 16, 1)
```

It's common to raise an error in the CATCH block. This message will be returned to the application that executed the script. Often, we can create an error message that is more intuitive than a default error message. If the error message would be used in more than one place, it makes sense to create a message that is permanently stored in the system.

The error can be logged into the application log by adding the clause WITH LOG at the end of the statement. This can be useful if the SQL Server Agent service is monitoring for that specific error number.

Severity and State are also included in the RAISERROR message. Severity levels are intended to indicate how serious an error is. Possible severity levels can be from 0 through 25, with 25 being the most severe. If you want a more detailed explanation of these error levels, see the Books Online article titled, "Database Engine Error Severities."

The state is an arbitrary number between 1 and 127. It is usually left as 1. It's useful only if the same error is being raised by different blocks of code and you want to identify specifically which block of code raised it. For example, in the usp_OrderParts stored procedure, you could have this statement in a CATCH block:

```
RAISERROR (50001, 16, 1) WITH LOG
```

And in the usp_UpdateCustomer stored procedure, you could have this statement in the CATCH block:

```
RAISERROR (50001, 16, 9) WITH LOG
```

If you came across the error, you could look at the value of the state. If it was a 1, it came from the usp_OrderParts stored procedure, and if it was a 9, the error was generated from the usp_upateCustomer stored procedure.

It's also possible to raise an error without first adding a message to the system. This can be done directly in the code. Instead of using an error number, specific text is added as follows:

```
RAISERROR ('Uh Oh.  Something bad happened.', 16, 1)
```

This will return the text you include in the error to the application that called the code.

Distributed Transactions

Distributed transactions are transactions that span two or more instances or servers. Distributed transactions are managed using a two-phase commit process. The two phases are Prepare and Commit. A transaction manager (such as Microsoft Distributed Coordinator) is used to track the progress of all distributed elements of a transaction.

 EXAM TIP If a transaction must commit on multiple servers or instances within the same transaction, you need to use a distributed transaction. If a transaction spans multiple databases within the same instance of SQL Server, a distributed transaction is not needed.

Remember, a transaction is used to ensure all elements of a transaction complete successfully, or none of them complete successfully. A distributed transaction simply means we ensure all elements of a transaction commit on each separate server, instance, or database involved in the transaction. If one of the transactions within the distributed transaction fails, they all fail.

During the Prepare phase, each server involved in the transaction attempts to make the transaction durable locally. It then reports success or failure to the transaction manager.

Once all elements of the transaction successfully complete the Prepare phase, then the transaction manager sends the Commit command to them all. Once again, each distributed element of the transaction reports success or failure. If any failures are reported, a rollback command is issued. Otherwise, a success is reported to all.

Distributed transactions are begun with the BEGIN DISTRIBUTED TRANSACTION command. They are completed with the COMMIT TRANSACTION, COMMIT WORK, ROLLBACK TRANSACTION, and ROLLBACK WORK commands.

As an example, a transaction could be written to write changes to a Sales database on one server and a Distributing database on another server. A business rule could state that we don't want to record the changes unless we are assured the changes have occurred in both databases. A distributed transaction could be used to enforce this business rule.

Transactions that span two separate databases in the same instance are technically referred to as distributed transactions, but can be managed as a regular transaction. Distributed transaction commands are NOT needed for transactions between different databases within the same instance.

User-Defined Stored Procedures

Within stored procedures, you can write hundreds of lines of T-SQL code that can be used to validate data, encase business rules, return specialized error messages, make complex decisions with IF and CASE statements, repeat processes a variable number of times with loops, and more. Can you tell I'm excited?

If you haven't done many stored procedures or don't feel comfortable with them, let's get past that right away. The only way to feel comfortable with most programming is to do it.

If you really want to learn how to create stored procedures, you have to create them. That means fingers on the keyboard, typos, errors, successes, and victories. In the following pages, you'll have the opportunity to do just that with a couple of exercises.

Creating Stored Procedures

As with other database objects, the command used to create a stored procedure is CREATE. Once created, the stored procedure can be removed from the database with the DROP command. Or, if the definition of the database needs to be changed, the ALTER statement can be used.

Stored procedures can reference tables, VIEWs, user-defined functions, and other stored procedures.

Very few T-SQL statements can't be included in a stored procedure. These include the statements listed in Table 9-3.

CREATE AGGREGATE	CREATE DEFAULT
CREATE (OR ALTER) FUNCTION	CREATE OR ALTER PROCEDURE
CREATE RULE	CREATE SCHEMA
CREATE (OR ALTER) TRIGGER	CREATE (OR ALTER) VIEW
SET PARSEONLY	SET SHOWPLAN_ALL
SET SHOWPLAN_TEXT	SET SHOWPLAN_XML
USE (database)	

Table 9-3 Commands that Cannot Be Included in a Stored Procedure

When creating a stored procedure, it must be the only statement in a batch. In other words, either this is the only code that is being executed, or it is separated with GO statements before and after the CREATE PROC statement.

In the following exercise, we'll create a simple stored procedure within the AdventureWorks database.

Exercise 9.5: Create a Simple Stored Procedure

1. If not already open, open an instance of SSMS and create a new query window.

2. Enter the following script and execute it to provide an e-mail listing of all employees in the AdventureWorks database:

```
USE AdventureWorks;
GO
SELECT pc.FirstName, pc.LastName, pc.EmailAddress
FROM Person.Contact pc
INNER JOIN HumanResources.Employee emp
ON pc.ContactID = emp.ContactID;
```

3. Now create a stored procedure using the following script:

```
CREATE PROC usp_EmployeeEmailList
AS
```

```
SELECT pc.FirstName, pc.LastName, pc.EmailAddress
FROM Person.Contact pc
INNER JOIN HumanResources.Employee emp
ON pc.ContactID = emp.ContactID
```

4. With the stored procedure created, we can now execute it with this statement:

```
EXEC usp_EmployeeEmailList
```

We'll build on this simple stored procedure in the next exercise.

Using Parameters

A core feature of stored procedures is the ability to accept parameters. By defining parameters in the stored procedure, we can configure it to dynamically construct T-SQL statements based on the data passed in.

Parameters of any SQL data type can be passed in. Common data types are text data types (char, varchar, and so on), integer or other numeric data types, and datetime data types.

As an example of a stored procedure that accepts a parameter, we could create a stored procedure that is designed to return a variable number of rows from a table. This requires a single variable of type integer.

```
USE AdventureWorks;
GO
CREATE Proc dbo.usp_ViewRows
  (@NumberOfRows int)
AS
SELECT TOP (@NumberOfRows) *
FROM Person.Contact
```

Once created, we could execute the stored procedure with the following statement to return only five rows:

```
EXEC usp_ViewRows 5
```

We can also provide defaults for parameters. Using the previous example, let's say users typically only want five rows, but occassionally they may want more. We can modify the stored procedure definition so the default is 5, but a parameter will be used if passed in.

```
ALTER Proc dbo.usp_ViewRows
  (@NumberOfRows int = 5)
AS
SELECT TOP (@NumberOfRows) *
FROM Person.Contact
```

Now the procedure can be executed without providing a parameter (and the default of 5 would be used), or with a parameter to specify the number of rows to be returned.

```
EXEC usp_ViewRows
EXEC usp_ViewRows 10
```

In the following exercise, we'll alter the simple stored procedure created earlier to accept parameters of LastName and FirstName. This will allow a user to execute it to retrieve a specific e-mail address, or retrieve all the addresses by not providing a parameter.

Exercise 9.6: Add Parameters to a Simple Stored Procedure

1. If not already open, open an instance of SSMS and create a new query window.

2. Enter the following script and execute it to alter the stored procedure created in the previous exercise.

```
ALTER PROC usp_EmployeeEmailList
  (@LastName varchar(50), @FirstName varchar(50))
AS
SELECT pc.FirstName, pc.LastName, pc.EmailAddress
FROM Person.Contact pc
INNER JOIN HumanResources.Employee emp
ON pc.ContactID = emp.ContactID
WHERE FirstName = @FirstName AND LastName = @LastName
```

3. Enter and execute the following line to retrieve the e-mail address of a specific employee.

```
EXEC usp_EmployeeEmailList  'Gilbert', 'Guy'
```

4. Enter and execute the following line to retrieve the e-mail address of all employees. Notice that this fails since the stored procedure is expecting parameters.

```
EXEC usp_EmployeeEmailList
```

5. Modify this slightly so the procedure will use defaults of NULL if parameter values aren't passed in. We can then check for NULL, and if both names are NULL, we can give an e-mail listing for all employees. Enter and execute the following script:

```
ALTER PROC usp_EmployeeEmailList
  (@LastName varchar(50) = NULL, @FirstName varchar(50) = NULL)
AS
IF (@LastName IS NULL and @FirstName IS NULL)
  SELECT pc.FirstName, pc.LastName, pc.EmailAddress
  FROM Person.Contact pc
  INNER JOIN HumanResources.Employee emp
  ON pc.ContactID = emp.ContactID
ELSE
  SELECT pc.FirstName, pc.LastName, pc.EmailAddress
  FROM Person.Contact pc
  INNER JOIN HumanResources.Employee emp
  ON pc.ContactID = emp.ContactID
  WHERE FirstName = @FirstName AND LastName = @LastName
```

6. Now we can execute the stored procedure with or without parameters. Enter and execute each of the two following lines to see the results:

```
EXEC usp_EmployeeEmailList  'Gilbert', 'Guy'
EXEC usp_EmployeeEmailList
```

Using Variables

While we've shown the use of variables in several examples, we should clarify a few concepts with variables. We can include variables in any type of T-SQL batches, not just stored procedures.

Variables must be first declared with the DECLARE statement, and the declaration must include the data type. Once declared, variables can be populated with the SELECT or SET statements.

To populate a variable with the SELECT statement, use syntax similar to the following script:

```
DECLARE @CustomerID int
SELECT @CustomerID = CustomerID
FROM Orders WHERE OrderID = 54
```

To populate a variable with the SET statement, use syntax similar to the following script:

```
DECLARE @myVar varchar(30)
SET @myVar = 'Hello World'
```

Variables are identified with the @ symbol. A local variable is only available in the current batch or until a GO statement. As an example, consider the following code:

```
DECLARE @str varchar(30)
SET @str = 'Hello'
Print @str + ' Before GO'
GO
Print @str + ' After GO'
```

The Print before the GO will execute, but the Print after the GO will result in an error since the variable has fallen out of scope and is no longer available.

Using Encryption

Just as with other database objects (such as VIEWs and functions), the definition of stored procedures can be encrypted. When specified, it causes the original text of the CREATE PROCEDURE to be stored in an unintelligible format. This does not affect the data, only the definition of the stored procedure. Additionally, this feature is not available for CLR-integrated stored procedures, or for stored procedures that are to be published as part of SQL Server Replication.

As an example, the procedure created and manipulated in the previous two exercises could be encrypted with the following script. The only thing modified is the text that has been added in bold.

```
ALTER PROC usp_EmployeeEmailList
  (@LastName varchar(50) = NULL, @FirstName varchar(50) = NULL)
WITH ENCRYPTION
AS
IF (@LastName IS NULL and @FirstName IS NULL)
  SELECT pc.FirstName, pc.LastName, pc.EmailAddress
  FROM Person.Contact pc
```

```
  INNER JOIN HumanResources.Employee emp
  ON pc.ContactID = emp.ContactID
ELSE
  SELECT pc.FirstName, pc.LastName, pc.EmailAddress
  FROM Person.Contact pc
  INNER JOIN HumanResources.Employee emp
  ON pc.ContactID = emp.ContactID
  WHERE FirstName = @FirstName AND LastName = @LastName
```

Now, if we try to view the definition by selecting one of the catalog views of the system stored procedure sp_helptext, it will not succeed. For example, if the following line was executed:

```
EXEC sp_helptext usp_EmployeeEmailList
```

the result would be:

```
The text for object 'usp_EmployeeEmailList' is encrypted.
```

Be aware, though, that this doesn't make the stored procedure definition completely inaccessible. Privileged users that can access system tables, and users that can attach a debugger to the server process can retrieve the decrypted procedure definition.

Creating a Stored Procedure with Built-in Functions

In the classroom, I use a learning exercise to combine the usage of functions with stored procedures. This allows students to gain a better knowledge of both. These seven steps will help you master both stored procedures and built-in functions:

1. Pick a category (such as Scalar Date and Time or Aggregate) from the "Functions (Transact-SQL)" BOL article. Pick a function in your chosen category.

2. Run the function to understand it. Use the BOL example if necessary.

3. Create a stored procedure (without any parameters) using the function.

4. Execute the stored procedure to make sure it works.

5. Alter the stored procedure to accept an input parameter.

6. Execute the altered stored procedure to make sure it works.

7. Tweak as desired.

1. Pick a category (such as Scalar Date and Time or Aggregate) from the Functions (Transact-SQL) BOL article. Pick a function in your chosen category. Let's start with the Date and Time functions in the Scalar Functions list. The first function is DATEADD. BOL shows that DATEADD allows us to add an interval (such as day, month, or year) to a date. For example, if I wanted to create a span of a single year, I could start with some date (such as today), and add negative one (–1) to subtract a year. The syntax for DATEADD is *DATEADD (datepart, number, date).*

datepart could be days, weeks, years, and so on. We'll use the "day" datepart to add some days to the date. Notice that BOL shows that day could be abbreviated as *dd* or *d.*

2. Run the function to understand it. Use the BOL example if necessary.
The example from BOL is shown next. It adds 21 days to the OrderDate from the Sales.SalesOrderHeader table in AdventureWorks and lists this as TimeFrame.

```
USE AdventureWorks;
GO
SELECT DATEADD(day, 21, OrderDate)AS TimeFrame
FROM Sales.SalesOrderHeader;
```

We could slightly modify it by adding OrderDate to the SELECT statement as shown next. This allows us to more clearly see that it is adding 21 days to the OrderDate.

```
SELECT OrderDate, DATEADD(day, 21, OrderDate)AS TimeFrame
FROM Sales.SalesOrderHeader;
```

Or, if you want to simplify the example, you don't have to use the AdventureWorks database at all. Change your query to:

```
SELECT DATEADD(day, 21, '11/03/2008');
```

Execute this and you'll see it returns a date of 11/24/2008, adding 21 days to the given date.

We'll expand both the modified BOL example and the simple example that is not using AdventureWorks in the following steps.

3. Create a stored procedure (without any parameters) using the function.
Now we simply wrap the SELECT statement within the required syntax to create a stored procedure. Notice the bolded text is all we need to add to create two new stored procedures.

```
USE AdventureWorks;
GO
CREATE Proc dbo.usp_AddDaysToOrder
AS
SELECT OrderDate, DATEADD(day, 21, OrderDate)AS TimeFrame
FROM Sales.SalesOrderHeader;
GO
CREATE Proc dbo.usp_AddDaysToDate
AS
SELECT DATEADD(day, 21, '11/03/2007');
```

4. Execute the stored procedure to make sure it works.

```
EXEC dbo.usp_AddDaysToOrder;
EXEC dbo.usp_AddDaysToDate;
```

TIP Note that the default schema is dbo. We don't have to execute it as dbo.usp_AddDays, but if it were defined with a different schema, we would need the two-part name.

Prefixing User-Defined Stored Procedures with usp

Many programming objects use prefixes to define what they are. For example, views are frequently named with a prefix of *vw_*.

A logical prefix for a stored procedure is *sp_*. However, system stored procedures have already taken this prefix. A best practice is to use a different prefix for stored procedures. For example, many DBAs use the prefix *usp_* for "user-defined stored procedures."

*xp_* is the prefix for extended stored procedures, which are still supported in SQL Server 2005, but have been deprecated.

5. Alter the stored procedure to accept an input parameter. Next we'll use the DDL ALTER statement to modify the structure of the stored procedure to accept an input.

Again, the bolded text is all we must modify to accomplish the task. Since the stored procedure exists, we use ALTER instead of CREATE. Next, we add the input parameter definition, and last we change the literal date to the defined input parameter:

```
USE AdventureWorks;
GO
--This will add a variable number of days to the OrderDate
ALTER Proc dbo.usp_AddDaysToOrder
        @InputDays integer


AS
SELECT OrderDate, DATEADD(day, @InputDays, OrderDate)AS TimeFrame
FROM Sales.SalesOrderHeader;
GO
--This will add 21 days to a given date
ALTER Proc dbo.usp_AddDaysToDate
        @InputDate datetime


AS
SELECT DATEADD(day, 21, @InputDate);
```

6. Execute the altered stored procedure to make sure it works. In the first example, we are passing in the number *21* to add 21 days to the OrderDate. In the second example, we are passing in the date. Notice our stored procedures are now flexible enough to accept any number of days for the first stored procedure, or any date for the second one.

```
EXEC usp_AddDaysToOrder 12;
EXEC usp_AddDaysToDate '12/03/2008';
```

7. Tweak as desired. Let's fine-tune the second example a little. Instead of always adding 21 days, you can give the user the option of entering the number of days. You can do this by adding another input parameter and using it. Notice that we add a comma after the first parameter.

```
USE AdventureWorks;
GO
--This will add a variable number of days to a given date
ALTER Proc dbo.usp_AddDaysToDate
      @InputNumberofDays int, @InputDate datetime

AS
SELECT DATEADD(day, @InputNumberofDays, @InputDate);
```

Execute the new procedure:

```
EXEC usp_AddDaysToDate 30,'11/03/2008';
```

Notice that with more than one parameter, we have to either enter the parameters in order (as we did earlier) or identify the parameters with an = operator. This would not work as desired if we entered it as:

```
EXEC usp_AddDaysToDate '11/03/2006', 30;
```

The stored procedure would try to interpret the date *'11/03/2006'* as a number of days (an integer) and the number *30* as a date.

However, we could do it this way:

```
EXEC usp_AddDaysToDate @InputDate = '11/03/2007', @InputNumberofDays = 30;
```

Now that you've done this with one DateTime function, repeat it with the next DateTime function, and then with the rest of the DateTime functions. And then the Aggregate functions. And then the String functions. And then... well, you get the idea.

Here's a warning, though. What I often notice students in class do is skip steps 1 through 6 and start creating a fancy tweaked stored procedure. It doesn't work and so they're faced with trying to debug all seven steps simultaneously, causing them to get frustrated and quit.

After you've done a couple dozen stored procedures, you'll probably be able to jump right to step 7, but for now, take your time and go through each step one at a time. As you succeed with each step, count it as a mini-victory, yell out "Woo-Hoo!" and move on to the next. There's a lot to be said for getting some positive feedback during the process.

Testing Stored Procedures

There may be times when you're required to test stored procedures. During development, this is easy enough. You simply execute them within a query window in SSMS. For serious problems in the logic, you may want to use a debugger.

If you're coming from a SQL Server 2000 background, you probably know that stored procedures previously could be debugged in the Query Analyzer. However, in

SQL Server 2005, there is no Query Analyzer. Instead, query windows can be created right in the SSMS environment. This might lead you to believe we must be able to debug stored procedures within SSMS. I've hunted for it. It's not there.

Instead, to debug stored procedures you need to use Visual Studio's development environment. The actual procedure of debugging a stored procedure is beyond the scope of this book; however, I did want to mention that it could be debugged in Visual Studio, not SSMS.

One of the problems you may be faced with is testing the stored procedures after an upgrade. This could be after a major upgrade of the entire server from SQL Server 2000 to SQL Server 2005, or a minor upgrade such as a service pack. In this situation, the use of test scripts is often the best solution.

 EXAM TIP　If tasked with testing stored procedures after an upgrade, consider the use of test scripts. Test scripts can easily control the input and test for a predicted output.

By using test scripts to test your stored procedures, you can control the input parameters and predict the stored procedure output.

Stored Procedures as a DBA

While the previous exercises help you get your hands on both stored procedures and functions, you may like to see something useful on the job.

We explored DBCC CheckDB in Chapter 7. It can be used to check the integrity of a database and all the objects in that database. In the following exercise, we'll create a stored procedure that will run DBCC CheckDB on all of our databases.

Exercise 9.7: Create a Stored Procedure to Check Database Integrity

1. Open a New Query window in SSMS.

2. Execute the following script to check the health of the AdventureWorks database. This script takes about 20 or more seconds to run.

```
USE AdventureWorks;
GO
DBCC CHECKDB;
```

3. As part of a maintenance plan, you may choose to create stored procedures that you will use on a regular basis. Instead of creating these in user databases or system databases, it's considered a best practice to create these objects in your own database. Create a database named Dba to hold your database administrator objects using the following script:

```
Use Master;
GO
CREATE DATABASE Dba;
```

4. Execute the following script to identify how many databases you have in your system:

```
SELECT MAX(dbid) FROM master.dbo.sysdatabases;
```

We can use this statement embedded into a script instead of the actual number of databases.

5. What we need to do is run DBCC CHECKDB on each database. However, there could easily be too many to do manually. By creating a script, we can automate it. Enter the following script to build the DBCC CHECKDB statement for each database:

```
--Declare variables
DECLARE @dbid integer;                  --Current database
DECLARE @DBName nvarchar(50);           --Database name
DECLARE @mySQL nvarchar(200);           --SQL Statement
--Start with first database
SET @dbid = 1;
--Loop through all databases
WHILE @dbid < (SELECT MAX(dbid) FROM master.dbo.sysdatabases)
BEGIN
  SELECT @DBName = name
    FROM master.dbo.sysdatabases
    WHERE dbid = @dbid;
  --Dynamically build statement to execute for each database
  SET @mySQL = 'DBCC CHECKDB(' + @DBName + ')';
  --Show dynamically built SQL statement
  SELECT 'Statement = ' + @mySQL AS 'Dynamically Built T-SQL Statement';
  --Increment database to do the same for the next database
  Set @dbid = @dbid + 1;
END;
```

When you run this script, notice that the SELECT statement that is output just shows us what the dynamically built statement looks like. It doesn't run it. Also notice that we're using the "+" to concatenate the string *'DBCC CHECKDB('* with the actual name of the database pulled from the SELECT statement.

6. Add the EXEC line (in bold next) after the SELECT statement:

```
SELECT 'Statement = ' + @mySQL AS 'Dynamically Built T-SQL Statement';
EXEC sp_executesql @statement = @mySQL
```

7. Execute the modified script. This will take a while. Afterward, you should see a result set similar to Figure 9-14.

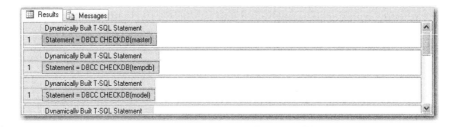

Figure 9-14 The results output of the script

8. Click the Messages tab. This lets you see the results of the CheckDB statement, which should look similar to Figure 9-15.

```
▦ Results  🗒 Messages

(1 row(s) affected)
DBCC results for 'master'.
Service Broker Msg 9675, State 1: Message Types analyzed: 14.
Service Broker Msg 9676, State 1: Service Contracts analyzed: 6.
Service Broker Msg 9667, State 1: Services analyzed: 3.
Service Broker Msg 9668, State 1: Service Queues analyzed: 3.
Service Broker Msg 9669, State 1: Conversation Endpoints analyzed: 0.
Service Broker Msg 9674, State 1: Conversation Groups analyzed: 0.
```

Figure 9-15   Messages from the CheckDB statement

9. We used the SELECT statement for debugging as we built the script, but we don't need it in the stored procedure, so remove it by adding two dashes to the beginning to comment it out, as shown next. Rerun your script again to ensure it still works correctly.

```
--SELECT 'Statement = ' + @mySQL AS 'Dynamically Built T-SQL Statement';
```

10. Now make this into a stored procedure. Add the bolded lines to the beginning of your script. Execute the script to create the stored procedure.

```
USE Dba;
GO
CREATE PROC usp_DBCC_CheckAllDB
AS
--Declare variables
DECLARE @dbid integer;
DECLARE @DBName nvarchar(50);
DECLARE @mySQL nvarchar(200);
--Start with first database
SET @dbid = 1;
--Loop through all databases
WHILE @dbid < (SELECT MAX(dbid) FROM master.dbo.sysdatabases)
BEGIN
  SELECT @DBName = name
    FROM master.dbo.sysdatabases
    WHERE dbid = @dbid;
  --Dynamically build statement to execute for each database
  SET @mySQL = 'DBCC CHECKDB(' + @DBName + ')';
--SELECT 'Statement = ' + @mySQL AS 'Dynamically Built T-SQL Statement';
  EXEC sp_executesql @statement = @mySQL
  --Increment database to do the same for the next database
  Set @dbid = @dbid + 1;
END;
```

11. Execute the following script to execute your stored procedure:

```
USE dba;
GO
EXEC usp_DBCC_CheckAllDB
```

In Chapter 13, we'll explore using SQL Server Agent to automate running stored procedures like the one we've just created. Not only can we automate the process, but we can also do things like save the output to a text file so we can examine it at our leisure.

Recompiling Stored Procedures

The SQL Server database engine optimizes and compiles a stored procedure the first time it's run. The result is stored in cache. Depending on variables such as how much memory is available to SQL Server and how often the stored procedure is run it may stay in cache indefinitely, or it may be optimized and recompiled each time it is run.

Occasionally, you will want to make sure it is recompiled. Often, this is due to a very active OLTP database. For example, let's say you have a stored procedure that queries several tables and produces a report. We run the report today, and SQL identifies the best plan to create the report. Since our server has a lot of memory, the compiled plan stays in cache.

The next day we run the plan again. However, between yesterday and today the updates to the database have made the original plan less than ideal. Running the plan today takes three times as long because the indexes used in the plan have been heavily modified.

If instead we were to force the stored procedure to be recompiled, SQL Server would identify the best plan based on the current state of the database. We would lose a little time in the initial recompilation, but in this example we save time in the long run.

Another reason why we may need to force a stored procedure to be recompiled is to counteract the effects of passing in significantly different parameter values. Normally, when a stored procedure is executed, parameter values are included as part of the query plan. As long as the parameters are typical ones, the compiled plan will work well.

However, if the parameters supplied are significantly different from one execution to another, then it may be beneficial to recompile the stored procedure each time it is executed. For example, one execution of the stored procedure may work well with one set of indexes, but the next execution may have different parameters that would work better with different indexes.

A new feature of SQL Server 2005 allows statement-level recompilation of stored procedures. In other words, instead of recompiling the entire stored procedure each time it is run, specific statements within the stored procedure can be targeted for recompilation. This is very useful if the parameters vary significantly from one execution to another. SQL will use the parameter values as they exist in the recompiled statement when regenerating a query plan.

EXAM TIP If a stored procedure performs poorly with different parameters, consider creating the stored procedure using the WITH RECOMPILE option. If the stored procedure has several queries but just one of the queries is performing poorly with different parameters, use the RECOMPILE option in just this query instead of the entire stored procedure. The latter option (RECOMPILE applied to individual queries within a stored procedure) is new to SQL Server 2005, and as a new feature you should be especially aware of it when taking the tests.

Let me stress, though, that forcing stored procedures to be recompiled each time they are run is the *exception*.

SQL Server will regularly look at different variables such as the statistics of indexes and if needed, it will automatically recompile stored procedures. Additionally, any time the UPDATE STATISTICS command is issued against a table or VIEW, stored procedures that use this table or VIEW will automatically be recompiled.

 TIP Ideally, stored procedures will stay in cache as long as they're being used. If you find they are regularly being recompiled, you might like to look for an automated script scheduled to run regularly and update all the statistics. Updating the statistics will immediately purge them from cache.

A stored procedure (or part of a stored procedure) can be made to recompile in four ways:

1. **Use the sp_recompile system stored procedure.**   This system stored procedure can be executed with any existing stored procedure as a parameter. The following script shows the syntax assuming a stored procedure named usp_ ShowOrders exists in your database:

```
EXEC sp_recompile 'usp_ShowOrders'
```

2. **Create the stored procedure using WITH RECOMPILE.**   This option is added in the definition of the stored procedure and will prevent SQL Server from storing the procedure in cache. The following script shows the syntax:

```
CREATE PROCEDURE dbo.usp_ShowOrders @CustomerID int
WITH RECOMPILE
AS
    SELECT *
    FROM Orders
    WHERE CustomerID = @CustomerID;
```

3. **Use the query hint RECOMPILE for a specific query in the stored procedure definition.**   When only a single query within a stored procedure needs to be recompiled instead of the entire stored procedure, the RECOMPILE query hint can be specified for the specific query. The following script shows the syntax:

```
CREATE PROCEDURE dbo.usp_ShowOrders2 @CustomerID int
WITH RECOMPILE
AS
    SELECT *
    FROM Orders
    WHERE CustomerID = @CustomerID;
--Only the following query will be recompiled each time the
--stored procedure is executed
    UPDATE CustomerQuery
    SET QueryCount = QueryCount + 1
    WHERE CustomerID = @CustomerID
    OPTION (RECOMPILE);
```

4. **Execute the stored procedure using the WITH RECOMPILE option.** When a stored procedure is executed, the WITH RECOMPILE clause can be added to force the stored procedure to be recompiled this time. SQL Server will create a new plan, and discard it immediately after the stored procedure is executed. If there is an existing plan for the stored procedure in cache, it will remain there. The following script shows the syntax:

```
EXEC usp_ShowOrders 101 WITH RECOMPILE
```

Security

While overall database security was covered in Chapter 8, stored procedures have some special security considerations that deserve to be mentioned here. One especially important concept to grasp is that we normally only have to grant Execute permission to a stored procedure without granting any permissions to underlying tables.

Permissions and Access

The basic permissions available with stored procedures are shown in Figure 9-16 and are outlined in the following bullets.

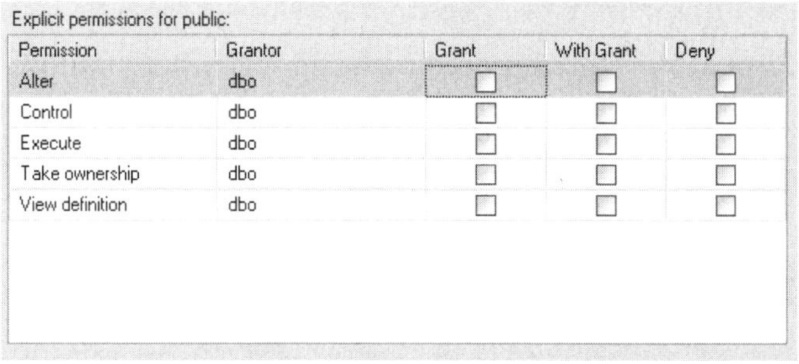

Figure 9-16

Stored procedure permissions

Explicit permissions for public:				
Permission	Grantor	Grant	With Grant	Deny
Alter	dbo	☐	☐	☐
Control	dbo	☐	☐	☐
Execute	dbo	☐	☐	☐
Take ownership	dbo	☐	☐	☐
View definition	dbo	☐	☐	☐

- **Alter** Allows the user or role to modify the properties (except ownership) of the stored procedure. This includes the ability to execute ALTER, CREATE, or DROP statements against the stored procedure.

- **Control** This can be thought of as full control and grants ownership-like capabilities.

- **Execute** Grants the ability to execute (or run) the stored procedure.

- **Take Ownership** Allows the user or role to take ownership of the object.

- **View Definition** When granted, enables the user or role to view the metadata (the statement that was used to create the stored procedure).

For each of the permissions, three possible permissions can be selected:

- **Grant** Allows this permission. Removing the grant permission is referred to as revoking the permission.

- **With Grant**   When accompanied by the grant permission, the *with grant* permission allows the user or role to also grant the permission to others.

- **Deny**   Explicitly prevents use of this permission. If a user is in one role that grants the permission and another role that denies the permission, deny takes precedence.

The Execute Permission

The stored procedure permission you'll be concerned with most often is the Execute permission. As we mentioned, this allows the user or role to execute or run the stored procedure. Often, this is the only permission that needs to be granted, even when underlying tables are read or modified.

By granting execute permission on the stored permission, the permission is chained to DML statements on the underlying table. Permission chaining was presented in Chapter 8. The ultimate effect of permission chaining is that by granting execute permission to a stored procedure, a user is able to execute it even if they don't have permissions to any underlying tables read or modified by the stored procedure.

As an example, consider a stored procedure named sp_AddEmployees used to add employee records to the Employees table. In order for Sally to use this stored procedure, she only needs Execute permission on the sp_AddEmployees stored procedure. She does NOT need any permissions on the Employees table.

EXAM TIP   You do *not* need permissions for underlying tables to execute a stored procedure that executes DML statements (SELECT, INSERT, UPDATE, and DELETE) against those tables. By granting the Execute permission on the stored procedure, the user can effectively read and/or modify the underlying table via the stored procedure without having any permission on the underlying tables.

To demonstrate how the Execute permission on a stored procedure is chained to the underlying table, the following exercise will create and execute stored procedures using a user account that has no permission on the table.

Exercise 9.8: Use Execute Permission to Read or Modify Data

1. Open an instance of SSMS and create a New Query window. We'll use this to set up the environment.

   a. Change the instance to mixed mode.

   b. Create a database named Chapter9 with the following script:

   ```
   USE Master;
   GO
   CREATE DATABASE Chapter9
   ```

   c. Create a table in the Chapter9 database named Gryffindor with the following script:

   ```
   USE Chapter9;
   GO
   CREATE TABLE Gryffindor (
   ```

```
                    StudentID int IDENTITY(100,1) NOT NULL,
                    LastName varchar(35) NULL,
                    FirstName varchar(35) NULL,
                    Points int NULL,
                    CONSTRAINT [PK_Gryffindor_StudentID] PRIMARY KEY CLUSTERED
                    (StudentID)
            )
```

d. Populate the table with some data by using the following script:

```
INSERT into Gryffindor VALUES('Longbottom','Neville',NULL)
INSERT into Gryffindor VALUES ('Thomas','Dean', NULL)
INSERT into Gryffindor VALUES ('Parvati','Patil', NULL)
```

e. Create a server login and a database user with the following script:

```
CREATE LOGIN Dumbledore
    WITH PASSWORD = 'P@ssw0rd';
USE Chapter9;
CREATE USER Dumbledore;
```

NOTE Note that we have created the user named Dumbledore, but we have NOT granted any permissions to the Gryffindor table. However, even without permissions on the table, this user will be able to execute a stored procedure that is using SELECT statements against it (as long as the user has Execute permissions on the stored procedure).

---

2. Now we want to create a stored procedure that will read the data in the Gryffindor table. Use the following script to create and execute the stored procedure:

```
CREATE PROC uspStudentList
AS
    SELECT * FROM Gryffindor;
GO
Exec uspStudentList;
```

3. We need the Dumbledore user to be able to execute this stored procedure. Use the following script to grant the Execute permission to the uspStudentList stored procedure:

```
GRANT EXECUTE ON uspStudentList to Dumbledore
```

If you use the SSMS Object Explorer and browse to the uspStudentList and view the Permissions page of the properties of the uspStudentList stored procedure, it will look similar to Figure 9-17.

4. With everything checked out, let's try to read the data with the Dumbledore database user we created earlier.

a. Try to read the data in the Gryffindor table using the Dumbledore user. We'll use EXECUTE AS to execute the stored procedure as Dumbledore.

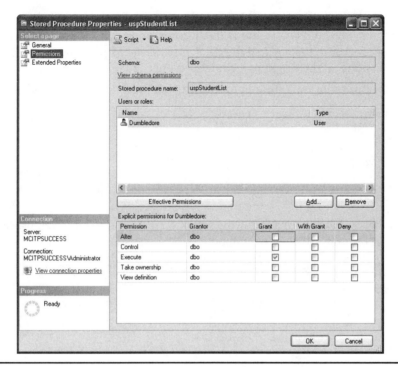

Figure 9-17   The permissions of the uspStudentList stored procedure

This will fail since Dumbledore does not have any direct access to the table.

```
EXECUTE AS LOGIN = 'Dumbledore';
   SELECT * FROM Gryffindor;
REVERT;
```

b. Now try to read the data using the stored procedure. Since Dumbledore has the Execute permission on the stored procedure, he is able to read the data in the underlying table. Thus, the following statement succeeds:

```
EXECUTE AS LOGIN = 'Dumbledore';
EXEC uspStudentList;
REVERT;
```

NOTE   The same concept applies to stored procedures that modify the data. In the following steps, we'll create stored procedures that INSERT, UPDATE, and DELETE data. By granting the Execute permission on the stored procedure, the underlying table can be modified.

5. Enter and execute the following script to create and test stored procedures that use the INSERT, UPDATE, and DELETE commands. Since you are logged on with the account that created the database and stored procedure, additional permissions on the stored procedure aren't needed.

   a. Use this script for a stored procedure using the INSERT command:

   ```
   CREATE PROC uspInsertStudent
      (@LastName varchar(35),@FirstName varchar(35))
   AS
      INSERT INTO Gryffindor
      VALUES(@LastName,@FirstName, NULL);
   GO
   Exec uspInsertStudent 'Finnegan', 'Seamus'
   EXEC uspStudentList;
   ```

   b. Enter and execute the following script to create and test a stored procedure that uses the UPDATE command:

   ```
   CREATE PROC uspAssignPoints (@LastName varchar(35),@points int)
   AS
   UPDATE Gryffindor
      SET Points = @Points
      WHERE LastName = @LastName
   GO
   Exec uspAssignPoints 'Longbottom', 5;
   Exec uspStudentList;
   ```

   c. Enter and execute the following script to create and test a stored procedure that uses the DELETE command:

   ```
   CREATE PROC uspDeleteStudent (@LastName varchar(35))
   AS
   DELETE FROM Gryffindor
      WHERE @LastName = LastName;
   GO
   EXEC uspDeleteStudent ' Finnegan '
   EXEC uspStudentList
   ```

6. Verify that Dumbledore can't execute INSERT, UPDATE, or DELETE statements against the Gryffindor table directly. Therefore, each of the following statements should fail.

   a. Try to INSERT data with the following script. This will fail:

   ```
   EXECUTE AS LOGIN = 'Dumbledore';
   INSERT INTO Gryffindor
      VALUES('Snape', 'Severus', NULL);
   REVERT;
   ```

   b. Try to UPDATE data with the following script. This will also fail.

   ```
   EXECUTE AS LOGIN = 'Dumbledore';
   UPDATE Gryffindor
      SET Points = 10
      WHERE LastName = 'Longbottom';
   REVERT;
   ```

c. Try to DELETE data with the following script. This will fail as well.

```
EXECUTE AS LOGIN = 'Dumbledore';
DELETE FROM Gryffindor
    WHERE LastName = 'LongBottom';
REVERT;
```

7. Grant the Dumpledore user the Execute permission on the uspInsertStudent, uspAssignPoints, and uspDeleteStudent stored procedures.

```
GRANT EXECUTE ON uspInsertStudent to Dumbledore;
GRANT EXECUTE ON uspAssignPoints to Dumbledore;
GRANT EXECUTE ON uspDeleteStudent to Dumbledore;
```

8. Try to execute each of these stored procedures as Dumbledore.

   a. Execute the uspInsertStudent stored procedure as Dumbledore using the following script. This will succeed.

```
EXECUTE AS LOGIN = 'Dumbledore';
EXEC uspInsertStudent 'Brown', 'Lavender';
EXEC uspStudentList;
REVERT;
```

   b. Execute the uspAssignPoints stored procedure as Dumbledore with the following script. This will succeed, also.

```
EXECUTE AS LOGIN = 'Dumbledore';
EXEC uspAssignPoints 'Longbottom', 5;
EXEC uspStudentList;
REVERT;
```

   c. Execute the uspDeleteStudent stored procedure as Dumbledore with the following script. This will succeed, too.

```
EXECUTE AS LOGIN = 'Dumbledore';
EXEC uspDeleteStudent 'Longbottom';
EXEC uspStudentList;
REVERT;
```

9. Taking this one step further, we can actually explicitly deny access to the underlying table (which is effectively the same as not granting any permissions to the table), but with Execute permissions on the stored procedure, the user can still read and modify the data.

   a. Use the following script to read or modify access to the table.

```
DENY DELETE ON Gryffindor to Dumbledore
DENY INSERT ON Gryffindor to Dumbledore
DENY UPDATE ON Gryffindor to Dumbledore
DENY SELECT ON Gryffindor to Dumbledore
```

   b. Now execute all of the stored procedures as Dumbledore. This succeeds for each one.

```
EXECUTE AS LOGIN = 'Dumbledore';
EXEC uspInsertStudent 'Brown', 'Lavender';
```

```
EXEC uspDeleteStudent 'Thomas';
EXEC uspAssignPoints 'Finnegan', 15
EXEC uspStudentList;
REVERT;
```

Execution Context

This topic came up in Chapter 6, but deserves some clarification here. In SQL Server 2005, we have the ability to specifically identify the execution context of stored procedures, triggers, and many functions. In other words, we can specify which user's account will be used when the module is run.

While execution context concepts apply to all these modules, let's focus our discussion on a stored procedure. It will work the same way for other modules.

Consider this scenario. On a regular basis, we import data into a staging table from an external database. Immediately before importing the data, we truncate the staging table. We use a stored procedure to do this, which is executed by a DBA.

In this case, either the DBA needs elevated permissions to truncate the staging table and import the data, or the stored procedure needs elevated permissions. However, since there isn't a Truncate permission available, we'd have to grant the DBA ALTER permissions on the database to allow him to truncate the table.

Instead of granting ALTER permissions, we use the EXECUTE AS clause to allow the user to execute the stored procedure with elevated permissions without actually granting the elevated permission to the user for any purpose other than this stored procedure.

The EXECUTE AS clause has several contexts that the stored procedure can be configured to run under. The choices are:

- User Name
- Caller
- Self
- Owner

User Name   User Name specifies that the stored procedure will run under the context of any specified database user or server login.

Caller   Caller specifies that the stored procedure will run as the user that executes the stored procedure. In this case, the user executing the stored procedures must have all the required permissions on all referenced objects. Caller is the default for stored procedures when the EXECUTE AS clause is not added.

Self   Self specifies that the stored procedure will run under the context of the user creating or altering the stored procedure. Self is the default for queues.

Owner   Owner specifies that the module will run under the context of the owner of the module. If the module doesn't have an owner, the owner of the schema of the module will be used.

EXAM TIP When elevated permissions are required to execute statements within a stored procedure, consider using the EXECUTE AS clause. Using the EXECUTE AS *Owner* clause, you can allow the user that executes the stored procedure to execute all statements within the stored procedure using the same permissions you have. This can allow them to access all objects within the database and execute statements with elevated permissions.

So how could we create our stored procedure for the staging table? We have multiple possibilities. Obviously, whoever executes the stored procedure needs Execute permissions on the stored procedure. Other permissions are shown next:

- **EXECUTE AS User_name** We would define the stored procedure using the EXECUTE AS User_name clause, and designate a user with appropriate permissions on the staging table. Anyone with Execute permission on the stored procedure could execute it.

- **EXECUTE AS Caller** Ensure the DBA executing the stored procedure has appropriate permission on the staging table. Only someone with ALTER permission on the staging table could successfully execute the stored procedure that truncates it.

- **EXECUTE AS Self** Ensure the person who created the stored procedure has appropriate permissions on the staging table. Anyone with Execute permission on the stored procedure could execute it.

- **EXECUTE AS Owner** Ensure that the owner of the schema of the stored procedure has appropriate permissions on the staging table. Anyone with Execute permission on the stored procedure could execute it.

With this explanation, let's connect some information back to Chapter 6, where we briefly mentioned the execution context of CLR-integrated assemblies and how it can be used to allow or restrict access to data. Here, we have expanded the explanation of the execution context for running the modules as other users.

As a reminder, the three execution context permissions we discussed in Chapter 6 for CLR assemblies are:

- **Safe** Only access to internal data is allowed.

- **External Access** This allows access to external resources such as files, network environmental variables, and the Registry.

- **Unsafe** Allows unrestricted access to resources within and outside SQL Server.

SQL Injection Attacks

SQL injection attacks are typically launched on web sites, but can also be directed at internal applications. They take advantage of weaknesses in dynamic SQL.

Consider Figure 9-18. This form is requesting a user's name and password. It looks simple enough.

Figure 9-18
Requesting
credentials

We could dynamically construct a statement based on user input. Within the code, it would look something like this:

```
SELECT *
FROM Users
WHERE login = 'txtLogin.Text' and password = 'txtPassword.Text';
```

With the user input, we dynamically create a SELECT statement that looks like the following:

```
SELECT *
FROM Users
WHERE login = 'darril' AND password = 'P@ssw0rd';
```

If it returns a result, we allow the user to log in.

This may work fine for that 99 percent of users who enter their username and password as expected. However, for the one attacker who tries to see what he can see, this can be disastrous.

As shown in Figure 9-19, the malicious attacker enters something different than what we'd expect.

Figure 9-19
A SQL injection
attack

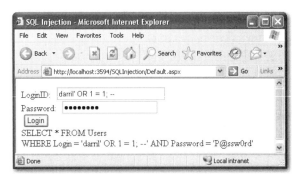

Changing the input for the loginID to the following input significantly changes what happens:

```
darril' OR 1=1; --
```

With this input for the login and password, our dynamically created script is changed to this:

```
SELECT *
FROM Users
WHERE login = 'darril' OR 1=1;
--AND password = 'P@ssw0rd';
```

Notice a couple of things. First, note that the user entered an apostrophe after the name *Darril* to signal the end of the character string. However, instead of ending it there, an *OR 1=1* phrase was added to ensure we always get a True from the statement; 1 will always equal 1, so we will always execute *SELECT * FROM Users*. Next, the attacker uses the comments command "- -" to force the rest of the statement to be ignored.

The attacker has gained access to your database. Depending on the content of your database, this could be rather benign or disastrous. What would happen if the user were to enter the data shown in Figure 9-20 instead, causing the Users table to be dropped?

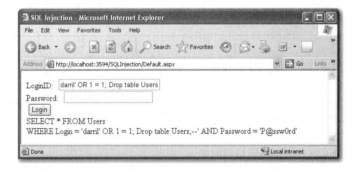

Figure 9-20   Malicious data entered into the form

```
SELECT *
FROM Users
WHERE Login = 'darril' OR 1=1;
Drop table Users;
--AND Password = 'P@ssw0rd';
```

You can color your Users table gone.

Using Parameterized Stored Procedures to Protect against SQL Injection

One of the primary protections against SQL injection is the use of parameterized stored procedures—stored procedures with parameters. Parameters that are passed in to a stored procedure with extra data (as the attacker would do) are taken wholly as a parameter. Within the stored procedure, this extra data will not execute as desired by the attacker.

EXAM TIP One of the primary protection strategies against SQL injection is to use parameterized stored procedures.

For example, let's look at the core SQL statement. We've seen how SQL injection with dynamic SQL can cause us problems.

```
SELECT *
FROM Users
WHERE login = txtLogin.Text AND password = txtPassword.Text;
```

However, we can change this to a parameterized stored procedure. The two parameters are the login and the password. We'll identify these as input parameters and compare them as parameters in the WHERE clause.

```
USE AdventureWorks;
GO
CREATE Proc dbo.usp_SQLInjection
     @login nvarchar(20),
     @password nvarchar(20)
AS
SELECT *
FROM Users
WHERE login = @login AND password = @password;
```

This use of a parameterized stored procedure protects us from SQL injection. Basic checking is done on the parameters as they're passed in. For example, if the parameter specifies 20 characters, only the first 20 characters will be passed on.

Additionally, instead of the parameters being used to dynamically construct a T-SQL statement, the parameters are plugged into the statement as specific values.

As an example, if the user entered *Darril OR 1=1'; - -*, instead of the malicious code changing the format of the SELECT statement, the malicious code will be interpreted literally as a value to be compared in the WHERE clause as follows:

```
WHERE login = [Darril OR 1=1';--].
```

Since we have no login that matches *[Darril OR 1=1';--]*, we won't have a match.

```
SELECT *
FROM Users
WHERE login = [Darril OR 1=1'; --]
AND password = [P@ssw0rd]
```

Just using stored procedures doesn't always protect us. If we create dynamic SQL within the stored procedure, we have the same problem. The following code shows an example of an *unprotected* stored procedure. The parameters aren't being compared within the script, but instead are being added completely within the dynamically built SQL statement.

```
CREATE Proc dbo.usp_SQLInjection2
     @login nvarchar(20),
     @password nvarchar(20)
```

```
AS
DECLARE @mySQL nvarchar(1000)
SET @mySQL = ' SELECT * FROM Users '
SET @mySQL = @mySQL + 'WHERE login = '  + @login
SET @mySQL = @mySQL + 'AND password = ' + @password + ';'
EXEC sp_executesql @statement = @mySQL
```

With any type of security, we should always look for defense in depth—in other words, we try to protect ourselves on many levels. Parameterized stored procedures are a great protection against SQL injection, but we should always look to implement security in many different ways, and on many different levels.

Dynamic SQL and sp_executeSQL
Dynamic SQL is used to dynamically construct a T-SQL statement based on user input. Later in this chapter, we discuss how dynamic SQL is susceptible to SQL injection attacks and needs certain precautions. However, dynamic SQL is still required in some instances.

For example, let's say we want a user to be able to specify which table they want to access at runtime. We can't put this into a stored procedure directly. The following would fail:

```
CREATE Proc dbo.usp_ViewTable
  (@TableName varchar (50))
AS
SELECT *
FROM @Tablename
```

Since the SELECT statement is expecting a table in the FROM clause, and the @Table is instead just a variable string, the syntax is recognized as incorrect. However, we could instead dynamically create the SQL statement as a string and then use one of the methods available to execute the dynamic SQL statement. The system stored procedure sp_executesql is the recommended method of executing dynamic SQL statements.

 EXAM TIP   If there is a need to dynamically create SQL statements, consider using the sp_executesql system stored procedure. As a best practice, especially when protecting against SQL injection attacks, input parameters should be validated before being used.

In the following exercise, we create a stored procedure that will be used by the technical writers. It accepts two parameters: an integer to identify the number of rows to return and the name of the table. Before using the table name, we validate it by checking for the existence of the table. Since the name of the table can't be used as a variable, we use the sp_executesql system stored procedure.

Exercise 9.9: Create a Stored Procedure Using Dynamic SQL

1. Connect to an instance of SSMS and create a new query window.

2. Enter the following script to create a stored procedure that will accept two parameters. Notice we are limiting the length of the table name to the length of the character count of any table in the database. If it was longer, we might be susceptible to a SQL injection attack.

```
USE AdventureWorks;
GO
CREATE Proc dbo.usp_ViewTable
   (@NumberOfRows int, @TableName varchar (25))
AS
--Before we do anything, validate the input
--Check to see if table exists
IF EXISTS
  ( SELECT * FROM sys.tables
    WHERE NAME = @TableName )
BEGIN          --If table exists we go on, if not we print an error
--Get the schema so we can build the two-part table name
  DECLARE @SchemaID int
  SET @SchemaID = (
    SELECT Schema_ID FROM sys.tables
    WHERE Name = @TableName    )
--Build two-part table name
  DECLARE @Table varchar (100)
  Set @Table = SCHEMA_NAME(@SchemaID) + '.' + @TableName
--Build dynamic SELECT statement
  DECLARE @DynamicSQLString nvarchar(200)
  SET @DynamicSQLString =
    'SELECT TOP ' + + CONVERT(varchar(2),@NumberOfRows) + ' * FROM ' +
@Table + ''
--Execute the dynamically built SQL string
  Execute sp_executesql @DynamicSQLString
END
ELSE --Validation of input failed
PRINT 'Table ' + @TableName + ' doesn''t exist'
```

3. Enter the following script to execute the stored procedure and get back valid data:

```
Exec usp_ViewTable 5, Contact
```

4. Enter the following script to execute the stored procedure with invalid data:

```
Exec usp_ViewTable 5, Contacts
```

You can experiment with different integers or different tables. If there was the possibility that tables had the same names within different schemas, this stored procedure could be modified to accept both the schema and the table name.

CLR-Integrated Stored Procedures

One great feature of SQL Server 2005 is that you can create Common Language Runtime (CLR)-based database objects. In other words, you can write the object in a language such as C#.Net or VB.Net using the .NET Framework.

The benefits of CLR-integrated Stored Procedures are:

- Provide significant performance gains in computation-intensive and string-comparison applications. CLR stored procedures are significantly better than Transact-SQL statements.

- You can leverage the power of the .NET Framework language from within SQL Server 2005

EXAM TIP   For any computation-intensive applications or applications requiring complex string comparisons, CLR-integrated objects provide significant performance gains. If you're faced with a scenario where complex calculations or string comparisons must be done quickly and efficiently, think about using a CLR-integrated object.

Three steps are required to create a CLR stored procedure:

1. Create a class in the .NET Framework language of your choice. Define your stored procedure as a static method in that class and build an assembly.

2. Register the assembly in SQL Server.

3. Create a SQL Server stored procedure that references the registered assembly.

Stored Procedures aren't the only database objects that can benefit from the CLR. Triggers, functions, and user-defined data types can also be programmed in a .NET Framework assembly.

CLR and COM

Component Object Model (COM) objects have existed for a long time and their usefulness is not going away. By creating COM objects, developers can create reusable components that can easily be shared between applications. It's fully expected that .Net technologies will continue to work with COM objects.

However, the integration of CLR with database objects in SQL Server 2005 makes it much easier to create CLR-integrated objects today. One of the strengths of this is that it is a little easier to create a CLR-integrated object to integrate with a COM object.

In other words, if you have existing COM objects used to accomplish different tasks, there is no need to rewrite these. If you need to interact with a COM object, this can often be done with the creation of a CLR-integrated object.

For new development needs, a logical question is, "should I create a COM object or a CLR object?" Since SQL Server 2005 can so easily integrate database objects such as stored procedures and functions with CLR objects, the answer today is usually to create a CLR-integrated object instead of a COM object. Certainly if you're taking a Microsoft exam and you're faced with the choice of creating a COM object or a CLR-integrated object, the best answer is to use the current technology and create a CLR-integrated object.

One last comment... Just because you can create a CLR-integrated object doesn't mean you always should. If you can create a stored procedure that will get the job done without using an assembly, by all means do so. It'll be more efficient and overall, simpler.

The MCITP tests don't require you to create a CLR Stored Procedure, only to know that they exist and what the benefits are. However, some concepts regarding CLR objects are easier to conceptualize if we see them in action. In the following exercise, we'll create a CLR assembly and integrate it with a stored procedure.

Exercise 9.10: Create a CLR Assembly

Video 9-10 shows the steps required to create a CLR stored procedure.

1. Press WINDOWS+E to open Windows Explorer. Browse to the root of C:\ and create a folder named **MCITPSuccess.**

2. In the MCITPSuccess folder, create a new text document. Double-click the New Text Document and enter the following code into it:

```
Imports System
Imports System.Data
Imports Microsoft.SqlServer.Server
Imports System.Data.SqlTypes
Public Class CLRClass
    <Microsoft.SqlServer.Server.SqlProcedure()> _
    Public Shared Sub HappyDays()
        Dim strWeekDay As String
        strWeekDay = WeekdayName(Weekday(Today()))
        SqlContext.Pipe.Send("Happy " & strWeekDay & "!")
    End Sub
End Class
```

 NOTE The CLRClass has only one subprocedure, named HappyDays. It uses three date functions (WeekdayName, Weekday, and Today) to determine what day of the week it is. It then outputs one line of "Happy Monday", or "Happy Tuesday", and so on depending on which day of the week it is.

3. In Notepad, select File | Save As…

4. In the Save As dialog box, enter the File name as **"happydays_dll.vb"**, including the quotes.

 NOTE By entering the quotes around the file name, you ensure it is saved with the extension of vb and not the extension of .txt. The Visual Basic file (happydays_dll.vb) will be compiled to create a dynamic link library (DLL) file. However, if it's saved as a file with a .txt extension it can not be compiled

5. Using Windows Explorer, browse to the C:\WINDOWS\Microsoft.NET\ Framework\ directory. Identify the full name of the folder that holds the v2 framework and write it down here: _____. In Figure 9-21, you can see it as v2.0.50727.

Figure 9-21

Framework v2

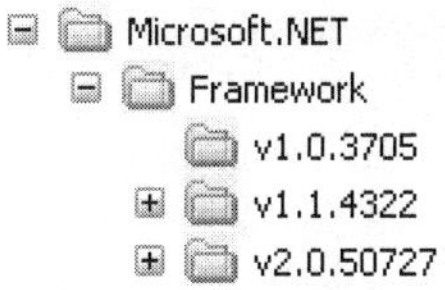

6. Press WINDOWS+R to open the run line. Enter **cmd to** access the command line.

7. At the command line, enter the following command. If your Framework version is different, substitute the correct directory identified in step 5. This directory holds the Visual Basic compiler (vbc) that we will use to compile our program.

```
cd c:\WINDOWS\Microsoft.NET\Framework\v2.0.50727
```

8. Enter the following command to compile the visual basic file you saved as happydays_dll.vb:

```
vbc /target:library c:\MCITPSuccess\happydays_dll.vb
```

9. Using Windows Explorer, verify that a file named Happydll.dll has been created in your MCITPSuccess folder.

10. Open SSMS and create a new query window.

11. If a Chapter9 database doesn't exist, create it using the following script:

```
USE Master;
GO
CREATE Database Chapter9
```

12. Enter the following query to create an assembly in the Chapter9 database:

```
USE Chapter9;
GO
CREATE ASSEMBLY CLR_MCITPSuccess
FROM 'c:\MCITPSuccess\happydays_dll.dll'
WITH PERMISSION_SET = SAFE
```

13. Using SSMS, browse to the Chapter9 | Programmability | Assemblies container. Right-click the Assemblies container and click Refresh. Your display should look similar to Figure 9-22, showing the CLR_MCITPSuccess assembly has been created.

Figure 9-22

The CLR_ MCITPSuccess assembly

14. Right-click the MCITP assembly and select Properties. Your display should look like Figure 9-23. Change the Permission Set to Unsafe and click OK. This will fail. Read the error and click OK. Click Cancel.

Figure 9-23 The CLR_MCITPSuccess assembly properties

NOTE Before the permissions can be changed, the owner of the assembly must have the appropriate permission, and the database must have the TRUSTWORTHY database property turned on, or the assembly must be signed with a certificate or key with the appropriate permission. TRUSTWORTHY can be turned on using the following command:

```
ALTER DATABASE Chapter9
    SET Trustworthy ON
```

15. Create a stored procedure that will access the assembly by entering the following script:

```
USE Chapter9;
GO
CREATE PROCEDURE uspSuccess
AS
EXTERNAL NAME
        CLR_MCITPSuccess.CLRClass.HappyDays;
```

Notice that the structure of the EXTERNAL_NAME is:

- The name of the assembly created in the database (CLR_MCITPSuccess)
- The name of the class within the actual DLL file (CLRClass)
- The name of the procedure within the class that you want to execute (HappyDays)

16. Before you can execute CLR-integrated objects, CLR must be enabled on the server. Use the following code to enable the execution of CLR on the server:

```
sp_configure 'show advanced options', 1;
GO
RECONFIGURE;
GO
sp_configure 'clr enabled', 1;
GO
RECONFIGURE;
```

17. Execute the stored procedure by using the following code:

```
Exec uspSuccess
```

Your display should look similar to Figure 9-24.

Figure 9-24

The result after executing the CLR-integrated stored procedure

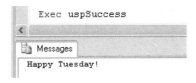

Chapter Review

In this chapter, we covered many of the details on stored procedures. We started with an overview, including some basics on the usage, types, and benefits of stored procedures.

It's common for stored procedures to include transactions, so we covered how to create begin, commit, and roll back transactions. A transaction that has begun must either be committed or rolled back. A transaction that is left open can allow the transaction log to grow uncontrollably, filling up the disk. To check for an open transaction, the DBCC OPEN TRAN command be used. While SQL Server works in autocommit mode by default (causing most T-SQL statements to commit when executed), it's possible to change settings so it works in implicit mode. When in implicit mode, many T-SQL statements need either a COMMIT TRAN before the actual commit to the database. We also covered distributed transactions, savepoints, marked transactions, and using the OUTPUT clause within a transaction.

A variety of error-handling tools are available. We covered the use of the @@ERROR function, TRY CATCH blocks, and even how to create our own error messages, which can be raised with the RAISERROR command.

As with most programming topics, there is no substitute for experience. This chapter included several exercises on how to create stored procedures, add parameters and variables, encrypt the definitions, and embed built-in functions with the stored procedures. We also demonstrated how to create a CLR-integrated stored procedure from beginning to end.

Lastly, we covered many of the security aspects that deal specifically with stored procedures. It's important to realize that by granting EXECUTE permission on a stored procedure, users have access to underlying tables through the stored procedure without having direct permissions to these tables. This can be used to prevent users from directly accessing base tables. We covered SQL injection attacks and the use of parameterized stored procedures to prevent SQL injection attacks. Occasionally, there's a need to use dynamic SQL, and we showed how the sp_executeSQL system stored procedure can be used to dynamically create a T-SQL statement, while still protecting against SQL injection attacks.

Additional Study

Self-Study Exercises

- Create a stored procedure that will retrieve all employees ordered by LastName.
- Create a stored procedure that accepts a date as a parameter and lists all the orders for that date.
- Create a stored procedure that includes a TRY CATCH block and will update the Person.Contact table. If the UPDATE fails, provide a user-friendly error message.
- Write a stored procedure to add a user to the person.contact table. Include a transaction that will roll back the transaction if a person already exists in the person.contact table with the same first and last names.
- Create a stored procedure with at least two different queries and one parameter passed to each. Write the stored procedure so that one of the queries (and only one) is recompiled each time the stored procedure is executed.
- Create a stored procedure that dynamically creates a T-SQL statement but also protects against SQL injection attacks.
- Create a CLR-integrated stored procedure. Change the permissions on the stored procedure so external files can be accessed.

BOL Topics

- System Stored Procedures (Transact-SQL)
- Transactions (Transact-SQL)
- Distributed Transactions (Database Engine)
- Transaction Savepoints
- Recompiling Stored Procedures
- Using EXECUTE AS to Create Custom Permission Sets
- OUTPUT Clause (Transact-SQL)
- Building Statements at Runtime
- CLR Stored Procedures

Summary of What You Need to Know

70-431

When preparing for the 70-431 exam, you should have a basic understanding of stored procedures. The 70-431 exam expects you to be very proficient with T-SQL and may ask you a question related to T-SQL syntax or format, but wrapped within a stored procedure. By doing the exercises in this chapter, you should have enough familiarity with stored procedures so this doesn't confuse you. You should be familiar with working with transactions, including BEGIN TRANSACTION, COMMIT TRANSACTION, and ROLLBACK TRANSACTION. You should also be familiar with TRY CATCH statements and how to catch errors within a T-SQL script.

70-441

For the 70-441 exam, ensure you understand the basics of stored procedures, including how to create them, how to use parameters, how to use transactions, and the various error-catching techniques. Additionally, make sure you understand how permission chaining works with stored procedures. This builds on the permission chaining topic in Chapter 8. For stored procedures, access to underlying tables can be controlled by granting Execute permissions to the stored procedure, but not granting permission to the base tables.

70-442

When preparing for the 70-442 exam, you should have a good understanding of all the concepts in this chapter. There is a lot of material in here that directly relates to this test. As a reminder, the 70-442 exam expects you to know the intricate details of T-SQL, and of course that's exactly what we put into stored procedures—T-SQL. Make sure you know everything about transactions (including savepoints, marks, and distributed transactions), how to follow the logic through a stored procedure, and the use of the execution context.

Questions

70-431

1. Your assistant has created a stored procedure designed to delete data from the Parts table in a SQL Server 2005 database. He shows you the following script used to create the procedure:

```
DECLARE @PartID int
BEGIN TRY
  BEGIN TRANSACTION
    DELETE From dbo.Parts
      WHERE PartID = @PartID
  COMMIT TRANSACTION
END TRY
BEGIN CATCH
  DECLARE @MyErrorMsg nvarchar(1000)
  SELECT @MyErrorMsg = ERROR_MESSAGE()
END CATCH
```

When testing, he finds it leaves open transactions and he asks you for help. What would you suggest?

A. Add a ROLLBACK TRANSACTION to the CATCH block.

B. Add a COMMIT TRANSACTION to the CATCH block.

C. Add a ROLLBACK TRANSACTION to the TRY block.

D. Add a COMMIT TRANSACTION to the TRY block.

2. You manage a database that has Sales data horizontally partitioned based on location at three different retail store locations. The Parts table needs to be modified to include a new column named Discontinued. In the future, instead of deleting parts, this column will be changed from 0 for false to 1 for true. You need to ensure that this column is added to all three Parts tables, or none of them. What set of T-SQL statements will achieve the objectives?

A.

```
BEGIN TRAN
  ALTER TABLE PartsVirginiaBeach
ADD Discontinued BIT NULL
  ALTER TABLE PartsNewportNews
ADD Discontinued BIT NULL
  ALTER TABLE PartsChesapeake
ADD Discontinued BIT NULL
COMMIT TRAN
```

B.

```
ALTER TABLE PartsVirginiaBeach
  ADD Discontinued BIT NULL
ALTER TABLE PartsNewportNews
  ADD Discontinued BIT NULL
ALTER TABLE PartsChesapeake
  ADD Discontinued BIT NULL
```

C.

```
BEGIN TRAN
  ALTER TABLE PartsVirginiaBeach
ADD Discontinued BIT NULL
  ALTER TABLE PartsNewportNews
ADD Discontinued BIT NULL
  ALTER TABLE PartsChesapeake
ADD Discontinued BIT NULL
  IF @@error <> 0
    ROLLBACK TRAN
  ELSE
    COMMIT TRAN
```

D.

```
BEGIN TRAN
  BEGIN TRY
    ALTER TABLE PartsVirginiaBeach
      ADD Discontinued BIT NULL
    ALTER TABLE PartsNewportNews
      ADD Discontinued BIT NULL
    ALTER TABLE PartsChesapeake
      ADD Discontinued BIT NULL
  END TRY
  BEGIN CATCH
    ROLLBACK TRAN
    RETURN
  END CATCH
COMMIT TRAN
```

3. You are tasked with creating a stored procedure that will be used within an application to perform some calculation-intensive operations and then return the results. Performance is important, so your solution should return the results as quickly and efficiently as possible. What would you do?

   A. Use parameters within the stored procedures.

   B. Use a TRY CATCH block within the stored procedure.

   C. Use a CLR-integrated stored procedure.

   D. Create the stored procedure so it recompiles each time it is run.

4. The StockPortfolio database recently had several stored procedures updated. Today it's giving a warning indicating that the transaction log file is almost full. You suspect that one of the stored procedures has left a transaction open. How can you verify your suspicions?

   A. Execute DBCC OPENTRAN against the StockPortfolio database.

   B. Execute DBCC OPENTRAN against the master database.

   C. Execute DBCC TLOGFULL against the StockPortfolio database.

   D. Execute DBCC TLOGFULL against the master database.

70-441

1. A web application is designed to allow a user to enter a keyword. This keyword is used in a T-SQL statement to search the product description and provide a listing of products that match keywords in the description. You need to redesign the process to improve both performance and security. What would you do?

   A. Pass the user input to a parameterized stored procedure.

   B. Use dynamic SQL to pass the user input into the T-SQL statement.

   C. Recreate the procedure as a CLR-integrated function.

   D. Use a text box on the web page and pass the user input to the database using a SQLCommand object.

2. You are creating a stored procedure that will access tables in both the Production schema and Sales schema in the AdventureWorks database. What permissions are needed?

   A. SELECT permission on the tables in the Production and Sales schemas

   B. Execute permission on the stored procedure and SELECT permission on the tables in the Production and Sales schemas

   C. Execute permission on the stored procedure only

   D. Execute permission on the tables in the Production and Sales schemas

3. An application will be used to access a database and underlying tables using stored procedures and views. Security requirements dictate that users will not have access to any underlying tables except through the client application, but they should still be able to read and modify the data. What permissions should users have on the underlying tables?

A. None

B. SELECT

C. SELECT, INSERT, UPDATE, and DELETE

D. Execute

4. You need to create a stored procedure that will be used to either insert a new customer (if the customer doesn't exist) or update the customer (if the customer does exist) with the most recent sale date. Customers provide their phone number, which is used as the CustomerID. Which one of the following queries could you use in the stored procedure?

A.

```
UPDATE Customers
  SET SaleDate = @SaleDate
  WHERE CustomerID = @CustomerID
IF(@@ROWCOUNT = 0)
  INSERT Customers (CustomerID, SaleDate)
  VALUES (@CustomerID, @SaleDate)
```

B.

```
BEGIN TRY
 UPDATE Customers
  SET SaleDate = @SaleDate
  WHERE CustomerID = @CustomerID
END TRY
BEGIN CATCH
INSERT Customers (CustomerID, SaleDate)
  VALUES (@CustomerID, @SaleDate)
END CATCH
```

C.

```
IF EXISTS
   (
   SELECT * FROM Customers
   WHERE CustomerID = @ CustomerID
   )
UPDATE Customers SET SaleDate = @SaleDate
  WHERE CustomerID = @ CustomerID
ELSE
 INSERT Customers (CustomerID, SaleDate)
  VALUES (@CustomerID, @SaleDate)
```

D.

```
IF NOT EXISTS
   (
   SELECT * FROM Customers
   WHERE CustomerID = @CustomerID
   )
   INSERT Customers (CustomerID, SaleDate)
   VALUES (@CustomerID, @SaleDate)
ELSE
    UPDATE Customers SET SaleDate = @SaleDate
    WHERE CustomerID = @ CustomerID;
```

5. You need to design a query that will provide a listing of total sales for different sales regions. The regions are known as North, South, West, and East and users will be able to choose one or more of the regions. Four different servers hold the different regional data. Your solution must minimize additional network utilization. What should you do?

   A. Create four views and allow users to query the views.

   B. Use an SSIS package to copy all the data to a central server.

   C. Implement replication to copy all the data to a central server.

   D. Create a parameterized stored procedure that queries the requested data and returns the results in a single result set.

6. You have just finished upgrading a SQL Server 2000 server to SQL Server 2005. Upgrade requirements have been stated as follows:

   • Servers must function with full SQL Server 2005 functionality.

   • All stored procedures must continue to work.

   • The migration must be validated within 48 hours.

   What would you do after the upgrade to comply with the requirements?

   A. Change the database compatibility level to 80.

   B. Change the database compatibility level to 90.

   C. Run test scripts for each stored procedure.

   D. Use the SSMS debugger to test the stored procedures.

7. You are assisting with the integration of two different database applications. You control the Customer database application, which accepts stock purchase orders and logs them for the customer. The second application (Stock application) accepts the stock purchase orders and executes the actual purchase of the stock. The Stock application has a Component Object Model (COM) object that accepts the data and enters it into the stock application. The stock application can also read XML files for new orders. What would you do to ensure the stock purchases are entered accurately?

   A. Create an SSRS package to pass the XML data to the stock application.

   B. Create an SSIS package to pass the XML data to the stock application.

    C. Write a CLR stored procedure to enter the customer's order into the Customer application and pass the information to the COM object.

    D. Create a COM object to pass the information to the COM object in the stock application.

8. Customer stock purchase orders are done through multiple different methods from within the StockPortfolio application. An analysis of the Stock database has uncovered many data consistency problems due to the different levels of details provided. You are tasked with ensuring that orders are entered with complete, consistent, and accurate information. What can you do?

    A. Write a trigger to check stock purchase orders and roll back any orders that don't meet the level of detail required.

    B. Write a COM object to enter the data and modify the application to only use the COM object

    C. Remove permissions to the base tables.

    D. Write a parameterized stored procedure and modify the application so it only uses this stored procedure to enter orders.

70-442

1. You need to design a solution that will add customer information for a stock portfolio database. A web application will accept all the appropriate information and then the customer needs to be created in the Customer's table. The customer must be informed if an error occurs. What would be the best method to create the new customer?

    A. Use dynamic SQL to build a query and submit it to the database to create the customer account. Check for errors, and if errors occur, report them to the web application.

    B. Create a parameterized VIEW to generate the customer account. Check for errors, and if errors occur, report them to the web application.

    C. Create a parameterized stored procedure to accept the customer information and insert the customer data into the Customers table. Check for errors, and if errors occur, roll back the insert.

    D. Create a parameterized stored procedure to accept the customer information and create the customer account. Check for errors, and if errors occur, report them to the web application.

2. You are tasked with implementing a solution with the existing usp_ CustomerStockOrder stored procedure to ensure that customer orders are entered accurately into an OrderHeader table and an OrderItems table. The purchase order is passed to the stored procedure as an XML parameter. You need to ensure the stored procedure does not enter a total of more than 10,000

shares of stock in any single order. What could you do within this stored procedure?

   A. When inserting into the OrderItems table, use the OUTPUT clause of the INSERT statement to verify at least one item is inserted. Roll the transaction back if not.

   B. Use CHECK constraints to ensure that orders are matched to existing customers.

   C. Implement an FK-to-PK relationship between the tables.

   D. Use a TRY CATCH block. Do the inserts within the TRY block, and if it fails, roll it back in the CATCH block.

3. You manage a database named StockPortfolio and are creating a stored procedure that requires elevated permissions. Users should have only minimal permissions within the database. What security context should you use within the stored procedure?

   A. EXECUTE AS Caller.

   B. EXECUTE AS Owner.

   C. EXECUTE AS Elevated.

   D. Add the user to the db_owner role.

4. An auditing table exists within a database on a MCITP1. Whenever a customer places an order, it should first be entered into the Orders table, which is located in the StockPortfolio database on MCITP2, and if successful it must be logged in the Auditing table. If the order is not logged in the auditing table, the order should be canceled. What two actions should be done? (Each correct answer presents part of the solution.)

   A. Use a local transaction.

   B. Use two local transactions.

   C. Use a distributed transaction.

   D. Commit the transaction after the INSERT for the auditing table.

   E. Commit the transaction after the INSERT for the Orders table.

5. Business requirements dictate that data within the StockPortfolio database must be transferred to the Archive database on the first of every month. If the transfer fails, you need to ensure that both databases can be restored to the same point in time. Both databases exist on the same server instance. You are writing the script to transfer the data. What command should you use first?

   A. Begin Distributed Transaction

   B. Begin Save Transaction

    C. Begin Transaction With Mark

    D. Begin Transaction T1 With Mark 'M1'

6. You are tasked with designing a stored procedure that will be used by the technical writers. They need to be able to retrieve a user-selected number of rows from any user-selected table within the StockPortfolio database. They should not have access to any underlying tables. How can this be accomplished? (Choose four. Each correct answer presents part of the solution.)

    A. Use the EXECUTE AS Owner clause.

    B. Use dynamic SQL with the sp_executeSQL system stored procedure.

    C. Specify the table name as a parameter for the stored procedure.

    D. Validate the table name as a valid table before execution.

    E. Specify the number of rows as a parameter for the stored procedure.

    F. Ensure users have access to all of the underlying tables.

7. You are designing a stored procedure for the StockPortfolio database that will allow customers to transfer money from their bank account to a money market account and then use that money to purchase stock. Both the transfer and the stock purchase must be within the same transaction. Occasionally, the stock purchase may not complete immediately, resulting in a failure. However, the money transfer should still succeed. How can this be accomplished?

    A. Specify a savepoint between the transfer and the stock purchase. If the stock purchase fails, roll back to the savepoint.

    B. Check for an error within the transaction, and if found, roll back the transaction.

    C. Utilize the @@Error function after the money transfer. If there's an error, roll back the transaction.

    D. Utilize the @@Error function after the stock purchase. If there's an error, roll back the transaction.

8. You are testing a stored procedure written by another DBA that includes the following code:

```
CREATE PROCEDURE usp_SellStock (@CustomerID int, @StockID int, @qty int)
AS
 SET IMPLICIT_TRANSACTIONS ON
 INSERT INTO SellOrder
 VALUES(@CustomerID int, @StockID int, @qty int)
```

You discover that the insert is not applied. What would you suggest to resolve the problem?

    A. Add logic to COMMIT or ROLLBACK the transaction.

    B. Add a BEGIN TRAN to the procedure.

C. Change the INSERT to an UPDATE.

D. Change SET IMPLCIIT_TRASACTIOS ON to SET IMPLICIT_
TRANSACTIONS OFF.

9. You are troubleshooting a stored procedure that includes several queries. The
stored procedure normally runs fine, but you discover that when one of the
queries executes with certain input parameters, the stored procedure runs much
slower. You discover that this query requires different indexes to run more
efficiently. What can you do?

A. Use the sp_recompile system stored procedure to recompile the stored
procedure before executing it.

B. Alter the stored procedure by adding the WITH RECOMPILE clause to it.

C. Alter the stored procedure by adding the RECOMPILE query hint option to
the problematic query.

D. Use the WITH RECOMPILE clause when executing the stored procedure.

10. A stored procedure has been started by another DBA that will be used to mark a
customer as inactive. Customers can only be marked as Inactive if they haven't
had a purchase in the past year. A DBA began with the following code and has
asked you for help:

```
CREATE PROCEDURE ups_MarkCustomerInactive
@CustomerID int
AS
DECLARE @datediff datetime
-- Help. What do I put here?
UPDATE Customer
Set ACTIVE ='Inactive'
WHERE CustomerID = @CustomerID
```

What code would you insert before the UPDATE statement?

A.

```
SELECT @datediff = datediff(yy,MostRecentOrderDate,getdate()),
FROM Sales WHERE CustomerID = @CustomerID
BEGIN TRY
IF @datediff < 1 RAISEERROR
END TRY
BEGIN CATCH
  RAISEERROR ('Customer cannot be marked inactive',16,1) WITH LOG
END CATCH
```

B.

```
SELECT @datediff = datediff(yy,MostRecentOrderDate,getdate()),
FROM Sales WHERE CustomerID = @CustomerID
BEGIN TRY
IF @datediff < 1 RAISEERROR
END TRY
```

```
BEGIN CATCH
  RAISERROR ('Customer cannot be marked inactive',16,1)
  RETURN
END CATCH
```

C.

```
SELECT @datediff = datediff(yy,MostRecentOrderDate,getdate()),
FROM Sales WHERE CustomerID = @CustomerID
IF @datediff < 1
  RAISERROR ('Customer cannot be marked inactive',16,1) WITH LOG
```

D.

```
SELECT @datediff = datediff(yy,MostRecentOrderDate,getdate()),
FROM Sales WHERE CustomerID = @CustomerID
IF @datediff < 1
BEGIN
  RAISERROR ('Customer cannot be marked inactive',16,1)
  RETURN
END
```

Answers

70-431

1. **A.** The purpose of the CATCH block is to catch errors. If the DELETE statement fails, we jump right out of the TRY block (without completing any other statements like the COMMIT TRANSACTION) and enter the CATCH block. We now have a BEGIN TRANSACTION without either a COMMIT or a ROLLBACK. Since we have an error that we're catching in the CATCH block, the right thing to do is roll it back with a ROLLBACK TRANSACTION statement.

2. **D.** The transaction first tries to modify each of the three tables, and if it succeeds, it commits the transaction. If an error occurs, the CATCH runs and rolls back the transaction. Answers A and B have no error checking, so they would commit the changes regardless of the success or failure of each of the statements. The @@ERROR global variable only holds the value of the result of the last statement, so answer C would only catch an error in the PartsChesapeake table, not the other two tables.

3. **C.** When performing calculation-intensive operations, use CLR-integrated database objects. Using parameters or TRY CATCH blocks with a stored procedure wouldn't make it handle calculation-intensive operations quicker. Recompiling it each time would cause it to run inefficiently.

4. **A.** The OPENTRAN Database Console Command (DBCC) can be used to identify open transactions in the database where it's executed. Since the problem is in the StockPortfolio database, we'd have to execute the command against the StockPortfolio database. There is no such thing as a DBCC TLOGFULL command.

70-441

1. **A.** The existing method is using dynamic SQL, which is susceptible to SQL injection attacks. Using parameterized stored procedures is one of the primary strategies used to protect against SQL injection attacks.

2. **C.** Only Execute permission on the stored permission is required. Permissions on the underlying tables are not needed.

3. **A.** Since data access is done through the stored procedures, and users are not to have access to any underlying tables directly, no permissions should be granted to the tables. By granting execute permissions on the stored procedures which access the tables, the user will be able to read and modify the data via the stored procedures.

4. **C.** This is mostly a logic question. The EXISTS function is used to check if the customer record exists. If it does, the customer record data is updated, and if not, the customer record is created. Answer A does not have any error checking, so if the row doesn't exist, the UPDATE statement will give errors. B is incorrect because it will try to do an INSERT for any type of error resulting from the UPDATE (not just if the customer doesn't exist). While D will work, it is not efficient (generally, any use of the word NOT should be avoided).

5. **D.** A key requirement is that network utilization must be minimized. One of the strengths of a stored procedure is the ability to minimize network utilization. The user can execute the stored procedure with a single line of code that includes the parameters, and the stored procedure then retrieves the data as a single result set. Copying all the data to a central server would significantly increase network utilization. A parameterized stored procedure would be easier to use than four different views.

6. **C.** The best way to test the stored procedures is with test scripts. SSMS does not include a stored procedure debugger. After the upgrade to SQL Server 2005, the compatibility level would be set to 90 (SQL Server 2005), so it wouldn't need to be changed. Changing the compatibility level to 80 (SQL Server 2000) would prevent full SQL Server 2005 functionality.

7. **C.** Only one answer enters the data in both applications (Customer application and Stock application). If a COM object exists that does the job, there's no reason why we shouldn't use it. Creating a COM object to pass the information to the other existing COM object would be much more difficult than creating a CLR-integrated stored procedure that can insert the data into the Customer application and pass the information to the Stock application.

8. **D.** A parameterized stored procedure can be used to check the data and consistently enter it each time data is entered. While a COM object can be used, it would be easier to create a stored procedure that is completely internal to the database. A trigger would cause additional work if anything needed to be rolled back. Removing permissions on the base tables could be done if a stored procedure was created, but removing the permissions only wouldn't meet the objectives.

70-442

1. **D.** A parameterized stored procedure would be the best choice, especially regarding a web application, to prevent vulnerability to a SQL injection attack. The scenario states the customer must be informed if an error occurs. This can be done by informing the Web application. If the INSERT fails, there is nothing to roll back. Dynamic SQL is susceptible to SQL injection, so this would not be recommended. VIEWs can not accept parameters.

2. **A.** The OUTPUT clause can be used to view the inserted table after the INSERT into the OrderItems table. If it includes too many rows, the entire transaction can be rolled back. A constraint (CHECK or FK) wouldn't be included in the stored procedure. TRY CATCH wouldn't work as described since there's no code that would cause an error.

3. **B.** When elevated permissions are required, the EXECUTE AS Owner clause can be used as long as the owner of the stored procedure has the appropriate permissions. Since you manage the database, you would have elevated permissions within it. Users should have only minimal permissions, so executing as the caller wouldn't work, and adding the user to the db_owner role would be granting too many permissions. EXECUTE AS Elevated doesn't exist.

4. **C, D.** Since the tables are on different servers, a distributed transaction is needed. The logic of the scenario dictates that the order must be logged into the Orders table first, and then the Auditing table. We should only commit after the INSERT into the Auditing table.

5. **D.** The With Mark clause can be used within a BEGIN Transaction to create a mark in the transaction log of each of the databases affected by the transaction. The correct syntax is only shown in the correct answer. Since both databases are in the same instance, a distributed transaction is not needed. Savepoints can be created, but there is no Begin Save Transaction.

6. **B, C, D, E.** Dynamic SQL must be used to supply the table name since the table name in the FROM clause fails with a variable as a string. Using the sp_executesql system stored procedure, a table name can be passed in as a parameter, and this can then be validated by checking the sys.tables catalog view to ensure the table exists. The number of rows can also be passed in as an integer. The EXECUTE AS clause and individual table permissions are not needed since execute permission on the stored procedure provides all the permissions necessary.

7. **A.** We need to be able to roll back part of the transaction in case of the failure of the stock purchase. Savepoints allow us to roll back part of a transaction. If we roll back the transaction, then both the money transfer and the stock purchase will be rolled back, but we need the money transfer to succeed.

8. **A.** When IMPLICIT TRANSACTIONS is set to ON, several statements (such as INSERT) implicitly begin a transaction and must be either committed or rolled back. If not, they will automatically be rolled back when the connection

is closed. The default for SQL Server 2005 is autocommit mode, so a SET IMPLICIT_TRANSACTIONS OFF is not needed by itself. With IMPLICIT TRANSACTIONS set to ON, a BEGIN TRAN is not needed.

9. **C.** Since the problem is only the specific query, we can use a query hint option to recompile only that query when the stored procedure is run. The other options would recompile the entire stored procedure, but normally the stored procedure runs fine so there is no reason to recompile the entire stored procedure.

10. **D.** This question can be broken down into two parts: 1) Should a TRY CATCH block be used within the code? and 2) Should it exit the stored procedure after checking? In this case, since the UPDATE is actually happening after we insert our code, there is nothing for the TRY CATCH to catch. The given IF statement would never generate an error, so the CATCH clause would never execute. If @datediff is less than 1 (indicating activity has occurred in the past year), we don't want to mark the customer as inactive. That is done in the UPDATE statement, so we must use the RETURN statement to exit the stored procedure. Without the RETURN (as in answer C), the UPDATE will execute. The WITH LOG clause just says to log the error but actually has no relevance to the question.

Disaster Recovery

In this chapter, you will learn about:

- Disaster recovery
- Transaction log
- Recovery models
- Backups
- Restores
- Detach and attach
- Log shipping
- Database snapshots
- Database mirroring

> *Insurance is something you always want to have, but never want to use.*
>
> —*Jack Grzena*

Disaster preparedness and business continuity are a significant part of any IT professional's overall strategy. We need to keep systems up and operational as much as possible when they are *expected* to be up and operational. When the unexpected happens, we need to be able to respond quickly and efficiently to restore the systems.

Just like having insurance, we want to be prepared for disasters, but we never want them to happen. Preparedness includes a combination of both backups and high-availability strategies.

A Disaster Recovery Overview

In the simplest terms, disaster recovery is the ability to recover system operations after a disaster. Disasters can take many forms. On a large scale, disasters may be fires, floods, hurricanes, earthquakes, or other major events that can affect an entire building. On a smaller scale, a disaster may be a hardware failure, a virus infection, accidental or purposeful deletion or some other event that affects only a single server or small group of servers.

Many organizations have Disaster Recovery Plans (DRPs) that identify specifics on backups and recovery procedures. DRPs also typically identify which systems are considered critical and need to be protected through high-availability strategies.

It's important to realize that backups and high-availability strategies are intended to work hand-in-hand and neither one negates the need for the other. Backups are intended to protect our data so that no matter what type of disaster we suffer through, we can always restore our data. High-availability strategies are intended to help us keep our systems up and operational so that if one server fails, for example, the user is still able to access the data via another method.

To fully describe backups and restores, we'll cover the following topics:

- Transaction Logs
- Recovery Models
- Backup Types, Devices, and Methods
- Restores
- Detach and Attach

For high-availability strategies, we'll cover the following topics. These don't cover all the possible high-availability strategies, but they do cover all the strategies you may come across in the 70-431 test.

- Log Shipping
- Database Snapshots
- Database Mirroring

The Transaction Log

We've discussed the transaction log in Chapters 4 and 7. By now, you should realize that the transaction log is very important for the functionality of the database.

As a reminder, all data modifications (INSERT, UPDATE, and DELETE statements) are recorded in the transaction log. Transactions can be singular statements—such as an INSERT, UPDATE, or DELETE—or they can be a combination of statements grouped together with BEGIN TRANSACTION and COMMIT TRANSACTION statements.

Internally, the transaction log is made up of several virtual logs. If you drill into the inner workings of SQL, you'll discover these virtual logs and how they work. For our discussion, we're going to keep it simple and just cover the log as a whole. Let's first take a look at the big picture of how the database is modified. It occurs in three steps:

1. The INSERT, UPDATE, or DELETE statement is issued.

2. Modification is recorded in the buffer (an area in memory reserved for this purpose) and the transaction log. We can see this in Figure 10-1. It might seem as though the database is being updated, but that doesn't occur right away.

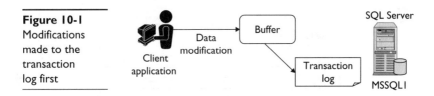

Figure 10-1 Modifications made to the transaction log first

3. A checkpoint event occurs. At this point, any committed transactions are read from the transaction log and written to the database. We can see this in Figure 10-2.

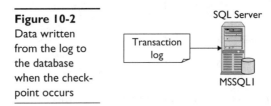

Figure 10-2 Data written from the log to the database when the checkpoint occurs

Step 1 was covered in Chapter 4 as we went through the different T-SQL statements. There should be no surprises there.

In step 2, we've added the buffer. It's used to speed things up. Data is brought into the cache a page at a time. Pages in cache are marked to indicate if they are "dirty" or not. A *dirty* page is one that has changed in memory but hasn't been written to the database yet. Additionally, the data is written to the transaction log. With each modification, the transaction log gets a little bigger.

Step 3 includes the checkpoint events. In short, during a checkpoint event the data in the transaction log is written to the database, and the transaction log is marked to indicate the data that has been written to the database.

NOTE People often ask, can I read the transaction log? After all, every other log we've talked about so far we can open in something like Notepad and read. So, what about transaction logs? The answer is a qualified "No." Microsoft does not provide any tools that allow transaction logs to be read. However, for several versions of SQL Server (including SQL Server 2005), third-party tools have been available that can be used to read the transaction log.

Checkpoints

Checkpoints deserve a little more explanation. Take a look at Figure 10-3.

This gives us an idea of how checkpoints work. I've put line numbers in the diagram so it's easier to understand. In line 1 we have an INSERT statement. INSERT, UPDATE, and DELETE statements don't need a specific commit statement since they are automatically committed, so they can be written to the database at the next checkpoint. Before the checkpoint occurs, we have three other transactions starting on lines 2, 3, and 4.

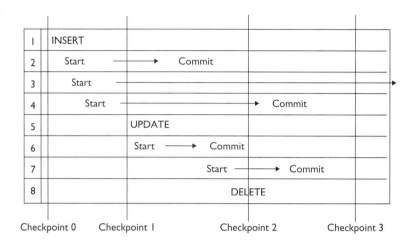

Figure 10-3
Checkpoints

At checkpoint 1, the system looks at all the activity since the last checkpoint (checkpoint 0). Any activity that is committed is written to the database. For example, the INSERT on line 1 would be written to the database here. There aren't any other committed transactions since the last checkpoint, so that's all that's done.

At checkpoint 2 the system looks at all the committed transactions since the last checkpoint. The transaction on line 2 that started before checkpoint 1 is committed, so this data would be written to the database. The UPDATE statement on line 5 would be committed to the database. Lastly, the transaction on line 6 started and committed before checkpoint 2, so it is written to the database. Notice the transaction on line 7 has started, as well as the DELETE statement on line 8, but neither has completed. Thus, they would not be committed.

Next is checkpoint 3. At checkpoint 3, the transactions on lines 4, 7, and 8 would be committed. Notice the transaction on line 3 is still open. This may be referred to as a *long-running transaction*, though long-running transactions typically span much more than just three checkpoints.

A logical question is "What causes a checkpoint to occur?" There's actually a long list of reasons, but be aware that checkpoints occur very frequently, often less than one per minute when the database is being modified.

Primarily, checkpoints are associated with the recovery interval option. This option is an advanced server option and is set to 0 by default. It allows the server to automatically adjust the interval, but generally, this means the checkpoints occur as often as needed to ensure that recovery can occur within a minute upon reboot if a server fails. During recovery, any committed transactions in the transaction log that haven't been written to the database are now written to the database.

Other events that cause checkpoints include the following:

- A database backup is about to start.
- The transaction log becomes 70 percent full and it's in log-truncate mode. Generally, log-truncate mode means the database is using the Simple recovery model.
- SQL Server service has stopped.

Recovery Interval

Recovery Interval is a server option that can be set to indicate how often to do checkpoints. Literally, the setting is indicating the maximum amount of time it would take to recover the database if a failure such as a power loss were to occur.

Indirectly, this setting tells the server how often to do checkpoints. If we do checkpoints every five minutes, then if the server were to experience a power failure and the database files weren't corrupted, the transaction log wouldn't have more than five minutes of data to recover once power returned.

This setting has always referred to minutes, though in practice, faster CPUs would perform more quickly. In other words, a setting of 10 indicates 10 minutes, but a server would generally recover much more quickly than 10 minutes.

It's rare to manipulate this setting. The only reason to do so is if you notice that frequent checkpoints are adversely affecting performance.

Checkpoints and Recovery

Checkpoints mark when data has been written to the database. This is especially useful if we suffer a server failure and need to recover from it. Consider Figure 10-4.

Figure 10-4
Using the transaction log to recover from a failure

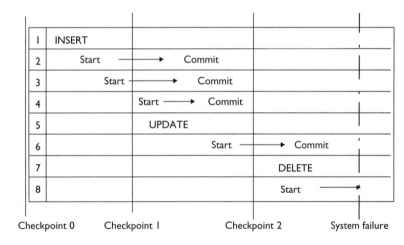

Let's say that all the shown checkpoints have occurred (checkpoints 0, 1, and 2). Then our system experiences a failure—and for whatever reason, the server loses power and goes down. Notice that on line 8, we have a transaction that has started but not committed. Additionally, note that on lines 6 and 7, we have transactions that have ended before a checkpoint. These have not been written to disk.

When SQL Server reboots, it looks at the checkpoint log and the transaction log and determines that it has work to do.

Lines 1 through 5 were all committed at or before checkpoint 2. At checkpoint 1, line was written to the database and at checkpoint 2, lines 2 through 5 were written to the database. The recovery process doesn't need to do anything with these lines.

However, on line 6, we have a transaction that started before checkpoint 2 and ended after checkpoint 2. It was not written to the database. The recovery process recognizes that this transaction was committed, so it will roll it forward and write all the modifications to the database. The same thing occurs for the DELETE on line 7; it is rolled forward and written to the database.

Line 8 is a little different. Here, we have a Start transaction without a Commit. Remember, the definition of a transaction is that all events in the transaction have to complete as a whole, or they all fail as a whole. In this case they haven't completed, so whatever was done after the start is rolled back.

Truncating the Transaction Log

Another important concept to grasp, especially when it comes to backups and restores, is *truncating* the transaction log. This is simply freeing up space in the log.

The transaction log is truncated when we back up the log. What does this mean? Take a look at Figure 10-5, which shows the same log from Figure 10-4. Instead of a system failure here, we've done a backup, which causes a checkpoint to occur immediately before the backup—something shown with checkpoint 3.

Figure 10-5
Truncating the log
during backup

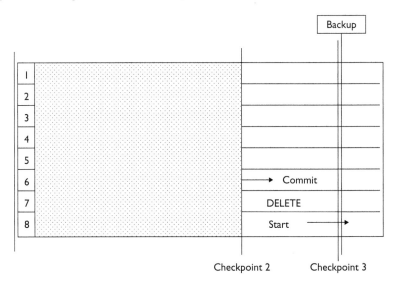

In the figure we can see that data between checkpoint 0 and checkpoint 2 (which has been committed, written to the disk, and backed up) is now blank. That space is truncated or freed up and now available to log additional transactions.

If we experienced a catastrophic failure the backup of the database, combined with the backup of the transaction log, would allow us to restore all committed transactions up to the point of the failure.

The only transaction that couldn't be reproduced from the backup is the transaction on line 8. We have a Start without a Commit. This also prevents us from truncating the portion of the log between checkpoint 2 and checkpoint 3.

 TIP To truncate the log, back it up. If the transaction log is growing too large, back it up more often.

This is a key point in any recovery model except simple: The transaction log will continue to grow until it's backed up. If not backed up, it could take over all your disk space. We will cover the different recovery models later in this chapter.

Restoring from the Transaction Log

We'll cover the details of how later, but in any recovery model except simple, the first step in recovering a database is backing up the transaction log. Take a look at Figure 10-6.

Figure 10-6
Using the transaction log for restore

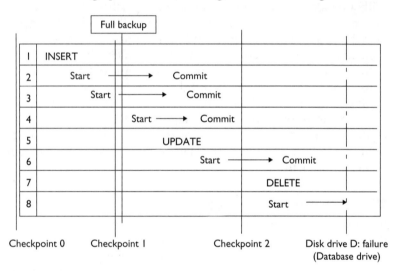

The database is configured as follows:

- Database on drive D:
- Transaction log on drive E:

The failure occurs on the drive holding the database (D:), but the drive holding the transaction log (E:) is still intact. With the full backup done at checkpoint 1, we have the data from line 1, but not from lines 2 through 8. Even though the data has been committed to the database, that's where the failure occurs. Since the changes are stored in the transaction log files on drive E:, we simply need to reapply the transaction log to reapply the changes to the database after restoring the database from backup.

EXAM TIP The first step in a restore for all recovery models except simple is to back up the transaction log. This allows us to restore all of the transactions that have occurred since the last backup.

What's the first step? Back up the transaction log. The transaction log that is backed up immediately after a failure is called the *tail log*. It holds all of the transactions since the last backup. We'll discuss the tail log more thoroughly later.

Next, we restore the full backup done with checkpoint 1 and include the INSERT on line 1.

Then, by restoring the tail log, we recapture all of the data changes that occurred on lines 2 through 7. Notice the data on line 8 is the start of a transaction without a commit transaction. This will not be restored to the database.

Recovery Models

With an understanding of the transaction log, what it contains, and how it's used, we can now jump into recovery models. Let me spell out what I'm implying here—recovery models are directly related to the transaction log.

SQL Server 2005 supports three recovery models: simple, bulk-logged, and full. Each of these deals with the transaction log differently and determines what we can use the transaction log for in our backup and restore strategies.

Often the choice of different recovery models depends on how much data you need to be able to restore. For example, let's say we do full backups of the database every night at midnight. At 2 P.M., the database fails. Can we accept the loss of data between midnight and 2 P.M.? Or do we need to be able to restore every possible transaction that occurred during the day?

The Full Recovery Model

In the full recovery model, all transactions are logged into the transaction log. The only time the log is truncated is when it is backed up. The full recovery model would be used when we want the capability to recover our data up to the point of failure.

Since everything is logged and the complete log is retained between backups, the full recovery model allows us to restore everything that occurred since the last backup. In the example where we did full backups every night at midnight but experienced a failure at 2 P.M., we can get all the data back.

The first thing we must do is back up the transaction log. We can then restore the database and the transaction log, letting us recover all of the committed data up to 2 P.M.

The full recovery model is the only recovery model that allows point-in-time recovery of data. In other words, it lets us use the transaction log to restore up to a specific time, such as 11 A.M. In contrast, the bulk-logged recovery model only allows us to completely restore up to the point of failure.

TIP   If point-in-time restores are required, you must use a full recovery model. The bulk-logged recovery model does *not* support restores using STOPAT to recover to a specific point in time if the log backup contains bulk-logged changes.

A subtlety is that STOPAT can be used if the bulk-logged recovery model is used and the transaction log does not contain any bulk-logged changes.

The Bulk-Logged Recovery Model

In the bulk-logged recovery model, most transactions are logged into the transaction log. Bulk-loads (a bulk import of data via methods such as SSIS packages or bcp scripts) are not recorded line by line, but are instead recorded as a single event. The only time the log is truncated is when it is backed up. The bulk-logged recovery model would be used when we want the capability to recover our data up to the point of failure, except for bulk-loads.

Similar to the full recovery model, everything is logged and the complete log is re-tained between backups. However, let's say that at 9 A.M. every day, we do a bulk import of thousands of lines of data that aren't otherwise modified during the day.

If we were to use the full recovery model, these thousands of lines would be recorded in the transaction log. It could impact the performance of the server during the bulk-load, and it could make the transaction log unacceptably large.

With the recovery model set to bulk-logged, the bulk-load of thousands of lines instead logs only a couple of lines such as "bulk-load started" and "bulk-load ended." The method of bulk-load isn't important. It could be from a legacy DTS package, an SSIS package, or even using the bcp command-line utility.

Figure 10-7
A disk failure on the drive holding the database after a bulk-load

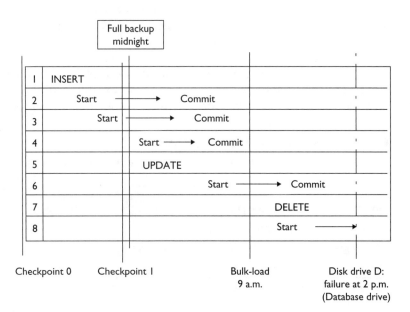

EXAM TIP Any time you want to ensure that a bulk-load event has minimal impact on the transaction log, set the recovery model to bulk-logged.

What happens if we have a disk crash? Take a look at Figure 10-7. It shows a backup last night at midnight, a bulk-load (at 9 A.M.), and a disk failure at 2 P.M.

The first thing we do is back up the transaction log. We can then restore the full backup and the transaction log. It gives us everything *except* the data loaded in at 9 A.M. We would now repeat the bulk-load, and find ourselves back to where we were before the disk crash.

So, we use the bulk-logged recovery model to allow recovery up to the moment of failure, but without logging bulk-loaded data.

The Simple Recovery Model

In the simple recovery model, only minimal amount of data is logged into the transaction log. It's still used for recovery purposes and to ensure the database can survive power failures, but the data in the transaction log is not available to us as database administrators. The log is truncated at every checkpoint. The simple recovery model would be used when we never need the capability to recover any data other than what was included in the last backup, such as in databases that don't have few changes.

In early versions of SQL Server, an option called "trunc. log on chkpt." existed. Setting this caused the transaction log to be truncated at every checkpoint. The simple recovery model replaces this.

With the simple recovery model selected, the log is continuously being truncated at every checkpoint. A benefit is that the database administrator (DBA) doesn't need to manage the transaction log—it will not grow out of control, taking over the disk. A drawback is that transactions recorded in the transaction log aren't available to be recovered if a disk failure occurs.

In other recovery models, the only time the transaction log is truncated is during backups. All transactions since the last backup are available. When we experience a disk failure, we back up the transaction log and have the transactions since the last backup available for the restore. This capability is not available in the simple recovery model.

Recovery Model Summary

Table 10-1 summarizes the important points of the recovery models.

Model	What's Logged	Available for Restore?	Log Truncated
Full	All transactions	Yes	At backup
Bulk-logged	All transactions except bulk-load events	Yes	At backup
Simple	Minimal for recovery operations	No	When checkpointed

Table 10-1 Recovery Model Summary

EXAM TIP Don't overlook the importance of the recovery model choices. You can expect many exam questions to mention the recovery model. Some of these may have nothing to do with the question, but are just added in to throw off the uneducated. Knowing the recovery model allows you to quickly and easily identify the relevance of the recovery model to the question.

Setting the Recovery Model

The recovery model can be set via the GUI in SSMS or via a script. You should know how to do it both ways for the exams. When setting it in SSMS, it's done via the Database properties page. It's set with T-SQL using an ALTER database statement. The syntax is:

```
ALTER DATABASE DatabaseName
SET RECOVERY FULL; (or BULK_LOGGED, or SIMPLE)
```

The following exercise will lead you through creating a database and then setting and observing the recovery model.

Exercise 10.1: Create a Database and Change the Recovery Model

View how to change the Recovery Model in SSMS in video 10-1.

1. Open an instance of SSMS.

2. Use the following script to create a database named Chapter10:

   ```
   USE Master;
   GO
   CREATE DATABASE Chapter10;
   ```

3. Right-click the Chapter10 database and click Properties.

4. In the Select A Page area, choose Options. View the recovery model. Your display should look similar to Figure 10-8.

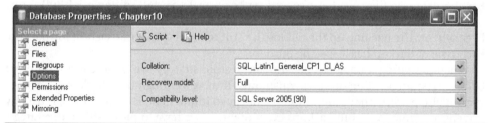

Figure 10-8 Viewing the recovery model

At this point, your recovery model may be different from the display. When the database is created, the recovery model is set the same as the model database. When I created Chapter10, my model database was set to the full recovery model.

5. Change the Recovery Model to Simple. Click OK. That's it. It's changed.

6. Enter the following script in the query window to change the recovery model to bulk-logged:

```
ALTER DATABASE Chapter10
SET RECOVERY BULK_LOGGED
```

7. When the query completes, use SSMS to look at the properties of Chapter10, and verify it has been changed to bulk-logged.

8. Enter the following script to return the recovery model to full:

```
ALTER DATABASE Chapter10
SET RECOVERY FULL
```

9. When the query completes, use SSMS to look at the properties of Chapter10 and verify that it has been changed to full.

Database Backups

Database backups are an integral part of any DBA's job. You need to know how to do them and ensure they are done. One of the decisions to make is what type of backups to do, so we'll start with backup types.

 EXAM TIP It's possible to do backups using the GUI within SSMS since the Backup wizard is very good and automates much of the process. On the job, companies often invest in third-party tools to make work easier. For the 70-431 test, you should understand both the T-SQL statements used for backups and restores and how to use the Backup and Restore wizards in case you're faced with a simulation question. The test questions focus mainly on the details that the Backup wizard or third-party tools would handle. To best prepare for the test, you need to know these details. In this chapter, we'll focus on doing backups and restores with T-SQL instead of with the wizards.

Backup Types

For the database files, we have several types of backups: full, differential, full (copy only), file, and filegroup. Transaction logs have only one type of backup: transaction. Even when we're backing up the tail log, it's still referred to as a transaction log backup. Each type of backup has a specific purpose.

When designing a database backup-and-restore strategy, we often choose different backup types depending on time constraints. If there's enough time to do full backups every night, perfect. That's the simplest strategy to implement. However, there is usually not enough time to do full backups every night, so we have to pick a different strategy.

It's important to understand the details of each of the strategies so you're able to pick the strategy that fits your needs.

Full

Everything starts with a full backup. Without a full backup, differential backups and transaction log backups are useless. The full backup provides a baseline, or a starting point.

Verifying the Transaction Log Is Truncated

Does a full backup truncate the transaction log? The answer is a resounding *no*, but it is a concept that many new DBAs miss. You can prove it to yourself on a database that has the full recovery model set, such as AdventureWorks. To ensure the database has the full recovery model, you can use the following command:

```
ALTER DATABASE AdventureWorks
SET RECOVERY FULL
```

First, use the following command in a new query window.

```
DBCC SQLPERF(LOGSPACE)
```

With this, you can see the size of the AdventureWorks transaction log, and how much space is actually used. For example, on my system the Log size is approximately 2MB and the log space used is about 30 percent, but yours may be different depending on the activity of AdventureWorks.

Write your percentage of log space used here: _____.

Next, generate some log activity. The following script can be used:

```
DECLARE @VendorID int, @CreditRating int, @i int
SET @i = 1
SET @VendorID = 1
While @VendorID < 105   -- Loop through all vendors
Begin
   USE AdventureWorks
     -- Store credit rating's original value
   SET @CreditRating =
     (SELECT CreditRating
       FROM Purchasing.Vendor
       WHERE VendorID= @VendorID)
While @i < 6
   BEGIN -- Set CreditRating to 1, 2, 3, 4 and then 5
     UPDATE Purchasing.Vendor
       SET CreditRating = @i
         Where VendorID=@VendorID
     SET @i = @i + 1
   END
   SET @i = 1
    -- Return credit rating to original value
   UPDATE Purchasing.Vendor
   SET CreditRating = @CreditRating
     Where VendorID=@VendorID
   SET @VendorID = @VendorID + 1
End
```

By using the DBCC SQLPERF(LOGSPACE) command again, we can see that the amount of space used has increased. The size of the log is still the same, but the space used is higher. Write your percentage of log space used here: _____.

We can now back up the full database. While this does back up log entries from the transaction log, it doesn't truncate it. Use this script to back up the database and then verify the amount of space used by the AdventureWorks log:

```
BACKUP DATABASE AdventureWorks
    TO DISK = 'C:\AW_Full.bak'
GO
DBCC SQLPERF (LOGSPACE)
```

Notice that the amount of space used by the log isn't reduced. However, if we back up the transaction log, it is truncated as part of the process. We can see that in the following script:

```
BACKUP LOG AdventureWorks
    TO DISK = 'C:\AW_Log.bak'
GO
DBCC SQLPERF (LOGSPACE)
```

You'll see the log space percentage has been reduced proving the log space was truncated.

Just as the word "full" implies, a full backup backs up the complete database. If the recovery model is full or bulk-logged, it also backs up the transaction log. Even though the transaction log is backed up as part of a full backup, it is not truncated.

As part of the process, the full backup marks all extents (eight 8KB pages) in the database to indicate they've been backed up. When data is changed, SQL Server marks the extent to indicate it is different. The differential backup needs this information to know what to back up.

The basic syntax to perform a full backup follows. As we move through the chapter, we'll add to this basic syntax.

```
BACKUP DATABASE DatabaseName
    TO DISK = 'Path'
```

Differential

A differential backup backs up all the data that has changed since the last full backup. Without a full backup, a differential backup is meaningless. In this case, the full backup is known as the base of the differential backup, or the *differential base*. Differential file backups can be very fast. SQL Server does a good job of tracking the changes made since the last full backup was created.

The differential backup backs up all the extents that have changed data within them. As a reminder, an extent is 64KB in size.

A common backup strategy includes a full backup once a week and differential backups each day of the week. Figure 10-9 demonstrates this.

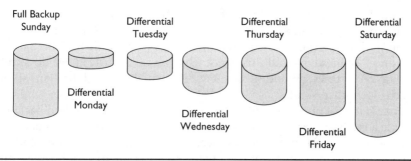

Figure 10-9 A full differential backup strategy

Notice how the differential is relatively small on Monday, but gets larger through the week. This shows how more and more of the data is being changed, so more and more of the data needs to be backed up. Figure 10-9 also helps show why we use differential backups.

A logical question is "Why not just do full backups every night?" Because, often when maintaining a database, we don't have the benefit of unlimited time for maintenance every night. We might have a lot of time one evening of the week, but are tasked with reducing the length of time backups take the rest of the nights.

In the scenario with Figure 10-9, the full backup on Sunday night might take four hours, but Monday's differential backup might take only 30 minutes, Tuesday's backup takes 60 minutes, Wednesday's backup takes 90 minutes, and so on.

The longer the time between full backups, the larger the differential backup becomes. By the time we get to Saturday, the length of the differential backup may be close to the length of the full backup. Remember, only a single row within the extent needs to change in order to mark the entire extent as needing to be backed up during the differential backup.

The basic syntax to perform a differential backup follows. It will fail if a full backup doesn't exist.

```
BACKUP DATABASE DatabaseName
    TO DISK = 'Path'
WITH DIFFERENTIAL
```

 NOTE There is no "incremental" backup type in SQL Server. While many traditional backup programs used for typical backups of files include incremental backup types, it is not included as a method type in SQL Server.

Full Copy-Only

A full copy-only backup is a full backup that does not affect a backup strategy. In other words, it will back up all the data, but will not mark the database to indicate it has been backed up.

For example, we could have a full differential backup strategy in place where we do full backups on Sunday and differential backups every other day. If we did a regular full backup on Wednesday, then subsequent differentials would only back up data that has changed since Wednesday—and this is not what we want. Instead, we do a full copy-only backup on Wednesday, and subsequent differentials will still back up all the data that has changed since Sunday.

Of course, a logical question is why we would do such a thing. Sound backup strategies include a method to store a copy of the database offsite. This prevents data loss in case of some major catastrophe, such as fire, flood, hurricanes, tornadoes, and so forth. In my town, a company called The Vault will actually come to your business and pick up full copy-only backups on a regular basis, such as every Wednesday.

Probably 95 percent of the companies that use The Vault never need to pull back the tapes to retrieve the data, but for the 5 percent that do need it, it can save their company. It's basically an insurance plan.

The significant difference between a full backup and a full copy-only backup is that the database is not marked to indicate it has been backed up. A full copy-only backup can occur at any time within a regular full/differential backup strategy.

The basic syntax to perform a full copy-only backup follows:

```
BACKUP DATABASE DatabaseName
    TO DISK = 'Path'
WITH COPY-ONLY
```

Transaction Log Backups

A transaction log backup will back up the transaction log only. It's backed up from the last successful full backup, differential backup, or log backup. Transaction logs are backed up for two reasons:

- To ensure the log is truncated periodically
- To reduce the amount of possible data loss in case of disk failure

 TIP For best performance, the transaction log should be placed on a different physical disk than the database files. We should also separate the transaction log file and the database files for backup purposes. Except for catastrophic server failure, it would be rare for both physical hard drives to fail at the same time. With the transaction log file and database files on separate drives (and a good backup plan in place, backing up both of them), we have a much better chance at restoring after a failure with minimal data loss.

Transaction logs can be backed up as part of a full/transaction log backup strategy, or as part of a full/differential/transaction log backup strategy. Transaction logs can only be backed up when the recovery model is set to full or bulk-logged. They cannot be backed up in the simple recovery model.

Look at Figure 10-10. In this figure, we have a full backup combined with transaction logs. The full backup is done once a day at 1 A.M., and the transaction log is backed up every six hours after that (7 A.M., 1 P.M., and 7 P.M.).

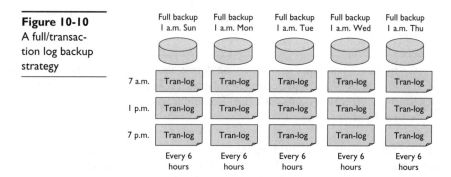

Figure 10-10
A full/transaction log backup strategy

Once we do a full backup on Monday, we no longer need the transaction log backups created on Sunday (except for possible archival purposes).

A more detailed backup strategy is a full/differential/transaction log backup strategy. Take a look at Figure 10-11.

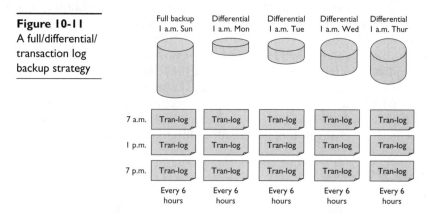

Figure 10-11
A full/differential/ transaction log backup strategy

In this figure, we're adding transaction log backups to the full/differential backup strategies. We'll cover restores in more depth later in this chapter, but for big-picture purposes, imagine a failure at 4 P.M. on Wednesday. What backups would be needed to restore your database to 3:59 P.M.? We'd need the full from Sunday, the differential from 1 A.M. Wednesday, and all the transaction logs since the differential.

The basic syntax to perform a transaction log backup follows. It will fail if a full backup doesn't exist.

```
BACKUP LOG DatabaseName
    TO DISK = 'Path'
```

File and Filegroup Backup

The last backup to discuss is a file or filegroup backup. In Chapters 3 and 7, we presented files and filegroups. Primarily in earlier chapters, we talked about using files and filegroups for optimization purposes—to help the database perform queries more quickly in very large databases. We can also use files and filegroups in a backup strategy for very large databases.

 NOTE If you don't remember the details about files and filegroups, take a look at the filegroups section in Chapter 7. We provided a full explanation there on when to use additional files and filegroups, and how they can be configured.

Let's state the obvious. File and filegroup backups are only relevant in databases that have multiple files or filegroups. This will occur in a very small percentage of databases. We could use a file or filegroup backup when the database size and performance requirements make a full database backup impractical. Instead, we separate the database into multiple files and filegroups, and then create a backup strategy to back up these files and filegroups.

Using file backups can increase the speed of recovery by allowing you to restore only damaged files without restoring the rest of the database. As an example, if you have a secondary file (second.ndf) stored on drive E: and drive E: fails, you can restore the secondary file only. You don't have to restore the entire database.

Filegroups can contain several files, so backing up a filegroup is the same as backing up each individual file within the filegroup. If the database is using the full or bulk-logged recovery model, the transaction log would also have to be backed up.

It's also possible to create file or filegroup differential backups. The same way a differential will back up all the changes since the last full backup, a file or filegroup differential will back up all the changes since the last file or filegroup backup.

Backup Devices

Up to now we've primarily discussed the backups using paths. However, instead of including the paths in each statement, we can create a backup device to identify the path.

You may think that a "backup device" refers to a physical device. I know I did when I first saw the term. But it doesn't, at least not directly. A *backup device* is a path to a file that is located on a hard disk or other disk storage media such as tape. Disk backup devices and tape backup devices work about the same; they just point to different media.

Backup devices can be on a local disk or tape, or on a shared network resource. The file identified by the backup device can be as large as the free disk space allows. To connect to a shared network resource, SQL must be aware of the resource by first mapping the Universal Naming Convention (UNC) path (*serverName**ShareName*\) to a drive using the xp_cmdShell program.

One of the great strengths of backup devices is that they allow us to use virtual paths in a development environment and easily convert them to actual paths in the production environment. For example, if we were creating backup scripts on an online server, we could test them using a device that points to one path on our test server, but another path on the online server. The scripts would be identical. Only the backup devices would be different.

When using a tape backup device, the tape must be physically connected to a computer running SQL Server when using SQL Server's backup and restore capabilities. We can't back up to a remote tape device, but we *can* back up to a remote disk device using the UNC path. If using third-party tools (and many good ones are available), we don't have this limitation. However, the test will focus on SQL Server 2005 capabilities.

Physical and Logical Devices

SQL Server identifies backup devices using either a physical or logical device name.

The *physical* name is the name of the path and the file used by the operating system to identify the backup device (such as *d:\SQLBackups\AdventureWorks.bak*).

The *logical* name is the alias used within SQL Server to identify the physical backup device. As an example, we could create a backup device with a logical name of *AdventureWorksBackupDevice* that points to the physical name of the file at *d:\SQLBackups\ AdventureWorks.bak*.

Either the physical or logical names can be used in backup and restore statements.

Creating Backup Devices

Backup devices can be created in SSMS or via T-SQL statements.

A Backup Devices container exists within the Server Objects container in SSMS. By right-clicking the Backup Devices container, selecting New Backup Device, and following the wizard, you can create a backup device.

To create backup devices in T-SQL, the sp_addumpdevice system stored procedure is used.

In the following exercise, we'll create a backup device that will be used in other exercises in this chapter.

Exercise 10.2: Create a Backup Device

1. Press WINDOWS+E to open Windows Explorer.

2. Browse to the root of C:, and create a new folder named **SQLBackups**. Close Windows Explorer.

3. Open SSMS and connect to the default instance of SQL Server.

4. Double-click the Server Objects container to open it. Right-click Backup Devices and select New Backup Device.

5. In the Backup Device window, enter **AW_SSMS_BackupDevice** as the Device Name.

6. Click the ellipsis button next to the filename. In the Locate Database Files dialog box, browse to c:\SQLBackups. In the File Name box, enter **AW_SSMS** and click OK. Your display should look similar to Figure 10-12. Click OK.

NOTE SQL Server automatically senses tape devices. If a tape device is not available on your system, the selection for a tape device as the destination will be dimmed.

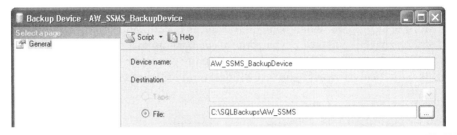

Figure 10-12 Creating a backup device in SSMS

7. Open a new query window in SSMS.

8. Enter the following script to create another backup device in the same folder:

```
EXEC sp_addumpdevice 'disk', 'AW_TSQL_BackupDevice',
'C:\SQLBackups\AW_TSQL.Bak'
```

9. Right-click the Backup Devices container and select Refresh. You should see both backup devices in this container.

Mirrors and Sets

SQL Server 2005 introduces a new concept to SQL Server 2005 known as *mirrored media sets*. In this section, we'll discover what a mirrored media set is and define some other relevant terms.

Media Set

The backups on a set of one or more backup media make up the media set. If multiple backups are spread across multiple tape drives, all the tapes make up the media set.

Since tape drives are slow, it is possible to add multiple tape drives and write to them in parallel. The media set is the ordered collection of backup media where we write a single backup. If three tapes were in the media set, the backup would actually be contained on three different tapes. Media sets can be on tapes or disks, but not both within the same media set.

Take a look at Figure 10-13. It shows a media set of four tapes: two tapes created on tape drive 1 and two tapes created on tape drive 2.

Figure 10-13
Media set

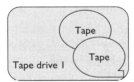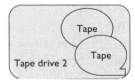

Mirrored Media Set

New to SQL Server 2005 is the capability to mirror backup media. If you're familiar with RAID-1 (mirroring) with disks, this works pretty much the same way. Whatever is written to one tape in the mirrored media set is written to the other tape. If one tape fails, we still have a copy on the other tape within the mirrored media set.

Look at Figure 10-14. We have added two additional tape drives. Whatever is backed up to the tape drives on one side of the mirror is also backed up to the tape drives on the other side of the mirror.

Figure 10-14
A mirrored
media set

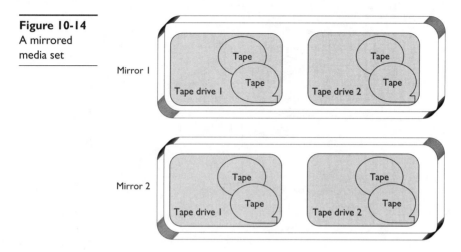

Unlike RAID-1, where only two sides of the mirror can exist, mirrored media sets allow the creation of from two to four mirrored media sets.

Media Family

Backups created on a set of mirrored devices constitute a media family. The number of backup devices used for the media set determines the number of media families in a media set.

Take a look at Figure 10-15. Here we're able to see that tape drive 1 and tape drive 3 will hold identical data and make up media family 1. Tape drives 2 and 4 also hold identical data and make up media family 2.

What's really significant about using mirrored media sets is that when it comes time to restore data, tapes from one mirrored set can be combined with tapes from another mirrored set. This is especially useful if one of the tapes in each set became corrupt. As long as they didn't hold the same data, tapes from different mirrored sets could be combined to produce a complete backup.

Take a look at Figure 10-16. As an example, let's say that the tapes from tape drive 1 failed, and the tapes from tape drive 4 failed. We can use the tapes from mirror 2, media family 1 (tape drive 3), and the tapes from mirror 1, media family 2 (tape drive 2), to restore our data.

NOTE Let's add a moment of realism. How many databases are going to have four mirrored media sets that are backed up to multiple tape drives resulting in a multiple media family backup? Not many. However, if the data you're working on is that important, there are multiple methods of making sure that not a single piece of data is ever lost. Mirrored media sets have become another tool added to the DBA's tool bag.

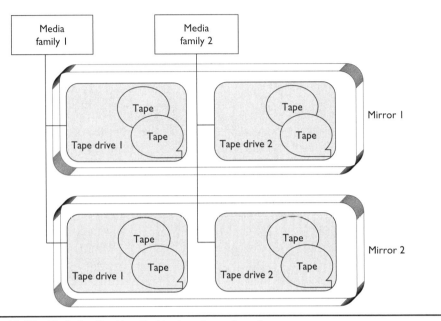

Figure 10-15   Media families identified in the mirrored media set

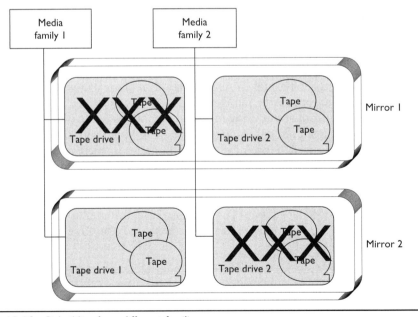

Figure 10-16   Rebuilding from different families

Backup Set

The backup files written to a media set as a group are referred to as a single backup set. If a media set is a single device, the backup set is the single file written to the device. If the media set comprises three devices, the backup set is the three different files, one for each of the three devices.

Media Header

The media header contains information required to identify the media. It is written onto each tape or media file and identifies the file's place within the media family where it belongs.

Some of the items in the media header include:

- The name of the media (optional).

- The unique identification number of the media set.

- The number of media families in the media set.

- The sequence number of the media family containing this media.

- The unique identification number for the media family.

- The sequence number of this media in the media family. For a disk file, this value is always 1.

- The date and time the label was written.

- The number of mirrors in the set (1–4); 1 indicates an unmirrored device.

 EXAM TIP To read the header from a tape, disk, or device, use the RESTORE HEADERONLY command. For example, if you backed up the AdventureWorks database, you could read the header with the RESTORE HEADERONLY command:

```
BACKUP DATABASE AdventureWorks
    TO DISK = 'C:\AW_Full.bak'
GO
RESTORE HEADERONLY
FROM DISK = 'c:\AW_Full.bak'
```

Backup and Restore Commands

The primary purposes of the Backup and Restore commands are to create backups and restore databases; however, you should know several subtleties of these commands. They lie in different categories, as outlined in Tables 10-2 through 10-7.

Backup and Restore Arguments The arguments in Table 10-2 identify what to back up (database, log, file, and so on), and where to back it up (tape, disk, and device) to or from.

Argument	Description
Database	Full database backup (or file or filegroup backup).
Differential	Specifies that the backup is a differential (instead of a full).
Log	Specifies the transaction log is backed up.
Copy_Only	Specifies creation of a Copy-Only backup. Does not affect a full/differential strategy.
File	Identifies a file to be backed up.
Filegroup	Identifies a filegroup to be backed up. This is the same as issuing several individual file backup commands—one for each file in the filegroup.
Disk/Tape	Path used instead of a backup device.
To	Identifies backup devices.
Mirror To	Indicates a set of backup devices is a mirror within a mirrored media set.

Table 10-2   Backup and Restore Arguments

Initialization Arguments   Table 10-3 shows the arguments used to initialize media sets and media headers.

Argument	Description
Format	Creates a new media set with a new media header. Existing data and headers are overwritten.
NoFormat	Specifies that the media header is not overwritten (default).
Init	Specifies that all backup sets are overwritten. Media headers are retained.
Name	The name of the backup set.

Table 10-3   Initialization Arguments

Informational and Safety   The arguments in Table 10-4 provide general information about the backup set or use basic checks to prevent data from being accidentally overwritten. Some are under the BACKUP command, but most are available with RESTORE.

Tape-Only Arguments   The arguments in Table 10-5 only apply to tapes, not disks.

Error-Checking Arguments   The arguments in Table 10-6 are used for error checking.

BACKUP LOG–Only Arguments   Arguments in Table 10-7 are used only with the BACKUP LOG and/or RESTORE LOG statements.

Before the Backup

It's recommended that any database maintenance activities that need to be done, be done before the backup.

Argument	Description
Description	Free-form text describing the backup set.
ExpiredDate	Specifies date when the backup set expires and can be overwritten.
RetainDays	Specifies number of days before the media can be overwritten.
Password	Deprecated (weak protection). Used to prevent incorrect restores. Instead of password security, the physical security of backups is recommended.
Skip	Does not check the expiration date before overwriting backup sets.
NoSkip	Checks the expiration date before overwriting any backup sets.
MediaDescription	Free-form text for the media set.
HeaderOnly	Returns information on all backups on the device or in the file.
LabelOnly	Returns information on the device (not detailed information on the backups within the device).
Stats	Displays a message each time another percentage completes. Without this, SQL Server displays a message after each increment of 10 percent completes.
VerifyOnly	Verifies that the backup set is complete and readable. Does not verify the structure or integrity.

Table 10-4   Informational Arguments

Argument	Description
NoRewind	Does not rewind tape once backup is complete. SQL keeps tape open.
Rewind	SQL rewinds tape and releases it (default).
NoUnload	Specifies tape is not unloaded automatically (default).
Unload	Automatically rewinds and unloads tape when backup is finished.

Table 10-5   Tape-Only Arguments

Argument	Description
Checksum	Used to verify pages prior to writing. This is different from the backup checksum created for the backup stream and stored on the backup media set.
NoChecksum	Disables page checksums (default).
Stop_On_Error	Stops if checksum errors are detected (default).
Continue_After_Error	Allows backup to continue even if checksum errors are detected.

Table 10-6   Error-Checking Arguments

Argument	Description
NoRecovery	Used when additional logs will be applied. Leaves the database in a recovering state.
Standby	Leaves the database in a standby state. Read access is allowed.
Recovery	Returns database to a fully functional state.
No_Truncate	Used to back up a log when the database is damaged. The database must be online.
No_Log | Truncate_Only	Deprecated. Removes an inactive part of the log without backing it up. It's recommended to use the simple recovery model instead.

Table 10-7   BACKUP LOG–Only Arguments

As an example, it could be that you've determined a need to rebuild one or two key indexes on a nightly basis. This is a time-consuming and resource-intensive activity. By completing the indexing before the backup, you have an optimized database that is backed up. In the case of failure, the database you restore is optimized.

Additionally, maintenance activities add to the transaction log. If maintenance were to be done immediately after the backup, the transaction log would start the day with all the maintenance activity logged. If a recovery were needed, the time would be lengthened due to a larger transaction log.

 TIP   As a best practice, do maintenance *before* any backups. Maintenance done after a backup would result in a larger transaction log and a longer restore.

In the following exercise, we'll create full, differential, and transaction log backups. This exercise assumes the previous exercise (creating backup devices) was done.

Exercise 10.3: Create Backups

1. Open SSMS while connected to the default instance of SQL Server.

2. Click the New Query button to open a new query window.

3. Enter the following script to add a line to the AdventureWorks database. We will later delete it and see it return when we restore the database.

```
USE AdventureWorks
INSERT INTO Person.Contact
(LastName, FirstName, PasswordHash, PasswordSalt)
VALUES ('Voldemort', 'Lord', 'P@ssw0rd','P@$$S@lt')
GO
USE AdventureWorks
SELECT * FROM Person.Contact
WHERE FirstName = 'Lord';
```

4. Enter the following script to back up the AdventureWorks database to the backup device created in the previous exercise:

```
BACKUP DATABASE AdventureWorks
   TO AW_TSQL_BackupDevice
```

5. After the backup completes successfully, enter the following command to view the header:

```
RESTORE HEADERONLY
FROM AW_TSQL_BackupDevice
```

Notice that you can tell a lot from this information. Look at the BackupStart-Date and BackupFinishDate columns. By subtracting one from the other, you can identify exactly how many seconds (or minutes, or hours) a backup takes. On my system it took about ten seconds.

6. Enter the following script to make a change to the database, and view the change:

```
USE AdventureWorks
UPDATE Person.Contact
Set LastName = 'He-who-can''t-be-named'
WHERE LastName = 'Voldemort'
GO
SELECT * FROM Person.Contact
WHERE FirstName = 'Lord'
```

7. Enter the following script to create a differential backup of the database:

```
BACKUP DATABASE AdventureWorks
    TO AW_TSQL_BackupDevice
        WITH DIFFERENTIAL
GO
RESTORE HEADERONLY
FROM AW_TSQL_BackupDevice
```

Notice that the differential backup is much quicker. Using the BackupStartDate and BackupFinishDate columns, I see that it finished in the same second it started—meaning the differential backup took less than a second. Only one extent (all of 64KB) changed, so that's all that needed to be backed up.

8. Enter the following script to make another change to the database, and then view the change:

```
USE AdventureWorks
UPDATE Person.Contact
Set FirstName = ' '
WHERE FirstName = 'Lord'
GO
SELECT * FROM Person.Contact
WHERE LastName = 'He-who-can''t-be-named'
```

9. Enter the following script to create a transaction log backup of the database:

```
BACKUP LOG AdventureWorks
    TO AW_TSQL_BackupDevice
GO
RESTORE HEADERONLY
FROM AW_TSQL_BackupDevice
```

Notice that another line has been added to the header. It now shows that we have three backups on this device—the full backup, the differential backup, and the transaction log backup.

You may have noticed that backups are listed by type in the RESTORE HEADERONLY display. Unfortunately, the type is displayed as an integer. Here's what some of the integers represent:

- 1 = Full
- 2 = Transaction log
- 5 = Differential

CHECKSUM and CONTINUE_AFTER_ERROR Option

It's possible to specify CHECKSUM when doing a backup. CHECKSUM requests that the backup operation verify each page and verify the backup as a whole.

When CHECKSUM is enabled and an error is encountered, the backup fails. If you want to allow the backup to continue even if an error is encountered, you can specify the CONTINUE_AFTER_ERROR option.

 TIP   If checksum is specified in the backup but you want to ensure that scheduled backups still complete, you must modify the jobs by adding the CONTINUE_AFTER_ERROR option if running the jobs via T-SQL statements. If you're using the Backup wizard within SSMS, these options are available in the Reliability section of the Backup options.

By default, the STOP_ON_ERROR is specified. The CONTINUE_AFTER_ERROR option is not available when using the GUI within SSMS to do backups and restores; the only way it can be chosen is by using T-SQL statements.

In this exercise, we'll create a full backup of the current database using the SSMS Backup wizard. Assuming that AdventureWorks was in the state we wanted it to be, we could easily use this backup to restore the AdventureWorks database somewhere else (on another server for example). This demonstrates one way that a database can be moved.

Exercise 10.4: Create Backups with the SSMS Backup Wizard

Video 10-4 walks you through the process of backing up a database in SSMS.

1. If not open, launch SSMS.
2. Open the Databases container and right-click AdventureWorks. Select Tasks | Backup.
3. Ensure the AdventureWorks database is selected. For the Backup Set Name, change the name to **AdventureWorksToMove**.

4. In the Destination section, if a destination path exists, click Remove.

5. Click Add. In the Select Backup Destination dialog box, click the ellipsis button and browse to the root of the C: drive. Enter the name of **AdventureWorksMoving**. Click OK, and then click OK again.

6. On the Select A Page pane, click Options.

7. In the Reliability section, click the check box next to Verify Backup When Finished. Click the Perform Checksum Before Writing To Media option and the Continue On Error option.

8. Click OK to start the backup.

9. Once finished, you can copy the backup file to another server and restore it.

Restores

The reason we do backups is so that when the time comes, we can do restores. Of course, the first time we do a restore should *not* be during a crisis. For a DBA, the knowledge of how to do a restore should be secondhand. We'll discuss doing test restores later in this section.

Restore's First Step

After we learn that a database has failed and we'll need to restore it the first step is to back up the transaction log. The transaction log holds all of the database modifications since the last backup. If we can back up the transaction log, we have a much better chance of restoring the database up to the moment of failure.

 NOTE Discussions on backing up and/or restoring the transaction log assume it is relevant to do so. In other words, any time we're talking about backing up and/or restoring the transaction log, assume that the recovery model is full or bulk-logged. If the recovery model is simple, there's no need to do anything with the transaction log.

Tail Log

This backup of the transaction log (immediately following a corruption of the database) is known as the tail log. Take a look at Figure 10-17. This shows that the tail log backup holds the transactions that occurred since the last backup.

While the figure shows that the tail log holds the transactions since the last transaction log backup, it could also be from the last differential or full backup. It doesn't have to be a transaction log backup. The important thing to understand is that the tail log captures all the database changes since the last backup.

By default, restore operations require the tail log to be backed up. If the tail log is not backed up, the subsequent restore will result in an error unless the RESTORE statement contains either the WITH REPLACE or WITH STOPAT clause.

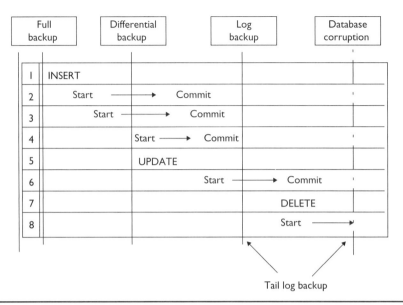

		Full backup	Differential backup	Log backup	Database corruption

1 | INSERT

2 | Start ———▶ Commit

3 | Start ——▶ Commit

4 | Start ——▶ Commit

5 | UPDATE

6 | Start ——▶ Commit

7 | DELETE

8 | Start ———▶

Tail log backup

Figure 10-17   Tail log backup

The tail log is backed up using either the NORECOVERY or NO_TRUNCATE options. NORECOVERY specifies that rollbacks not occur. NO_TRUNCATE ensures that data that may be needed for the restore is not erased from the transaction log.

Restoring with NORECOVERY and RECOVERY

To make the restore process easier to think through, let's create a scenario. Imagine that the AdventureWorks database has become corrupt. It's been recently backed up (in earlier exercises). You have a full backup, a differential backup, and a transaction log backup.

As the first step, you have backed up the tail log. Now you can begin the actual restore process. The first file to restore is the Full backup. However, since we have additional backups to restore, we would specify the NORECOVERY option.

At this point, the AdventureWorks database would no longer be online or accessible, but instead would be in the Restoring state.

The next step would be to restore the differential backup. Since we have more backups to restore after this, we would again use the NORECOVERY option.

We also have a transaction log to apply. Remember though, the last log to apply is the tail log. So when applying this transaction log, we'll still use the NORECOVERY option.

Finally, we'll apply the tail log. Since this is the last backup to apply, we use the RECOVERY option. This returns the database into a fully recovered state and brings it online.

EXAM TIP   Make sure you know the *order* of restore. First the full backup, then the differential backup, then the regular transaction log backup. All of these are restored using the NORECOVERY option. Lastly, the tail log backup is restored using the RECOVERY option.

Restore Strategies

Any restore strategy we use would match the backup strategy in place. Earlier in this chapter, we discussed different backup strategies using different combinations of full, differential, and transaction log backups. In the following section, we'll imagine a database failure and identify the steps used to restore the database.

Take a look at Figure 10-18. How many backups would be required to restore the database? What would the steps be?

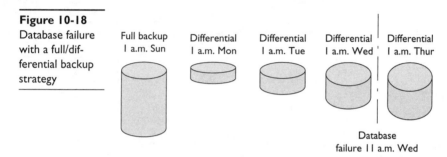

Figure 10-18
Database failure with a full/differential backup strategy

Full backup
1 a.m. Sun

Differential
1 a.m. Mon

Differential
1 a.m. Tue

Differential
1 a.m. Wed

Differential
1 a.m. Thur

Database
failure 11 a.m. Wed

This is a trick question—it depends whether the database is using the full, bulk-logged, or simple recovery model. In other words, do we need to worry about the transaction log?

If the database is using the simple recovery model, we restore the full backup from Sunday and the differential from Wednesday morning—two backups. Remember, in the simple recovery model we can't back up or restore the transaction log.

However, if the database is using the full or bulk-logged recovery model, then we need three backups to restore the database. The steps are:

1. Back up the tail log.
2. Restore the full backup from Sunday using NORECOVERY.
3. Restore the differential from Wednesday using NORECOVERY.
4. Restore the tail log using RECOVERY.

Looking at Figure 10-19, we see a failure occurring on Wednesday in the middle of our full/transaction log backup strategy. How many files would need to be restored here?

Since we're backing up the transaction logs, the recovery model must be full or bulk-logged. To fully restore the database, we'd need three backup files: the full, the 7 A.M. transaction log, and the tail log. The steps are:

1. Back up the tail log.
2. Restore the full backup from Wednesday using NORECOVERY.
3. Restore the 7 A.M. transaction log from Wednesday using NORECOVERY.
4. Restore the tail log using RECOVERY.

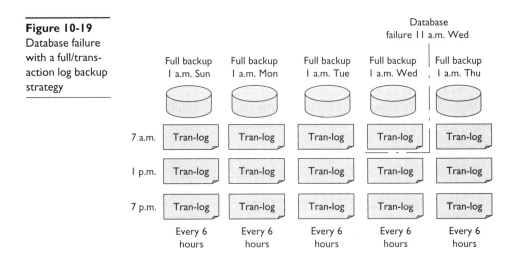

Figure 10-19
Database failure with a full/transaction log backup strategy

Figure 10-20 shows a failure with a full/differential/transaction log backup strategy in place. How many backups would be needed to restore this database?

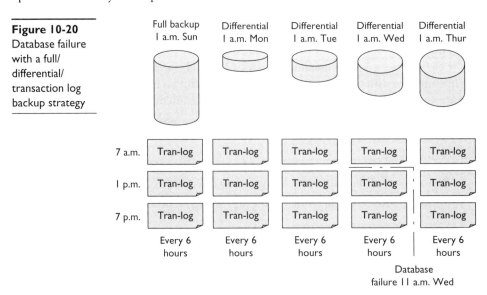

Figure 10-20
Database failure with a full/differential/transaction log backup strategy

As with the previous example, we can tell that the recovery model must be full or bulk-logged. To full restore from this failure, we'd need four backup files: the full on Sunday, the differential on Wednesday, the 7 A.M. transaction log, and the tail log. The steps are:

1. Back up the tail log.

2. Restore the full backup from Sunday using NORECOVERY.

3. Restore the differential backup from Wednesday using NORECOVERY.

4. Restore the 7 A.M. transaction log from Wednesday using NORECOVERY.

5. Restore the tail log using RECOVERY.

Restoring to a Point in Time (STOPAT)

It's also possible to restore up to a moment in time. Let's say that someone accidentally deleted some key records in a database at 3:30 P.M., but right now it's about 4:30 P.M.

If we did a full restore of all backups (full, differentials, and transaction logs) we'd restore the actions that deleted the data at 3:30 P.M. However, we can use the STOPAT option to identify a specific time to stop the restore. In this example, we'd use the STOPAT option to stop the restoration at 3:29 P.M.

It's also possible to create marks in transactions. For example, if we were preparing to do a risky operation such as a bulk import and wanted to ensure we had a way to return the database to exactly the way it was before the import, we could create a transaction with a mark.

Creating a transaction with a mark is done with the BEGIN TRANSACTION statement and then adding the WITH MARK clause. We could name the mark something like Beginning_Bulk_Import.

If things went bad, we could restore the database using the STOPATMARK = Beginning_Bulk_Import option.

In the following exercise, we'll delete some data from the AdventureWorks database and then restore the database. This exercise assumes the previous exercises in this chapter have been completed.

Exercise 10.5: Restore the Database

Watch video 10-5 to see how to restore a database.

1. Close all open connections with AdventureWorks, and open a new query window in SSMS.

 TIP Make sure all connections with AdventureWorks are closed. If connections still exist with AdventureWorks, some of the backup steps in this exercise will not work.

---

2. Use the following script to show that 'He-who-can't-be-named' still exists:

```
USE AdventureWorks;
GO
SELECT * FROM Person.Contact
WHERE LastName = 'He-who-can''t-be-named'
```

3. Execute the following script to delete this row:

```
DELETE FROM Person.Contact
WHERE LastName = 'He-who-can''t-be-named'
```

You may like to rerun the SELECT statement from step 2 to verify the row was successfully deleted.

4. Now we'll start the restore. The first step: Back up the tail log. Use the following command to back up the tail log:

```
USE Master;
GO
BACKUP LOG AdventureWorks
    TO AW_TSQL_BackupDevice
        WITH NORECOVERY
```

Notice that we specify the WITH NORECOVERY statement. This puts the database into a recovering state.

5. At this point, we could restore the database from the wizard. We *won't* do it, but let's try it partway:

a. Right-click the Databases container and select Restore Database.

b. On the Restore Database dialog box, select AdventureWorks in the To Database drop-down box.

c. On the From Database drop-down box, select AdventureWorks. Notice that the full, differential, and both transaction logs are automatically selected. Your display should look similar to Figure 10-21. Do not click OK. Click Cancel.

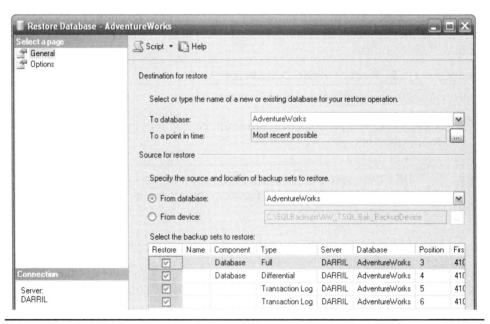

Figure 10-21 Looking at the Restore wizard in SSMS

TIP If things go awry while following the next scripts, you can always repeat steps I thru 5c, but instead of clicking cancel at the end of step 5c, click OK. This will return the database to square one.

6. Enter the following script to restore the full backup:

```
USE Master;
GO
RESTORE DATABASE AdventureWorks
    FROM AW_TSQL_BackupDevice
        WITH NORECOVERY
```

7. Use the RESTORE HEADERONLY line to identify the location of the files:

```
RESTORE HEADERONLY
FROM AW_TSQL_BackupDevice
```

Looking at Figure 10-22, we can see the differential file (backup type 5) is in location 2, and the first transaction log (backup type 2) is in location 3.

Figure 10-22
Partial result of
RESTORE
HEADERONLY

	BackupName	BackupDescription	BackupType	ExpirationDate
1	NULL	NULL	1	NULL
2	NULL	NULL	5	NULL
3	NULL	NULL	2	NULL
4	NULL	NULL	2	NULL

8. Enter the following script to restore the differential backup:

```
RESTORE DATABASE AdventureWorks
    FROM AW_TSQL_BackupDevice
    WITH FILE = 2, NORECOVERY
```

9. Enter the following script to restore the transaction log backup:

```
RESTORE LOG AdventureWorks
    FROM AW_TSQL_BackupDevice
    WITH FILE = 3, NORECOVERY
```

10. Enter the following script to restore the tail log backup:

```
RESTORE LOG AdventureWorks
    FROM AW_TSQL_BackupDevice
    WITH FILE = 4, RECOVERY
```

11. With everything restored, verify that the record you created, modified, and then deleted exists in the restored database. You can use the following script:

```
USE AdventureWorks;
GO
SELECT * FROM Person.Contact
WHERE LastName = 'He-who-can''t-be-named'
```

Verifying Backups

I was called in to help a company restore some data not too long ago. They were having problems and wanted some outside help. The lone overworked IT tech for the company walked through the restore procedure with me, and pretty soon it was clear the tape was corrupt. "Show me where you keep the tapes," I said. He took me to a storage room, where tapes were stacked on a shelf, without any formal record system that I could see.

One by one, we identified corrupt tape after corrupt tape. The tapes were well beyond their shelf life, and many probably should have been rotated out of service at least a year earlier. He complained about having no budget for new tapes, and no time to do testing. Ultimately, we were able to restore most of the database, though a couple of weeks of data were lost.

I had empathy for this tech since he was being expected to do a job but not given the resources to accomplish it. Still, this same story is repeated way too many times. Backups are done religiously but never checked. When it comes time to restore the data (due to a crisis), the tapes or backups are found to have problems due to faulty media, faulty procedures, or both.

Most data recovery strategies include schedules for doing test restores. A test restore is simply restoring the database to another location. This does a couple of things for us:

- **Tests the backups to ensure they are good.** If the backup fails, it's best to learn this during a test restore rather than during a crisis.

- **Allows us to practice the techniques to restore the database.** If we've restored a database 50 times previously during 50 test restores, when the database actually fails, we can easily, confidently, and competently restore the database.

Once the database has been restored, we can use scripts to verify that the database has been restored correctly. We can also use the trustworthy DBCC CheckDB statement to verify the integrity of the database.

 EXAM TIP   An easy way to verify the integrity of backups is to run the DBCC CheckDB statement on the database after doing a test restore of the database.

Torn Pages

A "torn page" refers to a problem with database pages. Remember, a page is 8KB. However, the operating system writes by sectors, and a sector is 512 bytes. So, it takes 16 sectors to make up a single 8KB page.

Imagine a system failure while a page is being written. The system successfully had written the first five sectors, but experienced a power failure before the remaining 11 sectors could be written. This page would now be inconsistent—in other words, a *torn page*.

By default, SQL Server is configured to detect torn pages. It reverses a bit in each sector as it's written. After the page is written, all sectors would have the bit the same. During recovery or restore operations, pages that don't all have this bit the same are detected and reported as torn pages.

If torn pages are detected, it's possible to use a recent database backup to restore only the torn page. Transaction logs can then be restored to bring the database to a fully consistent state.

 TIP If torn pages are detected, use database backups to restore only the torn page. Then restore all the transaction logs since the last backup.

Restoring Files and Filegroups

When restoring files or filegroups, all users must be disconnected from the database. Only the database administrator restoring the files or filegroups can be connected.

Either individual files can be restored, or a filegroup could be restored that would include all files within the filegroup. Just as full and full/differential restores can include transaction logs to restore up to a moment in time, files and filegroups can include transaction logs.

If a file or filegroup becomes corrupt and you need to restore it, follow these steps:

1. Back up the tail log.
2. Restore the file or filegroup using NORECOVERY.
3. Restore the tail log using RECOVERY.

Minimizing Restores

Why are there so many options and possibilities for backups and restores? The obvious truth is that every SQL Server 2005 implementation isn't the same. Some databases are online 24/7. Some databases are online from 9-to-5 Monday through Friday.

Maintenance requirements and the time available to do maintenance also vary. With these varied requirements, the DBA could be tasked with minimizing the time it takes to do backups, or with minimizing the time it takes to do a restore.

For example, you may be tasked with ensuring that the restore of a corrupt database takes as little time as possible. If your operation is a 9-to-5, Monday through Friday operation, you could probably do a full backup each night. If many transactions occur during the day, a differential or one or more transaction logs could be backed up.

On the other hand, for a 24/7 operation, we often don't have enough time to do full backups every night. In this case, we do a single full backup weekly and then do differential backups daily. We can add periodic transaction log backups to this.

Imagine doing just one full backup a week first thing every Sunday morning (no differentials) and then four transaction log backups each day (every six hours). If we had a failure Wednesday morning at 9 A.M., how many backups would need to be restored? Fifteen! The full backup is one backup. With four transaction log backups each for Sunday, Monday, and Tuesday, we'd have 12 more, bringing us to 13. A transaction log backup at 6 A.M. on Wednesday brings us to 14, and the tail log backup makes 15.

This backup strategy would be quick to execute, but the restores would be lengthy and complicated. The full backup would take the regular amount of time. Each transaction log backup would be relatively quick, holding no more than six hours of transactions.

To reduce the restore time in this scenario, we could add differential backups nightly. Now if we were to have a failure on Wednesday at 9 a.m., we only would need to restore four backups, instead of 15—the full from Sunday, the differential from the previous night, the transaction log at 6 a.m., and the tail log.

Detach and Attach

Often, a formal backup isn't needed to restore a corrupt or lost database if we have a fully functional database on another server. By simply detaching the database from SQL Server, we can then copy it as if it's a regular file to the different server. While attached, SQL Server has the files opened and they can't be copied. Detaching causes the SQL Server service to let the file go. Once copied, it can be attached to the new server and will begin functioning in seconds. When attached again, SQL Server opens the files and brings the database online and makes it available.

One of the great benefits of detaching and attaching databases is speed. It's often much quicker to do this instead of the lengthy process of doing backups and restores. Even if the size of the database was in the GB range, we could copy it to DVD relatively easily.

Let's say we have a SQL Server that is failing, and we need to move a critical database to another server. Detaching the database and copying it is much quicker than going through a backup procedure.

Another example could involve two servers replicating the entire database through transactional replication. The Publisher fails, but the Subscriber is up-to-date from the transactional replication. We could thus detach the database, make a copy, and quickly have the Publisher back in business.

 EXAM TIP The quickest way to move a database from one server to another is by detaching, copying it, and reattaching it.

Detaching a database simply forces SQL Server to release it. If you were to try to copy the database without detaching it, it would fail because SQL Server has it locked. Once it's detached, we can copy it locally and then quickly reattach the original. The time that the database is unavailable is only a moment. We then transport the copy to the server or instance that needs it and attach it there.

In the following exercise, we create a database, detach it, copy it, and then reattach it.

Exercise 10.6: Detach and Reattach a Database

1. Open SSMS and connect to the default instance. Create a new query window.

2. Open the Databases container and select the Chapter10 database.

3. Right-click Chapter10 and select Properties. In the Select A Page section, choose Files. In the Details pane, scroll over to the Path column. Your display should look similar to Figure 10-23.

4. Write down the location of the Chapter10.mdf file: _____. Click OK.

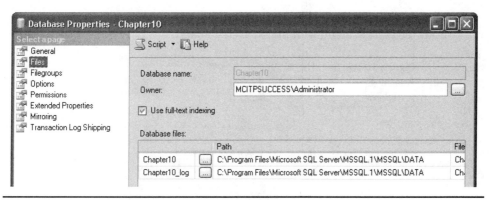

Figure 10-23 Viewing the path in database properties

5. Right-click the Chapter10 database and select Tasks | Detach.

6. On the Detach Database page, select OK. Notice that the Chapter10 database is no longer listed in the Databases section.

7. Press WINDOWS+E to open Windows Explorer. Browse to the path documented in step 5 earlier. Locate the two files associated with the Chapter10 database—one with an .mdf extension and one with an .ldf extension. Your display should look similar to Figure 10-24.

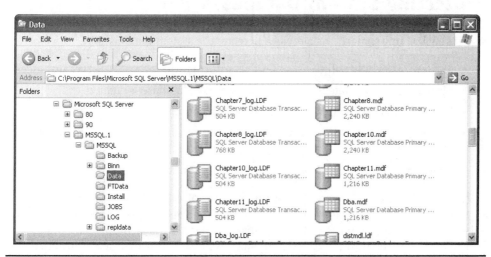

Figure 10-24 Locating the database files

8. Select both files and press CTRL+C to copy them.

9. Right-click in the details pane of the Data folder and click New | Folder. Name the new folder **Chapter10**.

10. Paste the two files into the Chapter10 folder by right-clicking it and selecting Paste.

11. Return to SSMS. Right-click the Databases container and select Attach. Figure 10-25 shows the context menu with the Attach command.

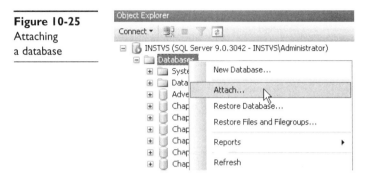

Figure 10-25
Attaching
a database

12. On the Attach Databases window, click Add. Browse to the location of the data folder you just created. Notice that only one file is listed—the .mdf file. Both files exist, but we only need to connect to the .mdf file.

13. Select the Chapter10.mdf file and click OK. Notice in the "Chapter10" database details section that both the .mdf and .ldf files are listed. Click OK.

14. The Chapter11 database is now reattached.

Protecting System Databases

Up until now, we've only covered user databases. However, system databases should also be backed up regularly. As a review, here are the system databases:

- **Master**   This holds all the system-level information for a SQL Server instance.
- **Model**   This template is used whenever a new database is created.
- **MSDB**   This holds all SQL Server Agent jobs and alerts.
- **Resource**   This is a read-only database that holds system objects included with SQL Server 2005.
- **Tempdb**   This is a workspace for holding temporary objects.

It's a good practice to keep at least one backup of each of these system databases. However, sometimes additional backups should be made of specific system databases. Table 10-8 outlines when each of the databases should be backed up.

The master is the most critical system database. If it is corrupt, a server instance may not be able to start. However, if the master database is damaged while the instance is running, you may be able to restore the master.

Rebuilding the Master

If the instance can't start due to a damaged master database, it can be rebuilt. However, this will revert all the system databases to their original state, requiring additional steps to restore each of the system databases. Additionally, all of the user databases will need to be restored to allow the rebuilt master database to learn of them.

Database	When to Back Up
Master	When the schema of any database changes, or a database is created. When any serverwide configuration options are changed. When logins are added or modified. When backup devices are created. When linked servers or remote logins are added.
Model	When the model is actually changed.
MSDB	When SQL Server Agent jobs, alerts, or operators are changed.
Tempdb	If the tempdb database size or other properties are changed.

Table 10-8 When to Back Up System Databases

The master must be rebuilt in two instances:

- A current backup of the master database is not available.
- The SQL Server instance won't start due to a corrupt master.

 NOTE The Rebuildm.exe program has been discontinued in SQL Server 2005. Notice this does not read "deprecated." If you have experience with a previous edition of SQL, you may have used rebuildm, but it is not available in SQL Server 2005.

Once the master database is rebuilt, it can be restored from a recent master database backup.

The tool used to rebuild the master database in SQL Server 2005 is setup.exe. Setup. exe is used to rebuild, verify, and repair a SQL Server instance, and to rebuild system databases. The most common use is to rebuild a corrupt master database, since a corrupt master will prevent the instance from starting. To rebuild the master, setup is run from the command line.

A corrupt master database is a little challenging to identify. However, let's go back to the logs we covered in Chapter 1. The error log records what's going on when an instance starts. It's also a good place to start. Remember, the error log is located in the C:\Program Files\Microsoft SQL Server\MSSQL.1\MSSQL\Log folder.

The following is a partial listing of an error log of an instance that won't start. Can you guess why?

```
2007-03-21 03:06:31.29 Server      Microsoft SQL Server 2005 - 9.00.3050.00
(Intel X86)
     Mar  2 2007 20:01:28
     Copyright (c) 1988-2005 Microsoft Corporation
     Developer Edition on Windows NT 5.1 (Build 2600: Service Pack 2)
2007-03-21 03:06:31.29 Server      (c) 2005 Microsoft Corporation.
2007-03-21 03:06:31.29 Server      All rights reserved.
2007-03-21 03:06:31.29 Server      Server process ID is 156.
2007-03-21 03:06:31.29 Server      Authentication mode is MIXED.
. . .
2007-03-21 03:06:31.29 Server           -d C:\Program Files\Microsoft SQL
Server\MSSQL.1\MSSQL\DATA\master.mdf
2007-03-21 03:06:31.29 Server           -e C:\Program Files\Microsoft SQL
```

```
Server\MSSQL.1\MSSQL\LOG\ERRORLOG
2007-03-21 03:06:31.29 Server          -1 C:\Program Files\Microsoft SQL
Server\MSSQL.1\MSSQL\DATA\mastlog.ldf
2007-03-21 03:06:31.32 Server Error: 17113, Severity: 16, State: 1.
2007-03-21 03:06:31.32 Server Error 2 (The system cannot find the file
specified) occurred while opening file 'C:\Program Files\Microsoft SQL
Server\MSSQL.1\MSSLQ\DATA\master.mdf to obtain configuration . . .
. . .
```

This error log shows we have a problem with the master database preventing the instance from starting. It must be rebuilt.

TIP   If the master is corrupt, preventing a SQL Server instance from starting, use the setup.exe program from the command line to rebuild it.

Single User Mode

Under certain circumstances you may be able to recover a damaged master database or other system database by starting SQL Server in single user mode. Consider single user mode an advanced tool that shouldn't be used lightly.

TIP   Single user mode should *not* be used for routine maintenance. It's an advanced tool that should only be used in extreme situations. Single user mode effectively locks out all users from the database.

To access single user mode, both the SQL Server service and the SQL Server Agent service must be stopped. With both those services stopped, you can open a command-line prompt and change the directory to **C:\Program Files\Microsoft SQL Server\ MSSQL.1\MSSQL\BINN**. This path is for the first instance installed (MSSQL.1). If you were trying to access a different instance, you'd change the path accordingly.

At this point, enter the following command to launch SQL Server in single user mode:

```
sqlservr - m
```

The following is a partial listing of the error log showing that the server was started in single user mode:

```
2007-03-22 06:22:30.50 Server       Microsoft SQL Server 2005 - 9.00.3050.00
(Intel X86)
      Mar  2 2007 20:01:28
      Copyright (c) 1988-2005 Microsoft Corporation
      Developer Edition on Windows NT 5.1 (Build 2600: Service Pack 2)
2007-03-22 06:22:30.50 Server       (c) 2005 Microsoft Corporation.
2007-03-22 06:22:30.50 Server       All rights reserved.
2007-03-22 06:22:30.50 Server       Server process ID is 6024.
2007-03-22 06:22:30.50 Server       Authentication mode is MIXED.
2007-03-22 06:22:30.50 Server       Logging SQL Server messages in file 'C:\
Program Files\Microsoft SQL Server\MSSQL.1\MSSQL\LOG\ERRORLOG'.
2007-03-22 06:22:30.50 Server       This instance of SQL Server last reported
using a process ID of 2792 at 3/22/2007 6:22:08 AM (local) 3/22/2007 10:22:08 AM
(UTC). This is an informational message only; no user action is required.
2007-03-22 06:22:30.50 Server       Registry startup parameters:
```

```
2007-03-22 06:22:30.50 Server              -d C:\Program Files\Microsoft SQL
Server\MSSQL.1\MSSQL\DATA\master.mdf
2007-03-22 06:22:30.50 Server              -e C:\Program Files\Microsoft SQL
Server\MSSQL.1\MSSQL\LOG\ERRORLOG
2007-03-22 06:22:30.50 Server              -l C:\Program Files\Microsoft SQL
Server\MSSQL.1\MSSQL\DATA\mastlog.ldf
2007-03-22 06:22:30.50 Server     Command Line Startup Parameters:
2007-03-22 06:22:30.50 Server         -m
2007-03-22 06:22:30.53 Server     SQL Server is starting at normal priority
base (=7). This is an informational message only. No user action is required.
```

The complete listing is displayed at the command prompt. Each of the databases in the server instance will be started, so it will take some time for the startup to complete.

At this point you can use the setup.exe program to rebuild the master database. Open another command prompt and identify the path where the setup command is located. In my system, the installation CD is in the D: drive, and the setup command is located in the Servers directory. The basic syntax is:

```
Start /wait d:\servers\setup.exe /qn instancename = instanceName reinstall =
SQL_Engine REBUILDDATABASE=1 sapwd = sapassword
```

 NOTE The previous half of this chapter primarily addressed database backup and recovery procedures. The rest of this chapter will cover high-availability strategies.

Log Shipping

Log shipping is a very simple way of keeping a full copy of your database on another system. While log shipping is typically used for a single database, it can also be configured for multiple databases.

Earlier in this chapter, we covered the transaction log. As a reminder, the transaction log records all data modifications. Any time an INSERT, UPDATE, or DELETE statement is issued, it is first written to the transaction log, and then when the log is checkpointed the data is written to the database.

The transaction log is helpful in maintaining the integrity of the database, but since it has a record of every change in the database, it can also be used to maintain a copy of the database on another server.

Look at Figure 10-26 for the big picture of using log shipping. It involves making a copy of the database and putting it on another SQL Server that we refer to as the *standby server*. Then, we simply copy or "ship" the transaction log over to the standby server and apply the logged changes to the standby server, and voilà! We now have another copy of our data.

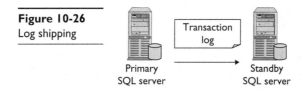

Figure 10-26
Log shipping

Primary
SQL server

Transaction
log

Standby
SQL server

ACID Tests

An ACID test is commonly referred to in many fields as a foolproof test that can prove something is sound. For example, in investing terminology, the ACID test ratio refers to the health of a company. With databases, it concerns the ability of the database to stay healthy.

ACID is an acronym for "atomicity, consistency, isolation, and durability."

Atomicity in this context refers to the ability of the database management system (DBMS) to ensure that transactions either succeed as a whole or fail as a whole. For example, if money is transferred from the savings account and passed to the checking account, both transfers must succeed for the transaction to succeed. If either fails, both are rolled back.

Consistency ensures that the database enforces all integrity constraints created within the database. This includes data types, PK-to-FK relationships, CHECK constraints, and UNIQUE constraints.

Isolation is the ability of the DBMS to hide or isolate elements of a transaction until the transaction is complete. For example, when transferring money from the savings account to the checking account, the change is isolated from other users. If a user were to look at either of these accounts during the transaction, it would either not be viewable (locked) or it would show the state before the transaction.

Durability is the ability of the DBMS to survive system failures while maintaining the integrity of committed transactions. In SQL Server 2005 this is done by writing the data into the transaction log and periodically checkpointing the log. Once written to the log, the DBMS has the capability to write the data to the database. If interrupted by a power failure, the DBMS recognizes this and rolls forward all committed transactions from the transaction log into the database once power is restored; uncommitted transactions are rolled back.

Benefits and Requirements

Log shipping offers several possible benefits. These include:

- Fault tolerance
- Offloading backups
- Offloading query processing

Log shipping gives us a full backup of the database on the primary server. If the primary server goes down we can bring up the standby server, and with minimal interaction we are back in business. While the convenience of automatic failover is *not* possible with log shipping, a standby server can be manually brought online to take the place of a primary server.

Backups could take an extraordinarily long time for a large database. For example, I worked on a very large database where it took over six hours to back up the database.

Our solution was not to back up the database on the production server. Instead, we used log shipping to create a complete copy of the database on a separate standby server. We were able to keep the primary server fully online at all times. The lengthy time-consuming backups were done on the separate standby server.

The standby server can be used as a read-only database for query processing. While useful in some instances, it can be problematic in others. Every time the transaction log is shipped over to the standby server and restored, all users must be disconnected. Depending on how often the transaction log is restored, this could be quite disruptive for the users.

For log shipping to work, several requirements must be met. These are:

- The databases in a log shipping configuration must be configured with the full or bulk-logged recovery model. They *cannot* be set to the simple recovery model.

- Each server involved in log shipping must be running one of the following versions of SQL Server:

  - SQL Server 2005 Standard Edition

  - SQL Server 2005 Workgroup Edition

  - SQL Server 2005 Enterprise Edition

- Each server involved in log shipping should have the same case-sensitivity settings.

 EXAM TIP   Make sure you're aware of the recovery model required for log shipping. We covered the details of the recovery models in detail earlier in this chapter. The simple recovery model logs very little in the transaction log, and therefore there would be very little to ship to the standby server. Log shipping requires the use of the full or bulk-logged recovery models.

To configure log shipping, you must be a sysadmin on both servers.

While the best use of log shipping is using two different servers, it's also possible to configure log shipping between a primary database and a secondary database on the same server, as long as separate instances are used.

Configuring log shipping is done in two steps:

1. Make a backup of the primary database and restore it on the secondary server.

2. Enable log shipping.

In the following exercise we'll combine both steps.

 TIP   This exercise requires a second instance of SQL Server installed on your system. If you don't have a second instance installed, consider this an ideal opportunity to practice this procedure. Chapter 1 has the procedure used to install an instance if you need a reference, but at this point in your studies, you can probably just pop in the DVD and follow the prompts. You can name the instance **MyNamedInstance**.

Exercise 10.7: Add a Secondary Database and Enable Log Shipping

1. Create two folders for the primary and secondary files and share them.

   a. Press WINDOWS+E to open an instance of Windows Explorer.

   b. Select the C: drive. If the display pane shows These Files Are Hidden, then click the link to Show The Contents Of This Folder.

   c. Right-click the display pane and select New | Folder. Rename the folder **LogPrimary**.

   d. Right-click the LogPrimary folder, and select Sharing and Security.... Click Share This Folder. Your display should look similar to Figure 10-27.

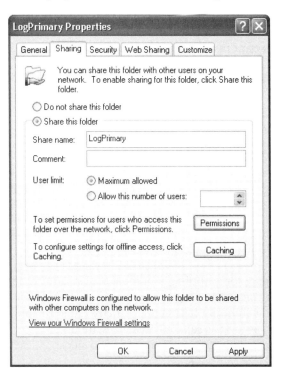

Figure 10-27
Sharing the
LogPrimary folder

   e. Click the Permissions button. With the Everyone group selected, click the check box to Allow Full Control. Click OK.

 TIP The permissions to be granted in the real world should be full control to the service account used by the SQL Server Agent service. However, to keep this lab focused on Log Shipping, we'll grant permissions to the Everyone group.

   f. Click the Security tab. Select the Users group and mark the check box next to Allow Full Control. Click OK.

g. Select the C: drive. Right-click the display pane and select New | Folder. Rename the folder **LogSecondary.**

h. Right-click the LogSecondary folder and select Sharing and Security.... Click Share This Folder.

i. Click the Permissions button. With the Everyone group selected, click the check box labeled Allow Full Control. Click OK.

j. Click the Security tab. Select the Users group and mark the check box next to Allow Full Control. Click OK.

2. Determine your computer name. Press WINDOWS+R to access the Run command. Enter **CMD** and click OK. At the command prompt, enter **Hostname** and press ENTER. Write down the name of your computer _____.

3. Open an instance of SSMS. Double-click Databases to expand the Databases container. Right-click the AdventureWorks database and select Properties.

4. Under Select A Page, choose Options. Change the Recovery Model to Full. Your display should look similar to Figure 10-28. Click OK to apply the change.

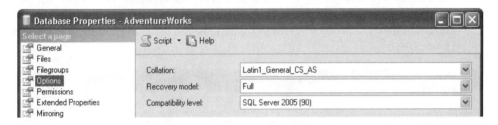

Figure 10-28   Changing AdventureWorks to the full recovery model

5. Right-click the AdventureWorks database and select Properties. Under Select A Page, choose Transaction Log Shipping. Select the box marked Enable This As A Primary Database In A Log Shipping Configuration.

6. Click Backup Settings. In the Network Path To Backup Folder box, enter **\\computerName\LogPrimary**, where *computerName* is the name of your computer.

7. *Enter* **c:\LogPrimary** as the backup folder path. Accept the defaults for the rest of the settings. Your display should look similar to Figure 10-29. Click OK.

8. Click Add. In the Secondary Database Settings dialog box, click Connect.

9. In the Connect To Server dialog box, change to your named instance and click Connect.

NOTE   In the real world, we'd connect to a different server. However, in this exercise, we will use the same server for both the primary and standby servers. This allows you to do your testing on a single box. The only catch is that it must be on separate instances.

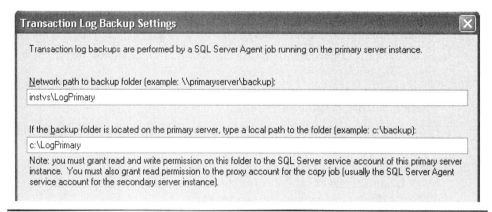

Figure 10-29   Configuring the transaction log backup settings

10. Change the name of the Secondary Database from AdventureWorks to **AWLogShipping**.

11. On the Initialize Secondary Database tab, click Yes, Generate A Full Backup Of The Primary Database And Restore It Into The Secondary Database (And Create The Secondary Database If It Doesn't Exist). Your display should look similar to Figure 10-30.

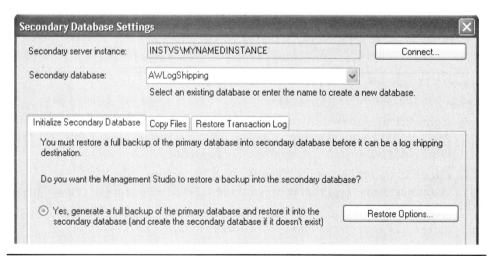

Figure 10-30   Configuring secondary database settings

12. Select the Copy Files tab. In the Destination folder for copied files, enter \\ **instvs\LogSecondary**.

13. Click the Restore Transaction Log tab.

14. Click Standby Mode. Select the check box for Disconnect Users In The Database When Restoring Backups. Leave the other defaults as they are. Click OK.

15. In the Database Properties page, click OK. This begins the process. It takes a moment, but once completed, you should see a display indicating success. Click Close.

At this point, we have configured log shipping on the primary server. This included:

- Backing up the primary database (AdventureWorks)

- Restoring the backup to the secondary database (INSTVS\ MYNAMEDINSTANCE.AWLogShipping)

- Saving the secondary destination configuration (INSTVS\MYNAMEDINSTANCE. AWLogShipping)

- Saving the primary backup setup

Monitor Server

While not required, log shipping supports a third server known as the monitor server. It records the history and status of log backup and log restore operations, and can be configured to raise alerts if any of the operations fail.

If configured, the monitor server tracks all of the details of log shipping such as when the transaction log was last backed up, when the secondary server last copied and restored the backup files, and information about any backup failure alerts.

Microsoft recommends using a different server from the primary or secondary servers for the monitor server. This way, if either the primary or secondary server goes down, the information will still be recorded on the monitor server.

In the first exercise, we configured log shipping. In the next exercise, we'll take a look at a few items that show that log shipping is working. Since the schedule was set to run every 15 minutes, you might like to take a short break before starting this exercise.

Exercise 10.8: Verify Log Shipping

1. If SSMS is not open, open it now. Connect to the named instance you created for the standby server. Select the AWLogShipping database and click the New Query button. This will open a new query window for the named instance.

2. Execute the following script to verify you don't have anyone in the Person. Contact table with the first name of Billy-Joe-Bob:

```
USE AWLogShipping;
GO
SELECT * FROM Person.Contact
WHERE FirstName = 'Billy-Joe-Bob'
```

Close this query window.

 CAUTION If you don't close this connection, when log shipping attempts to restore the backed up transaction log to the secondary server, it will fail and you won't see the results we're seeking.

3. If SSMS is only connected to the named instance of SQL Server, use SSMS to also connect to the default instance.

   a. Right-click the named instance and click Connect.

   b. In the Connect To Server dialog box, change the Server Name to the default instance (the name of your computer).

   c. Click Connect.

4. Open the instance, open the Databases container, and select AdventureWorks. Click the New Query button.

5. In the query window, execute the following script to show that AdventureWorks also does not have a person named Billy-Joe-Bob:

```
- Default Instance Query Window (primary)
USE AdventureWorks
SELECT * FROM Person.Contact
WHERE FirstName = 'Billy-Joe-Bob'
```

6. Now let's add Billy-Joe-Bob to the database with the following script in the default instance query window. The SELECT statement shows we were successful.

```
INSERT INTO Person.Contact
(FirstName, LastName,PasswordHash, PasswordSalt)
VALUES ('Billy-Joe-Bob', 'Smith', 'P@ssw0rd','P@$$S@lt')
GO
SELECT * FROM Person.Contact
WHERE FirstName = 'Billy-Joe-Bob'
```

 TIP   While we've modified the AdventureWorks database in the primary server, this change will not be reflected in the AWLogShipping database on the secondary server right away. Once log shipping has occurred (every 15 minutes with the schedule we've selected), we will be able to see the new entry in the Person.Contact table on the Secondary server. We'll do some other looking around and then come back to check the AWLogShipping database.

   Write down the time: _____.

7. Press WINDOWS+E to open an instance of Windows Explorer. Browse to the C:\LogPrimary folder.

8. Notice this folder has one or more files. The first file should be the AdventureWorks.bak file, which is the backup of the AdventureWorks database. Depending on how much time has passed, you should also see one or more transaction log backup files. These are labeled as AdventureWorks_*yyyymmddxxxxxx.trn*. If you look at the time these files were created, you'll see they were created on the quarter hour, as in 9:00, 9:15, 9:30, and 9:45 (or whatever the current hour is).

9. Browse to the LogSecondary folder. Here, you should see one or more transaction log backup files. The most recent file has the extension of .tuf. These are the transaction log backups that were shipped from the primary to the standby server. Your display should look similar to Figure 10-31.

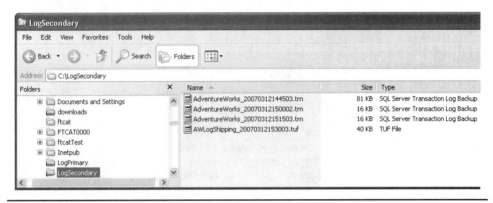

Figure 10-31 Windows Explorer showing shipped logs

10. Within the SSMS Object Explorer, select the named instance that is holding your standby server.

11. Open the Databases container and observe the AWLogShipping database. Notice that it is in Standby mode and is set to Read-Only. Your display should look similar to Figure 10-32. While you can't see it in the figure, the AWLogShipping database also has a dimmed icon to show it's in Standby/ Read-Only mode.

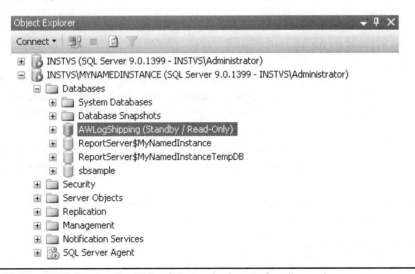

Figure 10-32 SSMS showing the AWLogShipping database in Standby mode

12. Still in the named instance of SQL Server, browse to SQL Server Agent and select Jobs. While we'll explore SQL Server Agent in more detail in Chapter 13, for now you can see that three jobs have been created for log shipping. Your display should look similar to Figure 10-33.

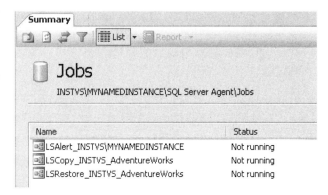

Figure 10-33
Three jobs created on the standby server

 NOTE If you followed the exercises in Chapter 1, SQL Server Agent should be configured to start automatically. However, if it's not, you will need to start it here. You can do this within SSMS by simply right-clicking SQL Server Agent and selecting Start.

13. Within the SSMS Object Explorer, select the default instance of SSMS. Browse to the SQL Server Agent container and select Jobs. Here, you should see at least two jobs created for log shipping.

14. Check the time. If it has been more than 15 minutes since you completed step 6 and wrote down the time, you can continue. Or, if it is simply past the quarter hour (:00, :15, :30, :45) since you did step 6, you can continue. In other words, if it was 9:20 when you did step 6 and it's now past 9:30, continue. If not, take a break.

 TIP In the next steps, we'll verify that the change to the AdventureWorks database has been shipped and applied to the AWLogShipping database. However, to avoid problems, we do not want to connect to the database until the update has been shipped and applied.

15. Within the SSMS Object Browser, select the AWLogShipping database in the named instance. With this database selected, click the button to open a new query window.

16. Execute the following query to verify that Billy-Joe-Bob has been shipped over to the secondary database:

```
USE AWLogShipping
SELECT * FROM Person.Contact
WHERE FirstName = 'Billy-Joe-Bob'
```

You should see a result set showing this entry has made it to the standby server.

Latency

In our exercises, we have accepted a default of 15 minutes for log shipping. This results in 15 minutes latency. At any given time, our secondary server could be as much as 15 minutes behind the primary server.

Latency isn't necessarily a problem. I worked with one customer that needed a full copy of a customer database at a remote office. Bandwidth wasn't available to constantly do log shipping throughout the day. However, bandwidth was available in the middle of the night for other maintenance tasks.

We configured log shipping to occur once a day in the middle of the night. The rest of the time, the office staff had access to a read-only database that they queried to their heart's content throughout the day. While the remote office never had access to customer's activities for the current day, this was rarely a problem.

 NOTE When talking about secondary servers and spares, you may come across the terms "cool," "warm," and "hot." A cool (or sometimes "cold") server is one that can be powered up and restored with a recent backup of the primary server in the event of a failure of the primary. A warm server (sometimes called a standby server) is online using an automated method to keep it up-to-date, while log shipping is a method used to keep a SQL Server warm and up-to-date. A hot server is not only kept up-to-date, but also allows for automatic failover to the secondary server in the event of a failure of the primary—for instance, a cluster is an example of a hot server. The hot server has the best response, but is also the most expensive.

On the other hand, if 15 minutes latency is too much, you can make the time frame shorter. For example, if you're using log shipping to create a standby server as a warm spare, you might want it more up-to-date than just 15 minutes. You can configure log shipping to occur every two minutes. This just entails changing the schedule in the jobs on both servers.

 EXAM TIP To decrease the latency between the primary and standby servers, simply change the timing in the schedules of the jobs. On the primary server, change the schedule of the backup job, and on the standby server, change the schedules of the copy and restore jobs.

Now if the primary server crashes, the maximum amount of data you might have lost is only two minutes' worth.

Of course, this begs the question: How do I change a standby server to a primary server? We'll explore this in the next section.

Procedures for Changing Roles

When the primary server has failed and you want to failover to the secondary server and make it your primary, several steps must be taken. I've outlined the steps in the following paragraphs, but one thing to really take away from this is that it's not automatic to swap roles. It takes some time and energy.

If you want a full and automatic failover solution of a server, clustering and database mirroring are the best solutions. We'll cover both of these later in this chapter.

One of the benefits of log shipping is that it doesn't require the specialized hardware a clustering solution does, and it can provide a full warm spare. The steps to change roles are:

1. Manually failover from the primary database to the secondary database.

2. Disable log shipping jobs.

3. Reconfigure log shipping (if desired) to swap the roles.

4. Bring the secondary database online.

Manually Failover from the Primary Database to the Secondary Database

It's unlikely the databases are fully synchronized when a failover is needed. So, to ensure as much data as possible is brought up on the new primary server, perform the following steps:

1. Check to see if any transaction log backup files on the primary server have not been copied to the secondary server. If so, either manually copy them or run the job that copies them.

2. Apply any unapplied transaction log backups to the secondary server (the server that will be the new primary).

3. If possible, create a backup of the transaction log on the original primary server (using NORECOVERY), and apply it to the new primary server.

Disable the Log Shipping Jobs

The second step in changing roles is to disable the log shipping jobs on both the primary and secondary servers. It's best to disable them instead of deleting them. If you want to switch roles back, one of the steps is to disable the new jobs and enable the ones we're disabling now.

Reconfigure Log Shipping (If Desired) to Swap the Roles

The third step in changing roles is to reconfigure Log Shipping. If the original primary server is operational and you want to make it a secondary server, simply repeat the steps to configure log shipping with the roles reversed.

Bringe the Secondary Database Online

The last step in changing roles is to manually issue RESTORE commands to bring the original secondary server online. If you have any transaction logs to apply, use the NORECOVERY clause for each restore except the last. We covered the restore process earlier in this chapter.

Database Snapshots

Database snapshots are a new feature available in SQL Server 2005. They are read-only and are only available in the Enterprise edition. If you think of the metaphor of a photo snapshot, you have a pretty good idea of database snapshots. They effectively give you the same result, though the process is a little different.

Database snapshots are created at a moment in time. They can be used for reporting purposes for that given time. In the event of some type of user or administrative error, you can easily revert the source database to the state it was in when the snapshot was created.

You won't be tested on how the database snapshots work internally. However, a little background knowledge will help you grasp how they are created and maintained.

Think of a picture of a field of sunflowers. In the background are white-peaked mountains with puffs of white clouds amidst a blue sky. If you took a snapshot of this with a regular camera, you would instantly have a full view of the scene.

However, if we could constantly monitor this scene and know what's going to happen just before it happens, we could record it a little differently. Instead of our photograph showing what it's like, it starts with a blank canvas. Then as the scene changes, we record the original state. A sunflower bends in the wind—we record the original sunflower in its original location. Clouds move away revealing blue sky—we record the original clouds. If we looked at the recorded picture, it would be like puzzle pieces of the original scene with many parts of the blank canvas showing.

This piecemeal picture may not seem very useful, but if we looked at the current scene and then overlaid our original puzzle pieces on top of it, we could see exactly what the original scene looked like. Imagine the field of sunflowers six months later. No flowers are blooming. But if we pasted our stored bits of sunflower pictures over the current scene, we could see exactly what it looked like six months ago.

Database snapshots work this way, based on a concept known as *copy-on-write*—meaning whenever data is written to a database the original page is copied to the snapshot just before the data is written. When you first take the database snapshot, the slate is clean. Empty. Almost nothing is recorded. When something in the database is changed, then the page holding the data just before the change occurred is recorded.

If we need to restore the database to where it was when the snapshot was taken, we first use the current state of the database with all the changes, and then overlay the original data from the snapshot files to show us exactly what it was originally. Pretty cool.

 TIP Snapshots vs. snapshots… *Database* snapshots are unrelated to snapshot *replication.* We will present snapshot replication later in Chapter 15.

Purpose and Benefits

Some of the primary purposes and benefits of using database snapshots are:

- Protecting data from user error
- Safeguarding data against administrative error

- Maintaining historical data for report generation
- Using a mirror database that you are maintaining for availability purposes

 TIP One of the great benefits of database snapshots is the ability to overcome user errors. By creating database snapshots on a regular basis, you can mitigate the impact of user errors such as inadvertently deleting data, or an administrative error such as what might occur during a manual bulk-load process.

Creating and Using a Database Snapshot

If users have permission to create a database, they have permission to create a snapshot. If you're comfortable with T-SQL, snapshots are quite easy to create. Unfortunately, SQL Server Management Studio does not have the tools available for the creation of database snapshots. It must be done through T-SQL statements.

Before creating the snapshot, consider the size of the source database. If you allow the snapshot to continue to grow, it can get as large as the source database, but no larger. Make sure you have enough disk space to support it.

Once a snapshot is created, it can be queried as easily as a regular database. We simply invoke the USE command to set the context of the snapshot.

The command to create the snapshot is a CREATE DATABASE command. In the following exercise, we'll create a snapshot of the AdventureWorks database, modify the original database, and then query the snapshot to show the original data is still available.

Exercise 10.9: Create a Database Snapshot

1. Open an instance of SSMS, and create a new query window.

2. Enter the following command to create a database snapshot of AdventureWorks:

```
CREATE DATABASE AdventureWorks_Snapshot_0900 ON
( NAME = AdventureWorks_Data, FILENAME =
'C:\Program Files\Microsoft SQL
Server\MSSQL.1\MSSQL\Data\AdventureWorks_Snapshot_0900.ss' )
AS SNAPSHOT OF AdventureWorks;
```

 NOTE Note that we have included the name "Snapshot" and the time "0900" in the snapshot name and in the name of the file. This is a common convention and especially useful if we have several snapshots and need to easily differentiate between them.

3. Select the Databases container. Right-click and select Refresh.

4. Open the Database Snapshots container. You should see the AdventureWorks_Snapshot_0900 snapshot.

5. Use the following query to read data from the snapshot:

```
USE AdventureWorks_Snapshot_0900
GO
SELECT * FROM Person.Contact
WHERE FirstName = 'Billy-Joe-Bob'
```

6. Use the following query to modify the AdventureWorks database by changing any persons with the first name of Billy-Joe-Bob to Mary-Joe-Marina. In the next exercise, we'll use the database snapshot to revert to the original names.

```
USE AdventureWorks;
UPDATE Person.Contact
SET FirstName = 'Mary-Joe-Marina'
WHERE FirstName = 'Billy-Joe-Bob'
GO
SELECT * FROM Person.Contact
WHERE FirstName = 'Billy-Joe-Bob'
```

7. Use the following query to read data from the snapshot and show that the original data is still available in the snapshot:

```
USE AdventureWorks_Snapshot_0900
GO
SELECT * FROM Person.Contact
WHERE FirstName = 'Billy-Joe-Bob'
```

Managing Snapshots

When creating snapshots, it's best to include the name of the original database, an indication that this is a snapshot, and some type of sequence number such as time of day. For example, in our exercise, we named the snapshot AdventureWorks_Snapshot_0900.

Just by looking at the name, even a casual observer would know that this is a snapshot of the AdventureWorks database taken at 9 A.M. (0900). Sure, we could name it *awss9*. For the next five minutes, I would probably be able to remember what this is, but there are no guarantees I'd have a clue what *awss9* meant by next week.

Because one of the primary reasons to use database snapshots is to safeguard against user or administrative errors, it makes sense to create several snapshots a day. Consider a travel agency where travel agents have accidentally deleted existing reservations in the past. By creating several snapshots throughout the day, a DBA could retrieve data that was created after the first snapshot but deleted in the original database.

If we were only concerned about protecting our database from risky operations such as a manual bulk-load process, we could choose to create a single snapshot immediately before the start of the bulk-load. If something were to go wrong during the bulk-load, we could use the database snapshot to quickly recover.

Since these database snapshots continue to grow, a strategy of managing snapshots must include dropping older snapshots. For example, if we did backups of the database every night, we could choose to drop the snapshots as soon as the backups were completed. This would free up the space for new snapshots throughout the day, and if data was lost, it could be retrieved from the backups.

Recovering Data from a Snapshot

At any time we can revert the database to the state it was in when the snapshot was created. This is done with a simple RESTORE command. We covered restores earlier in the chapter. Here we can see how simple it is to recover a database from a database snapshot.

The partial syntax of the RESTORE command is:

```
RESTORE DATABASE name_of_database_to_be_restored FROM
DATABASE_SNAPSHOT = 'name_of_database_snapshot';
```

When reverting to a snapshot, only one snapshot on the database can exist. If more than one snapshot exists, the revert will fail. However, it's common for several snapshots to exist on a server so before you can revert a database from a snapshot you must delete all but the desired snapshot.

The previous exercise erroneously changed the name "Billy-Joe-Bob" to "Mary-Joe-Marina." In the next exercise, we'll revert the database snapshot to the original state.

 TIP   This exercise assumes you have done Exercise 10.9, where the snapshot was created and the original AdventureWorks database was modified.

Exercise 10.10: Revert a Database Snapshot

1. Use this query to verify that the earlier change has occurred in the database:

   ```
   USE AdventureWorks;
   GO
   SELECT * FROM Person.Contact
   WHERE FirstName = 'Billy-Joe-Bob'
   ```

   You should not have any results since this name was changed to Mary-Joe-Marina.

2. Execute the following query to show that the original still exists in the snapshot:

   ```
   USE AdventureWorks_Snapshot_0900
   GO
   SELECT * FROM Person.Contact
   WHERE FirstName = 'Billy-Joe-Bob'
   ```

   You should have one row in the result set.

3. Enter the following query to revert to the original:

   ```
   USE master;
   RESTORE DATABASE AdventureWorks FROM
   DATABASE_SNAPSHOT = 'AdventureWorks_Snapshot_0900';
   ```

4. Use this query to verify that the original state of the database has been restored from the snapshot:

   ```
   USE AdventureWorks;
   GO
   SELECT * FROM Person.Contact
   WHERE FirstName = 'Billy-Joe-Bob'
   ```

   You should have one row in the result set.

5. To ensure other labs work, remove the database snapshot. Within the SSMS Object Explorer, select the AdventureWorks_Snapshot_0900 in the Database Snapshots container. Right-click the snapshot and select Delete. On the Delete Object page, click OK.

Database Mirroring

New to SQL Server 2005 is a feature called database mirroring. It is a software solution used to increase the probability that a database is highly available.

Database mirroring is similar to log shipping in concept. They both can be configured to provide high availability for databases, and they both use the transaction log to keep the copy up-to-date. While both can be configured for multiple databases, each configuration is for a single database.

One significant difference between log shipping and database mirroring is that database mirroring can be configured for automatic failover. Requirements must be met, but automatic failover is possible on a database mirror but not with log shipping.

The way that database mirrors communicate with each other is significantly different than log shipping. In log shipping, jobs are created on each server and run at appropriate times to copy and apply the transaction log.

In database mirroring, a database session is established where the two instances communicate with each other regularly through PING messages and the exchange of other state information, as shown in Figure 10-34.

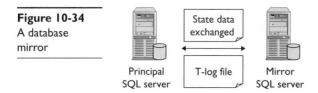

Figure 10-34
A database mirror

Principal SQL server — State data exchanged — T-log file — Mirror SQL server

Any time the principal server makes changes to the transaction log, it simultaneously sends a copy of the transaction log to the mirror server. The mirror server applies those changes as if they occurred on the mirror's database.

Requirements

Some basic requirements to use database mirroring are:

- At least the SQL Server 2005 Service Pack 1 should be installed.
  Database mirroring is disabled by default in the original release of SQL Server 2005.

- The recovery model must be set to full.
  Database mirroring will not work in simple or bulk-logged recovery models.

- Only databases can be mirrored, not servers.
  Mirroring is implemented on a per-database basis.

- They must be supported on SQL Server Standard and Enterprise editions.

NOTE Database mirroring wasn't a fully supported feature in the original release of SQL Server 2005. It was there, but disabled by default. It has been fully enabled since SP1. If you are running SQL Server 2005 without SP1 installed, you could enter **DBCC TRACEON (1400)** in a query window to enable it.

Any *user* databases can be configured with database mirroring. The master, msdb, tempdb, and model databases cannot be configured as database mirrors.

Benefits

One of the great benefits of database mirroring is that it's a simple solution to implement. It doesn't require any special hardware (such as a clustering solution would require), yet can provide high availability.

If configured with a witness server, database mirroring can provide high-availability benefits for a database.

While database mirrors can't be queried directly, when they are used with database snapshots users can query the mirror. In other words, if a database mirror is created without a database snapshot, it can't be queried. If you want the ability to query the database mirror, a database snapshot, can be created on the mirror and users will then be able to query the mirror via the snapshot. Without the snapshot you provide a layer of redundancy to your solution. With the snapshot you add high availability.

The Witness Server

A third server can also be configured with a database mirror, as shown in Figure 10-35. This third server is known as the *witness server*.

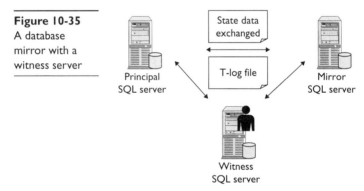

Figure 10-35
A database mirror with a witness server

Principal SQL server · State data exchanged · T-log file · Mirror SQL server · Witness SQL server

The only purpose of the witness server is to enable automatic failover, or to enable high-availability mode. If this is not your goal, it's recommended to leave the witness set to Off.

For the database mirroring session to support automatic failover with a witness server, the session must be in synchronous-operating mode. The two choices are synchronous and asynchronous. They are also referred to as "transaction safety on" (synchronous) and "transaction safety off" (asynchronous). Synchronous mode provides high availability, while asynchronous mode provides high performance. These modes are outlined in Table 10-9.

Mode	Transaction Safety	Result
Synchronous	On	High availability.
Asynchronous	Off	High performance.

Table 10-9 Database Mirror Operating Modes

TIP If you are implementing automatic failover on a database mirror, you must have a witness server configured. This is really the only reason to configure a witness server. High-availability mode (automatic failover) also requires the session to be set to synchronous mode.

The witness server monitors the state between the principal and mirror servers, and can initiate a change in roles if the principal server goes down. All three servers exchange PING messages with each other to verify connectivity and operation.

If a witness server is not implemented or the mode is not configured in synchronous mode, then automatic failover is not possible. However, the mirror still functions as a warm spare and can be manually switched over to the principal role.

Database Mirroring Endpoints

SQL Server 2005 uses endpoints to manage connections. An *endpoint* is a SQL Server object, and it is used by SQL Server to communicate over the network with other SQL Server instances. A database mirroring endpoint is used specifically to facilitate communication within database mirroring connections.

Database mirroring endpoints identify a unique listener port. A server instance can have only one database mirroring endpoint, but multiple database mirrors can use the same endpoint. In other words, if we create a second database mirror on an instance, we would not re-create a new endpoint, but instead use the first one.

Each database-mirroring server instance requires a unique listener port for mirroring connections. To identify the port for a server instance to use, you need a unique database mirroring endpoint for that instance. A server instance can have only one endpoint for mirroring, and all of the mirroring sessions to be supported by that server instance must use the same endpoint. When creating the endpoint, a system administrator specifies the authentication and encryption methods of the server instance.

Endpoints and Ports

If you're a system administrator, this language about ports may sound familiar. For example, you may know that port 80 is the well-known port for HTTP, 25 for SMTP, 20 and 21 for FTP, and so on. IANA.org has identified the protocols used with the first 1024 ports as well-known ports. However, the possible ports actually go up to 65,536.

An IP address combined with a port number is sometimes referred to as a *packet*. The IP address tells the packet how to get to the specific computer. However, once it gets to the computer, the port number tells the computer what to do with the data. For example, port 80 tells the computer to pass this onto the HTTP process to respond to the packet.

When we create a database mirroring endpoint, we're telling the computer that whenever a packet is received that is addressed to this port, pass it to the process managing the database mirroring session.

In the next exercise, we'll check for the existence of a database mirroring endpoint. Since one shouldn't exist, we'll then create one so we can later create a database mirror.

 TIP This exercise assumes you have multiple instances installed on your server. If you followed the previous exercises, you should have a default instance and a named instance.

Exercise 10.11: Create a Database Mirroring Endpoint

1. Open a new query window in the default instance of SSMS.

2. Enter the following query to determine if an endpoint exists:

```
--Default instance
SELECT * FROM sys.database_mirroring_endpoints
```

You shouldn't have any rows returned.

3. Enter the following query to create a database mirroring endpoint using port 5088:

```
CREATE ENDPOINT DB_Mirroring_Endpoint
    STATE = STARTED
    AS TCP ( LISTENER_PORT = 5088 )
    FOR DATABASE_MIRRORING (ROLE=PARTNER);
```

 NOTE If the CREATE ENDPOINT statement fails, double-check to ensure you're running SP1. You may remember from Chapter 1, one way you can verify that you have at least SP1 installed is by checking the four-digit release number in the first line of the Object Explorer in SSMS. For example, if it reads "SQL Server 9.0.1399," it indicates you're running the original RTM version. The number *2047* indicates SP1. SP2 was originally released as *3042*.

 TIP The default state of endpoints is stopped. If the state isn't included in the CREATE ENDPOINT statement, or if it is specified as STOPPED, then the endpoint won't be monitored and thus won't work.

4. Enter the following query to view the endpoint you created:

```
SELECT * FROM sys.database_mirroring_endpoints
```

You should have one row returned. If you scroll to see the details, you'll notice that encryption is automatically enabled on database mirroring endpoints.

5. Open a new query window from the named instance in SSMS.

   a. If the named instance is not available, right-click the default instance and select Connect. In the Connect To Server dialog box, select the named instance as the Server Name and click Connect.

   b. With the named instance selected, click the New Query button to create a new query window connected to the named instance.

6. Run the following query to see if any endpoints exist in the named instance:

```
--Default instance
SELECT * FROM sys.database_mirroring_endpoints
```

You shouldn't have any rows returned.

7. Enter the following query to create a database mirroring endpoint using port 5089. Since we are creating the database mirror on the same server (but different instances), we must use different port numbers for each instance. Otherwise, this is the same script you ran on the default instance.

```
CREATE ENDPOINT DB_Mirroring_Endpoint
    STATE = STARTED
    AS TCP ( LISTENER_PORT = 5089 )
    FOR DATABASE_MIRRORING (ROLE=PARTNER);
```

 TIP Note that the role is set as Partner. It can either be Partner or Witness. The database mirroring endpoint doesn't care whether it's a principal or a mirror; both are listed as Partner. Only the witness server is specified differently.

8. Enter the following query to view the endpoint you created:

```
SELECT * FROM sys.database_mirroring_endpoints
```

One row should be returned.

Implement Database Mirroring

With endpoints created, it's relatively easy to now implement database mirroring. As a reminder, database mirroring must use the full recovery model, so we want to check this.

Next, we make a backup of the database, restore the backup to the mirror, and then launch the wizard to configure the mirror.

In the following exercise, we'll create a database, ensure it's using the full recovery model, back it up and restore it to the mirror, and then implement database mirroring on the database.

Exercise 10.12: Implement Database Mirroring

1. If not already open, open a new query window connected to the default instance.

 TIP Make sure you pay attention to the specified instance in this exercise. We start in the default instance, and then continue in the named instance.

2. If the Chapter10 database doesn't exist in the default instance, use the following query to create a database named Chapter10 in the default instance:

```
CREATE Database Chapter10;
```

3. Use the following query to create a table named MirrorMe in the Chapter10 database:

```
USE Chapter10;
CREATE TABLE dbo.MirrorMe
(
      MirrorMeID int IDENTITY(1,1) NOT NULL,
      UserName varchar(50) NOT NULL,
      LoginTime datetime NULL,
      CONSTRAINT [PK_MirrorMe_MirrorMeID] PRIMARY KEY CLUSTERED
      (
            MirrorMeID
      )
);
```

4. Use the following script to ensure the recovery model is set to Full, and then back up the Chapter10 database and log to the C: drive.

```
USE master;
GO
ALTER DATABASE Chapter10
SET RECOVERY FULL;
GO
BACKUP DATABASE Chapter10
    TO DISK = 'C:\Chapter10_Full.bak'
    WITH FORMAT
GO
BACKUP LOG Chapter10
    TO DISK = 'C:\Chapter10_Log.bak'
    WITH FORMAT
```

5. Within the Object Explorer in SSMS, connect to the named instance by selecting it. Click the New Query button to open a new query window connected to the named instance.

6. Enter the following script to restore the Chapter10 database and log it to the named instance. Since we're restoring it to the same server (although a different instance), we need to specify a different location with the Move option. It's not necessary to restore it to the LogSecondary directory, but we can use the directory here since we created it in Exercise 10.7 earlier. (If you didn't create it earlier, create it now.)

```
RESTORE DATABASE Chapter10
    FROM DISK = 'C:\Chapter10_Full.bak'
    WITH NORECOVERY,
        MOVE 'Chapter10' TO
'C:\LogSecondary\ShipChapter10.mdf',
        MOVE 'Chapter10_Log'
TO 'C:\LogSecondary\ShipChapter10.ldf'
RESTORE LOG Chapter10
    FROM DISK = 'C:\Chapter10_Log.bak'
    WITH NORECOVERY
```

TIP The WITH NORECOVERY clause is critical. The mirrored database is not restored into a fully functional database, but is instead restored to a state that allows transaction logs to be constantly applied to it.

7. Return to the default instance within the SSMS Object Explorer. Right-click the Chapter10 database and select Properties.

8. In the Select A Page section, select Mirroring. Notice that the Principal information is already filled in with TCP://*Servername:port. The port is the same port number we configured in the endpoint.*

9. Click the Configure Security button to launch the Configure Database Mirroring Security wizard.

10. On the Configure Database Mirroring Security wizard page, click Next.

11. On the Include Witness Server page, click No so that a witness server is not included. Click Next.

12. On the Choose Servers To Configure page, verify the Mirror server instance is checked and click Next.

13. On the Principal Server Instance page, observe that the data is filled in. Click Next.

14. On the Mirror Server Instance page, select your named instance (where you created the second endpoint) from the Mirror Server Instance drop-down list, and click Connect.

 EXAM TIP It's also possible to create the mirror in a completely separate domain. If this is the case, though, we need a trust relationship between the domains. In the absence of a trust, instead of using Windows Authentication, we need to make sure SQL Server Authentication is selected in step 14, and that the SQL Server is configured for SQL Server Authentication.

15. In the Connect To Server dialog box, make sure your named server is listed in the Server Name drop-down list and click Connect. Notice that Listener Port is now listed as *5089*, and the Endpoint Name field is filled in. Your display should look similar to Figure 10-36. Click Next.

16. On the Service Accounts page, leave the spaces blank and click Next. If we were within a domain, we would use the domain accounts used to start the SQL Server services.

17. On the Complete The Wizard page, review what you've done. Your display should look similar to Figure 10-37. Click Finish.

18. On the Configuring Endpoints page, you should see "Success" for both actions—configuring the principal server and configuring the mirror server. Click Close.

Figure 10-36
The Mirror
Server Instance
page completed

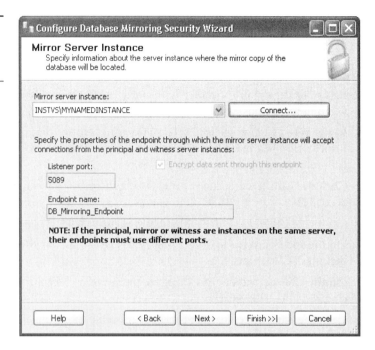

Figure 10-37
Finishing the
wizard

19. If everything was configured correctly, a Database Properties dialog box should appear showing what has been configured and asking if you want to start mirroring. It should look similar to Figure 10-38. Click Do Not Start Mirroring.

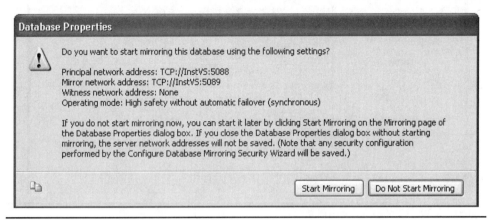

Database Properties

Do you want to start mirroring this database using the following settings?

Principal network address: TCP://InstVS:5088
Mirror network address: TCP://InstVS:5089
Witness network address: None
Operating mode: High safety without automatic failover (synchronous)

If you do not start mirroring now, you can start it later by clicking Start Mirroring on the Mirroring page of the Database Properties dialog box. If you close the Database Properties dialog box without starting mirroring, the server network addresses will not be saved. (Note that any security configuration performed by the Configure Database Mirroring Security Wizard will be saved.)

[Start Mirroring]   [Do Not Start Mirroring]

Figure 10-38   Almost ready to start mirroring

20. Since we have not configured a witness server, we need to select asynchronous mode. On the Database Properties page, select Asynchronous (High Performance).

21. In the real world, we'd be in a domain and we could put in a fully qualified domain name for the mirror server. However, it's likely you're using Windows XP as a learning platform, so instead of a fully qualified domain name, we need to put in the IP address.

   a. Press WINDOWS+R to access the Run command. Enter **CMD** to launch the command line.

   b. At the command line, type **Hostname** and press ENTER. Write down your hostname here: _____, type **IPConfig**, and press ENTER. Write down your IP Address here: _____. Type **exit** and press ENTER to exit the command line.

   c. In place of your hostname on both the Principal and the Mirror server, enter the IP address. Note that it still needs to be prefixed with *TCP://* and still needs to end with *:portnumber*. Don't delete the colon (:) right before the port number. Your display should look similar to Figure 10-39.

22. At this point, all we have to do is click the Start Mirroring button. After a moment, the databases are synchronized and the mirror is established.

Querying a Database Mirror

While a database mirror *cannot* be queried directly, a database snapshot can be created and used in conjunction with the database mirror. Users can query the snapshot for reporting purposes, and the database mirror can be maintained for high availability.

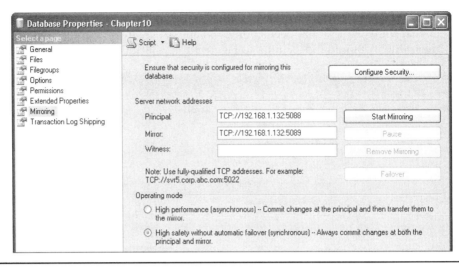

Figure 10-39   Configuring mirroring

High-Availability Comparisons

Having covered most of the high-availability methods available (we skipped clustering since it's not on the 70-431 test) it's worth taking the time to compare the different methods available for high availability. In Table 10-10, we list the four high-availability methods covered in this chapter, along with some of the requirements and features of each.

	Log Shipping	Database Mirroring	Database Snapshots
Recovery Model	Full or bulk-logged.	Full only.	Doesn't matter.
Failover	Not automatic.	Automatic if the witness server is configured. Manual if not.	No. Can be reverted (used to restore database).
Secondary Use for Queries	The standby server can be queried when logs are not being applied.	The database mirror can't be queried unless snapshots are used.	Snapshots can be queried.
Remarks	Uses the Monitor Server to observe.	Uses the Witness Server. Mirror can't be queried unless the database snapshot is also used.	Can be used with database mirroring to allow querying.
What Can Be Protected	One or more databases can be protected.	One or more databases can be protected.	One or more databases can be protected.
Difficulty to Implement	Medium	Simple	Simple.

Table 10-10   High-Availability Comparisons

Chapter Review

This chapter covered backups and restores, and high-availability strategies. We discussed the transaction log in great depth, including how it relates to the recovery models. We explored the three recovery models (full, bulk-logged, and simple), including when to use each, and how to configure a database.

We then discussed in depth the different backup types available in SQL Server 2005 (Full, Differential, and Copy-Only), and how to back up the database and the transaction log using either SSMS or T-SQL statements. We also covered different restore strategies, including exactly how to restore a database. The quickest way to restore a database if an existing database is functional is by simply using detach and attach, and we showed exactly how to do that within an exercise.

Several high-availability strategies are available with SQL Server 2005, and we covered many of the methods available. This included:

- **Log shipping** Log shipping was available in previous editions of SQL. It makes copies of the transaction log and ships them to the standby server. Failover is possible but not automatic. The standby server can be used as a read-only server for queries.

- **Database mirroring** New to SQL Server 2005, this allows databases to be mirrored on separate servers. When configured with witness servers in synchronous mode, they can be configured for automatic failover. This may be a good alternative to the high expense of clustering. If a database snapshot is configured on the mirror, it can be queried, but the mirror cannot be queried by default.

- **Database snapshots** New to SQL Server 2005, this feature is designed primarily to protect against user or administrative error. Snapshots can be queried.

Additional Study

Self-Study Exercises

Use these additional exercises to challenge yourself:

- Create a database named Ch10 and change the recovery model to simple, bulk-logged, and then full.

- Create a backup device named Ch10BackupDevice.

- Create three backups of the Ch10 database: a full, a differential, and a transaction log.

- Execute the command needed to view what is in the Ch10BackupDevice.

- Simulate a failure in the Ch10 database, and go through the steps required to restore it.

- Detach the Chapter10 database and move it to another location. Reattach it at the new location.

- Create a second instance on your SQL Server.
- Implement log shipping for a database and observe the jobs that are created.
- Create a database snapshot, query it, and then restore the original database from the database snapshot.
- Implement a database mirror.

BOL Topics

- Backup under the Full Recovery Model
- Backup under the Bulk-Logged Recovery Model
- Backup under the Simple Recovery Model
- Using Differential Backups
- Backup Devices
- Media Sets, Media Families, and Backup Sets
- Using Mirrored Backup Media Sets
- RESTORE (Transact-SQL)
- Reducing Recovery Time When Restoring a Database
- Backing Up the Master Database
- Understanding Log Shipping
- Log Shipping How-to Topics
- Changing Roles between Primary and Secondary
- Typical Uses of Database Snapshots
- Database Snapshots
- How Database Snapshots Work
- Overview of Database Mirroring
- Database Mirroring How-to Topics
- How to: Allow Database Mirroring Network Access Using Windows Authentication (Transact-SQL)

Summary of What You Need to Know

70-431

This entire chapter is devoted solely to the 70-431 test.

70-441

No objectives for the 70-441 are covered in this chapter.

70-442

No objectives for the 70-442 are covered in this chapter.

Questions

70-431

1. You are tasked with moving a SQL Server 2005 database named Hurricanes to a new database server. You need to minimize the amount of time the database is unavailable. What's the quickest way to move the database?

   A. Back up the database. Copy the backup file to the new server. Restore the database.

   B. Create a database mirror.

   C. Implement replication.

   D. Detach the database. Copy the files to the new server. Attach the files.

2. You maintain a SQL Server 2005 database that is updated with data from another database on a weekly basis using bulk imports. You want to ensure this import has minimal impact on the transaction log. What should you do?

   A. Set the database recovery model to Full.

   B. Set the database recovery model to Bulk-logged.

   C. Set the database recovery model to Simple bulk.

   D. Disable the transaction log before doing the import.

3. What command can be used to view all the backup sets on a particular backup device?

   A. Restore LabelOnly.

   B. Restore SetsOnly.

   C. Restore VerifyOnly.

   D. Restore HeaderOnly.

4. You maintain the Hurricane database that is configured to use the full recovery model. You learn that a developer has accidentally deleted some critical data in a table in the Hurricane database, and you need to restore this data without affecting the availability of any other data. What should you do?

   A. Restore the database using the last full backup.

   B. Create a database mirror, and restore the table from the mirror.

   C. Back up the transaction log. Restore the database with a different name using the last full backup and all transaction logs, and stop at the point just before the data loss. Copy the table back to the original database.

   D. Back up the transaction log. Restore the database using the last full backup and all transaction logs, and stop at the point just before the data loss.

5. You are tasked with configuring backup scripts for a SQL Server named MCITP1. Currently, backup scripts are written to a local tape drive, but in the future, they will be written to a hard drive on a new central backup server. How can you create the scripts so they will work on the new server with the least administrative effort?

   A. Configure the scripts to write to the local disk. When the new server arrives change the path of all the scripts.

   B. Configure the scripts to write to a UNC path. When the new server arrives name the server to match the UNC.

   C. Configure the scripts to write to the local tape drive. When the new server arrives, move the tape drive to the new server and change all the scripts to reflect the new location.

   D. Configure the backup jobs to write to backup devices for the local tape drive. When the new server arrives, change the devices to point to the new server.

6. You manage two SQL Server 2005 servers named MCITP1 and MCITPBackup. You have configured transaction log shipping to copy the logs from MCITP1 to MCITPBackup using the default SQL Server Agent schedule settings. You are tasked with reducing the latency between the two servers. What should you do?

   A. On MCITP1, reschedule the transaction log backup job so it occurs every two minutes. On MCITPBackup, reschedule the log shipping copy and log shipping restore jobs to occur every two minutes.

   B. On MCITPBackup, reschedule the transaction log backup job so it occurs every two minutes. On MCITP1, reschedule the log shipping copy and log shipping restore jobs to occur every two minutes.

   C. Delete the log shipping jobs and recreate them from scratch.

   D. Nothing. The default SQL Server Agent schedule already selects the minimum latency possible.

7. You are implementing transaction log shipping for a large database. What recovery model(s) can be used for transaction log shipping? (Choose all that apply.)

   A. Simple

   B. Bulk-logged

   C. Full

   D. Transaction

8. You manage a critical database named MCITP on SQL1 and are tasked with creating a database mirror on a second server named SQLMirror. Which recovery model should you choose for MCITP?

   A. Simple

   B. Bulk-logged

C. Full

D. Mirror

9. You manage a critical database named MCITP on SQL1 and are tasked with creating a database mirror on a second server named SQLMirror. MCITP is configured correctly. Which of the following two steps should you take?

    A. Back up MCITP on SQL1. Restore the backup on SQL2, and specify the NORECOVERY option.

    B. Back up MCITP on SQL1. Restore the backup on SQL2, and specify the STANDBY option.

    C. Create endpoints on all participating servers.

    D. Set the AutoMirror property of MCITP on SQL1 to True.

Answers

70-431

1. **D.** Since the database is being moved, the simplest and quickest method is to simply detach the database, copy it to the other server, and reattach it on the other server. Other methods would take a lot more steps.

2. **B.** Setting the recovery model to Bulk-logged will prevent each line item of the bulk import from being logged. The full recovery model logs everything. There is no such thing as a simple bulk recovery model, and it's not possible to disable the transaction log.

3. **D.** The Restore HeaderOnly shows all the backup sets on a backup device. The Restore LabelOnly shows a header for the entire device but no individual backup sets. The Restore VerifyOnly verifies the backup set is readable and valid, but does not list the backup sets. There is no such thing as a Restore SetsOnly command.

4. **C.** Since the goal is to restore the accidentally deleted data without affecting anything else, it's best to restore the database elsewhere and copy the data back to the original database. Just restoring the full backup doesn't account for the transaction logs. Creating a database mirror after the data loss wouldn't help. Restoring the database to a point in time just before the data loss would lose all data modifications to other tables that have occurred since the data loss.

5. **D.** The simplest answer is to use backup devices. When the new server is installed we just change the backup device, and now all scripts that use this device will use the server as the target.

6. **A.** The backup occurs on the primary server (MCITP1), and the copy and restore occur on the standby server (MCITPBackup). The schedule of all three jobs needs to be adjusted. Deleting them and starting from scratch is much more work than you want to do.

7. **B, C.** Log shipping requires the database to be in the bulk-logged or full recovery model. It will not work if in the simple recovery model. There is no such thing as a transaction recovery model.

8. **C.** For a database mirror, the recovery model must be set to Full. It will not work in the bulk-logged or simple recovery model. There is no such thing as a mirror recovery model.

9. **A, C.** Endpoints are required on all servers for database mirroring to work. The database mirror must be restored using the NORECOVERY option, not the STANDBY option. There is no AutoMirror property.

Data Access

In this chapter, you will learn about:

- Service Broker
- Web services and HTTP endpoints
- Linked servers
- Data access methods—MARS and more

> *I have traveled the length and breadth of this country and talked with the best people, and I can assure you that data processing is a fad that won't last out the year.*
>
> —*The editor in charge of business books for Prentice Hall, 1957*

So far in this book, we've talked about how to create the database, secure it, and create many different database objects. Generally, we create database objects such as stored procedures, VIEWs, and user-defined functions to limit direct access to the database tables. In this chapter, we'll cover some of the methods beyond traditional database objects used to provide access.

Service Broker, for instance, is used to provide reliable messaging services, especially when asynchronous messaging is required, while web Services offer a method for SQL Server to provide data to external web applications. Lastly, we'll cover some of the programmatic data access methods such as Multiple Active Result Sets (MARS). Both Service Broker and MARS are new to SQL Server 2005, proving once again that data processing is much more than a fad, and will continue to improve with each release.

Service Broker

New to SQL Server 2005 is a component called Service Broker. Service Broker provides reliable messaging services by guaranteeing that messages will be delivered exactly one time and delivered in the order sent. It includes fault tolerance, ensuring that messages are not lost. The message can be simply informative or can cause actions to take place within an application or service program.

Messages can be sent to applications that use a single SQL Server instance or that use different instances on different servers. They are asynchronous, meaning we don't have to have a continuous connection to send a message, and they can be queued and then sent when the infrastructure allows the messages to be sent.

Service Broker uses TCP/IP to exchange messages. It includes features to prevent unauthorized access and to encrypt the data when sent over the network.

As with many other topics in SQL Server 2005, Service Broker can fill a book on its own. The goal in this chapter is not to make you an expert on Service Broker, but to instead show you some of its capabilities. So, when a need for an asynchronous messaging capability arrives in a high-end database application, you'll remember Service Broker and can drill into the details to create a solution to meet your needs.

Service Broker Object Types

Service Broker applications have several database object types, as shown in Figure 11-1.

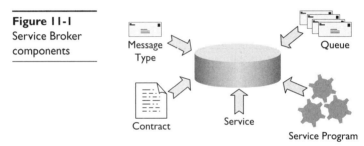

Figure 11-1
Service Broker
components

The object types are:

- **Message Type**   This is used to communicate as part of a conversation. The message type can be binary well-formed XML, or valid XML types. The message types are identical in each database that participates in a conversation. Each message forms part of a conversation between applications.

- **Contract**   A contract is an agreement between two services. It identifies the messages that will be sent between each. It also identifies whether a message can be sent (as an initiator) or received (as a target).

- **Queue**   The queue accepts messages for a specific service. Each service has one queue. Messages are placed in the queue by the Service Broker, and an application (or service program) then retrieves messages from the queue. Queues can be viewed by querying the sys.transmission_queue catalog view (SELECT * FROM sys.transmission_queue).

- **Service**   The service object represents the addressable endpoint for a service. A service is created on a queue related to a contract. It defines the name of the queue that holds the messages for the service and specifies the contract(s) that use this service.

- **Service Program or Application**   This is the program that provides the logic for the service. Service Broker can be configured to automatically activate the program when a message is in a queue, or the program can be scheduled to check for messages periodically. Service programs send response messages back to the initiator as a two-way conversation. Conversations are reliable asynchronous exchanges of messages.

Service Broker Applications

Applications use Service Broker to exchange messages as part of a conversation or dialog. Once the different components are created, two database applications can begin a conversation with Service Broker messages, as shown in Figure 11-2.

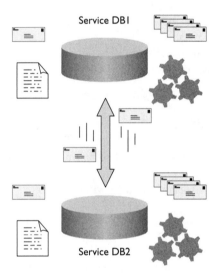

Figure 11-2
A Service Broker conversation

Service DB1

Service DB2

When discussing how to use Service Broker, two themes tend to recur. These are the benefit of asynchronous messages and guaranteed delivery. Let's define both of these phrases in the context of Service Broker.

Asynchronous Messages

If you and I were standing face to face, we could talk, and as you finish what you say, I could respond. I finish, you respond. As we talk, there wouldn't be large gaps between the time one person stops talking and another person starts talking. And, unless one of us was rude, we would not be engaged in other activities as we talked.

Asynchronous messages work like e-mail. If I send you an e-mail, I don't wait until you respond. As soon as I click Send, I can move on to other work. If either of our computers is having temporary connectivity problems, the e-mail infrastructure waits and eventually the sent message is received.

In asynchronous message processing, the application that sends the message is immediately free to work on something else without waiting for a result. When the message is delivered, the server can notify the application that the message was successfully processed.

EXAM TIP   For any application that requires asynchronous messaging, use Service Broker. This allows messages to be sent without waiting for other processes to complete.

Even though asynchronous messages may not be delivered immediately, they are still delivered and maintained in a specific order. The queue maintains the order of all the messages.

Guaranteed Delivery

Service Broker has built-in processes that ensure that messages sent from one service to another are actually sent. A conversation or dialog occurs between the two services when messages are sent.

If messages are undeliverable, they can be viewed in the sys.transmission_queue using the following statement:

```
SELECT * from sys.transmission_queue
```

Service Broker Uses

SQL Server Service Broker provides a database-oriented middleware (a communications layer that allows applications to interact across a network). This can be useful for any application that needs to perform processing asynchronously. Some typical Service Broker Uses are listed in the following bullets.

- **Asynchronous triggers**   A traditional trigger won't complete until all actions associated with the trigger complete. Sometimes we want the trigger to complete now, even if an additional action won't occur until later. The trigger can send a message to Service Broker. As soon as the message is sent by the trigger, the trigger considers the action complete. Service Broker provides guaranteed delivery, so even if the message was to be in a queue for a while; we know it would be delivered even if the remote system was currently unavailable or the communication link was down.

- **Reliable query processing**   Some applications need to guarantee a query is processed. The application can use Service Broker to combine the process of reading the message, running the query, and returning the results into a single transaction. If any part of the transaction fails, it all fails and the message can be returned to the queue to run again later.

- **Reliable data collection**   For applications that collect data from many different sources, it's possible to lose connectivity. With asynchronous message delivery, even if we occasionally lose connectivity, we still have guaranteed delivery.

- **Distributed server-side processing for client applications**   In large distributed applications such as online sales, it's possible for one of the links to break down. For example, the inventory database may be unavailable, but we may still want to accept orders. Instead of one process stopping all sales, Service Broker can be used to queue messages and process them later.

Now that we've completed an overview of Service Broker, let's see it in action. The following three exercises show you how to configure Service Broker and send and receive messages. Exercise 11.1 sets up the databases, Exercise 11.2 configures the Service Broker components, and Exercise 11.3 uses T-SQL scripts to mimic an application that would send and respond to messages.

In this first exercise, we'll create two databases that we'll use for Service Broker.

Exercise 11.1: Create Two Databases and Configure Them to Support Service Broker

1. Open a new query window in SSMS.

2. Create a database named Ch11SB1 for our first Service Broker database using the following code:

```
USE Master;
GO
CREATE DATABASE CH11SB1
WITH TRUSTWORTHY ON
```

 NOTE   For the Service Broker services to successfully talk between the databases, the TRUSTWORTHY property of the database must be set to ON. This indicates that the instance of SQL Server trusts the database and its contents and some services (such as Service Broker when sending messages between databases) are allowed to work.

3. Create a database named Ch11SB2 for our second Service Broker database using the following code:

```
USE Master;
GO
CREATE DATABASE CH11SB2
WITH TRUSTWORTHY ON
```

4. Create master database keys in both databases used for encryption. Encryption is required when starting a dialog between databases.

```
USE CH11SB1;
GO
CREATE MASTER KEY
ENCRYPTION BY PASSWORD = 'P@ssw0rd';
GO
USE CH11SB2;
GO
CREATE MASTER KEY
ENCRYPTION BY PASSWORD = 'P@ssw0rd';
```

 NOTE   If a database master key already exists, it won't be necessary to create another one. Since we've just created these databases, we know a database master key does not exist.

Our next step is to create Message Types, Contracts, Queues, and Services.

Message Types

A message type defines the name of a message and, if desired, the validation that Service Broker will perform on this message. The default validation is none, allowing the message to contain any data or be NULL. The message type in both sides of a conversation must be the same.

The syntax for the Message Type is:

```
CREATE MESSAGE TYPE message_type_name
    [ AUTHORIZATION owner_name ]
    [ VALIDATION = {   NONE
                     | EMPTY
                     | WELL_FORMED_XML
                     | VALID_XML WITH SCHEMA COLLECTION
schema_collection_name
                     } ]
[ ; ]
```

Contracts

With message types defined, a contract can be created. The contract defines the message types used in the conversation and also identifies which side of the conversation can send messages of that type. A contract is defined on both sides of the conversation and defines the initiator (the service that starts the conversation) and the target (the service that accepts conversations).

 EXAM TIP To configure messages to be sent between applications, we create a Contract. The Contract identifies the names of the messages and who they're sent by (initiator or target).

The syntax to create a contract is:

```
CREATE CONTRACT contract_name
    [ AUTHORIZATION owner_name ]
        (  {   message_type_name SENT BY { INITIATOR | TARGET | ANY }
          | [ DEFAULT ] } [ ,...n] )
[ ; ]
```

Queues

The queues store the incoming messages. The Service Broker service accepts the message and then places the message in the queue. Once a message is placed in a queue, it can be read with either a SELECT statement or a RECEIVE statement, as we'll see in Exercise 11.3. The SELECT statement performs a nondestructive read of the queue meaning that the message is not deleted when it is read. The RECEIVE statement will read it and delete it. Since Service Broker conversations are intended to be two-way conversations, queues are created in both databases.

 EXAM TIP Service Broker queues are matched to Service Broker services. For each service, a single queue is needed.

The syntax to create a queue is:

```
CREATE QUEUE <object>
  [ WITH
    [ STATUS = { ON | OFF }  [ , ] ]
    [ RETENTION = { ON | OFF } [ , ] ]
    [ ACTIVATION (
        [ STATUS = { ON | OFF } , ]
          PROCEDURE_NAME = <procedure> ,
          MAX_QUEUE_READERS = max_readers ,
          EXECUTE AS { SELF | 'user_name' | OWNER }
          ) ]
    ]
    [ ON { filegroup | [ DEFAULT ] } ]
[ ; ]
```

 EXAM TIP   To disable a Service Broker queue, set the STATUS of the queue to OFF. With the status off, the Service Broker service will not receive any messages.

Services

The Service Broker service oversees the entire conversation. It will route and deliver messages to the correct queue and enforce the contract for the conversation.

The syntax to create a service is:

```
CREATE SERVICE service_name
  [ AUTHORIZATION owner_name ]
  ON QUEUE [ schema_name. ] queue_name
  [ ( contract_name | [DEFAULT] [ ,...n ] ) ]
[ ; ]
```

In Exercise 11.2, we create the Service Broker objects on both databases that we'll use to send and receive messages.

Exercise 11.2: Create Service Broker Message Types, Contracts, Queues, and Services

1. Use the following script to create, send, and receive message types in the CH11SB1 and CH11SB2 databases. Notice that the message types are identical.

```
USE CH11SB1;
GO
CREATE MESSAGE TYPE [mySendMsg]
VALIDATION = WELL_FORMED_XML;
CREATE MESSAGE TYPE [myReceiveMsg]
VALIDATION = WELL_FORMED_XML;
GO
USE CH11SB2;
GO
CREATE MESSAGE TYPE [mySendMsg]
VALIDATION = WELL_FORMED_XML;
CREATE MESSAGE TYPE [myReceiveMsg]
VALIDATION = WELL_FORMED_XML;
```

2. The following script will create the message contract in both databases:

```
USE CH11SB1;
GO
CREATE CONTRACT myContract
(mySendMsg SENT BY INITIATOR,
myReceiveMsg SENT BY TARGET );
GO
USE CH11SB2;
CREATE CONTRACT myContract
(mySendMsg SENT BY INITIATOR,
myReceiveMsg SENT BY TARGET );
```

3. Now we create the queues. This script will create them in both databases:

```
USE CH11SB1;
GO
CREATE QUEUE FirstQueueDB1
WITH STATUS = ON;
GO
USE CH11SB2;
GO
CREATE QUEUE SecondQueueDB2
WITH STATUS = ON;
```

Notice we've specified the STATUS = ON. By default, the status is on, so this clause can be omitted. However, if we wanted to ensure the queue didn't receive any messages, we'd use the STATUS = OFF clause.

4. Lastly, we create the Service Broker services in both databases. The services need to have different names.

```
USE CH11SB1;
GO
CREATE SERVICE SB1Service1
ON QUEUE FirstQueueDB1 (myContract);
GO
USE CH11SB2;
GO
CREATE SERVICE SB2Service2
ON QUEUE SecondQueueDB2 (myContract);
```

With the Service Broker components configured, we can now start a conversation between the two databases—which is exactly what we'll do in the next exercise.

Exercise 11.3: Use Service Broker to Start a Conversation

1. Use the following script to start the dialog between the service in database 1 and the service in database 2:

```
USE CH11SB1;
GO
DECLARE @ConversationHandle uniqueidentifier;
DECLARE @XMLmsg xml;
--Start the conversation
BEGIN DIALOG CONVERSATION @ConversationHandle
    FROM SERVICE SB1Service1
```

```
         TO SERVICE 'SB2Service2'
            ON CONTRACT myContract;
SET @XMLmsg = '<MCITPSuccess/>';
SEND ON CONVERSATION @ConversationHandle
MESSAGE TYPE mySendMsg(@XMLmsg);
```

2. With the message sent, use the following script to see that the message has been received by CH11SB2:

```
USE CH11SB2;
GO
SELECT * from SecondQueueDB2;
```

Note that the SELECT statement is a nondestructive read of the queue; the message is not deleted when it is read. The RECEIVE statement will read the data off the queue and delete it at the same time.

3. Use the following script to read the message off the queue and then send a message back to the first database:

```
USE CH11SB2;
GO
DECLARE @receivedMsg XML;
DECLARE @ConversationHandle uniqueidentifier;
RECEIVE TOP(1) @receivedMsg = message_body,
               @ConversationHandle = conversation_handle
FROM SecondQueueDB2
SELECT @receivedMsg;
/*At this point the application can do something with the message.
For example, if the message is MCITPSuccess we could fire a stored
procedure named usp_Success. Of course, as an XML message we could have
much more than just a one line message. The logic is limited only by the
imagination of the database developer.*/
DECLARE @returnMsg XML;
SET @returnMsg = '<Success/>';
SEND ON CONVERSATION @ConversationHandle
      MESSAGE TYPE myReceiveMsg(@returnMsg);
```

4. View the message sent from CH11DB2 back to CH11DB1 by using the following script:

```
USE CH11SB1;
GO
SELECT * FROM FirstQueueDB1;
```

5. The service program would typically do something with the message. To read the message, use the following script:

```
USE CH11SB1;
GO
DECLARE @receivedMsg XML;
DECLARE @ConversationHandle uniqueidentifier;
RECEIVE TOP(1) @receivedMsg = message_body,
               @ConversationHandle = conversation_handle
FROM FirstQueueDB1
SELECT @receivedMsg;
```

6. To verify a message is not stuck in either of the transmission queues, use the following script:

```
USE CH11SB1;
GO
SELECT * from sys.transmission_queue
GO
USE CH11SB2;
GO
SELECT * from sys.transmission_queue
```

If a message is stuck in a queue, scroll over to the right to identify the transmission status. This usually gives a clear text explanation of the problem.

7. To close the conversation on each database, use the following script:

```
USE CH11SB1;
GO
DECLARE @ConversationHandle uniqueidentifier
SELECT TOP(1) @ConversationHandle = conversation_handle
FROM sys.conversation_endpoints;
END CONVERSATION @ConversationHandle;
GO
USE CH11SB2;
GO
DECLARE @ConversationHandle uniqueidentifier
SELECT TOP(1) @ConversationHandle = conversation_handle
FROM sys.conversation_endpoints;
END CONVERSATION @ConversationHandle
WITH CLEANUP
```

NOTE The WITH CLEANUP removes all messages from the queue and removes catalog view entries for this side of the conversation without notifying the other side.

Event Notifications

Event notifications can be used to capture events that have occurred either within a database or on a server. Both DDL statements and SQL Trace events can be captured. Once they're captured, it's relatively easy to record these events in their own table, or in their own database. Since the event notifications use Service Broker, they can be used to perform actions in response to events.

In Chapter 6, we covered triggers—in particular, DDL triggers. In Chapter 13, we'll cover SQL Trace. Event notifications provide an alternative to both DDL triggers and SQL Trace. One of the benefits of event notifications over triggers is that they run asynchronously, outside the scope of a transaction. In other words, the event notification occurs whether the transaction commits or not. Unlike SQL Trace, event notifications can be used to cause another action to occur in response to an event.

For a closer comparison of event notifications compared with DDL triggers, check out the BOL article "Understanding Event Notifications vs. Triggers." A discussion comparing event notifications with SQL Trace can be found in the BOL article, "Understanding Event Notifications vs. SQL Trace."

TIP A key to deciding whether to use triggers or event notifications is understanding that triggers run synchronously and event notifications run asynchronously. In other words, the trigger is processed within the scope of the transaction that caused it to occur. If the transaction is rolled back, the trigger is rolled back. However, event notifications do not run in the scope of the transaction, so they will still occur, even if the original transaction is rolled back. In some situations you may want to do both. For example, if you want to roll back DDL changes you can use a DDL trigger. However, if you want to ensure the event is recorded, you can also create an event notification for the DDL change.

Some common uses of event notifications by DBAs include:

- **Monitor for schema changes** Any and all DDL commands can be captured.
- **Auditing security events** Includes login, logout, impersonation, permission usage, and so on.
- **Auditing server operations** Includes system starts and stops.

Once an event is captured, SQL Server uses the Service Broker architecture to send the notification. We covered some of the basics of Service Broker (including creating message types, contracts, and sending messages between two databases) earlier in this section. SQL Server 2005 includes message types and contracts specifically designed for event notifications. The Service Broker objects that need to be created are a queue, a service, and a route.

Implementing Event Notifications

To implement an event notification, follow these steps:

1. Identify a target service used to receive event notifications.
2. Create the event notification:
   a. Create a QUEUE.
   b. Create a SERVICE on a QUEUE.
   c. Create a ROUTE for the SERVICE.
   d. Create an EVENT NOTIFICATION to a SERVICE.
3. Create a SERVICE PROGRAM to process notification events in the QUEUE.

Identifying a Target Service

The predefined message types are listed next as target services used to receive event notifications. While this is the first step in implementing an event notification, they are built-in and are accessed with the http:// target. The following bulleted items show some of the more commonly used message types, but in this chapter, we'll only use the first one—PostEventNotification.

- http://schemas.microsoft.com/SQL/Notifications/Post**EventNotification**
- http://schemas.microsoft.com/SQL/Notifications/**EventNotification**

- http://schemas.microsoft.com/SQL/Notifications/**QueryNotification**
- http://schemas.microsoft.com/SQL/ServiceBroker/**DialogTimer**
- http://schemas.microsoft.com/SQL/ServiceBroker/**EndDialog**
- http://schemas.microsoft.com/SQL/ServiceBroker/**Error**
- http://schemas.microsoft.com/SQL/ServiceBroker/**ServiceDiagnostic/Query**
- http://schemas.microsoft.com/SQL/ServiceBroker/**ServiceDiagnostic/Status**
- http://schemas.microsoft.com/SQL/ServiceBroker/**ServiceEcho/Echo**

Creating the Event Notification

Before actually creating the event notification, we need to create a queue, create a service on the queue, and then create a route for the service. With these basic Service Broker components created, we can then create the event notification associated with the service.

The basic syntax used to create an event notification is:

```
CREATE EVENT NOTIFICATION event_notification_name
ON { SERVER | DATABASE | QUEUE queue_name }
FOR { event_type | event_group } [ ,...n ]
TO SERVICE 'broker_service' ,
{ 'broker_instance_specifier' | 'current database' }
```

Notice that syntax defines a few distinct parts of the event notification:

- *Define the event notification.* Give it a name.
- *Specify the scope.* Choose either server or database.
- *Specify the event.* Choose either a specific event type or an event group.
- *Specify the service.* List the specifics for the Service Broker service created previously.

Events and Event Classes   Events can be DDL events or Trace events. Generally, any statement that starts with CREATE, ALTER, or DROP is a DDL event that can be captured. You can use the following statement to see a full listing of event types supported by event notifications:

```
SELECT * FROM
sys.event_notification_event_types
```

Trace events are more commonly used for auditing purposes and can capture a wide array of security-related events. This includes events such as a database or database object being accessed; a user, login, or role being added; logins and logouts, and much more. Other Trace events include lock and deadlock events, various warnings, errors and exceptions, and more. For a full listing, view the "Trace Events for Use with Event Notifications" Books Online article.

In addition to capturing individual events, it's also possible to capture all the events within a class or group of events.

The following list shows a few of the auditing classes that are more commonly used. They show that we can monitor overall activity on the server and many of the security events, such as when a user's logon or permissions are used.

- **Audit Server Starts and Stops Event Class**   This indicates that the SQL Server service state has been modified.
- **Audit Database Management Event Class**   This indicates that a database has been created, altered, or dropped.
- **Audit Database Principal Impersonation Event Class**   This indicates that an impersonation has occurred within the database scope.
- **Audit Broker Conversation Event Class**   This reports audit messages related to Service Broker dialog security.
- **Audit DBCC Event Class**   This indicates that a DBCC command has been issued.
- **Audit Backup/Restore Event Class**   This indicates that a backup or restore statement has been issued.

For a full listing of all auditable event classes, you can look at the Books Online article "Security Audit Event Category (SQL Server Profiler)."

Service Programs

Lastly, we'll need to create a program that can process notification events in the queue. One of the good things about a queue is that the messages remain there until retrieved. The program could be a simple stored procedure that was fired regularly by SQL Server Agent or a complex application that queries the queue based on other activity within the program.

In the following two exercises, we'll lay the groundwork for an event notification and then create one. Once it's created, we'll perform an event that will fire the event notification and then process it with a script masquerading as the service program.

In this exercise, we create a database, the components required for an event notification, and then create an event notification.

Exercise 11.4: Create a Database, a Queue, a Service, and an Event Notification

1. Open an instance of SSMS and create a new query window.

2. Create a database named EventNotifications with the following script:

```
USE Master;
GO
CREATE DATABASE EventNotifications;
```

3. Use the following script to ensure that the Service Broker is enabled for the database:

```
USE EventNotifications;
GO
ALTER DATABASE EventNotifications SET ENABLE_BROKER;
```

4. Create a table named LogEvents within the EventNotifications database with the following script:

```
CREATE TABLE LogEvents
 (
 Command NVARCHAR(1000),
 PostTime NVARCHAR(24),
 HostName NVARCHAR(100),
 LoginName NVARCHAR(100)
 )
```

5. Create a Service Broker queue with the following script:

```
CREATE QUEUE AuditQueue WITH STATUS = ON
```

6. Create the service with the following script. Notice it uses the predefined message type PostEventNotification, which will post an event to the AuditQueue.

```
CREATE SERVICE AuditService
ON QUEUE AuditQueue
([http://schemas.microsoft.com/SQL/Notifications/PostEventNotification])
```

7. Create a route on the service to define the address where the Service Broker will send the messages with the following script:

```
CREATE ROUTE rtNotify
WITH SERVICE_NAME = 'AuditService',
ADDRESS = 'LOCAL'
```

8. Create the event notification with the following script:

```
CREATE EVENT NOTIFICATION Audit_CREATE_TABLE_Events
ON DATABASE
FOR CREATE_TABLE
TO SERVICE 'AuditService','current database'
```

Leave SSMS open for the following exercises.

In the next exercise, we'll verify that there aren't any events logged, and then we'll create an event and view it in the queue. Lastly, we'll execute a script that is similar to what may be implemented in a service program.

Exercise 11.5: Invoke an Event Notification

1. Enter the following command to view the contents of the queue:

```
SELECT * FROM AuditQueue
```

Notice that there aren't any rows in our queue at this time.

2. Create a table within the database with the following statement. This will create a Create_Table event.

```
CREATE TABLE MCITP
(
Success char
)
```

3. Enter the following command to verify a row within the queue has been created:

```
SELECT * FROM AuditQueue
```

 NOTE You may remember from earlier in the chapter that the SELECT statement is a nondestructive read of the queue; the message is not deleted when it is read. The RECEIVE statement will read the data off the queue and delete it at the same time.

4. The message body is what we're really interested in and it's in XML format. Use this command to read it:

```
SELECT CAST(message_body AS xml) FROM AuditQueue
```

When you click the XML display, you should see something similar to the following XML document:

```
<EVENT_INSTANCE>
  <EventType>CREATE_TABLE</EventType>
  <PostTime>2008-04-15T14:22:31.703</PostTime>
  <SPID>51</SPID>
  <ServerName>DARRIL</ServerName>
  <LoginName>DARRIL\DarrilGibson</LoginName>
  <UserName>dbo</UserName>
  <DatabaseName>EventNotifications</DatabaseName>
  <SchemaName>dbo</SchemaName>
  <ObjectName>MCITP</ObjectName>
  <ObjectType>TABLE</ObjectType>
  <TSQLCommand>
    <SetOptions ANSI_NULLS="ON" ANSI_NULL_DEFAULT="ON" ANSI_PADDING="ON"
QUOTED_IDENTIFIER="ON" ENCRYPTED="FALSE" />
    <CommandText>CREATE TABLE MCITP
(
Success char
)</CommandText>
  </TSQLCommand>
</EVENT_INSTANCE>
```

Notice that the command is contained within the CommandText node. Later in this exercise, we'll extract the CommandText data using the query command.

5. Use the following script to extract the data out of the queue and input it into the LogEvents table:

```
--Declare variables to pull data from queue
DECLARE @messageTypeName NVARCHAR(256), @messageBody XML ;
--Pull data from queue
RECEIVE TOP(1)
    @messageTypeName = message_type_name,
    @messageBody = CAST(message_body AS xml)
  FROM AuditQueue;
IF @@ROWCOUNT = 0        --Nothing in queue
    RETURN              --Exit
--Declare variables to INSERT data into LogEvents table
DECLARE @cmd NVARCHAR(1000), @posttime NVARCHAR(24), @spid NVARCHAR(6)
```

```
DECLARE @hostname NVARCHAR(100), @loginname NVARCHAR(100)
--Populate variables
SET @cmd = CONVERT(NVARCHAR(100),
     @messagebody.query('data(//TSQLCommand//CommandText)'))
SET @posttime =
CONVERT(NVARCHAR(24),@messagebody.query('data(//PostTime)'))
SET @spid = CONVERT(NVARCHAR(6),@messagebody.query('data(//SPID)'))
SET @hostname = HOST_NAME()
SET @loginname = SYSTEM_USER
--Insert data into LogEvents table
INSERT INTO LogEvents(Command,PostTime,HostName,LoginName)
VALUES(@cmd, @posttime, @hostname, @loginname)
```

6. To view the inserted data in the LogEvents table, use the following command:

```
SELECT * FROM LogEvents
```

Web Services and HTTP Endpoints

Web services are a broad range of technologies that allow different applications to communicate with each other. They are based on a core set of standards:

- XML provides the common syntax used to represent the data.

- Simple Object Access Protocol (SOAP) is used to exchange the data. SOAP normally travels over HTTP (or HTTPS when secure communication is required).

- Web Services Description Language (WSDL or "whiz-dull") provides a mechanism to describe the capabilities of a web service.

Web services are used heavily in Internet applications. For example, when you purchase a product online, web services are used to validate and approve your credit card. The credit card company has created a web service with a WSDL that describes the service and the specifics of what can be requested and how. Appropriate data (name, credit card number, expiration date, and so on) is formatted into an XML document and sent to the credit card company using SOAP. A response comes back either approving or rejecting the request.

Other common uses of web services include weather, shipping companies, financial companies, and much more. For example, some news sites include weather data (temperature, humidity, and forecast) on pages within their site. These news sites don't have their own weather service, but instead subscribe to a national weather service that provides the information via a web service.

A key point is that the web service makes the data available externally as long as the external developer follows the proper format of the web service. With this in mind, almost any external application can be used to access the web service. If the format of the web service is not followed exactly, data isn't shared.

The web service allows queries of a database using Internet technologies. One of the beauties of web services is that they are platform-independent. Since the data requests (and the data responses) are formatted in XML, the back-end databases can be any database that understands XML. Today, we'd be hard pressed to find a current database that doesn't understand XML.

Just as importantly, the client consuming the web service can be anything. For example, it could be a Windows-type application that is accessing the Internet and pulling the data from the web service. It can also be a web browser running on any client that is accessing the web service.

Figure 11-3 shows how an application would go through the Internet and through the firewall to SQL Server to retrieve data. The application could be initiated by a web browser accessing a third-party web application or a regular Windows application with Internet access—either way, the user has access to the Internet. The user or application issues a command activating a web method that ultimately executes a stored procedure on the SQL Server's endpoint.

Figure 11-3
Web services
accessing a SQL
Server endpoint

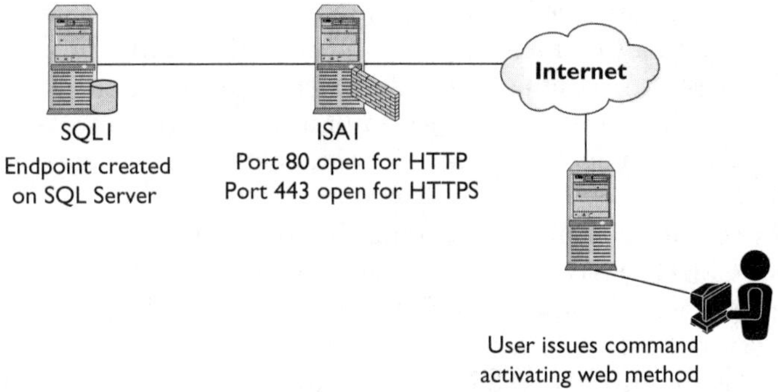

SQL1
Endpoint created
on SQL Server

ISA1
Port 80 open for HTTP
Port 443 open for HTTPS

Internet

User issues command
activating web method

EXAM TIP If you need to provide external access to your database via the Internet, the most common method is via a web service. With a web service, applications created by external developers can access the data that we choose to make available via the web service. Since a web service can accept parameters, we can also accept data via a web service.

The firewall (Microsoft's Internet Security Accelerator [ISA] in this figure) would have the necessary ports open to access the endpoint. This is typically done by creating a web publishing rule on ISA, mapping traffic from the Internet to the internal SQL Server computer.

By default, HTTP uses port 80 and HTTPS uses port 443. Different ports could be chosen if desired; the HTTP endpoint, the web service, and the firewall all need to be configured with the same port.

When the traffic reaches the SQL Server computer, the system looks at the port and recognizes that the SQL Server endpoint is configured to handle it. The traffic is passed to the endpoint. If the web method is executing a stored procedure, the stored procedure then executes on SQL, and the results are sent back to the Internet and the application that issued the command.

As we can see, the web services aren't created in the database. Instead, the web service is created by the developer in one of the .NET programming languages such as C# or VB. With this in mind, it's beyond the scope of the MCITP test objectives to actually create a web service, but you should understand when an application can benefit from the creation of such.

On the other hand, the HTTP endpoint is created within SQL Server and you should know how to create and configure the HTTP endpoints. We'll do that in the next section.

HTTP Endpoints

An HTTP endpoint is simply a designed port where SQL Server listens for specific traffic. HTTP endpoints include one or more web methods that are queried by a web service. With an endpoint created, SQL Server will then listen for queries using the specified web method. As long as the web method is formatted accurately, SQL Server will respond with the data specified in the web method.

Typically, a web method is associated with a stored procedure that executes within a database, retrieves the results, and then sends the results back to the requestor. While a web method could be a function or a stored procedure, stored procedures are much more common due to the flexibility and better performance of a stored procedure over functions.

We created a database mirroring endpoint in Chapter 10. An HTTP endpoint uses the same CREATE ENDPOINT command, except it specifies it as an HTTP endpoint. Just as the database mirroring endpoint identifies a port, the HTTP endpoint identifies a port. However, the default port for HTTP is 80, so if the port isn't identified port 80 is used. If SSL is specified, HTTPS is assumed and the default port is 443.

 EXAM TIP If you need to ensure data is securely transmitted over the Internet, specify SSL in the HTTP endpoint definition. SSL will encrypt the data during transmission over the Internet. (This does require extra steps by the system administrator to configure the IIS web server, but our responsibility is in the configuration of the HTTP endpoint only.)

The partial syntax to create an HTTP endpoint follows:

```
CREATE ENDPOINT endPointName
STATE = { STARTED | STOPPED | DISABLED }
AS HTTP (
  PATH = 'url'
      , AUTHENTICATION =( { BASIC | DIGEST | INTEGRATED | NTLM | KERBEROS }
[ ,...n ] ),
   PORTS = ( { CLEAR | SSL} [ ,... n ] )
  [ SITE = {'*' | '+' | 'webSite' },]
  [, CLEAR_PORT = clearPort ]
  [, SSL_PORT = SSLPort ]   )
FOR SOAP(
  [ { WEBMETHOD [ 'namespace' .] 'method_alias'
    (   NAME = 'database.owner.name'
      [ , SCHEMA = { NONE | STANDARD | DEFAULT } ]
      [ , FORMAT = { ALL RESULTS | ROWSETS_ONLY } ]    )
  }
    [ , WSDL = { NONE | DEFAULT | 'sp_name' } ]
  [ , DATABASE = { 'database name' | DEFAULT }
  [ , NAMESPACE = { 'namespace' | DEFAULT } ] )
```

State

The state identifies whether the endpoint will respond to connections when created. The default is STOPPED.

 EXAM TIP If the state is not specified when the endpoint is created, it will default to STOPPED. The status of the endpoint can be checked using SQL Server Surface Area Configuration Tool | Surface Area Configuration For Features | Native XML Web Services.

AS HTTP

The AS HTTP section identifies the path, authentication method, and ports.

The path identifies the path under the root and starts with a forward slash (/). For example, if we were creating an endpoint with a path of /GetProducts available on a server named mcitpsuccess.com, the full path would be:

`http://mcitpsuccess.com/GetProducts`.

Authentication choices are outlined in Table 11-1.

Authentication Method	Comments
Basic	Authentication is sent in clear text. This is typically used with SSL to encrypt the authentication on the Internet.
Digest	Introduced in Windows 2000 but rarely used.
NTLM	Used for backward compatibility for Windows 95, Windows 98, and NT 4.0 clients.
Kerberos	Used as an Internet authentication mechanism supported in Widows 2000 and later. When Kerberos is used, the instance of SQL Server must associate a service principal name (SPN) with the account used to start SQL Server.
Integrated	Used in a domain environment. With Integrated authentication, the endpoint can respond with either NTLM or Kerberos, depending on the client. When Kerberos is used, the instance of SQL Server must associate a service principal name (SPN) with the account used to start SQL Server.

Table 11-1 Endpoint Authentication Methods

The default port for HTTP is 80 and for HTTPS, 443. Setting the port to CLEAR sets the port to use HTTP and port 80. Setting the port to SSL uses HTTPS and sets it to 443. If the default ports are being used, different ports can be set with the CLEAR_PORT argument and the SSL_PORT argument.

For SOAP

In the For SOAP section, we identify the web methods, the WSDL, and the database.

Web methods are used to identify stored procedures that can be called via the endpoint. It's possible to include multiple web methods. Stored procedures are identified with a three-part name: (*databasename.owner.storedprocedure*).

The WSDL allows the web service consumer to understand what is being provided by the endpoint. While the default WSDL has a lot of extras, it will suffice for many purposes.

Reserving an HTTP Namespace

In some situations, it's necessary or desirable to reserve an HTTP namespace when creating endpoints for web service applications. Reserving a namespace guarantees that other applications cannot bind to it. This gives an application sole ownership of the namespace.

Reserving an HTTP namespace is recommended by Microsoft when a web service application is running under a non-administrative account or if SQL Server is running under the local system account. The requirement to reserve the HTTP namespace is typically given as part of the web service application technical requirements.

The namespace can be reserved when creating the HTTP endpoint or later with the sp_reserve_http_namespace.

Permissions

The last step is to grant connect permissions to the endpoint to any logins that will need to access it. Connect permission can be granted to SQL Server logins, Windows logins, or logins created from a certificate.

Connect permission to the endpoint can only be done through T-SQL statements. The basic syntax is:

```
GRANT connect ON ENDPOINT::endPointName TO login;
```

Additionally, execute permissions for the stored procedure(s) identified in the web method need to be granted.

Imagine that AdventureWorks decides to make their current product listing available to resellers. In the following exercise, we'll accomplish that by creating a stored procedure, then making the stored procedure accessible via an HTTP endpoint.

Exercise 11.6: Create the HTTP Endpoint

1. Open a new query window in SSMS.

2. Create a stored procedure that we'll use within the endpoint with this script:

```
USE AdventureWorks;
GO
CREATE PROCEDURE dbo.GetProductList
AS
BEGIN
    SELECT ProductID, Name, ProductNumber, ListPrice
        FROM Production.Product
        WHERE ListPrice > 0
END
```

You can test your stored procedure with:

```
EXEC dbo.GetProductList
```

3. With the stored procedure in place, we can now create the HTTP endpoint. Use the following script:

```
CREATE ENDPOINT AW_Products
    STATE = Started
AS HTTP
    (
        PATH = '/Products',
        AUTHENTICATION = (INTEGRATED),
        PORTS = (CLEAR),
        SITE = '*'
    )
FOR SOAP
    (
        WEBMETHOD 'GetProductList'
            (NAME = 'AdventureWorks.dbo.GetProductList'),
        WSDL = DEFAULT,
        DATABASE = 'AdventureWorks',
        NAMESPACE = DEFAULT
    )
```

CAUTION   If you get an error when you try to create the endpoint that includes "One or more of the ports specified in the CREATE ENDPOINT statement may be bound to another process," something else, such as IIS, is already using port 80 on your system. You can shut down IIS or you can modify the following line:

```
PORTS = ( CLEAR ),
```

To become:

```
PORTS = ( CLEAR ), CLEAR_PORT = 8080
```

This simply uses a different port (in this case 8080) instead of the default port of 80 for the HTTP endpoint.

4. Now you can view the WSDL on your server. Enter the following path into your web browser:

```
http://localhost/products?WSDL
```

Localhost works for your local computer. In a production environment, we would need a server name that was available on the Internet, or an intranet.

5. Launch the SQL Server Surface Area Configuration tool. Click Surface Area Configuration For Features. Select the Native XML Web Services entry. Your display should look similar to Figure 11-4.

6. At this point, our job is done. We've created the stored procedure and the endpoint. However, what makes this valuable is the ability of the consumer of the web service to be able to access it.

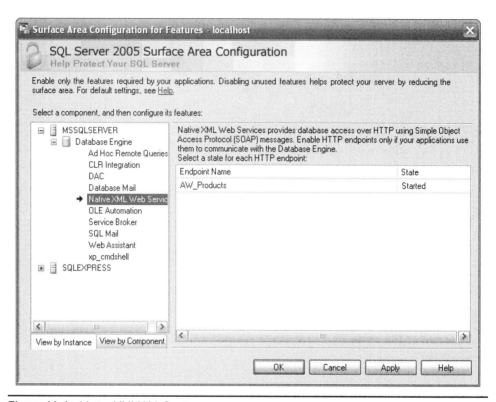

Figure 11-4   Native XML Web Services

To demonstrate consuming a web service, I created a small C# program within Visual Studio. After registering the web service in Visual Studio, I was able to add about four lines of code to populate the data grid from the web service. It looks like Figure 11-5.

 NOTE   If you have Visual Studio and want to recreate this C# Windows application, the following are the four lines added to the new project after adding a button and a data grid VIEW named dataGridView1:

```
 Add this to the beginning of the class
using System.Net;
/*Add these lines to the button click event
procedure*/localhost.AW_Products Products = new localhost.AW_Products();
Products.Credentials = CredentialCache.DefaultCredentials;
dataGridView1.DataSource = (Products.GetProductList()[0] as _
            DataSet).Tables[0];
```

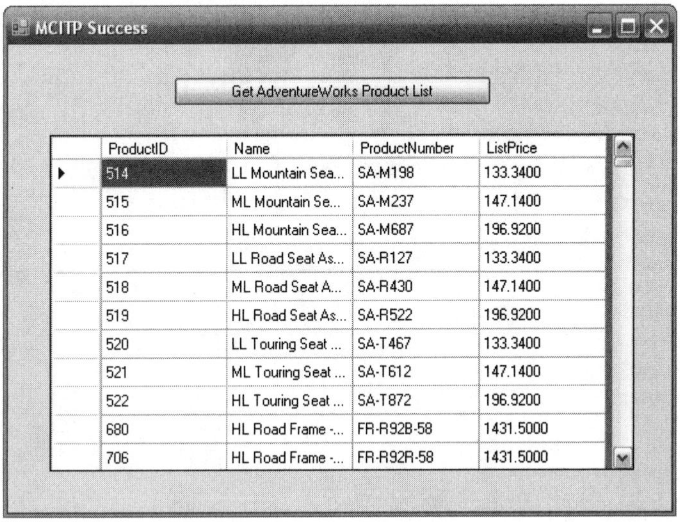

Figure 11-5   Consuming a web service

Linked Servers

Linked servers are created when we need to use distributed queries. A distributed query simply means that we want to execute queries on more than one server. The remote server can be another SQL Server, an Access database, an Oracle server, or any other server as long as we have an OLE DB provider as the remote database.

In Figure 11-6, we can see how this works once it's configured. The client application still submits the queries to the front-end SQL Server. However, any distributed queries are forwarded to the remote servers holding the remote databases. Microsoft offers many OLE DB providers, but often a vendor will update their DLL and make it available for download. In other words, if you don't see the OLE DB provider you need included in SQL Server, check with the vendor to see if they have a DLL that can be downloaded.

Without a linked server, our query can be executed with OPENROWSET or OPENDATASOURCE. While that's fine for an ad hoc query, if you plan on executing the query more than a few times, you could create a linked server.

A linked server allows us to reference database objects in a remote server using the four-part name *server.database.schema.object*.

A linked server can be created in two steps. First, we create the linked server, and next we configure the logins.

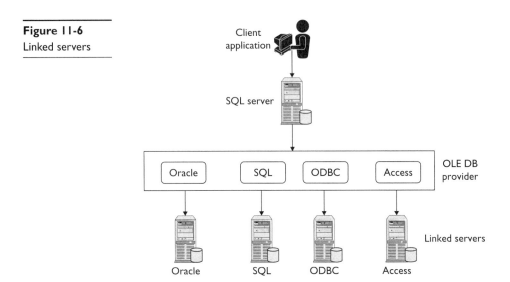

Figure 11-6
Linked servers

Creating a Linked Server

It's very important to understand where we are creating the linked server. Take a look at Figure 11-7. We configure the linked server on MSSQL1. Another way of saying this is that we add Oracle1 as a linked server to MSSQL1.

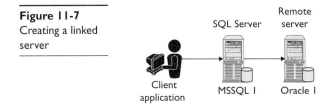

Figure 11-7
Creating a linked
server

EXAM TIP Make sure you understand the perspective of where the linked server is created. We add the definition of the linked server to the local server, not the other way around. Often we don't have administrative control of the remote server, so we can't create anything on the remote server.

You can use two possible methods when you want to create a linked server:

- Use the stored procedure sp_addlinkedserver
- Use the GUI in SSMS

sp_addlinkedserver

The syntax for the system stored procedure sp_addlinkedserver is:

```
sp_addlinkedserver [ @server= ] 'server' [ , [ @srvproduct= ] 'product_name' ]
    [ , [ @provider= ] 'provider_name' ]
    [ , [ @datasrc= ] 'data_source' ]
```

```
[ , [ @location= ] 'location' ]
[ , [ @provstr= ] 'provider_string' ]
[ , [ @catalog= ] 'catalog' ]
```

Table 11-2 shows the parameters available with sp_addlinkedserver.

Parameter	Comments
@Server	Name of linked server. Network or DNS hostname if SQL Server.
@srvproduct	OLE DB data source.
@provider	OLE DB provider friendly name.
@datasrc	Data source (different for different OLE DB providers).
@location	Location of database (different for different OLE DB providers).
@provstr	Connection string required by some OLE DB providers (different for different OLE DB providers).
@catalog	Catalog (default database in SQL) to use when connecting (different for different OLE DB providers).

Table 11-2   sp_addlinkedserver Parameters

What's not apparent is that many of the parameters are used differently, or not used at all, depending on what provider is being used. For example, an Access provider will use the data source parameter to identify the name of the database, including the path. For another SQL Server, the data source parameter will hold the instance name, or may even be blank for the default instance.

Adding another SQL Server as a linked server can be accomplished quite easily. The following script shows that only the server name and the product name are needed to add another SQL Server as a linked server:

```
USE master;
GO
EXEC sp_addlinkedserver
    'MCITP2',
    'SQL Server'
GO
```

Adding a Linked Server via the GUI

If you open SSMS and look at Server Objects\Linked Servers\Providers, you can see that Microsoft offers 19 providers out of the box (see Figure 11-8).

The primary provider for other SQL Server 2005 servers is the SQLNCLI provider. It will use this as the native client OLE DB provider if no provider name is specified, or if SQL Server is specified as the product name.

To create a linked server in SSMS, simply right-click Linked Servers and select New Linked Server. Type in the name of the linked server and select the provider. Depending on which provider you select, different parameters will be available or dimmed.

In the following exercise we'll create a linked server within SSMS.

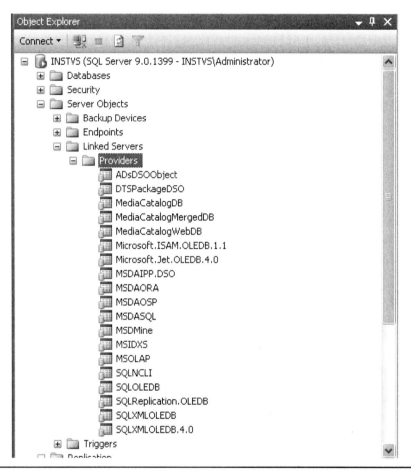

Figure 11-8 Providers within SQL Server

Exercise 11.7: Create a Linked Server via SSMS

1. Open SSMS.

2. Double-click Server Objects to open this container.

3. Double-click Linked Servers to open this container.

4. Right-click Linked Servers and select New Linked Server.

5. In the New Linked Server dialog box, enter **MCITP1** as the Linked Server.

6. For the Server type, select SQL Server. Click OK.

Configuring Logins for a Linked Server

For the distributed queries to work, access to the different servers must be granted via SQL Server logins. As discussed in Chapter 8, SQL Server logins allow access to SQL Server the same way a system login (username and password) allows access to a domain or individual computer. If SQL is configured to use Windows Authentication, the Windows account can be added to SQL Server, granting login access to the server.

Let's say Sally is a user in the MCITPSuccess.com domain. She has a user account and has logged into the domain. Next, we can add Sally's domain user account as a login to any servers she needs to access. When Sally accesses the SQL Server, instead of being challenged and having to enter her credentials again, SQL Server verifies her Windows login exists in the sysLogins table, and she is granted access.

Impersonation and Delegation

Authentication can be simplified with linked servers. Consider this scenario. Sally connects to SQL on MCITP1 and executes a query on a linked SQL server named LinkedSQL2. It's actually MCITP1 that's running the query on LinkedSQL2, but we can configure it so Sally's credentials are used.

This is referred to as delegation or impersonation.

TIP Though *delegation* and *impersonation* are often spoken of as different concepts, they actually refer to the same process. The only thing that is different is the perspective. If we're talking about the server, it impersonates the user. If we're talking about the client or the user, the user delegates credentials to the server.

MCITP1 is impersonating Sally for the query running on LinkedSQL2. Said another way, Sally delegates her account credentials to MCITP1 to run the query on LinkedSQL2.

After configuring a linked server, we still must ensure several conditions are met in order for impersonation to work correctly. First, all players (the client and both servers) must be using TCP/IP.

Additional requirements are listed next.

The Client:

- Must have permissions on both servers (MCITP1 and LinkedSQL2).

- The following Active Directory property must be *unchecked* for the user account: Account Is Sensitive And Cannot Be Delegated. (You can see this in Figure 11-9.)

Both Servers:

- Must have a service principal name (SPN) registered by the domain administrator.

NOTE A service principal name (SPN) is the name a client uses to uniquely identify an instance of a service. When SQL Server is running under the local system account, setup automatically registers the SPN. In a domain, the Kerberos authentication service can use an SPN to authenticate a service; however, when SQL Server is running under a domain account, the SPN is not registered automatically. This must be done by a domain administrator using the SQL Server Active Directory Helper (MSSQLServerADHelper) in order for linked servers to work correctly.

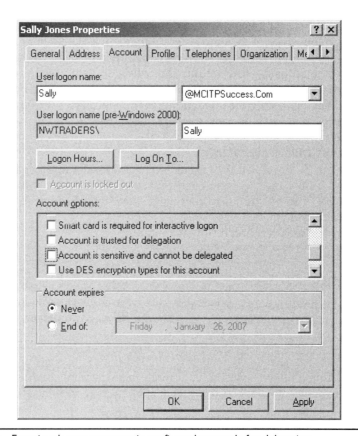

Figure 11-9 Ensuring the user account is configured correctly for delegation

On MCITP1:

- Linked server logins must be configured for self-mapping. This can be done with sp_addlinkedsrvlogin.

- The SQL Server Service must have the account option labeled Account Is Trusted For Delegation checked. This is the account we configured in Chapter 1. You can see this in Figure 11-10.

Mapped Logins

Impersonation and delegation is the preferred method of accessing linked servers. However, sometimes this isn't possible. If you're unable to configure the SQL Server service account so it's trusted for delegation, or unable to configure the user account so it can be delegated, or if impersonation simply isn't desired, you'll need to configure mapped logins.

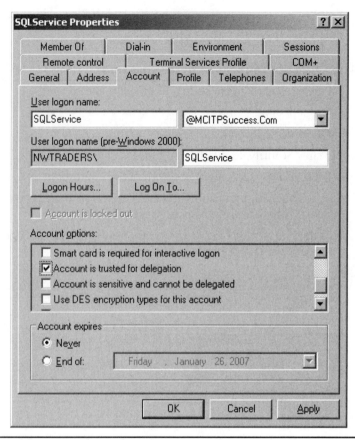

Figure 11-10 Ensuring the SQL Server service account (named SQLService) is configured correctly

A mapped login sounds fancier than it is. All you are doing is specifying the login account and password that will be used when the linked server is used.

The system stored procedure sp_addlinkedsrvlogin can be used to create the mapped login. When the distributed query is executed, the username and password created as a mapped login is sent to the linked server to execute the query.

Mapped logins can also be created via SSMS. Table 11-3 shows how we can map a local SQL Server login named DBA to the RemoteDBA account on the linked server.

MCITP1 Local Login	MCITP2 Remote User	Remote Password
DBA	RemoteDBA	P@ssw0rd

Table 11-3 Mapping Logins

In the next exercise, we'll create this mapped login and also identify an account to be used if the local DBA account isn't being used.

Exercise 11.8: Create Mapped Logins in SSMS

Watch video 11-8 to see how to create and configure a linked server.

1. If necessary, open SSMS.

2. Create a SQL Server login named DBA:

   a. Double-click Security. Right-click Logins and select New Login.

   b. In the Login–New page, enter **DBA** as the Login name.

   c. Select SQL Server authentication and enter a password of **P@ssw0rd** in both the Password and Confirm Password boxes.

   d. Uncheck the box labeled User Must Change Password At Next Login. Click OK.

Figure 11-11   Mapping logins

3. Access the security properties of the linked server you created earlier:

   a. Double-click Server Objects to open the container.

   b. Double-click Linked Servers to open the container.

   c. Right-click the MCITP1 linked server you created earlier and select Properties.

   d. In the Select A Page section, choose Security.

4. Click Add to add a mapped login.

5. In the Local Login section, select DBA.

6. In the Remote User section, enter **RemoteDBA**. In the Remote Password, enter **P@ssw0rd**.

7. In the bottom section labeled For A Login Not Defined In The List Above, Connections Will:, select Be Made Using This Security Context.

8. Enter **RemoteGuest** in the Remote Login box and **P@ssw0rd** in the With Password box. You should now have a display similar to Figure 11-11. Click OK.

OPENQUERY

Once a linked server is created, the OPENQUERY statement can be used to execute pass-through queries on the linked server.

OPENQUERY returns a result set so it can be referenced in the FROM clause of a query as if it were a table name. It can also be referenced as a table in an INSERT, UPDATE, or DELETE statement.

The use of OPENQUERY is limited to linked servers. It will not function if a linked server has not been created.

OPENDATASOURCE and OPENROWSET

It's also worth mentioning that if we choose not to create a linked server, we can use the OPENDATASOURCE or OPENROWSET commands. This will make queries much more complex, but if you're only executing a query once or twice, it may be easier than going through the process of creating and deleting a linked server.

The syntax for OPENDATASOURCE is listed next:

```
OPENDATASOURCE ( provider_name, init_string )
```

init_string is the connection string and can be quite complex, depending on the provider used.

The following query shows how to use OPENROWSET in a query. The query is pulling data from an Access database.

```
SELECT CustomerID, CompanyName
   FROM OPENROWSET('Microsoft.Jet.OLEDB.4.0',
      'C:\Program Files\Microsoft Office\OFFICE11\SAMPLES\Northwind.mdb';
      'admin';'',Customers)
```

In contrast, look at a query that is pulling data from a linked server (named MCITP2) using the four-part name. It is much simpler.

```
SELECT * from MCITP2.AdventureWorks.Sales.SalesOrderHeader
```

Data Access Methods

While this book has focused on accessing SQL Server directly and doing most everything within SQL Server Management Studio (SSMS), that's not what applications do. Instead, applications provide their own user interface and interact with the database behind the scenes. The actual method they use to interact with the database depends on several factors.

Within Microsoft's world, we use one of the .NET Framework applications such as C# .NET or Visual Basic .NET. Many more .NET development languages can be used, but the point is to use one of the languages that employ the .NET Framework.

The two data access providers used with the current .NET Framework for SQL Server 2005 are SQLNCLI and ADO .NET 2.0. These use the System.Data.sqlClient namespace to connect to SQL Server. They have been specifically designed to access the new features of SQL Server 2005. Some of the specific functionality supported by each includes:

- Support for user-defined data types
- Support for the new XML data type
- Support for new large value types, such as varchar(max) and varbinary(max)
- Support for snapshot transaction isolation level
- Support for Multiple Active Result Sets (MARS)
- Support for asynchronous operations

Within the data access providers, we have different data access methods we can use to interact with the data. For the 70-442 test, you should know these and when to use one over another. The three data access methods you can expect to be tested on are:

- Multiple Active Result Sets (MARS)
- DataSets
- DataReaders

The following sections explain each and when to use them.

Multiple Active Result Sets (MARS)

A new feature available with SQL Server 2005 is the ability to simultaneously maintain the results of multiple queries. Previously, as soon as we retrieved a new result set, the previous result set would be lost. Now, not only can we maintain multiple result sets, but we can also easily switch from one to another without conflicts.

Take a look at Figure 11-12. This shows how an application could access multiple results sets simultaneously without Multiple Active Result Sets (MARS). Each time the application needed a new result set, the system would open a new connection and create a new execution context within SQL Server.

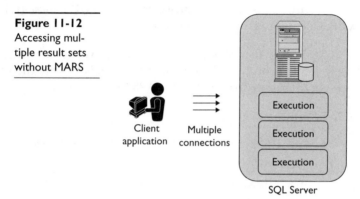

Figure 11-12
Accessing multiple result sets without MARS

While this gives the illusion of multiple result sets, it has an inherent problem if any of the same data is being accessed. Each connection creates its own locks on the data it is accessing and would prevent other connections from accessing the same data.

Now let's see how it would work with MARS. Take a look at Figure 11-13. This shows how multiple execution contexts are all contained within a single connection. We can easily switch between different result sets without worrying about locks, because the one connection holds any locks on the data.

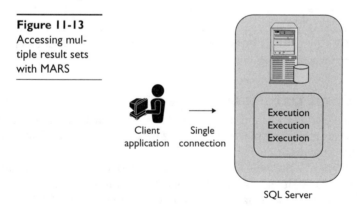

Figure 11-13
Accessing multiple result sets with MARS

 EXAM TIP Any time you want to minimize the number of connections to a database and will be issuing multiple queries against the database, use Multiple Active Result Sets (MARS).

The possible commands within a Multiple Active Result Set include stored procedures, SELECT, INSERT, UPDATE, DELETE, FETCH, and RECEIVE.

The data access client libraries that support MARS are:

- **ADO .NET 2.0 SqlClient**
- **SQL Native Client provider**   This includes SQL Native Client for Open Database Connectivity (ODBC), SQL Native Client for OLE Database (OLE DB), and SQL Native Client for ActiveX Data Objects (ADO).

It's relatively easy to enable MARS for any connection. While the syntax of the full connection string for each of the different client libraries is beyond the scope of this book, the following list shows how to enable MARS for a connection.

- ADO.NET 2.0 SqlClient

```
multipleActiveResultSets = true | false (connection string setting)
```

- SQL Native Client ODBC
  Set SQLSetConnectAttr with:

```
SQL_COPT_SS_MARS_ENABLED = SQL_MARS_ENABLED_YES |
SQL_MARS_ENABLED_NO
```

- SQL Native Client OLE-DB

```
SSPROP_INIT_MARSCONNECTION = VARIANT_TRUE | VARIANT_FALSE (data source
initialization property)
```

- SQL Native Client ADO

```
Mars_Connection = true | false (connection string setting)
```

 TIP   By default, MARS functionality is not enabled. It must be enabled in the connection string.

DataSets and DataReaders

Another choice you'll face when designing data access is whether to use a DataSet or a DataReader. Both have their places, but before we can really dig into which one to use, we need to describe them.

A DataSet is an in-memory (cached) representation of the data. DataSets are specific to .NET and use a DataAdapter to fill the DataSet after connecting to the database. Multiple data tables can be added to a DataSet and the relations between the different data tables can mimic the relations in the actual database.

DataSets use a disconnected architecture. In other words, they connect to the database, fill the DataSet with the requested data and then disconnect from the database. Because of this, it's possible for the cached data to become out-of-date, depending on how often the data in the database is updated and how long we keep the data in cache.

Data within the DataSet can be queried and updated by an application and when desired, the DataAdapter can reconnect to the database and update data that has been modified within the DataSet.

EXAM TIP   If the data will be repeatedly queried, and especially if the data only rarely changes, use a DataSet. This creates an in-memory (cached) representation of the data and it limits round trips to the database from your application.

In contrast, DataReaders are much simpler. A DataReader is a read-only representation of the data. Data retrieved through the DataReader is forward-only and once the data has been read, the DataReader is closed. The only way to access the data again is by opening another DataReader. DataReaders use a connected architecture. In other words, they connect and stay connected to the database until the DataReader has reached the end of the data and the DataReader has been closed. DataReaders are faster than DataSets.

 EXAM TIP   If data will not be modified and speed is the most important factor when designing your data access strategy, use a DataReader. DataReaders are quicker than DataSets.

Table 11-4 outlines the differences between DataSets and DataReaders.

DataSet	DataReader
Disconnected architecture. Uses in-memory representation of data (cached).	Connected architecture. Forward-only reads.
Takes up memory resources	Does not consume much memory, but keeps connection open.
Can include multiple related tables.	Returns a single result set. Has no concept of relationships.
Slower than a DataReader.	Fast.
Read-write capabilities.	Read-only.

Table 11-4   Comparison of DataSets and DataReaders

Chapter Review

In this chapter, we covered many different data-access methods. These included:

- **Service Broker**   Service Broker is used when we need an asynchronous messaging system that provides guaranteed delivery of messages. By configuring Service Broker in two different databases, we can create a conversation or a dialog between the databases. Service Broker includes messages, queues, contracts, services, and an application or service program. Messages are added to a service with the CREATE CONTRACT command, and are sent with the BEGIN DIALOG CONVERSATION command.

- **Web services and HTTP endpoints** Web services is a well-established technology that makes data available to applications over the Internet. By creating HTTP endpoints on SQL Server, we allow SQL Server to answer web services. Endpoints are created using the CREATE Endpoint command.

- **Linked servers** When your data is scaled out to multiple servers, very often you will be using distributed queries. Linked servers allow us to optimize distributed queries. Further, if configured correctly we can use impersonation and delegation to manage some rudimentary security.

- **Data access methods** Multiple Active Result Sets (MARS), DataSets, and DataReaders all provide their own specific strengths when connecting to a database. We learned that MARS can help us limit connections when we need to query the database multiple times. DataSets provide a cached representation of data that can be read or written. They are useful at reducing round trips to the database, especially if the data changes infrequently. DataReaders are fast read-only representations of the data that take up little memory resources.

Additional Study

Self-Study Exercises

- Configure Service Broker in two different databases.

- Add the SalesNotification message to each service.

- Send messages between the two databases.

- Configure an event notification to notify you when SQL Server is stopped, started, or paused. Use the AUDIT_SERVER_OPERATION_EVENT.

- Create an HTTP endpoint that will be started immediately.

- Configure authentication for the endpoint to support NT 4.0 and Windows XP clients.

- Configure a linked server on your test system for an external SQL Server named MCITP2.

BOL Topics

- Service Broker Programming
- CREATE QUEUE (Transact-SQL)
- CREATE CONTRACT (Transact-SQL)
- CREATE SERVICE (Transact-SQL)
- CREATE MESSAGE TYPE (Transact-SQL)
- CREATE ENDPOINT (Transact-SQL)
- Endpoint Authentication Types
- GRANT Endpoint Permissions (Transact-SQL)

- Configuring Linked Servers for Delegation
- Using Multiple Active Result Sets (MARS)

Summary of What You Need to Know

70-431

When preparing for the 70-431 test, make sure you understand these topics:

- Service Broker
- Event notifications
- Web services
- HTTP endpoints
- Linked servers

70-441

When preparing for the 70-441 test, you should focus on the Service Broker and Web Services sections in this chapter.

70-442

When preparing for the 70-442 test, you only need to focus on parts of this chapter. The Data Access Methods section is the most important. Make sure you understand the decision points between Multiple Access Result Sets (MARS), DataSets, and DataReaders. You should also understand when to use web services and HTTP endpoints.

Questions

70-431

1. You maintain a web-based application that connects to a SQL Server 2005 database named Stocks. A Service Broker connection has been created between Stocks and another database named StockPurchases. You are tasked with adding two new message types to the service, so you create messages named StockInfo and StockPurchase in each of the databases. How do you add the messages to the service?

   A. Create the services by using the command CREATE SERVICE on each database.

   B. Create a contract by using the command CREATE CONTRACT.

   C. Create a conversation between the databases by using the command BEGIN DIALOG.

   D. Enable the messages by using the command ENABLE MESSAGE.

2. You manage a SQL Server 2005 server that is using Service Broker to manage data requests between databases. You need to modify objects for an existing

server, but want to ensure that no messages can be received by the service until the changes are complete. What should you do?

A. Set the queue STATUS to OFF. Set it to ON when the service is ready.

B. Set the queue STATUS to DISABLED. Set it to ENABLED when the service is ready.

C. Disable Service Broker on each server by entering the command SET SERVICE _ BROKER_ENABLED = FALSE.

D. Accept the defaults when created. When the service is restarted, the changes will take effect.

3. What is the default state of an HTTP endpoint when created?

A. Enabled

B. Disabled

C. Stopped

D. Running

4. You manage a SQL Server named MCITP1. You are tasked with creating a stored procedure and HTTP endpoint that will be used to provide parts listings to external customers. You create a stored procedure named usp_GetParts to retrieve the data in the Parts database. To create the endpoint, you use the following code:

```
CREATE ENDPOINT Parts_PartsListing
    AS HTTP (PATH = '/PartsListing',
    AUTHENTICATION = (INTEGRATED),
    PORTS = (CLEAR),
    SITE = ' MCITP1')
FOR SOAP (WEBMETHOD 'GetPartsListing'
    (NAME='Parts.dbo.usp_GetParts'),
    BATCHES = DISABLED,
    WSDL = DEFAULT,
    DATABASE = 'Parts' )
```

Unfortunately, the web service developer says he is unable to retrieve any data. What should be done?

A. Change BATCHES to ENABLED.

B. Specify the STATE as STARTED.

C. Specify a Namespace.

D. Have the developer try again.

5. You manage two SQL Servers named MCITP1 and MCITP2. You've created a stored procedure on MCITP1 that uses the OPENQUERY statement to access data on MCITP2 but it fails. How can you solve this problem?

A. Add MCITP1 as a linked server on MCITP2.

B. Add MCITP2 as a linked server on MCITP1.

C. Ensure that you have permission to execute stored procedures on MCITP2.

D. Change the stored procedure to a function using the OPENQUERY statement.

6. You manage several SQL Servers and are tasked with writing a query that joins data on MCITP2 with data from MCITP1. You will execute the query on MCITP2. What's the best authentication choice to ensure your query executes properly?

   A. Configure MCITP2 as a linked server on MCITP1 to impersonate the remote login.

   B. Configure MCITP1 as a linked server on MCITP2 to impersonate the remote login.

   C. Configure MCITP2 as a distributed server on MCITP1 to delegate the remote login.

   D. Configure MCITP1 as a distributed server on MCITP2 to delegate the remote login.

7. Sally needs to frequently run queries against databases on MCITP1 and MCITP2. She has a login on MCITP1, but the DBA of MCITP2 says she can't be granted access to MCITP2. What can be done to allow her to run queries against MCITP2?

   A. Nothing. Without access, she can't run queries against MCITP2.

   B. Create a linked server on MCITP1 to MCITP2. Configure the linked server to use delegation.

   C. Create a linked server on MCITP1 to MCITP2. Configure the linked server to use impersonation.

   D. Create a linked server on MCITP1 to MCITP2. Configure the linked server to use mapped logins.

70-441

1. Customers place orders for stocks via the stockportfolio web application. The stock purchase request is a time-consuming process that might take over a minute to complete. Customers should immediately receive a message indicating the process has begun and indicating they can check the status later. You need to design a stored procedure that meets these requirements. What would you use?

   A. A stored procedure that uses a SQL Server Integration Services (SSIS) package.

   B. A stored procedure that uses Service Broker.

   C. A stored procedure that uses a distributed transaction.

   D. A stored procedure that uses a linked server.

2. You are designing a Service Broker application. Four different client applications will be used to submit requests to the Service Broker application. Two different Service Broker services will be created to support the application. How many queues should be used?

   A. One queue.

   B. Two queues.

   C. Four queues.

   D. Six queues.

3. Your company sells office supplies over the Internet through several different resellers. The resellers have their own custom applications that run via their web site applications. After customers place orders, they want to be able to track the status of the order. You need to design a process that will allow customers to track the status of their orders. What would you do?

   A. Create a stored procedure to return status information.

   B. Create a user-defined function to return status information.

   C. Create a SQL Server Integration Services (SSIS) solution to return status information.

   D. Create a web service to return status information.

4. You are designing an application named Developers where independent external contractors write code for different applications and submit the code via a web site. The code is then tested and integrated into the appropriate application. You need to provide for secure transmission of the code and ensure the contractors will not access the database directly. How can you do this?

   A. Use a MARS connection.

   B. Create a web service method by using HTTP endpoints.

   C. Create a web service method by using HTTP endpoints specifying SSL.

   D. Use Service Broker.

70-442

1. Your company matches job applicants with job opportunities on a contract basis. The company has partners around the country that share information on potential job opportunities. These partners need to be able to use their own applications to upload job opportunities into your database. What could you design to support this?

   A. Design an HTTP endpoint with a stored procedure.

   B. Design a MARS query.

   C. Allow access via SSIS.

   D. Allow access via SSL.

2. You are designing the data access strategy for a computer accessories web site. In addition to buying the accessories from your web site, customers can also purchase from a national retail store chain. When displaying accessories, the local store inventory is queried and displayed before displaying the next accessory. The solution must minimize the number of connections to the database. What data access strategy should you use?

A. System.Data.DataReader

B. System.Data.DataWriter

C. MARS

D. A web service

3. You are designing the data access strategy for a computer accessories web site. When a customer searches a specific category, the results of this search should be used for future searches in the same session to minimize round trips to the database. Which strategy should you use?

A. Multiple Active Result Sets (MARS)

B. System.Data.DataReader

C. System.Data.DataSet

D. A web service

4. You are designing the data access strategy for an application that matches up job candidates with available jobs. In-house job brokers occasionally need to retrieve a listing of available jobs. This data must be returned as quickly as possible. What strategy should you use for this query?

A. Multiple Active Result Sets (MARS)

B. System.Data.DataReader

C. System.Data.DataSet

D. A web service

5. You are designing the data access strategy for an application that matches up job candidates with available jobs. Available jobs are offered by a core group of external partners, and changes to data on these partners are infrequent. Additionally, round trips to the database should be limited. What strategy should you use for this query?

A. Multiple Active Result Sets (MARS)

B. System.Data.DataReader

C. System.Data.DataSet

D. A web service

Answers

70-431

1. **B.** To add messages to the service, we create a contract. To send the messages, we use BEGIN DIALOG CONVERSATION. CREATE SERVICE isn't used to add messages. There is no such command as ENABLE MESSAGE.

2. **A.** The queue status can be set to OFF or ON. If the status is omitted, the status is ON by default. There is no DISABLED or ENABLED setting for the queue. There is no such command as SET SERVICE _BROKER_ENABLED = FALSE.

3. **C.** The default state of an HTTP endpoint is STOPPED. Since it wasn't specified in the script creating the endpoint, it is stopped and would need to be started.

4. **B.** The default state is STOPPED. Since there is no STATE line in the script, it is not started. Setting BATCHES to ENABLED would allow ad hoc SQL requests, but only the stored procedure is called for. The namespace wouldn't stop it from working completely.

5. **B.** OPENQUERY is used with linked server definitions. If a linked server definition has not been created, it will fail. We would want to create the linked server definition on the server where we are running the distributed query—MCITP1.

6. **A.** We can't configure a distributed server, only linked servers. Since we're running the query on MCITP2, we configure MCITP1 as a linked server on MCITP2.

7. **D.** If impersonation or delegation can't be done (and it can't because Sally doesn't have a login on MCITP2), then mapped logins can be used. A login account on MCITP1 can be used to execute the queries.

70-441

1. **B.** Since we want the process to continue, but a message to be sent immediately, we would use Service Broker. Service Broker allows asynchronous messages to be sent. SSIS can be used to extract and transform data, but this isn't needed. There is no indication we have more than one server involved in a transaction so distributed transactions or linked servers aren't needed.

2. **B.** Since two Service Broker services are being used, two queues should be created—one for each service. One queue wouldn't be enough, and four and six queues would be too many.

3. **D.** A web service is the ideal solution. We can publish the WSDL that can be used by the different resellers. A stored procedure or function by itself wouldn't work because the different resellers couldn't access these database objects without a web service. SSIS would be used to transform the data, not return information.

4. **C.** First, since the contractors are submitting the code via a web site, the only possible choice from those given is a web service. A MARS connection or Service Broker wouldn't be used for a web site solution. Second, since secure transmission of the code is required, SSL would be specified.

70-442

1. **A.** It's not stated, but since the partners are around the country, the only feasible way they could connect is via the Internet. Since partners are using their own applications to upload, the only possible solution is to design a web service with a designated HTTP endpoint. It's common to use stored procedures with endpoints. Neither MARS nor SSIS could support this solution. If a secure connection was required, we could design an HTTP endpoint with SSL, but this was not specified.

2. **C.** The scenario requires multiple reads of the database to first identify the accessories, and then determine the inventory at the local store. It also requires a minimum number of connections. MARS can do this with a single connection. Since it's our web site, a web service isn't needed.

3. **C.** Since we want to minimize round trips and reuse the results of the original query, we would use the caching benefit of a System.Data.DataSet. A DataReader is forward-only, so it could not be reread. MARS allows us to do multiple queries to the database in the same connection, but this isn't needed. Since everything is happening on our web site, a web service is not necessary.

4. **B.** Since the data must be returned as quickly as possible, we would use a DataReader. The DataReader is quicker than the DataSet. It's just a single query, so MARS isn't needed. The job brokers are in-house, so a web service isn't needed either.

5. **C.** Since the changes are infrequent and round trips should be limited, a DataSet is the best solution. The DataReader would require a round trip for each query. It's just a single query, so MARS isn't needed. The job brokers are in-house, so again a web service isn't needed either.

Support Services

In this chapter, you'll learn about:

- SQL Server Reporting Services (SSRS)
- Notification Services
- An intro to SQL Server Analysis Services

> *Ask not for a lighter burden, but for broader shoulders.*
>
> *—Jewish Proverb*

As the popularity and usefulness of high-end databases continues to grow, the need for more sophisticated services to meet the needs of users also continues to grow. Reporting Services allows us to create quality reports and make them available to end users with just a few clicks of the mouse. Moreover, we can create Report Models to allow users to fine-tune their own reports on an ad hoc basis. For users that need to be notified of events as they happen, Notification Services allows us to match events, subscribers, and subscriptions and easily deliver notifications via delivery methods such as e-mail and Short Message Delivery (SMS) systems.

Yes, as user needs grow, our burden as database administrators and database developers doesn't get lighter. But with the support services available, our ability to meet these demands becomes much easier.

SQL Server Reporting Services (SSRS)

One of the significant holes in SQL Server in the past was the lack of ability to pull out the data in a meaningful format for the end users. SQL Server has long been a powerful database engine, but the tools to access the data have always only been available outside of SQL Server.

To access the data, dedicated programs were written by developers. Microsoft Access has provided many tools for creating reports, and Microsoft Access devotees have often used it as a front-end with SQL Server working as a back-end database. If you've used Access to create reports, some of what you see in Reporting Services will likely seem familiar.

Crystal Reports, currently owned by Business Objects, has long been a powerful tool used to access a wide variety of databases. Microsoft Visual Studio has included an OEM version of Crystal Reports in the last few versions.

SQL Server Reporting Services (SSRS) came out late in the lifetime of SQL Server 2000. It was available as a separate download. In SQL Server 2000, Reporting Services required the installation of Visual Studio, but with SQL Server 2005, SSRS can now be installed as a component of SQL Server 2005, and reports can be created with the Business Intelligence Development Studio (BIDS).

With the inclusion of Reporting Services, SQL Server 2005 is becoming a much more comprehensive platform for business intelligence solutions. Before we get too far into this chapter, let's introduce the major components of Reporting Services

- **Business Intelligence Development Studio (BIDS)** BIDS is the primary development environment for Reports and Report Models. It uses the same interface as Visual Studio 2005 but is used for Business Intelligence projects. In addition to Reporting Services projects, BIDS is used for SQL Server Analysis Services projects and SQL Server Integration Services projects.

- **Report Server** Report Server is where the reports will be hosted. It uses Internet Information Services (IIS) to serve the reports as web pages. Reports created in BIDS can be deployed to the Report Server, where they can be made accessible to any users with access to the Report Server.

- **Report Manager** Report Manager is the primary interface users can use to view, search, and subscribe to reports. For example, Report Models can be deployed to here and users can then use the Report Builder in the Report Manager to create their own reports. It can also be used to administer the Report Server remotely.

- **Report Model** Report Models are the bare bones skeletons of reports. They include the data source definitions (such as which server and which database to connect to for the model) and data source view definitions (such as which tables or views to include in the model). A model doesn't actually show any data in a report, but instead is the foundation of creating a report with Report Builder.

- **Report Builder** Report Builder is a tool designed for end users so they can easily create ad hoc reports. Reports can be created from either published data sources or Report Models.

The tasks involved in deploying a Reporting Services solution include:

- Installing and configuring Reporting Services components
- Designing and creating reports
- Deploying reporting solutions

We'll cover each of these tasks in this chapter.

Reporting Services Databases

When Reporting Services is installed, it installs two databases. These are the reportserver and reportservertempdb databases. The reportserver database is used for persistent storage of all Reporting Services objects. The reportservertempdb database is used for temporary storage requirements while running.

 CAUTION These databases should not be modified or tuned directly. Microsoft warns that doing so may result in future service packs or upgrades conflicting with your changes and impairing the operations of the report server. Make all changes using report server management tools such as Report Manager and SSMS.

Unlike the SQL Server tempdb database, the reportservertempdb database is not recreated automatically. It is recommended that you include the reportservertempdb database in your backup strategy, along with the reportserver database.

Session Caching

Since the report server temporary database is used to store cached reports, it may become large. If you discover that this database has become abnormally large, check to see if you have any large reports that are using session caching. By disabling session caching on the reports, you can control the size of the report server temporary database size.

 TIP To minimize the size of the report server temporary database, reduce the use of session caching in your reports.

Requirements

SSRS has a few requirements. First and foremost, the reports are served by the Internet Information Services (IIS) web server. You must be running at least IIS version 5.0 or later with ASP .NET 2.0. SQL Server 2005 installs the Microsoft Windows .NET Framework 2.0, so that isn't an additional concern when installing IIS. Let's clarify something here, though. IIS is needed for users to access the reports, but the reports are actually developed and tested in BIDS.

Additionally, the SQL Server Reporting Services service for the instance needs to be running. This is installed and configured as part of a typical installation.

 NOTE Requirements for SQL Server Reporting Services beyond the SQL Server Reporting Services service are IIS and ASP .NET 2.0. If you will use Reporting Services, ensure these services are installed. However, if Reporting Services is not required, you should ensure that IIS is *not* enabled (unless it's being used for a different solution).

In Chapter 1 we went through the process of installing Reporting Services as part of the installation. This did install the SQL Server Reporting Services service. However, we did not install IIS, so the installation gave us a warning. While we could develop reports without IIS, IIS is needed to deploy reports. So, as promised, we'll go through the steps to install it here.

CAUTION As with all exercises in this book, it's assumed you are doing the install on Windows XP or Windows Vista. While you can install IIS on Windows XP or Vista and these exercises will work, once you're done with these exercises, it's recommended you either uninstall IIS or disable the World Wide Web Publishing service.

In the following exercise, we will install Internet Information Services (IIS).

Exercise 12.1: Install IIS

1. Launch the Control Panel.

2. In the Control Panel, start the Add Or Remove Programs applet.

3. In the Add Or Remove Programs applet, click the Add/Remove Windows Components button on the left pane. This may take a moment to launch.

4. On the Windows Components page, click the check box for IIS. Your display should look similar to Figure 12-1. You may notice that the check box is dimmed. All components of IIS do not need to be installed. The default components are acceptable. Click Next. You may be prompted to insert your installation CD. If so, insert it and click OK.

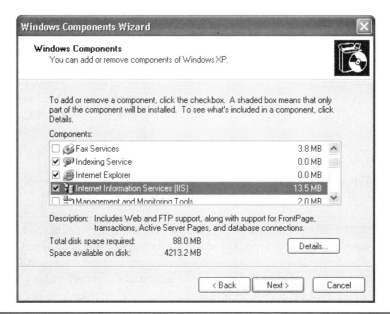

Figure 12-1 Installing the Internet Information Services Windows component

5. When the Windows Components Wizard completes, click Finish. Close the Add Or Remove Programs applet and the Control Panel.

CAUTION   Occasionally, you may receive various errors when installing IIS after the Framework has been installed, such as the following:

```
Visual Studio .NET has detected that the specified Web
server is not running ASP.NET version 1.1. You will be
unable to run ASP.NET Web applications or services.
```

If this occurs, you can run the aspnet_regiis command with the –i switch to fix the problem. Microsoft KB article 306005 explains how to do this, but in short it is: `C:\Windows\ Microsoft.Net\Framework\v2.0.50727\aspnet_regiis.exe -i`

6. At this point, you should have Reporting Services installed (from Chapter 1) and IIS installed. However, IIS is not configured for Reporting Services. Launch the Reporting Services Configuration Manager from Start | All Programs | Microsoft SQL Server 2005 | Configuration Tools | Reporting Services Configuration.

7. Select the Report Server Virtual Directory page from the left pane. Click New… to create a new Report Server virtual directory. Click OK to accept the defaults. At this point, your display should look like Figure 12-2.

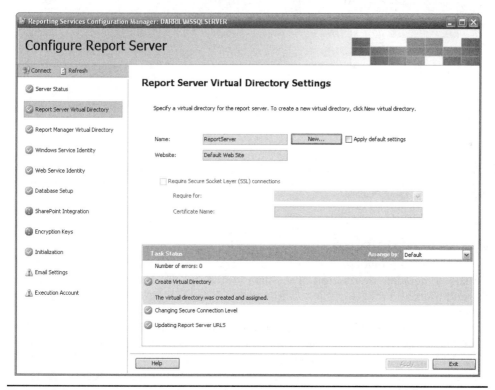

Figure 12-2   Configuring a Report Server virtual directory

8. Select the Report Manager Virtual Directory page. Click New… and click OK to accept the defaults. Click Exit to close the Reporting Services Configuration Manager tool.

9. Launch the Report Manager by opening Internet Explorer and typing the following URL into the address bar: **http://localhost/reports**. At this point, we don't have any reports to manage, so it will be blank, but you should see a display similar to Figure 12-3.

Figure 12-3 Report Manager

Report Models

A Report Model provides the foundation for end users to create their own reports. It's actually a metadata description of the data source, but the complexity is hidden from the end users and they are able to easily create their own ad hoc reports using the Report Model.

Once a Report Model is created, end users can then use Report Builder to build their own reports based on the available data in the Report Model. The first step in building a model is to create a report model project.

EXAM TIP If users need the capability of building their own ad hoc reports, the primary solution is to create a Report Model and let users create their own reports from this model using Report Builder.

Report Models are created within the Business Intelligence Development Studio (BIDS). In the following exercise, we'll create a Report Model that will later be used to create an ad hoc report using Report Builder.

Exercise 12.2: Build a Report Model

1. Launch the Business Intelligence Development Studio by clicking Start | All Programs | Microsoft SQL Server 2005 | SQL Server Business Intelligence Development Studio.

2. Select File | New | Project. The New Project dialog box will appear. Select the Report Model Project. In the Name field, enter **Ex12ReportModel**, and for the location, select C:\MCITPSuccess. If a MCITPSuccess directory doesn't exist on your system, you can use the Browse button to browse to the root of C:\ and create the directory. Your display should look similar to Figure 12-4. Click OK.

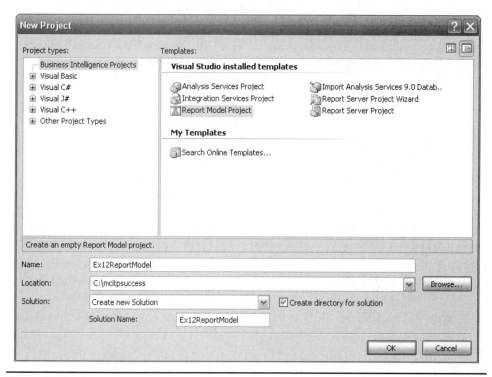

Figure 12-4 Creating a new project in BIDS

TIP If you're familiar with Visual Studio, you're familiar with BIDS. It the same interface. If you're not familiar with it, the Solution Explorer (on the top right side of the screen) includes containers for all of the objects in your project. Right below it is the Properties page. Most of our will work will be done in the center pane, even though it begins as a start page, often with links to MSDN articles.

3. Our first step in the project is to create a data source. We'll be using the AdventureWorks database as our data source. In the Solution Explorer, right-click Data Sources and select Add New Data Source. This will launch the Data Source Wizard.

   a. On the Welcome To The Data Source Wizard page, click Next.

   b. On the Select How To Define The Connection page, click New.

   c. On the Connection Manager page, enter **localhost** as the Server name. Accept the default of Use Windows Authentication. On the Connect to a Database section, select the AdventureWorks database. Click the Test Connection button. You should see a Connection Manager dialog box indicating success. Click OK on the Success dialog box. Click OK in the Connection Manager page. Click Next on the Select How To Define The Connection page.

   d. On the Completing The Wizard page, verify the data source name is AdventureWorks and click Finish.

4. We now need to define a Data Source View. This is a logical data model that we create from the data source. It includes tables and views from the data source, but can also include additional information as we deem appropriate.

   a. Right-click Data Source Views and click Add New Data Source View.

   b. On the Welcome To The Data Source View Wizard page, click Next.

   c. On the Select A Data Source page, ensure AdventureWorks is selected. This is the Data Source we created in step 3. Click Next.

   d. On the Select Tables And Views page, select the Person.Contact table and click the > button to move this table into the Included Objects column. Click the Add Related Tables button to add all tables related to the Person.Contact table to the Included Objects column. Select the HumanResources.vEmployee view and click the > button to move it into the Included Objects column. Click Next.

   e. On the Completing The Wizard page, change the name to **Contacts**. Click Finish.

5. With the Data Source and the Data Source View created, we can now create the Report Model.

   a. In the Solution Explorer, right-click Report Models and select Add New Report Model.

   b. On the Welcome To The Report Model Wizard page, click Next.

   c. On the Select Data Source View page, select Contacts. This is the Data Source View we created in step 4. Click Next.

   d. On the Select Report Model Generation Rules page, accept the defaults and click Next.

e. On the Collect Model Statistics page, change the section to Use Current Model Statistics Stored In The Data Source View. Click Next.

f. On the Completing The Wizard page, click Run. After a moment, the wizard will complete and the Report Model will be generated. Click Finish. Your display should look similar to Figure 12-5.

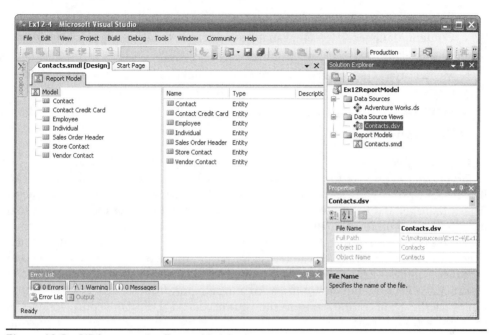

Figure 12-5 BIDS open with a Report Model

6. To make this Report Model available to users, we must publish it to the Report Server. Within the Solution Explorer, right-click the Ex12ReportModel project (the top line in the Solution Explorer) and select Deploy.

7. Launch Internet Explorer and enter **http://localhost/Reports** to access the Report Manager. You will see that this now includes a new Data Source and a new Model from the deployment in step 6.

Report Manager

Report Manager is one of two web sites that users can use to access reports. (The other one is the Reporting Services web site—http://localhost/ReportServer, if you followed the previous exercises.)

By accessing the Report Manager web site, users can view reports deployed to the Reporting Services web site, build reports from Report Models using the Report Builder, create subscriptions for reports, and view a history of the reports (if a history exists).

If a user can access the Reporting Services (http://localhost/ReportServer) web site, you can also grant them access to the Report Manager (http://localhost/Reports) web site. If they don't have access to the Reporting Services site, they won't have access to the Report Manager site. Based on what role we place users into, they will have a varying amount of permissions. The roles are:

- **Browser**   Users may view folders, reports, and subscribe to reports.
- **Content Manager**   Users may manage content in the Report Server. This includes folders, reports, and resources.
- **My Reports**   Users may publish reports and linked reports, and manage folders, reports, and resources in a users' My Reports folder.
- **Publisher**   Users may publish reports and linked reports to the Report Server.
- **Report Builder**   Users may view report definitions.

Two tools used to create reports are Report Designer and Report Builder.

Report Builder is a basic tool intended for users who want to create basic reports easily without writing queries. Users can also use it for ad hoc reporting. It's accessible via Report Manager and comes with several predefined report models and templates that have drag-and-drop functionality.

Report Designer is a full-featured report authoring tool that is run in Business Intelligence Development Studio. It can be used to create simple or complex reports. Report Designer includes a Report wizard that can be used to create the general framework of a report, and a Report template for use in creating a report from scratch. With both, you can tweak the details of the report to suit your needs. We'll explore Report Designer in the next section. Reports from Report Designer are typically created on a client computer (not the report server) and then published, or deployed, to the report server.

In the following exercise, we'll create a report using Report Builder.

Exercise 12.3: Build a Report Using Report Builder

1. Launch Internet Explorer and enter **http://localhost/Reports** into the address line to access Report Manager.

2. Once we create a report, we want to save it in our folder, so click New Folder. In the Name box, enter **Chapter12**. In the Description box, enter **Reports created in Chapter 12**. Click OK.

3. Click the Report Builder button. If this is the first time you clicked the button, an Application Run—Security Warning dialog box will appear. Click Run. If the Report Server was on a different server, this would download and install the Report Builder on your system. Since we have the Report Server on the same system we're using to develop the reports, it simply installs and launches Report Builder.

4. In the right pane, the Getting Started Wizard appears. We have only one data source (Contacts). Select it. We'll create a report in the Table format, so leave Table (columnar) selected and click OK.

5. At this point, we have a blank report. We can drag and drop items from the left side of the page onto our report.

6. First, let's give our report a title. Click the box labeled Click To Add Title And Enter AdventureWorks Employee Phone And Email Listing.

7. Select the vEmployee view from the Entities box.

8. Next, we want to populate the report with the desired fields:

   a. In the Fields: box, select LastName and drag it into the box labeled Drag And Drop Column Fields.

   b. Select the FirstName field and drag it just to the right of LastName. While dragging the FirstName field, hover within the LastName field on the report. A blue cursor will appear to indicate whether it will be inserted to the left or right of the LastName field.

   c. Select the EmailAddress field and drop it next to the FirstName field.

   d. Select the Phone field and drop it next to the EmailAddress field.

   e. Since the EmailAddress field is longer, resize it by hovering over the line between EmailAddress until the resize cursor appears. Click the line and drag it to the right. Your display should look similar to Figure 12-6.

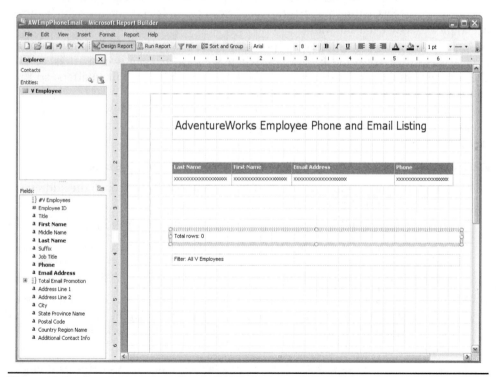

Figure 12-6   Creating a report in Report Builder

9. Click Run Report. After a moment, the report will be generated and appear in Report Builder.

10. Let's save this report. Select File | Save. Since we created this report from a Report Model, the Save dialog box defaults to the http://localhost/ReportServer/ Models address. Click the Up button to move up to the root. You should now see the Chapter12 folder you created earlier in this exercise. Double-click the Chapter12 folder. In the Name box, enter **AWEmpPhoneEmail** and click Save.

11. This report is now available to be viewed in the Report Manager. Launch Internet Explorer and enter **http://localhost/Reports**.

12. Select the Chapter12 folder by clicking it. Select the AWEmpPhoneEmail report by clicking it. This will display the report we just created.

Matrix Reports

A matrix report (also called a cross-tab report) is one where the user can interact with it and pick and choose the data desired. Similar tables in Microsoft Excel are referred to as pivot tables.

Let's say a manager wants to view the average sales for any given territory during any given timeframe. Perhaps she first wants to know what the annual sales were, but once that question is answered she wants to be able to drill into specific quarters or even specific months. By creating a matrix report, she can get an overall picture, which allows her to pick exactly what she wants.

An interesting attribute of matrix reports is that the columns vary depending on the data. For example, we could have a year where we have sales in two quarters, so two columns are shown, and another year where we have sales in four quarters, so four columns are shown.

I've found that students often have problems conceptualizing how a matrix (cross-tab) report works, so the following exercise shows us how to create a simple report using a matrix.

Exercise 12.4: Build a Matrix Report Using Report Builder

1. Launch Internet Explorer and enter **http://localhost/Reports** into the address line to access the Report Manager.

2. Click the Report Builder button. This will launch the Report Builder.

3. In the right pane, the Getting Started Wizard appears. We have only one data source (Contacts). Select it. We'll create a report in the Matrix format, so select Matrix (cross-tab) and click OK.

4. At this point, we have a blank report. We can drag and drop items from the left side of the page onto our report. Notice how the format of the report is different than the columnar report. Instead of a single cell, we have two rows with two columns each.

5. Add a title to your report. Click in the box labeled Click To Add Title And Enter AdventureWorks Sales By Territory.

6. Select the Sales Order Header table from the Entities box.

7. Next, we want to populate the report with the desired fields

   a. In the Fields box, select the + next to OrderDate to show the fields available. Select Order Year and drag it into the top right cell of the box labeled Drag And Drop Column Groups.

   b. Again in the Fields box, select the + next to OrderDate to show the fields available. Select Order Quarter and drag it into the same cell as the Order Quarter.

   c. Select the Territory ID field and drag it into the bottom left cell labeled Drag And Drop Row Groups.

   d. In the Fields box, select the + next to Total Total Due to show all the fields available. Select the Avg Total Due and drag it to the bottom right cell labeled Drag And Drop Totals. Your display should look similar to Figure 12-7.

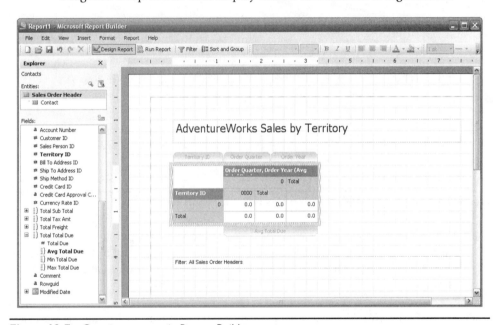

Figure 12-7   Creating a report in Report Builder

8. Click Run Report. After a moment, the report will be generated and appear in Report Builder.

9. Select File | Save to save the file. In the Save As Report dialog box, browse to the Chapter12 folder in http://localhost/ReportServer. In the Name box, enter **AWSalesByTerritory** and click Save.

10. This report is now available to be viewed in the Report Manager. Launch Internet Explorer and enter **http://localhost/Reports**.

11. Select the Chapter12 folder by clicking it. Select the AWSalesByTerritory report by clicking it. This will display the report we just created. It should look similar to Figure 12-8.

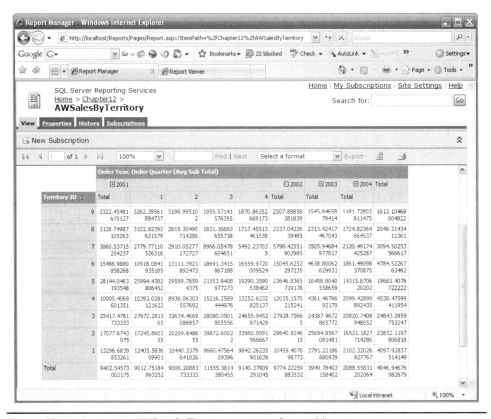

Figure 12-8 Viewing the AWSalesByTerritory report in Report Manager

12. Notice that by clicking the + next to a year, we can open up that year and view the totals for each individual quarter. Click the year 2002 and notice that data is available for four quarters. Click the year 2001 and notice that data is available for two quarters.

EXAM TIP When designing matrix reports, the number of columns available will change according to the data.

Report Properties and Options

With the creation of a couple of reports under our belt, let's discuss some of the options available with reports. When viewing a report via Report Manager, four pages can be viewed. These are:

- **View**   The rendered report is viewed here.

- **Properties**   Five properties pages are available through here: General, Data Sources, Execution, History, and Security. We can create linked reports here, set report caching properties, view the report history, and set security on the report.

- **History** This allows you to view report snapshots that are generated and stored over time.

- **Subscriptions** New subscriptions and new data-driven subscriptions can be created from this page.

Properties

The Properties tab includes five or six items depending on whether parameters are included in the report. Figure 12-9 shows one of the sample reports that has parameters available. If parameters are not included in the report, there won't be a parameters section.

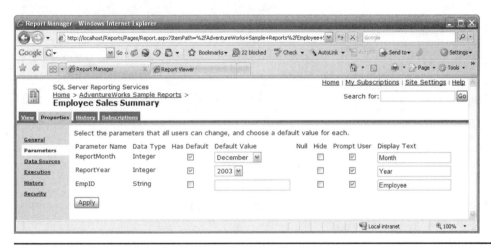

Figure 12-9 Employee Sales Summary sample report Properties page

The General property page shows general information on the report, such as when it was created or modified.

By selecting the Data Sources property page, you can modify both the data source and credentials. By default, the data source is set to a shared data source. If you want to specify the data source, you must use the connection string. A sample connection string for the AdventureWorks on the server named MCITP1 is shown in the following code:

```
Data Source=MCITP1;Initial Catalog=AdventureWorks
```

One of the primary reasons to specify the connection string is because you want to specify the credentials to be used to run the report. Credentials can be supplied by the user, stored securely on the server, or Windows integrated security can be selected to use the credentials of the user running the report.

TIP Before setting your server to cache copies of your report, creating history snapshots, or creating subscriptions, you must set credentials for your report. When using Windows credentials, they must be specified in the format of Domain\UserName or ComputerName\UserName.

The Execution property page allows you to create cached copies of your report, also referred to as session caching. With a cached copy created users can repeatedly request a viewing of the report, but instead of reprocessing the report for every request, it will show the cached copy. Figure 12-10 shows settings configured to have the cached copy of the report expire in 30 minutes.

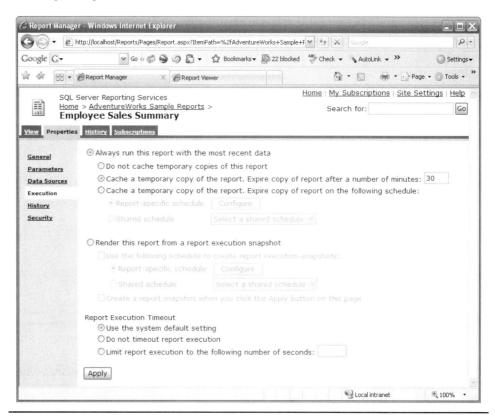

Figure 12-10 Configuring your report to use cached copies

Notice that enabling session caching for a report allows us to specify the number of minutes a report will be cached, but it doesn't allow us to specify the time of day when a report will run. Instead, the first time the report is requested by a user, it will be created and cached. For any users that access that report afterwards, the cached copy will be used as long as the cached copy hasn't expired. If the report expires, then the next time it is requested, a new report will be created and cached.

EXAM TIP By enabling session caching for a report, you can minimize the response time for the creation of the report, and minimize the impact of running the report on the overall performance of your servers. Consider using this for reports that are frequently queried but allow the use of aged data.

In addition to creating cached copies of the report, we can also create report snapshots from the Execution property page. Report snapshots allow us to specify exactly when a report is run based on the time of day. With report snapshots created, users that access the report will view the snapshot instead of the report being rerun. For example, for a processor-intensive report, we can configure it to run every day at 2 A.M.

Report snapshots can be saved over time to create a history of the report, including the data. The History property page allows us to configure how a history of reports can be saved. We can see this page in Figure 12-11.

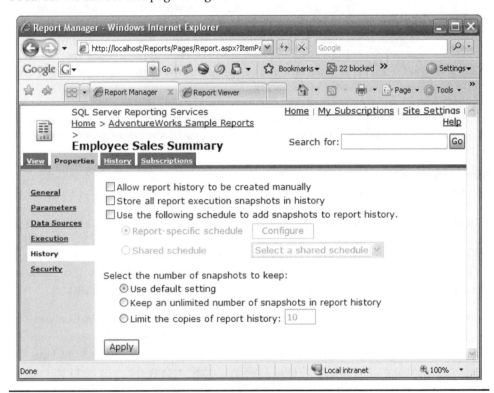

Figure 12-11 The History properties page of a report

The Store All Report Execution Snapshots In History option allows us to save any snapshots we've scheduled to be created in the Execution property page. Even if we haven't configured snapshots to run, we can also configure a schedule to regularly run snapshots specifically to be stored in history.

User permissions and roles can be specified in the Security properties page. By default, these are inherited by the parent.

Report Snapshots

A report snapshot is just what it sounds like. It contains layout information and data from a specific point in time just as a camera snapshot captures what something looks like at a particular moment in time. Report snapshots are typically processed based on a set schedule and then saved to a report server.

You may want to use report snapshots for several reasons:

- To improve the performance of large reports by running them during off-peak time
- To capture and retain report history
- To ensure the consistency of data to end users

 TIP If you have reports that are draining your resources on a Reporting Server, consider using report snapshots. By scheduling these to occur during off-peak times (such as in the middle of the night), you can control when the report is run and subsequently control some of the load on your server. While this won't work for all reports, it can be done for some of the larger reports where data doesn't need up-to-the-minute accuracy.

By clicking the History tab in Report Manager, you can view any report snapshots that have been created by a snapshot schedule or created simply to generate a history of the reports.

Subscriptions

The Subscriptions tab allows you to create either New Subscriptions or New Data-driven Subscriptions.

Instead of just waiting for users to come and retrieve the reports, Reporting Services can also send reports based on subscriptions. Reports can be sent via e-mail or to a share. When creating a Reporting Services subscription, you can specify when a report will be delivered, such as every Monday at 8:00 A.M. or every weekday at noon. Reporting Services supports two kinds of subscriptions—standard and data-driven:

- **Standard subscriptions** A standard subscription has static values that are defined at design time and can't be changed at runtime.
- **Data-driven subscriptions** Data-driven subscriptions are dynamic and are modified as part of the subscription process. Presentation, delivery, and parameter values are retrieved at runtime. These are useful when you have a very large recipient list with varying report needs.

 TIP Use data-driven subscriptions when it's desirable to have reports sent automatically even though the values for presentation, delivery, or parameters may change at runtime. By using parameters, you can even modify who receives the subscription based on the data.

Subscriptions have several components. These include:

- Conditions for processing the subscription (such as a schedule)
- Parameters used when running the report (used with parameterized reports)

- Delivery method and settings (e-mail details or share details)

- A rendering extension that allows the report to be presented in a specific format

- Credentials to allow the report to run unattended

The ReportViewer Control

While the ReportViewer control is not part of SQL Server 2005, it's worth noting because it provides a simple way to view reports hosted on a SQL Server 2005 Report Server from within any .NET application. The ReportViewer control is a control within Visual Studio.

The ReportViewer control doesn't connect to the data source itself, but instead relies on the SQL Server 2005 Report Server to connect to the data. An important feature of this is that you're able to allow access to the reports from within an application using a single application user for permissions. Additional users don't need to be added to the Server.

 EXAM TIP If you need to provide access to reports served from SQL Server Reporting Services from within a .NET application, use a ReportViewer control.

Creating and Modifying Reports in BIDS

So far we've created a Report Model in BIDS and used it to explore the Report Manager. We also created a report from the Report Model using the Report Builder. Next, we'll explore some of the possibilities of creating and manipulating reports in BIDS.

Microsoft includes many sample reports in the Sample Applications package.

In the following exercise, we'll install the Sample applications. These will be used for Reporting Services exercises.

Exercise 12.5: Install Sample Applications

1. Check to see if Samples are available for installation. Click Start | All Programs | Microsoft SQL Server 2005 | Documentation and Tutorials | Samples | Microsoft SQL Server 2005 Samples (English). If available, go to step 2. If not available, install them using the following steps:

   a. Launch the Add Or Remove Programs applet in the Control Panel.

   b. Find Microsoft SQL Server 2005 and click the Change button.

   c. On the Component Selection page, select Workstation Components and click Next.

   d. On the Welcome page, click Next.

   e. On the System Configuration Check page, click Next.

   f. On the Change Or Remove Instance page, click Change Installed Components.

g. On the Feature Selection page, open the Documentation, Samples, And Sample Databases item. For the Sample Code And Applications entry, change it to Will Be Installed On Local Hard Drive. Click Next.

h. On the Error And Usage Report Settings page, review the choices and click Next.

i. On the Ready To Update page, click Install.

j. On the Setup Progress page, click Next.

k. On the Completing Microsoft SQL Server 2005 Setup page, click Finish.

2. Install the Samples:

a. Click Start | All Programs | Microsoft SQL Server 2005 | Documentation and Tutorials | Samples | Microsoft SQL Server 2005 Samples (English).

b. On the Welcome page, click Next.

c. On the Destination Folder page, click Next.

d. On the Ready To Install page, click Install.

e. On the Completion page, click Finish.

With the basics out of the way, we can now start looking at some of the sample reports and creating our own. The next exercise launches the Sample Reports solutions.

Exercise 12.6: View and Deploy Sample Reports

1. Launch Windows Explorer and browse to the C:\Program Files\Microsoft SQL Server\90\Samples\Reporting Services\Report Samples\AdventureWorks Sample Reports folder. This includes a solution that has been created, and which includes several reports.

2. Double-click the AdventureWorks Sample Reports.sln Solution file. This will launch the SQL Server Business Intelligence Development Studio (BIDS) with this solution installed. Be patient. It does take a little time to load.

3. On the right side of BIDS, look at the Solution Explorer. You will have two shared data sources, and several reports. Double-click the Company Sales report to open it. Your display should look similar to Figure 12-12.

 NOTE Notice that you have a project with two folders: Shared Data Sources and Reports. Shared data sources describe data source connections and are required by report models. They are optional for reports and data-driven subscriptions. A shared data source is reusable across many reports and subscriptions. The Reports folder will hold all the reports you create in this project.

4. Above the report are three tabs: Data, Layout, and Preview. The Data tab identifies the dataset. Click the Data tab. You can see this is just a SELECT statement (albeit a complex SELECT statement).

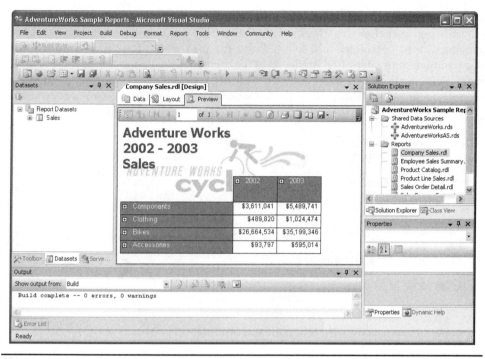

Figure 12-12 A sample report loaded into BIDS

5. Click the Layout tab. The Layout tab has the layout of the report. You can think of the layout as a group of cells that can be manipulated individually. An individual cell's appearance and data can be changed without affecting other cells.

6. Click the Preview tab. The Preview tab lets you see what the report will ultimately look like. With the Company Sales report, we see that a matrix is being used to allow the report user to drill down to any specific data needed. Play around with clicking the + on the report to see the result. If a manager needs a macro view of sales, all the pluses can be compressed to show just the totals. If a micro view is needed, any of the pluses can be pressed to provide the details needed.

7. To deploy the Employee Sales report to the Reporting Services server, right-click the report in the Solution Explorer and select Deploy.

Feel free to look at all the reports. In this chapter, we'll just scratch the surface of using Reporting Services, but by looking at these reports, you'll get a good idea of what's possible.

Parameterized Reports

Reports can be configured to accept parameters. With a parameterized report, the user is given the opportunity to select parameters and the value selected is then plugged into the SELECT statement as variables.

If you open the Employee Sales Summary report, you'll notice that no data is displayed when you click the Preview tab. This report is a parameterized report. It isn't generated until parameters are selected and the user selects the View Report button. The parameters are identified in the SELECT statement as @ReportYear (for the selected year), @ReportMonth (for the selected month), and @EmpID (for the selected employee). Figure 12-13 shows what the report looks like once the parameters of Month (December), Year (2003), and Employee (Garrett Vargas) are provided.

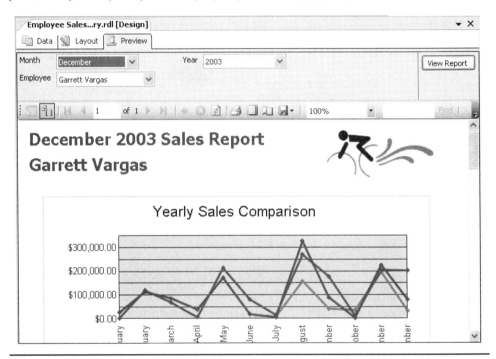

Figure 12-13   A parameterized report

 TIP   Parameterized reports are useful in providing the same type of data to multiple users, but filtering it to exactly what individual users need. For example, if a regional office has a dedicated web site, regional sales reports can use the parameter of a specific region code. In this manner, headquarters can use the identical report with a different parameter to view all regional sales offices, while each regional sales office would see only data related to their region.

Linked Reports

A linked report provides an access point to an existing report. Think of a linked report as a shortcut used to run the actual report. Furthering our example with the Employee Sales report, we can deploy a linked report to the regional offices that need it by linking the report to the primary Employee Sales report. Using parameters, we can specify which data the regional offices are able to view.

Linked reports retain the original report's definition and always inherit the layout and data source properties of the original report. Other property settings such as security, parameters, location, subscriptions, and schedules can be set individually on the linked report.

While linked reports are typically based on parameterized reports, this is not required. Linked reports can be done any time any of the individual properties needs to be different from the primary report.

Report Server Projects

Using BIDS, it's possible to create our own Reports and then deploy them to the Reporting Services server. The Report Server Project Wizard leads you through the creation of a report, but you can also create reports without the Report Wizard.

In the following two exercises, we'll create a simple report using the Report Server Project Wizard, and then another report without the wizard.

Exercise 12.7: Create a Report with the Report Server Project Wizard

Take a mini-tour of SSRS in video 12-7.

1. Launch BIDS.

2. Select File | New Project.

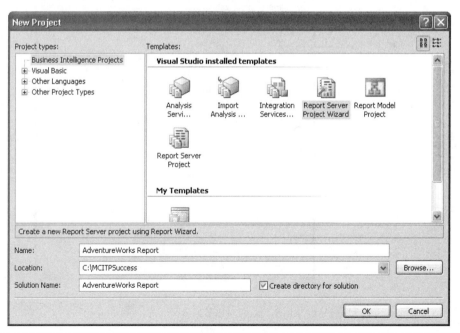

Figure 12-14   Creating a report from the Report Server Project Wizard

3. On the New Project page, choose Business Intelligence Projects, and select the Report Server Project Wizard. In the Name, enter **AdventureWorks Report**. For the Location, enter **c:\MCITPSuccess** (a folder created in an earlier exercise). Your display should look similar to Figure 12-14. Click OK.

4. On the Welcome To The Report Wizard page, click Next.

5. On the Select The Data Source page, enter **AW_Employees** as the Name. Ensure the Type is selected as Microsoft SQL Server. Click Edit.

   a. On the Connection Properties page, enter **localhost** as the Server Name. Press TAB.

   b. Select the drop-down box under Select Or Enter A Database Name, and then choose AdventureWorks. Your display should look similar to Figure 12-15.

   c. Click Test Connection. Click OK for the dialog box stating Test Connection Succeeded. Click OK.

Figure 12-15
Configuring
the connection
properties for the
report dataset

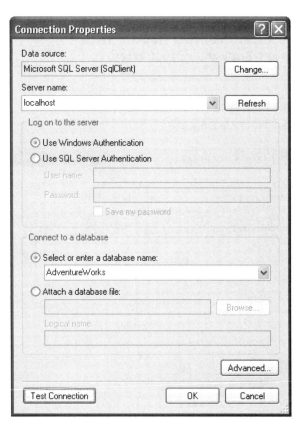

6. On the Select The Data Source page, click Next.

7. On the Design The Query page, enter the following query string:

```
SELECT * FROM HumanResources.vEmployeeDepartment
```

Click Next.

8. On the Select The Report Type page, ensure Tabular is selected and click Next.

9. On the Design The Table page, select Department and click the Group> button. This will group the employees into their respective departments. Click Next.

10. On the Choose The Table Layout page, ensure Stepped is selected and click Next.

11. On the Choose The Table Style page, select Corporate and click Next.

12. On the Choose The Deployment Location page, accept the default report server (http://localhost/ReportServer) and the default folder (AdventureWorks Report). Click Next.

13. On the Completing The Wizard page, name the report **Employees by Department**. Select the Preview Report check box, and then click Finish.

14. After a moment, BIDS will launch with the report generated in the Preview tab. This doesn't have all the bells and whistles of the sample reports, but it does show us how to create simple reports that can be deployed to an IIS server.

Exercise 12.8: Create a Report without the Report Wizard

1. If not open, launch BIDS.

2. Select File | New Project. On the New Project page, select the Business Intelligence Projects project type. Select the Report Server Project template. Change the name to **AdventureWorks**. Browse to a directory on your system, but leave the other defaults as they are. Your display should look similar to Figure 12-16. Click OK.

3. Create a new blank report. Right-click Reports and select Add | New Item. In the Add New Item page, select Report. Name the report **Customers.rdl**. (RDL documents use the Report Definition Language, which is translated into XML by Report Builder.) Click Add. A Customers.rdl document will be opened, showing three tabs: Data, Layout, and Preview.

4. Create a dataset to be used by the report:

   a. Click the drop-down box next to Dataset on the Data tab and select New Dataset.

   b. Click the Edit button. On the Connection Properties dialog box, enter **localhost** as the Server Name to connect to the default instance. If you wanted to connect to a named instance, you could enter it as *serverName\instanceName*. In the Connect To A Database section, select AdventureWorks from the drop-down box. Click Test Connection to verify the connection is valid. Click OK in response to the Test Connection Succeeded message. Click OK on the Connection Properties page.

   c. On the Data Source page, click OK to create the data source.

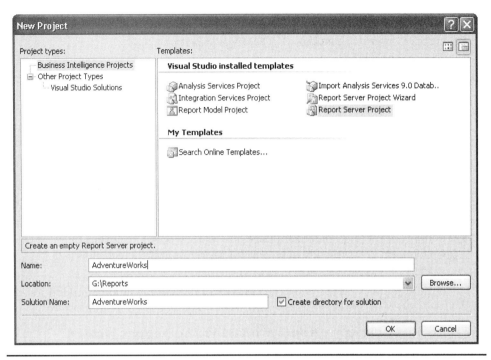

Figure 12-16   Creating a report project

   d. Modify the dataset. Click the ellipsis button next to the AdventureWorks dataset you just created. Change the name from AdventureWorks to **dsSales**.

   e. Enter the following command into the Query String box:

```
SELECT c.LastName, c.FirstName, Phone, c.EmailAddress
FROM Sales.Individual i
      INNER JOIN Person.Contact c
   ON c.ContactID = i.ContactID
ORDER BY c.LastName
```

5. Lay out the report elements:

   a. Click the Layout tab. Resize the grid so it fills the Layout window with BIDS maximized. You can resize it by hovering over the bottom line of the grid until a double-headed arrow appears. Then, click and drag downward to resize it.

   b. At this point, we want to drag some elements from the Toolbox into the report. The Toolbox is on the left, but more than likely, the Datasets window is visible. Click the tab at the bottom to make the Toolbox appear. Your display should look similar to Figure 12-17.

   c. Select a Textbox from the Toolbox, and drag it onto the report. Position it at the top-left corner. We will use this for a header for the report.

   d. Select a second Textbox, and drag it to the top-right corner. We will use this text box to add a date to the report.

Figure 12-17
The BIDS Report
Items Toolbox

e. Select the List item from the Toolbox, and drag it onto the report. Resize the List item to the width of the grid with a little bit of a margin around it. This list item will hold rows.

f. Select the Datasets window (below the Toolbox). Click the + next to dsCustomers to open it. Drag and drop each of the columns from the dsCustomers onto the List item in the report. Resize the height of the List item so the columns fit without a lot of extra space. Your display should look similar to Figure 12-18.

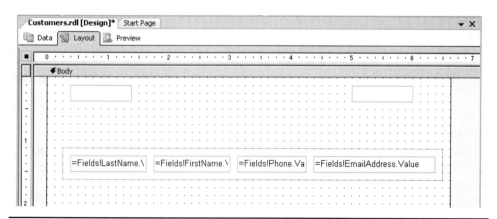

Figure 12-18 Building the report

6. Add some formatting to the report:

   a. Select the text box in the upper-left corner and type in **AdventureWorks Customers**. If you look at the properties window at the bottom right of BIDS, you will see that the Value property has changed to AdventureWorks Customers.

   b. With the first text box still selected, select the Font in the Properties window. Click the + to open the Font. Change the FontSize to **24pt**. Change the FontWeight to **Bold**. Resize the text box so the text shows.

   c. With the second text box selected, choose the Value property. Click the down arrow and select *<Expression…>*.

   d. In the Edit Expression window, select the + next to Common Functions to open it. Select Date & Time. Double-click Now to add the Now function to the above window with the = prefix. Click OK. Note the Value is *=Now*. Your display should look similar to Figure 12-19.

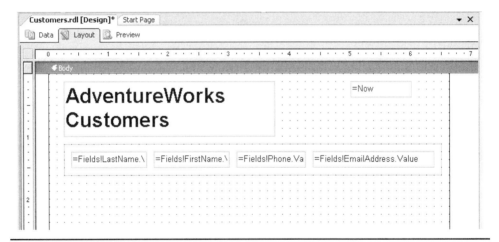

Figure 12-19   Formatted Customers report

7. Click the Preview tab to view the report. It's very likely this isn't exactly how you want the final report to look, so you can move back and forth between the Layout tab and the Preview tab as you make adjustments. The height of the list item can be adjusted, as well as the widths of the individual columns.

Report Formats

While the traditional method of serving web pages from a web server is an HTML format, SQL Server Reporting Services supports many more formats for reports. Supported formats include:

- HTML
- MHTML
- PDF
- XML

- CSV   • Excel
- TIFF

SSRS Server Placement

SQL Server Reporting Services (SSRS) was originally designed to allow internal users to access reports on an intranet web server. However, it is possible to use SSRS to make reports available to a much larger audience. Some other possibilities include:

- **Extranet**   Deploying Report Server on an Extranet using either Windows Authentication or Custom Authentication. Extranets are used for trusted partners and sometimes trusted customers depending on the business model. An extranet allows authorized users to access part of your internal network via the Internet.

- **Internet**   A public Report Server configured for anonymous access.

- **Embedded reports**   These are hosted in a ReportViewer control in custom applications that you create and deploy.

Figure 12-20 shows these possibilities. IIS1 would be used internally as an intranet server. IIS2 could be used as an extranet web server requiring authentication, while IIS3 could be used as an Internet web server using anonymous access.

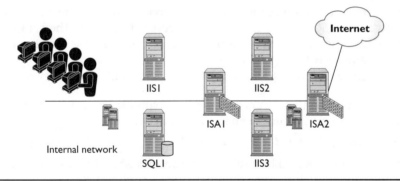

Figure 12-20   Different scenarios for hosting an SSRS Report Server

Notification Services

Notification Services is a set of services that allow users to subscribe to events, and when the event occurs they are notified. Notification Services was available in a post-release version of SQL Server 2000, but is fully integrated in SQL Server 2005.

As a simple example, a subscriber may want to be notified when a specific stock price goes above $50.00. The subscriber subscribes to the event, and when the event occurs, the subscriber is notified via a notification channel.

Multiple delivery methods of notification exist depending on what notification channels are configured. These include:

- E-mail
- Short Message Service (SMS), commonly used with personal digital assistants (PDAs)
- Instant messaging
- .NET Alerts, using a custom delivery channel
- File

The bulk of programming Notification Services occurs within a .NET application such as C# or Visual Basic. As a matter of fact, all of the sample applications are Visual Studio solutions with all the different components of Notification Services. This is similar to CLR-integrated objects.

If you remember in Chapter 9, we created a CLR-integrated stored procedure. First, we created a DLL assembly. This was a simple Visual Basic file that we compiled from the command line but which could have been much more complex. Once it was created, we then integrated the DLL assembly into SQL Server 2005, and afterward created a stored procedure to use it.

For Notification Services, we create and compile the application in Visual Studio (or using another development tool). The SQL Server 2005 samples include many sample applications for Notification Services and other services. Next, we create a Notification Services instance in SQL Server 2005 and configure it to point to the compiled .NET application. Lastly, we run the application. In this section, we'll use exercises to explore one of these samples from beginning to end.

Before we get too far into Notification Services, let's identify some key terms:

- **Event**   An action that occurs and affects the specified data. In our previous example, the event occurs when the stock price exceeds $50.00.

- **Subscriber**   A user that wants to be notified when a specific event occurs.

- **Subscription**   Created by a subscriber. Specifies what the user wants to be notified about, such as when the stock price exceeds $50.00.

- **Notification**   Generated by Notification Services. This is the actual message that is delivered to the subscriber.

- **Event provider**   An event provider collects event data and submits it to Notification Services. Notification Services comes with standard event providers that can be used with applications, or specialized event providers can be created.

- **Generator**   The generator matches events with subscribers and subscriptions. Notifications are then passed to the distributor. This is identified as the name of SQL Server 2005 server.

- **Distributor**   The distributor converts the raw notifications received from the generator into the specified delivery methods (such as e-mail or SMS notifications). This is identified as the name of SQL Server 2005 server.

Notification Application

To support Notification Services, a Notification Services application must be created. Figure 12-21 shows the general capabilities of a Notification Services application. It monitors for events. Users can create subscriptions to subscribe to an event. Once an event occurs, the Notification Services application sends notifications based on a specified delivery method such as e-mail or an SMS message to a smart phone.

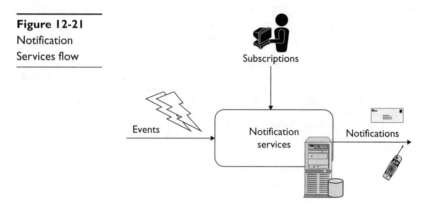

Figure 12-21
Notification
Services flow

Subscriptions

Events

Notification services

Notifications

A Notification Services application uses XML files to specify many of the properties and capabilities of the application. Two key XML files are the application definition file (ADF) and the instance configuration file (ICF).

The Application Definition File

The application definition file (ADF) is used to define the application. This includes the structure of events it will monitor, subscriptions it will accept, and the structure of the notifications it produces. The ADF file for the StockInstance application would fill three pages if we included it here. If you're interested in what it looks like, you can find it here:

```
C:\Program Files\Microsoft SQL Server\90\Samples\Notification Services\Stock\
AppDefinition\appADF.xml
```

The primary elements within this file are:

- **EventClasses**   Identifies events that the instance can monitor.
- **SubscriptionClasses**   Subscriptions that are accepted. This includes the event and schedule rules, which are actually T-SQL scripts that interact with the database.
- **NotificationClasses**   Defines the notification methods used by the application.
- **Providers**   Identifies the event providers used by the application.

- **Generator**   Identifies generators used by the application.

- **Distributors**   Identifies distributors used by the application.

- **ApplicationExecutionSettings**   Includes multiple elements that specify properties and settings for the application. These are explored in more depth later in this chapter.

The Instance Configuration File

The instance configuration file (ICF) identifies several of the elements of the Notification Services instance. The following partial ICF comes from the Stock sample Notification Services application. When the application is deployed to SQL Server as a new Notification Services instance, parameters will be provided to fill in the variables (identified with leading and trailing percent [%] symbols).

The following example shows two delivery channels: File and Email.

```xml
<?xml version="1.0" encoding="utf-8" ?>
- <NotificationServicesInstance xmlns:xsd="http://www.w3.org/2001/XMLSchema"
xmlns:xsi="http://www.w3.org/2001/XMLSchema-instance"
xmlns="http://www.microsoft.com/MicrosoftNotificationServices/
ConfigurationFileSchema">
  <InstanceName>StockInstance</InstanceName>
  <SqlServerSystem>%SqlServer%</SqlServerSystem>
- <Applications>
- <Application>
  <ApplicationName>Stock</ApplicationName>
  <BaseDirectoryPath>%SampleDirectory%\AppDefinition</BaseDirectoryPath>
  <ApplicationDefinitionFilePath>appADF.xml</ApplicationDefinitionFilePath>
- <Parameters>
- <Parameter>
  <Name>_BaseDirectoryPath_</Name>
  <Value>%SampleDirectory%</Value>
  </Parameter>
. . .
  </Parameters>
  </Application>
  </Applications>
- <DeliveryChannels>
- <DeliveryChannel>
  <DeliveryChannelName>FileChannel</DeliveryChannelName>
  <ProtocolName>File</ProtocolName>
- <Arguments>
- <Argument>
  <Name>FileName</Name>
  <Value>%SampleDirectory%\Notifications\FileNotifications.txt</Value>
  </Argument>
  </Arguments>
  </DeliveryChannel>
- <DeliveryChannel>
  <DeliveryChannelName>EmailChannel</DeliveryChannelName>
  <ProtocolName>SMTP</ProtocolName>
  </DeliveryChannel>
  </DeliveryChannels>
  </NotificationServicesInstance>
```

If you did Exercise 12.5, you have all of the sample applications installed on your system. Previously, we worked with the Reporting Services application. In the next set of exercises, we're going to build the Stock Notification Services solution that we can use to demonstrate the capabilities of Notification Services.

The next exercise creates a strong name key file (used for encryption in the application) and builds the sample solution from the command line. We'll then build the Stock Notification solution.

Exercise 12.9: Build a Sample Notification Services Solution

1. Launch the Microsoft .NET Framework command prompt. Click Start | All Programs | Microsoft .NET Framework SDK v2.0 | SDK Command Prompt. This command prompt sets the Software Development Kit (SDK) environment variables that allow you to easily use the .NET Framework tools.

2. Change the path to the location of the sample files using the Change Directory (cd) command. If you installed the samples in the default directory, these are located at C:\Program Files\Microsoft SQL Server\90\Samples. The command to change the directory is:

```
cd Program Files\Microsoft SQL Server\90\Samples
```

3. Create the strong name key file with the following command in the command prompt:

```
sn -k SampleKey.snk
```

4. Change the path to the location of the Stock Notification solution with the following command in the command prompt:

```
cd Notification Services\Stock
```

Alternatively, you can type in the full path, as shown in the following command:

```
cd Program Files\Microsoft SQL Server\90\Samples\Notification Services\
Stock
```

5. Now we want to build the Visual Studio solution. At the same command prompt, enter the following command:

```
msbuild Stock_VB.sln
```

After a moment, the build of the solution will be completed with a message stating "Build succeeded."

6. Close the SDK Command Prompt by entering **Exit**.

In the previous exercise, we built the Notification Services solution. If you have Visual Studio installed on your system and you're interested in the details of how the solution is put together, you can browse to the Notification Services\Stock folder and double-click one of the solution files. The file named Stock.sln is the C# version, while the file named Stock_VB.sln is the Visual Basic version.

Deploying and Registering an Instance of Notification Services

Once a Notification Services application is created, we need to deploy and register it in SQL Server 2005.

To deploy it, we use SSMS and create a new Notification Services instance. Here we need to fill in the parameters required by the application. Parameters are identified in the InstanceConfig.xml file in the Parameters section. Parameters have both leading and trailing percent (%) symbols. Different Notification Services instances will have different parameters.

In the samples, you need to identify the server name hosting SQL Server 2005, the SQL Server instance, and the path to the application.

After the Notification Services instance is deployed, you need to register it. By registering it the instance name, version, and database server information is added to the Windows Registry.

Exercise 12.10: Deploy the Stock Notification Services Sample Solution to SQL Server 2005

1. Launch SQL Server Management Studio (SSMS) and connect to the default instance.

2. Using Object Explorer, right-click Notification Services and select New Notification Services Instance….

3. In the New Notification Services Instance dialog box, click Browse. Browse the Stock sample directory (C:\Program Files\Microsoft SQL Server\90\Samples\ Notification Services\Stock) and select the InstanceConfig.xml file.

4. The SqlServer parameter identifies the server name and instance of SQL Server. If you're using the default instance (instead of a named instance), enter your server name only. If you're unsure of the name of your computer, you can launch a command prompt by using the WINDOWS+R keys, typing **CMD**, and pressing ENTER. At the command prompt, enter **HOSTNAME** and press ENTER.

5. For the SampleDirectory parameter, enter the path to the directory holding the Stock sample Notification Services application: **C:\Program Files\Microsoft SQL Server\90\Samples\Notification Services\Stock**.

 TIP When entering the path, make sure the trailing slash (\) is entered. The ICF uses this path to locate relative paths from here, and without the trailing slash the paths are interpreted incorrectly, causing you to receive errors saying the files can't be located.

---

6. For the NotificationServicesHost, enter the name of your computer.

7. Select the check box to Enable instance after it is created. Your display should look similar to Figure 12-22. In this figure, the name of the system I'm using is Darril. Click OK.

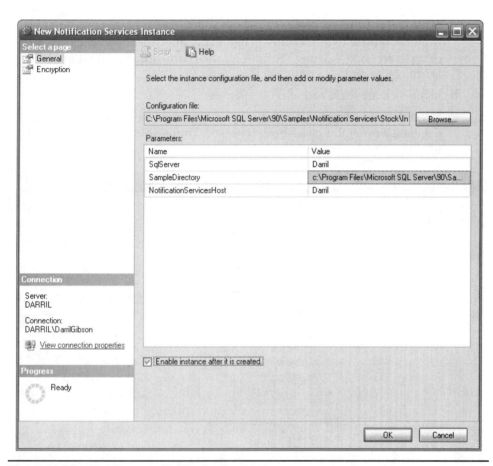

Figure 12-22 Creating a new Notification Services instance

8. After a moment, the Notification Service creation should complete. Click Close on the Creating New Notification Services Instance dialog box. At this point, you should see a new Notification Service named StockInstance in the Notification Services container in the SSMS Object Explorer. In addition to creating the StockInstance, it also creates two databases named StockInstanceNSMain and StockInstanceStock, which will be used for the NotificationServices application.

9. We're not done yet. Next, we need to register the instance of Notification Services in SSMS. Right-click the StockInstance Notification Service and select Tasks | Register. Accept the defaults (nothing selected) and click OK. Once the Registering Instance dialog box has completed and indicates success, click Close.

10. Next, we need to grant the required permissions for the Notification Services instance.

   a. Identify the login you're using to access SQL Server. Within the SSMS Object Explorer, browse to the Security | Logins container. Identify the login you're using to access SQL Server. (For me, it's the DarrilGibson account on the Darril computer.)

   b. Right-click the login and select Properties.

   c. Select the User Mapping property page. Choose the StockInstanceNSMain database. Ensure this check box is checked. Your display should look similar to Figure 12-23. Click OK.

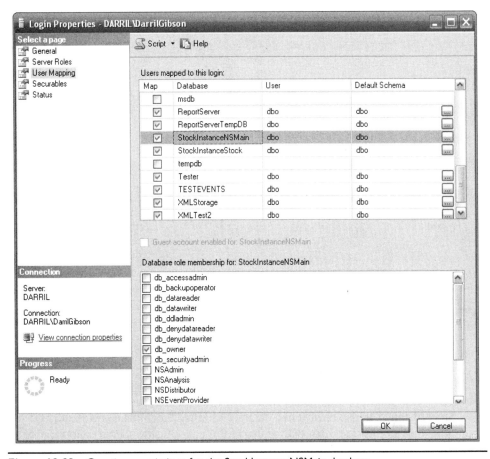

Figure 12-23   Granting permissions for the StockInstanceNSMain database

11. Grant the required NTFS permissions.

   a. Launch Windows Explorer by pressing WINDOWS+E. Browse to the Events folder for the sample application: C:\Program Files\Microsoft SQL Server\90\ Samples\Notification Services\Stock\Events.

b. Right-click the Events folder and select Properties. Select the Security tab. Ensure the account you're logged onto your system with has at least Read and Modify permissions. Click OK.

c. Browse to the Notifications folder for the sample application: C:\Program Files\Microsoft SQL Server\90\Samples\Notification Services\Stock\ Notifications.

d. Right-click the Notifications folder and select Properties. Choose the Security tab. Ensure the account you're logged onto your system with has at least Write permissions. Click OK.

e. Browse to the Notifications Services folder: C:\Program Files\Microsoft SQL Server\90\Samples\Notification Services.

f. Right-click the Notifications Services folder and select Properties. Choose the Security tab. Ensure the account you're logged onto your system with has at least Read and Read & Execute permissions. Click OK.

Application Databases

The Notification Services application typically creates a database used to hold event and subscription data, resulting notification data, and application metadata. It's also possible to use an existing database.

When creating the database, you should consider the size based on how many notifications you expect and how long the notifications will be retained.

The application XML file includes a <Vacuum> element, which is used by the data removal process. The data removal process is also called the vacuumer. Child elements include the Vacuum Schedule, which specifies when the vacuumer is run, and the RetentionAge element, which specifies the minimum age when event and notification data is considered obsolete. Obsolete data is available for removal by the data removal process.

 EXAM TIP   To prevent your Notification Services application database from growing out of control, make sure you configure the <Vacuum> and <RetentionAge> elements. This will allow you to specify when notifications are considered obsolete and can be automatically deleted.

Subscribing to an Event

Subscribing to a Notification Services event is done within a .NET application. It isn't done with SQL Server 2005, though ultimately the data is added to tables within the database. In the following exercise, a console application is used to add subscribers and subscriptions.

To allow users to subscribe, it's not uncommon to create a Windows form or a web form that gives them the option of subscribing. The interface would typically include drop-down boxes and/or text boxes. For example, a user that logs in to the application could enter the stock they're interested in, and the stock price they want to be notified about.

Once the stock reaches the user's target price, the user can be notified and then allowed to decide whether to buy or sell the stock.

Within the application, the System.Data.SqlClient.SqlDependency object can be used to register and receive notifications via the System.Data.SqlClient.SqlDependency .OnChanged event handler. The .OnChanged event handler is similar to a trigger within SQL Server 2005 where INSERTs, UPDATEs, and DELETEs can be monitored, and when one occurs, the event handler fires. The SQLDependency object manages the complexity involved in setting up the notification in the database.

 EXAM TIP When configuring subscriptions within a Notification Services application, consider using the System.Data.SqlClient.SqlDependency object and the System.Data.SqlClient.SqlDependency.OnChanged event handler. The SqlDependency object is used to create a notification subscription.

To see this in action, you can review the ReviewWatcher sample available from the MSDN Codeplex samples site:

```
http://www.codeplex.com/MSFTEEProdSamples/Wiki/View.aspx?title=SS2005!Readme_
ReviewWatcher&referringTitle=Home.
```

The ReviewWatcher sample demonstrates the SqlDependency object to subscribe to Query Notifications.

Once a subscription is generated, rules are created within Notification Services that fire in response to the event and match the event, subscriber, and subscription. These are commonly referred to as rule firings.

In the following exercise we'll start the instance Notification Services that we've created, add subscribers and subscriptions, and submit events.

Exercise 12.11: Run the Stock Notification Services Sample Application

1. Using the SSMS Object Explorer, browse to the Notification Services | StockInstance. Right-click StockInstance and click Enable. On the dialog box, click Yes.

2. Open Windows Explorer and browse to the following folder:

```
C:\Program Files\Microsoft SQL Server\90\Samples\Notification Services\
Stock\HostableExecutionEngine\vb\HostableExecutionEngine\bin\Debug
```

3. Double-click the HostableExecutionEngine.exe file. This will open a console application that will start the StockInstance. Pressing any key will stop the instance, so simply minimize the command prompt window to leave it open and keep StockInstance running.

4. Using Windows Explorer, browse to the following folder:

```
C:\Program Files\Microsoft SQL Server\90\Samples\Notification Services\
Stock\AddSubscribers\vb\AddSubscribers\bin
```

5. Double-click the AddSubscribers.exe file. A console application will open and indicate that four subscribers have been added. You should see something similar to Figure 12-24. Press ENTER from within the console application.

Figure 12-24

Adding subscribers

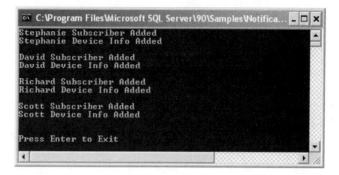

6. Using Windows Explorer, browse to the following folder:

```
C:\Program Files\Microsoft SQL Server\90\Samples\Notification Services\
Stock\AddSubscriptions\vb\AddSubscriptions\bin
```

7. Double-click the AddSubscriptions.exe file. A console application will open and indicate that four subscriptions have been added. You should see something similar to Figure 12-25. Press ENTER from within the console application to close it.

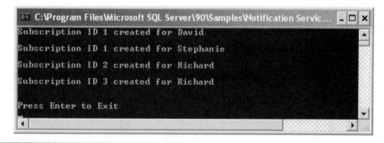

Figure 12-25 Adding subscriptions

8. Using Windows Explorer, browse to the following folder:

```
C:\Program Files\Microsoft SQL Server\90\Samples\Notification Services\
Stock\NonHostedEventProvider\vb\NonHostedEventProvider\bin
```

9. Double-click the NonHostedEventProvider.exe file. A console application will open and indicate that Event StockEvents has been added and committed. Press ENTER from within the console application to close it.

10. Using Windows Explorer, browse to the following folder:

```
C:\Program Files\Microsoft SQL Server\90\Samples\Notification Services\
Stock\Notifications
```

11. Double-click the FileNotifications.txt file. Notice it is formatted as an e-mail with an embedded HTML message. If displayed in a web browser, or a PDA that can accept and display HTML messages, it would look similar to Figure 12-26.

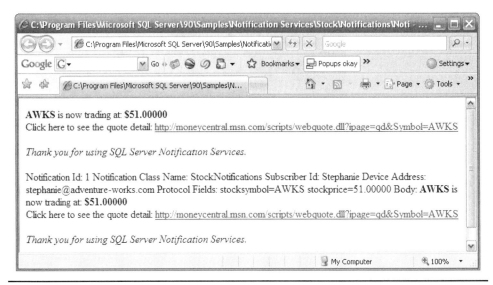

Figure 12-26   Viewing a notification

Application Properties

Application properties are contained within an XML file. For our stock application, the name of the file is appADF.xml and the path is:

```
C:\Program Files\Microsoft SQL Server\90\Samples\Notification Services\Stock\
AppDefinition
```

If you open up this file, you will see several elements for the application, including:

- EventClasses
- SubscriptionClasses
- Providers
- Generator
- Distributors
- ApplicationExecutionSettings

Most of the elements provide the definitions for the Notification Services instance. However, the ApplicationExecutionSettings element provides us with the capability to set several properties for the application. The properties include:

- **QuantumDuration**   The QuantumDuration element determines the length of time for various work processes. For example, this is used to determine the delay between when an event occurs and when an event batch is used for notifications. The default is 60 seconds.

- **PerformanceQueryInterval**   The PerformanceQueryInterval specifies how often the application updates its performance counters. Performance counters are used by Performance or System Monitor to measure the overall performance of a system. System Monitor will be covered in more depth in Chapter 13.

- **SubscriptionQuantumLimit**   The SubscriptionQuantumLimit specifies how far behind Notification Services can be before it skips subscription rule firings. For example, if Notification Services is down for a while, it will be behind, and it will skip subscription rule firings to catch up. The default is 30 minutes.

- **Vacuum**   The Vacuum element contains settings used by the data removal process that remove obsolete event and notification data from the application database. It includes the RetentionAge element, which can be used to specify when event notification data is considered obsolete and available for removal.

Notification Services vs. SQL Server Agent

We'll cover SQL Server Agent in Chapter 13, but a logical question that arises is, "Why not use the functionality of SQL Server Agent instead of Notification Services?" After all, SQL Server Agent can be configured to send e-mail alerts. Unfortunately, SQL Server Agent doesn't work as well for a couple of reasons.

First, SQL Server Agent was designed to send messages to administrators and/or perform tasks based on server or database conditions. Notification Services can collect data from just about any source, match events to subscriptions for millions of users, and send millions of notifications per day. SQL Server Agent simply can't scale to millions of users.

Analysis Services

SQL Server Analysis Services (SSAS) is used to analyze data using online analytical processing (OLAP) and data mining. Though the majority of this book deals with online transaction processing (OLTP), we should still point out several differences that exist between OLAP and OLTP.

- OLAP is generally static data, while OLTP includes active INSERTs, UPDATEs, and DELETEs.

- OLAP is highly denormalized data that is optimized for data retrieval, while OLTP is generally normalized data that is optimized for data modification.

- OLAP data is reorganized into different dimensions (cubes) allowing the data to be easily viewed in various ways. When necessary, OLTP data can be presented using cube-like qualities (for example, using GROUP BY WITH CUBE), but this relies on the processor to reorganize the data.

Data mining is known as the extraction of previously unknown, but potentially useful information from a data source. As the amount of available data and the size of databases have grown, the need for methods to sort through and pick out only the relevant information required has also grown. Analysis Services helps fill this need.

Objects used within SSAS include:

- **Data Sources**   This is typically a back-end database such as SQL Server 2005, though other data sources are possible.

- **Data Source Views**   This is similar to VIEWs created within SQL Server 2005, but that are instead created within SSAS. The VIEWs often contain denormalized data (such as calculated columns) that make data retrieval quicker.

- **Cubes**   A cube is a multidimensional structure that contains dimensions and measures. Similar to a square cube that you can pick up and look at from different perspectives, cubes within SSAS allow views of the data from different perspectives.

- **Dimensions**   Dimensions are used to organize data within a cube depending on the area of interest. They contain attributes that correspond to columns within dimension tables and can be organized into multilevel hierarchical structures.

If you pursue the MCITP: Business Intelligence Developer certification, you will need to know much more about SSAS. However, for the MCITP: Database Developer certification, a short introduction is all that's required. If you're interested in learning more about SSAS, start with the Books Online article, "SQL Server Analysis Services (SSAS)" and follow the links for additional information.

Chapter Review

In this chapter, we covered SQL Server Reporting Services (SSRS) and Notification Services in some depth and provided a short introduction to SQL Server Analysis Services (SSAS).

SSRS provides reporting capabilities for SQL Server and allows us to deploy reports via a web server. Internet Information Services (IIS) is required to support the deployment of Reporting Services. The Report Manager can be used by users to view reports, and also to create their own ad hoc reports if Report Models have been created and deployed to Reporting Services. Using SSRS within BIDS, sophisticated reports can be created, such as parameterized reports that provide specific data depending on the parameters provided. Snapshot reports can be created to limit the processing time of reports, and report subscriptions can provide users with any specific reports when needed.

Notification Services is used to provide users with notifications of events to which they subscribe. Notifications can be sent via a variety of means, including e-mail and Short Message Services (used with PDAs). The majority of a Notification Services application is created in a .NET application, but once created it is deployed to SQL Server 2005.

Within SQL Server 2005, databases are used in conjunction with an instance of Notification Services. Two XML files are used to provide many of the definitions for XML: the application definition file (ADF) and the instance configuration file (ICF).

SQL Server Analysis Services (SSAS) is used for online analytical processing (OLAP) and data mining. SSAS lets us create highly denormalized versions of the database in the form of cubes. An OLAP database is optimized for queries.

Additional Study

Self-Study Exercises

- Install IIS to install Reporting Services.
- Launch BIDS and create a Report Model
- Launch the Report Manager and create a report using Report Builder and one of the Report Models you've created.
- Follow the tutorial to create an instance of Notification Services using the following tutorial:

```
C:\Program Files\Microsoft SQL Server\90\Samples\Notification Services\
Flight\Readme_Flight.htm
```

BOL Topics

- SQL Server Reporting Services
- SQL Server Reporting Services (How Do I)
- Report Server Database
- Distributing Reports through Subscriptions
- What Does Notification Services Do?
- How Does Notification Services Work?
- Using SqlDependency to Subscribe to Query Notifications
- SQL Server Analysis Services (SSAS)

Summary of What You Need to Know

70-431

There are no topics in this chapter for the 70-431 test.

70-441

When preparing for the 70-441 test, you should know all of the concepts presented in both the Reporting Services and Notification Services sections.

70-442

When preparing for the 70-442 test, you should know all of the concepts presented in the Notification Services section.

Questions

70-441

1. Analysts within your company frequently ask for minor changes to reports, but database developers often can't respond quickly. The analysts ask if there is any way they can create their own ad hoc reports without having to wait for a developer to create the report. What would you do?

   A. Create a Report Model and allow the analysts to create their own reports using Report Builder.

   B. Create a Report Builder and allow the analysts to create their own reports using Report Model.

   C. Create a report and allow the analysts to create their own reports using Report Builder.

   D. Create a report and allow the analysts to create their own reports using Report Model.

2. You need to design a report using SQL Server Reporting Services that will have a different number of columns based on the actual data used by the report. What will you use within your report?

   A. A grouping level

   B. A columnar list

   C. A matrix

   D. A filer

3. Business analysts frequently access the DailySalesReport in SQL Server Reporting Services throughout the day. You are asked to minimize the response time in creating this report, and also minimize the overall impact on the production servers' performance. The data can be up to 30 minutes old. What would you do?

   A. Create snapshots of the report every two hours.

   B. Enable session caching on the report with the cached copy set to expire after 30 minutes.

   C. Create a matrix report.

   D. Create the report to run with credentials stored within the report server.

4. You have hosted a SQL Server Reporting Services (SSRS) solution making reports available to internal users. You do not want to grant unnecessary privileges to the Reporting Server. A developer is creating a Windows application and asks you for the best method to allow users to view reports on the SQL Server Reporting Services server available within his application. What should you suggest?

   A. Add a hyperlink to SSRS within the application.

   B. Add a hyperlink to Report Manager within the application.

   C. Add a Report Viewer control to the application.

   D. Create a web service and access it from the application.

5. Your company sells plumbing supplies to a core group of resellers. The resellers have asked for a method where they can view weekly activity on their orders. The resellers will be accessing the data from locations around the country. What do you suggest?

   A. Create an SSRS solution on your intranet and serve reports from here.

   B. Create an SSRS solution on an extranet and serve reports from here.

   C. Create an SSRS solution on the Internet and serve reports from here.

   D. Send the reports to the resellers via e-mail.

6. Users within your company need to be able to view sales reports on a monthly basis. Sales reports need to be generated on a weekly, monthly, and quarterly basis. Most users will access the reports with Internet Explorer, but some users need the reports in PDF format. What solution would you recommend?

   A. Use SSRS.

   B. Use SSIS.

   C. Send the reports via e-mail.

   D. Make the reports available via a specialized ASP .NET web site.

7. You are designing a Notification Services solution for the StockPortfolio database. It will be used to send confirmation notices to customers once requested stock purchases are configured. You need to minimize the size of the Notification Services database. How can you do this?

   A. Specify a maximum size for the TempDB database.

   B. Specify the Simple Recovery Model so the transaction log is truncated regularly.

   C. Specify a retention age of one week for events.

   D. Run a SQL Server Agent job regularly to shrink the database.

8. You manage a database for an automobile parts store. Most of the parts have a populated column named Low-Inventory that identifies when a part must be reordered, though most parts are reordered before this Low-Inventory number is reached. The manager has asked to be notified via e-mail when any item reaches the Low-Inventory column. What do you suggest?

   A. Create an SSRS report and send this report to the manager via e-mail on a regular basis.

   B. Create a Notification Services application that sends e-mail messages when the Low-Inventory event occurs.

   C. Create a SSIS application and e-mail the application to the manager.

   D. Create a stored procedure check for Low-Inventory and then e-mail the results to the manager.

70-442

1. You are creating a solution that matches job candidates with available jobs. A client application is being developed to run on employees' client computers. During business hours, both job candidates and available jobs sometimes change frequently. You want to ensure that these changes are relayed to the client application as they occur. The client application can display data that is up to 30 minutes old.

   A. Design the client application to refresh the data every 30 minutes.

   B. Use the SqlDependency.OnChanged event to notify the client applications when a change occurs. Refresh the data when this event occurs.

   C. Use the SqlDependency.OnChanged event to notify the client applications when a change occurs. Refresh the data if the last refresh was done more than 30 minutes ago.

   D. Configure an SSRS to send reports to the client application every 30 minutes.

2. You manage an application used by authors to submit written articles to your publications. Articles are stored in a varbinary(max) data type within the application database. Once articles are reviewed, they are commented on, and then reposted for the authors to retrieve and incorporate the changes into a final copy. You need to ensure that the authors are notified when commented articles are posted. What can you do?

   A. Use SSRS to send reports to the authors when the change occurs.

   B. Use SSIS to send packages to the authors when the change occurs.

   C. Use Notification Services to send an e-mail when the change occurs.

   D. Task the editor with sending an e-mail when the change occurs.

Answers

70-441

1. **A.** By creating a Report Model, users can create their own ad hoc reports with Report Builder, using the available data in the Report Model. The Report Model must be created first, and afterward only the Report Builder can be used to create ad hoc reports.

2. **C.** A report configured with a matrix will have a varying number of columns based on the data. A columnar list will have a set number of columns. Neither the grouping level nor filters affect the columns.

3. **B.** By enabling session caching, we can set the report to expire after 30 minutes. Snapshots can be specified to run on a daily basis and we can specify the time to run the snapshot, but we don't have the ability to specify the minutes or hours between snapshots.

4. **C.** The Report Viewer control (available in Visual Studio) is ideally suited for this need. By adding it to the application, users can view reports from the SSRS server without the need to access the SSRS server directly. While hyperlinks will be possible, user permissions would need to be added for each user that accesses a report. With the ReportViewer, a single application user can be added and used by all users that use the application.

5. **B.** Since it's a core group of resellers, we could make the data available via Internet technologies. However, since it's data we wouldn't want just anyone to see, we'd use an extranet, requiring the resellers to provide authentication before access to the reports is granted.

6. **A.** SQL Server Reporting Services (SSRS) can be configured to serve reports in multiple formats, including PDF. An ASP .NET web site could also work, but the solution would take more time to develop and maintain. Reports could be sent via e-mail, but this would be time-intensive unless configured as subscriptions with SSRS. SQL Server Integration Services (SSIS) is used to extract and transform data but wouldn't be used to create and distribute reports.

7. **C.** The RetentionAge element is a child element of the Vacuum element and specifies when notifications are considered obsolete and can be automatically deleted when the vacuumer (data removal process) is run. The size of the TempDB database doesn't affect the Notification Services database. Truncating the transaction log won't affect the size of the actual database file. Shrinking the database can't shrink it to a size smaller than the actual data.

8. **B.** The only solution that can immediately send an e-mail to the manager when the Low-Inventory event occurs is a Notification Services solution. While a report subscription could be created, it would only run when scheduled, not as soon as the event occurred. An SSIS application could be used to extract or transform data, but wouldn't be able to capture this event. A stored procedure could check for the event and send an e-mail, but couldn't capture the event in real time.

70-442

1. **C.** The SqlDependency object can be used to create a notification subscription and the .OnChanged event can monitor for specific changes. Since the requirement states that data can be 30 minutes old, we wouldn't refresh with every change, but instead only when the last refresh was more than 30 minutes previous. Having the client application refresh every 30 minutes would cause needless traffic when no changes occur. SSRS isn't a good solution for this problem, and subscriptions cannot be set to run every 30 minutes; instead, subscriptions would have to be created for specific times, which could lead to needless traffic.

2. **C.** Notification Services can be configured to watch for the change and then automatically send an e-mail. Neither SSRS nor SSIS can be configured to watch and respond to the change. It would be possible to task the editor, but an automated method would be more reliable.

Maintenance Tools

In this chapter, you will learn about:

- System Monitor
- SQL Server Agent
- The Maintenance Plan Wizard
- SQL Server Profiler and SQL Trace

> *You can't control what you can't measure.*
>
> —*Tom DeMarco*

In a perfect database, nothing ever goes wrong. Then again, if nothing ever went wrong, there wouldn't be much need for database administrators (DBAs) and database developers. Thankfully, there's no such thing as a perfect database and things do go wrong. Successful database administrators and database developers know the tools available help us measure, monitor, and troubleshoot a database application when things do go wrong.

The tools in this chapter will help you measure and monitor your databases. And with proper metrics, we can control our databases.

System Monitor

System Monitor is a built-in tool within Windows. In Windows operating systems, the overall tool is officially called Performance—and often, informally, Performance Monitor.

Performance uses objects and counters. Each object within Performance has multiple counters that can be measured to determine the operation and health of the server. When SQL Server is installed, additional SQL objects are added that can be monitored to identify specific activity within SQL Server.

Counters can be monitored in real time with System Monitor, or they can be monitored over a span of time in counter logs. Additionally, we can create alerts to respond when a counter exceeds a certain threshold.

In this section, we'll explore several of the counters available for the core four resources. We'll also go through the process required to measure them, and then create a baseline.

Performance can be launched in several ways. One way is to enter **perfmon** at the command or run line. If you do so, you should see a display similar to Figure 13-1.

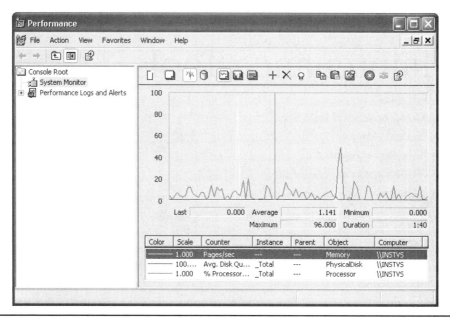

Figure 13-1 Performance

Notice that, by default, three counters are automatically added. System Monitor adds the most popular counter for each of the following three objects: Memory, Physical Disk, and Processor (as shown in Table 13-1).

Object	Counter
Memory	Pages/sec.
Physical Disk	Avg. Disk Queue Length.
Processor	% Processor Time.

Table 13-1 Default Counters Added to System Monitor

Additional counters can be added if desired by clicking the + icon on the System Monitor toolbar. You would then select the Performance object desired and the specific counter desired for that object. In Figure 13-2, we've clicked the + icon on the toolbar and are getting ready to add additional Processor object counters.

Measuring Counters in System Monitor

When measuring the performance of any server (SQL Server 2005, or any other server), we start by measuring the core four resources. These are:

- CPU or processor usage
- Memory usage

Figure 13-2
Adding Processor
object counters

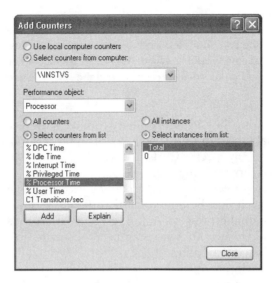

- Disk usage
- Network bandwidth

Then, depending on what server we are monitoring, we add additional counters related to the specific service the server is hosting. For example, if it's a SQL Server, we can use some of the SQL Server counters to measure performance of the SQL Server. If it was a Domain Name System (DNS) server, or domain controller, or Dynamic Host Configuration Protocol (DHCP) server (or hosting just about any other server role), we would then add additional counters to monitor the performance of the appropriate role.

Is It Performance, Performance Monitor, or System Monitor?
Among system administrators, Performance, Performance Monitor, and System Monitor are sometimes used interchangeably. Performance is the name of the tool on the Start menu. It can be launched by clicking Start | All Programs | Administrative Tools | Performance on systems with administrative tools installed on the main menu. It can also be launched by entering **perfmon**—short for "Performance Monitor"—at the run line. Books Online says that System Monitor replaced Performance Monitor after Windows NT 4.0—thus, it's technically *not* accurate to refer to Performance by using the name *Performance Monitor*, but you may hear administrators do it often. Performance includes *System Monitor* and *Performance Logs and Alerts*. If we want to view real-time data, we'd use System Monitor. If we want to create a baseline or an alert, we'd use Performance Logs and Alerts.

EXAM TIP When measuring the performance of any server, start by measuring the core four resources. These are processor usage, memory usage, disk usage, and network bandwidth. Next, add additional counters for the server role to gather information on how well the server is performing in its specific role.

CPU

When measuring the CPU, the primary counter is the % Processor Time. You can measure the total processor time (meaning for all processors), or you can measure the processor time of any specific CPUs. This can be useful if you've used the affinity to limit which processors are being used by SQL.

If the *Processor:% Processor Time* counter exceeds 80 percent on a regular basis during operation, it may be time to either offload processes, upgrade your processor(s), or add additional processors. At the very least, it deserves further investigation. When the processor reaches 100 percent, expect the queues to start backing up and users to experience longer wait times.

Sometimes the processor is especially busy due to specific processes that are running. A rudimentary way to identify which processes are taking up the most CPU time is by launching Windows Task Manager and clicking the Processes tab. A more sophisticated method is using System Monitor and the Process object. Here, you can collect detailed data on individual processes.

Memory

If we don't have enough memory, we'll experience excessive paging. It's common to see a symptom of *disk thrashing*, where the disk is extremely busy swapping data between physical and virtual RAM and the system slows to a crawl.

One of the easiest counters to check for excessive paging is the Pages/sec counter in the Memory Performance object. You can see this in Figure 13-3.

Figure 13-3
Adding Memory object counters

The Memory:Pages/sec counter identifies how much paging is taking place on your system. Some will always be occurring, but you want to keep it as low as possible. You would typically measure this against your baseline to see if it is excessive.

Any time you're not sure what a counter actually measures, you can click the Explain button for an explanation. A small window pops up and includes an explanation of the selected counter, as we can see in Figure 13-4.

Figure 13-4

The Explanation page in System Monitor

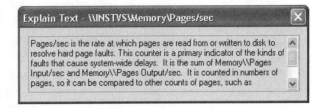

Explain Text - \\INSTVS\Memory\Pages/sec

Pages/sec is the rate at which pages are read from or written to disk to resolve hard page faults. This counter is a primary indicator of the kinds of faults that cause system-wide delays. It is the sum of Memory\\Pages Input/sec and Memory\\Pages Output/sec. It is counted in numbers of pages, so it can be compared to other counts of pages, such as

An additional memory counter to monitor is the Available Bytes counter. This indicates the amount of physical memory that is available to be used. You never want to see less than 5 percent of your total RAM listed in Available Bytes. If it is, your memory will be a bottleneck for the workload.

Disk

Two disk objects can be used to measure disk activity: *physical* disk and *logical* disk. A physical disk can be divided into partitions such as C:, D:, and so on. If you want to measure the C: drive only, use the Logical Disk counters. If you're interested in all the drives on the spindle, or the entire disk, use the Physical Disk object.

Physical Disk counters that can give you insight into the performance of your disk subsystem include *PhysicalDisk:% Disk Time* and *PhysicalDisk:Avg. Disk Queue Length*. The same counters are available on the Logical Disk object. If the % Disk Time counter is over 90 percent, it deserves further investigation. As with most queues, if the Avg. Disk Queue Length is more than two, then you probably want to investigate further.

TIP As a general rule, if a queue is more than two, it may be a bottleneck. This goes for counters with any objects such as *System object: Processor Queue Length* counter, *Server Work Queues object:Queue Length* counter, *Network Interface object:Output Queue Length* counter, and more. A *queue* is a waiting line. Any time more than two of anything are waiting in line, it deserves further investigation. At the very least, it deserves a comparison with the baseline.

One of the counters available in the Logical Disk object is the *Logical Disk:% Free Space* counter. This can be used to identify any time a disk drive space falls below a given threshold.

NIC

You can use the Network Interface object to measure activity on any Network Interface Cards (NICs) you have installed. The *NetworkInterface:Bytes Total/sec* counter measures the rate at which data is sent and received over the NIC. As with many counters, if measured against the baseline, it can give you insight into how activity is increasing over time.

As with many tasks, sometimes the simplest way is the easiest way. You can press CTRL+SHIFT+ESC to launch Task Manager and look at the Networking tab. This tells you what the link speed is, and the percentage that's being utilized.

SQL Counters

Several counters are added when you install SQL Server, as you can see in Figure 13-5.

Figure 13-5

SQL Server objects in System Monitor

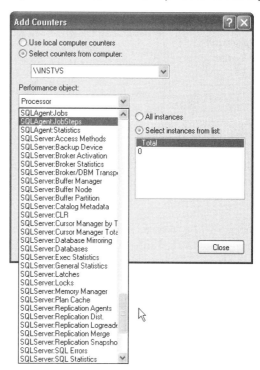

Different performance objects provide the ability to measure different performance characteristics of SQL Server. All of the performance objects are listed in the following groups of bullets, but they are organized based on what you're trying to measure.

The following performance objects are used to measure the overall performance of SQL Server for the end user. As an example, some of these counters can be used to measure query response times for the SQL Server.

- **SQLServer:SQL Statistics**   These statistics provide information about T-SQL queries such as the number of batches, and the number of compilation and recompilations.

- **SQLServer:General Statistics**   These counters provide information on server-wide activity, such as the number of users connected to an instance, or the number of currently blocked processes.

- **SQLServer:Exec Statistics**   These counters provide information on executions, such as distributed queries and OLE DB calls.

EXAM TIP By monitoring the number of query compilations and recompilations, and the number of batches received, it gives you an indication of how quickly SQL Server is processing user queries and how effectively the query optimizer is processing the query. All of these counters are available in the SQL Server:SQLStatistics object.

For example, you may be interested in how efficiently SQL Server is using the memory, or want to be alerted when a transaction log exceeds a certain size. The following performance objects have many counters that can be very useful when you need to measure this. Some of these are:

- **SQL Server:Buffer Manager** This object provides information about memory buffers used by SQL Server, such as free memory and the buffer cache hit ratio.

TIP The buffer cache hit ratio indicates the percentage of pages that are read from the cache (memory) without having to read the page from disk. Reading from cache is significantly quicker than reading from disk, so the higher the number is, the quicker the system is performing. If this number is low, adding more memory can increase the hit ratio and improve the performance.

- **SQL Server:Buffer Partition** Use this to measure how frequently SQL Server requests and accesses free pages.
- **SQL Server:Memory Manager** Use this to monitor overall server memory usage.
- **SQLServer:Plan Cache** This object provides information on the cache used to store compiled objects, such as stored procedures, triggers, and query plans.

Locks are created by SQL Server to prevent concurrent use of data when it should be prevented. For example, when a row is being modified by one transaction, a lock would prevent the row from being read or modified from another transaction. Cursors are used to open a result set and process it one row at a time. Cursor and lock information can be obtained from the following objects.

- **SQLServer:Cursor Manager Total** Use to obtain information on cursors.
- **SQLServer:Cursor Manager by Type** For more detailed information, such as how many are active, or the number of cursor requests per second, use this object.
- **SQLServer:Locks** If excessive locks or deadlocks are suspected, use this object to determine information on locks or deadlocks. SQL Profiler can then be used to obtain more detailed information.
- **SQLServer:Latches** This object provides information on latches used on internal resources such as database pages.

The following SQL Server objects don't fall into categories as easily as the previous ones, but can still be valuable in measuring items of specific interest.

- **SQLServer:Access Methods** Measures the allocation of SQL Server database objects, such as the number of index searches or the number of pages allocated to indexes and data.

- **SQLServer:Backup Device** This is used to obtain information on backup and restore operations.

- **SQLServer:CLR** This object provides information on execution time for CLR-integrated objects.

- **SQLServer:Database Mirroring** This object provides information about database mirroring.

- **SQLServer:Databases** The SQL Server Databases object can be used to measure specifics on individual databases. A couple of the individual counters that can be used to measure sizes of files are listed next:

- **SQLServer:SQL Errors** This object can be used to track errors within SQL Server, such as the number of errors per second.

- **SQLServer:Transactions** Counters within this object are used to measure transactions such as identifying the length of time for the longest running transaction.

- **SQLServer:User Settable** Custom counters can be created and used within SQL Server using this performance object. Values for these counters must be set through the use of the sp_user_counter1 through sp_user_counter10 system stored procedures. The syntax is shown in the following line of code. The value is any integer value.

```
EXEC sp_user_counter1 value
```

- **SQLServer:Wait Statistics** This object provides information on waits within SQL Server.

In the following exercise, we'll explore the real-time measurement capability of System Monitor.

Exercise 13.1: Explore System Monitor

1. Choose Start | Administrative Tools | Performance. Alternatively, you could type **perfmon** from the command line or the run box. Notice that the default counters for the CPU, memory, and disk objects have been added.

2. Click the plus (+) in the toolbar. Select the Process Performance object. The % Processor Time counter is selected by default. Under Select Instances From List, choose the sqlservr process, as shown in Figure 13-6. Click Add.

Figure 13-6
Monitoring the sqlservr process in the Process object

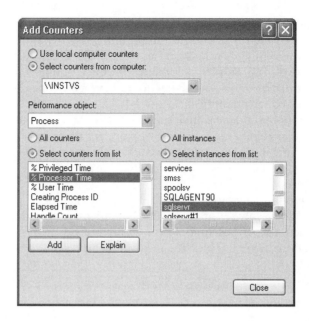

3. Select the SQL Server:Buffer Manager object. The Buffer Cache Hit Ratio counter is chosen by default. Click Add.

4. In the Add Counters dialog box, click Close to return to the graph display.

5. Click the Pages/sec counter in the bottom pane of System Monitor. Record the Last, Average, Minimum, and Maximum values for this counter. The default Duration (length of time the graph will display) is 1 minute and 40 seconds (1:40).

6. Click the Avg. Disk Queue Length counter and record the values.

7. Click the % Processor Time counter and record the values.

8. Launch a few programs—such as Word, Internet Explorer, Outlook, or something else—on the computer you're using. Now look at the counters again, and notice that the average and maximum values have changed.

9. You decide you want to remove the Pages/sec counter. Select the Pages/sec counter in the bottom pane of System Monitor and press DELETE.

Baselines

We've mentioned baselines a few times in this chapter already, but haven't really explained them. In this context, a *baseline* is a set of measurements for a server created in a counter log.

A baseline log would be captured over a period of time, often a week. We capture data during peak time and off-peak time to ensure we truly know the load at any given moment. However, rather than capture the data every minute of every day, we would instead take snapshots throughout the day or week to create a baseline. Snapshots are typically taken at intervals of 15, 30, or 45 minutes. The goal is to find a balance where we can measure the server without dumping much additional load on it.

For a server in any role—such as an application server (running Microsoft Exchange or Microsoft SQL Server), a domain controller, or a network infrastructure server (like DHCP or DNS—it's a sound practice to have a baseline. At the very least, the core four resources (CPU, memory, disk, and NIC) are measured. Then, based on the role, additional counters are measured, such as Buffer Manager counters on a SQL Server.

For example, if I came into a company as a new hire and was tasked with managing and maintaining a set of SQL Servers, I might be interested in viewing the baseline. Let's say one doesn't exist. No problem. I'd make it a priority to create a baseline for each of the servers.

Six months later, users begin complaining that one of the servers is responding sluggishly. "Sluggishly" is pretty hard to quantify, but if we take measurements and compare them to our baseline, we can easily put our finger on the problem. Table 13-2 shows the current and baseline measurements.

Counter	Baseline	Today
Pages/sec	9	515
% Processor Time	40%	45%
% Disk Time	35%	85%
Bytes Total/sec	5,036,241	9,324,438

Table 13-2   Comparing the Baseline to Current Measurements

Notice the significant increase in the Pages/sec counter. We also see an increase in the % Disk Time, but this is likely due to the increase in paging. The processor time has only a moderate increase of 5 percent. Paging has increased because we don't have enough RAM for the processes on this server.

I can't say what has caused the increased load on RAM, but I can clearly see that paging has increased. Increasing the amount of physical RAM in this system would likely solve the problem.

Bytes Total/sec (transferred) has increased from 5MB to 9MB, which in itself is a moderate increase, but if I had a 10-Mbps NIC, I'd be very concerned and would be looking to upgrade this NIC to a 100-Mbps NIC as soon as possible. If it's a 10-Mbps NIC, we've significantly increased the usage. However, if it's a 100-Mbps NIC or a 1-Gbps NIC, the increase is only moderate compared with the total capability.

An additional benefit is that communicating this successfully to management is much easier with numbers. It's one thing to go to management and ask for money to add RAM because you're pretty sure you don't have enough and it's causing the system to act sluggishly. It's something completely different when you can tell them that increases in the server load have resulted in a paging increase from an average of 9 per second to over 500 per second (a 5000 percent increase) over a six-month period—something which has more than doubled the load on the disk and resulted in a noticeable slowdown of the server's response.

Likewise, if you wanted to replace the 10-Mbps NICs, you could say that the load on the NIC on this server has increased from about 50 percent to about 93 percent, and if the NIC is not replaced soon, an increase in usage of this server will result in more slowdowns.

 TIP I often find that when people haven't been exposed to baselines before, or haven't actually created a baseline, the concept easily slips past them. When teaching baselines in the classroom, I have students create a 24-hour baseline on any computer—whether it's their home computer or a server they manage. Use the following exercise as a guide to create your own baseline.

Exercise 13.2: Create a Baseline

Watch video 13-2 to see how to create a baseline on the core four resources.

1. Launch System Monitor.

2. Double-click Performance Logs And Alerts to open it. Right-click Counter Logs and select New Log Settings.

3. In the New Log Settings dialog box, enter **MCITP Baseline** and click OK.

4. In the MCITP Baseline dialog box, click Add Counters. It should default to the Processor Performance object and the % Processor Time counter. Click Add.

5. Select the Memory Performance object. Ensure that Pages/sec is selected, and then click Add.

6. Select the Physical Disk Performance object. Ensure that % Disk Time is selected, and then click Add.

7. Select the Network Interface Performance object. Ensure that Bytes Total/sec is selected, and then click Add. Click Close.

8. In the Sample Data Every section, change the Units from *seconds* to *minutes.*

9. In the Run As box, enter the username of an account that has administrative permissions. Click Set Password and set the password for this account. Your display should look similar to Figure 13-7.

10. Click the Log Files tab. Note that a binary file will be created.

11. Click the Schedule tab. In the Start Log section, change At to *12:00:01 AM* and On to the next Sunday. Your display should look similar to Figure 13-8.

12. In the Stop Log section, set After to 7 and Units to "days." Click OK. If prompted to create a C:\Perflogs folder, click Yes.

The counter log is now scheduled to automatically start on the next Sunday morning and automatically stop after seven days.

Figure 13-7
Adding counters
to the baseline

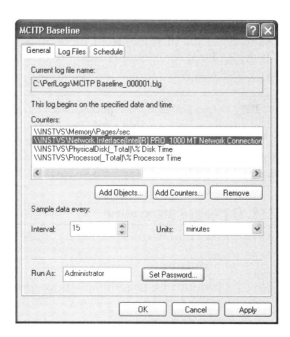

Figure 13-8
Configuring the
schedule for the
baseline log

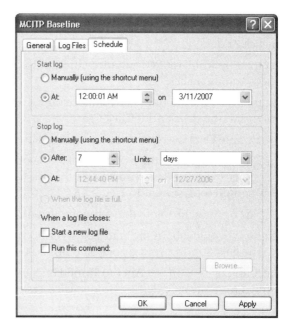

Performance Alerts

Alerts allow us to configure our system to monitor for specific events, or thresholds, and once they occur, to fire an alert. The alert can then log the event in the application log, send a network message, start another log, or run any program we identify.

NOTE Performance alerts are different from SQL Server Agent alerts, which will be covered later in this chapter. While a Performance alert monitors a specified counter, SQL Server Agent alerts will monitor (and can fire based on) SQL Server events, SQL Server performance conditions, and Windows Management Instrumentation (WMI) events.

As an example, we can configure a Performance alert to track the transaction log. One of the dangerous things that can happen with a database is for the transaction log to fill up. If it does become full and can't resize itself, the database becomes read-only. Recall from Chapter 11 that the proper response to a full transaction log is to back it up. This truncates the log and frees up space.

TIP You may remember from Chapter 10 that by backing up a transaction log, you truncate it. What this means is that *committed* transactions (transactions already written to the database) are deleted from the transaction log, freeing up space.

In this exercise, we create a database with a single table. We'll then create an alert to notify us when the transaction log is more than 50 percent full. To see the alert fire, we'll add data to our table until the transaction log is 50 percent full.

Exercise 13.3: Create a Performance Alert

1. Launch SSMS and open a New Query window.

2. Use the following query to create a new database named Chapter6 and a table named TestTransactions within the database:

```
USE Master;
GO
CREATE DATABASE Chapter13;
GO
USE Chapter13;
CREATE TABLE dbo.TestTransactions
(
   TestTransactionsID int IDENTITY(1,1) NOT NULL,
   UserName varchar(50) NOT NULL,
   UserDate datetime NULL,
   CONSTRAINT [PK_AuditAccess_AuditAccessID] PRIMARY KEY CLUSTERED
   (
        TestTransactionsID
   )
);
```

3. The database is created from the model database and should be using the Full Recovery model by default, but to ensure it is using the Full Recovery model (and to ensure this exercise works), use the following script:

```
ALTER DATABASE Chapter13
SET RECOVERY FULL, PAGE_VERIFY CHECKSUM;
GO
```

4. Launch Performance by entering **perfmon** from the run line.

5. Double-click Performance Logs And Alerts to open it. Right-click Alerts and select New Alert Settings.

6. In the New Alert Settings dialog box, enter **MCITPTransactionLogFull** and click OK.

7. Click Add to add a counter. For the Performance Object, select SQLServer: Databases. For the counter, choose Percent Log Used. For the instance, select Chapter13. Your display should look similar to Figure 13-9. Click Add. Click Close.

Figure 13-9
Adding the Percent Log Used counter to the alert

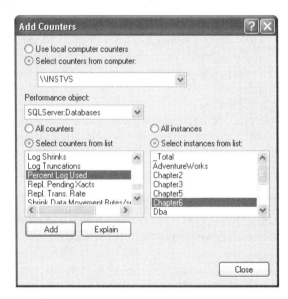

8. For the limit, enter **50** to indicate 50 percent.

9. Click the Action tab. Ensure that Log An Entry In The Application Event Log is checked. Click OK. Your alert should be green, indicating it is running. If not, right-click it and select Start.

10. We'll use the following script to add 1000 rows to our table and log some activity in the transaction log:

```
DECLARE @intCounter int
DECLARE @myDate datetime
Set @intCounter = 1
While @intCounter < 1000
```

```
Begin
  Set @myDate = DATEADD(day, 1, GetDate())
  INSERT INTO TestTransactions VALUES(SUSER_SNAME(),@myDate);
  Set @intCounter = @intCounter + 1
End
```

11. Now, let's take a look at the application log. Click Start, point to My Computer, right-click My Computer, and select Manage. This will launch Computer Management.

12. Within Computer Management, double-click Event Viewer and select the Application log. Your display should look similar to Figure 13-10.

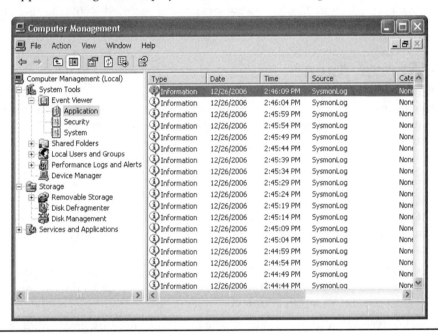

Figure 13-10   Viewing alerts in Event Viewer

13. Double-click one of the SysmonLog entries. You can see that these entries are from your alert.

TIP   Instead of just logging an entry in the Event Viewer application log, we would typically cause another action to occur to resolve the problem. In our example of identifying a transaction log file that is filling up, we could run a SQL Server Agent job that would back up the transaction log. When a transaction log is backed up, the log space is truncated and unused space is reclaimed. We'll see this in an exercise in the SQL Server Agent section later in this chapter.

We could just as easily cause a different diagnostic tool to start. For example, if the NIC reached some threshold indicating excessive network activity, we could start a network capture with Microsoft's Network Monitor or a freeware tool such as Ethereal.

Or, if manual intervention is required, we could run a script that could send an e-mail, or even page someone if our mail server is configured to do so.

Obviously, many counters could be used to create alerts on. A couple of popular counters used to measure the amount of space on hard drives are the *LogicalDisk:% Free Space* and *LogicalDisk:Free Megabytes* counters. If we have a partition (for example, the D: drive) that is in danger of filling up, we could create an alert on the LogicalDisk:% Free Space counter to fire when the drive is over 80 or 90 percent full. Or we could create the alert on the LogicalDisk:Free Megabytes counter to fire when the number of free megabytes is less than 100MB (or whatever threshold we choose).

SQL Server Agent

SQL Server Agent is the DBA's friend. With it, you can create jobs, operators, and alerts to automate many configuration and routine administrative tasks. Much of a DBA's job can be tedious and repetitious. By automating the repetitious tasks, the DBA can focus her energies on more proactive tasks, such as planning database changes or optimizing performance.

SQL Server Agent has three primary components. They are:

- **SQL Server Agent Jobs** A job is a scheduled administrative task that is run by SQL Server Agent. In past chapters, we've created SQL Server Agent jobs for log shipping, database mirroring, and replication. The associated wizards automatically set up these jobs for use.

- **Operators** An operator identifies who will be notified by an alert. Operators can be a computer or a logged-on user (notified with a net send message), an e-mail recipient, or a page recipient.

- **SQL Server Agent Alerts** An alert is an automated response to an event. Events generated by SQL Server are entered into the Windows application log. SQL Server Agent monitors the application log, and if an alert has been specified for the event, SQL Server Agent fires the alert. Additionally, SQL Server Agent can monitor performance conditions and Windows Management Instrumentation (WMI) events and can fire alerts in response.

SQL Server Agent Service

For the SQL Server Agent to run, its service must be started. When jobs are configured, SQL Server Agent service is typically configured to start automatically. We can ensure this automatic start with the SQL Server 2005 Surface Area Configuration tool.

As a reminder, we can launch the SQL Server 2005 Surface Area Configuration tool by pointing to Start | All Programs | Microsoft SQL Server 2005 | Configuration Tools and then clicking SQL Server Surface Area Configuration. Since we want to manipulate a service, we would then select Surface Area Configuration For Services And Connections.

The SQL Server Agent service can be selected, as shown in Figure 13-11.

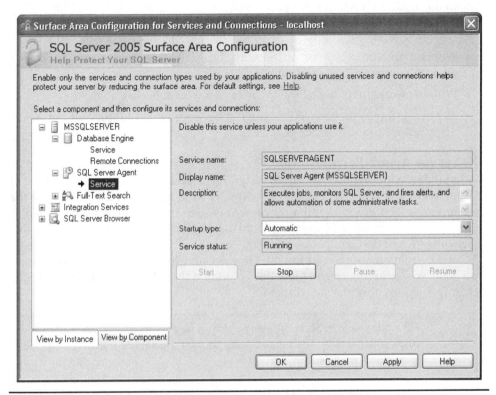

Figure 13-11   Configuring SQL Server Agent service to start automatically

Notice that the Startup Type is set to Automatic. This will cause the service to start automatically when the server starts. It could also be set to Manual or Disabled. Manual requires the service to be started manually when needed. Disabled prevents it from starting. We would set it to Disabled if we weren't using the SQL Server Agent service.

NOTE   To ensure that SQL Server Agent service starts when the server starts, you must set the service to start automatically.

The Startup Type setting could also be configured via the Services applet in Administrative Tools.

Identifying an Account for SQL Server Agent Service

In Chapter 1, we mentioned that accounts are needed to start services. For the SQL Server Agent service to start, it needs an account. It's important to give serious consideration to which account you will use and how you'll configure it.

As a reminder, the following are some highlights we mentioned in Chapter 1 that relate to the SQL Server Agent service account:

- Use the same account for the SQL Server Agent service and the SQL Server service.

- Within a domain, use a domain account. This will allow the accounts to access domain resources.

- Within a workgroup, use a local account or the Local Service account.

- As Microsoft recommends, do *not* use the Network service for the SQL Server Agent service or the SQL Server service.

SQL Server Agent Permissions

As a reminder, Windows uses groups to assign rights and permissions. For example, if we want to give someone full access to a system, we would add their user account to the local administrators group. A full array of permissions and rights has been granted to the administrators group, and any user placed in this group automatically has the rights and permissions of that group.

In many situations, we would use the same account for the SQL Server service and the SQL Server Agent service and place this account in the Administrators group. Based on some situations, this may be required.

 TIP For the SQL Server Agent service to be able to restart automatically if it stops unexpectedly, the account used to start the service must be a member of the local administrators group.

However, if we're looking for extra security, we may choose to use different accounts for each of the services. The SQL Server service would still be placed into the local administrators group, but not the account for the SQL Server Agent service.

For the SQL Server Agent service to function correctly, it needs to have certain rights and permissions. When SQL Server was installed, a group called *SQLServer2005SQLAgentUser$serverName$instanceName* was created. This is created exactly as shown except that the *serverName* and *instanceName* are the actual server name and actual instance name, respectively. For the default instance, it would be MSSQLSERVER.

If security restrictions prevent us from placing the SQL Server Agent service account into the administrators group, we can place the service account into the SQL Agent User group and grant it the minimum permissions needed to do regular maintenance jobs.

By placing the service used to start the SQL Server Agent service into this group, we grant it the necessary rights and permissions. This can be done in Computer Management, as shown in Figure 13-12.

Notice that built-in groups are created for each instance. To add a user to the group, we'd simply double-click the group and add the user. If this is not done, some SQL Server Agent jobs may not run as desired.

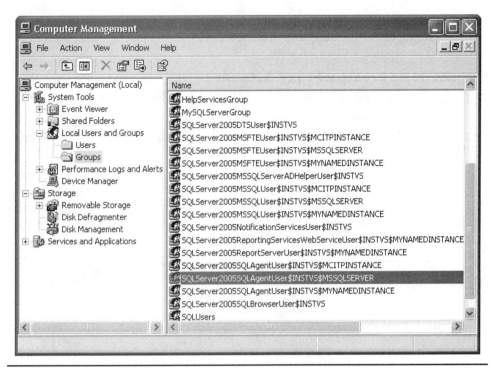

Figure 13-12 Computer Management showing SQL local groups

Proxy Account Some job steps can require elevated permissions that you may not wish to grant to the SQL Server Agent on a routine basis. Instead, you have the ability to create proxy accounts that can be used for specific job steps.

The account could be a local or domain user account. It would be granted the appropriate privileges, and then when the job step is run, this account would be used for that job step.

This is not an entirely new feature. Proxy accounts were available in SQL Server 2000. However, they were handled differently, and it's important to realize how they're migrated. If you upgraded from SQL Server 2000, all user proxy accounts that existed before upgrading are changed to the temporary global proxy account *UpgradedProxyAccount*. These can be used to run ActiveX scripts or CmdExec commands that can access the command line.

With SQL Server 2005, the proxy accounts can be assigned to individual job steps, providing a lot more security control. It's very likely you'll want to remove the access granted to these legacy proxy accounts. To do so, use the sp_revoke_proxy_from_subsystem stored procedure.

To assign proxy accounts to job steps, we must first create credentials, and then create proxies for the specific job step types. A credential is a record that contains the authentication information required to connect to a resource outside SQL Server. Most credentials include a Windows user and a password. It's a little tricky, so let's show the steps in an exercise.

In the following exercise, we'll create a user account in Windows, create a SQL credential pointing to the user account, and then use the credential to create a proxy account that can execute ActiveX job steps.

Exercise 13.4: Create a Proxy Account

1. Launch Computer Management. You can do this by clicking Start, right-clicking My Computer, and selecting Manage.

2. Double-click Local Users And Groups to open the container. Select Users. Right-click Users and select New User.

3. In the New User dialog box, enter **AgentActiveXProxy** as the User Name, **Proxy for ActiveX steps** as the Description, and **P@ssw0rd** in the Password and Confirm Password blocks. Since this is a service account, uncheck the User Must Change Password At Next Logon check box. Your display should look similar to Figure 13-13. Click Create. Click Close.

Figure 13-13
Creating an
account to use as
an ActiveX Proxy

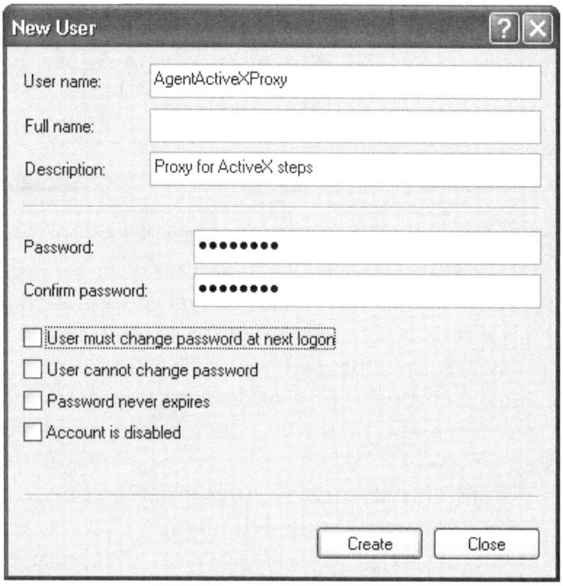

4. Add the AgentActiveXProxy account to the local Administrators group:

   a. Double-click the AgentActiveXProxy account to access the properties page. Click the Member Of tab.

   b. Click Add on the Select Groups page and click Advanced.

   c. Click Find Now. Select the Administrators group and click OK. Click OK on the two screens that follow.

5. Open SSMS and use the Object Explorer to browse to the Credentials container within the Security container.

6. Right-click the Credentials container and select New Credential.

7. In the Credential Name box, enter **ActiveXProxy**.

8. For the Identity, click the ellipsis button. Choose Advanced | Find Now. Select the AgentActiveXProxy account and click OK. Click OK.

9. Enter **P@ssw0rd** in the Password and Confirm Password boxes. Your display should look similar to Figure 13-14. Click OK.

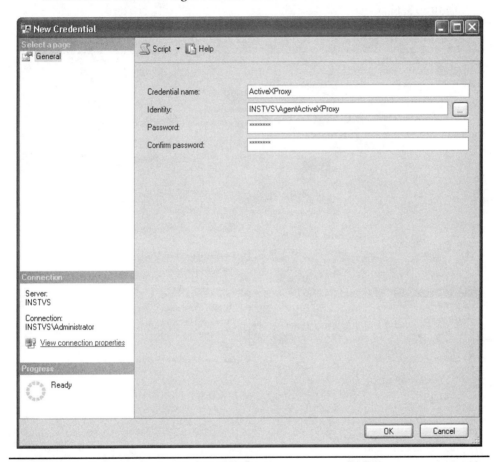

Figure 13-14   Creating a credential within SQL Server

10. Open the SQL Server Agent container.

 TIP   If the SQL Server Agent is not running, you will not be able to open the container. If it's not running, you can right-click the SQL Server Agent within SSMS and select Start.

11. Open the Proxies container, right-click ActiveX Script, and select New Proxy.

12. On the New Proxy Account page, enter **ActiveXProxy** as the Proxy Name.

13. For the Credential Name box, click the ellipsis button. On the Select Credential page, click Browse. On the Browse For Objects page, click the check box next to ActiveXProxy. Click OK, and then click OK again on the following screen.

14. Verify that the ActiveX Script box is checked. Your display should look similar to Figure 13-15. Click OK.

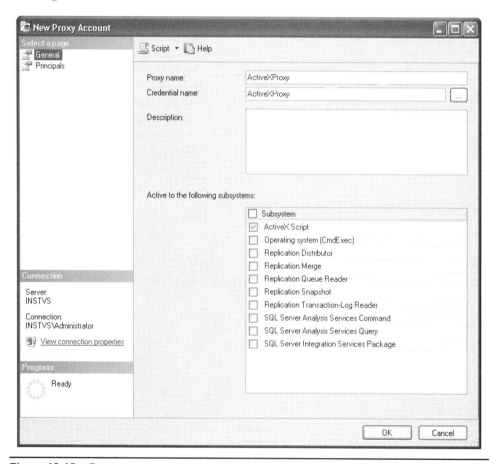

Figure 13-15   Creating a new proxy account

15. At this point, we could use the proxy account to run ActiveX job steps.

Remember that while creating proxy accounts for specific job steps can be done, it's not necessary if the SQL Server Agent service account is a member of the local administrators group. If the service is in the local administrators group, then it is mapped to the sysadmin role of SQL Server and has full permissions.

SQL Server Agent Properties

To access the SQL Server Agent Properties, right-click SQL Server Agent in SSMS and click Properties. The six property pages listed include:

- **General** You can configure the SQL Server Agent service to restart if the SQL Server service stops unexpectedly or if the SQL Server Agent service restarts unexpectedly. You can also configure where to locate the error logs.

- **Advanced** If you have a central SQL Server collecting all events, event forwarding can be configured on this page. Also, the idle CPU condition is defined here. Note that the idle CPU condition is not defined by default.

 NOTE The idle CPU condition deserves a special note since jobs can be configured to run when the CPU is idle, but will never run if this setting is not defined. If you select the check box to Define Idle CPU Condition, by default it defines the CPU as idle if the CPU usage falls below 10 percent for more than 600 seconds (10 minutes). In other words, the CPU idle feature is used to have a job execute if the CPU is not busy for a certain amount of time. Both the percentage and the timing can be modified if desired.

- **Alert System** Use this page to configure mail session information, pager e-mails, and the fail-safe operator.

- **Job System** A shutdown time-out interval (how long SQL gives a job to finish before forcibly shutting it down) and a global proxy account can be configured on this page.

- **Connection** An alias local host server can be configured here.

- **History** The size of history logs (in rows) can be configured here. Additionally, SQL Server Agent can be configured to remove old logs automatically.

Creating Operators, Alerts, and Jobs

SQL Server Agent jobs can be created to automate many tasks, such as backing up databases or logs, monitoring transaction logs, rebuilding indexes, updating statistics, and much more. Jobs can be configured to respond to alerts and can also be configured to notify operators.

Creating Operators

An operator is an alias for either people or groups that can receive a notification. We define operators, and then we identify alerts to notify the operators. As with jobs and alerts, operators are stored in the msdb database.

Operators can be created to send messages via the net send command, e-mail messages, or via pages.

NOTE For operators to send e-mail messages, Database Mail must be configured. We will cover the process and requirements for Database Mail later in this section.

There are some system requirements for operators to fully function. For example, the net send command requires the Messenger service be started on both the computer sending the message and the computer receiving the message, but it is disabled by default on Server 2003 and Windows XP. The Messenger service is not supported on Windows Vista. E-mail requires Database Mail to be enabled and the SMTP service to be running. For pages to work, an e-mail server such as Microsoft's Exchange must be configured to accept e-mail messages and send them as pages.

In the following exercise, we'll create a SQL Server operator that we'll use in later exercises.

Exercise 13.5: Create a SQL Server Agent Operator

1. Launch SSMS.

2. Using Object Explorer, browse to the SQL Server Agent. If it isn't running, right-click the SQL Server Agent and click Start. Double-click the SQL Server Agent to open the container. Your display should look similar to Figure 13-16.

Figure 13-16
SQL Server Agent

3. Right-click the Operators container and select New Operator.

4. On the New Operator page, enter **Darril** as the Name. In the E-Mail Name box, enter **Darril@mcitpsuccess.com**. For the Net Send Address, enter the name of the user account you used to log on to your local computer.

   a. If you're unsure of the name of the account you are using, press CTRL+ALT+DELETE. In the dialog box that appears, the logon information identifies the account being used. Do not enter the computer name and the backslash, but instead just enter the account name. For example, I am logged on as Administrator on the InstVS computer. I would enter only Administrator (not instvs\ Administrator).

b. After you create the operator, click OK. Right-click the Operators container and select Refresh. Double-click the Darril operator to re-enter the Properties page.

5. Your display should look similar to Figure 13-17. Click OK.

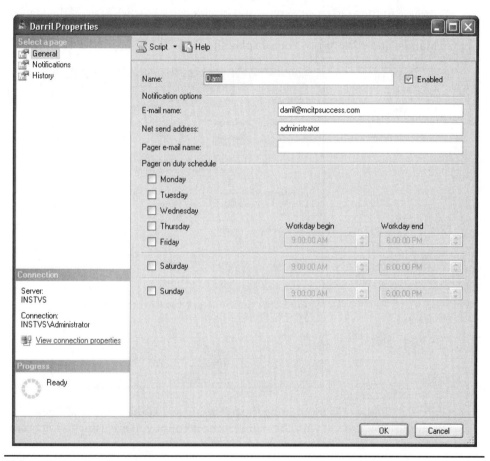

Figure 13-17   Creating an operator

   NOTE   The Messenger service is not available on Windows Vista. If you are performing this exercise on a system running Vista, you won't be able to perform step 6. Likewise, the SQL Server Agent operator will not be able to perform Net Send messages on a Vista system.

6. Since we are using a Net Send, we need to start the Messenger service from the Services applet:

   a. Launch Computer Management. Click Start, right-click My Computer, and choose Manage.

   b. Click the + next to Services And Applications to open the container. Click Services.

   c. Browse to the Messenger Service and double-click it. Click Start. If the Startup Type is set to Disabled, you first will need to change this to Automatic or Manual and click Apply. Your display should look like Figure 13-18.

Figure 13-18
Configuring
the Messenger
service

7. Verify Net Send works by entering the following text at the command line. Substitute *administrator* with the name of the account you are using to log on to your computer.

```
Net Send administrator "MCITP Success"
```

Fail-Safe Operator   If pages are configured, we can create schedules for the pages. Let's say that Joe has pager duty from 7 A.M. to 3 P.M., Maria has it from 3 to 11 P.M., and Sally has it from 11 P.M. to 7 A.M. Based on when the alert is fired, the proper page will be sent to the right person having standby duty at that time.

It's also possible to configure a fail-safe operator—someone to be notified if no one is scheduled to receive the pages. For example, perhaps we have pager duty configured for Monday–Friday, but no one is on duty during Saturday and Sunday. If an alert occurs when no one is scheduled to be paged, the alert will be sent to the fail-safe operator instead of it being ignored.

Creating Alerts

An alert is a predefined response to an event. They can notify an operator or execute a job.

A big part of understanding alerts is realizing that SQL Server Agent is constantly monitoring the application log. Consider Figure 13-19.

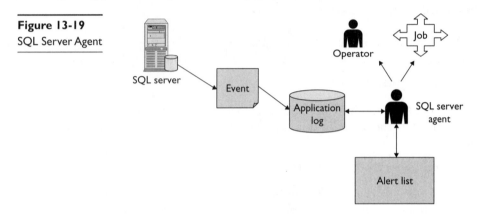

Figure 13-19
SQL Server Agent

Events are generated by SQL Server and entered into the Windows application log. SQL Server Agent is constantly watching the application log. When an event is logged, Agent reads it and compares it to the alert list. If an alert is defined for the logged event, then SQL Server Agent goes into action. It checks to see if either an operator or a job is configured for the alert. If so, SQL Server Agent notifies the operator or executes the job.

Some errors are logged by the system, and user-defined errors can be logged with the raiserror command within a T-SQL script. When using the raiserror command, you can append it with the WITH LOG option to force the error to be logged into the application log. This allows the SQL Server Agent to inspect it.

Error messages have severity levels. Severity levels from 0 through 18 can be specified by any user, while severity levels from 19 through 25 can only be specified by members of the sysadmin fixed server role. Severity levels from 20 through 25, on the other hand, are considered fatal. Error messages with a severity level of 10 are informational, and severity level 11 through 16 messages indicate errors that can be corrected by the user.

SQL Server includes many predefined messages. Message numbers 0 through 50,000 are reserved with these predefined messages. Database administrators can create their own messages, but they must start with message numbers over 50,000.

The syntax to create a message is:

```
exec sp_addmessage 50100, 16, 'Users cannot be deleted from the database',
'us_english','True','Replace'
```

Notice the message number is *50100*, a number greater than 50,000. The severity level is *16*—an error that can be addressed by the user. The text can be whatever we want, but it's best to make it as clear as possible to the user. The *'True'* indicates the message will be logged in the application log, and the *'Replace'* indicates that if a 50100 message exists, replace it with this one.

 EXAM TIP In order to have SQL Server Agent respond to an event, it must be logged. There are two ways to have an event logged. One is by using the WITH LOG clause with a RAISERROR statement. The second is by creating a message (using sp_addmessage) and specifying that the message will be logged—so when the created message is raised it will be logged.

Once the error message has been created, you raise the error in your application logic at any time. To raise the error, we can use the raiserror statement as follows:

```
raiserror (50100, 16,1)
```

If the message wasn't created with True to force the message to be logged, we can use the WITH LOG statement in the raiserror statement to force it to be logged. It would look like this:

```
raiserror (50100, 16,1) WITH LOG
```

SQL Server Agent can also be configured to respond to Performance events and Windows Management Instrumentation events, as shown in Figure 13-20.

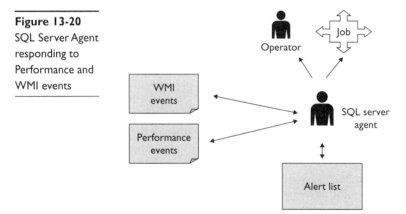

Figure 13-20
SQL Server Agent responding to Performance and WMI events

Performance events are based on the same objects and counters in System Monitor, but instead of creating Performance alerts, we create SQL Server Agent alerts.

In the previous lab, we created an operator. In this lab, we'll create a SQL Server Agent alert.

Exercise 13.6: Create a SQL Server Agent Alert

Take a tour of the SQL Server Agent Alert Video in 13-6.

1. If SSMS is not open, open it and create a new query window by clicking the New Query button.

2. Enter the following T-SQL script to create an error message:

```
exec sp_addmessage 50101, 16, 'Part number %d needs to be reordered.',
'us_english','true','replace'
```

Notice that we have added the *%d*. This allows a decimal variable to be passed into the message when the error is raised.

3. Right-click Alerts and select New Alert.

4. In the Name box, enter **Order Parts**. Leave the SQL Server event alert selected.

5. Change the Database Name to **AdventureWorks**. In the Error Number box, enter **50101**. Your display should look similar to Figure 13-21.

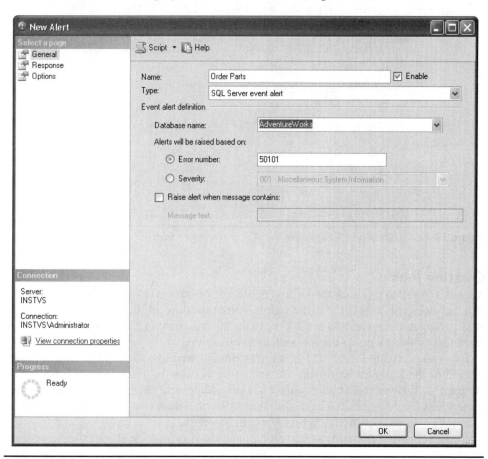

Figure 13-21 Creating an alert

6. Select the Response properties page. Check the Notify Operators box, and in the Operator list, select Net Send for the Darril operator.

7. Click the Options properties page. Click the check box to Include Alert Error Text In Net Send. In the text box for Additional Notification Message To Send, enter **The inventory for the part is low. Please reorder**. Click OK.

8. To see the alert fire, enter the following text in the query window and execute it:

```
USE AdventureWorks;
GO
raiserror (50101, 16,1, 55);
```

The raiserror should log the error into the application log. SQL Server Agent then will recognize the event and check for the alert. Since we just created an alert on message 50101, Agent will check the alert and see that it needs to send a net send. You should see a Net Send message similar to Figure 13-22.

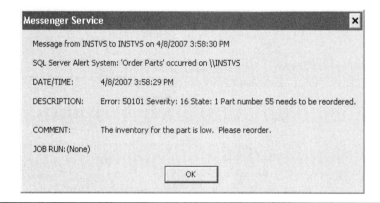

Figure 13-22   A Net Send message from the SQL Server Agent alert

Creating Jobs

A job is a specified series of operations (or a single operation) performed sequentially by SQL Server Agent. Jobs can execute scripts, command-line applications, ActiveX scripts, SSIS packages, or replication tasks. Once jobs are run, they can be configured to notify operators of the results of the job and/or to raise alerts.

Jobs can be created in SSMS via several different wizards, such as the Linked Server Wizard or the Database Mirroring Wizard, as we've done in past chapters. Later in this chapter, we'll cover the Maintenance Plan Wizard, which can be used to create automated jobs for many routine administrative tasks on a database server. Jobs can also be manually created within SQL Server Agent in SSMS.

In the following exercise, we'll create an alert to monitor the size of the Adventure-Works transaction log. We'll create a job to back up the transaction log. We'll then connect the two by setting the alert to execute the job if the transaction log grows to more than 70 percent full. Lastly, we'll run a script to force the log to grow and eventually fire the alert while running System Monitor to watch it all in action.

CAUTION This exercise assumes that AdventureWorks is not using the simple recovery model. Before starting, you might like to check the Options properties page of the AdventureWorks database and verify it is set to either the full or bulk-logged recovery model.

Exercise 13.7: Create a SQL Server Agent Job

Take a tour of the SQL Server Agent Job in video 13-7.

1. If SSMS is not open, open it and browse to the SQL Server Agent container. Verify SQL Server Agent is running.

2. Create a Performance alert:

   a. Right-click Alerts and select New Alert.

   b. In the Name box, enter **AW TLog 70% Full**.

   c. In the Type box, change the drop-down box to select SQL Server Performance Condition Alert.

   d. In the Object box, select SQLServer:Databases.

   e. In the Counter box, select Percent Log Used.

   f. In the Instance box, select AdventureWorks.

   g. In the Alert If Counter box, select Rises Above.

   h. In the Value box, enter **70**.

   i. Your display should look like Figure 13-23.

   j. In the Select A Page area, choose Response. We will configure this alert to execute a job, but not until we create the job. Click OK.

3. Create a SQL Server Agent Job to back up the transaction log:

   a. Right-click Jobs and select New Job.

   b. In the Name box, enter **Backup AW TLog**.

   c. Leave the Owner as you, assuming you have permission to execute a BACKUP statement.

   d. Change the Category to Database Maintenance.

   e. On the Select A Page area, click Steps.

   f. Click New to create a new step.

   g. In the Step Name, enter **Backup TLog**. Ensure the Type selected is Transact-SQL Script (T-SQL). Change the Database to AdventureWorks.

   h. For the command, enter the following script:

```
BACKUP LOG AdventureWorks
    TO DISK = 'C:\AW_Log.bak'
```

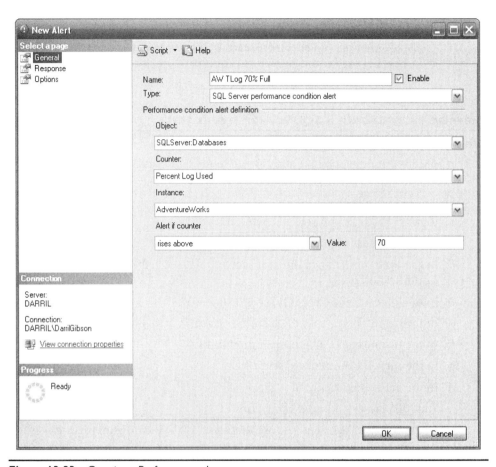

Figure 13-23   Creating a Performance alert

    i. Click Parse to verify the command is syntactically accurate. On the Parse Command Text dialog box, click OK. Your display should look similar to Figure 13-24.

    j. We won't change anything else on this job, but let's take a look at the options. On the Job Step Properties page, in the Select A Page area, click Advanced. Here we can choose what to do on success, on failure, how many times to retry the step, and we can configure outputs. Click OK.

    k. On the New Job Properties page, in the Select A Page area, click Schedules. Here we can configure a recurring schedule for a job.

    l. On the Alerts page, we can connect a job to an alert, but we won't do this yet.

    m. On the Notifications page, we can configure what to do when the job completes.

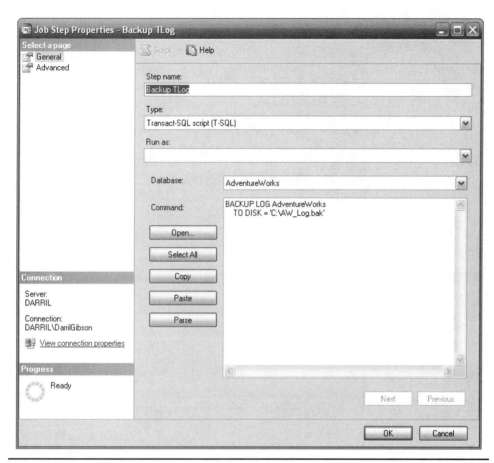

Figure 13-24   Creating a job step

TIP   If you're coming from a SQL Server 2000 background, you may notice something here. In SQL Server 2000, the default was for a job to be written to the Windows Application event log. In SQL Server 2005, you need to select the check box.

    n. On the Targets page, we can configure the job to be used on multiple servers.

    o. Click OK to save the job.

  4. Configure the alert to execute the job:

    a. Double-click the AW TLog 70% Full alert you created earlier.

    b. Click the Response page in the Select A Page area.

    c. Select the check box for Execute Job. In the drop-down box, select Backup AW TLog (Database Maintenance). Check the Notify Operators check box. Mark the check box for Net Send for the Darril operator. Your display should look like Figure 13-25. Click OK.

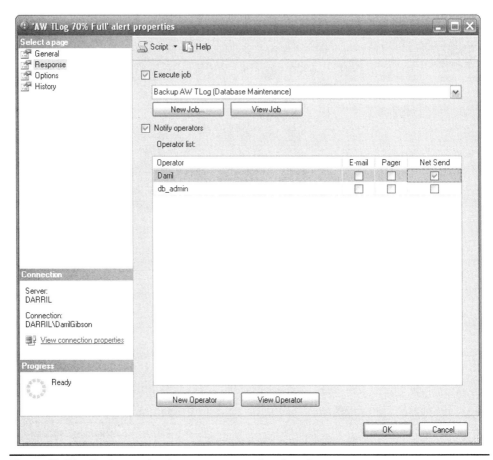

Figure 13-25   Configuring the alert to execute a job and notify an operator

5. Now we want to launch Performance so we can see the counter:

   a. Click Start | Run. Enter **Perfmon**.

   b. In System Monitor, click the + button.

   c. In the drop-down box under Performance Object, select SQL Server:Databases.

   d. In the list box under Select Counters From List, select Percent Log Used.

   e. In the list box under Select Instances From List, select AdventureWorks. Your display should look similar to Figure 13-26. Click Add, and then click Close.

TIP   When Performance is launched, it will automatically have the Pages/sec, Avg Disk Queues, and % Processor counters added. This allows you to view the Memory, Disk, and Processor objects. For this exercise, it'll be worthwhile to leave these counters in.

Figure 13-26

Configuring
System Monitor
to observe the
AdventureWorks
transaction log

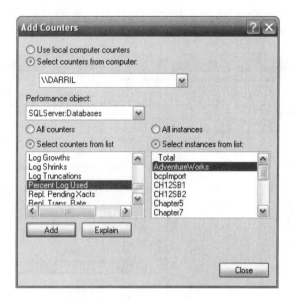

6. Now we want to generate some log activity in the AdventureWorks transaction log. As the log fills, the alert should fire. The alert causes the job to execute, which backs up and truncates the transaction log. We'll see all the activity in System Monitor.

a. In SSMS, click the New Query button to create a new query window.

b. Create some activity in the transaction log with the following script. As the script runs, observe System Monitor.

```
USE AdventureWorks;
GO
DECLARE @i int
SET @i = 1
While @i < 1000
Begin
  SET @i = @i + 1
      INSERT INTO Person.Contact
      (FirstName, LastName,PasswordHash, PasswordSalt)
      VALUES ('Mickey', 'Mouse', 'P@ssw0rd','P@$$S@lt')
End
```

TIP   By selecting Percent Log Used and then pressing CTRL+H, you can highlight the Percent Log Used counter in the performance console screen.

c. By running the script once, you can see the percentage of the log has increased. Press F5 to rerun the script. Wait a second or two, and then press F5 again. Keep doing this while observing System Monitor. You will see that the transaction log continues to fill up. When it reaches 70%, the alert will fire and execute the job. You will see the percentage of the log used reduce significantly, and the alert will pop up on the screen. Your display of System Monitor will look similar to Figure 13-27.

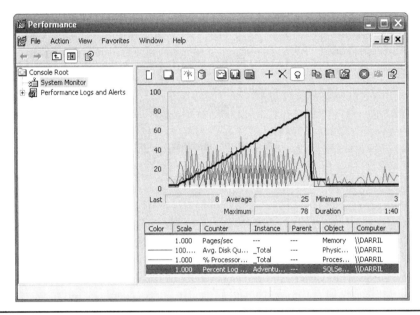

Figure 13-27   Observing the transaction log in System Monitor

Notice that the heavy black stair-stepped line is the Percent Log Used counter. Each stair-step increase reflects a time of running the script. When the log reached 70% full, the alert fired and the job ran. We can see that the Avg Disk Queue Length counter suddenly shot up as the transaction log was backed up, and the Percent Log Used counter fell back close to zero.

7. Clean up the extra data you entered with this script:

```
DELETE FROM Person.Contact
WHERE FirstName = 'Mickey' AND LastName = 'Mouse'
```

8. Close System Monitor.

Scheduling Jobs

When scheduling jobs, you have four possibilities. These are:

- **Recurring**   This is a regular schedule such as once a week.
- **One time**   This is to occur once and once only.
- **Start automatically when SQL Server Agent starts**
- **Start whenever the CPUs become idle**

The recurring and one-time schedules are easy to understand. The other two need a little explanation.

For any job that you want to run as soon as a system is rebooted or restarted, select the option to start automatically when SQL Server Agent starts. During normal operation, SQL Server Agent won't be restarting on its own. If it does restart, the system has probably been restarted.

Lastly, you can choose to have some jobs run only when the CPU(s) become idle. There's a caveat, though. This is not available until you define what idle is for the CPU. This is done in the Advanced tab of the SQL Server Agent properties.

Disabling Jobs, Alerts, and Operators

Sometimes you may want a job, alert, or operator to be disabled. It is relatively simple to do so and much preferred to deleting and then recreating them.

For jobs and alerts, you can simply right-click the object within SSMS and select Disable. Operators, jobs, and alerts can all be disabled by accessing the properties page and clearing the Enabled check box. Once disabled, the entry appears with a small red down-arrow.

Disabled jobs, alerts, and operators won't function until enabled again.

SQL Server Agent Mail

When creating alerts, we have the capability of configuring e-mail. While earlier we only entered the e-mail address, a little more is involved in making it work.

SQL Server 2005 supports two mechanisms for sending e-mail: SQL Mail (for legacy support) and Database Mail.

In previous versions of SQL Server, the method of sending e-mail was SQL Mail. While it is still supported for purposes of backward-compatibility, Microsoft is pushing the usage of Database Mail as a better substitute.

SQL Mail

SQL Mail is Messaging Application Programming Interface (MAPI)-based, meaning that it uses a MAPI client to send the e-mail. The MAPI client uses Exchange Server to send and receive e-mail. To use it, you must configure a MAPI profile on the SQL Server computer, which requires the installation of a MAPI client such as Microsoft Office Outlook.

SQL Mail is deprecated and will be removed in a future version of SQL Server.

 NOTE If you are upgrading to SQL Server 2005 from SQL Server 2000, and SQL Mail was in use, it's recommended to enable Database Mail to convert all of the SQL Mail functions to Database Mail. Once this is done, the MAPI client used with SQL Mail (probably Microsoft Outlook) should be removed from the server.

Database Mail

Database Mail allows e-mail to be sent through any Simple Mail Transport Protocol (SMTP) server. It does not require installing a MAPI client on the SQL Server.

Once Database Mail is configured, SQL Server Agent jobs can be configured to send e-mail. It's possible to configure multiple Database Mail profiles within a single SQL Server instance and pick which profile will be used when a message is sent.

Some benefits of Database Mail include:

- Messages are sent asynchronously via a Service Broker queue.
- Queries can be sent and result sets returned via e-mail.
- It includes multiple security features, including filters to prevent unwanted attachments and a governor to limit the size of attachments.
- The component that delivers e-mail runs outside of SQL Server in a separate process. Even if the destination SMTP Server was not online, the component would not load down SQL Server, but instead the queued messages would be sent when it came back online.

In line with Microsoft's SD³+C (Secure by Design, Secure by Default, and Secure in Deployment and Communication) philosophy, Database Mail is off by default. It can be enabled in the SQL Server Surface Area Configuration tool and also requires some additional steps.

In the next exercise, we'll configure Database Mail in SQL Server. The overall steps to configure it are:

- Enable Database Mail in the SQL Server Surface Area Configuration tool.
- Create a Database Mail profile.
- Add the SQL Server Agent service account to the DatabaseMailUserRole in the msdb database.
- Configure the alert properties of SQL Server Agent to use Database Mail.
- Restart the SQL Server Agent service.

In the following exercise, we'll configure Database Mail to work with a fictitious SMTP mail server.

Exercise 13.8: Enable Database Mail

1. Launch the SQL Server 2005 Surface Area Configuration tool. Click Start | All Programs | Microsoft SQL Server 2005 | Configuration Tools | SQL Server Surface Area Configuration.

2. Click the Surface Area Configuration For Features link.

3. In the SQL Server 2005 Surface Area Configuration page, click Database Mail. Select the check box to Enable Database Mail Stored Procedures. Click OK. Close the SQL Server 2005 Surface Area Configuration tool.

4. Open SSMS.

5. In the Object Explorer, browse to Management. Select Database Mail.

6. Right-click Database Mail and click Configure Database Mail.

7. On the Welcome To Database Mail Configuration Wizard page, click Next.

8. On the Select Configuration Task page, ensure that the box labeled Set Up Database Mail By Performing The Following Tasks is selected, and then click Next.

9. On the New Profile page, enter **MCITP Profile** in the Profile Name box. Click Add.

10. On the New Database Mail Account page, enter **MCITP** as the Account Name.

11. In the Outgoing Mail Server (SMTP) area, enter **mcitpAgent@mcitp.com** for the E-Mail Address.

12. In the Display Name, enter **MCITP SQL Server Agent**.

13. In the Reply E-Mail, enter **mcitpAgent@mcitp.com**.

14. In the Server Name, enter **MCITP1**.

 NOTE While actually configuring an SMTP Server is beyond the scope of the test and this book, if you want to do so, look up KB 308161. It shows how to do this in Windows 2000, but the directions can be used to enable SMTP on other operating systems as well.

15. Your display should look similar to Figure 13-28. Click OK.

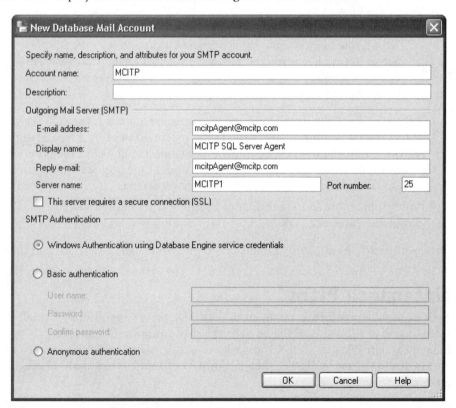

Figure 13-28 Configuring the Database Mail profile

16. On the New Profile page, click Next.

17. On the Manage Profile Security page, click the MCITP Profile to make it available to all users of any mail-host database. Click Next.

18. On the Configure System Parameters page, observe the properties, and click Next.

19. On the Complete The Wizard page, click Finish. Once it has been created, click Close.

20. Configure SQL Server Agent to use Database Mail:

    a. Using the SSMS Object Explorer, browse to the msdb database within the Databases\System Databases container.

    b. Browse to the Database Roles container within the Security\Roles\Database Roles container.

    c. Double-click the DatabaseMailUserRole object to access the properties page. Click Add.

    d. On the Select Database User Or Role page, click Browse.

    e. On the Browse For Objects page, select the user account used to start the SQL Server Agent service.

 TIP If you can't remember which account is used to start the SQL Server Agent service, you can access the services applet (Control Panel | Administrative Tools) and select the Log On tab on the properties of the SQL Server Agent service.

---

    f. If you followed the installation procedure from Chapter 1, the SQL Server Agent service is running under the Local System account. In a typical domain account, it would be running under a domain account. Select the NT Authority\System account if it is running under the Local System account. Click OK, and then click OK again on the next screen.

    g. Your display should look similar to Figure 13-29. On the Database Role Properties page, click OK.

Once configured, the sp_send_dbmail stored procedure can be used to send mail.

Maintenance Plans

While it's certainly possible to create all of your SQL Server Agent jobs manually, the Maintenance Plan Wizard is designed to make this process much simpler. Using the Maintenance Plan Wizard, a DBA can easily schedule many core maintenance tasks to ensure the database is backed up, performs well, and is regularly checked for inconsistencies.

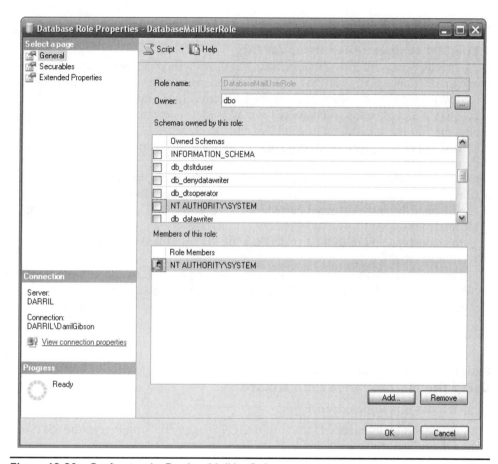

Figure 13-29 Configuring the DatabaseMailUserRole

Common maintenance tasks that can be created with the Maintenance Plan wizard include:

- Backing up databases and transaction logs
- Reorganizing and rebuilding statistics
- Checking database integrity
- Updating statistics
- Deleting old history logs

Just as with all other SQL Server Agent data, maintenance plans are stored in the msdb database. The wizard is fairly straightforward, so let's jump right into an exercise.

In the following exercise, we'll create a maintenance plan to reorganize an index and then back up the AdventureWorks database.

The SP2 Maintenance Interval Bug

When SQL Server 2005 was first released, the shortest interval for scheduling tasks in a maintenance plan was "days." As often happens, admins in the field provided feedback to Microsoft asking for a change. Specifically, many DBAs wanted to be able to schedule tasks in intervals of "hours." With the release of SQL Server 2005 SP2, the "hours" scheduling interval was added.

This would have been perfect except for a minor bug. When the service pack was deployed, the minimum interval was now "hours" instead of "days," and existing maintenance plans that were previously scheduled with the minimum interval of "days" were now scheduled in the interval of hours. For example, a plan that occurred every day, now occurred every hour. Needless to say, this caused a problem for many DBAs.

Microsoft quickly released a critical update and modified SP2, giving it a new version number.

You can tell which version you have installed by looking at the version number (listed in Object Explorer in SSMS). The original release of SP2 was version 9.0.3042.00. After the critical update, SP2 was re-released as version 9.0.3050.00.

Exercise 13.9: Create a Maintenance Plan Using the Maintenance Plan Wizard

1. If SSMS is not open, launch it.

2. Browse to Maintenance Plans within the Management container in the SSMS Object Explorer.

3. Right-click Maintenance Plans and select Maintenance Plan Wizard.

4. On the SQL Server Maintenance Plan Wizard page, click Next.

5. On the Select Plan Properties page, enter **Weekly AdventureWorks maintenance** as the Name. Ensure Single Schedule For The Entire Plan is selected. Click the Change button.

6. On the Job Schedule Properties page, configure the properties so it looks like Figure 13-30. Notice the time of occurrence is 12:01 A.M. Sunday morning. Click OK.

7. On the Select Plan Properties page, click Next.

8. On the Select Maintenance Tasks page, select the check boxes next to Reorganize Index and Back Up Database (Full). Your display should look like Figure 13-31. Click Next.

9. On the Select Maintenance Task Order page, ensure that Reorganize Index is first in the list. Click Next.

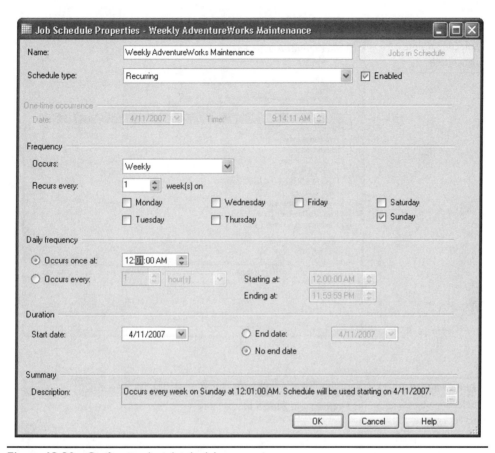

Figure 13-30 Configuring the job schedule properties

 TIP Remember, as a best practice it is recommended to perform maintenance on a database before doing the backup. This ensures our backup is optimized, and if we have to do a restore, we restore an optimized database.

10. On the Define Reorganize Index Task page, in the Databases drop-down box, select AdventureWorks and click OK.

11. While we could reorganize all tables and VIEWs by selecting Tables And Views as the object, it is more realistic to pick and choose the specific tables and/or VIEWs we want to reorganize based on usage. For example, in a database that has a lot of sales transactions, it makes sense to reorganize tables or VIEWs that have a lot of transaction activity. Select the Object as Table.

12. In the These Objects list, select the Sales.SalesOrderDetail and Sales. SalesOrderHeader tables. Your display should look similar to Figure 13-32. Click OK, and then click Next.

Figure 13-31

Selecting maintenance tasks

Figure 13-32

Selecting objects to reorganize

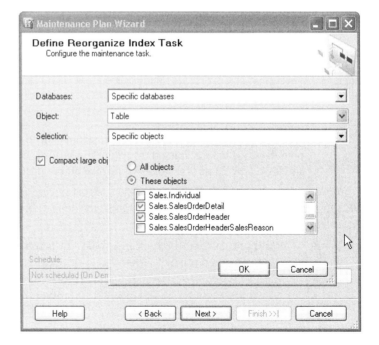

13. On the Define Backup Database (Full) Task page, select AdventureWorks as the Database. Mark the Verify Backup Integrity check box. Click OK, and then click Next.

14. On the Select Report Options page, ensure that Write A Report To A Text File is selected. Note that, by default, the path is set to C:\Program Files\Microsoft SQL Server\MSSQL.1\MSSQL\LOG, and the name of the report file is the name of the maintenance plan appended with the date and time. For example, after this maintenance plan ran, we could look at the Weekly AdventureWorks_ *yyyymmddhhmmss*.log file in this directory. Click Next.

15. On the Complete The Wizard page, review the plan and click Finish. After a moment, the Maintenance Plan Wizard should complete indicating success. Click Close.

16. In the Maintenance Plans container, observe that the Weekly AdventureWorks maintenance plan has been created. Right-click the plan and select Modify.

17. Right-click the Object:Table task and click Edit. In the Reorganize Index Task, notice that you can modify this task. For example, if you wanted to add or remove specific tables, you could do so within the plan. Click the View T-SQL button. This shows the Transact-SQL generated by the wizard. If desired, you could also just execute this T-SQL code as part of a SQL Server Agent job. Click Close, and then click Cancel.

18. Right-click the Back Up Database task and click Edit. Notice this is the same screen that appeared in the wizard and that it can also be modified. Click Cancel.

19. Close the maintenance plan.

Viewing Job History

SQL Server 2005 maintains a rich set of logs related to SQL Server Agent and maintenance plans. These allow you to review what jobs are running, what jobs aren't, and any problems you may have with them.

We can view the history the following ways:

- Right-clicking a maintenance plan and clicking View History.
- Right-clicking Jobs within SQL Server Agent and selecting View History.
- Looking in the C:\Program Files\Microsoft SQL Server\MSSQL.1\MSSQL\LOG directory.

In the following short exercise, we'll take a look at some of the maintenance logs available to us.

Exercise 13.10: View History of Maintenance Plans and SQL Server Agent

1. Open an instance of SSMS.

2. Browse to the Maintenance Plans container within Management.

3. Right-click the Weekly AdventureWorks Maintenance plan and click View History.

Since the maintenance plan was just created in the previous exercise, we don't have any log entries. Notice, however, that we can also access Database Mail, Job History, Remote Maintenance Plans, and SQL Agent logs from this menu. Select the + next to SQL Agent to open it.

4. Select Current to access the current SQL Agent log. Your display should look similar to Figure 13-33. Notice these logs follow the same icon format as the Event Viewer, with an *X* for an error, an exclamation mark for a warning, and an *i* for information.

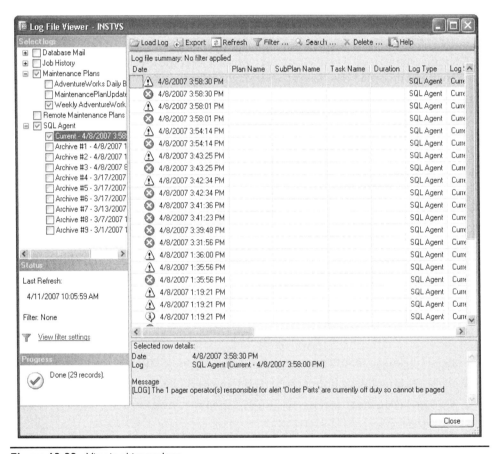

Figure 13-33 Viewing history logs

5. Close this Log File Viewer. Browse to the Jobs container within the SQL Server Agent container. Right-click Jobs and select View History.

6. Notice that from here you can view the history of all the jobs, and some other logs are available to choose.

SQL Server Profiler

SQL Server Profiler is an invaluable tool that can be used to track down long-running queries and stored procedures.

Remember, the most important resources of any server are CPU, memory, disk, and network—the core four. We can measure these with System Monitor. However, let's say you have an extraordinarily high level of disk activity measured with System Monitor. You know it's high because you've compared the measurements against your baseline. Now you can use SQL Server Profiler to trace or capture the specific activity that has high read or write values to the disk drive.

Profiler includes many built-in templates that can be used to capture activity and measure performance of the SQL Server. Additionally, user-defined templates can be created to meet specific needs.

SQL Profiler can be useful in several situations. Some typical scenarios where SQL Profiler can be used are to:

- Find the worst-performing queries
- Identify poorly performing adhoc queries
- Identify deadlocks and associated connections
- Monitor stored procedures
- Audit activity on SQL Server
- Monitor activity on a per-user basis
- Collect data for tuning

 EXAM TIP   A classic purpose of SQL Profiler (and SQL Trace) is identifying the worst-performing queries. In some environments, database users have the capability to create their own queries and execute them on an adhoc basis. These queries can sometimes be constructed without performance in mind and can bog down the system. SQL Profiler, using the TSQL_Duration template, is ideally suited to easily find problematic queries.

Templates

SQL Server Profiler has several templates that are designed to capture specific data. New templates can also be created. These templates include:

- **Standard**   This captures all stored procedures and Transact-SQL batches. It's used to monitor general database server activity.
- **Tuning**   This captures information about stored procedures and Transact-SQL batches. It's used to produce trace output for the Database Engine Tuning Advisor.
- **TSQL**   This captures all Transact-SQL statements and the time issued. It's used to debug client applications.

- **TSQL_Duration**   This captures all Transact-SQL statements with their execution time (in milliseconds) and groups them by duration. It's used to identify slow queries.

- **TSQL_Grouped**   This captures all Transact-SQL statements with the time they were issued. It groups the information by the user or client that submitted the statement. It's used to investigate queries from a particular client or user.

- **TSQL_Replay**   This captures detailed information about Transact-SQL statements used to replay a trace. It's good for performing iterative tuning, such as benchmark testing.

- **SP_Counts**   This captures stored procedure execution behavior over time. It's used to monitor stored procedures.

- **TSQL_SPs**   This captures detailed information about all executing stored procedures. It's used to analyze the individual steps of stored procedures.

Trace Events

Templates have preselected Trace events. Each trace can be modified by adding additional Trace events and renaming the template. Table 13-3 shows a partial listing of the available Trace events.

While we covered auditing in the security chapters earlier in this book, it's important to realize that the Security Audit event class holds a full set of events that can be used to audit events from the simple login and logout to the more complex impersonation of various management events.

With the basics covered, let's take a look at SQL Profiler and create a trace that we can use to tune a database.

In the following exercise, we will launch SQL Profiler and create a trace that can be used as a workload file by the Database Tuning Advisor.

Exercise 13.11: Create a Trace Using the Tuning Template

Video 13-11 shows how to create a trace in SQL Server Profiler.

1. Launch SQL Profiler by selecting Start | All Programs | Microsoft SQL Server 2005 | Performance Tools | SQL Server Profiler.

2. Select File | New Trace or click the New Trace button on the far left of the toolbar.

3. On the Connect To Server dialog box, ensure the Server Name is set to your local server and click Connect.

4. In the Use The Template drop-down box, select Tuning.

5. Click the check box for Save To File. In the Save As dialog box, enter **TuningTrace** as the name of the file to save. Click Save.

6. Click the Events Selection tab. Notice that two Stored Procedures events and one T-SQL event have been selected in this template. Click Run.

7. Launch SSMS and create a new query window by clicking the New Query button.

Event Class	Description
Broker	Produced by Service Broker.
CLR	Produced by .NET common language runtime (CLR objects within SQL Server).
Cursors	Produced by cursor operations.
Database	Produced when data or log files grow or shrink automatically.
Deprecation	Includes deprecation related events.
Errors and Warnings	Produced whenever a SQL Server error or warning is issued.
Full Text	Produced when full-text searches are started, interrupted, or stopped.
Locks	Produced when a lock is acquired, canceled, released, or has some action performed on it.
OLEDB	Produced by OLE DB calls.
Objects	Produced by DDL statements (CREATE, ALTER, DROP).
Performance	Produced by DML statements (INSERT, UPDATE, and DELETE).
Progress Report	Shows progress of online index operations.
Query Notifications	Produced by query notifications processing.
Scans	Produced when tables or indexes are scanned.
Security Audit	Used to audit server activity.
Server	Includes general server events.
Sessions	Includes server session events.
Stored Procedures	Produced by the execution of stored procedures.
TSQL	Produced by execution of T-SQL statements.
Transactions	Produced by statements writing to the transaction log, or by Microsoft Distributed Transaction Coordinator transactions.

Table 13-3 SQL Profiler Trace Events

8. Enter the following script to create a little activity on the server:

```
USE AdventureWorks;
GO
SELECT * FROM Person.Contact
```

 NOTE It's very possible, based on previous exercises, that you have additional activity on your server that will be captured by SQL Profiler. This could include maintenance plans or SQL Server Agent jobs or alerts.

9. Stop the trace. You can select File | Stop Trace or click the red square Stop Trace button on the toolbar.

10. Scroll toward the top of the trace and find the query you executed. How long did the query take on your system? Looking at Figure 13-34, you can see this query had a duration of 2978 on my system. This is given in milliseconds, so it equates to almost three seconds.

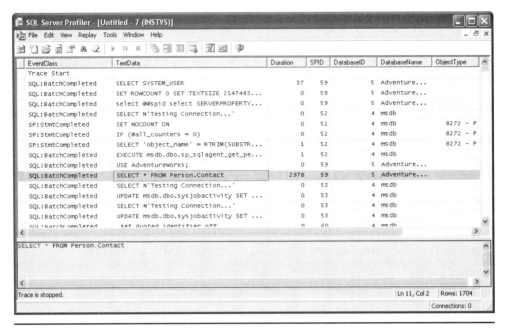

Figure 13-34 A SQL Profiler trace output

11. By scrolling to the right, you can see the Login Name of the user that executed the query.

NOTE Since this trace was already named, it has been saved. We could now use it as a workload file in Database Tuning Advisor if desired. However, our trace is very small with very little activity, so it wouldn't be very useful. A trace that has captured a full day's worth of activity would be much more valuable (and much larger).

12. You can also filter out extra information that you're not interested in. For example, in the bottom-right corner of Figure 13-34, you may have noticed my trace had over 1700 rows. Due to other activity on my server, SQL Profiler captured a lot of activity. If I were just interested in the amount of time taken by queries from a specific application, I could use a filter. Select File | Properties or click the Properties icon on the SQL Profiler toolbar.

13. Click the Events Selection tab. Click the Show All Columns check box to allow all the columns to appear. Select the ApplicationName for each of the events. Deselect the Show All Columns check box. Your display should look similar to Figure 13-35.

14. Click the Column Filters button.

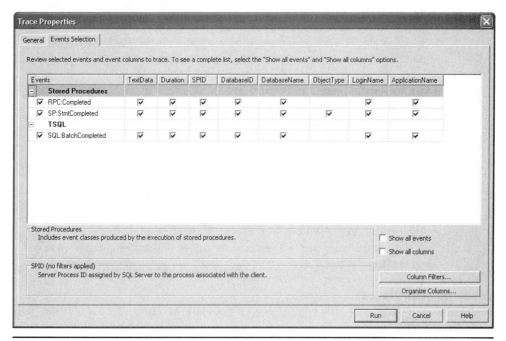

Figure 13-35 Configuring Trace Properties by adding an ApplicationName column

15. In the Edit Filter dialog box, ensure ApplicationName is selected and click the plus sign next to Like. Enter **Microsoft SQL Server Management Studio – Query** in the blank box under Like. Spelling counts here. Any typo will result in zero rows returned. Your display should look similar to Figure 13-36. Click OK.

Figure 13-36
Editing filters in
a SQL Profiler
trace

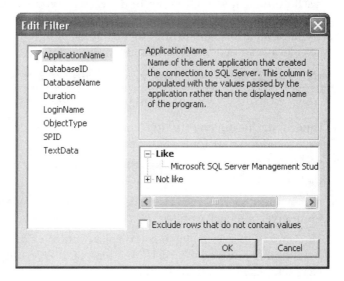

EXAM TIP   Filters can be implemented within SQL Profiler to capture specific data. This includes filtering by application name, database name, duration (measured in milliseconds), login name, and more.

16. Click Run to start the trace, and return to SSMS and rerun the query:

```
USE AdventureWorks;
GO
SELECT * FROM Person.Contact
```

17. Return to SQL Profiler. You should see two lines and only two lines. The first line is from the USE command, and the second line is from the SELECT command.

TIP   If you don't have any lines displayed, check your spelling in the filter. A single letter mistyped will result in zero lines of data being captured in the trace. Stop the trace, correct anything that is wrong, and then restart it.

Creating Templates

By default, each template holds a specific set of Trace events. However, any template can be slightly modified, creating a completely different template. Additionally, templates can easily be exported to be used on other SQL Server computers.

For example, let's say we want to monitor a specific application and especially pay attention to disk reads and writes from this application. The Standard template may have many of the events we want (including reads and writes), but lacks the application name. We can start with the Standard template, modify it by adding an application filter, save it with a different name, and then export it.

In the following exercise, we will create a template, export it, and then import it. While we'll do this on a single server in the exercise, you would do it between different servers on the job. In a production environment, you may create a template on one server and want to share it with other database developers. You can export it from your server, give it someone else, and let them import it.

Exercise 13.12: Create, Export, and Import a Template

Watch video 13-12 to see how to create a SQL Server Profiler template.

1. Launch SQL Profiler by clicking Start | All Programs | Microsoft SQL Server 2005 | Performance Tools | SQL Server Profiler.

2. Select File | New Trace or click the New Trace button on the far left of the toolbar.

3. On the Connect To Server dialog box, ensure the Server Name is set to your local server and click Connect.

4. The Trace Properties dialog box is displayed. If you close a trace and want to start another one, you can click File | Templates | New Template, or click the New Template icon on the toolbar.

5. On the Trace Template Properties page, ensure that Microsoft SQL Server 2005 is set as the Server Type. In the New Template Name box, enter **MCITP Application Trace**.

6. Click the check box next to Base New Template On Existing One. In the drop-down box, select the Standard template.

7. Click the Events Selection tab. Ensure that Reads and Writes are checked for each event possible. Reads monitors the number of logical disk reads, and Writes monitors the number of physical disk writes.

8. Click the Column Filters button. Click the + next to Like and enter **MCITP**. This assumes the application we want to measure is named MCITP. Click OK. Since we don't have an MCITP application, this trace won't actually do anything, but the exercise does show how to create a template.

 TIP You may notice that the Standard template includes a Not Like box with SQL Server Profiler listed. This is so the trace does not capture data generated from SQL Profiler.

9. Click Save to save the template. The template will be saved and closed.

10. Click File | Templates | Export Template.

11. In the Select Template Name dialog box, ensure that Microsoft SQL Server 2005 is chosen as the Server Type. Select MCITP Application Trace (User), and then click OK.

12. In the Save As dialog box, enter **MCITPApplicationTrace**. Ensure the Save As Type is set to SQL Server Profiler Template Files (*.tdf). Click Save. On the SQL Server Profiler dialog box, click OK.

13. Delete the template. Select File | Templates | Edit Template. In the Trace Template Properties dialog box, select the item labeled MCITP Application Trace (User) in the Select Template Name drop-down box. Click Delete, and then click Cancel.

14. Import the template. Select File | Templates | Import Template.

15. In the Open File dialog box, select the MCITPApplicationTrace.tdf file. Click Open, and then click OK.

Where to Run Traces

Traces can be run on the same computer you are measuring, or run on different SQL Server computers separate from the production databases.

There's an old story about an experiment at a manufacturing plant. They wanted to see the impact on production if lights were turned up. They turned up the lights, and all the scientists and managers watched. Production went up. They turned the lights up some more and watched again. Production went up. On a hunch, they turned the lights down and watched. Production went up. It turns out that the increased production had nothing to do with the lights, but instead was due to all the attention the workers were getting.

With everyone watching them, the workers worked harder. The measuring affected the measurements.

We have the same challenge when measuring servers. Through the process of measuring it, we have the potential of adding a load on the server we are measuring. This may make the server appear to be loaded down, but without measuring it, it works fine. One way to avoid this problem is to run the trace on a test bed server. We still connect to the production server and capture the trace data running on the production server; however, the data is saved and processed on the test bed server.

Locks

SQL Profiler is very valuable in capturing lock and deadlock activity. However, before we can meaningfully discuss capturing information on locks, we need to define locks. In Chapter 14, we'll talk about locks and deadlocks and revisit SQL Profiler.

SQL Trace

New to SQL Server 2005 is SQL Trace. SQL Trace allows you to launch SQL stored procedures that can be used from within an application to create traces manually. While SQL Server Profiler is valuable and very useful, it can't be launched from within an application to measure specific trace data. But SQL Trace can.

As an example, if we wanted to track how often stored procedures are executed from within an application, we could use SQL Trace to capture Stored Procedures:SP:Starting or Stored Procedures:SP:Completed events. A filter could be used to only capture events from a specific application.

 EXAM TIP SQL Trace can be used as an alternative to SQL Profiler, especially when an automated solution is required. The significant benefit of SQL Trace over SQL Profiler is that it can be started automatically, such as within a SQL Server Agent job or within an application. SQL Profiler can only be started manually.

Traces can be created on any traceable events. In other words, any events that can be captured in SQL Profiler can be captured with SQL Trace.

Since SQL Trace uses stored procedures, it's relatively easy to create jobs that use T-SQL to execute the stored procedures. Jobs can be scheduled to start when the SQL Server Agent starts, or essentially when the server starts. Used this way, SQL Trace can have jobs start each time the system is booted.

As an example, let's say you want to configure auditing of all login events associated with a specific application. A SQL Server Agent job could be configured to run SQL Trace, accessing the appropriate Trace events. The job could be configured to start each time the SQL Server Agent service started, and the SQL Server Agent service could be configured to start each time the SQL Server service started.

SQL Trace is launched and managed with a group of stored procedures, which include sp_trace_create, sp_trace_setevent, sp_trace_setfilter, sp_trace_setstatus, and more. In the next exercise, we'll enter the code to create a SQL Trace and then view the output. Afterward, we'll use these system stored procedures. First, let's introduce them and the basic syntax.

sp_trace_create

The sp_trace_create system stored procedure is used to create a trace. The basic syntax is:

```
sp_trace_create [ @traceid = ] trace_id OUTPUT
        , [ @options = ] option_value
        , [ @tracefile = ] 'trace_file'
    [ , [ @maxfilesize = ] max_file_size ]
    [ , [ @stoptime = ] 'stop_time' ]
    [ , [ @filecount = ] 'max_rollover_files' ]
```

Three parameters must be specified:

- **@traceid** The @traceid is an integer assigned by the system but a variable is used to identify the traceid in the rest of the batch.

- **@options** Three options are available: TRACE_FILE_ROLLOVER (creates multiple trace files once one trace file reaches the maximum size), SHUTDOWN_ON_ERROR (used for auditing and shuts down SQL Server if an error occurs in the trace), and TRACE_PRODUCE_BLACKBOX (specifies that the last 5MB of trace activity is always saved by the server). Choosing a value of 0 will select none of these options.

- **@tracefile** Specifies the name and location of the file created by the trace.

sp_trace_setevent

The sp_trace_event system stored procedure identifies the events we want to capture. Each event that is available in SQL Profiler can be specified here, although only one event can be added at a time. The basic syntax is:

```
sp_trace_setevent [ @traceid = ] trace_id
        , [ @eventid = ] event_id
        , [ @columnid = ] column_id
        , [ @on = ] on
```

With over 200 possible events and more than 60 possible columns, we won't list them here. If you want to see them all, look in the BOL article, "sp_trace_setevent." A few of the events are:

- 12 SQL:BatchCompleted
- 13: SQL:BatchStarting
- 42 SP:Starting
- 44 SP:Completed

A few of the columns are:

- 6   NTUserName
- 10 ApplicationName
- 14 StartTime
- 18 CPU

The @on value is used to turn the event on or off. A bit value must be passed to this parameter with a 1 turning it on and a 0 turning it off.

sp_trace_setfilter

The sp_trace_setfilter system stored procedure can be used to filter the events that the SQL trace captures. As an example, you can capture traffic only associated with a specific application name. The basic syntax is:

```
sp_trace_setfilter [ @traceid = ] trace_id
        , [ @columnid = ] column_id
        , [ @logical_operator = ] logical_operator
        , [ @comparison_operator = ] comparison_operator
        , [ @value = ] value
```

The traceid is the integer identifying the trace that was created in the sp_trace_create stored procedure, while the @column is the integer identifying the column we want to compare. All of the integers for specific columns can be viewed in the BOL article, "sp_trace_setevent." The @logical_operator specifies the AND (a 0) or OR (a 1) operators to be used when multiple filters are added. Even with a single filter. The logical operator must be specified.

The @comparison_operator uses integers between 0 and 7 to specify one of the following comparison operators: =, <>, >, <, >=, <=, LIKE, and NOT LIKE, respectively. Lastly, the @value specifies the value we're interested in comparing.

sp_trace_setstatus

The sp_trace_setstatus system stored procedure is used to start, stop, or delete the trace. The basic syntax is:

```
sp_trace_setstatus [ @traceid = ] trace_id
        , [ @status = ] status
```

Status has three possibilities:

- **0** This starts the trace.
- **1** This stops the trace.
- **2** This closes the trace and deletes its definition from the server.

Exercise 13.13: Create a SQL Trace to Capture How Often Stored Procedures Are Started

1. Launch SSMS and connect to the default instance. Click the New Query button to create a new query window.

2. Use the following code to create a SQL trace. This code assumes the existence of the MCITPSuccess folder on your C:\ drive. If it doesn't exist, create it before running the code.

```
DECLARE @mySQLTrace int
DECLARE @traceid int
EXEC @mySQLTrace=sp_trace_create @traceid=@traceid output,
```

```
   @options=0,
   @tracefile=N'C:\MCITPSuccess\myTraceFile'
IF @mySQLTrace > 0
   PRINT 'sp_trace_code failed with error ' + cast(@mySQLTrace as char)
ELSE
   PRINT 'traceid for the trace is ' + cast(@traceid as char)
```

The number of the traceid should print out in your Messages tab. Write the number of the traceid here _____. At this point, we've created the trace, but it doesn't have any events assigned to it and isn't running.

3. Use the following code to set the trace to capture SP:Starting events (event number 42) with the application name column (column number 10). If your traceid identified in step 2 was something other than 4, then modify the *@traceid* = ___ code to reflect the number of your traceid.

```
DECLARE @on bit
SET @on = 1
EXEC sp_trace_setevent @traceid = 4, -- the number of our trace
   @eventid = 42, --SP_Starting events
   @columnid = 10, -- Application name column
   @on = @on       -- turn it on
```

4. Use the following code to add an additional column to the SP:Starting events (event number 42). The additional column is the start time (column number 14). Again, if your traceid is something other than 4, then substitute 4 with the number of your traceid.

```
DECLARE @on bit
SET @on = 1
EXEC sp_trace_setevent @traceid = 4, -- the number of our trace
   @eventid = 42, --SP_Starting events
   @columnid = 14, -- Start time column
   @on = @on       -- turn it on
```

Additional columns could be added depending on the data you want to collect. We'll just collect data on these two columns (Application Name and Start Time).

5. Use the following code to add a filter to your trace. This code will only capture events generated from the SSMS query window. Other events will be ignored. We can use this to filter the trace to capture data from a specific application.

```
sp_trace_setfilter  @traceid = 4, -- the number of our trace

     @columnid = 10, --application name

     @logical_operator = 0, -- 0 is for AND, but with only one filter it
doesn't matter

     @comparison_operator = 6, -- 6 is for LIKE

     @value = N'Microsoft SQL Server Management Studio - Query'
```

6. We're now ready to start the trace. Use the following code to start it:

```
sp_trace_setstatus @traceid = 4 -- the number of our trace
        , @status =    1         -- start the trace
```

7. Now let's execute a stored procedure from within the query window. Use the following code:

```
USE AdventureWorks;
GO
EXEC dbo.uspGetEmployeeManagers 1
```

8. Stop the trace with the following code:

```
sp_trace_setstatus @traceid = 4 -- the number of our trace
          , @status =   0       -- stop the trace
```

9. Use Windows Explorer to browse to the C:\MCITPSuccess folder, and once there, double-click the myTraceFile.trc file. This should open the trace file within SQL Profiler. You should see something similar to Figure 13-37.

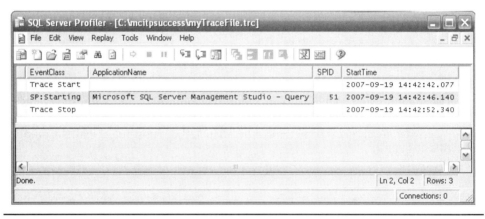

Figure 13-37   Trace opened showing one captured event

Notice the bottom-right corner shows three rows have been captured. One is to start the trace, one is to stop it, and the remaining rows represent our captured data. In this example, we can see that our application (the SSMS query window) only executed one stored procedure while the trace was running.

10. Use the following script to delete the trace:

```
sp_trace_setstatus @traceid = 4 -- the number of our trace
          , @status =   2       -- delete the trace
```

Dynamic Management VIEWs and Functions

Dynamic management VIEWs (DMVs) and functions were mentioned briefly in Chapter 7 in the index maintenance section. Here, we'll provide a more comprehensive coverage in a central location.

These VIEWs and functions are used to provide information on the health of a server instance, to diagnose problems, and to tune performance. Interestingly, Microsoft warns that these may change in future releases of SQL Server. This means any scripts you create with dynamic management VIEWs and functions may not port over well to the next version of SQL Server. So this is a warning to limit your use of them in scripts.

The VIEWs and functions are created in the master database within the sys schema. Since it is a schema other than dbo, the sys schema must be specified in any queries.

The 12 categories of dynamic management VIEWs and functions are listed next. Notice the first eight are VIEWs only, while the last four are VIEWs and functions.

Dynamic Management VIEWs

- Common Language Runtime Related
- Database Mirroring Related
- Query Notifications Related
- Database Related
- Replication Related
- Service Broker Related
- Full-Text Search Related
- SQL Operating System Related

Dynamic Management VIEWs and Functions

- Index Related
- Execution Related
- Transaction Related
- I/O Related

The syntax to query any of the dynamic VIEWs is the same as querying from any VIEW. We can do a SELECT * FROM VIEW, or use a column list. For example, the following query can be used to tell us how often indexes are used by presenting the usage statistics:

```
USE MASTER;
GO
SELECT * FROM sys.dm_db_index_usage_stats
```

Index-Related Dynamic Management VIEWs and Functions

The following DMVs and functions were covered more extensively in Chapter 7 in the indexes section.

- **sys.dm_db_index_usage_stats**   This returns counts of different types of index operations and the time each type of operation was last performed. The user_ updates counter indicates the level of maintenance on the index (caused by INSERT, UPDATE, and DELETE commands against the table). The seeks, scans, and lookups counters show how often the index is used for the queries.

- **sys.dm_db_index_physical_stats**   This returns size and fragmentation information for the data and indexes of the specified table or VIEW.

- **sys.dm_db_index_operational_stats**   This returns current low-level I/O, locking, latching, and access method activity for each partition of a table or index in the database.

EXAM TIP   The *index-related* dynamic management VIEWs and functions are ideal tools to check the health and usefulness of indexes. The sys.dm_db_index_usage_stats is ideal for identifying whether an index is being used, while the sys.dm_db_index_physical_stats is excellent for checking fragmentation of an index.

While the sys.dm_db_index_usage_stats DMV does identify how often indexes are used, a quirk about it is that if an index has never been used, it won't be listed in this VIEW. The following query can be used to locate unused indexes:

```
DECLARE @dbid int
SELECT @dbid = db_id('AdventureWorks')
SELECT objectname=object_name(i.object_id),
       indexname=i.name, i.index_id
FROM sys.indexes i, sys.objects o
WHERE objectproperty(o.object_id,'IsUserTable') = 1
AND i.index_id NOT IN
  (SELECT us.index_id
   FROM sys.dm_db_index_usage_stats AS us
   WHERE us.object_id=i.object_id AND
         i.index_id=us.index_id AND database_id = @dbid )
AND o.object_id = i.object_id
```

Execution-Related Dynamic Management VIEWs and Functions

- **sys.dm_exec_cached_plans**   This returns information about the query execution plans that are cached by SQL Server for faster query execution.

- **sys.dm_exec_query_stats**   This returns aggregate performance statistics for cached query plans.

- **sys.dm_exec_requests**   This returns information about each request that is executing within SQL Server. It can be useful when tracking locks and deadlocks.

- **sys.dm_exec_sessions**   This returns one row per authenticated session on Microsoft SQL Server.

SQL Server Operating System–Related DMV

- **sys.dm_os_sys_info**   This returns a miscellaneous set of useful information about the computer and about the resources available to, and consumed by, SQL Server.

- **sys.dm_os_wait_stats**   You can use this VIEW to diagnose performance issues with SQL Server and also with specific queries and batches. It records information since the last restart or since the data was cleared.

NOTE The counters reported from the sys.dm_os_wait_stats can be reset to 0 with the following command:

```
DBCC SQLPERF ('sys.dm_os_wait_stats', CLEAR);
```

Database Mirroring–Related Dynamic Management VIEWs

- **sys.dm_db_mirroring_connections** This returns a row for each database mirroring network connection.

In the following exercise, we'll execute some dynamic management VIEWs and evaluate the output.

Exercise 13.14: Execute Dynamic Management VIEWs

1. Open SSMS and create a new query window by clicking the New Query button.

2. Execute the following script to observe statistics on wait time. Notice that we are using the ORDER BY...DESCending clause to give us the highest wait times first.

```
SELECT * FROM
sys.dm_os_wait_stats
ORDER BY Wait_time_ms DESC
```

Depending on how long your server has been running, some of these numbers may be very high.

3. Right-click within the results grid and click Save Results As. In the Save Grid Results dialog box, enter **WaitStats** and click Save.

4. Reset the statistics with the following script:

```
DBCC SQLPERF ('sys.dm_os_wait_stats', CLEAR);
```

5. Check the statistics again with the following script:

```
SELECT * FROM
sys.dm_os_wait_stats
ORDER BY Wait_time_ms DESC
```

Notice that the majority of the counters are now 0, and a couple of the counters have already begun counting again.

6. Execute the following script to check the generic statistics on the server:

```
SELECT * FROM sys.dm_os_sys_info
```

Look at the physical_memory_in_bytes column to identify how much memory the server has available.

7. Execute the following script to identify any indexes that have more than 10 percent fragmentation in the AdventureWorks database:

```
SELECT * FROM sys.dm_db_index_physical_stats
    (DB_ID ('AdventureWorks'), NULL, NULL, NULL, NULL)
WHERE avg_fragmentation_in_percent > 10
ORDER BY avg_fragmentation_in_percent DESC
```

8. While this does identify the indexes, it doesn't give meaningful names. Use the following script to identify the common names of these indexes, but substitute the object_id with the index you want to identify:

```
SELECT * FROM sys.objects
WHERE object_id = 1435152158
```

   a. Of course, we could combine both queries into a single query if desired. The following script combines the desired columns from both the sys.dm_db_index_physical_stats DMV and the sys.objects table to give us exactly what we need:

```
SELECT name, index_id, index_type_desc,
       avg_fragmentation_in_percent, page_count
FROM sys.dm_db_index_physical_stats
     (DB_ID ('AdventureWorks'), NULL, NULL, NULL, NULL) AS S
JOIN sys.objects AS O
ON S.object_ID = O.object_id
WHERE avg_fragmentation_in_percent > 10
ORDER BY avg_fragmentation_in_percent DESC
```

9. Execute the following script to check the usage of indexes within the AdventureWorks database:

```
USE AdventureWorks;
GO
SELECT * from sys.dm_db_index_usage_stats
WHERE database_id = DB_ID ('AdventureWorks');
```

   When I did this on a test system that had been running less than 24 hours, three indexes showed up. When I ran it on a SQL Server with an uptime of 12 days, 50 indexes appeared. The number that appears for you may differ, considering this shows the indexes that have been used since the server was last started and reflects the activity of the server.

10. Restart the SQL Server service. Within SSMS, right-click the instance name, and then select Restart.

11. When SQL is restarted, enter the following script again to verify that zero indexes are listed:

```
USE AdventureWorks;
GO
SELECT * from sys.dm_db_index_usage_stats
WHERE database_id = DB_ID ('AdventureWorks');
```

   You should have zero rows returned. This is an important point—indexes that are never used simply don't appear in this query.

12. To force an index to be used, enter the following script:

```
USE AdventureWorks;
GO
SELECT * FROM
Person.Contact;
```

13. Use the following script to show that an index is now showing usage:

```
SELECT * from sys.dm_db_index_usage_stats
WHERE database_id = DB_ID ('AdventureWorks');
```

Dashboard Reports

While they aren't in the objectives, the dashboard reports are derived directly from dynamic management VIEWs, so they could creep into the tests. These reports were a pleasant surprise to many DBAs after having installed SQL Server 2005 Service Pack 2.

Once you install SP2, additional menu items appear in the context menus with SSMS, as you can see in Figure 13-38. The only requirements are that SP2 is installed on the instance you are monitoring, SP2 is installed on the instance of SSMS you are using to monitor it, and SQL Server Agent is running. Reporting Services is not required.

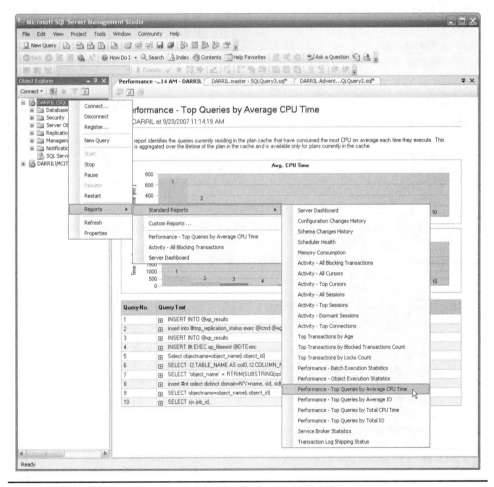

Figure 13-38   Dashboard reports available in SQL Server 2005 SP2

Since these reports use existing data from the dynamic management VIEWs, they have very little overhead. Performance counters aren't polled, and tracing doesn't need to be enabled. Instead, they just query existing data when you request a report.

These dashboard reports can help you diagnose the following common performance problems:

- CPU bottlenecks (and what queries are consuming the most CPU)
- IO bottlenecks (and what queries are performing the most IO)
- Index recommendations generated by the query optimizer (missing indexes)
- Blocking
- Latch contention

Figure 13-39 shows part of one of the reports: Server Dashboard.

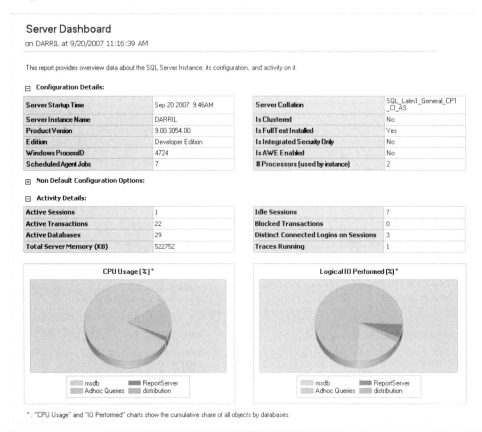

Figure 13-39   The Server Dashboard report

This report is representative of many of the reports. The title includes when and where it was run, and graphs are used to display the data along with tables of the details you need. By right-clicking anywhere in the report, you can either print the report or export it to a PDF file.

There's no substitute for experience, so I suggest you take a look at a few of these reports on your own.

Chapter Review

In this chapter, we covered several maintenance tools. These included:

- System Monitor
- SQL Server Agent
- The Maintenance Plan Wizard
- SQL Server Profiler
- Dynamic management VIEWs and functions

System Monitor allows us to measure the basic resources of any server (processor, memory, disk, and NIC). Additionally, once SQL Server is installed on a server, we have several SQL Server–specific objects and counters, as well as counters that can be used to measure the performance of SQL. By using Performance Logs and Alerts we can create a log that can be used as a baseline. By comparing new measurements to the baseline, we can determine trends, and the impact of increased load on the server.

The SQL Server Agent is an invaluable tool when it comes time to automate jobs. It includes jobs (that do the work), alerts (that can monitor for events), and operators (that can be notified). An integral part of configuring SQL Server Agent security is configuring the service account that will launch it.

While SQL Server Agent allows us to automate jobs, the Maintenance Plan Wizard takes things a step further by automating the creation of many common maintenance plans. It can be used to back up databases, manage indexes, rebuild statistics, and more.

For troubleshooting that requires capturing activity, SQL Profiler is the tool of choice. It includes many default templates that can be used to capture and examine SQL Server Profiler. If these templates aren't enough, you can create your own, and even export the templates to other servers.

SQL Trace provides a group of stored procedures that can be used in place of SQL Profiler when an automated method is needed to capture trace data. SQL Trace stored procedures can be started with a SQL Server Agent job.

Lastly, we covered the 12 different categories of dynamic management VIEWs and functions a little more fully. To see them all, however, you'll have to do some exploring on your own.

Additional Study

Self-Study Exercises

- Create a 24-hour or 7-day baseline on any computer.

- Create an alert that will notify you if the disk space on your C: drive falls below 1GB.

- Create an operator with your e-mail address and computer name.

- Create an alert to notify you if the space of the C: drive falls below 100MB of free space (use the Logical Disk object, Free MB counter).

- Create a job to back up the AdventureWorks database.

- Create a maintenance plan to do differential backups of AdventureWorks every day except Sunday.

- Create a maintenance plan to shrink the AdventureWorks database every Saturday morning.

- Create a SQL Profiler template named MyTemplate from the Replay template. Export it. Import it. Delete it.

- Run the dynamic management VIEW that will tell you if the indexes within AdventureWorks are fragmented.

- Install SP2 and view the Server Dashboard report.

BOL Topics

- Setting Up Windows Service Accounts

- SQL Server Agent

- Implementing SQL Server Agent Security

- Creating SQL Server Agent Proxies

- RAISERROR (Transact-SQL)

- Database Engine Error Severities

- Database Mail

- Introducing SQL Server Profiler

- SQL Server Profiler Templates

- Dynamic Management VIEWs and Functions

Summary of What You Need to Know

70-431

This entire chapter includes objectives for the 70-431 test.

70-441

When preparing for the 70-441 exam, make sure you are familiar with the following topics from this chapter:

- System Monitor
- Performance Logs and Alerts
- SQL Profiler
- SQL Trace

70-442

When preparing for the 70-442 exam, ensure you are familiar with the following topics from this chapter:

- System Monitor
- SQL Profiler
- SQL Trace
- Dynamic management VIEWs (DMVs)

Questions

70-431

1. You maintain a server named MCITP1 running SQL Server 2005 Enterprise Edition on Microsoft Windows Server 2003. The server has 3GB of RAM. The databases grow at a rate of about 200MB per month. Users have been complaining that queries are running slower, and your assistant has suggested it's because the server does not have enough RAM. What performance object could you monitor to help you decide whether to add RAM?

   A. SQLServer:Buffer Manager

   B. SQLServer:SQL Statistics

   C. SQLServer:General Statistics

   D. SQLServer:Locks

2. You have configured a SQL Server Agent job with multiple steps. After running the job for several weeks, you discover that the job does not complete all the steps if one of the intermediate steps fails; however, you still need the job to complete. What should you do?

   A. Re-create the job as a maintenance plan.

   B. Change the On Success action to "Go to the next step."

   C. Change the On Failure action to "Go to the next step."

   D. Configure the SQL Server Agent to restart automatically.

3. To aid in maintenance of your SQL Server 2005 server, you decide to use SQL Server Agent. You want three tasks to run every Saturday, and three tasks to run on the 15th day of every month. How would you schedule these tasks?

    A. Create a single job schedule to run daily. Assign jobs to this schedule. Have the job check if it is either a Saturday or the 15th, and then run the job if so.

    B. Create two job schedules. One job schedule would run every Saturday and would include the tasks to run every Saturday. The other schedule would run on the 15th and include the tasks to run on the 15th.

    C. Create six job schedules. Create one job for each task and schedule the jobs individually.

    D. Create one maintenance plan for all the tasks.

4. You created a maintenance plan (named MarketingCheck) to check the integrity of your Marketing database and scheduled it to run over the weekend. Now you want to view the detailed results of this maintenance plan. How can you do this? (Choose two of the following.)

    A. View the application log using Event Viewer.

    B. In SSMS, right-click the MarketingCheck maintenance plan and select View History.

    C. View the text file that starts with "MarketingCheck" in the C:\Program Files\ Microsoft SQL Server\MSSQL.1\MSSQL\LOG folder.

    D. Select the MarketingCheck report using Reporting Services.

5. Which one of the following dynamic management VIEWs will show you which indexes have not been used by any queries since the last time SQL Server 2005 was started?

    A. sys.dm_db_null_index_usage

    B. sys.dm_index_query_stats

    C. sys.dm_db_index_usage_stats

    D. sys.dm_db_index_physical_stats

6. Developers have recently modified several scripts within an application named Hurricanes running on MCTIP1. Now the system is running slowly, and you suspect some of the updated scripts are the cause. You want to capture only the scripts running on this application that take longer than three seconds. What do you do?

    A. Filter by application name of MCITP1 and with duration greater than three.

    B. Filter by application name of Hurricanes and with duration greater than three.

    C. Filter by application name of MCITP1 and with duration greater than 3000.

    D. Filter by application name of Hurricanes and with duration greater than 3000.

70-441

1. You manage a SQL Server 2005 server. You've added additional production databases to the server and these databases are expected to have an increased load in the coming months. You want to identify if and when the server hardware approaches full utilization. What can you do?

   A. Use SQL Profiler to regularly measure the activity.

   B. Use SQL Server Agent to regularly measure the activity.

   C. Use SQL Trace to regularly measure the activity.

   D. Use Performance Logs and Alerts to regularly measure the activity.

2. You manage a SQL Server 2005 server. A new application solution is being added to the server. You've determined that if it adds more than 30 percent processor or disk overhead, the server will need to be upgraded or other applications on the server will need to be migrated to a different server. How can you determine the load the new application adds to the server?

   A. Use Task manager to measure the CPU utilization.

   B. Measure CPU and Disk objects before and after the new application is installed.

   C. Use SQL Profiler to measure the response times of queries.

   D. Use SSIS to measure the utilization before and after the application is added.

3. You are tasked with creating a baseline for a SQL Server used as a back-end database by a web-based application hosted by your company. You should monitor only the necessary counters. Of the following, which should you include in your baseline? (Choose four.)

   A. Disk usage

   B. Processor usage

   C. Network packet size

   D. HTTP authenticated requests

   E. Query response time

   F. Memory usage

4. There are some concerns about the performance of the StockPortfolio database and you are tasked with automatically monitoring and storing some performance measurements. You need to track CPU utilization and how often stored procedures are executed from within the application. What would you use to track CPU utilization?

   A. Use SQL Profiler.

   B. Use SQL Trace.

   C. Use Performance Logs and Alerts.

   D. Use SQL Server Agent.

5. There are some concerns about the performance of the StockPortfolio database and you are tasked with automatically monitoring and storing some performance measurements. You need to track CPU utilization and how often stored procedures are executed from within the application. What would you use to track how often stored procedures are executed?

   A. Use SQL Profiler.

   B. Use SQL Trace.

   C. Use Performance Logs and Alerts.

   D. Use SQL Server Agent.

70-442

1. You manage a SQL Server 2005 server named MCITP1 that hosts a database named Stocks. Users report slow response times from the database. You are confident the hardware on MCITP1 is adequate but want to investigate what else may be the problem. What tool would you use?

   A. SQL Server Agent

   B. SQL Server Trace

   C. System Monitor

   D. Database Engine Tuning Advisor

2. You suspect some problematic queries are bogging down the Sales database on your SQL Server 2005 server and you decide to design an automated solution to log the performance metrics of the Sales database. What could you use?

   A. Run SQL Profiler at various intervals to find the problematic queries.

   B. Schedule SQL Trace to run at various intervals to find the problematic queries.

   C. Run System Monitor at various intervals to find the problematic queries.

   D. Schedule Network Monitor to run at various intervals to find the problematic queries.

3. You took over the management of a SQL Server 2005 server that is having some performance problems. Using System Monitor, you gather the following data:

Object:Counter	Min	Max	Avg
Memory:Pages/Sec	0	139	3
Physical Disk:Avg. Disk Queue Length	0	2	.06
Processor:Percent Processor Time	39	100	95
Network Interface:Bytes Total/Sec	21501.9	41290.4	35348.7

What should you do to resolve the problems?

A. Upgrade the NIC.

B. Upgrade the processor.

C. Upgrade the disk subsystem.

D. Add additional memory.

4. You are attempting to identify query performance problems with an application using SQL Server 2005. What would be the best tool to identify the problem queries?

A. System Monitor

B. SQL Profiler

C. Database Engine Tuning Advisor (DTA)

D. SQLCmd

5. You manage a Sales database on a SQL Server 2005 server. Queries against the Sales database are very slow. DTA was recently used to optimize the indexes, but provided only moderate improvement. You need to analyze the queries. You want to identify the longest running queries first. How can you do this?

A. Use SQL Server Profiler and group the trace by duration.

B. Use SQL Server Profiler and group the trace by user.

C. Use System Monitor and capture counters in the SQLServer:Databases object.

D. Use System Monitor and capture counters in the SQLServer:General Statistics object.

6. You are analyzing the indexes in use on the Sales database on a SQL Server 2005 server you manage. The server has been continuously running since the last scheduled downtime almost 30 days ago. You want to identify how often each of the existing indexes has been used. What tool would you use?

A. SQL Trace

B. SQL Profiler

C. The sys.dm_db_index_usage_stats DMV

D. The sys.dm_db_index_operational_stats DMV

Answers

70-431

1. A. The Buffer Manager object helps us identify how well SQL Server is using the amount of RAM. (Memory:Pages/sec would be the primary server counter to measure to see if the server has enough RAM.) Statistics are used to measure the effectiveness of indexes. Locks help us identify performance issues often related to the application.

2. **C.** Currently, when a step fails, the job stops. Each step should be configured to continue ("Go to the next step") on failure. Recreating the job as a maintenance plan isn't necessary. Manipulating the SQL Server Agent service wouldn't cause failed steps to continue.

3. **B.** Since we have two recurring schedules (one every Saturday and one on the 15th of the month), we can create two job schedules, one for each recurring schedule. Within each job, we can add the tasks for that job. Scheduling a job daily and then scripting it to check the date would be more work. Creating six jobs instead of two would also be more work. With two recurring schedules, one maintenance plan would not be sufficient.

4. **B, C.** To view the logs, you can right-click the maintenance plan and select View History, or look in the default folder for the name of the maintenance plan. Results neither are sent to the application log nor are available via Reporting Services.

5. **C.** The sys.dm_db_index_usage_stats VIEW shows statistics on indexes, while the sys.dm_db_index_physical_stats VIEW checks for fragmentation. The sys. dm_db_null_index_usage and sys.dm_index_query_stats aren't valid VIEWs.

6. **D.** To filter by the application, we would use the name of the application (Hurricanes), not the name of the server (MCITP1). Duration is shown in milliseconds—thus, 3 seconds would be a duration of 3000 milliseconds.

70-441

1. **D.** Performance Logs and Alerts can be used to create a baseline of the core four hard resources (CPU, memory, disk, and network) and then regularly measure the changes from the baseline. None of the other tools can measure the performance of the hardware resources.

2. **B.** CPU and Disk objects can be measured using Performance or System Monitor. By measuring them before *and* after the application is installed, we can determine the additional load created by the new application. Task Manager wouldn't be the best choice because it can only be viewed in real time. Additionally, the Task Manager answer only says to measure the CPU, but the scenario requires measurement of the CPU and disk. Measuring the queries wouldn't provide information on the CPU or disk usage. SSIS doesn't provide the ability to measure the CPU and disk usage.

3. **A, B, E, F.** Generally, the core four resources to measure are processor, memory, disk, and NIC. However, network packet size doesn't measure the usage (instead we should measure bytes total/sec, received/sec, or sent/sec). Since this is a back-end server, we could measure the query response time by measuring SQL Statistics. The web server would be handling HTTP authenticated requests, not the SQL Server.

4. **C.** Performance Logs and Alerts can be used to create either a log file or an alert to track CPU utilization. SQL Profiler and SQL Trace could be used to monitor and track activity but can't capture overall CPU utilization. SQL Server Agent is useful to run jobs and maintenance tasks, but can't be used to track overall CPU utilization.

5. **B.** SQL Trace can be used to *automatically* track how often stored procedures are executed. While SQL Profiler can also do the job, it requires manual intervention. In contrast, SQL Trace stored procedures can be configured in a batch to start and monitor these events. Neither Performance Logs and Alerts nor SQL Server Agent can measure how often stored procedures are executed.

70-442

1. **C.** There are many reasons why the response times are slow. System Monitor allows you to measure many counters specifically related to SQL Server. Since the hardware is considered adequate, the core four resources (processor, memory, disk, and network) may not need to be measured, but System Monitor can do much more than measure the core four. SQL Trace (and SQL Profiler) can be used to look for things like long-running queries, but there's no indication of the source of the problem without some measurements from System Monitor. SQL Server Agent can run jobs and alerts, but can't troubleshoot general problems. The Database Engine Tuning Advisor can help us create indexes, but at this point, we don't know that the lack of indexes is the problem.

2. **B.** SQL Profiler and SQL Trace are ideally suited to identify problematic queries. Once the trace is captured, we can search for high duration times (for CPU times). Since the design requires an automated solution, we'd use SQL Trace since scripts can be written and SQL Server Agent can be configured to run the scripts when desired. SQL profiler can't be automated. Neither System Monitor nor Network Monitor can easily find problematic queries.

3. **B.** The processor average processor time is 95. Generally, when this exceeds 80 percent, it's time to consider either upgrading the processor to a faster one or adding an additional processor. An average of three pages/sec is low; generally, we would compare this to a baseline on the server to see if there's a significant change. An average queue length less than two is acceptable, so the disk subsystem isn't causing the bottleneck. The counters for the NIC need to be compared to the bandwidth of the NIC (such as 10MB, 100MB, or 1GB). However, these numbers are low even for a 10MB NIC.

4. **B.** SQL Profiler is ideally suited to identify problem queries. System Monitor can be used to capture performance metrics, but can't narrow the capture to identify problem queries. The DTA is helpful identifying indexes, but can't find useful queries. The SQLCmd utility allows you to enter T-SQL statements from the command prompt, but can't capture problem queries.

5. **A.** SQL Server Profiler is ideally suited to locate long-running queries. The longest running queries will have the highest duration in SQL Server Profiler. Grouping by the user won't help in finding the longest running queries. System Monitor doesn't have any objects that can identify the longest running queries.

6. **C.** The sys.dm_db_index_usage_stats DMV is ideal in identifying usage of an index. The sys.dm_db_index_operational_stats DMV returns current low-level I/O, locking, latching, and access method activity for each partition of a table or index in the database, but not actual usage. Neither SQL Trace nor SQL Profiler has simple methods to track index usage.

Locks and Cursors

In this chapter, you will learn about:

- Locks
- Deadlocks
- Transaction isolation levels
- Hints
- Cursors

Complex problems have simple easy-to-understand wrong answers.

—Grossman's Law

A good database is always seeking a balance between:

1. Allowing as many users as possible to use the database at the same time (high concurrency) and,
2. Preventing problems from multiple users accessing the same data when one or more users are trying to modify the data (through the judicious use of locks).

For the many SQL Server databases, locks occur automatically within the database, and database developers often don't need to know how to troubleshoot locks. However, blocking locks cause problems, and when they do occur you need to know how to find and kill them. For high-end databases we sometimes need to create our own locks. We can establish our own locks by setting individual transaction isolation levels, or by using query or table hints.

Deadlocks occur primarily due to the way objects are accessed within an application. Implementing good programming practices within an application can often eliminate almost all possible deadlock conditions. However, when they do occur you need to know how to find them.

Cursors are used to retrieve a result set and process it one row at a time. While developers still often use cursors because they are easy to use and easy to conceptualize, they can often be rewritten as queries or batches that perform much more efficiently. Not always, but very often, the use of cursors are simple easy-to-understand wrong solutions for complex problems. Still, they're on the 70-442 exam, so you need to know them.

Locks and Deadlocks

From an optimization perspective, locks and deadlocks become very important to understand, identify, and manage. Many times I've been asked about a "slow" database that often seems to just "lock up." After investigation, I've often found that locks and deadlocks were the culprit. Because of this, whenever I hear about a slow database that is periodically unresponsive, I almost always suspect locks or deadlocks.

For the MCITP tests, you need to understand what locks and deadlocks are and how to identify them once you suspect they're occurring. Once identified, you need to know how to kill them, or in other words be able to stop the processes causing the lock. Thankfully, SQL Server 2005 has many tools that can be used to help you track down and manage locks. These include:

- Activity Monitor
- System Monitor
- SQL Profiler
- Dynamic management VIEWs

What Are Locks?

Locks occur when a process needs to prevent access to data by another process. Let's consider a simple example where data is updated without locks:

```
EmpID   FName        LName        Phone        Email
101     Sally        McGirk       555-1212     Sally@mcitp.com
```

Sally gets married, changes her last name to Johnson, and her phone number changes to 555-3434. Now let's say that one person executes an UPDATE statement to change her last name to Johnson. At the same time, another person enters an UPDATE statement to change her phone number.

Since each person is updating only one column of data, all the other data should stay the same with a regular UPDATE. However, what's not apparent is that when an UPDATE is issued, the entire row (all columns) is rewritten, not just the changed column.

When the statement is executed to change her name, it would result in the following row. Notice that only the last name has changed.

```
EmpID   FName        LName        Phone        Email
101     Sally        Johnson      555-1212     Sally@mcitp.com
```

When the second statement is executed at the same time to change her phone number, it would result in the following row. Remember, both statements were executed at the same time, but let's say that the second statement took a millisecond longer so it was saved last. Notice that since the original last name of McGirk existed when the phone UPDATE started, McGirk is retained. The update of the last name is lost.

```
EmpID   FName        LName        Phone        Email
101     Sally        McGirk       555-3434     Sally@mcitp.com
```

Obviously, this is unacceptable. Without locks on data, it becomes a case of the "last one who saves, wins," and the consistency of the data isn't guaranteed. To ensure this doesn't happen, database management systems implement different locking modes to ensure that other access doesn't occur simultaneously.

The common lock modes are:

- **Shared (S)**   This mode is used for read operations that do not change or update data. While I'm reading data using a SELECT statement, you can also read data using a SELECT statement because a shared lock is placed on the table. However, we typically don't want someone modifying the data while we're reading it.

- **Exclusive (X)**   This is used for data modification (INSERT, UPDATE, or DELETE). This type of lock would be used when two processes are trying to update data at the same time. In our earlier example with Sally Johnson, an exclusive lock would be created on the row until the name was successfully changed to Sally McGirk. Once done, the second process could update the phone number. By creating the locks, the two processes are separate and independent; the locks ensure that both changes occur without affecting the previous change.

- **Update (U)**   This mode is used on resources that can be updated. Note that the Exclusive (X) is done for INSERT, UPDATE, and DELETE statements; the Update(U) is only for UPDATE statements. This is used to prevent a common deadlock condition when multiple sessions are reading a resource, and then they try to upgrade the lock to an exclusive lock.

- **Intent**   This is used to establish a lock hierarchy and to signal intent on creating a higher lock soon. Types of intent locks are intent shared (IS), intent exclusive (IX), and shared with intent exclusive (SIX).

- **Schema**   This mode is used when performing a Data Definition Language (DDL) operation. The types of schema locks are schema modification (Sch-M) and schema stability (Sch-S).

Many locks are compatible with each other and allow concurrent access to the data. For example, if one user is executing a SELECT statement using a shared lock, other users can also execute SELECT statements with shared locks.

Some locks are not compatible with each other. An exclusive lock is just that—exclusive. With an exclusive lock on a resource, other processes are blocked from access until the exclusive lock is released.

Lock Granularity
Exactly what is locked? The entire database? Just the row? The database management system (DBMS) makes a determination on what needs to be locked and then locks it at the lowest level needed to ensure consistency.

If one user is updating the Person.Contact table, and another user is updating the Sales.Products table, clearly there is no connection between these updates. Locks on either of these actions should not prevent the other from occurring.

Locks can be created and held at different resource levels from an individual row up to the entire database. Some of the locking levels are:

- **RID**   This is used to lock single rows by use of a row identifier.
- **KEY**   This is used to lock a row within an index. It protects key ranges in serializable transactions.
- **PAGE**   This is used to lock an 8KB page in a database.
- **EXTENT**   This is used to lock a contiguous group of eight pages.
- **TABLE**   This is used to lock an entire table, including all data and indexes.
- **FILE**   This is used to lock an entire database file.
- **DATABASE**   This is used to lock the entire database.

Blocks

A process that is being stopped by a lock is referred to as being "blocked." Often, we learn of a problem through a block. While the block isn't the source of the problem, it does help us understand there is a problem and then search for the source.

When troubleshooting locks, we often look for processes that are "Blocked By" or that are "Blocking" a certain process. The Blocked By data tells us which process is causing the problem, and the Blocking data tells what other processes are being affected by this process.

What Are Deadlocks?

Deadlocks occur when two different processes have a lock on one resource but are trying to access a second resource, which is already locked by the other process. Let's use an example.

Sally is executing a statement that first locks the Employees table, and then is waiting for access to the Customers table to update it (see Table 14-1). At the same time, Joe is executing a statement that first locks the Customers table and then is waiting for access to the Employees table to update it (see Table 14-2).

Sally	
Employees table	Locked
Customers table	Waiting

Table 14-1   Tables Accessed by Sally

Joe	
Customers table	Locked
Employees table	Waiting

Table 14-2   Tables Accessed by Joe

This is a Catch-22 condition. Sally needs the Customers table, but can't get it until Joe releases it. Joe will release Customers once he accesses the Employees table, but he can't access the Employees table until Sally releases it. Sally won't release the Employees table until she accesses the Customers table. And around and around we go.

Thankfully, SQL Server 2005 will detect deadlock conditions and automatically stop them. The deadlock detection process runs by default every five seconds, but will run more frequently if deadlocks are detected more often.

Once a deadlock is detected, SQL Server tries to determine which transaction is the least expensive to roll back. That transaction becomes the deadlock victim. The transaction is rolled back and a 1205 error is returned to the application.

 EXAM TIP A 1205 error indicates a deadlock has occurred. Results of deadlock errors (and deadlock victims) are recorded in the SQL Server error log.

Preventing Locks and Deadlocks

Locks and deadlocks can often be prevented by following some best practices in relation to transactions. This is referred to as *reducing lock contention*.

Use transactions only to modify the data. Before entering the transaction that creates the lock, get all required data. This is especially true of user input. Starting a transaction and then asking for a user to enter data is a recipe for disaster. Nothing stops that user from going on a coffee break, heading off for lunch, or departing for vacation. While the system waits for the user, everyone else waits for the system to release the lock.

One of the easiest ways to avoid deadlock errors is to ensure that all database developers access tables in the same order. In other words, transactions that need to access the Customers and Employees tables would all access the Customers table first, and then access the Employees table. This requires some planning and coordination on the part of the developers, but certainly pays for itself in the long run.

Troubleshooting Locks and Deadlocks

When locks or deadlocks occur, the DBA's challenge is to identify them and kill them if necessary. While the DBA typically is not involved in development work, the DBA does need to be able to identify problems with the server or with the development of the application. This is not always an easy task.

Growing up in a family-owned restaurant, I remember feuds between the waitresses and cooks. There was a lot of finger pointing. Later, as a sous chef, I noticed the same type of finger pointing between the bakers and the chefs. In the Navy, blame-storming occurred between maintenance techs and operators. In the IT world with databases, often the developers blame the hardware or the server, and the administrator (responsible for the hardware and the server) blames the software. The key to successful resolution of problems in all these situations was, and is, having an understanding of the opposite side.

As a DBA, you probably won't be responsible for much of the programming. If lock or deadlock issues arise, the task of fixing the problem will fall to the developer. Likewise, if the problem is with the hardware, such as there not being enough memory, or the hard drives are not optimized, the database developer won't be doing much. The task of fixing hardware issues falls to the administrator.

As an administrator, you can probably easily prove or disprove that the problem lies with hardware. If you suspect the problem is not enough memory, you can use System Monitor to prove your case, present the numbers to management, and get a purchase order approved for more memory.

If you suspect the problem is locks, your best course of action is to prove that's the case, present the database developers with the numbers, and let them fix the problem(s). However, simply proving that the hardware is *not* the problem doesn't prove that the software *is* the problem. I have witnessed a couple of heated blame-storming sessions between DBAs and database developers where fingers are pointed:

"The problem is memory."

"It's the application."

"It's the hardware."

"It's the software."

The hero in this situation is the one who understands both sides of the issue and has enough technical savvy that she can prove exactly what the problem is. She doesn't need to know how to fix the problem, only to definitively identify it.

Understanding the following tools will help you definitively prove whether locks are the problem.

Activity Monitor

Activity Monitor is built into SQL Server Management Studio and can quickly give you a view of locks in your system. Since activity can be very dynamic, the Activity Monitor takes a snapshot of activity when it's accessed. You can take your time viewing the data, and if desired, refresh it.

To access the Activity Monitor, look in the Management container of SSMS. After right-clicking Activity Monitor, you can choose among the following:

- View Processes
- View Locks by Process
- View Locks by Object

Some of the Activity Monitor icons may not be intuitive. The following is a short explanation of what they mean:

- **Running—Green arrow**   The system is currently performing work.
- **Runnable—White check on green circle**   The process is connected to the server and has run in the past, but is not currently doing anything.
- **Sleeping—Red down-arrow on white circle**   The process has work to perform, but is currently waiting for something (such as user input or a lock to be released).
- **Background—Gray curved up- and down-arrows on white circle**   This is a background process that periodically wakes up to do work.
- **Suspended—Hourglass**   This is a stopped process that has work to perform. Look at the Wait Type field for a clue as to what has caused it to stop.
- **Other—Blue left-right two-way arrow on white circle**   This indicates a status that is not one of the other statuses (such as Running, Runnable, Sleeping, and so on).

Once Activity Monitor is showing, any of the three views can be selected in the Select A Page section. Activity Monitor is shown in Figure 14-1.

Activity Monitor - DARRIL						
Select a page	Refresh Filter ... Help					
Process Info						
Locks by Process	Displayed 13 items from a total of 31 items.					
Locks by Object						
		Process ID	System Process	User	Database	Status	Oper
		51	no	NT AUTHORITY\SYSTEM	ReportServer	Sleeping	0
		52	no	DARRIL\DarrilGibson	master	Sleeping	0
		53	no	NT AUTHORITY\SYSTEM	msdb	Sleeping	0
		54	no	DARRIL\DarrilGibson	AdventureWorks	Sleeping	0
Status		55	no	DARRIL\DarrilGibson	AdventureWorks	Sleeping	0
Last Refresh:		56	no	DARRIL\DarrilGibson	Chapter6	Sleeping	0
9/22/2007 7:19:09 AM		57	no	DARRIL\ASPNET	ReportServer	Sleeping	0
Next Refresh:		58	no	NT AUTHORITY\SYSTEM	msdb	Sleeping	0
Manual		59	no	DARRIL\DarrilGibson	AdventureWorks	Sleeping	0
		60	no	NT AUTHORITY\SYSTEM	msdb	Sleeping	0
View refresh settings		61	no	DARRIL\DarrilGibson	Chapter6	Sleeping	0
		62	no	DARRIL\ASPNET	ReportServer	Sleeping	0
Filter: Applied		63	no	DARRIL\DarrilGibson	tempdb	Runnable	2
View filter settings						

Figure 14-1 Activity Monitor

So that we can see some meaningful information, let's do an exercise. We'll use SSMS to create some locks and then use the Activity Monitor to view and kill a lock.

Exercise 14.1: Find and Kill Locks

See how to identify and kill a lock in video 14-1.

1. Launch SSMS and connect to the default instance.

2. Click the New Query button to create a new query window. As the very first line, enter the following comment so we know this is Query Window 1:

```
-- Query Window 1
```

3. Enter the following script and execute it to start a transaction. Notice that we have begun a transaction, but have not committed it or rolled it back.

```
USE AdventureWorks;
GO
BEGIN Transaction
  INSERT INTO Person.Contact
    (FirstName, LastName, PasswordHash, PasswordSalt)
      VALUES ('Old', 'McDonald', 'P@ssw0rd','P@$$S@lt')
```

4. Within SSMS, open the Management container. Right-click Activity Monitor and select View Processes. If you look at the Database column, you should see one process for the AdventureWorks database. Write down the Process ID for this process here: _____. Leave the Activity Monitor open.

5. Go back to SSMS and create another new query window by clicking the New Query button again. As the first line, enter the following comment so we know this is Query Window 2:

```
-- Query Window 2
```

6. In Query Window 2, enter the following T-SQL statement to query the Person. Contact table and then execute it:

```
USE AdventureWorks;
GO
SELECT *
FROM Person.Contact
```

Notice that the script never completes. Instead, at the bottom of the window, a green circle continues to be drawn and redrawn with the status message of "Executing query."

7. Go back to the Activity Monitor. Click the Refresh button. Notice that the original AdventureWorks process is not changed, but an additional process accessing the AdventureWorks database has appeared. It is in a Suspended state with the hourglass as the icon. We have created a lock.

8. Scroll to the far right to observe the Blocked By column as shown in Figure 14-2. Notice that the suspended process is blocked by the Process ID identified in step 4.

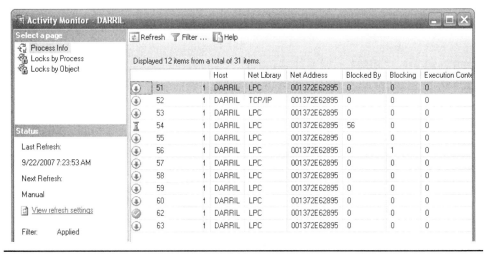

Figure 14-2 Identifying the blocking process

9. Another way a blocking process can be identified is with the sys.dm_exec_requests dynamic management VIEW (DMV). Execute the following script in the first query window:

```
SELECT *
FROM sys.dm_exec_requests
WHERE blocking_session_id <> 0
```

The blocking_session_id identifies the process that is causing the block. If you scroll to the right, you should see the blocking_session_id column and identify the process as the same one from step 4.

10. Enter the following command to identify how many total locking requests are active:

```
SELECT * FROM sys.dm_tran_locks
```

Look at the status line of the query window and identify how many rows were returned. If you run this query again after the process is killed, you will notice that the number of rows is significantly reduced.

11. Right-click the process identified in step 4. Notice you can choose Kill Process, as shown in Figure 14-3.

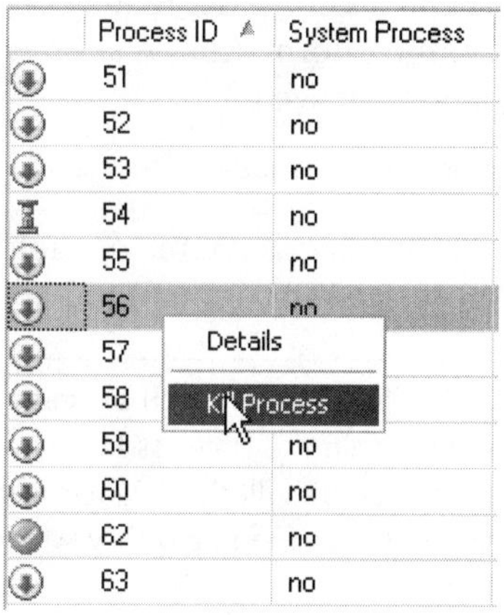

Figure 14-3

Killing a process in Activity Monitor

	Process ID	System Process
⊕	51	no
⊕	52	no
⊕	53	no
I	54	no
⊕	55	no
⊕	56	no
⊕	57	Details
⊕	58	Kill Process
⊕	59	no
⊕	60	no
⊘	62	no
⊕	63	no

12. Go back to SSMS and create a third query window by clicking the New Query button again. As the first line, enter the following comment so we know this is Query Window 3:

```
-- Query Window 3
```

13. In Query Window 3, enter the following command to kill the process from the open transaction in Query Window 1. In my system, the Process ID from step 4 was 54. It may be different for you.

```
Kill 54
```

14. Switch to Query Window 2. Notice the query has now completed successfully. You can verify this from the status bar at the bottom of the query window.

15. Switch to Activity Monitor and click the Refresh button. You can see that the suspended process has completed and is now sleeping.

16. Run the following script to identify how many total locking requests are active now. Compare this with what you observed in step 10.

```
SELECT * FROM sys.dm_tran_locks
```

17. Close all open SSMS query windows.

Killing Locks

As we saw in the previous exercise, a lock can be killed in a couple of ways. First, we need to identify which process is causing the lock. This can be done in Activity Monitor or in a query window.

For any process, we can check the Blocked By column within Activity Monitor in the Process Info view. This verifies two things. First, it verifies the process is being blocked. Second, it identifies the process doing the blocking.

We can also query the sys.dm_exec_requests DMV and view the Blocking_Session_id column to gain the same information. A simple SELECT statement querying the DMV gives all the information we need:

```
SELECT * from sys.dm_exec_requests
```

To kill the lock, we also have a couple of choices. We either right-click the process in Activity Monitor, or use the Kill command to kill the specific Process ID.

EXAM TIP   To identify which process is blocking another, check the Blocked By column within the Process Info view of Activity Monitor. Once identified, the process can be killed by right-clicking the process and selecting Kill Process, or by entering **Kill <PID>** in a query window with the process ID number substituted for **<PID>**.

Dynamic Management VIEWs

In Chapter 13, we covered dynamic management VIEWs and functions. In the following, we've listed a few DMVs that are helpful when troubleshooting locking and contention issues:

- **sys.dm_exec_requests**   This includes a Blocking_Session_ID column, which can be used to identify a process that is blocking another.

- **Sys.dm_tran_locks**   This returns information about currently active lock manager resources. It includes several columns about the resource that is being requested (resource group) and several columns on the lock request (request group). This can be useful in identifying locks as they occur.

EXAM TIP   The sys.dm_exec_requests DMV can be useful in identifying processes that are blocked. The blocking_session_id column holds the ID of the session that is blocking the request. If the blocking_session_id is NULL, the request is not blocked.

- **Sys.dm_os_wait_stats** This returns information about waits encountered by threads. The wait_time_ms column reports the total wait time. The max_wait_time_ms reports the maximum of any individual waits. After modifying an application, we can reset these counters to zero and see if our modifications have an impact. The command to reset these counters is:

```
DBCC SQLPERF ('sys.dm_os_wait_stats', CLEAR)
```

sp_who

If you've been around SQL Server for a while, you probably recognize sp_who. This can be used to identify details on processes. Without any parameters, sp_who can be used to identify details on every process that is interacting with SQL Server. If you provide an integer representing a specific process ID (SPID), you can find out details on that process.

For example, let's say you're informed by users that your system is occasionally unresponsive. One day you notice the problem occurring and run the *SELECT * FROM sys.dm_tran_locks* statement to see if it's a locking problem. You identify many locks and want to know where they're coming from.

You notice that many locks are being generated by *request_session_id 64* (SPID 64). But who is *request_session_id 64*? *Sp_who* knows. By using the sp_who stored procedure with *64* as the parameter, you can find out. The command looks like this:

```
Sp_who 64
```

The result shows the hostname of the computer, where the command came from, the user that issued the command, and more.

System Monitor

Another tool useful in the hunt for locks is System Monitor. We covered the usage of System Monitor in Chapter 13, but here we'll add some information on locks and deadlocks. SQL Server includes the SQL Server Locks object. It has several counters that can be used to determine the level of contention in your system.

Counters in the SQL Server Locks object include:

- **Lock Requests/sec** This is the total of the locks and lock conversions requested from the lock manager.

- **Number of Deadlocks/sec** This is the total of the lock requests that resulted in a deadlock.

- **Average Wait Time (ms)** This is the average amount of wait time in milliseconds for each lock request that resulted in a wait.

- **Lock Waits/sec** This is the total lock requests that couldn't be satisfied immediately and required a wait before being granted a lock.

NOTE When an application is slow and/or periodically stops responding, suspect locks and deadlocks. Use System Monitor to identify if excessive locks are occurring. System Monitor can quickly give you quantifiable data on how many locks and deadlocks are occurring and how they are impacting wait time. Once locks or deadlocks are identified as being a problem, other tools such as Activity Monitor, DMVs, and SQL Profiler can be used to get more detailed information on who or what is causing the problem.

A certain level of locking is normal in any functioning database. Just because locks are detected does not indicate a problem. The easiest comparison is to check current locks against the number of locks in the baseline.

Deadlocks are not common. In a fully functioning database application, the goal is to have zero deadlocks. The application development team can implement different methodologies to reduce or eliminate deadlocks. These include:

- **Have all developers access objects in the same order.** For example, if the Currency table and the CurrencyRate table both need to be accessed within a transaction, having all developers access the Currency table first and then the CurrencyRate table next will help prevent deadlocks. As we'll see in Exercise 14.2, when one developer accesses tables in one order and another developer accesses them in another order, we create the potential for a deadlock.

- **Limit the number of long-running queries as much as possible.**

SQL Profiler

In Chapter 13, we also covered SQL Profiler. However, we limited the discussion on the use of SQL Profiler to capture information on locks until we could define locks. SQL Profiler has a full Locks Event class that can be used to trace information on locks.

CAUTION Remember, SQL Profiler can be very resource-intensive. Running Profiler on the production server may load it down unacceptably. Ideally, you would run SQL Profiler on a completely separate system used for testing. When starting a new trace the first step is to connect to a server, and you can connect to any SQL Server in your network.

Individual lock events that can be captured are listed in Table 14-3.

Most of these events are self-explanatory, but let's add a few words to the deadlock events. Again, the goal for deadlocks is to have zero. If System Monitor shows that deadlocks are occurring, a logical choice is to use SQL Profiler to capture these deadlock events to get more details.

The three most important events in the Lock Events class are:

- **Lock:Deadlock** This provides some generic information on the deadlock, such as application name, database name, and duration.

Event Class	Description
Lock:Deadlock Graph	Provides an XML description of a deadlock.
Lock:Acquired	Indicates that a lock has been acquired on a resource, such as a row in a table.
Lock:Cancel	Tracks requests for locks that were canceled before the lock was acquired (for example, due to a deadlock).
Lock:Deadlock Chain	Produced for each of the events leading up to a deadlock. Used to monitor when deadlock conditions occur and which objects are involved.
Lock:Deadlock	Tracks when a transaction has requested a lock on a resource already locked by another transaction, resulting in a deadlock.
Lock:Escalation	Indicates that a finer-grained lock has been converted to a coarser-grained lock.
Lock:Released	Tracks when a lock is released.
Lock:Timeout (timeout > 0)	Tracks when lock requests cannot be completed because another transaction has a blocking lock on the requested resource.
Lock:Timeout	Tracks when lock requests cannot be completed because another transaction has a blocking lock on the requested resource.

Table 14-3 SQL Profiler Lock Events

- **Lock:Deadlock Graph**   This provides more detailed information, such as Login Name, Session Login Name, Server Name, and SPID.

- **Lock:Deadlock Chain**   This includes information on the events leading up to the deadlock.

EXAM TIP   When using Profiler to track down and identify the causes of deadlocks, use the Deadlock, Deadlock Graph, and Deadlock Chain events. The Deadlock Graph event can capture a full XML file of data on the deadlock, and the Deadlock Chain event can capture data on the events leading up to the deadlock, including all participants.

In the following exercise, you will create a deadlock condition and use SQL Profiler to identify the cause and details of the deadlock.

Exercise 14.2: Use SQL Profiler to Identify a Deadlock

1. Start SQL Profiler by clicking Start | All Programs | Microsoft SQL Server 2005 | Performance Tools | SQL Server Profiler.

2. Click the New Trace button. Click Connect to connect to the default instance of SQL Server 2005.

3. In the Trace Properties page, select Blank in the Use The Template section.

4. In the Trace Properties page, select the Events Selection tab. Click the + next to Locks to open it. Select Deadlock Graph, Lock:Deadlock, and Lock:Deadlock Chain. Your display should look similar to Figure 14-4. Click Run.

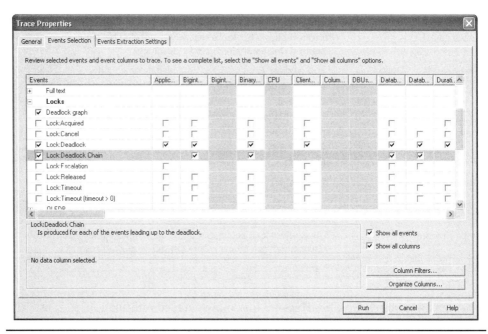

Figure 14-4   Creating the trace to capture deadlock events

5. If not open, launch SSMS.

6. Create a new query window by clicking the New Query window button. At the top of this window, type in the following comment so we know this is Query Window 1:

```
--Joe Query Window 1
```

7. Enter the following script and execute it to begin a transaction to insert a row into the Currency Rate table. Notice there is no commit, so the transaction will remain open.

```
USE AdventureWorks;
GO
BEGIN TRANSACTION
INSERT INTO Sales.CurrencyRate
    (CurrencyRateDate, FromCurrencyCode,ToCurrencyCode,
         AverageRate, EndOfDayRate)
VALUES (GetDate(), 'USD', 'CAD',1.585, 1.583)
```

8. Create another new query window by clicking the New Query window button. At the top of this window, type in the following comment so we know this is Query Window 2:

```
--Sally Query Window 2
```

9. Type in the following script to create a locking condition. Notice this is just a lock, not a deadlock.

```
USE AdventureWorks;
GO
BEGIN TRANSACTION
INSERT INTO Sales.Currency
    (CurrencyCode, Name)
VALUES ('VUC', 'Vulcan Cha')
--
UPDATE Sales.CurrencyRate
    SET EndOfDayRate = 1.584
    WHERE Year(ModifiedDate) = Year(GetDate()) AND
        Month(ModifiedDate) = Month(GetDate()) and
            Day(ModifiedDate) = Day(GetDate())
```

 NOTE By looking at the status bar, you can see that the query continues to execute but never completes.

At this point, let's review what we have:

- Joe in Query Window 1 has created a lock on the Currency Rate table.
- Sally in Query Window 2 has created a lock on the Currency table and is trying to access the Currency Rate table.

  If Joe finishes the work and releases the lock on the Currency Rate table, then Sally can complete her work. However, what we'll do now is have Joe try to do some work on the Currency table that Sally has locked.

10. View the SQL Server Profiler trace. Notice that nothing has been logged. We don't have any deadlocks at this point.

11. Return to the query window labeled Joe Query Window 1. Enter the following script:

```
UPDATE Sales.Currency
    SET Name = 'Vulcan Sha'
    WHERE CurrencyCode = 'VUC'
```

 NOTE You can enter this text below the existing text in Query Window 1. Once it's typed in, simply highlight it, and then press F5 to execute it.

This runs successfully.

12. Return to the query window labeled Sally Query Window 2. Notice that the message has returned a 1205 error. You should see something like the following message:

```
Msg 1205, Level 13, State 51, Line 2
Transaction (Process ID 56) was deadlocked on lock resources with
another process and has been chosen as the deadlock victim. Rerun the
transaction.
```

13. Switch to SQL Profiler. You should see something similar to Figure 14-5.

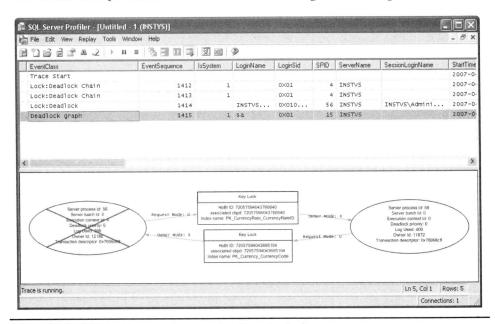

Figure 14-5 SQL Profiler capturing trace data for a deadlock

Notice that you have four events captured: two Deadlock Chain events, one Deadlock, and one Deadlock Graph.

14. Select the Deadlock Graph event. Looking in the diagram area, you can see one of the events has an *X* over it indicating it was the deadlock victim. Hover over either of the circles in the diagram. You will see data on the statement that was a part of the deadlock. You can view this in Figure 14-6.

Profiler and System Monitor

In Chapter 13, we covered System Monitor. System Monitor and Profiler can be configured to work together in some interesting ways to monitor performance and, more specifically, to detect locks and deadlocks.

Using System Monitor, we can create a counter log to capture the data. At the same time, we can create a trace log within SQL Profiler. Once the data is captured and saved,

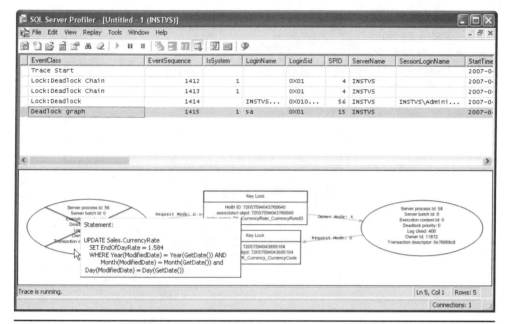

Figure 14-6   Viewing details in SQL Profiler

we can view both the trace data and the System Monitor graph within SQL Profiler. This can be useful in quickly identifying deadlocks and capturing the actual statements that are causing the deadlocks.

In the following exercise, we'll set up System Monitor and SQL Profiler to capture deadlock events. We'll then create a deadlock event in SSMS and use SQL Profiler to view the data.

Exercise 14.3: Use SQL Profiler with System Monitor

Video 14-3 shows how to use SQL Profiler with System Monitor.

1. Set up the counter log:

   a. Click Start | Run and enter **perfmon** to launch System Monitor.

   b. Open the Performance Logs And Alerts to access Counter Logs. Right-click Counter Logs and select New Log Settings. In the New Log Settings dialog box, enter **Capture Deadlocks**. Click OK.

   c. In the Capture Deadlocks dialog box, click Add Counters. For the Performance Object, select SQL Server:Locks. Select the Number of Deadlocks/sec counter. Your display should look similar to Figure 14-7. Click Add, and then click Close.

Figure 14-7

Adding the Number of Deadlocks/sec counter in System Monitor

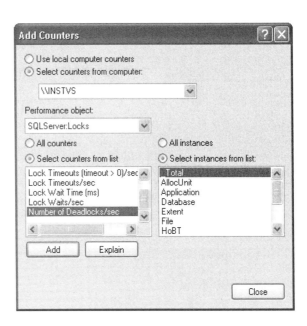

d. While still on the General tab of the Capture Deadlocks dialog box, change the sample data interval to 1 second.

e. Click the Log Files tab. Change the Log File Type to *Text File (Comma Delimited)*. By default, this will be created in the c:\PerfLogs directory.

f. Click the Schedule tab. Verify that the log file is scheduled to start and stop manually.

g. Click OK. If prompted to create the PerfLogs directory, click Yes.

h. Select the Capture Deadlocks counter log. If it doesn't turn green to indicate it's started, right-click it and select Start.

2. Set up SQL Profiler to capture the trace:

a. Start SQL Profiler by clicking Start | All Programs | Microsoft SQL Server 2005 | Performance Tools | SQL Server Profiler.

b. Click the New Trace button. Click Connect to connect to the default instance of SQL Server 2005.

c. In the Use The Template area, select the TSQL_Replay template.

d. Click the Save To File check box. In the Save As dialog box, browse to the C:\ PerfLogs directory. Enter **CaptureDeadlocks** as the filename and click Save.

e. At this point, your display of SQL Profiler should look similar to Figure 14-8. Click the Run button to start the trace.

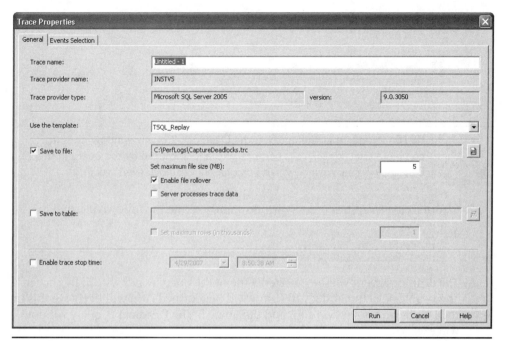

Figure 14-8 Setting up SQL Profiler to capture the trace

3. If not already open, start an instance of SSMS, and then connect to the default instances.

4. Open a new query window by clicking the New Query button. At the top of the window, enter the following comment so we can identify it as the Deadlock 1 query window:

```
--Deadlock 1 query window
```

5. In the Deadlock 1 window, enter the following script and execute it:

```
USE AdventureWorks;
GO
BEGIN TRANSACTION
INSERT INTO Sales.CurrencyRate
    (CurrencyRateDate, FromCurrencyCode,ToCurrencyCode,
          AverageRate, EndOfDayRate)
VALUES (GetDate(), 'USD', 'CAD',1.585, 1.583)
```

6. Open a new query window by clicking the New Query button. Enter the following script, including the comment to identify it as the Deadlock 2 query window. Execute the script.

```
--Deadlock 2
USE AdventureWorks;
GO
BEGIN TRANSACTION
INSERT INTO Sales.Currency
```

```
       (CurrencyCode, Name)
VALUES ('VUC', 'Vulcan Cha')
--
UPDATE Sales.CurrencyRate
   SET EndOfDayRate = 1.584
   WHERE Year(ModifiedDate) = Year(GetDate()) AND
         Month(ModifiedDate) = Month(GetDate()) and
              Day(ModifiedDate) = Day(GetDate())
```

 NOTE Notice that the query in the Deadlock 2 query window does not complete executing. This is because of the lock caused by the query in the Deadlock 1 query window. We don't have a deadlock event yet.

7. Return to the Deadlock 1 query window and execute the following script:

```
UPDATE Sales.Currency
   SET Name = 'Vulcan Sha'
   WHERE CurrencyCode = 'VUC'
```

8. The deadlock event will be detected. One of the query windows will be chosen as a deadlock victim and a 1205 error will be returned. You will likely see this in the Deadlock 2 query window, and the query in the Deadlock 1 query window will execute.

9. Return to System Monitor and stop the Capture Deadlocks counter log by selecting it, right-clicking, and choosing Stop.

10. Return to SQL Profiler. Click the red button to stop the trace.

11. Open the captured trace file in SQL Profiler. Click File | Open | Trace File. Select the CaptureDeadlocks.trc file in the C:\Perflogs directory.

12. Import the counter log data into SQL Profiler. Choose File | Import Performance Data. Select the Capture Deadlocks_000001.csv file and click Open. In the Performance Counters Limit dialog box, mark all the check boxes to import all the data. Click OK.

13. Your display should look similar to Figure 14-9. Notice that the graph shows one spike. We only captured deadlock events, so this spike shows clearly where the deadlock occurred.

14. Click at the spike in the graph. Notice in the top pane that details on the command occurring at the time are displayed. In the bottom pane, the full text of the command being executed is displayed.

15. In the top pane, select the line above the line originally selected. Notice the text changes in the bottom pane. Select the line below the first line originally selected. Once you are close to the deadlock event, you can easily look at what was happening immediately before and after the event.

16. Close System Monitor. Close SQL Profiler.

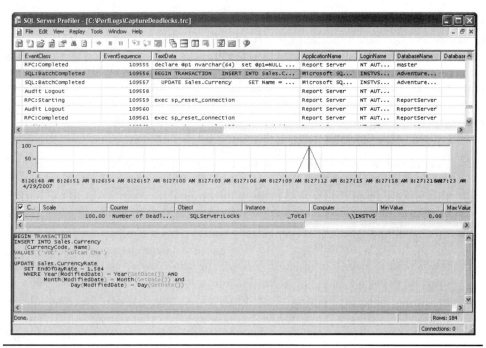

Figure 14-9 Viewing performance data in SQL Profiler

Transaction Isolation Levels

Transactions can specify an isolation level that defines how much one transaction is isolated from another. These are used to control whether locks are employed when the data is read, what types of locks are requested, how long read locks are held, and how a read operation treats rows modified by another transaction.

The isolation level doesn't affect the locks required to modify the data. Instead, transaction isolation levels are used for read operations and to define the level of isolation (or protection) from the effects of modifications made by other transactions.

The isolation levels are:

- Read committed (default)
- Read uncommitted
- Repeatable read
- Serializable
- Snapshot

The ultimate goal is to provide some level of isolation while also allowing multiple users to simultaneously access the data—concurrently. However, when users access data concurrently, some concurrency side effects come into play.

Concurrency Effects

Concurrency effects are important when considering available transaction isolation levels. Is it acceptable for data being read by one transaction to be modified by another? Is it a requirement for data read once to be the same if it's read again within a transaction? Dirty reads and nonrepeatable reads are a couple of the side effects we need to consider. Sometimes, these side effects are acceptable for a given situation, and sometimes they are not.

Side effects resulting from concurrency issues are listed next:

- **Uncommitted dependency (dirty read)**   One transaction is modifying data. Before the transaction is done, a second transaction reads the modified data. This is considered a dirty read because the original transaction could roll back the data, but the second transaction still treats the data as valid.

- **Inconsistent analysis (non-repeatable read)**   This is similar to a dirty read except there are multiple reads of a row, and the data is changing each time the row is read. A second transaction accesses the same row several times and reads different data each time due to modifications from other transactions.

- **Phantom reads**   A phantom read occurs when a delete is performed by one transaction against a range of rows being read by another transaction. The first read shows it exists, but due to a deletion, subsequent reads show it is no longer there—a phantom. Or, the first read shows the row does not exist, but subsequent reads show the row is there.

- **Lost Updates**   Last one who saves, wins. If two transactions are allowed to modify the same row at the same time (though on different columns), then the second transaction will overwrite the first one.

Picking a Transaction Isolation Level

With a better understanding of the concurrency side effects, we can now explore the transaction isolation levels a little better. These are not restricted to Microsoft's SQL Server, but instead are part of the SQL-99 standard.

Read Committed (Default)

This is the default if a transaction isolation level is not specified in SQL Server 2005.

Read Committed specifies that statements cannot read data that has been modified but not committed. Nonrepeatable reads or phantom reads are possible with the Read Committed transaction isolation level since data can be changed by other transactions between individual statements within the current transaction.

A new feature in SQL Server 2005 is the READ_COMMITTED_SNAPSHOT option. This option slightly modifies the behavior of the Read Committed transaction isolation level.

- If READ_COMMITTED_SNAPSHOT is set to OFF, shared locks prevent other transactions from modifying rows while the current transaction is running a read operation. This is the default in SQL Server.

- If the READ_COMMITTED_SNAPSHOT option is ON, then *row versioning* is used to provide a transactionally consistent snapshot of data as it existed when first queried. While the read still views the original unchanged data, locks are not used to protect the data from updates.

Row versioning is a new feature supported in SQL Server 2005. When used, every time a row is modified by a specific transaction, the database engine stores a version of the previously committed image of the row in tempdb. Versions of the row are marked with the transaction sequence number of the transaction that made the change. One of the benefits of row versioning is that it allows a transaction to view the original data even though the original data has been modified. Row versions are only held temporarily.

EXAM NOTE To reduce excessive locks without changing the default transaction isolation level of Read Committed, set the READ_COMMITTED_ SNAPSHOT option to ON. This will use row versioning to ensure the transaction has a record of the data when the transaction began, even if the data actually changed. It will also protect against dirty reads while minimizing locking contention.

Read Uncommitted

Read Uncommitted specifies that transactions or statements can read data that has been modified but has not been committed. A simpler way of saying this is that dirty reads are allowed with the Read Uncommitted transaction isolation level.

Transactions using the Read Uncommitted transaction isolation level do not issue shared locks to prevent other transactions from modifying data. They are also not blocked from exclusive locks that would prevent the transaction from reading uncommitted data. This is the least-restrictive isolation level.

TIP If dirty reads are acceptable, use the Read Uncommitted transaction isolation level whenever possible. This will result in fewer locks and better performance.

Repeatable Read

Repeatable Read prevents statements or transactions from reading data that has been modified but not committed. Additionally, other transactions cannot modify data being read by the current transaction until the current transaction is done. The primary problem this is designed to prevent is one of inconsistent analysis (nonrepeatable read). As an example, you may find that reading the data once within a transaction shows one result, while reading the data again within the same transaction with the same query produces different results. The repeatable read transaction isolation level will prevent this problem.

EXAM NOTE To prevent the problem of inconsistent analysis (a nonrepeatable read), use the repeatable read transaction isolation level.

Shared locks are used to protect any data read by the transaction until the transaction completes. Repeatable Read provides a low level of concurrency and is recommended for use only when necessary.

Serializable

The Serializable transaction isolation level can't read uncommitted data from other transactions, other transactions can't modify data being read by this transaction, and other transactions can't insert new rows in the range of rows being read by this transaction. These restrictions are in place until the transaction completes. This is the most restrictive of the isolation levels, creating the most locks within the database. It provides the lowest level of concurrency.

Snapshot

The Snapshot transaction isolation level specifies that data read by a statement in a transaction must stay transactionally consistent within the transaction. However, it uses a snapshot method to record what the data was at the beginning of the transaction instead of using locks to prevent other transactions from modifying the data.

Other transactions can make modifications to the data. As they do so, they do not block Snapshot transactions from reading the data. The ALLOW_SNAPSHOT_ISOLATION database option must be set to ON.

Table 14-4 compares the different isolation levels. Notice that the only isolation level that allows dirty reads is Read Uncommitted. To prevent phantom reads, you would select the Snapshot or Serializable isolation level.

Isolation Level	Dirty Read	Nonrepeatable Read	Phantom
Read Uncommitted	Yes	Yes	Yes
Read Committed	No	Yes	Yes
Repeatable Read	No	No	Yes
Snapshot	No	No	No
Serializable	No	No	No

Table 14-4 A Comparison of Transaction Isolation Levels

EXAM TIP To prevent phantom reads, select either the Snapshot or Serializable isolation levels. Serializable is the most restrictive, providing the lowest level of concurrency, while Snapshot can prevent phantom reads while also allowing more concurrency.

Setting a Transaction Isolation Level

To set the transaction isolation level, we would use a SET statement. Typically, a script would set a transaction isolation level just before beginning a transaction.

As an example, the following partial script shows how to set the transaction isolation level to Read Uncommitted (or allow dirty reads):

```
USE AdventureWorks;
GO
SET TRANSACTION ISOLATION LEVEL READ UNCOMMITTED;
GO
BEGIN TRANSACTION;
-- Transaction work here
COMMIT TRANSACTION;
```

Hints

The query optimizer, shown in Figure 14-10, does a great deal of work under the hood in SQL Server. When a query is submitted to a database, the query optimizer parses it (makes sure it's syntactically correct), resolves it (makes sure database objects exist), and then optimizes it (picks the best indexes, the join types, and more).

Figure 14-10
The query optimizer

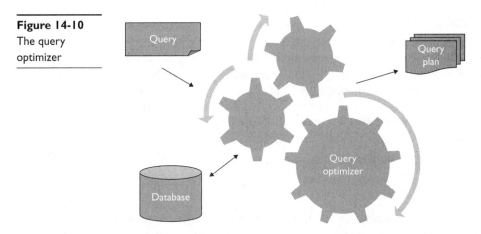

In the optimization phase, the query optimizer analyzes the query against the existing database, including tables and indexes. It tries to determine the most efficient method to retrieve the data. We saw in Chapter 7 how indexes are used to optimize queries. The query optimizer uses the statistics available on indexes to pick the best indexes for the query.

As a reminder on how indexes work, let's say you were looking for information on VIEWs. You thought there was information in this book, but you weren't sure. One method would be to start at page 1 and look on every page until you came to a topic on VIEWs. You'd find some information in Chapter 2, but would you be done? No. There's more information on VIEWs in other parts of the book, so you would have to continue looking at every page in the book.

However, it's a common practice to put an index in the back of the book. Instead of checking every page in the book, you could look up VIEW in the index and find all the places within the book where VIEW topics are discussed. The index makes it much more efficient when searching for a topic.

That's also how indexes are used within a database. Let's say a table within a database takes up 2MB of space. An index may take up only 60KB of space. It's obviously quicker to search 60KB than it is to search 2MB.

The difference between a book and a database is that tables within a database can have multiple indexes. The query optimizer determines which indexes are most appropriate for the query and then includes them in the query plan.

The query optimizer does a great job of quickly identifying the best way to run a query, but it hasn't always been this way. In SQL Server 6.5, the query optimizer left a lot to be desired. Database administrators then had to help out the query optimizer by telling it what index or indexes to use.

In other words, DBAs had to provide hints. Hints still exist, though today it's quite difficult to consistently come up with a better plan than the query optimizer. Hints can be provided for queries, for joins, and for tables. We'll limit our discussion to table hints.

Table Hints

Table hints are used to direct the query optimizer to use a specific index or to use a specific lock strategy when running the query. Most queries can be run by the query optimizer without any hints. Said another way, use hints only when absolutely required. They are used to optimize queries, but often simply aren't needed.

Consider a query that is heavily tested on January 5, when it is determined that it runs best using a specific index and a specific locking strategy. By giving the query optimizer the hint to use this index, it no longer has to analyze the script and pick what it considers the best query plan. However, on January 15, as data and indexes have changed, the chosen plan is no longer the best choice. Since the hint exists, the query optimizer no longer analyzes the query, and we live with a poorly performing query.

In contrast, if hints aren't added to queries, the query optimizer continuously analyzes the queries against existing indexes and picks the best strategy at any given time. Today, it may pick one index or one table locking strategy, but as the database dynamically changes, it may pick another index or locking strategy on another day.

Table hints can be added to any Data Manipulation Language (DML) statement (INSERT, UPDATE, DELETE, or SELECT).

A hint embedded into a query to direct it to use a specific index that exists for a table may look like the following script:

```
SELECT Author, Title, Price, PublishDate
FROM Books WITH (INDEX(1))
WHERE PublishDate > '2001'
```

EXAM TIP Microsoft has spent a lot of time and effort improving the Query Optimizer with every release of SQL Server. Every time a DBA is forced to use a query hint, it's like a slap in the face to the Microsoft SQL Server developers. Well, maybe not that bad, but you get the idea. Microsoft recommends that hints be used only as a last resort by experienced developers and database administrators. Index hints are almost never needed, and removing them is generally a good idea, but table hints may occasionally provide improvement.

All of the available table hints can be viewed in the "Table Hint (Transact-SQL)" Books Online article. Some of the more popular table hints are listed in the following bullets. Note that setting the isolation levels of a transaction will achieve the same results of many of the table hints.

- **HoldLock** This is the same as setting the transaction isolation level to serializable. This is the most restrictive transaction isolation level.

- **ReadCommitted** Specifies that read operations comply with the rules for the read committed transaction isolation level by using locking or row versioning depending on the value of the Read_Committed_Snapshot option. If OFF, locking is used; if ON, row versioning is used.

- **ReadCommittedLock** Specifies that read operations comply with the rules for the read committed transaction isolation level by using locking. This ignores the Read_Committed_Snapshot database option.

- **ReadPast** ReadPast tells the database engine to skip rows that are locked by other transactions. This can sometimes be very useful in a heavily queried and updated table that is experiencing long delays and frequent deadlocks, but should be tested thoroughly to ensure that the skipped rows do not affect the integrity of the database.

- **ReadUncommitted** Specifies that read operations comply with the rules for the read uncommitted transaction isolation level. This allows dirty reads.

- **RepeatableRead** Uses the same locking as the Repeatable Read isolation level.

- **TabLock** Specifies that a lock is obtained and held on the table until the end of the statement. A SELECT statement causes a shared lock. Other DML statements cause exclusive locks.

- **UpdLock** Specifies that Update locks are to be obtained and held until the transaction completes.

- **NoLock** This is the same as setting the transaction isolation level to read uncommitted; allows dirty reads.

Query Plan Guides

Query Plan Guides are a new feature available in SQL Server 2005 that allow you to create a specific query plan, or specific query hints, to be used by the query optimizer. By using a query plan guide, we can provide hints to the query for a specific execution without modifying the original query. The primary hints you'll come across with plan guides are:

- OPTIMIZE FOR
- RECOMPILE
- USE PLAN

Both OPTIMIZE FOR and RECOMPILE are useful when a query has a cached query plan whose parameter values are substantially different from the query you want to optimize it for. OPTIMIZE FOR directs SQL Server to use your value as the parameter during the optimization phase. RECOMPILE tells it to discard the cached query plan as soon as the query is run.

As an example, consider the following script, which is used to created a stored procedure. Notice the stored procedure accepts the parameter of @Country, which is used in the WHERE clause.

```
CREATE PROCEDURE Sales.uspGetSalesOrderByCountry (@Country char(2))
AS
SELECT *
FROM Sales.SalesOrderHeader h, Sales.Customer c, Sales.SalesTerritory t
WHERE h.CustomerID = c.CustomerID AND c.TerritoryID = t.TerritoryID
AND CountryRegionCode = @Country
```

Normally, the country passed into the stored procedure is 'US' for the United States. When the query is optimized for 'US', it performs well. However, if the query plan is not cached and the parameter passed in is something other than 'US' (such as 'DE' for Germany), then the query will no longer be optimized for the majority of queries which use 'US'. Instead, it's optimized for 'DE', and as long as it remains in cache, it will use the plan for 'DE' even when the actual parameter passed in is 'US'.

In this case, we may want to create a query plan guide and optimize it for the parameter of 'US'. The code to do this is shown in the following script. Notice the plan guide is created from the system stored procedure sp_create_plan_guide.

```
sp_create_plan_guide N'PlanGuideGetSalesOrderByCountry',
--The following is the query to optimize
N'SELECT *
FROM Sales.SalesOrderHeader h, Sales.Customer c, Sales.SalesTerritory t
WHERE h.CustomerID = c.CustomerID AND c.TerritoryID = t.TerritoryID
AND CountryRegionCode = @Country',
--Object indicates the query is embedded in an object (such as a stored
procedure)
N'OBJECT',
N'Sales.uspGetSalesOrderByCountry',
NULL,
--The OPTION with OPTIMIZE FOR specifies the parameter to use when optimizing
the query
N'OPTION (OPTIMIZE FOR(@Country = N''US''))'
```

EXAM TIP When a query (or stored procedure) occasionally runs poorly only after receiving a parameter outside of what's considered normal for the parameter, consider creating a plan guide using the OPTIMIZE FOR hint. This allows you to specify the parameter you want to use when the query is optimized.

A Query Plan Guide uses a special type of hint (USE PLAN) to tell the query optimizer how to execute the query. With what we've discussed about hints so far, you should have an idea that using a hint should only be used as a last resort. However, let's say an external application is frequently executing a query against your database. Testing shows that the query is performing poorly, but the designers of the application are either unwilling, or unable, to modify the query.

In SQL Server 2005, we have the ability to provide hints for this query to improve its performance without actually modifying the query. This is frequently useful when a query or small subset of queries in an application is performing poorly.

To do this, we create a plan guide and apply it to the specific query. The USE PLAN hint takes XML_Plan as an argument. XML_plan is a string literal used to produce the query plan.

XML plans can be created in two ways:

- Using the SET SHOWPLAN_XML ON statement before the query
- Applying a trace event on the query using SQL Server Profiler

As an example, the following query uses SET SHOWPLAN_XML ON to begin the creation of an XML document for the query. We then run the query and then turn SET SHOWPLAN_XML off.

```
SET SHOWPLAN_XML ON
GO
SELECT h.SalesOrderID, h.OrderDate, h.Comment
FROM Sales.SalesOrderHeader h, Sales.Customer c,
    Sales.SalesTerritory t
WHERE h.CustomerID = c.CustomerID AND c.TerritoryID = t.TerritoryID
    AND CountryRegionCode = N'US'
GO
SET SHOWPLAN_XML OFF
```

The following XML fragment shows a small part of the plan created:

```
<ShowPlanXML xmlns="http://schemas.microsoft.com/sqlserver/2004/07/showplan"
Version="1.0" Build="9.00.3054.00">
  <BatchSequence>
    <Batch>
      <Statements>
        <StmtSimple StatementText="SELECT h.SalesOrderID, h.OrderDate,
h.Comment&#xD;&#xA;FROM Sales.SalesOrderHeader h, Sales.Customer c,&#xD;&#xA;
Sales.SalesTerritory t&#xD;&#xA;WHERE h.CustomerID = c.CustomerID AND
c.TerritoryID = t.TerritoryID&#xD;&#xA;    AND CountryRegionCode =
N'US'&#xD;&#xA;" StatementId="1" StatementCompId="1" StatementType="SELECT"
StatementSubTreeCost="0.897611" StatementEstRows="15996.7"
StatementOptmLevel="FULL" StatementOptmEarlyAbortReason="GoodEnoughPlanFound">
          <StatementSetOptions QUOTED_IDENTIFIER="false" ARITHABORT="true"
```

```
CONCAT_NULL_YIELDS_NULL="false" ANSI_NULLS="false" ANSI_PADDING="false"
ANSI_WARNINGS="false" NUMERIC_ROUNDABORT="false" />
          <QueryPlan CachedPlanSize="29" CompileTime="58" CompileCPU="36"
CompileMemory="392">
              <RelOp NodeId="0" PhysicalOp="Hash Match" LogicalOp="Inner Join"
EstimateRows="15996.7" EstimateIO="0" EstimateCPU="0.267483"
AvgRowSize="151" EstimatedTotalSubtreeCost="0.897611" Parallel="0"
EstimateRebinds="0" EstimateRewinds="0">
. . .
```

This entire XML document can then be cut and pasted into the sp_create_plan_guide system stored procedure execution statement. The following code shows the syntax. Notice this is almost the same code as used in the OPTIMIZE FOR example, except that the OPTION in this example is the USE PLAN option.

```
EXEC sp_create_plan_guide N'UsePlan_PlanGuide',
   N'SELECT h.SalesOrderID, h.OrderDate, h.Comment
    FROM Sales.SalesOrderHeader h, Sales.Customer c,
        Sales.SalesTerritory t
    WHERE h.CustomerID = c.CustomerID AND c.TerritoryID = t.TerritoryID
        AND CountryRegionCode = @Country',
   N'OBJECT',
   N'Sales.GetSalesOrderByCountry',
   NULL,
   N'OPTION (USE PLAN
            N''<ShowPlanXML
xmlns="http://schemas.microsoft.com/sqlserver/2004/07/showplan"
Version="0.5" Build="9.00.1079">
  <BatchSequence>
. . . - XML plan guide document goes here.
  </BatchSequence>
```

Cursors

A cursor within T-SQL is an in-memory representation of data pulled from a SELECT statement. Cursors are actually an extension of a result set that provides the ability to work with one row, or a small block of rows, at a time.

When you execute a SELECT statement, you receive a result set. If you execute the command in a query window, you have a viewable copy of the result set. However, many applications cannot always work effectively with the result set as an entire entity. Instead, they need to be able to go through the results set one row (or group of rows) at a time. Cursors provide that ability.

Cursors are typically used in stored procedures, triggers, and batch files. The basic syntax of a T-SQL cursor is:

```
DECLARE cursor_name CURSOR
    [ LOCAL | GLOBAL ]
    [ FORWARD_ONLY | SCROLL ]
    [ STATIC | KEYSET | DYNAMIC | FAST_FORWARD ] --Cursor Options
    [ READ_ONLY | SCROLL_LOCKS | OPTIMISTIC ]
    [ TYPE_WARNING ]
    FOR select_statement[ FOR UPDATE [ OF column_name [ ,...n ] ] ]
```

Of the listed cursor arguments, the most important to understand for the 70-442 exam are the four cursor options. These are identified in the following bullets:

- **STATIC**   Think of this as a snapshot of the result set. A static cursor does not reflect any types of changes to the underlying database, such as INSERTs, UP-DATEs, or DELETEs. This is a read-only cursor that can go forward or backward.

- **FAST_FORWARD**   This will create a fast forward-only, read-only cursor. As the name implies, the cursor can only go from the first row forward to the last row. Unlike a STATIC cursor, rows are not retrieved from the database until they are fetched. Any changes to a row (from INSERT, UPDATE or DELETE statements) before the row is fetched, will be reflected in the fetched row.

- **DYNAMIC**   All changes made to the underlying data via INSERT, UPDATE, or DELETE statements will be visible in the cursor. By default, uncommitted data is not shown unless the transaction isolation level is set to read uncommitted.

- **KEYSET**   This creates a fixed order of rows in a keyset-driven cursor. The keyset is built in the tempdb when the cursor is opened. While the order of the rows can not change, any UPDATEs to the underlying data are reflected in the cursor. INSERTs to the underlying data are not visible unless the cursor is closed and reopened. If a row has been deleted the @@FETCH_STAUS will return a-2 for a "row missing" status.

 EXAM TIP   When preparing for the 70-442 test, make sure you know the four different cursor types, their capabilities, and when to use each of them. Static and Fast_forward cursors are read-only cursors; static can move forward and backward while fast_forward moves forward only. The Dynamic cursor will reflect all changes. Keyset is updateable, but also maintains a fixed order of rows in the tempdb database.

The Local and Global arguments identify the scope of the cursor. Local specifies the cursor as only available within the batch, stored procedure, or trigger where it is created. Global specifies that the cursor is available to any batch or stored procedure executed in the same connection.

Forward_only and Scroll arguments are used to identify the FETCH options available. Forward_only allows FETCH NEXT only and allows the cursor to scroll from the first to the last row only. Static and Scroll allows any FETCH option (First, Last, Prior, Next, Relative, and Absolute).

The read_only, Scroll_locks, and Optimistic options are used to specify options related to updates. Read_only prevents updates made through the cursor. Scroll_locks locks rows as they are read into the cursor so that UPDATEs and DELETEs are guaranteed to succeed. Optimistic does not lock the rows, but instead operates on the premise that it is optimistic that UPDATEs and DELETEs will succeed without a lock. If the row was updated or deleted since the row was read into the cursor, then any UPDATE or DELETE through the cursor will fail.

Building a Cursor

Building a cursor generally is accomplished in five steps.

1. Declare variables or each column in the cursor.

2. Declare the cursor and associate it with a SELECT statement. This is where you would also define the type of the cursor, such as read-only or forward-only if desired.

3. Use the OPEN statement to populate the cursor from the SELECT statement.

4. Use the FETCH statement to fetch individual rows and populate the columns of the cursor.

5. Clean up by using the CLOSE and DEALLOCATE statements to close the cursor and free resources associated with the cursor.

The following code shows these steps:

```
--Step 1. Declare variables used by cursor
DECLARE @ContactID int, @First varchar(50), @Last varchar(50), @Email
varchar(50)
--Step 2. Declare the cursor and associate with a SELECT statement
DECLARE EmpCursor CURSOR FOR
SELECT pc.FirstName, pc.LastName, pc.EmailAddress
 FROM Person.Contact pc INNER JOIN
       HumanResources.Employee e ON pc.ContactID = e.ContactID
--Step 3. Open cursor
OPEN EmpCursor;
--Step 4. Use FETCH to get first row.  WHILE END loops through all rows in
cursor
FETCH NEXT FROM EmpCursor INTO @ContactID, @First, @Last, @Email;
WHILE(@@FETCH_STATUS = 0)
BEGIN
  --do code to process the cursor
  -- get next row from cursor
  FETCH NEXT FROM EmpCursor INTO @ContactID, @First, @Last, @Email;
END
--Step 5. Cleanup by closing and deallocating the cursor
CLOSE EmpCursor
DEALLOCATE EmpCursor
```

Cursor Performance

Cursors are inherently slow. Several factors contribute to why cursors are slow.

- Each FETCH is the same as a single SELECT statement. As an example, consider a cursor that returns 10,000 rows. It's the equivalent of 10,000 SELECT statements. A single result set-oriented operation would be much more efficient.

- Cursors consume a large amount of resources, especially memory. This takes memory resources away from other processes that need it, such as cache.

- Cursors create locks on the rows that are contained within the cursor and can cause locking problems within the database.

Recognizing that each FETCH within the cursor is the same as a single SELCT statement, one of your goals when creating the cursor is to reduce the number of rows in the cursor. This is done by using effective filters in the WHERE clause of the SELECT statement. Filtering should not be done in the processing code of the cursor if it can be done in the SELECT statement.

For example, if you create a cursor using the following SELECT statement, it will create a cursor of over 19,000 rows.

```
SELECT ContactID, FirstName, LastName, EmailAddress
FROM Person.Contact
```

If you use code similar to the following snippet within your cursor to check to see if the ContactID exists in the Employee table, then you have to look at each of the 19,000 rows in the cursor:

```
IF EXISTS (SELECT @ContactID
   FROM HumanResources.Employee)
```

On the other hand, if you built your SELECT statement similar to the following code, your cursor would only be 290 rows and would perform much better:

```
SELECT pc.FirstName, pc.LastName, pc.EmailAddress
FROM Person.Contact pc INNER JOIN
HumanResources.Employee e ON pc.ContactID = e.ContactID
```

Both code choices would achieve the same objective, but creating a cursor using only 290 rows would be much more efficient than a cursor of over 19,000 rows.

 EXAM TIP When creating cursors, use a SELECT statement that will filter the cursor to the minimum number of rows needed. Larger cursors take more resources and will perform significantly slower.

Replacing Cursors with Result Set-Oriented Operations

While the use of cursors is common in many database solutions, Microsoft stresses that the use of cursors often ignores the power of a relational database engine and so generates code that performs poorly in comparison to code that will accomplish the same objective without a cursor. Using a cursor is generally much more resource-intensive (and slower) than using a result set-oriented operation. A result set-oriented operation is just a fancy way of saying a SELECT statement is used to return a result set.

While developing cursors is sometimes easier for a developer than working with a complex result set, Microsoft frequently repeats in SQL Server 2005 documentation that replacing cursors with result set-oriented operations is more efficient.

 EXAM TIP When a cursor-based operation is performing slowly and consuming a large amount of resources on your SQL Server 2005 server, consider rewriting the cursor using result set-oriented operations.

Generally, when replacing a cursor with a result set-oriented operation, you can use one of three strategies:

- Rebuild the logic as multiple queries.
- Rebuild the logic as a user-defined function.
- Rebuild the logic as a complex query using a case expression.

Let's take a look at a single example.

In the following query, we'll create a simple cursor to pull the FirstName, Lastname, and EmailAddress out of the Person.Contact table. Of particular note in this exercise is how long the query takes to run. We'll then rewrite the cursor as a query and compare the times.

Exercise 14.4: Create a Cursor and Refactor a Cursor

1. Launch SSMS and create a new query window.

2. Enter the following script to create and execute a cursor:

```
USE AdventureWorks;
GO
--Step 1. Declare variables used by the cursor
DECLARE @Start datetime, @end datetime
SET @Start = GetDate()
DECLARE @FirstName varchar(50), @MiddleName varchar(50),
        @LastName varchar(50), @EmailAddress varChar(50)
--Step 2. Declare the cursor and associate it with the SELECT statement
DECLARE curMidName CURSOR FOR
SELECT FirstName, MiddleName, LastName, EmailAddress FROM Person.Contact
--Step 3. Open the cursor
OPEN curMidName;
--Step 4. Use FETCH NEXT to get the first row
FETCH NEXT FROM curMidName
  INTO @FirstName, @MiddleName, @LastName, @EmailAddress
--The WHILE .. END construct will loop until we've retrieved every row
WHILE (@@FETCH_STATUS = 0)
--@@FETCH_STATUS = 0 indicates success.  It will be -1 after the last
row
BEGIN
  IF (@MiddleName is NOT Null)
    BEGIN
     PRINT @FirstName + ' ' + @MiddleName + ' ' +
              @LastName + ' ' + @EmailAddress
    END
  ELSE
    BEGIN
     PRINT @FirstName + ' ' + @LastName + ' ' + @EmailAddress
    END
  FETCH NEXT FROM curMidName INTO
     @FirstName, @MiddleName, @LastName, @emailAddress
END
--Step 5. Cleanup by closing and deallocating the cursor
CLOSE curMidName
DEALLOCATE curMidName
SET @end = GetDate()
PRINT 'Query took ' + CONVERT(varchar(10), datediff(ms, @start, @end)) +
' milliseconds'
```

3. The last line in the messages tab indicates how long the script takes to run. On my system, this took 1810 milliseconds or almost 2 seconds. Record how long it took on your system here _____.

4. Now let's refactor the cursor, or in other words, let's rewrite the cursor to use a result set-oriented operation. The following script uses the ISNULL function to replace NULL values for the middle name with a zero length string:

```
USE AdventureWorks;
GO
DECLARE @Start datetime, @end datetime
SET @Start = GetDate()
SELECT FirstName, ISNULL(MiddleName,'') AS MiddleName, LastName,
EmailAddress
FROM Person.Contact
SET @end = GetDate()
PRINT 'Query took ' + CONVERT(varchar(10), datediff(ms, @start, @end)) +
' milliseconds'
```

5. Click the Messages tab to see how long the second query took. On my system, it took 703 milliseconds. That's less than half the time it took for the cursor to provide the same results. Generally, if you can rewrite a query without the use of a cursor, you will get better performance.

Chapter Review

In this chapter, we covered some basics on locks, deadlocks, transaction isolation levels, hints, and cursors. While some level of locks in any database application is normal, excessive locking can significantly slow down an application.

Deadlocks are uncommon and the goal should be zero deadlocks in an application. Deadlock events can normally be avoided by modifying the logic within an application. Error 1205 indicates a deadlock event.

If deadlocks are occurring, DBAs need to be able to identify the source of the problem, even if they aren't responsible for rewriting the application causing the deadlocks. This can be done using a combination of tools such as System Monitor, Activity Monitor, dynamic management VIEWs, and SQL Profiler.

Transaction isolation levels can be set on a transaction level to increase or decrease the ability of multiple users to access data concurrently. If more users can access the data at the same time, fewer locks occur and the application generally performs better. The isolation levels are Read Committed (default), Read Uncommitted, Repeatable Read, Serializable, and Snapshot.

However, concurrent access has side effects such as dirty reads, nonrepeatable reads, phantom reads, and lost updates. Choosing transaction isolation levels becomes a trade-off between accepting some of the concurrency side effects for better performance, or reducing the side effects at the expense of performance. Read Committed is the default isolation level. However, if dirty reads are acceptable, this can be changed to Read Uncommitted.

The query optimizer picks the best query plan (such as which indexes to use, what types of joins to use, and so on) based on the information available, and almost always does a better job than we could manually. Sometimes, we may want to provide hints with our queries. We can also direct what to do when creating the query plan. The three choices in this are to tell the query plan to OPTIMIZE FOR a specific parameter, RE-COMPILE each time the query is executed, or USE PLAN (use a specific plan provided via an XML document).

Lastly, we explored some basics with cursors. Generally, poorly performing cursors can be rewritten as queries to enjoy significant performance gains. If a cursor must be used, make sure you know the difference between the four cursor types. Static and Fast_forward cursors are read-only cursors. A Static cursor takes a snapshot of the data when the cursor is executed (so data modifications aren't reflected in the cursor), but the Fast_forward cursor reads the data from the database when the row is read, so data modifications are reflected in the cursor. Dynamic and Keyset cursors are both update-able. A Dynamic cursor reflects all changes (INSERT, UPDATE, or DELETE), while a Keyset cursor only reflects changes made by UPDATE statements. Additionally, Keyset cursors create a fixed order of rows and hold them in the tempdb database.

Additional Study

Self-Study Exercises

- Create a lock and use Activity Monitor to view it.
- Use a DMV to view the locks.
- Use Activity Monitor to kill a process.
- Kill a process within a query window.
- Reset the counters for OS_wait_stats.
- Launch SQL Profiler and add the counters to capture a deadlock event.
- Launch System Monitor and add the counters to capture a deadlock event.
- Create the script for a transaction that will allow dirty reads.

BOL Topics

- Lock Modes
- Lock Compatibility (Database Engine)
- Isolation Levels in the Database Engine
- SET TRANSACTION ISOLATION LEVEL (Transact-SQL)
- Using Row Versioning-Based Isolation Levels
- Concurrency Effects
- Table Hint (Transact-SQL)
- Cursor Concurrency (Database Engine)
- DECLARE CURSOR (Transact-SQL)

Summary of What You Need to Know

70-431

When preparing for the 70-431 test, you should know how to:

- Monitor and resolve locks and deadlocks.
- Use the sys.dm_exec_requests DMV to troubleshoot locks and deadlocks.
- Use SQL Profiler to capture lock activity.

70-441

No topics for the 70-441 exam are contained in this chapter.

70-442

When preparing for the 70-442 exam, you should have a good understanding of:

- Transaction isolation levels
- Hints and plan guides
- Cursors

Questions

70-431

1. Sally is using the MCITP application and complains that it stopped responding as she was processing an order. You suspect it's a blocking problem. You identify Sally's session ID as 73. What can you use to identify the problem?

   A. View the Locks By Process page in Activity Monitor. View the Blocked By column for session 73.

   B. View the Process Info page in Activity Monitor. View the Blocked By column for session 73.

   C. View the Locks By Object page in Activity Monitor. View the Blocked By column for session 73.

   D. View the Process Info page in Activity Monitor. View the Blocking column for session 73.

2. Sally is using the MCTIP application and complains that it stopped responding as she was processing an order. You suspect it's a blocking problem. You identify Sally's session ID as 73. What can you use to identify the problem?

   A. Execute the following script:
   ```
   SELECT * FROM sys.dm_exec_requests WHERE session_id =73
   ```
   View the blocking_session_id column.

   B. Execute the following script:
   ```
   SELECT * FROM sys.dm_exec_requests WHERE session_id =73
   ```
   View the blocked_by column.

C. Execute the following script:

```
SELECT * FROM Sys.dm_tran_locks WHERE session_id =73
```
View the blocking_session_id column.

D. Execute the following script:

```
SELECT * FROM Sys.dm_tran_locks WHERE session_id =73
```
View the blocked_by column.

3. How can a blocking process be killed?

A. Find the process in System Monitor and select Kill Process.

B. Find the process in Activity Monitor and select Kill Process.

C. Find the process in SQL Profiler and select Kill Process.

D. Find the process in SSRS and select Kill Process.

4. A process with a process ID of 101 is being blocked by a process ID of 76. How can the blocking process be killed?

A. Execute the command Kill 76.

B. Execute the command Kill 101.

C. Execute the command Kill Process 76.

D. Execute the command Kill Process 101.

5. Users are reporting many instances of 1205 errors. You want to gather information on all participants of the error. What should you do?

A. Use System Monitor to capture transaction isolation level data.

B. Change the transaction isolation level to Repeatable Read for the server.

C. Use SQL Profiler to capture Lock:Deadlock Chain events.

D. Use SQL Profiler to capture Lock:Deadlock events.

70-442

1. You are developing some stored procedures that will use transactions to add and modify rows based on searches in the Sales database. Business requirements state that phantom rows are not allowed. However, any method used to prevent phantom rows should have a minimum amount of negative impact on concurrency. What should you do?

A. Use a cursor with the keyset operator.

B. Use the read committed transaction isolation level.

C. Use the snapshot transaction isolation level.

D. Use the serializable transaction isolation level.

2. You have migrated a SQL Server 2000 database and associated application to SQL Server 2005. Monitoring the activity on SQL Server after the migration, you discover there are excessive read locks being created on some key tables. You want to reduce these. What can you do?

A. Set the READ_COMMITTED_SNAPSHOT database option to OFF.

B. Set the READ_COMMITTED_SNAPSHOT database option to ON.

C. Set the transaction isolation level to repeatable read.

D. Set the transaction isolation level to serializable.

3. You notice that excessive table locks are being created when the uspEmployeeSales stored procedure is executed. You investigate and discover the stored procedure was created with the following script:

```
CREATE PROC uspEmployeeSales (@StartDate datetime, @EndDate datetime)
AS
SET TRANSACTION ISOLATION LEVEL SERIALIZABLE
SELECT SalesPersonID, TotalDue, OrderDate
FROM Sales.SalesOrderHeader
WHERE OrderDate BETWEEN @StartDate and @EndDate
ORDER BY OrderDate
```

It is being executed with scripts such as the following:

```
EXEC EmployeeSales '2002', '2003'
```

What can you do to reduce the number of table locks?

A. Set the READ_COMMITTED_SNAPSHOT database option to OFF.

B. Set the READ_COMMITTED_SNAPSHOT database option to ON.

C. Change the transaction isolation level to READ COMMITTED.

D. Rewrite the query using a table hint.

4. The following stored procedure is being used to pull transaction information and populate a report.

```
CREATE PROCEDURE uspGetTransactions (@TransDate datetime)
AS
SET TRANSACTION ISOLATION LEVEL READ UNCOMMITTED
SELECT TransactionID, ProductID, TransactionDate, Quantity
FROM Production.TransactionHistory
WHERE TransactionDate = @TransDate
```

However, you've found that executing the stored procedure twice within a single transaction occasionally produces different results even when using the same parameter. What can you do to correct this problem?

A. Set the READ_COMMITTED_SNAPSHOT database option to OFF.

B. Set the READ_COMMITTED_SNAPSHOT database option to ON.

C. Set the transaction isolation level to repeatable read.

D. Use a keyset-driven cursor.

5. An intranet web site is used to provide information for employees about the AdventureWorks company. One page displays the ten most recent transactions, but you must modify it to display all transactions for the past week. Management has specified that this page can not include dirty reads. Additionally, you want to minimize locking. What transaction isolation level should you use?

A. read committed

B. read committed with the read committed snapshot option turned on

C. read uncommitted with the read committed snapshot option turned on

D. repeatable read

6. You've used SQL Profiler to identify the slowest running queries and you identify the following query as running exceptionally slow:

```
SELECT Author, Title, Price, PublishDate
FROM Books WITH (INDEX(0))
WHERE PublishDate > @PubDate
```

You notice that the query is always using a clustered index scan. What can you do to improve this query?

A. Change the INDEX(0) clause to INDEX(1).

B. Remove the INDEX(0) clause.

C. Add a READPAST locking hint to the query.

D. Set the transaction isolation level to read committed.

7. You manage a database for a large multiple-ship cruise line. Customer reservations are created in the Bookings table, which is heavily queried and updated. Users have complained that queries frequently take a long time to complete and deadlocks regularly occur. Using available tools, you identify a single query that is frequently being blocked. Of the available choices, what may be done to improve the performance of the query?

A. Use the UpdLock hint.

B. Use the ReadCommitted hint.

C. Use the ReadUncommitted hint.

D. Use the ReadPast locking hint.

8. You manage a database for a large travel agent. One table named Hotels holds millions or rows of data which reservation agents use to search for recommended hotels in cities around the world. New hotels are only added once a month during scheduled downtime. During busy tourist seasons, as many as 1000 agents are actively searching for hotels simultaneously. You are designing a query strategy for the Hotels table. Of the following, which query hint would best meet your needs?

A. NoLock

B. UpdLock

C. TabLock

D. ReadCommitted

9. You manage a Sales database running in SQL Server 2005. You've identified a stored procedure that occasionally runs extremely slow, but at other times runs within acceptable time frames. The stored procedure normally accepts a parameter of @TotalSale, which is greater than $200. When it runs slowly, it does so after accepting a parameter significantly less than $200, and continues to run slowly even with a parameter in the normal search scope. You want to ensure the stored procedure performs as fast as possible when the parameter is greater than $200. What should you do?

A. Create a plan guide and use the OPTIMIZE FOR hint.

B. Create a plan guide and use the RECOMPILE hint.

C. Create a plan guide and use the USE PLAN hint.

D. Create a plan guide and use the USE PARAMETER hint.

10. A development team has completed the creation of queries, batches, and stored procedures to be used for a Sales application. One of the stored procedures uses a cursor. The test team reports that this stored procedure runs slowly and consumes a significant amount of resources on the database server. What could be done to improve the performance of this stored procedure?

A. Rewrite the cursor using result set-oriented operations.

B. Change the cursor to a Keyset-driven cursor.

C. Change the cursor to a Static cursor.

D. Change the cursor to a Dynamic cursor.

11. You have come across the following cursor that is performing slowly.

```
. . .
DECLARE @ContactID int, @First varchar(50), @Last varchar(50), @Email
varchar(50)
DECLARE EmpCursor CURSOR FOR
SELECT ContactID, FirstName, LastName, EmailAddress FROM Person.Contact
OPEN EmpCursor;
FETCH NEXT FROM EmpCursor INTO @ContactID, @First, @Last, @Email;
WHILE(@@FETCH_STATUS = 0)
BEGIN
IF EXISTS (SELECT @ContactID
   FROM HumanResources.Employee)
 --do code
ELSE
 -- do else code
FETCH NEXT FROM EmpCursor INTO @ContactID, @First, @Last, @Email;
END
. . .
```

You need to optimize this cursor for better performance. What would you do? (Choose two of the following.)

A. Change the SELECT statement in the cursor to filter only employees.

B. Use a Static cursor.

C. Use a Keyset-driven cursor.

D. Remove the IF EXISTS clause.

12. You are creating a stored procedure that will use a cursor. Data in the rows retrieved by the cursor needs to be updatable, with the updates viewable after they are made. The cursor needs to have a fixed membership where the order of the rows does not change. Which option should you use when creating the cursor?

A. Static

B. Fast_forward

C. Dynamic

D. Keyset

13. You are rewriting a stored procedure that was originally created with a dynamic cursor. After the rewrite, the cursor should be read-only and the only Fetch command that will be used is Fetch Next. How should you define the cursor?

A. Change the cursor to Forward_Only.

B. Change the cursor to Forward_Only with the Optimistic option.

C. Change the cursor to Fast_Forward.

D. Change the cursor to Fast_Forward with the Optimistic option.

Answers

70-431

1. **B.** Of the three pages in Activity Monitor, the only one that has Blocked By or Blocking columns is the Process Info page. The Locks By Object and Locks By Process pages do not have these columns. Since you suspect Sally is being blocked, you would check the Blocked By column.

2. **A.** The sys.dm_exec_requests DMV can be used to identify details of specific sessions. The blocking_session_id column would identify the source of the block if one exists. The sys.dm_tran_locks DMV does not have a blocked_by or blocking_session_id column.

3. **B.** The Kill Process menu selection is available in the Activity Monitor, located in the Management container of SSMS. It is not available in the other tools mentioned.

4. **A.** We want to kill the process that is doing the blocking—76 in this question. The T-SQL command is Kill with the number of the process. There is no such T-SQL command as *Kill Process xx*.

5. **C.** A 1205 error indicates deadlocks. To capture data on all participants in the deadlock event, use the Lock:Deadlock Chain event class in SQL Profiler. The Lock: Deadlock event class doesn't capture information on participants leading up to the deadlock. System Monitor doesn't have any counters for transaction isolation levels, and it isn't possible to set transaction isolation levels for the server.

70-442

1. **C.** Both the snapshot and serializable transaction isolation levels will prevent against phantom reads. However, the serializable transaction isolation level is the most restrictive on concurrency, so snapshot fully meets the business requirements. Neither the read committed transaction isolation level nor a Keyset cursor will prevent phantom reads.

2. **B.** New to SQL Server 2005 is row versioning, supported when the READ_COMMITTED_SNAPSHOT option is set to ON. Instead of using locks to keep the original data, row versioning keeps a record of the original data in the tempdb database. The default is OFF and it will not use row versioning. Both transaction isolation levels of repeatable read and serializable will increase the locks on the data.

3. **C.** The serializable transaction isolation level is the most restrictive and creates the most locks. Of the choices given, the best choice is to change the isolation level to READ COMMITTED (or simply remove the SET TRANSACTION ISOLATION LEVEL SERIALIZABLE line from the stored procedure and allow the default of READ COMMITTED). The READ_COMMITTED_SNAPSHOT database option only applies to the read committed transaction isolation level. It wouldn't apply to serializable. Rewriting the query using a table hint wouldn't affect the isolation level or the number of locks.

4. **C.** Getting different results when reading the same data within a single transaction is known as inconsistent analysis (a nonrepeatable read). Setting the transaction isolation level to repeatable read will prevent this problem. Both read committed and read uncommitted transaction isolation levels allow nonrepeatable reads. Using a cursor wouldn't prevent the problem of inconsistent analysis.

5. **B.** A dirty read is one where it's possible to read uncommitted modifications (modifications that haven't been committed to the database yet). Both read committed and read uncommitted allow dirty reads, but the read committed transaction isolation level also supports the read_committed_snapshot option. With this option turned on, dirty reads are prevented and locking contention is minimized. Repeatable read should be used to prevent nonrepeatable read problems, but this is not part of this scenario.

6. **B.** Removing the index hint will generally improve performance since it allows the query optimizer to pick the best index. Changing the index hint from 0 to a 1 will only change it from a clustered index scan to a clustered index scan or seek. It still prevents the query optimizer from picking the best index. Setting the readpast locking hint will cause the query to skip locked rows, but won't override the index hint. The READ COMMITTED transaction isolation level is the default.

7. **D.** Of the available choices, the only one that would be used to improve query response time and reduce deadlocks is the ReadPast locking hint. This will skip rows that are locked. Thorough testing should be done to ensure the skipped rows do not affect the integrity of the database. UpdLock would increase the locks by specifying that Update locks be created and held until the end of the query. Read committed is the default. Read uncommitted would allow dirty reads, which wouldn't affect the locks.

8. **A.** Since the table is only modified during scheduled downtimes, locks aren't necessary. Everyone should be able to read the data at the same time without causing any concurrency problems. NoLock is the same as read uncommitted, which allows dirty reads, but since the data isn't changed while users access it, there will be no dirty reads. UpdLock and TabLock will needlessly add locks reducing concurrency. Read Committed isn't needed since the data is only updated during downtimes.

9. **A.** In the scenario, occasionally when a parameter smaller than $200 is provided, the plan is created and cached based on this smaller parameter. Since the plan is cached, when normal parameters (greater than $200) are provided, the cached plan is still used, resulting in poor performance. The solution is to create a plan guide and force it to OPTIMIZE FOR a parameter greater than $200. Using the RECOMPILE hint would prevent it from being in cache at all, which wouldn't provide any improvement for the majority of the queries. The USE PLAN hint would be useful if the query was problematic, but we couldn't rewrite it. There is no indication this is the problem. Also, there is no such thing as a USE PARAMETER hint.

10. **A.** Cursors that perform slowly can enjoy significant improvements if rewritten as a result set–oriented operation. Based on the information in the scenario, it doesn't matter which option is used to create the cursor. It's performing slowly and can be improved by refactoring the cursor.

11. **A, D.** As written, the SELECT statement returns over 19,000 rows. If the SELECT statement is rewritten with a join on the HumanResources.Employee table, the cursor will include only employees and will only have 290 rows. With the SELECT statement rewritten, the IF EXISTS clause will no longer be needed within the cursor. Filtering the rows within the cursor is not recommended. Based on the data given, the type of cursor needed cannot be determined.

12. **D.** A keyset-driven cursor is updateable and maintains a fixed order or rows (created in the tempdb database). Static and Fast_forward cursors are read_only. A dynamic cursor does not have a fixed membership; INSERT and DELETE statements will be reflected in the cursor.

13. **C.** A Dynamic cursor allows updates. To make it read-only, the dynamic option must be changed and the only other option choices are Static, Fast_forward, and Keyset. Of these, only Static and Fast_forward are read-only. Optimistic would be specified to identify how updates are handled, but updates will not be used if Optimistic is not needed. A Forward_only cursor isn't read-only.

Transferring Data

In this chapter, you will learn about:

- Replication
- SQL Server Integration Services (SSIS)
- Bulk Imports and Exports, including bcp

> *The pessimist sees the difficulty in every opportunity; the optimist,*
> *the opportunity in every difficulty*
>
> —*L.P. Jacks*

Many times, we're tasked with getting data from here to there—from one database to another database, or from one server to another server. For the simplest tasks, we have our old friend bcp—the command-line bulk copy program that's been in SQL Server since before SQL Server 7.0.

For more complex tasks, we have SQL Server Integration Services (SSIS), which replaces Data Transformation Services (DTS) from SQL Server 2000. SSIS can be used for extract, transform, and load (ETL) functions and can perform some very sophisticated data transformations during the transfer.

To keep data in one database in sync with data in another database, we can use replication. This allows us to replicate data in one database to another database either in real-time or on a schedule.

Replication

Replication is one of those topics that could fill a book—and if you were to do a search, you would easily find several books on replication. Microsoft doesn't expect you to know everything about replication in order to become an MCITP: Database Administrator. Instead, you need to know what replication does from a big-picture perspective, and then you need to know about the different types of replication.

When a challenge presents itself on the job where high availability is required, you should know where replication fits in and some of the decision points to decide which method to choose.

The big picture of replication is that it's a set of technologies used to copy and distribute data among multiple users or consumers. The users can be local or in multiple remote locations connected via a LAN, a WAN, the Internet, or any other connection method.

Unlike other methods of high availability, replication often doesn't distribute entire databases, but instead distributes parts of the database, such as tables or VIEWs. These are referred to as *articles* and are distributed as part of a *publication*.

 EXAM TIP   Replication is not new to SQL Server 2005, and was available in previous editions of SQL Server. Because of this, don't expect it to be heavily tested. However, you should still know the basics of the Publisher metaphor and the three different types of replication: merge, transactional, and snapshot. On the other hand, Replication Monitor offers significant improvements (such as using Tracer Tokens to measure latency) and you can expect to see a couple of questions related to the Replication Monitor.

By distributing only parts of the database, we have the capability to make key data available to users that need it, and to effectively offload some of the processing. We use it in its simplest form to replicate heavily queried tables to a different server and direct the queries to that server.

The Publisher Metaphor

Replication centers on a Publisher metaphor. It includes Publishers, Distributors, Subscribers, articles, publications, and subscriptions. Figure 15-1 shows the relationship of Publishers, Distributors, and Subscribers. Notice that Subscriber 1 has a two-way arrow to the Distributor. It's not as common, but Subscribers can sometimes publish data back to the Publisher.

Figure 15-1
A Publisher,
Distributor, and
Subscribers

Publisher   Distributor   Subscriber 1

Subscriber 2

Subscriber 3

For example, consider a company that has a very large database (over 20GB). The billing department needs only the information on the customers and invoices from the past year. The primary database can be configured as a Publisher. A publication can be created that includes articles such as the Customers table and a filtered view on the Invoice table. The publication can be sent to the Distributor (a process on the same server as the primary database) and then sent to the Subscribers in the billing department.

Of course, the question "Why?" comes to mind. "What's the benefit?"

Instead of sending the entire 20GB database to the billing department, we can send them just the articles they need—the customer table and an invoice view (shown in Figure 15-2). This allows us to save on bandwidth and other resource usage on the server used by the billing department.

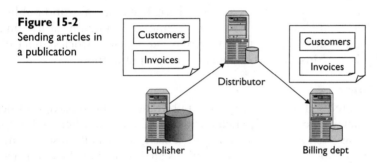

Figure 15-2
Sending articles in a publication

The Publisher

The Publisher is the source of the data. This is the database that makes its data available to others through replication, and Publishers define what they publish through a publication. Just as in the real world, a Publisher can have more than one publication.

The Distributor

The Distributor is often the same as the Publisher, but could be a different database instance and could even be on a different server than the Publisher. The Distributor knows who to send the data to and sometimes acts as a queue for data being sent from the Publisher to the Subscribers.

Subscribers

Subscribers receive the replicated data. This is a database that uses publications from the Publisher to keep itself up-to-date. Just as in the real world, Subscribers can subscribe to multiple publications from multiple Publishers.

Subscribers can also send data back to the Publisher or publish data to other Subscribers.

Articles

Articles are the actual database objects included in the publication, such as tables, VIEWs, stored procedures, indexes, and more. In the real world, a magazine can have multiple articles; a publication can also have multiple articles.

EXAM TIP When choosing articles for publication, you should also consider the objects you've created to optimize them. For example, if indexes were created to optimize the performance of queries against specific tables, you should consider including these indexes in the publication. If they are omitted, the queries could perform poorly on the Subscribers.

Articles can be filtered when sent to Subscribers. Filtering can be used to restrict the columns and/or the rows of data sent to Subscribers. You can even filter out all the data in specific tables so the only thing replicated is the database and table definitions.

Publications

A publication is a group of articles for a database. Just as a real-world publication will group SQL Server articles in a SQL Server magazine, and gardening articles in a gardening magazine, publications are used to group like articles. Articles aren't distributed individually, but are instead distributed as part of a publication.

Subscriptions

Subscriptions are used to request specific publications. The subscription defines the publication that will be received, when it will be received, and where. Subscriptions can be configured as push subscriptions or pull subscriptions. *Pull* subscriptions are initiated by the Subscriber, while *push* subscriptions are initiated by the Publisher.

- **Push subscription**   Initiated by the Publisher. The Publisher sends changes to the Subscriber either continuously or on a frequently recurring schedule. This is most often used with snapshot or transactional replication since the subscription would be pushed based on transactions, or based on when a snapshot is created.

- **Pull subscription**   Initiated by the Subscriber. The Subscriber requests changes made at the Publisher, either on demand or on a schedule, rather than continuously. This is most often used with merge replication.

EXAM TIP When deciding whether to use a push or pull subscription, follow the type of replication. For snapshot or transactional replication, use a push subscription. For merge replication, use a pull subscription.

Replication Methods

The three methods of replication are *snapshot, merge,* and *transactional.* Each method has its own strengths. The method you choose depends on the physical replication environment, the type and quantity of data to be replicated, and whether the Subscriber can update the data.

All replication types begin by synchronizing objects between the Publisher and Subscriber(s). This is often done with a *snapshot,* which is a copy of all the objects and data specified by the publication. The snapshot quickly gets the Subscriber up to speed with the data, and the rest of the replication process is involved with keeping it up-to-date as the Publisher data changes.

It's possible to only do snapshot replication. If the data rarely changes, perhaps a new snapshot once a month is enough to keep it up-to-date. *Transactional replication* tracks changes through the transaction log, while *merge replication* tracks changes through triggers and metadata tables.

Snapshot Replication

Snapshot replication is probably the easiest to do and involves very little overhead. It starts with a snapshot or a complete copy of the publication at a moment in time. When the data changes substantially (or if a particular replication schedule is in place), another snapshot is taken and distributed to the Subscribers. Snapshots completely overwrite the previous snapshot.

It makes sense to use snapshot replication when one or more of the following is true:

- **Data rarely changes.**   For this reason, the snapshot would rarely be out-of-date. For example, a parts catalog may change only monthly. Using snapshot replication, the catalog is replicated to Subscribers only monthly.

- **It's acceptable to have data on the Subscriber that is out-of-date from the Publishers data.**   For example, in a college setting, new students are added and signed up for future courses. However, some school administrators may only need to be able to access the records of students that have attended past or current courses.

- **Only small amounts of data are replicated.**   Trying to replicate a 10GB snapshot regularly over a partial T1 simply won't work. However, replicating a 5MB snapshot publication over a T1 would easily work, especially if it could be scheduled to occur in the middle of the night when a lot of bandwidth is available.

- **A large volume of data changes occurs in a short period.**   For example, if on the last day of every month, a bulk import modifies the database, but for the rest of the month hardly any changes occur, snapshots would work well. In this example, we'd do snapshot replication after the bulk import.

Since incremental changes are not tracked, snapshot replication has a lower overhead on the Publisher than other methods of replication.

Transactional Replication

Transactional replication uses the transaction log. As with all types of replication, it starts with a snapshot. Once the snapshot is applied, all changes at the Publisher are quickly delivered to the Subscriber. Transactional replication occurs in near real time.

It makes sense to use transactional replication when one or more of the following is true:

- **You want changes to be sent to Subscribers as they occur.** A stock listing service is a good example of data that you want to be sent to all Subscribers as soon as they occur. Even if it's just a change to a single stock price—send it.

- **Low latency is required.** You need the Subscribers to have up-to-date data as soon as possible.

- **Access to intermediate data states is required.** For example, if a company has 100 MCITP books on hand and they sell 20 books to five different customers for five different classes, the quantity is reduced from 100 to 80, 80 to 60, 60 to 40, 40 to 20, and then 20 to 0. If the application requires the knowledge of the intermediate quantities, transactional replication would be used. In contrast, snapshot and merge replication would show a quantity of 100, then a quantity of 0 without the intermediate data states.

- **The Publisher has a high volume of transactional activity.** In other words, there's a large volume of INSERT, UPDATE, and DELETE statements against the database.

- **The Publisher or Subscriber is not a Microsoft SQL Server database.** For example, one of the players could be running a different DBMS such as Oracle.

While Subscribers in transactional replication typically do *not* send changes back to the Publisher, it is possible to configure transactional replication so the updates occur at the Subscriber and are submitted to the Publisher.

Merge Replication

Just like the other two methods, merge replication starts with a snapshot. However, since updates are typically done at both the Publisher and Subscribers in merge replication, it can't simply rely on the transaction log to replicate the changes. Instead, triggers are used to track all data changes and schema modifications.

It makes sense to use merge replication when one or more of the following is true:

- **Multiple Subscribers can update the same data.** For example, a series of car parts stores may need to access the primary database, but must also be able to update this database as it pertains to their store.

- **Subscribers need to be able to change data offline and then later synchronize changes with the Publisher.** As an example, on-the-road sales personnel may need to be able to make changes to their database on their computer, and then at some point (perhaps at the end of the day) connect to the primary database and merge their changes into the primary database.

- **If Subscribers require a different partition of data.** For instance, each of the different car parts stores may need to be able to manage the inventory in their store, but not other stores. This can be achieved by horizontally partitioning the data via merge replication.

- **Conflict detection and resolution must be possible.** For example, in the car parts store, let's say Store 1 sells a battery from their inventory. At the same time, Store 2 sells the same battery from Store 1's inventory. If we started with five batteries, we would now have three. However, each of these transactions would do the math as 5–1, leaving an inventory of four batteries. Merge replication can detect conflicts like this, and rules can be set up to resolve them.

- **Access to intermediate data states is not required.** Remember our earlier example of a company selling 100 books in 5 sets of 20? Merge replication would just replicate the end state with zero books on hand, not the intermediate states of 80, 60, 40, and 20 books on hand.

Probably the biggest thing to remember about merge replication is that it allows multiple Subscribers to update data. In distributed data scenarios, this is often needed. Additionally, with multiple Subscribers updating the data, the possibility of conflicts exists. Merge replication provides many different ways to handle conflicts.

In the following exercise, we'll configure the Publisher and Distributor for replication.

Exercise 15.1: Configure the Publisher and Distributor

1. If not already open, open an instance of SSMS.

2. Right-click the Replication container and select Configure Distribution.

3. On the Configure Distribution Wizard page, click Next.

4. On the Distributor page, ensure that the box titled '*Yourcomputername*' Will Act As Its Own Distributor; SQL Server Will Create A Distribution Log Database And Log is selected. Your display should look similar to Figure 15-3. Click Next.

Figure 15-3
Selecting the local computer as the Distributor

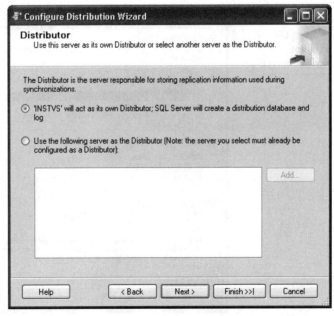

5. On the Snapshot Folder page, accept the default location and click Next.

TIP If SQL Server Agent isn't configured to start automatically, you'll receive a notification from the Distribution Wizard with a prompt to configure it to start automatically. Select Yes, and then click Next to continue.

6. On the Distribution Database page, accept the defaults and click Next.

7. On the Publishers page, verify the local computer is listed and selected, and then click Next.

8. On the Wizard Actions page, verify that the Configure Distribution check box is checked and click Next.

9. On the Complete The Wizard page, click Finish. Your display should indicate success.

We can now configure the publication. We'll do this in the next exercise.

Exercise 15.2: Configure the Publication

Take a mini-tour of SSIS in video 15-2.

1. Right-click the Local Publication container within the Replication container, and then select New Publication to launch the New Publication wizard.

2. On the New Publication Wizard page, click Next.

3. On the Publication Database page, select AdventureWorks and click Next.

4. On the Publication Type page, select Snapshot Publication. Your display should look similar to Figure 15-4. Click Next.

Figure 15-4
Selecting the Snapshot replication type

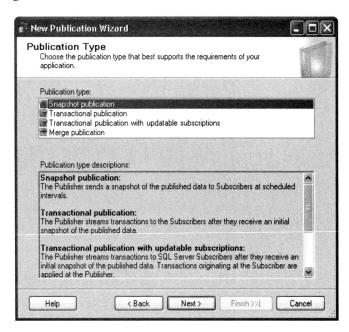

5. On the Articles page, we will select the individual database objects to include in the snapshot:

   a. Open the Tables container and select Address (Person) and Contact (Person).

   b. Open the Stored Procedures container and select uspGetEmployeeManagers (dbo).

   c. Open the Views container and select vAdditionalContactInfo(Person).

   d. Your display should look similar to Figure 15-5. Click Next.

Figure 15-5
Selecting objects
to replicate

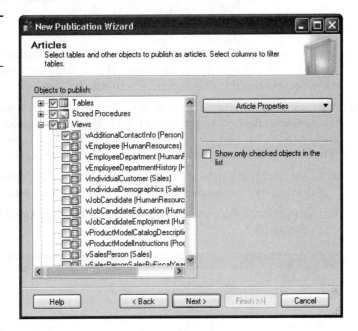

6. On the Article Issues page, acknowledge that other objects are required by the vAdditionalContactInfo VIEW and will automatically be included. Click Next.

7. On the Filter Table Rows page, we could add filters for both horizontal partitioning (with a WHERE clause) and vertical partitioning (by selecting the columns to replicate). For our example, we won't provide a filter. Click Next.

8. On the Snapshot Agent page, select the check boxes for Create A Snapshot Immediately… and for Schedule The Snapshot Agent…. Your display should look similar to Figure 15-6. Click Next.

9. On the Agent Security page, click Security Settings. Select Run under the SQL Server Agent service account. In a real-world environment, we would use a dedicated service account for this purpose. On our test bed, this account will work. Click OK, and then click Next.

10. On the Wizard Actions page, ensure Create The Publication is checked and click Next.

Figure 15-6
Configuring the
Snapshot Agent

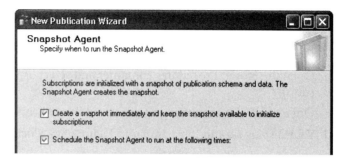

11. On the Complete The Wizard page, enter **AdventureWorksContacts** for the Publication name, and click Finish. The wizard should start, and after a moment you should see a Success screen. Click Close.

12. After the Snapshot Agent is configured, you may find that some items aren't replicating as desired. In particular it's a good practice to double-check and ensure all the indexes you've created to optimize these tables are also replicated. If not, the performance of the Subscriber may not be acceptable.

   a. Open the Local Publications folder. Right-click the [AdventureWorks]: AdventureWorksContacts publication and click Properties.

   b. In the Select A Page pane, choose Articles. Your display should look similar to Figure 15-7.

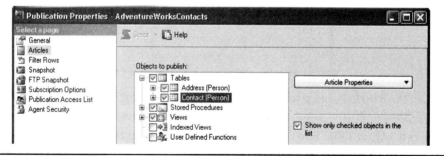

Figure 15-7   Modifying the publication properties

   c. Right-click the Contact[Person] table and select Set Properties Of This Table Article.

   d. On the Article Properties page, scroll to the top of the page. Change the Copy Nonclustered Indexes entry from False to True. Change the Copy Full Text Indexes entry from False to True. Change the Copy XML XSD entry from False to True. Change the Copy XML Indexes entry from False to True. Your display should look similar to Figure 15-8. Click OK. On the Publication Properties page, click OK.

Figure 15-8
Changing the
article properties
to copy all
indexes

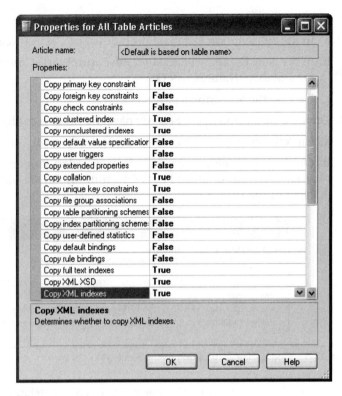

We now have the publication configured. The last step is to configure the Subscriber. We'll do that in the next exercise.

Exercise 15.3: Configure the Subscriber

1. Connect to the named instance in SSMS:

   a. Right-click over the default instance within the Object Explorer in SSMS and click Connect.

   b. In the Connect To Server page, select the named instance and click Connect.

2. Browse to the Replication container, and select the Local Subscriptions container.

3. Right-click the Local Subscriptions container and select New Subscription.

4. On the New Subscription Wizard page, click Next.

5. On the Publication page, select Find SQL Server Publisher from the Publisher drop-down box. In the Connect To Server dialog box, select the default instance and click Connect.

6. The publication AdventureWorksContacts created in the previous exercise should be available and selected. Click Next.

7. On the Distribution Agent Location page, select Run All Agents At The Distributor and click Next.

8. On the Subscribers page, we need to create a new database:

   a. In the Subscription Database drop-down box, select New Database.

   b. In the New Database page, enter **AdventureWorksContactsRepSnapshot** as the Database Name. Click OK.

   c. Back on the Subscribers page, click Next.

9. On the Distribution Agent Security page, we need to configure security:

   a. Click the ellipses (…) button under Connection To Subscriber.

   b. On the Distribution Agent Security page, select Run under the SQL Server Agent service account and click OK. Your display should look similar to Figure 15-9. Click Next.

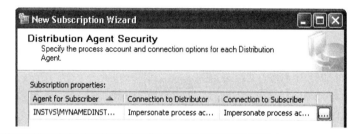

Figure 15-9   Configuring Distribution Agent Security

10. On the Synchronization Schedule page, accept the defaults and click Next.

11. On the Initialize Subscriptions page, accept the defaults and click Next.

12. On the Wizard Actions page, ensure the Create The Subscription(s) check box is checked and click Next.

13. On the Complete The Wizard page, click Finish. You should see a Success page indicating the subscription has been successfully created.

Replication Monitor

 Take a mini-tour of the Replication Monitor in video 15-RepMon.

In a perfect world, replication would work and you'd never have to worry about it. Of course, none of us live there, so thankfully we have the Microsoft SQL Server Replication Monitor that can be used to monitor replication.

Replication Monitor allows us to monitor the overall health of the replication topology. We can view status and performance indicators to determine basic performance issues. Basic questions that can be answered with the Replication Monitor include:

- Is the replication system healthy?
- Are any subscriptions slow?

- How far behind is a transactional subscription?

- How long will it take a committed transaction to reach a Subscriber?

- Why is a merge subscription slow?

- Why isn't an agent running?

- What's the average replication time (or the worst replication time) among many Subscribers?

To launch Replication Monitor, right-click a publication and select Launch Replication Monitor. It takes a moment to launch, so be patient or you may end up with several instances running. If you did the previous three exercises in this chapter and select the AdventureWorks publication, your display should look similar to Figure 15-10.

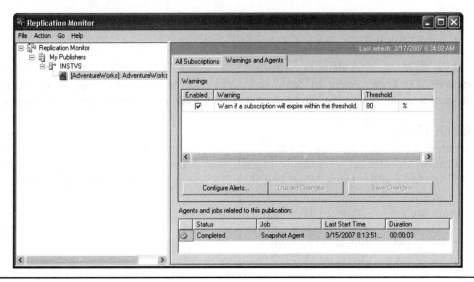

Figure 15-10   Replication Monitor

Configuring Warnings and Alerts

Replication allows you to configure many warnings and alerts. By clicking the Warnings And Agents tab and selecting Configure Alerts, you are given a choice of many warnings and alerts to choose from.

Warnings are listed next:

- Long merge over dialup connection

- Long merge over LAN connection

- Slow merge over dialup connection

- Slow merge over LAN connection

- Subscription expiration
- Transactional replication latency

Other alerts are:

- Agent custom shutdown
- Agent failure
- Agent retry
- Agent success
- Expired subscription dropped
- Subscriber has failed data validation
- Subscriber has passed data validation
- Subscription reinitialized after validation failure

These warnings and alerts tap into the SQL Server Agent service infrastructure. We explored SQL Server Agent in detail in Chapter 13. Be aware that SQL Server Agent allows us to create alerts that can be used to send e-mail, pages, and Net Send messages.

Watch Lists

If desired, the Replication Monitor can be set up with different watch lists. The way that Replication Monitor achieves this is through agents. The details of how this is done are better left for another book. What you should know is that watch lists can be created, and also know what they can be created for.

As we can see in Figure 15-11, watch lists can be created on:

- Worst performing subscriptions
- Errors and warnings
- Only subscriptions that are running, or not running

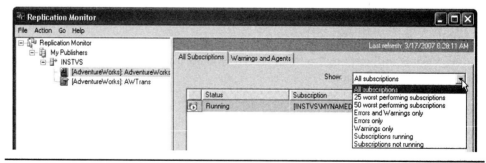

Figure 15-11   Watch lists in Replication Monitor

Tracer Tokens

A new feature in SQL Server 2005 is the Replication Monitor's ability to use tracer tokens. When I think of tracers, I think of the old war movies (and some new ones, too); tracer bullets light up the path they take, giving immediate feedback as to where they end up. Tracer tokens work similarly, without the destruction of the bullets.

Within SQL Server 2005, a tracer token is a small amount of time-stamped data that is inserted into the publication database transaction log. When it reaches the Distributor and/or Subscribers, it can be examined to determine how long it took to get there. Of course, if the tracer token never reaches the destination, that gives you some good information, too.

The technical term for this is *latency*. Tracer tokens can be used to easily measure latency.

 EXAM TIP To measure and record latency for Subscribers, configure tracer tokens. Tracer tokens are accessed via the Tracer Tokens tab in Replication Monitor.

The Tracer Tokens tab appears in transactional replication publications, but not in merge or snapshot publications. In Figure 15-12, I have configured a transactional replication publication and launched Replication Monitor to show it.

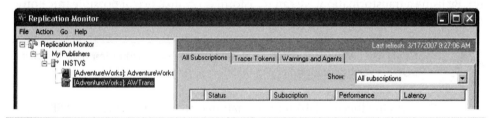

Figure 15-12 Replication Monitor with the Tracer Tokens tab

SQL Server Integration Services (SSIS)

New to SQL Server 2005 is SQL Server 2005 Integration Services (SSIS). This is a powerful tool to help database administrators build higher-performance data integration solutions to extract, transform, and load data from a wide array of sources.

SSIS allows the creation of sophisticated packages that can perform extract, transform, and load (ETL) workflow functions, including FTP operations, executing SQL statements, and sending e-mail messages. It can transform data by cleaning, aggregating, merging, copying, and standardizing data.

While SQL Server 7.0 and 2000 had Data Transformation Services (DTS), in SQL Server 2005 the service that does everything DTS did, and more, is SSIS. DTS is still supported for purposes of backward-compatibility, but new packages should be created in SSIS.

SSIS is a huge add-on to SQL Server 2005—so huge it actually has another interface to access most of the features: Business Intelligence Development Studio (BIDS).

If you've used Microsoft Visual Studio, this will be familiar because BIDS has a similar interface to Visual Studio.

There's no way this chapter will be able to make you a master of SSIS. Instead, the goal is to expose you to some of the features. When it comes time to dig deeper, you can pick up one of the many SSIS books available.

ETL

An important element of many Business Intelligence (BI) solutions is the ability to extract, transform, and load (ETL) data. Often, the data exists somewhere. We just need the right tools to access it and bring it into our database in the correct format. In SQL Server 2005, the right tool is SSIS.

Extract is the process of pulling data out of a source database. *Load* is the process of putting it into the target database. *Transform* is where the magic happens. Frequently, we receive data in a wide variety of formats, and we need to transform that data to cleanse and standardize it.

For example, a table could have a column meant to be true or false. However, over time, the data has been entered as *True, true, T, t, 1, Yes, Y,* and *y* for "True" and *False, false, F, f, 0, No, N,* and *n* for "False." If we're trying to filter based on whether the column is true or false, all these possible entries need to be included in a complex OR clause. This makes the query harder to write and more processor-intensive when it's run. By using a transformation, we can transform every instance of possible true entries into a single Boolean True, providing standardization of the data.

 EXAM TIP When you need to cleanse and/or standardize imported data, use SQL Server Integration Services (SSIS).

Some Business Intelligence (BI) transformation categories supported by SSIS are:

- **Row transformations** These are used to update column values and to create new columns. They are applied to each row. As an example, string functions could be applied to character data to eliminate leading or trailing spaces.

- **Rowset transformations** These create new rowsets based on aggregated, sorted, sampled, pivoted, or unpivoted rowsets. A simple example of a rowset transformation is to sort the data.

- **BI transformations** These are used to clean data and to perform data mining operations. As an example, a BI transformation could perform a fuzzy lookup (identify close matches instead of exact matches) on a text column to mine relevant data.

- **Split and Join transformations** These can be used to split single tables into multiple tables, or to join multiple tables into single tables. As an example, a wide customer table could be split into two narrower tables.

- **Miscellaneous and custom transformations** These can be used to import, export, add audit information, and do just about anything else you want to the data.

Requirements

For SQL Server Integration Services to run, the SQL Server Integration Services service must be running. SSIS is shared among all instances on the server. In other words, if we have two instances installed on a server, we would have two instances of the MSSQLServer service and two instances of the SQL Server Agent service. However, we would only have one instance of the SQL Server Integration Services service running.

All versions of SQL Server 2005 have the Import/Export wizard, which we'll cover later in this chapter. This is a very basic feature of SSIS. SQL Server 2005 Standard Edition offers many SSIS features within BIDS. All features are available in the Enterprise edition, including data mining and fuzzy lookup transformations.

32-Bit vs. 64-Bit

If you're running a 64-bit version of SQL Server 2005, you need to be aware of a compatibility issue with DTS packages created in SQL Server 2000. While most DTS packages will run without any problem within SSIS, they are all 32-bit packages and won't run automatically on a 64-bit installation of SQL Server 2005.

If you are running a 64-bit installation of SQL Server 2005, you need to change the Run64BitRuntime to False to force the solution to run the packages in 32-bit emulation mode. This page is accessed from the properties of the SSIS solution and is shown in Figure 15-13. While this is in the debugging section, this setting affects the package when run at any time.

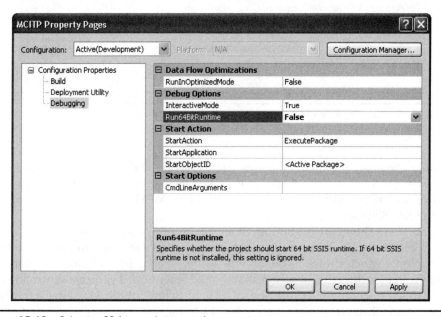

Figure 15-13   Selecting 32-bit emulation mode

Business Intelligence Development Studio (BIDS)

Let's take a look at the Business Intelligence Development Studio (BIDS) to get an idea of the big picture. To launch it, click Start | All Programs | Microsoft SQL Server 2005 | SQL Server Business Intelligence Development Studio.

With it launched, you have a blank slate. This is Visual Studio, which is used for a lot of different development tasks, such as Visual Basic or C#, not just SQL Server 2005. To start an SSIS project, you would select File | New Project. If you were to select Business Intelligence Projects, your display would now look like Figure 15-14.

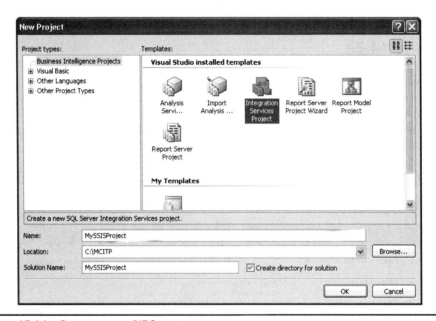

Figure 15-14   Creating a new BIDS project

Notice the many installed templates. In this section, we'll focus on the Integration Services projects. Later in the chapter, we'll take a look at the Report Server Project Wizard. I've named the project MySSISProject in the C:\MCITP directory with a solution name of MySSISProject.

Figure 15-15 shows the beginnings of an SSIS project within BIDS.

To the left is the Toolbox. In the center is the Package Designer. To the right is Solution Explorer, which shows all the objects in this project. To configure the properties of the project (such as the 32-bit emulation mode mentioned earlier), we would right-click MySSISProject and select the properties here. Below Solution Explorer is the Properties page of whatever object currently has the focus.

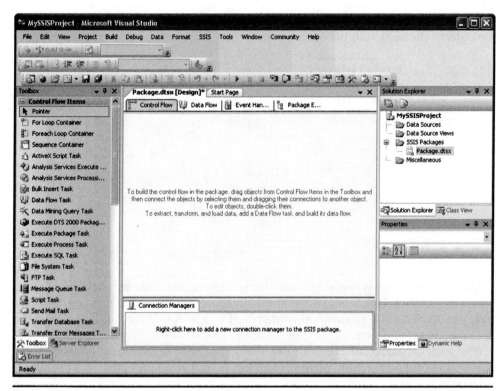

Figure 15-15 Creating an SSIS project within BIDS

Packages

Except for using the Import/Export Wizard within SSMS, we use the Business Intelligence Development Studio to create packages. Packages can be simple with just a single task or complex with multiple tasks.

The best way to think of a package is as a Windows executable. BIDS allows us to create and deploy the packages within manifest files, which will be discussed in the "Deploying Packages" section later in the chapter.

Packages have multiple components. These include:

- Constraints
- Tasks
- Containers
- Connections

Take a look at Figure 15-16. Notice that it has multiple tasks. We are able to control the order of the tasks with the connections.

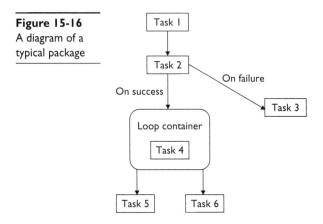

Figure 15-16
A diagram of a typical package

When the package is executed, Task 1 runs. Upon successful completion of Task 1, Task 2 is executed. Task 2 has two possible outcomes configured. If it succeeds, it will pass execution control to the loop container. If it fails, it will execute Task 3, and the package will be complete.

The loop container allows us to loop through Task 4 as many times as we wish. Upon successful completion, we have two tasks (Task 5 and Task 6) that will run simultaneously.

Constraints

Constraints allow some basic flow control. When a task completes, there are three possible outcomes: success, failure, or completion (with an error). These are the most commonly used constraints.

Tasks

Tasks define units of work that are performed in a package, and a package can contain one or more tasks. If more than one task is contained within a package, they are connected with control flow constraints such as On Success, On Completion, or On Failure.

Tasks are broken down into different categories:

- **Maintenance tasks**   These tasks are used to perform administrative functions, such as backing up SQL Server databases, rebuilding or reorganizing indexes, and running SQL Server Agent jobs. They include the Back Up Database, Check Database Integrity, Execute SQL Server Agent Job, Execute T-SQL Statement, History Cleanup, Notify Operator, Rebuild Index, Reorganize Index, Shrink Database, Update Statistics, and Maintenance Cleanup tasks.

- **Data Flow task**   This task extracts data, applies simple column transformations, and loads data. Only the Data Flow task is included in this category.

- **Data Preparation tasks** These tasks copy files and directories, download files and data, execute web methods, and apply operations to XML documents. They include File System, FTP, web service, and XML tasks.

TIP With the high availability of the Internet, it's very common for companies to make data accessible via FTP sites, or more often, via a web service. We saw in Chapter 11 that an HTTP endpoint can be consumed by a web service. It's also possible to configure a web service task to retrieve data from a web service available on the Internet.

- **Workflow tasks** These tasks communicate with other processes to run packages, run programs, send and receive messages, send e-mail, and interact with Windows Management Instrumentation (WMI) data and events. They include Execute Package, Execute DTS 2000 Package, Execute Process, Message Queue, Send Mail, WMI Data Reader, and WMI Event Watcher tasks.

NOTE While packages can't be nested within packages, they can be executed from within a package. This is done with the Execute Package task. Legacy DTS packages can be executed with the Execute DTS 2000 Package task.

- **SQL Server tasks** These tasks access, copy, insert, delete, and modify SQL Server objects and data. They include Bulk Insert, Execute SQL, Transfer Database, Transfer Error Messages, Transfer Jobs, Transfer Logins, Transfer Master Stored Procedures, and Transfer SQL Server Objects tasks.
- **Scripting tasks** These tasks extend functionality of packages with scripts. They include the ActiveX and Script tasks.
- **Analysis Services tasks** These tasks are used to create, modify, delete, and process online analytical processing (OLAP) objects. They include the Analysis Services Processing, Analysis Services Execute DDL, and Data Mining Query tasks.

Containers
Instead of just connecting tasks so they occur in sequence based on control flow (success, completion, or failure), it's also possible to place tasks within containers. The primary purpose of doing this is to perform looping.

In any programming language, loops allow us to perform an operation (or sequence of operations) repeatedly. Sometimes that's a set number of iterations such as 100 times, and other times it's a conditional set of iterations such as those based on a variable measured within the loop.

The two loops we have within SSIS are a For Loop and a ForEach Loop. The For Loop repeats the control flow until a specified expression is false. A ForEach Loop enumerates a collection and repeats the control for each member of the collection. A Sequence Container allows us to group multiple tasks and manage them as a unit.

As an example, let's say we run an auto parts chain. Each night, many of the stores send us text files that need to be imported into the database, but on any given night, we don't know how many text files we have. So, we can put a Bulk Import task within a container, and the Bulk Import task will identify the files in a certain directory and run the Bulk Import task for each file in the directory.

 TIP To repeat tasks within an SSIS package, use a For Loop or a ForEach Loop container. The loop can then be configured to repeat as many times as desired.

Package Designer

Having reviewed this information on constraints, tasks, and containers, let's take a closer look at the Package Designer within BIDS. Figure 15-17 shows the beginnings of a project with several tasks dragged over from the Toolbox.

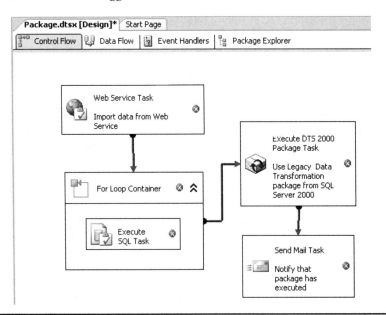

Figure 15-17   Looking at a package in the Package Designer

In the first box, you can see I dragged over the Web Service task. This could connect to a web service and import data from it. I then added a For Loop container with an Execute SQL task within it. Depending on how much data I received from the Web Service task, I could loop through it until a condition was met. Next, I could use the Execute DTS 2000 task to execute a legacy DTS task from SQL Server 2000. Lastly, I've added the Send Mail task to send e-mail, including the results of the package.

Connections

Connections allow us to identify data sources and data destinations. We can connect to many different types of databases such as SQL Server, Access, Oracle, or any database type that has an OLEDB provider. Many common OLEDB providers are included within BIDS. We can also connect to flat files—simple text files with common delimiters such as a comma or tab.

Package Storage

Packages are stored within SQL Server in the msdb database. If you want to ensure you have a full backup of all SQL Server SSIS packages, back up the msdb database. Any time SSIS packages are added or modified, the msdb database should be backed up to ensure these changes are retained. Without a good copy of the msdb database, all SSIS packages, SQL Server Agent jobs, alerts, and operators will be lost.

It's also possible to store SSIS packages in files. If stored in files, they can be backed up just as any other files are backed up.

Package Protection Levels

In line with Microsoft's SD^3+C (Secure by Design, Secure by Default, and Secure in Deployment and Communications) philosophy, package security has been seriously considered. Multiple protection levels are available for SSIS packages.

A couple of the package protection levels refer to sensitive data. For all values, sensitive information is defined as:

- The password part of a connection string.
- The task-generated XML nodes that are tagged as sensitive. Tagging of XML nodes is controlled by SSIS and cannot be modified by users.
- Any variable that is marked as sensitive. Marking of variables is controlled through SSIS.

The different package protection levels available are:

- **Rely on server storage for encryption.**   Packages are protected based on role security to the msdb database. This is not supported if the packages are saved as a file.
- **Do not save sensitive.**   Sensitive data is not saved and must be supplied by the user each time the package is used.
- **Encrypt all with password.**   This level encrypts the entire package. To open the package (or to run it with Dtexec), the password must be supplied.
- **Encrypt all with user key.**   This level encrypts the entire package using a key associated with the logged-on user. This key is kept in the user's profile so only the same user logged with the same profile will be able to access the package.
- **Encrypt sensitive with password.**   This level encrypts only the sensitive information with a password. Information is marked as sensitive by the package developer. For example, information such as social security numbers or credit card numbers may be marked as sensitive.

- **Encrypt sensitive with user key.** This level encrypts only the sensitive information with the logged-on user's key. This key is kept in the user's profile so
only the same user logged with the same profile will be able to access the sensitive data within the package.

TIP To protect a package so only a group of users (such as a group of
database administrators) can access and/or execute the package, you would
encrypt it with a password using the Encrypt All With Password option. A
password can be shared among many DBAs, but a key cannot be shared.

Executing Packages

With the Business Intelligence Development Studio (BIDS), it's rather easy to execute packages. Simply right-click the package and select Execute Package, as shown in
Figure 15-18.

Figure 15-18
Executing a
package in BIDS

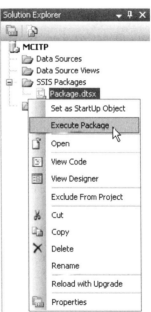

It's also possible to execute packages from the command line (or from a script accessing the command line). The utility used to execute packages from the command
line is Dtexec. Dtexec can also be used to configure SSIS packages.

The Dtexec utility provides access to all the package configuration and execution
features, including connections, properties, variables, logging, and progress indicators.
It can load packages from a SQL Server database, the SSIS service, and package files.

We can also create deployment packages and use them to deploy our SSIS packages
on another system.

In the following exercise, we'll look at the Import/Export wizard a little more closely
in relation to the SSIS properties.

Exercise 15.4: Examine the Import/Export Wizard

1. Launch SSMS. Browse to the AdventureWorks database in the Databases container.

2. Right-click AdventureWorks and select Tasks | Export Data.

3. On the Welcome To SQL Server Import And Export Wizard page, click Next.

4. On the Choose A Data Source page, verify it is using the SQL Native Client as the Data Source, your server as the Server Name, and AdventureWorks as the Database. Click Next.

5. On the Choose A Destination page, accept the default of SQL Native Client for the Destination and Local as the Server Name. Click the New button. On the Create Database page, enter **Chapter15** as the Name and accept the defaults for the rest of the values. Click OK, and then click Next.

6. On the Specify Table Copy Or Query page, ensure the box labeled Copy Data From One Or More Tables Or Views is selected and then click Next.

7. On the Select Source Tables And Views page, select the check box next to the AdventureWorks.Person.Contact table.

8. Double-click the icon next to *[Chapter15].[Person].[Contact]* in the Destination column. Select the Drop And Re-create Destination Table check box.

9. In the Column Mappings page, observe that many options can be changed. Click the Edit SQL button. This shows the SQL statement that will be used to create the new table. Click OK. Your display should look similar to Figure 15-19.

Figure 15-19
Configuring the export to delete existing data in the Destination table

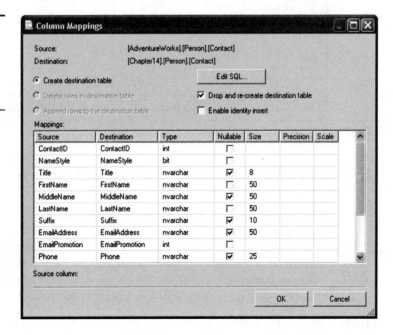

10. On the Select Source Tables And Views page, click the Preview button to see the data that will be exported. Click OK, and then click Next.

11. On the Save And Execute Package page, ensure the Execute Immediately check box is checked. Check the Save SSIS Package box, and ensure the SQL Server radio button is selected to save the package in the msdb database. For the Package Protection Level, select Encrypt All Data With Password, as shown in Figure 15-20. Enter **P@ssw0rd** in both the Password and Retype Password boxes. Click Next.

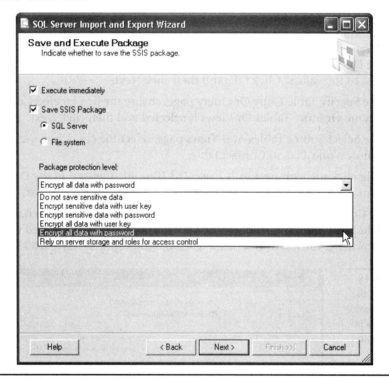

Figure 15-20   Configuring the package with a password

12. On the Save SSIS Package page, enter **SSISExport** as the Name. Enter **Chapter 15 Exercise 4** as the Description, and then click Next.

13. On the Complete The Wizard page, click Finish.

TIP   Note that the steps will execute, and one of the steps will fail with an error. This is normal. Since the database has just been created and the Person. Contact table doesn't exist yet, the step to drop this table fails. For the second time this package is executed, as well as those thereafter, this will succeed.

14. On the Report page showing the execution is completed, click Close.

In the following exercise, you will launch Business Intelligence Development Studio and create a solution using the existing package. You will then run it within BIDS and from the command line using Dtexec.

 Take a mini-tour of SSIS in video 15-2.

Exercise 15.5: Launch BIDS and View the Package Created from the Import/Export Wizard

1. Launch the SQL Server 2005 Business Intelligence Development Studio. Select Start | All Programs | Microsoft SQL Server 2005 | SQL Server Business Intelligence Development Studio.

2. Select File | New Project to create a new project.

3. On the New Project page, select Business Intelligence Projects. In the Visual Studio installed templates, select Integration Services Project. In the Name text box, enter **Chapter15**. For the Location, enter **c:\MCITPSuccess**. The Solution Name should be **Chapter15** (the same as the name). Click OK.

4. After a moment, Visual Studio should appear with the Chapter15 solution in place, and a single SSIS Package named Package.dtsx. In Solution Explorer, right-click SSIS Packages, and select Add Existing Package.

5. On the Add Copy Of Existing Package page, ensure the Package Location is set to SQL Server. Select (Local) from the drop-down menu for the Server. Ensure the Authentication is set to Windows Authentication. For the package path, click the button to the right of the text box.

6. A dialog box should appear showing the SSIS Packages that are currently held in the msdb database. It should look similar to Figure 15-21. Select SSISExport and click OK.

Figure 15-21
SSIS Packages held in the msdb database

7. On the Add Copy Of Existing Package page, click OK. When prompted to enter a password, enter **P@ssw0rd**. Click OK. This will take a moment. Double-click the SSISExport.dtsx package to open it in the Package Designer. In the Package Password box, enter **P@ssw0rd** and click OK.

8. Delete the Package.dtsx package. Since we won't be doing anything with the default package, right-click Package.dtsx and select Delete. On the Microsoft Visual Studio dialog box, click OK to confirm the deletion.

9. Ensure the Control Flow tab is selected in the Package Designer. Your display should look similar to Figure 15-22.

Figure 15-22
Control Flow tasks

Drop table(s) SQL Task

Preparation SQL Task

Data Flow Task

10. Select the Preparation SQL task. Right-click the task and select Edit. This shows all the properties for the Execute SQL task. It sets up the connection information and also has a T-SQL statement that truncates the table. Click Cancel.

11. Right-click the arrow between the Preparation SQL task and the Data Flow task and then select Edit. Notice that the constraint is set to Success. On the success of the Preparation SQL task, the Data Flow task will execute. Click Cancel.

12. Right-click the Data Flow task and click Edit. Notice that now the Data Flow tab is selected. Your display should look like Figure 15-23. The Source is the Contact table in the AdventureWorks database, and the Destination is the Contact table in the Chapter15 database.

Figure 15-23
A Data Flow task

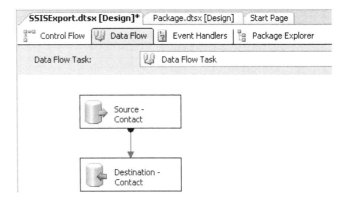

SSISExport.dtsx [Design]* Package.dtsx [Design] Start Page

Control Flow Data Flow Event Handlers Package Explorer

Data Flow Task: Data Flow Task

Source - Contact

Destination - Contact

13. Right-click the SSISExport.dtsx package in the SSIS Packages container in Solution Explorer. Select Execute Package. After a moment, an information link will appear saying:

```
Package execution completed. Click here to switch to design mode,
or select Stop Debugging from the Debug menu.
```

Additionally, each of the tasks will turn green, indicating they have run successfully. Click the information link (toward the bottom of the window with an "i" bubble) to stop debugging.

14. Run the package from the command line using Dtexec with the following steps:

    a. Open a command prompt by pressing WINDOWS+R. Then, type **cmd**.

    b. At the command prompt, enter the following command:

    ```
    Dtexec /sql ssisexport /decrypt
    ```

    c. After a moment, you will be prompted to enter a password. Enter **P@ssw0rd**.

    The package will then run successfully.

15. Leave the instance of BIDS open for the next exercise where a deployment utility will be created for this package.

Deploying Packages

We've created a package, but what if we want to run it on another SQL Server? We certainly don't want to have to reconfigure everything from scratch. Instead, we can create a deployment utility and use it to deploy the package on the other server.

The deployment utility is run on the same server where SSIS is installed and the package was created. This creates a deployment package that includes the SSIS package and a manifest file.

Often, when we deploy or install something, we have a setup file. For SSIS packages, the file that does the work is the manifest file. The manifest file lists the packages, the package configurations, and any miscellaneous files in the project. Once the SSIS packages and manifest files are copied to a destination server, the installation is started by double-clicking the manifest file.

 NOTE You don't need two SQL Servers to create and deploy an SSIS package in the following exercise. It's possible to deploy SSIS packages from one instance to another. And, even if you only have one SQL Server instance available, you can still create the deployment utility and install it on the same server.

In the following exercise, we create a deployment utility for our package and deploy it.

Exercise 15.6: Create a Deployment Utility

1. Return to BIDS and the solution that you have open from the previous exercise.

2. Right-click the Chapter15 solution and select Properties. Select the Deployment Utility in the Configuration Properties.

3. Ensure the AllowConfigurationChanges property is set to True. Change the CreateDeploymentUtility to True. Notice the path is set to bin*Deployment*. Your display should look similar to Figure 15-24. Click OK.

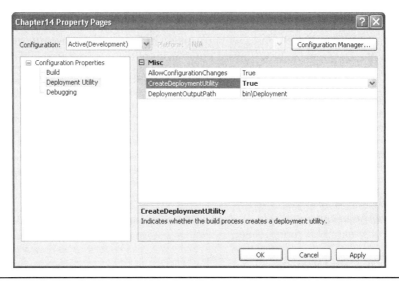

Figure 15-24   Changing the solution property page to allow deployment

4. In Solution Explorer, right click the project and select Build. After a moment, the status bar at the bottom left should indicate the build succeeded.

5. Launch Windows Explorer and browse to the C:\\MCITPSuccess\\Chapter15\\ Chapter15\\bin\\Deployment directory. You should see two files. One file is the package with the .dtsx extension, while the other file is named Chapter15.SSISDeploymentManifest.

NOTE   If you have another server, you can run the following steps on the other server. Otherwise, you will be repeating the same steps on the same server where you created the package.

6. Copy the files to a USB or floppy drive.

7. Log onto another SQL Server, and launch Windows Explorer. Make a directory named **SQL**, and then copy the two files into the SQL directory.

8. Double-click the manifest file (Chapter15.SSISDeploymentManifest). This will start the installation of the package.

9. After a moment, the SSIS Package Installation Wizard will launch. Click Next.

10. On the Deploy SSIS Packages page, select SQL Server Deployment to install this package onto this server's msdb database. Click Next.

11. On the Specify Target SQL Server page, accept the defaults and click Next. If we were deploying this to a separate instance, we could choose the different instance here.

12. On the Encrypted Packages page, select your package and enter the password of **P@ssw0rd**. Click Next.

13. On the Select Installation Folder page, accept the default and click Next.

14. On the Confirm Installation page, click Next.

15. On the Finish The Package Installation Wizard page, click Finish.

16. Use Dtexec to verify the package has been installed. Enter the following command at a command prompt on the destination server:

    ```
    Dtexec /sql ssisexport /decrypt
    ```

17. Enter the password of **P@ssw0rd** when prompted.

Optimizing an SSIS Solution

An important step in finalizing any SSIS solution is to ensure optimal performance of each SSIS package. This includes monitoring SSIS packages, and designing solutions that will scale to meet your requirements.

When testing and monitoring any SSIS solution, you should test on a system that at least mimics the load of your production server. This doesn't mean you test the deployment on a production server, but instead, you create a test-bed server that has similar data and a similar load (even if simulated).

By creating a test-bed server, you ensure you can test the solution, without impacting your live server.

TIP When testing SSIS packages, it's best to test on a realistic environment. However, deploying untested SSIS packages to your production server is not a good idea. Instead, create a test-bed server and add actual data to the test-bed to test your packages. Using actual data (instead of just sample data) will provide more realistic measurements.

Monitoring SSIS in System Monitor

SSIS can be monitored using a familiar tool that we covered in Chapter 13—Performance or System Monitor. When Integration Services is installed, a set of performance counters is also installed that can be used to monitor the performance of the data flow engine.

The two groups of counters that are installed with SSIS are:

- Pipeline counters
- Service counters

Pipeline Counters   The SQL Server:SSIS Pipeline object has the majority of counters available for measuring SSIS. These counters can be used to measure the performance of the data flow engine.

Table 15-1 lists the pipeline counters associated with the SSIS data flow engine. Many of these counters are related to buffers. If you suspect SSIS is performing slowly due to not enough memory, these counters can usually prove or disprove your suspicions.

Counter	Description
BLOB bytes read	Number of bytes of binary large object (BLOB) read.
BLOB bytes written	Number of bytes of BLOB data written.
BLOB files in use	Number of BLOB files being used for spooling.
Buffer memory	Amount of memory buffers in use. Compare to the amount of physical memory to identify excessive paging.
Buffers in use	Number of buffer objects currently being used.
Buffers spooled	Number of buffers written to disk.
Flat buffer memory	Total amount of memory used by flat buffers (large blocks of memory for data that is accessed byte by byte).
Flat buffers in use	Number of flat buffers being used.
Private buffer memory	Total amount of memory in use by all private buffers (buffers used for temporary work during a transformation).
Private buffers in use	Number of buffers being used for transformations.
Rows read	Number of rows read from a source.
Rows written	Number of rows offered to a destination. Does not reflect rows written to the destination data store.

Table 15-1   Pipeline Counters to Measure SSIS in System Monitor

If the performance of an SSIS package is slow, use System Monitor to measure the core four resources of the server (memory, processor, disk, and NIC) first, and then use the pipeline counters for specific information on SSIS.

Service Counter   There is only one counter in the SQL Server:SSIS Service performance object. This is the SSIS Package Instance, and it only reports the number of package instances currently running.

SSIS Logs

In addition to using System Monitor for monitoring packages, you can use SSIS logs. SSIS packages include LogProvider objects that can create log information. Most SSIS objects support logging and have a Logging Mode property. After changing this to Enabled (as shown in Figure 15-25), you can then specify the LogProvider object to use.

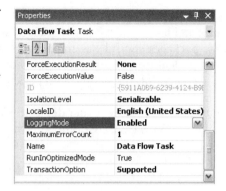

Figure 15-25
Setting the
Logging Mode to
Enabled

Log Providers can be added by selecting SSIS | Logging…. The dialog box shown in
Figure 15-26 will appear. The following LogProvider objects are available:

- **SQL Server Profiler** This LogProvider object creates a SQL Trace (with .trc
  extension) that can be viewed in SQL Server Profiler.

- **SQL Server** Writes event log entries to the sysdtslog90 table.

- **Text File** Writes events into an ASCII text file in a comma-separated value
  (CSV) format.

- **Windows Event Log** Writes events to the Application Log.

- **XML File** Writes events to an XML formatted file.

Figure 15-26
Picking a Logging
Provider

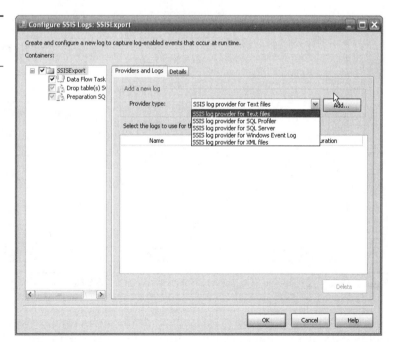

Scheduling SSIS Packages

Once you've completed testing of the SSIS packages, when should you run them? Ideally, running your packages should not impact the operation of your database. Understanding this, the ideal time to run packages is during off-peak hours. To do this, you can use SQL Server Agent to schedule SSIS packages to run exactly when you need them to run.

We covered SQL Server Agent in greater depth in Chapter 13, but the basic steps to create a job to run an SSIS package are outlined next:

- Create a SQL Server Agent job
- Add a job step to the SQL Server Agent job
- Add a Job Schedule for the SQL Server Agent job

Figure 15-27 shows the selections for a new SQL Server Agent job step. Notice that we can select the type of SQL Server Integration Services Package.

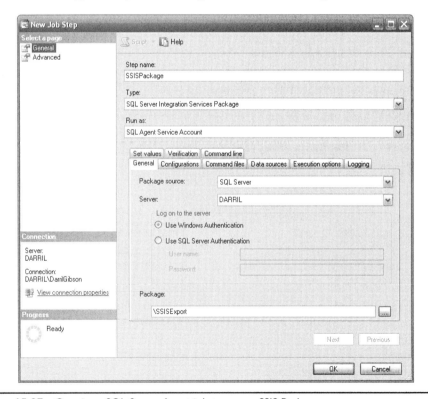

Figure 15-27　Creating a SQL Server Agent job to run an SSIS Package

Once a job step is created, we can schedule the job to run by creating a Job Schedule within the SQL Server Agent job. We can see this in Figure 15-28.

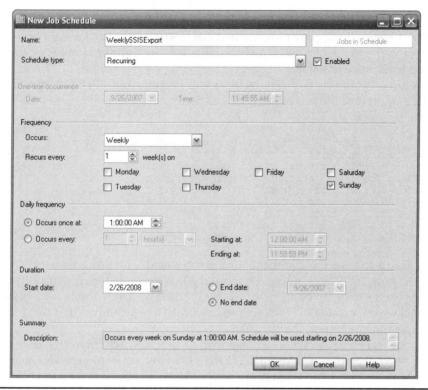

Figure 15-28   Creating a Job Schedule for a SQL Server Agent

EXAM TIP   To schedule SSIS packages, use SQL Server Agent. Some packages can be resource-intensive, so scheduling them outside of normal working hours can ensure they don't negatively impact the performance of the online database.

Bulk Imports and Exports

Frequently, we need to import a lot of data into a database quickly. It's important for a DBA to know what is available to do this and what the basics are of each method. When the time comes to bulk import a large amount of data, you'll know which tools to choose from.

SQL Server 2005 supports several bulk-import methods. These include:

- The bcp Utility
- SQL Server Integration Services (SSIS)
- BULK INSERT
- INSERT … SELECT * FROM OPERNROWSET

The bcp Utility

The bcp utility is a bulk-copy program that can be used to bulk copy data from, or to, a file in a user-specified format. The bcp utility has been around for a long time, but don't underestimate its value.

For advanced imports and exports, SSIS will be your tool of choice, but for basic imports and exports, the bcp utility is easy to use.

The basic syntax is:

```
bcp {[[database_name.][owner].]{table_name | view_name} | "query"}
    {in | out | queryout | format} data_file
    [-mmax_errors] [-fformat_file] [-x] [-eerr_file]
    [-Ffirst_row] [-Llast_row] [-bbatch_size]
    [-n] [-c] [-w] [-N] [-V (60 | 65 | 70 | 80)] [-6]
    [-q] [-C { ACP | OEM | RAW | code_page } ] [-tfield_term]
    [-rrow_term] [-iinput_file] [-ooutput_file] [-apacket_size]
    [-Sserver_name[\instance_name]] [-Ulogin_id] [-Ppassword]
    [-T] [-v] [-R] [-k] [-E] [-h"hint [,...n]"]
```

Let's take a look at the arguments in the command. The first argument is a table, VIEW, or an actual T-SQL query. Tables and VIEWs are identified with a three-part name. A T-SQL query can be specified when exporting data. Just about any T-SQL statement that we can execute in SSMS we can execute in a bcp command. If using a query, the *queryout* argument must be specified.

The next argument can be *in*, *out*, *queryout*, or *format*. When importing data, we use *in*, and when exporting data we use *out*. Here is where we would specify the *queryout* argument if we were using a T-SQL query. The *format* argument is used to bulk import data selectively to specific columns in a table. The format command can be used to create a format file for a table.

The last argument is the name of the data file. Depending on the previous argument, this data file can be a target or a source.

Next are the switches. Just as with any command-line programs, the bcp utility has many switches that can be used to modify the functionality of the command. Table 15-2 outlines many (though not all) of the switches available. Most are optional. Notice that the case is important: *-t* and *-T* each mean something completely different.

A basic bcp command would look like this:

```
bcp AdventureWorks.Sales.Currency out Currency.dat -T -c
```

With the bcp command, we are first identifying the table or VIEW that is the target with the three-part name. We then specify *out* for an export (though it could also be *in* for an import, or *queryout* for a T-SQL query). We're using two common switches: *-T* indicates we're using a trusted connection, and *-c* indicates the file is using the character data type.

While the example does show the basic syntax, with the number of switches available, bcp isn't always basic.

Switch	Name	Comment
-c	Char	Uses char type for each column separated with tabs.
-t	Field_term	Specifies a field terminator. The default is tab, but it can be changed to anything, such as a comma or a semicolon.
-r	Row_term	Specifies a different row terminator instead of newline \n.
-S	Server_name\instance	Can specify the server name and instance used for a connection.
-U	LoginID	Specifies the login ID to use to connect to SQL Server.
-P	Password	The password for login.
-T	Trusted connection	Uses the user account that is currently logged on. This user account needs a login in SQL. If -T is not used, -U and -P must be used.
-f	format_file	Specifies the full path of the format file.
-x	XML format	Used with a format-file for an XML-based format.
-e	err_file	Specifies the use of an error file and path.

Table 15-2   Some bcp Switches

Field Terminator

A feature that many DBAs find handy is the ability to specify different field terminators. While it's common to separate fields with commas or tabs, using the -t (notice that's a lowercase *t*, not uppercase *T*) switch, we can specify any field terminator we desire. The following exercise uses different field terminators.

EXAM TIP   The -t switch in the bcp utility allows a field terminator to be specified. While a comma is most common (such as in a comma separated value file), the field terminator can be any readable character.

Imagine a database user has a need for a text file holding products we sell. This information is in the Production.Product table. In the following exercise, we'll use the bcp command to export this data to a text file.

Exercise 15.7: Export Data with bcp

See a demonstration of importing and exporting data with bcp in video 15-7.

1. Launch a command line.
2. Enter the following command at the command line to create the products.txt file and populate it with the contents of the Production.Product table:

   ```
   Bcp AdventureWorks.Production.Product out products.txt -T -c
   ```
3. To view the table contents, enter:

   ```
   Notepad products.txt
   ```

The command-line window should look similar to Figure 15-29.

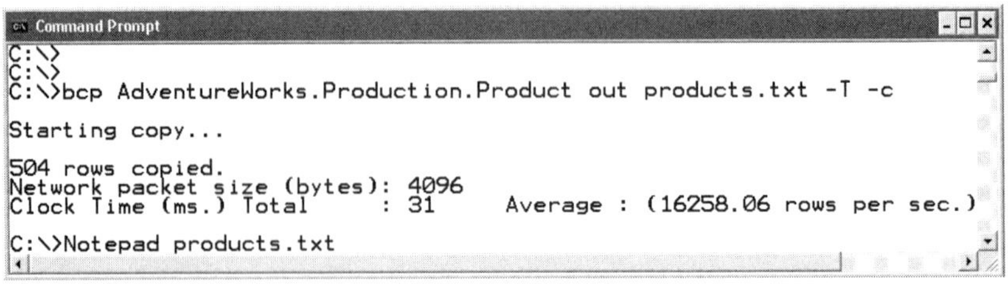

Figure 15-29 Using the command line to access bcp

4. Close Notepad. Instead of separating the columns with the default of tab, use the *-t* switch to change the delimiter to a semicolon:

```
Bcp AdventureWorks.Production.Product out products.txt -T -c -t;
```

5. To view the table contents, enter:

```
Notepad products.txt
```

You can see that instead of columns being separated by tabs, now they are separated by semicolons. Close Notepad.

6. You have been tasked with providing an e-mail listing of people in the Person. Contact table. However, only specific columns are required. Use the following command with the queryout command to create the e-mail list:

```
bcp "SELECT Title, FirstName, LastName, EmailAddress FROM
   AdventureWorks.Person.Contact" queryout emaillist.txt -T -c
```

7. View the e-mail list with the following command:

```
Notepad emaillist.txt
```

Close Notepad.

8. Change the delimiter to a comma in the output with the following command:

```
bcp "SELECT Title, FirstName, LastName, EmailAddress FROM
   AdventureWorks.Person.Contact" queryout emaillist.txt -T -c -t,
```

9. View the output in Notepad, and then close it when you're done.

```
Notepad emaillist.txt
```

10. If the user needs the e-mail list in a specific order, perhaps ordered by last name, we can slightly modify the query. Use this query to modify the output:

```
bcp "SELECT Title, FirstName, LastName, EmailAddress FROM
   AdventureWorks.Person.Contact ORDER BY LastName"
   queryout emaillist.txt -T -c -t,
```

11. View the output in Notepad, and close it when you're done:

```
Notepad emaillist.txt
```

In the following exercise, we'll create a table in the database and then use bcp to import data from a text file into the table.

NOTE This exercise assumes that the previous exercise has been done and that an e-mail list exists in the emaillist.txt file.

Exercise 15.8: Import Data with bcp

1. Open a new query window within SSMS.

2. Create a database named bcpImport with the following command:
   ```
   USE Master;
   GO
   CREATE Database bcpImport
   ```

3. Use the following script to create a table named emailList within the database:
   ```
   USE bcpImport;
   GO
   CREATE TABLE dbo.emailList
   (
           Title nvarchar(6) NULL,
           FirstName nvarchar(50)  NULL,
           LastName nvarchar(50)  NULL,
           email nvarchar(50)  NULL,
   );
   ```

4. With the table created, we can now use the bcp utility to import the data. Launch a command line and enter the following command:
   ```
   Bcp bcpImport.dbo.emailList in emaillist.txt -T -c -t,
   ```

   Note that since we created the emaillist.txt file with a comma as the delimiter, we must specify the comma as the delimiter when importing the file. The output should look similar to Figure 15-30.

```
Command Prompt                                                          _ □ x
1000 rows sent to SQL Server.  Total sent:  15000
1000 rows sent to SQL Server.  Total sent:  16000
1000 rows sent to SQL Server.  Total sent:  17000
1000 rows sent to SQL Server.  Total sent:  18000
1000 rows sent to SQL Server.  Total sent:  19000

19977 rows copied.
Network packet size (bytes): 4096
Clock Time (ms.) Total     : 28062  Average : (711.89 rows per sec.)

C:\>bcp bcpImport.dbo.emailList in emailList.txt -T -c -t,_
```

Figure 15-30 bcp output when importing data to SQL Server

5. Switch back to the query window in SSMS and enter the following command:
   ```
   USE bcpImport;
   GO
   SELECT * FROM emailList
   ```

You can see that over 19,000 rows have been added to the emailList table quicker than you can say "I'm going to be an MCITP."

BULK INSERT Statement

The BULK INSERT statement is similar to the bcp utility except that it's a T-SQL statement. In other words, we execute the bcp utility from the command line, but would execute the BULK INSERT statement in a query window in SSMS or from a program that executes T-SQL statements.

 TIP Since bcp works from the command line, it can be created as a batch file (.bat) and then scheduled to run when desired. However, it's possible you may need the same functionality of bcp, but from within a T-SQL script. The BULK INSERT statement can provide the same functionality as a bcp command, but be embedded within a T-SQL script or even a stored procedure.

The basic syntax of the BULK INSERT is:

```
BULK INSERT object with three part name
 FROM 'file with path'
```

As a simple example, let's say we created a new table in the bcpImport database we created earlier:

```
CREATE TABLE dbo.BulkInsert
(
     Title nvarchar(6) NULL,
     FirstName nvarchar(50)  NULL,
     LastName nvarchar(50)  NULL,
     email nvarchar(50)  NULL,
);
```

Now, instead of importing the emaillist.txt into the table with bcp, we'll use the BULK INSERT statement:

```
BULK INSERT bcpImport.dbo.BulkInsert
 FROM 'c:\emaillist.txt'
   WITH
     ( FIELDTERMINATOR = ',',
       ROWTERMINATOR = '\n' )
```

The primary benefit of the BULK INSERT task is that it can be run within a script. We don't have to access the command-line interface.

OPENROWSET and OPENDATASOURCE

The OPENROWSET and OPENDATASOURCE commands can be used to connect to remote data sources. They both depend on the existence of OLE DB providers that provide the framework for the connection.

Both OPENROWSET and OPENDATASOURCE appear as functions (and are referred to as functions), though internally they work as macros. The limitation is that we can't pass T-SQL variables into them as we can with regular functions.

These commands would be used for connections that occur infrequently. If the queries needed to be executed more than a few times (and there aren't any specific restrictions against doing so), we would typically create a linked server, as described in Chapter 11.

For both to work, we would need to enable the feature using the SQL Server 2005 Surface Area Configuration tool, Surface Area Configuration for Features. We can see it enabled in Figure 15-31.

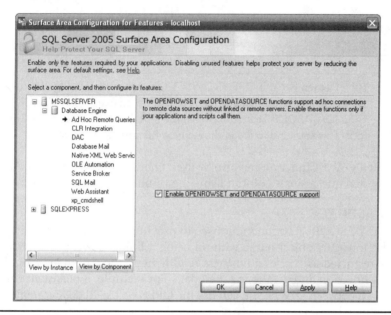

Figure 15-31   Enabling OPENROWSET and OPENDATASOURCE

OPENROWSET

The OPENROWSET function can be used to connect to non-Microsoft SQL Server remote data sources and to access data from those data sources. It uses an OLE DB provider. As long as we have a provider for the remote database (and we have the permissions), we can connect and access the data.

As a function, OPENROWSET works like other functions. Since the result of the function is in a table format, we can include the OPENROWSET function in statements that expect a table, such as within VIEWs or SELECT statements.

The basic syntax of the OPENROWSET function is:

```
OPENROWSET
( { 'provider_name' , { 'datasource' ; 'user_id' ; 'password'
  | 'provider_string' }
    , {   [ catalog. ] [ schema. ] object
    | 'query'
  }
} )
```

OLE DB providers are available for many Microsoft products (such as other SQL Servers or Access databases) and many non-Microsoft products (such as Oracle or IBM's DB2).

Let's say we had an Access database named Sales that had a Customers table we wanted to query. The OLE DB provider for a Microsoft Access database is 'Microsoft.Jet .OLEDB.4.0'. The following query could be executed against SQL Server. As long as the path of the Sales.mdb database was correct, we'd get our result set.

```
SELECT *
    FROM OPENROWSET('Microsoft.Jet.OLEDB.4.0',
        'C:\data\Sales.mdb';
        'admin';'',Customers)
```

 TIP Remember, the OPENROWSET function is disabled by default. In order for this statement to run, you need to enable OPENROWSET and OPENDATASOURCE statements in the SQL Server Surface Area Configuration tool. This setting is found in the Ad Hoc Remote Queries section.

The OPENROWSET function can also be used to bulk import XML data. An XML file can be imported into a single column using the varbinary(max) data type.

OPENDATASOURCE

The OPENDATASOURCE command is used to provide ad hoc connection information as part of a four-part object name without using a linked server name. When linked servers are restricted as part of a business requirement, the command can be used to make the connection and get the required data. For example, if persistent connections aren't allowed between servers, you can use the OPENDATASOURCE statement instead of creating linked servers.

Remember the four-part name is *server.database.schema.object*. If we had created a linked server, we could include the four-part name within our query. However, without a linked server defined, we substitute the server portion of the four-part name with the OPENDATASOURCE function.

The basic syntax is:

```
OPENDATASOURCE ( provider_name, init_string )
```

Different OLE DB providers have different string requirements.

Let's take a look at the function in the context of a SELECT statement. The following statement will allow us to connect to a named instance (MyNamedInstance) on a remote SQL Server named MCTIP1 using the SQL provider ('SQLNCLI'):

```
SELECT * FROM
    OPENDATASOURCE('SQLNCLI',
      'Data Source=MCITP1\MyNamedInstance;Integrated Security=SSPI')
      .AdventureWorks.Person.Contact
```

NOTE *SSPI* stands for "Security Support Provider Interface." It's used for obtaining integrated security services for authentication, message integrity, and privacy for distributed applications.

After the OPENDATASOURCE statement closes, we then have the other three remaining parts of the four-part name.

The Import/Export Wizard

While we're talking about imports and exports, we can't forget the easiest way to get copies of data from one database to another. This was previously done as part of Data Transformation Services (DTS) in previous versions of SQL Server.

SQL Server 2005 has replaced DTS with the SQL Server 2005 Integration Services (SSIS), and the Import/Export Wizard is part of SSIS. Exercise 15.4 demonstrated an example of how to use this wizard.

The primary purpose of the wizard is to copy data from a source to a destination. The source and destination data sources can be:

- Any data source with an OLE DB driver (such as Oracle, Outlook, and Analysis Services)

- Any data source with a .NET provider driver (such as Oracle, ODBC, and SQL Server)

- Microsoft SQL Server

- Microsoft Project

- Microsoft Excel

- Microsoft Access

- Flat file (text file)

Chapter Review

In this chapter, we covered some basics on transferring data using Replication, SQL Server Integration Services (SSIS) packages, and bulk import and export tools.

Replication is patterned after a publisher metaphor with Publishers, Distributors, and Subscribers. Subscriptions are composed of articles that can be the entire database, or a portion of the entire database. The three primary types of replication are transactional (used for real-time replication), merge (used when multiple subscribers are also publishers and all changes need to be merged into a common database), and snapshot (used for scheduled replication). While replication has been available in previous editions of SQL, Replication Monitor has been completely redesigned in SQL Server 2005 and can be used to measure and monitor replication. A new feature is the use of Tracer Tokens to measure latency.

SSIS in SQL Server 2005 replaces DTS from SQL Server 2000. It can be used for simple imports and exports or for sophisticated data transformations, including fuzzy lookups. SSIS is accessed via the Business Intelligence Development Studio (BIDS). With BIDS, complex packages can be created using multiple tasks to individually act on the data, and even to loop through tasks if desired. Packages can be protected with encryption either via keys or via passwords. Once created, packages can be deployed by creating deployment packages that can be run on target servers. To launch a deployment package, the manifest file is executed.

With bulk imports and exports, several methods are available for use. We covered the bcp utility, which is like an old friend to many DBAs. We also learned how to use the OPENROWSET and OPENDATASOURCE functions when linked servers aren't allowed or required. Lastly, we saw how easy imports and exports are when using the SSIS Import/Export wizard.

Additional Study

Self-Study Exercises

- Implement a transactional replication.
- Launch Replication Monitor and observe the performance of your replication.
- Find the tracer tokens tab and insert a tracer token.
- Create a package with SSIS.
- Create a deployment package and deploy it.
- Use bcp to export selected columns from AdventureWorks.person.contact to create a phone listing in a text file. Use the semicolon as a separator, and order the results by last name.

BOL Topics

- SQL Server Replication
- Snapshot Replication Overview
- Merge Replication Overview
- Transactional Replication Overview
- Integration Services Tasks
- Setting the Protection Level of Packages
- The Dtexec Utility
- The bcp Utility
- Overview of Bulk Import and Bulk Export
- Introducing bcp, BULK INSERT, and OPENROWSET(BULK)
- OPENDATASOURCE (Transact-SQL)

Summary of What You Need to Know

70-431

When preparing for the 70-431 exam, you should have a basic understanding of the following topics:

- Replication
- Replication Monitor (including the new feature of Tracer Tokens)
- Bulk Import and Export methods (including the bcp utility)

70-441

When preparing for the 70-441 exam, you should have a solid understanding of the Replication and SSIS topics presented in this chapter.

70-442

When preparing for the 70-442 exam, you should know the Replication topics presented in this chapter.

Questions

70-431

1. You have configured replication between two SQL Server 2005 servers named MCITP1 and MCITP2 with similar hardware. MCITP1 holds the source database named Hurricane, while MCITP2 holds the replicated database named HurricaneRepl. While the performance of Hurricane is acceptable, users find that running similar queries against HurricaneRepl is unacceptably slow. What's a likely reason?

   A. All the properties are not being replicated.

   B. All the indexes are not being replicated.

   C. All the partitioning schemes are not being replicated.

   D. This is normal operation for a replicated database.

2. You manage two SQL Servers that have replication configured between them. MCITP1 is the Publisher and Distributor, while MCITP2 is the Subscriber. Only one publication (SalesData) is configured. You want to measure latency between MCITP1 and MCITP2. What tool could you use?

   A. Use the Subscription Watch List in Replication Monitor.

   B. Use Tracer Tokens in Replication Monitor.

   C. Use the Subscription Watch List in System Monitor.

   D. Use Tracer Tokens in System Monitor.

3. You are tasked with importing data into a SQL Server 2005 database. The data is received as a text file containing temperature readings for recent hurricanes. Columns in the data are separated by an asterisk (*). What should you do to import the files into your database?

    A. Import the data as is, and then use a script to strip out the *.

    B. Use a search and replace feature of a text editor, and change the * to a comma. Use the bcp command to import the modified text file.

    C. Use the bcp command with the default arguments.

    D. Use the bcp command with the * as a field terminator.

70-441

1. Your company hosts a SQL Server 2005 server at the headquarters office in Virginia Beach, VA. The server acts as the back-end for company web sites. Branch offices are located in Brussels and Manila and each of these branch offices hosts their own web site using the headquarters SQL Server 2005 server for the data. All data changes can only be done at the Virginia Beach office. Customers searching the web site using the Brussels or Manila web sites complain that the searches are painfully slow. What can you do to improve the performance of these web sites while ensuring the data is up-to-date? (Choose three. Each answer is part of the solution.)

    A. Create a snapshot replication publication in Virginia Beach.

    B. Create a transactional replication publication in Virginia Beach.

    C. Create a merge replication publication in Virginia Beach.

    D. Create a pull subscription for the offices in Brussels and Manila.

    E. Create a push subscription for the offices in Brussels and Manila.

    F. Configure the Brussels and Manila web sites to use a locally configured SQL Server.

2. You manage a SQL Server 2005 database named StockPortfolio. This database is heavily accessed during normal business hours by customers from a web application. Business analysts also heavily query this database and the combined load is nearing the capacity of the server. Business analysts do not need to be able to see the current week's data, but they do need to be able to see any data that's more than a week old. You are asked to create a solution for the business analysts. What would you suggest?

    A. Create a second database on the server to be used by the business analysts. Create an SSIS package to copy the appropriate data to the second database on a weekly basis.

    B. Create a second database on the server to be used by the business analysts. Use transactional replication to replicate the appropriate data to the second server on a weekly basis.

    C. Create a second server to be used by the business analysts. Use replication to replicate the appropriate data to the second server on a weekly basis.

    D. Create a second server to be used by the business analysts. Use transactional replication to replicate the appropriate data to the second server on a weekly basis.

3. An auto parts dealer currently has three stores, but plans on opening three additional stores in the next year. Each store holds its own database with its own data, but they all share a common data set for lookup tables. They've asked you for the method with the minimum number of steps that could be used to deploy the database to new stores as they are opened. What do you recommend?

    A. Detach the database from one of the live servers, copy it, and attach it to the new server for the new store.

    B. Create an SSIS package to copy the entire database from one of the live servers to the new server for the new store.

    C. Back up the database from one of the live servers and restore it to the new server for the new store.

    D. Use replication to replicate the database definition and all lookup tables from one of the live servers to the new server for the new store.

4. You manage a database that inputs data from external sources. Frequently the received data isn't standardized (for example, true is identified as True, T, t, and 1). What can you use to standardize data before it's put into your database?

    A. SSRS

    B. SSMS

    C. SSIS

    D. A CLR-stored procedure

5. You've created an SSIS package that will be used to import large amounts of stock analysis data into your StockPortfolio database. You want to test the package to ensure it doesn't affect your production database. What would you do?

    A. Create a test bed and add sample data. Run the package on this test bed.

    B. Create a test bed and add actual data. Run the package on this test bed.

    C. Run the packages only after doing a full backup of the StockPortfolio database.

    D. Run the packages on the StockPortfolio database using transactions that can be rolled back.

6. You've created an SSIS package that will be used to import large amounts of stock analysis data into your StockPortfolio database. You want to ensure that when this package is run, it has the least impact on the performance of

the database and the associated application for users. Which of the following actions would you take?

A. Schedule packages to run during off-peak hours using SQL Server Agent.

B. Schedule packages to run during off-peak hours using the schedule properties of the SSIS package.

C. Use Task Manager and set the priority of the SQL Server service to Low.

D. Use Task Manager and set the priority of the SQL Server Agent service to Low.

7. You manage a StockPortfolio database that will be migrated from SQL Server 2000 to SQL Server 2005. The database copies data from a legacy database that is in a difficult-to-use format. Data is copied monthly into an existing table within the StockPortfolio database. What should you use to copy this data after the migration?

A. Create a DTS package and use it to import the data after the upgrade.

B. Create a SQL Server Integration Services (SSIS) package to import the data.

C. Use bcp to import the data.

D. Use transactional replication.

70-442

1. You are tasked with designing a method to improve performance of reports run against the StockPortfolio database. The reports often take 20 or more minutes to run, and they bog down the Sales database. Data must be no more than ten minutes old, and the report processing should be offloaded. What would you recommend?

A. Use transactional replication.

B. Use database mirroring.

C. Use database snapshots.

D. Use log shipping.

2. The Accounts Payable (AP) and Accounts Receivable (AR) departments are located in a separate building that is connected via a slower WAN connection. Both departments need read access to elements of the sales database. The AP department needs their data refreshed on a monthly basis, but the AR department must have the most current information available to them. You are tasked with designing solutions for each department. Which of the following should you recommend?

A. Database mirroring for the AP department, and snapshot replication for the AR department

B. Merge replication for the AP department, and transactional replication for the AR department

C. Transactional replication for the AP department, and snapshot replication for the AR department

D. Snapshot replication for the AP department, and transactional replication for the AR department

Answers

70-431

1. **B.** Since the hardware is similar on both, the problem must be elsewhere. Indexes are created to improve the performance of queries against tables or VIEWs. If the indexes aren't included in the publication, then the queries on the Subscribers will run more slowly.

2. **B.** Tracer Tokens in Replication Monitor are new to SQL Server 2005 and can be used to measure latency between a Distributor and Subscriber. They are only available for Transactional Replication. A Subscription Watch List will not measure latency. While System Monitor has objects and counters for replication, there aren't any counters that will measure the latency between the Distributor and Subscriber.

3. **D.** The -t switch in the bcp utility allows a field terminator to be specified. While a comma is common, the field terminator can be any readable character including and asterisk (*).

70-441

1. **B, E, F.** By configuring a local SQL Server in the branch offices, the web site performance will be greatly improved. Transactional replication is the best choice for replication to make the data to the branch office servers up-to-date. Since the data must be up-to-date, snapshot replication isn't viable. Since all changes occur at one location, merge replication isn't needed. Push replication is used with transactional replication.

2. **C.** Since the server is nearing capacity, we need to offload processing to a different server (not just a second database on the same server). Snapshot replication will be the best choice (even though it wasn't listed as a specific answer) since the data can be a week out-of-date. Transactional replication is not appropriate since this will unnecessarily bog down the server while doing constant updates to the second database.

3. **D.** Since new stores will use their own data (except for lookup tables), we only want to replicate the database definitions for most tables, and the accompanying data for lookup tables. This can be done with replication by using filters on the tables where we don't want the data. All the other given solutions result in a full copy of the database and all the data to the new store's server.

4. **C.** SQL Server Integration Services (SSIS) is the best choice to cleanse and standardize data. Neither SQL Server Reporting Services (SSRS) nor SQL

Server Management Studio (SSMS) have any automated data transformation capabilities. While a CLR-integrated stored procedure could be created to transform data, it would be much more difficult than creating an SSIS package.

5. **B.** Creating a test bed with actual data and running your packages here is the best choice for testing your SSIS packages. Running the package against sample data won't provide a realistic test. Testing packages on the production database to ensure the packages don't impact the production database is not a sound testing practice.

6. **A.** SSIS packages can be scheduled to run at specific times by creating a SQL Server Agent job and then scheduling the job. By running the job during off-peak hours, you will have the least impact on users. SSIS packages do not have schedule properties. By changing the priority of the SQL Server service to Low, you cause SQL Server to run slower than any other applications or services. By changing the priority of the SQL Server Agent service to Low, you cause all of the SQL Server Agent jobs to run slower than any other applications or services, not just the SSIS package.

7. **B.** SSIS packages can be used to extract, transform, and load data from one data source to another. DTS packages were used in SQL Server 2000 and more than likely one exists to handle this job now. While DTS packages can be executed within an SSIS package, it wouldn't be the best choice. The bcp utility is useful for simple import and exports, but the scenario is beyond "simple." Transactional replication would be used to replicate similar database data on a real-time basis. Since the databases are not similar and the import is only needed on a monthly basis, transactional replication wouldn't work.

70-442

1. **A.** Using transactional replication, the data can be replicated to a second server in near real time. Reports can then be run on the second server. A database mirror can't be queried (unless it is combined with a database snapshot). A database snapshot can be queried, but it still queries the primary data, so it doesn't provide gains in this example. Log shipping can be used to reduce the load on the primary server by using a secondary server for read-only query processing, but every time the shipped log is restored, all users must be disconnected—thus, a report could never be done since log shipping must occur at least every 10 minutes and reports take 20 minutes to run.

2. **D.** Since the AP department only needs data once a month, snapshot replication is the best choice. The AR department needs data updated almost continuously so transactional replication is the best choice for them. Database mirroring does not allow users to query the data unless a database snapshot is also configured. Since a database snapshot is not mentioned, a database mirror is not appropriate. Merge replication is only called for if the Subscribers will be updating the data, but since the departments only need read access, merge replication is not needed.

About the CD

The CD-ROM included with this book comes complete with MasterExam, CertCam video clips, and the electronic version of the book. The software is easy to install on any Windows 98/NT/2000/XP/Vista computer and must be installed to access the MasterExam and MasterSim features. You may, however, browse the electronic book and CertCams directly from the CD without installation. To register for the second bonus MasterExam, simply click the Online Training link on the Main Page and follow the directions to the free online registration. The author has also made some of the scripts from the book available on the CD-ROM for your use.

System Requirements

Software requires Windows 98 or higher, Internet Explorer 5.0 or above, and 20MB of hard disk space for full installation. The electronic book requires Adobe Acrobat Reader.

Installing and Running MasterExam

If your computer CD-ROM drive is configured to auto run, the CD-ROM will automatically start up upon inserting the disk. From the opening screen you may install MasterExam by pressing the MasterExam button. This will begin the installation process and create a program group named LearnKey. To run MasterExam use Start | Programs | LearnKey. If the auto run feature did not launch your CD, browse to the CD and click on the LaunchTraining.exe icon.

About MasterExam

MasterExam provides you with a simulation of the actual exam. The number of questions, the type of questions, and the time allowed are intended to be an accurate representation of the exam environment. You have the option to take an open book exam, including hints, references, and answers; a closed book exam; or the timed MasterExam simulation.

When you launch MasterExam, a digital clock display will appear in the upper left-hand corner of your screen. The clock will continue to count down to zero unless you choose to end the exam before the time expires.

70-441 and 70-442 MasterExam

The MasterExam featured with this book includes case-study based exam formats intended to represent Microsoft's format for the 70-441 and 70-442 exams. Each case study presents a different scenario. You must click the Case Study button at the bottom of the MasterExam interface to view the scenario before you answer the exam questions related to that scenario. Each case study may have a variety of tabs. Each tab displays particular information related to that scenario. Use the down arrow key to scroll through the different tabs of each scenario.

MasterExam will not alert you when you have reached the end of each case study section, so be sure to click the Case Study button again when you complete each scenario so you can move on to the next set of exam questions and the next scenario.

Your actual exam may contain other exam question types not featured in the MasterExam. Be sure to visit the Microsoft Learning web site for the most up-to-date information available on the different types of questions you may see on the real exam.

Electronic Book

The entire contents of the Exam Guide are provided in PDF. Adobe's Acrobat Reader has been included on the CD.

CertCam

CertCam .avi clips provide detailed examples of key certification objectives. These video clips walk you step-by-step through various system configurations. You can access the clips directly from the CertCam table of contents by pressing the CertCam button on the Main Page.

The CertCam .avi clips are recorded and produced using TechSmith's Camtasia Producer. Since .avi clips can be very large, ExamSim uses TechSmith's special AVI Codec to compress the clips. The file named tsccvid.dll is copied to your Windows\System folder during the first auto run. If the .avi clip runs with audio but no video, you may need to re-install the file from the CD-ROM. Browse to the Programs\CertCams folder and run TSCC.

Some of the .avi clips available with this book have been posted for download from the LearnKey Online Learning site and can be downloaded by following the same directions used to download the bonus MasterExams (see the previous section "About MasterExam").

Help

A help file is provided through the Help button on the main page in the lower left-hand corner. An individual help feature is also available through MasterExam.

Removing Installation(s)

MasterExam is installed to your hard drive. For *best* results, remove the program by choosing Start | Programs | LearnKey | Uninstall.

Technical Support

For questions regarding the content of the electronic book, MasterExam, or CertCams, please visit www.osborne.com or email customer.service@mcgraw-hill.com. For customers outside the 50 United States, email international_cs@mcgraw-hill.com.

LearnKey Technical Support

For technical problems with the software (installation, operation, removing installations), and for questions regarding downloads, please visit www.learnkey.com or email techsupport@learnkey.com.

Exam 70-431: What You Need to Know to Pass

It's got to be the going, not the getting there that's good.

—Harry Chapin

70-431 TS: Microsoft SQL Server 2005— Implementation and Maintenance

Introduction

While the 70-431 exam covers a wide range of topics, many of the questions center on surface-type subjects. In other words, they require you to know the basics of a topic instead of in-depth details. There are exceptions of course, but this is generally the case.

One of the biggest exceptions for a database developer may be mastering some of the database administrator tasks, such as high availability, backups, security, and some of the tools. Knowing this, you can adjust your study time appropriately and spend more time on Chapters 8, 10, 11, and 13.

It's expected that you'll probably do the 70-431 test first since it's the easiest of the three. Plus, there's a lot to be said for the psychological advantage of being able to pass one test and earn the Microsoft Certified Technology Specialist (MCTS) certification as a first step in getting your MCITP certification. However, if you choose to study and take the other two tests first, you probably won't have much more to study to pass this one.

Picking a Date

I suggest you pick a date 60 to 90 days from now as your target to take the 70-431 exam. You may be ready sooner and take the exam early, or life events may intrude and you may not be ready in time. But pick a date. Marking the calendar this way can be a great motivator in helping you get ready.

Consider actually registering for the test. Being registered adds that extra layer of commitment. You can always reschedule the test later if needed.

When teaching some certification courses in the college classroom, I've had students register for a test on the first night of a class. They pick a date about a week after the course ends, and we walk down to the test center en masse allowing everyone to register. The percentage of students taking and passing these tests has been over 70 percent.

In contrast, I've taught the same course to other students and provided encouragement to take and pass the test, but didn't have them register on the first night of class. Following up three months later (at the end of a six-month track), I've found that only 10 to 20 percent of the students had taken and passed the test.

This concept isn't unique to test taking. For any goal you are pursuing, you are much more likely to achieve it by writing it down. Goals not written down become forgotten daydreams.

So, pick a date to take the 70-431 exam and write it down here: _____.

What You Can Expect

You can expect primarily multiple-choice questions on the 70-431 exam. Also, a mix of simulation exams (where you need to accomplish a task) will likely appear, along with one or two "point-and-click" or "drag-and-drop" questions, which are really just testing whether you're familiar with the interfaces.

For the multiple-choice questions, pay attention to the wording. Sometimes you're required to pick more than one answer, as in cases where it tells you to "Select two" or "Select all that apply."

Simulation exam questions are a great new addition to certification exams. They prevent someone from just memorizing test questions and answers. One good thing about simulations from a test-taker's perspective is that it takes a lot of programming to make the simulation complex. Because of this, expect simulations on the exams to be straightforward, with a limited number of steps.

You can do two things to help you prepare for these simulations: do the exercises in the book, and watch the videos on the CD. These show you how to do certain tasks and allow you to put that knowledge into action.

The 70-431 exam is designed for professionals who are either working as, or pursuing careers as, database administrators or database developers. This is the first test in both the MCITP: Database Administrator and the MCITP Database Developer certifications on SQL Server 2005.

Because of this, the 70-431 exam crosses the three different fields. You will see topics from both of these MCITP certifications, though not to the depth of the full MCITP certification.

For those not working directly with databases as their primary job function, achieving the Microsoft Technical Specialist Certification demonstrates your ability to branch out beyond your core functions. When this is deemed valuable by your employer, it increases your worth to the company.

The number of questions on the test is not published by Microsoft and sometimes changes from one test to the next. A score of 700 is required to pass. You typically have about 90 minutes to complete roughly 50 questions.

Some tests include beta test questions, because the test developers are testing the question before it goes live. Beta test questions don't count for or against you, and you are given extra time to answer them. You could leave even them blank, and it wouldn't impact your score at all. Unfortunately, you never know if a question is live or beta, so you have to answer them all.

What's Expected of You

Someone who has successfully passed this test is expected to be an expert in the following topics:

- Tools usage

- UI navigation

- Wizard usage

- Writing code in different languages (T-SQL, CLR, and other scripting languages)

- Code debugging or syntactic issue resolution

- Troubleshooting

 EXAM TIP As a reminder, test objectives are listed at the beginning of the book with an objectives map showing which chapter contains the appropriate information. However, remember that these objectives might change. The legalese on Microsoft's site says, "This preparation guide is subject to change at any time without prior notice and at Microsoft's sole discretion." Before taking the test, take a look at Microsoft's web site for the current objectives.

Chapters Covering 70-431 Topics

All chapters within this book have something covered by the 70-431 test. The following is a list of the chapters with specific topics you should focus on when studying for the 70-431 test.

Chapter 1: Installing and Configuring SQL Server 2005

Know the entire chapter, paying particular attention to the following topics:

- Installing and configuring SQL Server 2005 instances and databases

- Protocols and their uses

- Ports used by SQL Server 2005

- Tools used to troubleshoot the install or operation of SQL Server, such as SQL Server startup logs and error messages in event logs

- Dedicated Administrator Connection

Chapter 2: SQL Server 2005 Database Basics

Know the entire chapter, paying particular attention to the following topics:

- VIEWs and tables
- Data types
- Nulls and defaults
- Configuring database properties, including log files and data files

Chapter 3: Database Design

Know all the topics, with particular emphasis on:

- CHECK constraints
- Partitioning tables

Chapter 4: Transact-SQL

Know the basics of DML statements and transactions. Advanced query techniques are not required for this exam. The following topics outline what you should know thoroughly:

- Using and interpreting SELECT statements
- Using and interpreting other DML statements
- Using aliases
- Using Group By and Having statements

Understand transactions.

- BEGIN TRANSACTION
- COMMIT TRANSACTION
- ROLLBACK TRANSACTION
- TRY CATCH constructs

Chapter 5: XML

Know the basics of XML, including:

- How to store XML data (which data type to use)
- Use of the For XML statement (including XSINIL parameter)
- XML methods (such as Nodes and Value)

Chapter 6: Advanced Database Objects

Know all topics, with particular emphasis on:

- Triggers (understand DDL, DML, and options such as how to disable a trigger)
- Functions (built-in and user-defined)
- CLR (functions and stored procedure usage)

Chapter 7: Optimizing Databases

Know this entire chapter, focusing especially on the following topics:

- Indexes
- Indexed VIEWs
- Statistics, updating statistics
- Full-text catalogs and full-text indexes
- Database Tuning Advisor

Chapter 8: Database Security

Know the basic principles in the following topics:

- Authentication modes (Windows Authentication, SQL Server, and Windows Authentication)
- Security principals
- Securables
- CLR permissions
- Encryption

Chapter 9: Stored Procedures

Know the following topics from this chapter:

- The basic usage and purpose of stored procedures
- How to create stored procedures, including using parameters, using transactions, and using error-catching techniques
- How permission chaining applies to stored procedures (permissions to underlying tables do NOT need to be granted if the Execute permission is granted on the stored procedure)

Chapter 10: Disaster Recovery

Know this entire chapter, and focus especially on the following topics:

- Recovery models
- Backups and backup devices
- Restore commands
- Steps for restore
- Detach and attach

Chapter 11: Accessing Data

Know the following topics from this chapter:

- Service Broker
- Event notifications
- HTTP endpoints and Web services
- Linked servers

Chapter 12: Support Services

This chapter has no topics relating to the 70-431 exam.

Chapter 13: Maintenance Tools

Know the following topics from this chapter:

- System Monitor
- Performance Logs and Alerts (including creating a baseline)
- SQL Profiler
- SQL Trace

Chapter 14: Locks and Cursors

Know the following topics from this chapter:

- How to monitor and resolve locks and deadlocks
- How to use the sys.dm_exec_requests DMV to troubleshoot locks and deadlocks
- How to use SQL Profiler to capture lock activity

Chapter 15: Transferring Data

Know the following topics from this chapter:

- Replication
- Replication Monitor (including Tracer Tokens)
- Bulk imports and exports (bcp, the SSIS Import/Export Wizard)

Inside the Design Exam

The Design Exam

Microsoft's design exams are a little different from most exams you may have taken. To answer the exam questions, you need to read and understand a lengthy scenario and apply the knowledge from the scenario to the questions. They remind me of language comprehension tests I took in high school.

When approaching a database design exam, think of yourself as a database consultant coming in to help a company solve a problem or implement some type of improvement to their existing environment. You need to interview people to learn what they have, what they need, and what they want. As you talk to everyone, you'll take notes. A case scenario in the database design exam is a compilation of all of your notes put into a professional format.

Now you'll be faced with questions. In a database design exam, you'll have anywhere from 4 to 15 exam questions in each scenario, asking specifics about the design. To answer these questions, you typically have to refer back to the scenario. You can jump back and forth from the scenario to the questions as much as you desire.

However, once you answer all the questions in one scenario and go to the next scenario, you can't go back. Your answers are final.

Occasionally, a design exam will also include a set of multiple-choice questions that are separate from any scenario. The 70-442 exam has separate questions in this format. These work the same as any other multiple-choice exams, except that they are often treated as a scenario. In other words, while working on these questions, you can go back and forth within them, but you can't go to other scenarios. Once you finish these questions and move to another scenario, you can't return to these questions.

Design Exam Success Tips

Design exams need to be approached a little differently to successfully master them. Use the following tips when taking a design exam:

- Read the questions first.
- Skim the scenario after reading the questions.
- Answer one question at a time while looking back at the scenario.
- Look for Microsoft solutions.
- Take your time.

Read the Questions First

Before reading the scenario, read the questions. There are two reasons to do this:

- Occasionally, you can answer an exam question without any knowledge of the scenario.

- By knowing what the questions are, you know what to focus on in the scenario.

For example, you may have a question that ends as:

"What tool would you use to measure the duration of the problem queries?" It really doesn't matter what problem queries are described in the scenario. The ideal tool to measure the duration of queries is SQL Profiler. If SQL Profiler is one of the answers, select it and you're done with this question.

The following is another example that looks like an in-depth question requiring knowledge of the scenario, but is actually asking a simple straightforward question:

1. You review the permissions in the MCITP database and see that there are no permissions granted to the following objects:

    - A table named dbo.Employees.

    - A table named dbo.EmployeeRegions.

    - A VIEW named dbo.EmpByRegion that retrieves data from the preceding two tables.

    - A stored procedure named dbo.GetEmployees that retrieves data from the preceding view.

    You need to allow the Managers database role to retrieve data using the dbo .GetEmployees stored procedure. What should you do? (Choose all that apply.)

    A. Grant the SELECT permission on the dbo.Employees object to the Managers role.

    B. Grant the SELECT permission on the dbo.EmployeeRegions object to the Managers role.

    C. Grant the SELECT permission on the dbo.EmpByRegion object to the Managers role.

    D. Grant the EXECUTE permission on the dbo.GetEmployees object to the Managers role.

This question could be worded more directly as "You've granted a user execute permission on a stored procedure. Do you also need to grant permissions to the underlying objects accessed by that stored procedure?" The answer is no. Don't expect any of the questions to be as straightforward as this yes or no answer, but it does show you how a design question can be worded to test your knowledge.

The questions are intentionally deeper, requiring you to analyze what's being asked and to apply the knowledge you have to the problem. By the way, the answer for the previous question is D.

The second reason to read the questions first is that they give you an idea of what to look for in the scenario. For example, you may have a statement like this:

1. You need to ensure that the XML data is stored according to the technical requirements.

In this case, you know to look for references to storing XML data in the Technical Requirements section of the scenario. When you come to it, pay more attention to the Technical Requirements section to identify what is needed related to storing XML data.

Skim the Scenario after Reading the Questions

Try to understand the big picture. Typically, scenarios have a large number of issues that need resolution in the real world, but that can be ignored to answer the questions. Don't let yourself get bogged down in unnecessary details.

Answer One Question at a Time while Looking Back at the Scenario

This is where you start answering the questions in earnest. The questions should make more sense to you after having read the scenario, but you'll probably need to refer back to the scenario to make sure you understand the details completely.

Look for Microsoft Solutions

If Microsoft spent a lot of time and money developing features that make this product better, you can bet that feature is going to be the correct answer in some questions.

For example, if one of the problems you are faced with is how to transform and cleanse data when transferring it from one data source to another, SQL Server Integration Services (SSIS) should jump to the forefront of your mind. Since DTS is deprecated, it's highly unlikely it will ever be a correct answer, even though it was a great solution for transferring and transforming data in SQL Server 2000.

Some features that Microsoft has touted and that you can bet will be on the exam are included on the objectives and are listed next. Often, you don't have to be an expert in the features, but you should still know what they all are, what problems they solve, and when it is appropriate to use each.

- SQL Server Management Studio (SSMS)
- SQL Server Reporting Services (SSRS)
- SQL Server Integration Services (SSIS)
- Notification Services
- Database Engine Tuning Advisor
- Service Broker
- HTTP Endpoints
- DDL Triggers

Take Your Time

There's no need to sweat about the time. You typically have three to four minutes per question. As long as you don't spend too much time trying to absorb all the details in the scenario before reading the questions, you should have more than enough time. The key is about digging into the details for what you need in order to answer the questions.

Scenario Topics

Scenarios are broken into different categories, just as a consultant may create a report for any given project. Each of these categories can have one or several subcategories composed of just a paragraph or two, or multiple screens. The following represent sample category topics that you may or may not see in every scenario:

- **Background**   This gives an overview of the company, the current issue(s) they are facing, and possibly what they are planning to do in the future. Problems and issues may be listed here. Possible subtopics might include Company Overview, Planned Changes, or Problem Statements.

- **Existing Environment**   The Existing Environment category gives the technical details of what exists today, such as servers, operating systems, versions of SQL Server, and applications being used. Problems and issues may also be listed here. By comparing this to what is planned for the future, it's possible to get an idea of the scope of the project. Possible subtopics might include Existing Application Environment, Existing Infrastructure, Database Information, or Server Information

- **Business and Technical Requirements**   Business requirements are those that are imposed from business rules such as how data is added to databases, or how it's made available. Technical requirements are those imposed by technical limitations. Similar requirements can be imposed in both the business requirements section and the technical requirements section. They may include subtopics such as Application Solution Requirements, Maintainability, Performance, Scalability, Availability, Recoverability, and Interoperability.

Sample Scenario Questions

1. You need to create a query that shows the parent and child relationships between any parts. Data will be pulled from the Parts table. What should you use to create this output?

   A. The Nodes and Value method of the XML data type

   B. FOR XML PATH

   C. A SELECT statement with a WHERE clause

   D. The Query method of the XML data type

2. After the migration, you need to import the data submitted from external companies. What tool would you use?

A. Create a stored procedure and use the BULK INSERT statement.

B. Create a CLR-integrated stored procedure.

C. Use SSIS.

D. Use bcp.

3. You need to provide ad hoc reporting capabilities to your customers as described in the Problem Statements section. What could be done?

A. Create reports and serve them with SSRS.

B. Create an SSRS Report Model and allow customers to create their own reports using Report Builder.

C. Create reports and serve them with SSIS.

D. Create a SSIS Report Model and allow customers to create their own reports using Report Builder.

4. What can you use to monitor processor utilization in accordance with the technical requirements?

A. SQL Profiler

B. SQL Trace

C. Performance Logs and Alerts

D. SSRS

Sample Scenario: MCITPSuccess Corporation

Company Overview

MCITPSuccess is a plumbing supply company that sells plumbing supplies to vendors and contractors around the world. They sell supplies both through software applications on the Web and through desktop applications that create supply lists based on user input, which can then be submitted via the web application (named OrderApp) by customer or sales personnel. Using the desktop application, plumbing for an entire new building can be laid out using building blueprints. The output file can be submitted via the Internet. DTS is used to convert the output file and add it to the database.

The company also accepts order files created from external applications. Before these files can be imported, however, the data must be cleansed and standardized.

Planned Changes   The company is running SQL Server 2000 on its database server, but plans to upgrade to SQL Server 2005. The primary database (named Plumber) is being optimized and will be renamed PlumberDesign. It will include sales data that can be used by sales personnel to generate reports. Business analysts will frequently generate a report that lists products sold (by highest quantity) and in which cities these products are shipped. The DTS package will be converted to the SQL Server 2005 server handling ETL.

Problem Statements The web site has been attacked several times. The sources of the attacks are unknown, but attempts were made to access data in back-end databases, and Denial of Service attacks resulted in the web site being unavailable for several hours during two of the attacks. The CEO wants to improve the security to minimize these risks.

Customers have requested the ability to access their past and current orders. You want to give customers the ability to view these orders via a web site in a report format. Additionally, you want to allow customers to modify these reports on their own.

Existing Data Environment

Databases

The following databases exist:

Database	Comments
Plumber	Will be replaced with PlumberDesign. Holds product, sales, and customer information.
Employees	Holds employee data (including salary data).

Both databases are set to use the full recovery model.

Approximately 300 tables are in the Plumber database, and about the same number are expected to be in the PlumberDesign database. However, users that access the database typically only access a small number of the tables related to their job or function.

Current transactions result in about 5000 new records added to the Plumber database daily. These are from the web application that generates the parts listing. Approximately 10 percent of the records from the orders are modified after originally being entered.

Servers Both the Plumber and Employees databases are hosted in the default instance of SQL Server 2000 running on a Windows Server 2000 operating system. The name of the server is SQL1.

Two IIS servers exist. IIS1 is used internally to access the Employees database, while IIS2 is in the DMZ and is used to access the Plumber database.

Database Access The Employees database is accessed via an intranet web application using ASP .NET technologies running on IIS1. The majority of access is limited to the EmpAppRole application role, but all users in the HR department can access the database directly.

Access to the OrderApp application is available to any Internet users. Customers create accounts that once validated allow customers to submit orders via the web application. The OrdAppRole application role is used to access the database.

Business Requirements

Availability If the Plumber database (or the PlumberDesign database after the upgrade) fails, it needs to be able to automatically failover as quickly as possible. The company wants to use database mirroring, if possible.

Recoverability The backup and recovery strategy for the Plumber database must meet the following requirements:

- Allow full recovery in the event of catastrophic hardware failure.

- Allow the database to be restored with a maximum loss of one hour of database activity.

- Minimize the overhead caused by backup and restore operations.

General Requirements The PlumberDesign database will include an XML column named PartsRelations in the Parts table. This column will be used to show inter-relationships between parts. For example, some connectors and pipes connect together to form an elbow joint. The elbow joint is the parent part and the XML column shows all the parts needed to create it. The connectors and pipes that create the elbow joint are child parts, and the XML column shows all of the parent parts that a child part can used in.

Performance The new servers must not reach more than 75 percent processor utilization. You are tasked with ensuring any individual application does not add more than 30 percent processor utilization.

Technical Requirements

Maintenance Maintenance plans will be created whenever possible to automate tasks. SQL Server Agent will be used to run regular maintenance jobs.

Performance You need to ensure that the upgrade does not add more than 30 percent processor utilization. Additionally, administrators need to be able to identify when the server hardware is approaching full utilization.

Sample Scenario Answers

1. **A.** In the Business Requirements | General Requirements section, the PartsRelations column in the Parts table is described. Parent and child relationships are in an XML column. The nodes method can be used to shred XML data into relational data. It can be combined with the value method to pull individual elements from an XML column. FOR XML is used to return the data in an XML format. A SELECT statement without a method to pull the XML data won't work. The Query method will only pull individual elements. See Chapter 5 for information on XML methods.

2. **C.** In the Company Overview section, it says "The company also accepts order files created from external applications. Before these files can be imported, the data must be cleansed and standardized." The best tool to cleanse and standardize data is SQL Server Integration Services (SSIS). See Chapter 15 for information on SSIS.

3. **B.** The scenario states, "Customers have requested the ability to access their past and current orders. You want to create the ability for customers to view these orders via a web site in a report format. Additionally, you want to allow customers to modify these reports on their own." By creating a Report Model, you provide customers with the ability to create their own reports using Report Builder. SSIS does not provide reporting capabilities. See Chapter 12 for more information on SSRS.

4. **C.** You don't need the scenario for this. The only tool from those given that can measure processor utilization is Performance Logs and Alerts. The scenario states "You need to ensure that the upgrade does not add more than 30 percent processor utilization. Additionally, administrators need to be able to identify when the server hardware is approaching full utilization." Using Performance Logs and Alerts, you can create a baseline log both before and after the upgrade to measure the impact on processor load, and then create logs regularly afterwards to measure processor load.

Final Notes

Notice that the scenario talks about a lot more than the questions ask about. This is the primary reason why you shouldn't spend the necessary time to fully understand every nuance about the scenario. Instead, only focus on the parts of the scenario that are necessary to answer the questions. To do this, you need to read the questions first.

On the CD are two test banks for each of the 70-441 and 70-442 exams (both of which are design exams). Each of these test banks has multiple scenarios and questions related to the scenario that are similar to what you saw in this appendix. Use them to practice for the actual exams.

Good luck.

Exam 70-441: What You Need to Know to Pass

There are three ingredients in the good life: learning, earning, and yearning.

—*Christopher Morley*

70-441: Designing Database Solutions by Using Microsoft SQL Server 2005

Introduction

The 70-441 exam focuses heavily on designing databases from the ground up. This includes data types, constraints, tables and relationships between tables, VIEWs, stored procedures, triggers, database security, and more. While the preparation guide indicates that you need to be an expert in T-SQL, the exam doesn't directly test this knowledge. Instead of coding, you need to have a solid knowledge of the underlying concepts.

What You Can Expect

This is a design exam. Unless you've taken a design exam before, you may be surprised by the format. Make sure you check out Appendix C for a full description of Microsoft's design exam format. Be prepared to read a lengthy scenario before you're presented any questions. Afterwards, you'll encounter some multiple-choice questions asking about the scenario. You will probably also see a mix of some "point and click" or "drag and drop" questions.

The number of questions on the exam is not published by Microsoft and sometimes changes from one exam to the next. A score of 700 is required to pass the exam, and you typically have about 180 minutes to complete around 45 to 50 questions. Notice this is twice as much time as you have with the 70-431 exam. This is because you'll need extra time to absorb those scenarios.

Some exams include beta test questions, where the exam developers are testing particular questions before they go live. Beta test questions don't count for or against you, and you are given extra time to answer them. You could even leave them blank and it wouldn't impact your score at all. Unfortunately, you never know if a question is live or beta, so you have to answer them all.

What's Expected of You

Someone who has successfully passed this exam is expected to be an expert in the following topics:

- Programming databases
- Troubleshooting programming objects (stored procedures, triggers, user-defined functions, user-defined data types, and queries)
- Performing database performance tuning and optimization
- Designing databases, at both the conceptual and logical levels
- Implementing databases at the physical level
- Designing and troubleshooting the data access layer of the application
- Gathering business requirements
- Writing Transact-SQL queries (though this knowledge is not tested directly)

 EXAM TIP As a reminder, exam objectives are listed at the beginning of the book with an objective map showing which chapter contains the appropriate information. However, remember that these objectives might change. The legalese on Microsoft's web site says "This preparation guide is subject to change at any time without prior notice and at Microsoft's sole discretion." Before taking the exam, take a look on Microsoft's web site for the current objectives.

Chapters Covering 70-441 Topics

Chapter 1: Installing and Configuring SQL Server 2005
This chapter contains no objectives for the 70-441 exam.

Chapter 2: SQL Server 2005 Database Basics
This entire chapter includes material that will be covered on the 70-441 exam, so make sure you focus on the following topics:

- Designing user-defined data types
- Designing tables
- Designing VIEWs
- Using data types
- Nulls and defaults

Chapter 3: Database Design

Know all the topics in this chapter, but focus especially on the following:

- The purpose and use of a PRIMARY KEY (PK)
- The purpose and use of a FOREIGN KEY (FK)
- Normalization
- Designing tables using one-to-many and many-to-many relationships
- Partitioning tables

Chapter 4: Transact-SQL

Not covered on this exam directly.

Chapter 5: XML

Know the following XML topics when preparing for this exam:

- XML data type versus (n)varchar(max)—and when to use each
- XML methods (nodes, value, query, modify, exist)
- How to optimize XML queries with XML indexes

Chapter 6: Advanced Database Objects

Know all the topics in this chapter, but focus especially on the following topics:

- Creating user-defined functions
- DML triggers
- DDL triggers

Chapter 7: Optimizing Databases

Know all the topics in this chapter, but focus especially on the following topics:

- Clustered indexes
- Nonclustered indexes
- Covering indexes

Chapter 8: Database Security

Make sure you know the following topics when preparing for the 70-441 exam:

- Permission chaining and database chaining
- Use of permissions on objects to control access (for example, granting permission to a VIEW, function, or stored procedure while denying direct access to underlying tables)
- The use of roles to control access
- The methods of encrypting data (and source code)

Chapter 9: Stored Procedures

The entire chapter contains material for this exam, but focus particularly on the following topics:

- The basics of stored procedures, including how to create them
- How to use parameters in stored procedures
- How to use transactions in stored procedures
- How to implement error-catching techniques in stored procedures
- Permission chaining (how access to underlying tables can be controlled by granting Execute permissions to the stored procedure but not to the base tables)

Chapter 10: Disaster Recovery

This chapter does not cover any objectives on the 70-441 exam.

Chapter 11: Data Access

When preparing for this exam, focus on the following topics:

- Service Broker
- Web services

Chapter 12: Support Services

When preparing for this exam, focus on the following topics:

- Reporting Services
- Notification Services

Chapter 13: Maintenance Tools

When preparing for this exam, focus on the following topics:

- System Monitor
- Performance Logs and Alerts
- SQL Profiler
- SQL Trace

Chapter 14: Locks and Cursors

This chapter does not cover any objectives on the 70-441 exam.

Chapter 15: Transferring Data

When preparing for this exam, focus on the following topics:

- Replication
- SQL Server Integration Services (SSIS)

Exam 70-442: What You Need to Know to Pass

> *The measure of success is not whether you have a tough problem to deal with, but whether it's the same problem you had last year.*
>
> —*John Foster Dulles*

70-442: Designing and Optimizing Data Access by Using Microsoft SQL Server 2005

Introduction

The 70-442 exam focuses heavily on coding using Transact-SQL. If you start off as an expert in T-SQL, you're ahead of the game, but don't skip Chapter 4. You'll find that some of the new T-SQL features will definitely be on the exam. Additionally, any T-SQL programmer should know how to create, implement, and troubleshoot stored procedures, so you're bound to see these topics on the exam.

You can also expect some advanced developer concepts to appear, such as use of cursors, locks, query plans and hints, notification services, data access strategies, and more.

What You Can Expect

This is a design exam. Unless you've taken a design exam before, you may be surprised by the format, so make sure you check out Appendix C for a full description of Microsoft's design exam format. Be prepared to read a lengthy scenario before you're presented with any questions. Afterwards, you'll have some multiple-choice questions asking about the scenario. You will probably also see a mix of some "point and click" or "drag and drop" questions.

The number of questions on the exam is not published by Microsoft and sometimes changes from one exam to the next. A score of 700 is required to pass the exam. You typically have about 180 minutes to complete around 45 to 50 questions. Notice this is twice as much time as you have with the 70-431 exam. It'll take some time to absorb those scenarios.

Some exams include beta test questions, where the exam developers are testing particular questions before they go live. Beta test questions don't count for or against you, and you are given extra time to answer them. You could even leave them blank and it wouldn't impact your score at all. Unfortunately, you never know if a question is live or beta, so you have to answer them all.

What's Expected of You

Someone who has successfully passed this exam is expected to be an expert in the following topics:

- Writing Transact-SQL queries
- Programming databases
- Troubleshooting programming objects (stored procedures, triggers, user-defined functions, user-defined data types, and queries)
- Carrying out database performance tuning and optimization
- Designing databases, at both the conceptual and logical levels
- Implementing databases at the physical level
- Designing and troubleshooting the data access layer of the application
- Gathering business requirements

 EXAM TIP As a reminder, exam objectives are listed at the beginning of the book with an objective map showing which chapter contains the appropriate information. However, remember that these objectives might change. The legalese on Microsoft's web site says "This preparation guide is subject to change at any time without prior notice and at Microsoft's sole discretion." Before taking the exam, take a look at Microsoft's web site for the current objectives.

Chapters Covering 70-442 Topics

Chapter 1: Installing and Configuring SQL Server 2005
This chapter contains no objectives for the 70-442 exam.

Chapter 2: SQL Server 2005 Database Basics
Ensure you focus on the following topics from this chapter:

- Use of appropriate data types (including appropriate use of varchar)
- Large values types: varchar(max), nvarchar(max), varbinary(max)
- Computed columns

Chapter 3: Database Design

Know all the topics in this chapter. Focus especially on the following:

- The purpose and use of a FOREIGN KEY (FK)
- Cascading updates and deletes
- Partitioning large tables

Chapter 4: Transact-SQL

Know all the topics in this chapter, but pay special attention to the following:

- SELECT
- WHERE
- NULL
- ORDER BY (including TOP)
- GROUP BY (including Having)
- CUBE
- PIVOT and UNPIVOT
- EXCEPT and INTERSECT
- WITH (common table expressions, including recursive common table expressions)
- RANK

Chapter 5: XML

Know all the topics in this chapter.

Chapter 6: Advanced Database Objects

While you can expect questions from any topic in this chapter, you probably will not see many.

Chapter 7: Optimizing Databases

Know all the topics in this chapter. Focus especially on the following topics:

- Clustered indexes
- Nonclustered indexes
- Full-text indexes
- Covering indexes
- Statistics
- Filegroups

Chapter 8: Database Security

This chapter contains no objectives for the 70-442 exam.

Chapter 9: Stored Procedures

The entire chapter involves material used on this exam, but you should focus heavily on:

- T-SQL topics
- Savepoints and marks
- Distributed transactions
- Execution context

Chapter 10: Disaster Recovery

This chapter does not cover any objectives that will appear on the 70-442 exam.

Chapter 11: Data Access

When preparing for this exam, focus on the following topics:

- Web services and HTTP endpoints
- Multiple Access Results Sets (MARS)
- DataSets and DataReaders

Chapter 12: Support Services

When preparing for this exam, focus on the Notification Services topic.

Chapter 13: Maintenance Tools

When preparing for this exam, focus on the following topics:

- System Monitor
- SQL Profiler
- SQL Trace
- Dynamic management VIEWs (DMVs)

Chapter 14: Locks and Cursors

When preparing for this exam, focus on the following topics:

- Transaction isolation levels
- Hints and plan guides
- Cursors

Chapter 15: Transferring Data

When preparing for this exam, focus on the Replication topic.

SQL Database Design Object Summary

> *Bloom where you're planted.*
>
> —*St. Francis DeSales*

This appendix has an abbreviated listing of many database objects. It includes:

- Constraints
- Views
- Functions
- Stored procedures
- Triggers
- CLR-integrated objects
- Indexes and indexed VIEWs

In early chapters of this book, we covered some basic database design objects such as constraints and views. Later, we introduced some advanced database objects, such as user-defined functions, stored procedures, and triggers. When we talked about optimizing databases, we brought indexes into the mix.

All of the objects work together to produce a cohesive database solution. One of your goals as a DBA is to understand what the available objects are, and to pick the right object for the right task. In this appendix, you'll find a reference to identify the key points of the major database design objects to help you compare them side by side.

This appendix is not meant to teach you all there is to know about these objects, but instead to provide some sparks to help you realize what you do know, and perhaps more importantly, what you need to study more before tackling the MCITP: Database Administrator tests.

Constraint (PK)   Example: You want to ensure all rows are unique in a table. You create a PRIMARY KEY (PK) that enforces entity integrity. [*Use to enforce entity integrity.*]

- A UNIQUE index is automatically created with the PK to enforce uniqueness.
- The PK defaults to a clustered index, but this can be changed.
- PKs are typically named after the table with *ID* as a suffix. For example, the PK for the Employee table would be named EmployeeID.
- NULL values are not allowed.
- A PK can be a single column or multiple columns (composite PK).

Constraint (FK)   Example: You want to create a relationship between the Employee table and the Address table. You would create a FOREIGN KEY (FK) in the Address table with the same data type (and often the same name) as the PK in the Employee table. [*Use to enforce referential integrity.*]

- Indexes are *not* automatically created on FOREIGN KEYs.
- Nonclustered indexes are commonly created on FKs to improve the performance of queries.
- Referential integrity can also be used to enforce data entry.
  - For example, a single-column State table could be created with the 50 states listed by the two-letter abbreviation in the PK named State. We could create a relationship between the Employee table state column (by creating an FK) and the State table state column (the PK). Any entries into the Employee table state column would be checked against the State table state column. If the state doesn't exist in the State table, the data entry is rejected.
- Constraint checking is done BEFORE the data is entered.

Constraint (CHECK)   Example: You want to check a phone number entered into the Phone column to ensure it is entered in the proper format. You could create a CHECK constraint on the column to ensure the format is always (###) ###-####. [*Use to enforce domain, or referential integrity.*]

- Invoked with INSERT and UPDATE statements.
- Can reference other columns or functions (built-in or user-defined including CLR integrated functions).
- *CHECK constraints* can be used to restrict values in a column. Considered the preferred, standard way of restricting values in a column.
- Checks data *before* it's entered into a table.

Constraint (DEFAULT)   Example: You want to ensure that the sales price of any product is always 10 percent off the regular price if it is not specified when the row is inserted. By creating a DEFAULT, you can check for data in the SalesPrice column.

If none is given, it will default to Price * 0.9, or 90 percent of the regular price. [*Use to enforce business rules.*]

- Only used during INSERT statements.
- The DEFAULT constraint provides data when none is input.
- Can also be used when creating a new column while specifying NOT NULL for the column.
  - Since the new column has no data, all the existing rows are NULL. This would cause the creation of the new row to fail. By using DEFAULT when creating the new column, you can specify what all the existing rows will default to when the column is created.

VIEWs   Example: You need to provide access to employee information such as a birthday or phone number, but you don't want to expose sensitive data such as salary or SSN. You can create a VIEW and provide access to the VIEW without granting access to the underlying table. [*Use to focus data, hide data, or mask complexity of SELECT statements.*]

- Provides access to select a column in table(s) instead of the actual table(s).
- Can be used for horizontal partitioning (row-level security).
- Cannot accept parameters (use functions for a parameterized view).
- WITH CHECK prevents data modifications from allowing data to fall out of view.
- WITH SCHEMABINDING prevents the modification of underlying objects, such as tables, from breaking the VIEW.
  - For example, if a view were created on the Employee table using the LName, FName, and Phone columns and someone later changed the name of the Phone column to HomePhone, the VIEW would break. Using WITH SCHEMABINDING would prevent the modification to the Employee table.
- WITH ENCRYPTION encrypts the definition of the VIEW, but not the data displayed.

EXAM TIP   VIEWs seem to be often misunderstood by new DBAs, especially regarding the use of the basic options (WITH CHECK, WITH SCHEMABINDING, and WITH ENCRYPTION). When preparing for the tests, make sure you understand VIEWs and their options well.

Functions (Built-In)   Example: You need the average price of all the products in the products table. The AVG built-in function can be used in a SELECT statement to calculate and retrieve the average price. SQL Server provides a rich set of built-in functions in several different categories. [*Use existing built-in functions instead of creating your own.*]

- Can be accessed in a SELECT statement or a VIEW.
- Different functions accept varying input.

- Output can be scalar (single value) or a result set that can be used as a derived table.
- The BOL topic, "Functions (Transact-SQL)" has a category listing of built-in functions. Two examples are:
  - String functions can be used to manipulate character data such as LTRIM to remove leading spaces.
  - Date functions can be used to retrieve or manipulate dates such as GetDate() to get the current date.

Functions (User-Defined Functions)   Example: You want to accept a ZIP code as input and retrieve the state and/or city. You can create a user-defined function that accepts the ZIP code and retrieves the ZIP code from an existing table. [*Use to hide details of calculations that are to be used in a SELECT statement.*]

- Can be accessed in a SELECT statement or a VIEW.
- Can accept input parameters.
- Output can be scalar (single value) or a result set that can be used as a derived table.
- CLR-integrated functions can be created.
  - Allows use of any .NET programming language such as C# or VB.
  - Useful when calculation-intensive operations are required.
  - Can combine sophisticated technologies, such as calling a Web service that is passing data via SOAP.

Stored Procedures   Example: You need to automate the process of pulling data out of a database, performing calculation-intensive operations on the data, and then returning information to the user based on the actions. This might take dozens or hundreds of T-SQL lines, but could be embedded in a single stored procedure. Since the example calls for calculation-intensive operations, you would probably create it as a CLR-integrated stored procedure. [*Use for complex queries and/or to implement business rules.*]

- Can have hundreds of statements. Can be very complex and can include error messages.
- *Cannot* be called from a SELECT statement.
- Used to reduce network traffic (for instance, one statement calling a stored procedure instead of hundreds of lines sent to the server).
- Provides a layer of security.
  - Users can execute stored procedures to read data without the need for permissions to underlying tables. (When modifying data, underlying table permissions are needed.)

- Can be executed with the EXECUTE AS clause, causing it to be executed with permissions of any designated user.

- Parameterized stored procedures are considered a core defense against SQL injection attacks.

- Can accept input parameters and can provide output (scalar or derived tables).

- Can include BEGIN TRANSACTION, COMMIT TRANSACTION, and ROLLBACK TRANSACTION statements.

- Can include TRY CATCH blocks for error catching.

- CLR-integrated stored procedures can be created.

  - Allows use of any .NET programming language such as C# or VB.

  - Useful when calculation-intensive operations are required. Can combine sophisticated technologies such as calling a Web service that is passing data via SOAP.

DML Triggers   Example: After an update to a table, an UPDATE trigger logs the data modification to a separate auditing table. DML triggers are placed on tables. DML triggers can respond to UPDATE, DELETE, or INSERT events. [*Use to enforce business rules such as auditing data changes.*]

- A specialized stored procedure.

- Can contain complex processing logic using T-SQL statements or CLR integration.

- Can do all that constraints can do, but with overhead.

- Associated with a table. Cannot be called directly.

- Triggers (and only triggers) have access to temporary updated and deleted tables that hold data based on the last INSERT, UPDATE, or DELETE statement.

- Can be disabled with ALTER TABLE *tableName* TRIGGER *triggerName* or DISABLE TRIGGER *triggerName* on *tableName*.

- Similar to constraints, triggers will capture all modifications no matter how the modification is made. For example, a DELETE trigger on a table will capture all DELETE statements against the table no matter what executes the DELETE statement (stored procedure, application, ad hoc queries, and so on).

- Can also be used to roll back modifications that are considered unacceptable.

  - For example, if you don't want to delete customers or employees, a DELETE trigger can roll back the deletion and instead somehow mark the row as inactive.

DDL Triggers   Example: Management wants to know whenever the definitions of any database objects (tables, VIEWs, and so on) or any databases are modified. You can create a DDL trigger on the database to monitor all ALTER events and log them to an audit table contained within an auditing database.

DDL triggers can be created for a server or for a database. DDL triggers can respond to CREATE, ALTER, or DROP events. [*Use to enforce business rules such as auditing changes to database objects.*]

- A specialized stored procedure.
- Can contain complex processing logic using T-SQL or CLR.
- Can do all that constraints can do, but with overhead.
- Associated with a server or a database.
  - Server scope—Can audit DDL events occurring at the server level (such as CREATE DATABASE or DROP DATABASE).
  - Database scope—Can audit DDL events occurring at the database level (such as ALTER TABLE).
- DDL triggers cannot be called directly, but only respond to events such as CREATE, ALTER, or DROP.

TEST TIP DDL triggers are new to SQL Server 2005. Microsoft often heavily tests new features to make sure people are aware of them. Know these well.

DML INSTEAD OF Triggers Example: You want to monitor UPDATE statements on the Parts table and see if a record exists. If the part exists in the Parts table, the UPDATE occurs naturally. If the part does not update, the trigger executes an INSERT statement instead of the UPDATE statement.

INSTEAD OF triggers can only be defined as DML triggers, not DDL triggers. DML triggers can respond to UPDATE, DELETE, or INSERT events. [*Use to cause a separate statement to fire instead of the statement causing the trigger.*]

- A specialized stored procedure.
- Can contain complex processing logic using T-SQL or CLR.
- Can do all that constraints can do, but with overhead.
- Associated with a table based on one of the three DML statements.
- Cannot be called directly.
- Can be disabled with ALTER TABLE *tableName* TRIGGER *triggerName* or DISABLE TRIGGER *triggerName* on *tableName*.
- Can be used to catch invalid data. Instead of trying to INSERT it into a table where a failure is certain, the INSTEAD OF trigger can INSERT the bad data to an alternate table.
- Will catch all data modifications no matter how the modification is done (via stored procedure, application, or T-SQL statements).
- Can be used to create an updateable view on a view that isn't updateable (due to the inclusion of a UNION clause).

CLR-Integrated Objects   Example: An application needs to frequently perform processor-intensive operations and return results as quickly as possible. A CLR-integrated stored procedure would be a perfect choice. [*Use when calculation-intensive operations are required.*]

- Can be created with any .NET programming language.
- Created assemblies are registered with SQL.
- Registered assemblies can be embedded in:
  - Stored procedures
  - Triggers
  - Many functions
  - User-defined data types

Clustered Indexes   Example: Users frequently query the database with a query that requires the Customers to be sorted in the order of their Last Name. You are tasked with optimizing this query. If you create a clustered index on the Customer table on the last name, the data is already in the order of last name. The query doesn't have to re-sort the data. [*Use to optimize queries where data needs to be ordered in the same order as the index.*]

- Similar to a dictionary. Using a dictionary, when you find the word, you've found the data. The data is ordered based on the clustered index.
- You can have only one clustered index on a table.
- The clustered index has an index ID of 1 in the system tables. (Nonclustered indexes have an index ID of 2–249.)
- Database Tuning Advisor can be used to identify the best columns to create clustered indexes upon based on workload. This includes keeping or dropping existing indexes.

Nonclustered Indexes   Example: The Orders table is frequently searched for order information based on the OrderDate column. By creating a nonclustered index on the OrderDate column, you can optimize these queries. [*Use to optimize searches in queries. This includes columns that are frequently included in queries, included in WHERE clauses with range values, or frequently grouped together in aggregations.*]

- Similar to the index in the back of the book. Instead of having to search every page of a book (or every page of a database), by looking at the index we can determine exactly which page(s) the data is located on and go right to that page.
- Nonclustered indexes have an index of between 2 and 249.
- Database Tuning Advisor can be used to identify the best columns to create nonclustered indexes upon based on workload. This includes keeping or dropping existing indexes.

Indexed VIEWs   Example: Users frequently use a VIEW, and you are tasked with optimizing its use. You can create an index on the VIEW and make it an indexed VIEW. [*Use to optimize frequently used views.*]

- The indexed VIEW *must* contain a clustered index.
- To create an indexed VIEW, several requirements exist. They are:
  - The VIEW must be created using WITH SCHEMABINDING.
  - The VIEW can only reference tables, not other VIEWs.
  - The VIEW must be deterministic. In other words, the VIEW cannot contain any nondeterministic functions.
  - Tables must be referenced by two-part names.
  - Included functions must be referenced by two-part names.
- Database Tuning Advisor can be used to identify the best VIEWs to create indexes upon based on workload. This includes keeping or dropping existing indexed VIEWs.

Full-Text Indexes   Example: Your table has a varchar(max) column holding employee résumés in Word documents. You are tasked with optimizing searches of the résumés. You create a full-text catalog on the database, and a full-text index on the Resume column. [*Use to optimize searching of textual data, including char, varchar, XML, and image.*]

- Before creating a full-text index, you must create a full-text catalog.
- After creating full-text index(es), you can use the CONTAINS predicate in queries.
- Without a full-text index, you can only use the LIKE clause.

ad hoc query   A query that is executed infrequently. Ad hoc queries can sometimes be troublesome because untrained users can create queries that are inefficient, causing the server to suffer significant performance degradation.

aggregate   A group such as grouped data. For example, when aggregating data, we are grouping data. A common aggregate function is Avg (average). It looks at a group of data (an aggregate) and provides an average.

alerts, Performance   A Performance alert is an alert configured within the operating system Performance Logs and Alerts tool. Performance alerts can be configured to log an entry into the application event log, send a network message, start a performance log, or run a program. They are not directly connected to SQL Server Agent.

alerts, SQL Server Agent alerts   A SQL Server Agent alert is an automated response to an event. SQL Server Agent monitors the application log and if an alert has been specified, the SQL Server Agent fires the alert. Alerts can notify operators or launch jobs.

alias   Within SELECT statements there are two possible definitions of an alias. First, the column header on the output can be labeled with something different than the name of the column in the SELECT statement by using an alias. Second, tables can be identified with an alias. This is useful in a SELECT statement joining multiple tables.

ALTER   A DDL statement used to modify objects within a database, or objects on the server.

baseline   A baseline is a known starting point for something. In the context of the MCITP Database Developer certification, it's a known starting point for a server. For example, when creating a performance baseline, we would measure the four core resources of a system: CPU, memory, disk, and network. A performance baseline would take a snapshot of the resources (perhaps every 30 minutes) over a period of about a week. Six months later, another counter log could be created, and by comparing it to the baseline, an administrator can identify what has changed.

bcp   The Bulk Copy Program (bcp) utility bulk copies data between SQL Server 2005 and a data file, using the format specified by the user (such as commas or other characters employed to separate the fields). It is intended to be an easy-to-use tool, but not when using the queryout option.

BI Business Intelligence (BI) is a group of different applications and technologies used to collect data, access data, and analyze data about the business. BI is used to help decision makers make better business decisions.

BIDS Business Intelligence Development Studio (BIDS) is installed with SQL Server 2005. It's used to create SQL Server Integration Services (SSIS) packages and SQL Server Reporting Services (SSRS) reports.

BLOB A binary large object. Large value data types [varchar(max), nvarchar(max), and varbinary(max)] are stored as BLOBs. Within SQL Server 2005, BLOBs can be as large as 2GB.

blocking lock A lock that blocks another process is called a blocking lock. Locks are placed on data to prevent it from being viewed or modified by one process as it is being viewed or modified by another process. Locks and blocking locks are not necessarily a problem. It's only when blocking locks are held for a long period of time and stopping a process from moving forward that they become problematic.

BOL Books Online (BOL) is a built-in help resource for SQL Server 2005. It can be read as a book using chapters from the contents tab, or searched for specific information. When connected to the Internet, BOL also returns information from MSDN Online, the Codezone Community.

bulk-logged recovery model In the bulk-logged recovery model, all transactions are logged into the transaction log EXCEPT bulk-logged operations. It is used when we want the capability to recover our data up to the point of failure, including all transactions in the transaction log, except for bulk-logged operations that either take up too many resources to log, or are easily reproduced.

CLR Common language runtime (CLR) is an execution environment for program code developed by Microsoft. Programs are written and developed in any language, and then compiled to a Microsoft Intermediate Language (MSIL). When run, they are submitted to the CLR to be fully compiled and run. CLR code can be integrated into SQL and it's highly recommended to do so for computation-intensive purposes.

clustered index A special type of index used to optimize queries. Tables can have only one clustered index. The data is ordered the same way the index is ordered. It's similar to a dictionary or a phone book. When you find the word or name, you're pointed right at the data.

collation Identifies how data is stored, sorted, compared, and presented. A collation is a set of rules and can be set at the database and column levels. It includes locale, sort order, and case sensitivity.

Common Table Expression (CTE) A temporary result set that is defined and used within the execution scope of another T-SQL statement. It is similar to a derived table in that it isn't persisted beyond the query. Unlike a derived table, a CTE can reference itself recursively within the same query.

composite index   An index that is composed of more than one column. Both clustered and nonclustered indexes can be created as composite indexes.

computed column   A column in a table that displays the result of an expression instead of stored data. For example, InventoryCost = QuantityOnHand * ProductCost. A calculated column could be calculated on-the-fly with the results not being stored, or the data can be persisted, where the computed data is held within the table.

concurrency   Provides multiple users with the ability to access data simultaneously. Locks are used automatically by SQL Server and can be configured by setting transaction isolation levels.

constraint   Constraints are special database objects used to enforce different types of integrity on data. While data types enforce basic data integrity (domain integrity), constraints allow much more sophisticated checking (entity integrity and referential integrity). Types of constraints include PRIMARY KEY, FOREIGN KEY, CHECKS, and DEFAULTS.

CREATE   A DDL statement used to create new objects within a database, or objects on the server.

cross-tab report   A cross-tab report is one where the results have been rotated so the rows are displayed as columns, or the columns are displayed as rows.

DAC   A dedicated administrator connection (DAC) is used to connect to a SQL Server instance that is otherwise unresponsive. Needs SQL Server Browser service to run remotely.

DatabaseMail   A service that can be used to send e-mail messages from within SQL Server 2005. It uses SMTP. Intended to replace SQL Mail, which has been deprecated.

database mirror   A new feature of SQL Server 2005 where a database can be mirrored on another instance or another server. When configured with a witness server and the mirror session placed in synchronous mode, automatic failover can be achieved.

database securable   Any object within a SQL Server database that can have access regulated. Securables include tables, VIEWs, stored procedures, functions, and even security principals.

database snapshot   A new feature of SQL Server 2005 where a snapshot of a database can be created at any given time to preserve the state of the database. The snapshot can be queried if desired and/or the entire database can be restored from the snapshot.

data mining   The process of extracting valid, authentic, and actionable information from large databases. The primary tool for data mining in SQL Server 2005 is SQL Server Analysis Services (SSAS), though SQL Server Integration Services (SSIS) can often be used also.

DBA A database administrator (DBA) is typically responsible for administering a database and the database server, as opposed to a database developer, who does much of the development work for a database. Administering responsibilities often include recoverability (backups and restores), maintaining integrity, managing security, ensuring availability, and maximizing performance.

DBCC Database Console Command (DBCC) was previously known as Database Consistency Checker. Four categories of DBCC commands include many methods that check on the various elements of a database.

DBMS A database management system (DBMS) is composed of software necessary to organize, store, and retrieve data in a database. Access, SQL Server, Oracle, and DB2 are all database management systems.

DDL Data Definition Language (DDL). This includes the statements of CREATE, ALTER, and DROP and applies to database objects (not data) such as tables, triggers, functions, stored procedures and more.

DDL trigger A trigger that fires in response to a DDL statement. DDL triggers can only be configured as AFTER triggers, not INSTEAD OF triggers. DDL triggers are configured at the database level or server level.

deadlock A locking condition where two processes both have locks on a resource and are waiting for the other process to release a resource before they can continue. For example, Sally could have a lock on the Sales table and be waiting to obtain a lock on the Product table. At the same time, Joe has a lock on the Product table and is waiting to obtain a lock on the Sales table. As a result, neither process can move forward. SQL Server automatically detects deadlocks and picks one of the processes as a deadlock victim and rolls it back.

DELETE A DML statement used to delete data within a table or VIEW. Note that data is deleted, but objects are dropped.

denormalized Process of optimizing a database by adding redundant data. A normalized database typically conforms to first normal form, second normal form, and third normal form, though more normal forms exist. By denormalizing a database, performance gains can sometimes be achieved.

deterministic Typically refers to functions such as deterministic functions. A deterministic function always returns the same result when called with the same input values. Indexed VIEWs require any functions used within the indexed VIEW to be deterministic. As a comparison, see nondeterministic.

differential backup A backup type that backs up all the changes since the last full backup. Since the differential backup only backs up the changes, it can be done much quicker than a full backup. A possible backup strategy might include performing a full backup once a week and doing differential backups daily.

Distributor Used in replication. In the Publisher metaphor, a Distributor is the process that transfers data from the Publisher to the Subscriber.

DMF   Dynamic management function (DMF). Dynamic management VIEWs and functions are new to SQL Server 2005. They are used to return server state information to monitor the health of a server instance, diagnose problems, and tune performance. There are about 12 different categories of both DMVs and DMFs.

DML   Data Manipulation Language (DML) includes the statements SELECT, INSERT, DELETE, and UPDATE and applies to data (not database objects) within tables and VIEWs.

DML trigger   A trigger that fires in response to a DML statement on a table or view. DML triggers can be AFTER triggers on a table, or INSTEAD OF triggers on a table or a VIEW.

DMV   Dynamic management VIEWs (DMVs) and functions are new to SQL Server 2005. They are used to return server state information to monitor the health of a server instance, diagnose problems, and tune performance. About 12 different categories of both DMVs and DMFs exist.

DROP   A DDL statement used to delete objects within a database, or objects on the server. Note that data is deleted, but objects are dropped.

DTA   The Database Engine Tuning Advisor (DTA) is used to analyze the performance effects of T-SQL statements and provide recommendations to add, remove, or modify indexes, indexed VIEWs, and partitioning (physical design structures).

DTS   Data Transformation Services (DTS) was the ETL tool available in SQL Server 7.0 and SQL Server 2000. SQL Server Integration Services (SSIS) is the successor to DTS. Legacy DTS packages can be migrated into SSIS, or run using the Execute DTS 2000 Package task.

dynamic SQL   A SQL statement built and executed at runtime by concatenating different parts of the statement based on provided variables. Generally, dynamic SQL is not recommended, especially in web sites, due to SQL injection attacks. The solution is to use parameterized stored procedures that build the SQL statement differently.

endpoints   A new feature in SQL Server 2005 used to manage connections. An endpoint is a SQL Server object used by SQL Server to communicate over the network. In database mirroring, a SQL Server instance uses a special purpose endpoint to receive database mirroring connections with other server instances. The two primary endpoints are HTTP endpoints and database mirroring endpoints.

ETL   This is a Business Intelligence (BI) term representing Extract, Transform, and Load. We extract data out of one database or table, transform it to conform to the standards in the destination, and load it into the target database or table. SSIS is the primary tool used for ETL in SQL Server 2005.

EXCEPT   The EXCEPT operator can be used within a SELECT statement. It will return any distinct values from a query to the left of the EXCEPT operator that are not also returned from the query to right of the EXCEPT operator.

federated database A database that is spread across multiple servers, often in multiple geographical locations, is called a federated database. The servers that hold the different parts of a federated database are referred to as a federation, or federated database servers. A federation of database servers is used to spread the processing load across a group of servers. The data is horizontally partitioned allowing each of the servers to be independently managed, but distributed queries can be used to process requests on the entire database.

filegroups A method of optimizing the performance of a database by controlling the placement of database files and database objects. By default, all data and database objects are placed into a single file, in a single filegroup. Unlike files, which can be viewed on the disk, a filegroup is conceptual.

fillfactor An index option that identifies how full an index will be when it is created. For tables that have a lot of INSERTS, setting an indexes fill factor to something other than 0 (indicating 100 percent full) will prevent excessive page splits and the resulting fragmentation of indexes.

FOREIGN KEY (FK) An FK is used to create a relationship between two tables, and typically points to a PK (PRIMARY KEY) in another table. The relationship enforces integrity between the two tables, allowing only entries in the FK table that exist in the PK table, and preventing deletions from the PK table if a related entry exists in the FK table.

fragmentation In databases, indexes can be fragmented similar to how a hard drive can be fragmented. A fragmented index results in slower performance of the database. Fragmentation can be reduced by setting a fill factor on an index so it has empty space. Fragmented indexes can be defragmented by using REORGANIZE (keeps the index online) or by using REBUILD (which defaults to offline but can be run online).

full backup A full backup backs up the complete database. This includes all data, all objects, and all files. A full backup also backs up the transaction log, but does not truncate it. Both differential and transaction log backups need to have a full backup done first.

full recovery model In the full recovery model, all transactions are logged into the transaction log. It is used when we want to be able to recover our data up to the point of failure, including all transactions in the transaction log.

full-text catalog Used to hold full-text indexes. A full-text catalog holds zero, one, or more full-text indexes.

full-text index A separate file that stores information about significant words in a column. Noise words (such as *the*, *and*, *a*, and so on) are not included in the index. Full-text indexes are used for complete full-text searches.

full-text search Allows faster searches of text columns (char, varchar, and nvarchar) and columns that include formatted binary data such as Microsoft Word documents held in a varbinary(max) column. A full-text search is only possible on a column that has a full-text index created on it.

function Functions are routines that can accept parameters, perform an action, and return the result of that action. SQL Server includes many built-in functions. User-defined functions can be created to meet specific needs.

index A database object used to provide faster access to data in a table. SQL Server 2005 has two types of indexes: clustered and nonclustered. Indexes are also used to enforce uniqueness.

INSERT A DML statement used to add new rows to a table.

INSTEAD OF trigger A trigger configured to fire instead of the action that caused it to fire. INSTEAD OF triggers are commonly used for updateable views and are only available with DML statements.

INTERSECT The INTERSECT operator can be used within a SELECT statement. It returns any distinct values from a query that are returned by the queries on both sides of the INTERSECT operator.

job SQL Server Agent workflows. A job can have one or more tasks within the workflow.

join Used to combine the contents of two or more tables. The most common join is an inner join. Other joins are left, right, full, and cross.

linked server A definition that specifies an external OLE DB database source, such as another SQL Server, or an Oracle server. Once defined, the linked server can be used for distributed queries using only the four-part name in the query.

lock A lock is an access restriction placed on part of a database to prevent other users or processes from viewing or modifying data as it is being viewed or modified by one process. Locks can be placed on rows, pages, extents, tables, or databases.

log shipping A high availability strategy where a copy of a database is created on another server or instance. The transaction log is periodically copied or shipped over to the standby server to keep it up-to-date.

lookup table In SQL Server databases, a lookup table is a table with relatively static data that can be used as a source for verifying data. For example, a table that includes the 50 states with their full spelling and two-letter abbreviations could be used as a lookup table.

maintenance plan A workflow of one or more maintenance tasks. Maintenance plans can be created manually or with the Maintenance Plan Wizard. Maintenance plans create jobs that are managed by the SQL Server Agent.

manifest file The installation file that is part of a deployment utility created by SSIS. Launching the manifest file will start the installation of the SSIS package and a server.

many-to-many table relationship   A many-to-many relationship is between *three* tables where many rows in one table can link to many rows in a related table. A many-to-many relationship can't be created directly, but instead requires a third table (often referred to as a junction table) that connects the two tables. When looking at table diagrams, the one is typically identified with a key icon, and the many is typically identified with an infinity icon.

master database   The primary system database that controls all the system-level operations of SQL Server. It records instance-wide metadata, such as logon accounts, endpoints, linked servers, and system configuration settings.

merge replication   A replication strategy used when multiple subscribers are also acting as publishers. In other words, the data is updated from multiple sources.

Model database   The template used when creating new databases. Any new database is created from a copy of the Model database and then modified from there.

msdb database   Used by SQL Server Agent to store information on jobs, alerts, and operators. It also holds all historical data.

nonclustered index   A nonclustered index is added to optimize queries. Tables can have multiple nonclustered indexes. A nonclustered index is similar to the index in the back of a book. By finding it in the index, you know specifically where to look in the book for the information.

nondeterministic   Typically refers to functions such as nondeterministic functions. A nondeterministic function returns different results when called with the same input values. As an example, GETDATE() would return different results at different times. Indexed views can not include nondeterministic functions.

normalized   A normalized database is where the tables in the database are reduced to their simplest terms. The concept came from a paper written by Dr. E. F. Codd in 1970 where the first three normal forms were defined.

ODBC   Open Database Connectivity (ODBC) is an application programming interface (API) that supports access to any data source as long as an ODBC driver is available.

OLAP   Online analytical processing (OLAP) refers to the process of creating multiple dimensions (or cubes) of a database and then performing the multidimensional analysis of business data. OLAP is part of the broader category of business intelligence and is supported by SQL Server Analysis Services (SSAS) in SQL Server 2005. This book's focus has been primarily on OLTP, not OLAP.

OLE DB   Object Linking and Embedding Database (OLE DB) is an application programming interface (API) used for accessing data. OLE DB supports accessing data in many formats besides database (such as spreadsheets and text files).

OLTP   Online transaction processing (OLTP). An OLTP database is optimized for changing data, as opposed to an OLAP database, which is optimized for data that is relatively static. Data is changed via DML statements (INSERT, UPDATE, DELETE).

one-to-many table relationship   A one-to-many relationship is between two tables where a single row in one table can link to many rows in the related table. When looking at table diagrams, the one is typically identified with a key icon, while the many is typically identified with an infinity icon.

one-to-one table relationship   A one-to-one table relationship is between two tables where a single row in one table is linked to a single row in another table. When looking at table diagrams, the one is typically identified with a key icon, and the many is typically identified with an infinity icon.

OPENDATASOURCE   A command that can be used to query external servers. OPENROWSET provides similar functionality. If the queries are to be repeated, it is recommended to create linked servers to make the queries less complex.

operator   In SQL Server Agent, an operator identifies who is notified. It can be configured to send e-mails, pages, or Net Send messages.

parameterized report   A SQL Server Reporting Services (SSRS) report that accepts input values (parameters) is known as a parameterized report. Parameters are used to complete a query used for the report so the report can be selective based on user input.

password policy   New to SQL Server 2005, a password policy applies password security policies to SQL logins. This feature is only fully supported on Windows Server 2003. The CHECK_POLICY option should be set to ON to enable this feature.

Performance   Also called Performance Monitor and System Monitor, though technically it is called simply Performance. Performance includes System Monitor, which can be used to measure system objects and counters in real time. Common objects measured on any server include CPU, memory, disk, and NIC. Performance also includes Performance Logs and Alerts which can be used to create counter logs or traces and performance alerts.

persisted computed column   A computed column of data that is physically stored in the table. For example, a Products table could have an On_Hand_Cost calculated from the On_Hand_Inventory and Cost columns. A computed column is calculated every time the data is queried, but is not stored. This has a performance cost if the column is heavily queried. A persisted computed column can store the new value each time the On_Hand_Cost or On_Hand_Inventory value is changed using a DML trigger at a lower performance cost.

physical design structure   Physical design structures (PDSs) include items such as indexes, indexed VIEWs, and partitioning. These are referenced in the Database Engine Tuning Advisor, which is used to evaluate a database and can recommend the implementation of different types of physical design structures for better performance.

PIVOT   The PIVOT operator is used within a SELECT statement. It is used to create cross-tab reports (similar to a spreadsheet) from normalized data.

predicate An expression that can be used in search conditions of WHERE clauses, HAVING clauses, and join conditions of FROM clauses. Predicates evaluate to true, false, or unknown.

PRIMARY KEY (PK) This is a special column, or columns, within a table that's used to enforce uniqueness. Typically, the first column is created as a PRIMARY KEY and often it is the name of the table appended with ID. For example, the Employees table would have a PK of EmployeeID. A table can have only one PK. A unique clustered index is created by default when the PK is created.

Publication In the Replication Publisher metaphor, the Publication identifies that the data is replicated. Publications can include multiple articles.

Publisher In the Replication Publisher metaphor, the Publisher is the database that is the source of the data.

query optimizer An optimization process running within SQL Server. Any queries submitted to SQL Server are first processed by the query optimizer. It determines the best way to run the query, including what indexes to use and what types of joins to use. The output is a query execution plan, sometimes called a query plan or just a plan.

query plan Once the query optimizer determines the best way to execute a query, it creates a query plan. This identifies all the elements of the query, including what indexes are used, what types of joins are employed, and more. The query execution plan can be observed in SSMS by pressing CTRL+L or by selecting Query | Display Estimated Execution Plan.

recovery models Identifies how the transaction log is used and what can be recovered in the case of database failure. The three recovery models in SQL Server 2005 are simple, bulk-logged, and full.

recursion Occurs when one process calls itself to run again. With triggers, it's the process of a trigger firing itself. Indirect recursion is where an update to Table1 fires a trigger that affects Table2 that fires a trigger that updates Table1 again. Direct recursion is where an update to Table1 fires a trigger that affects Table1 again that fires the trigger again.

replication A group of technologies within SQL Server 2005 that are used to copy and distribute data and database objects from one database to another. Data is then regularly synchronized to maintain consistency. Replication uses a publishing metaphor with Publishers (data source), Distributors (process responsible for replicating the data and/or objects), and Subscribers (data target).

Replication Monitor Tool used to monitor replication. Can observe real-time activity, troubleshoot problems, and analyze past replication activity.

Report Builder Report Builder is a tool designed to let end users create reports from a report model. A great strength with Report Builder is that users can modify their reports, effectively creating ad hoc reports without the need to ask developers to modify the report.

Report Designer   Report Designer is the tool used within Business Intelligence Development Studio (BIDS) to create reports. This is not available to most end users. Wizards are available to make the process of creating reports easier.

Report Manager   Report Manager is the primary interface users can use to view, search, and subscribe to reports. For example, report models can be deployed, and users can then use the Report Builder in Report Manager to create their own reports. It can also be used to administer Report Server remotely.

report models   Report models are templates used to create reports with Report Builder. They include the data source definitions (such as which server and which database to connect to for the model) and data source VIEW definitions (such as which tables or VIEWs to include in the model). Reports can't be viewed from a report model. Instead, the report model must be used to create a report using Report Builder.

report snapshot   A report that contains data captured at a specific point in time. Since report snapshots hold datasets instead of queries, report snapshots can be used to limit processing costs by running the snapshot during off-peak times.

resource database   A read-only database that contains system objects included with SQL Server 2005.

role   Roles exist at both the server level and the database level. By adding logins to roles, they are automatically granted the permissions of that role. For example, by adding a user to the sysadmin role, the user can do anything on the instance of the server. By adding a user to the db_owner role, the user can do anything in the database.

roll back   The process of undoing uncommitted transactions. As a part of the recovery process, uncommitted transactions are rolled back to ensure the database is recovered in a consistent state.

roll forward   The process of applying committed transactions. As a part of the recovery process, committed transactions are rolled forward to ensure the database is recovered in a consistent state with the changed data in the database.

SAN   Storage area network (SAN) architecture is used to attach remote computer storage hardware in such a way that servers recognize it as local storage. SANs are typically very expensive, so they are only used in large applications.

scalar   A scalar result is a single result. Some functions are referred to as scalar because they return a single answer. For example, MAX and MIN are considered scalar functions. While they look at a group of data, they return only a single answer.

schema   In SQL Server 2000, the schema identified the model of the database. For example, the tables, VIEWs, data types, and so on would be identified as the schema. In SQL Server 2005, the term schema is used to identify a collection of database entities within a single namespace. Schemas are the owners of the objects, and one or more users can be the owners of schemas.

schemabinding An option that allows an object (such as a VIEW) to prevent referenced tables or VIEWs from being modified in such a way that would cause the original object to no longer work.

SD³+C Microsoft's security mantra. It started as SD³ (Secure by Design, Secure by Default, and Secure in Deployment) and then evolved to SD³ + C (Secure by Design, Secure by Default, and Secure in Deployment and Communications)

security principal SQL logins or Windows logins that are granted access to the server, and users or roles granted access to a database.

SELECT A DML statement used to retrieve data from tables or VIEWs.

Service Broker A new service in SQL Server 2005 that allows developers to build asynchronous applications by exchanging messages. Contracts identify messages used by a Service Broker service and create an agreement between two services. Messages are held in queues if they can't be sent right away. Conversations between two applications are referred to as dialogs.

Service Broker contract A contract is an agreement between two services. It defines the message types an application uses.

Service Broker conversation An exchange of messages between two services. Also referred to as a dialog.

Service Broker queues Where messages are stored until delivered or retrieved.

simple recovery model In the simple model, transactions logged into the transaction log are not available for restore purposes. Simple recovery is used for internal recovery purposes and to maintain database consistency. It is automatically truncated and doesn't need to be backed up or otherwise maintained.

snapshot replication Replication of data taken at a moment of time. With snapshot replication, the entire data set is replicated at the same time.

SOAP Simple Object Access Protocol (SOAP) is a protocol used to exchange XML messages, typically using HTTP.

SQL Pronounced as *es-que-el* or *sequel*, SQL is commonly understood to be an abbreviation of Structured Query Language—a language used to retrieve, update, insert, and delete data in tables and VIEWs. SQL Server 2005 uses a version of SQL referred to as Transact-SQL.

SQL injection attack An Internet attack against a database accessible via a web page. Automated programs are available to launch attacks, and successful SQL injection attacks can obtain the entire layout of a database and all the data.

SQL login A login created to provide access to SQL Server. Unlike Windows logins which are associated with local or domain users or groups, a SQL Server login is not associated with any outside user or group. SQL logins are needed for users accessing SQL Server from non-Microsoft systems.

SQL Profiler   Used as the GUI equivalent of the command line SQL Trace. Monitors SQL Server by capturing (or tracing) activity and saving it into a file or table. SQL Profiler can save traces used by DTA, and saved traces can also be imported into System Monitor with corresponding counter logs. It is effective in identifying slow-running queries and deadlocks.

SQL Server Agent   A management tool used to create jobs, fire alerts, and notify operators. All SQL Server Agent data is stored in the msdb system database.

SQL Server Configuration Manager   The tool for providing basic configuration management for SQL Server services and protocols. Services can be configured, enabled, and disabled in this tool. Protocols such as Shared Memory, TCP/IP, and Named Pipes can be enabled or disabled.

SSAS   SQL Server Analysis Services (SSAS) includes tools and features for OLAP that are used to design, deploy, and maintain cubes.

SSIS   SQL Server Integration Services (SSIS) is used to build data integration packages, including ELT packages. It is the replacement for DTS in SQL Server 2000.

SSMS   SQL Server Management Studio (SSMS) is the primary GUI to access, configure, manage, administer, and maintain SQL Server 2005 components. It combines the features of Enterprise Manager and Query Analyzer from SQL Server 2000.

SSRS   SQL Server Reporting Services (SSRS) is a server-based reporting platform used to create and manage a wide variety of reports, including parameterized reports, report snapshots, and more. Reports can be deployed to an IIS server so they are easily accessible to users.

statistics   Statistics are a small sample of a whole used to represent the whole. In SQL Server, statistics are maintained on indexes and used by the query optimizer to determine which indexes to use for a given query. Instead of scanning an entire index (the entire population), statistical data (a sampling) is maintained on the index.

Subscriber   In the Replication Publisher metaphor, the Subscriber is the database that receives the data.

synonyms   Synonyms are used as an alternative name for a schema-scoped object. Objects can be referenced using the single-part synonym name, or the two-part, three-part, or four-part name.

System Monitor   An operating system tool that allows the measurement of counters and objects. Key operating system objects are the CPU, memory, disk drive, and NIC. When SQL Server is installed, additional objects are added that can be measured, such as SQL Agent:Statistics, SQL Server:Buffer Manager, SQL Server:Locks, SQL Server:SSIS Pipeline, and many more.

table   A two-dimensional storage location of data. Databases within SQL Server 2005 are composed of multiple related tables.

tail-log   The transaction log that is backed up from a possibly damaged database is called the tail-log. It holds all of the transactions since the last backup.

tempdb   One of the system databases. The tempdb database is used for temporary storage of data, including temporary objects created in normal operation, and results from temporary sorts when creating or rebuilding indexes using the SORT_IN_TEMPDB option. Since it is recreated each time SQL Server is restarted, it should be set to the size needed instead of allowing frequent auto growth operations.

trace   A trace is a collection of events and data. SQL Profiler is used to collect and monitor events. Creating a trace is sometimes referred to as capturing events.

transaction   One or more T-SQL statements grouped together. In a transaction, either all operations must succeed or they all fail. Transactions are identified with the BEGIN TRAN statement, and ended with either a COMMIT TRAN or ROLLBACK TRAN statement.

transactional replication   Replication that starts with a snapshot and then keeps the Subscribers up-to-date by using the transaction log. Transactions are recorded on the Publisher, distributed to the Subscribers, and then applied to keep the Subscribers up-to-date.

transaction log   The file that holds a record of all transactions (INSERTS, UPDATES, DELETES) in a database. Data modifications are first recorded in the transaction log, and then periodically (at checkpoints) the data is written to the database. The transaction log functions differently depending on which recovery model is being used: simple, full, or bulk-logged.

TRIGGER   A type of stored procedure that fires in response to action on a table. DML triggers are associated with INSERT, UPDATE, and DELETE statements. DDL triggers are associated with CREATE, ALTER, and DROP statements.

T-SQL   Transact-SQL (T-SQL) is Microsoft's version of SQL. It is an extension of the SQL language defined by the International Standards Organization (ISO) and the American National Standards Institute (ANSI).

UNPIVOT   The UNPIVOT operator is used within a SELECT statement to create a normalized data report from data that is stored as a spreadsheet.

UPDATE   A DML statement used to modify data within a table or VIEW.

user-defined function   Functions are routines that can accept parameters, perform an action, and return the result of that action. SQL Server includes many built-in functions, but user-defined functions can be created by any user with permission to do so. User-defined functions can be T-SQL functions or CLR-integrated functions.

VIEW   A virtual table that represents data in one or more tables in an alternate way. Almost any SELECT statement can be converted to a VIEW.

witness server   When using database mirroring, automatic failover can be configured by adding a witness server that monitors the status of the principal and mirror servers.

XML   Extensible Markup Language (XML) is an offshoot of the Standard Generalized Markup Language (SGML), just as HTML is, and is designed to be relatively human-legible. Within SQL Server, XML is a data type that allows full XML documents to be stored unmodified within a SQL Server database.

XML methods   SQL Server 2005 provides five different XML methods that can be used to query and manipulate XML data stored in an XML data type column. The five methods are Value, Nodes, Query, Modify, and Exist.